TIDE TABLES 2020

Summer time figures are enclosed within a shaded box. See title to each table for necessary adjustments.

○ Full Moon
● New Moon
☾/☽ Half moon – first or last quarter

PLYMOUTH (DEVONPORT)
LAT 50°22′N
LONG 4°11′W

TIMES AND HEIGHTS OF HIGH AND LOW WATER (Heights in Metres)

TIME ZONE UT
For Summer Time (area enclosed in shaded box) add 1 hour

2020

JANUARY

Date	Day	Time	m
1	W	0309 0911 1537 2136	1.8 5.0 1.8 4.6
2	TH	0344 0952 1616 2221	2.0 4.8 2.0 4.5
3	F ☽	0427 1039 1705 2315	2.2 4.6 2.2 4.4
4	SA	0525 1136 1808	2.4 4.5 2.3
5	SU	0020 0637 1246 1915	4.3 2.4 4.5 2.2
6	M	0133 0747 1359 2019	4.4 2.3 4.5 2.0
7	TU	0240 0850 1504 2117	4.6 2.0 4.7 1.8
8	W	0336 0946 1601 2210	4.9 1.7 4.9 1.5
9	TH	0427 1038 1652 2300	5.1 1.4 5.1 1.3
10	F O	0513 1128 1739 2347	5.3 1.2 5.2 1.1
11	SA	0558 1215 1826	5.5 1.0 5.3
12	SU	0033 0642 1302 1911	1.0 5.6 0.9 5.3
13	M	0119 0727 1347 1956	0.9 5.6 0.8 5.3
14	TU	0203 0812 1431 2041	0.9 5.6 0.8 5.3
15	W	0246 0857 1515 2127	1.0 5.5 1.0 5.1
16	TH	0331 0944 1601 2214	1.2 5.4 1.2 5.0
17	F ☾	0418 1034 1650 2308	1.4 5.1 1.5 4.8
18	SA	0511 1131 1749	1.7 4.9 1.7
19	SU	0011 0617 1241 1901	4.6 1.9 4.7 1.9
20	M	0124 0738 1355 2021	4.6 2.0 4.6 1.9
21	TU	0234 0856 1504 2130	4.7 1.9 4.7 1.7
22	W	0336 1001 1604 2227	4.9 1.6 4.8 1.5
23	TH	0430 1055 1656 2317	5.1 1.3 5.0 1.3
24	F ●	0517 1142 1742	5.3 1.1 5.1
25	SA	0001 0558 1225 1822	1.1 5.4 1.0 5.1
26	SU	0041 0637 1304 1859	1.0 5.4 1.0 5.1
27	M	0117 0711 1339 1932	1.1 5.4 1.0 5.1
28	TU	0149 0745 1410 2004	1.1 5.3 1.1 5.0
29	W	0217 0817 1438 2036	1.3 5.2 1.3 4.9
30	TH	0243 0849 1504 2109	1.5 5.1 1.5 4.8
31	F	0307 0922 1530 2143	1.6 4.9 1.7 4.6

FEBRUARY

Date	Day	Time	m
1	SA	0336 0957 1602 2222	1.8 4.7 1.9 4.5
2	SU ☽	0415 1040 1648 2313	2.1 4.5 2.1 4.3
3	M	0513 1138 1802	2.3 4.4 2.2
4	TU	0020 0644 1254 1927	4.3 2.3 4.3 2.2
5	W	0141 0807 1419 2040	4.4 2.2 4.4 2.0
6	TH	0257 0916 1532 2144	4.6 1.8 4.7 1.7
7	F	0359 1017 1631 2242	4.9 1.5 4.9 1.3
8	SA	0452 1113 1723 2335	5.2 1.1 5.2 1.0
9	SU O	0541 1204 1812	5.5 0.8 5.3
10	M	0024 0629 1252 1859	0.7 5.7 0.5 5.5
11	TU	0110 0716 1337 1945	0.5 5.8 0.4 5.5
12	W	0154 0801 1420 2028	0.5 5.8 0.4 5.5
13	TH	0235 0845 1501 2110	0.6 5.7 0.6 5.3
14	F	0315 0927 1541 2151	0.8 5.5 0.9 5.1
15	SA ☾	0356 1011 1622 2235	1.1 5.2 1.3 4.9
16	SU	0441 1059 1710 2329	1.5 4.8 1.7 4.6
17	M	0537 1205 1813	1.9 4.5 2.0
18	TU	0046 0654 1330 1944	4.4 2.1 4.3 2.2
19	W	0208 0836 1447 2115	4.4 2.1 4.4 2.0
20	TH	0317 0950 1551 2216	4.6 1.8 4.6 1.7
21	F	0413 1044 1643 2305	4.9 1.4 4.8 1.4
22	SA	0500 1130 1726 2347	5.1 1.1 5.0 1.1
23	SU ●	0540 1210 1804	5.3 0.9 5.1
24	M	0026 0617 1247 1838	0.9 5.4 0.8 5.2
25	TU	0100 0651 1320 1910	0.9 5.4 0.8 5.2
26	W	0129 0724 1347 1941	0.9 5.4 0.9 5.1
27	TH	0153 0755 1410 2011	1.1 5.3 1.1 5.0
28	F	0215 0825 1431 2040	1.2 5.1 1.3 4.9
29	SA	0236 0853 1453 2107	1.4 4.9 1.4 4.8

MARCH

Date	Day	Time	m
1	SU	0300 0920 1520 2136	1.5 4.7 1.6 4.6
2	M ☽	0334 0956 1558 2221	1.8 4.5 1.9 4.4
3	TU	0421 1052 1655 2327	2.0 4.3 2.2 4.3
4	W	0540 1208 1837	2.3 4.2 2.3
5	TH	0049 0730 1342 2009	4.3 2.2 4.3 2.1
6	F	0221 0851 1508 2122	4.5 1.8 4.5 1.7
7	SA	0333 0959 1612 2225	4.9 1.4 4.9 1.3
8	SU	0431 1056 1705 2319	5.2 0.9 5.2 0.8
9	M O	0522 1148 1754	5.5 0.5 5.4
10	TU	0008 0610 1236 1841	0.5 5.7 0.2 5.6
11	W	0054 0658 1320 1925	0.3 5.9 0.1 5.7
12	TH	0137 0743 1401 2007	0.2 5.9 0.1 5.6
13	F	0217 0826 1440 2047	0.3 5.7 0.4 5.5
14	SA	0255 0906 1517 2123	0.5 5.5 0.8 5.2
15	SU	0333 0945 1555 2200	0.9 5.1 1.2 4.9
16	M ☾	0414 1027 1638 2244	1.4 4.7 1.7 4.5
17	TU	0506 1130 1736	1.9 4.3 2.2
18	W	0007 0618 1311 1904	4.3 2.2 4.1 2.4
19	TH	0144 0819 1430 2058	4.2 2.2 4.2 2.2
20	F	0255 0935 1533 2158	4.5 1.8 4.4 1.8
21	SA	0350 1025 1622 2244	4.8 1.4 4.7 1.4
22	SU	0436 1108 1703 2325	5.0 1.1 4.9 1.1
23	M	0515 1146 1739	5.2 0.9 5.1
24	TU ●	0002 0551 1222 1812	0.9 5.3 0.8 5.2
25	W	0035 0625 1252 1844	0.8 5.3 0.8 5.2
26	TH	0103 0658 1318 1915	0.9 5.3 0.9 5.2
27	F	0126 0730 1340 1944	1.0 5.2 1.0 5.1
28	SA	0147 0759 1401 2011	1.1 5.1 1.1 5.0
29	SU	0209 0826 1424 2036	1.2 4.9 1.3 4.9
30	M	0234 0853 1452 2105	1.4 4.8 1.5 4.7
31	TU	0307 0929 1529 2149	1.6 4.6 1.8 4.6

APRIL

Date	Day	Time	m
1	W ☽	0353 1026 1623 2254	1.9 4.3 2.1 4.4
2	TH	0507 1142 1800	2.2 4.2 2.3
3	F	0016 0702 1316 1944	4.3 2.1 4.3 2.1
4	SA	0150 0829 1446 2101	4.5 1.8 4.5 1.7
5	SU	0308 0938 1550 2204	4.9 1.3 4.9 1.2
6	M	0407 1035 1643 2258	5.3 0.8 5.2 0.7
7	TU	0459 1126 1731 2347	5.6 0.4 5.5 0.4
8	W O	0549 1213 1818	5.8 0.1 5.6
9	TH	0032 0635 1257 1901	0.2 5.8 0.1 5.7
10	F	0115 0721 1338 1942	0.1 5.8 0.2 5.7
11	SA	0155 0803 1417 2021	0.3 5.6 0.4 5.5
12	SU	0233 0843 1454 2055	0.6 5.3 0.8 5.2
13	M	0311 0920 1531 2127	1.0 5.0 1.3 4.9
14	TU ☾	0353 0959 1614 2205	1.5 4.6 1.8 4.6
15	W	0444 1058 1709 2314	1.9 4.2 2.2 4.3
16	TH	0552 1247 1827	2.2 4.0 2.4
17	F	0113 0738 1404 2019	4.2 2.2 4.1 2.3
18	SA	0224 0902 1502 2124	4.4 1.9 4.4 1.9
19	SU	0318 0953 1550 2211	4.7 1.5 4.7 1.5
20	M	0403 1035 1630 2252	4.9 1.2 4.9 1.2
21	TU	0443 1113 1706 2329	5.1 1.0 5.1 1.0
22	W	0521 1147 1741	5.2 0.9 5.2
23	TH ●	0002 0556 1218 1815	1.0 5.2 0.9 5.2
24	F	0031 0632 1246 1848	0.9 5.2 0.9 5.2
25	SA	0057 0705 1311 1918	1.0 5.2 1.0 5.2
26	SU	0122 0736 1336 1946	1.1 5.1 1.1 5.1
27	M	0148 0805 1403 2014	1.2 4.9 1.3 5.0
28	TU	0218 0837 1434 2048	1.3 4.8 1.5 4.9
29	W	0254 0918 1515 2134	1.5 4.6 1.8 4.7
30	TH ☽	0343 1014 1612 2236	1.8 4.4 2.0 4.6

MAY

Date	Day	Time	m
1	F	0459 1126 1742 2352	2.0 4.3 2.2 4.5
2	SA	0640 1255 1918	2.0 4.3 2.0
3	SU	0121 0803 1419 2034	4.7 1.7 4.6 1.7
4	M	0240 0911 1523 2138	4.9 1.2 5.0 1.2
5	TU	0341 1009 1616 2233	5.3 0.8 5.3 0.8
6	W	0434 1101 1705 2323	5.5 0.5 5.5 0.5
7	TH O	0525 1148 1752	5.6 0.3 5.6
8	F	0009 0612 1233 1836	0.3 5.7 0.3 5.7
9	SA	0053 0658 1315 1917	0.3 5.6 0.4 5.6
10	SU	0134 0741 1355 1956	0.4 5.4 0.6 5.5
11	M	0214 0822 1433 2031	0.7 5.2 1.0 5.2
12	TU	0253 0900 1511 2103	1.1 4.9 1.4 5.0
13	W	0336 0938 1554 2141	1.5 4.5 1.8 4.7
14	TH ☾	0424 1031 1646 2235	1.8 4.2 2.1 4.4
15	F	0524 1203 1750	2.1 4.1 2.3
16	SA	0017 0637 1320 1909	4.3 2.2 4.2 2.3
17	SU	0137 0759 1418 2026	4.4 2.0 4.3 2.1
18	M	0234 0901 1507 2122	4.6 1.7 4.6 1.8
19	TU	0322 0948 1549 2207	4.8 1.5 4.8 1.5
20	W	0405 1029 1629 2247	4.9 1.3 5.0 1.3
21	TH	0447 1106 1708 2324	5.0 1.1 5.1 1.2
22	F ●	0527 1141 1746 2358	5.1 1.1 5.2 1.1
23	SA	0606 1214 1822	5.1 1.1 5.2
24	SU	0031 0642 1247 1855	1.1 5.1 1.1 5.2
25	M	0103 0717 1319 1927	1.1 5.1 1.2 5.2
26	TU	0136 0752 1352 2001	1.2 5.0 1.3 5.1
27	W	0212 0830 1430 2040	1.3 4.8 1.5 5.0
28	TH	0254 0914 1515 2127	1.4 4.7 1.6 4.9
29	F	0346 1008 1612 2225	1.6 4.6 1.8 4.8
30	SA ☽	0454 1114 1726 2333	1.8 4.5 1.9 4.7
31	SU	0614 1231 1847	1.7 4.5 1.9

JUNE

Date	Day	Time	m
1	M	0053 0732 1347 2002	4.8 1.6 4.7 1.6
2	TU	0209 0841 1451 2108	4.9 1.3 4.9 1.3
3	W	0313 0941 1548 2206	5.1 1.0 5.2 1.0
4	TH	0409 1035 1639 2259	5.3 0.8 5.3 0.8
5	F O	0502 1125 1728 2347	5.4 0.7 5.5 0.6
6	SA	0552 1211 1813	5.4 0.6 5.5
7	SU	0033 0638 1255 1856	0.6 5.4 0.7 5.5
8	M	0117 0723 1337 1935	0.7 5.2 0.9 5.4
9	TU	0158 0805 1416 2012	0.9 5.1 1.1 5.2
10	W	0238 0843 1455 2046	1.1 4.8 1.4 5.0
11	TH	0319 0921 1535 2123	1.4 4.6 1.7 4.8
12	F	0402 1004 1619 2207	1.7 4.4 2.0 4.6
13	SA ☾	0450 1058 1710 2304	1.9 4.3 2.1 4.5
14	SU	0546 1205 1810	2.0 4.2 2.2
15	M	0017 0647 1313 1914	4.4 2.0 4.3 2.2
16	TU	0130 0750 1411 2017	4.4 1.9 4.4 2.0
17	W	0231 0847 1503 2113	4.6 1.8 4.6 1.8
18	TH	0323 0938 1550 2202	4.7 1.6 4.8 1.6
19	F	0412 1024 1635 2247	4.8 1.4 5.0 1.4
20	SA	0458 1106 1717 2329	5.0 1.3 5.1 1.2
21	SU ●	0541 1148 1758	5.0 1.2 5.2
22	M	0010 0623 1228 1836	1.1 5.1 1.1 5.3
23	TU	0051 0704 1308 1915	1.1 5.1 1.1 5.3
24	W	0131 0745 1349 1954	1.0 5.1 1.2 5.3
25	TH	0213 0827 1431 2037	1.1 5.0 1.3 5.2
26	F	0257 0912 1516 2123	1.2 4.9 1.4 5.1
27	SA	0346 1002 1607 2215	1.3 4.8 1.5 5.0
28	SU ☽	0441 1059 1705 2314	1.5 4.7 1.7 4.9
29	M	0544 1203 1813	1.6 4.6 1.7
30	TU	0023 0655 1313 1927	4.8 1.6 4.7 1.7

SUNRISE AND SUNSET TIMES

PLYMOUTH
At 50°22′N 4°11′W

		Sunrise	Sunset
UT			
Jan	01	0817	1623
	15	0811	1641
Feb	01	0752	1709
	15	0729	1733
Mar	01	0700	1759
	15	0630	1822
BST			
Apr	01	0653	1949
	15	0623	2012
May	01	0552	2037
	15	0529	2058
Jun	01	0511	2119
	15	0505	2130
Jul	01	0510	2131
	15	0523	2122
Aug	01	0545	2100
	15	0606	2035
Sep	01	0632	2001
	15	0653	1930
Oct	01	0717	1854
	15	0740	1824
UT			
Nov	01	0708	1652
	15	0731	1631
Dec	01	0755	1616
	15	0811	1613

PLYMOUTH (DEVONPORT)
LAT 50°22′N
LONG 4°11′W

TIMES AND HEIGHTS OF HIGH AND LOW WATER (Heights in Metres)

TIME ZONE UT
For Summer Time (area enclosed in shaded box) add 1 hour

2020

JULY

Day	Time	m
1 W	0138 0808 1421 2038	4.8 1.5 4.8 1.6
2 TH	0247 0914 1522 2142	4.9 1.4 5.0 1.4
3 F	0349 1013 1617 2240	5.0 1.2 5.1 1.1
4 SA	0444 1107 1708 2331	5.1 1.0 5.3 1.0
5 SU ○	0536 1155 1755	5.2 0.9 5.4
6 M	0019 0623 1241 1838	0.9 5.2 0.9 5.4
7 TU	0104 0707 1323 1918	0.8 5.1 1.0 5.4
8 W	0145 0747 1401 1954	0.9 5.0 1.1 5.3
9 TH	0223 0824 1437 2028	1.1 4.9 1.3 5.1
10 F	0259 0857 1511 2101	1.3 4.8 1.5 5.0
11 SA	0334 0933 1545 2138	1.5 4.6 1.7 4.8
12 SU ☾	0410 1013 1623 2219	1.7 4.5 1.9 4.6
13 M	0452 1100 1710 2309	1.9 4.4 2.1 4.5
14 TU	0545 1157 1811	2.1 4.3 2.2
15 W	0011 0647 1304 1918	4.4 2.1 4.3 2.2
16 TH	0126 0751 1411 2023	4.4 2.0 4.5 2.0
17 F	0238 0851 1511 2122	4.5 1.8 4.7 1.8
18 SA	0339 0947 1604 2216	4.7 1.6 4.9 1.5
19 SU	0432 1039 1652 2306	4.8 1.4 5.1 1.3
20 M ●	0520 1127 1737 2354	5.0 1.2 5.3 1.1
21 TU	0607 1214 1821	5.1 1.0 5.4
22 W	0040 0652 1300 1904	0.9 5.2 0.9 5.5
23 TH	0125 0736 1344 1947	0.8 5.2 0.9 5.5
24 F	0209 0820 1426 2030	0.8 5.2 0.9 5.5
25 SA	0251 0904 1508 2114	0.8 5.1 1.0 5.4
26 SU	0334 0949 1552 2200	1.0 5.0 1.2 5.2
27 M ☽	0420 1037 1640 2251	1.2 4.9 1.5 5.0
28 TU	0512 1133 1738 2353	1.5 4.7 1.7 4.7
29 W	0617 1241 1851	1.7 4.6 1.9
30 TH	0111 0735 1354 2013	4.6 1.9 4.6 1.9
31 F	0228 0854 1503 2128	4.6 1.8 4.7 1.7

AUGUST

Day	Time	m
1 SA	0336 1000 1602 2229	4.7 1.5 5.0 1.4
2 SU	0434 1056 1654 2322	4.9 1.3 5.2 1.1
3 M ○	0524 1144 1740	5.0 1.1 5.3
4 TU	0008 0608 1228 1821	0.9 5.1 1.0 5.4
5 W	0051 0649 1308 1858	0.8 5.1 0.9 5.4
6 TH	0129 0725 1343 1932	0.9 5.1 1.0 5.4
7 F	0203 0757 1414 2004	1.0 5.0 1.1 5.3
8 SA	0232 0828 1441 2035	1.1 4.9 1.3 5.1
9 SU	0259 0900 1506 2107	1.3 4.8 1.5 4.9
10 M	0323 0934 1531 2140	1.6 4.7 1.8 4.7
11 TU ☾	0350 1011 1602 2219	1.8 4.5 2.0 4.5
12 W	0427 1057 1651 2310	2.0 4.4 2.2 4.4
13 TH	0532 1157 1817	2.2 4.3 2.4
14 F	0020 0701 1315 1941	4.2 2.3 4.3 2.3
15 SA	0151 0815 1433 2050	4.3 2.1 4.5 2.0
16 SU	0310 0919 1536 2152	4.5 1.8 4.8 1.6
17 M	0410 1017 1629 2248	4.8 1.5 5.1 1.2
18 TU	0501 1111 1717 2339	5.0 1.2 5.4 0.9
19 W ●	0549 1200 1803	5.2 0.9 5.6
20 TH	0027 0635 1247 1849	0.7 5.4 0.7 5.7
21 F	0112 0721 1331 1933	0.5 5.4 0.6 5.7
22 SA	0155 0804 1412 2017	0.5 5.5 0.6 5.7
23 SU	0235 0846 1452 2059	0.6 5.4 0.7 5.5
24 M	0315 0927 1531 2140	0.8 5.2 1.0 5.3
25 TU ☽	0355 1010 1615 2225	1.2 5.0 1.4 4.9
26 W	0440 1100 1707 2324	1.6 4.7 1.8 4.6
27 TH	0540 1210 1819	2.0 4.5 2.1
28 F	0051 0707 1335 1959	4.3 2.2 4.4 2.2
29 SA	0219 0846 1450 2123	4.3 2.1 4.6 1.9
30 SU	0329 0953 1550 2221	4.5 1.8 4.9 1.5
31 M	0424 1045 1639 2309	4.8 1.4 5.1 1.2

SEPTEMBER

Day	Time	m
1 TU	0510 1129 1722 2352	5.0 1.1 5.3 0.9
2 W ○	0549 1210 1800	5.1 0.9 5.4
3 TH	0030 0625 1247 1834	0.8 5.2 0.9 5.5
4 F	0105 0657 1319 1906	0.8 5.2 0.9 5.4
5 SA	0135 0728 1346 1937	0.9 5.2 1.1 5.3
6 SU	0200 0757 1408 2007	1.1 5.1 1.2 5.2
7 M	0220 0827 1427 2036	1.3 5.0 1.4 5.0
8 TU	0239 0856 1447 2104	1.5 4.8 1.6 4.8
9 W	0301 0927 1514 2137	1.7 4.7 1.9 4.6
10 TH ☾	0333 1008 1555 2226	2.0 4.5 2.2 4.4
11 F	0422 1107 1704 2336	2.3 4.3 2.4 4.2
12 SA	0605 1224 1907	2.5 4.3 2.4
13 SU	0109 0745 1356 2026	4.2 2.3 4.5 2.1
14 M	0247 0857 1510 2132	4.5 1.9 4.8 1.6
15 TU	0350 0958 1606 2229	4.8 1.5 5.2 1.1
16 W	0441 1052 1655 2320	5.1 1.1 5.5 0.7
17 TH ●	0528 1142 1743	5.4 0.7 5.7
18 F	0007 0614 1228 1828	0.5 5.6 0.5 5.9
19 SA	0052 0659 1311 1913	0.3 5.7 0.4 5.9
20 SU	0134 0742 1352 1957	0.3 5.7 0.4 5.8
21 M	0213 0822 1431 2038	0.5 5.6 0.6 5.6
22 TU	0251 0902 1509 2118	0.8 5.3 1.0 5.2
23 W	0329 0941 1551 2200	1.3 5.0 1.5 4.8
24 TH ☽	0413 1027 1642 2257	1.8 4.7 1.9 4.4
25 F	0510 1141 1755	2.2 4.4 2.3
26 SA	0040 0643 1319 1953	4.2 2.5 4.4 2.3
27 SU	0210 0836 1434 2112	4.2 2.3 4.6 2.0
28 M	0317 0937 1532 2204	4.5 1.9 4.9 1.5
29 TU	0407 1024 1618 2247	4.8 1.5 5.1 1.2
30 W	0447 1106 1658 2327	5.1 1.2 5.3 1.0

OCTOBER

Day	Time	m
1 TH ○	0523 1144 1733	5.2 1.0 5.4
2 F	0003 0556 1219 1806	0.9 5.3 0.9 5.5
3 SA	0035 0627 1249 1838	0.9 5.3 1.0 5.4
4 SU	0102 0657 1314 1910	1.0 5.3 1.1 5.4
5 M	0125 0728 1335 1939	1.1 5.3 1.2 5.2
6 TU	0145 0756 1354 2007	1.3 5.1 1.4 5.1
7 W	0204 0824 1416 2034	1.5 5.0 1.6 4.9
8 TH	0228 0853 1444 2107	1.7 4.8 1.8 4.6
9 F	0301 0933 1524 2158	2.0 4.6 2.1 4.4
10 SA ☾	0347 1033 1628 2309	2.3 4.4 2.4 4.2
11 SU	0514 1148 1835	2.5 4.4 2.4
12 M	0038 0717 1319 2002	4.3 2.4 4.6 2.1
13 TU	0221 0834 1441 2109	4.5 2.0 4.9 1.6
14 W	0326 0935 1540 2205	4.9 1.5 5.3 1.1
15 TH	0417 1029 1631 2256	5.3 1.0 5.6 0.7
16 F ●	0504 1118 1719 2343	5.5 0.7 5.8 0.4
17 SA	0550 1205 1806	5.7 0.4 5.9
18 SU	0028 0634 1248 1851	0.3 5.8 0.4 5.9
19 M	0110 0717 1330 1935	0.4 5.8 0.5 5.8
20 TU	0150 0758 1410 2017	0.6 5.7 0.7 5.5
21 W	0228 0837 1449 2057	1.0 5.4 1.1 5.1
22 TH	0307 0915 1532 2139	1.4 5.1 1.6 4.7
23 F ☽	0351 0959 1623 2237	1.9 4.8 2.0 4.4
24 SA	0447 1111 1734	2.3 4.5 2.4
25 SU	0022 0612 1253 1923	4.2 2.6 4.4 2.4
26 M	0146 0804 1406 2042	4.2 2.4 4.6 2.0
27 TU	0248 0906 1502 2133	4.5 2.0 4.8 1.7
28 W	0336 0953 1548 2216	4.8 1.7 5.1 1.4
29 TH	0416 1034 1627 2254	5.0 1.4 5.3 1.1
30 F	0451 1112 1703 2329	5.2 1.2 5.4 1.0
31 SA ○	0525 1146 1738	5.3 1.1 5.4

NOVEMBER

Day	Time	m
1 SU	0000 0557 1216 1811	1.0 5.4 1.1 5.4
2 M	0028 0630 1243 1844	1.1 5.4 1.2 5.3
3 TU	0053 0701 1307 1916	1.2 5.3 1.3 5.2
4 W	0117 0731 1331 1945	1.3 5.3 1.4 5.1
5 TH	0141 0759 1357 2015	1.5 5.1 1.6 4.9
6 F	0209 0831 1429 2052	1.7 5.0 1.8 4.7
7 SA	0245 0914 1513 2143	1.9 4.8 2.0 4.5
8 SU ☾	0334 1011 1617 2250	2.2 4.7 2.3 4.4
9 M	0454 1121 1802	2.4 4.6 2.3
10 TU	0011 0642 1244 1931	4.4 2.4 4.7 2.0
11 W	0144 0803 1406 2040	4.6 2.0 5.0 1.6
12 TH	0253 0907 1510 2138	4.9 1.6 5.3 1.2
13 F	0348 1003 1605 2230	5.3 1.1 5.5 0.8
14 SA	0438 1054 1655 2319	5.5 0.8 5.7 0.6
15 SU ●	0525 1141 1744	5.7 0.6 5.8
16 M	0004 0610 1227 1831	0.5 5.8 0.5 5.8
17 TU	0048 0654 1310 1916	0.6 5.8 0.6 5.6
18 W	0130 0736 1352 2000	0.8 5.7 0.8 5.4
19 TH	0210 0817 1434 2042	1.1 5.5 1.2 5.1
20 F	0250 0857 1518 2125	1.5 5.2 1.6 4.7
21 SA	0334 0940 1607 2218	1.9 4.9 1.9 4.4
22 SU ☽	0426 1037 1707 2340	2.2 4.6 2.2 4.3
23 M	0532 1204 1822	2.5 4.5 2.3
24 TU	0100 0655 1319 1944	4.3 2.5 4.5 2.2
25 W	0202 0813 1418 2045	4.4 2.2 4.7 1.9
26 TH	0253 0908 1507 2132	4.7 2.0 4.9 1.7
27 F	0336 0954 1550 2214	4.9 1.7 5.0 1.5
28 SA	0416 1034 1631 2251	5.1 1.5 5.2 1.3
29 SU	0453 1110 1710 2325	5.2 1.4 5.2 1.3
30 M ○	0530 1144 1748 2357	5.3 1.3 5.3 1.2

DECEMBER

Day	Time	m
1 TU	0606 1216 1824	5.4 1.3 5.2
2 W	0028 0640 1248 1859	1.3 5.4 1.3 5.2
3 TH	0059 0713 1319 1932	1.4 5.3 1.4 5.1
4 F	0130 0745 1352 2007	1.5 5.2 1.5 5.0
5 SA	0204 0821 1429 2047	1.6 5.1 1.6 4.8
6 SU	0244 0904 1515 2135	1.8 5.0 1.8 4.7
7 M	0334 0957 1613 2234	2.0 4.9 2.0 4.6
8 TU ☾	0439 1059 1728 2343	2.1 4.8 2.0 4.5
9 W	0601 1210 1851	2.2 4.8 1.9
10 TH	0101 0723 1327 2004	4.6 2.0 4.9 1.7
11 F	0215 0834 1437 2108	4.9 1.7 5.1 1.4
12 SA	0317 0935 1538 2204	5.1 1.4 5.3 1.1
13 SU	0412 1030 1634 2256	5.4 1.1 5.4 0.9
14 M ●	0503 1122 1726 2345	5.5 0.9 5.5 0.8
15 TU	0551 1210 1815	5.7 0.8 5.5
16 W	0031 0637 1256 1902	0.8 5.7 0.8 5.4
17 TH	0115 0721 1340 1947	0.9 5.6 0.9 5.3
18 F	0157 0803 1423 2030	1.1 5.5 1.1 5.1
19 SA	0238 0842 1505 2110	1.4 5.3 1.4 4.8
20 SU	0318 0921 1548 2151	1.7 5.1 1.7 4.6
21 M ☽	0401 1004 1633 2238	1.9 4.8 1.9 4.4
22 TU	0449 1054 1725 2337	2.2 4.6 2.1 4.3
23 W	0546 1158 1825	2.3 4.5 2.2
24 TH	0046 0652 1309 1930	4.3 2.4 4.5 2.2
25 F	0151 0801 1412 2031	4.5 2.2 4.6 2.0
26 SA	0247 0900 1507 2124	4.6 2.0 4.7 1.8
27 SU	0337 0951 1557 2210	4.8 1.8 4.9 1.6
28 M	0422 1035 1643 2252	5.0 1.6 5.0 1.5
29 TU	0505 1117 1727 2332	5.2 1.4 5.1 1.4
30 W ○	0546 1156 1808	5.3 1.3 5.1
31 TH	0010 0624 1235 1847	1.3 5.4 1.3 5.1

PORTLAND
LAT 50°34'N
LONG 2°26'W

TIMES AND HEIGHTS OF HIGH AND LOW WATER (Heights in Metres)

TIME ZONE UT
For Summer Time (area enclosed in shaded box) add 1 hour

Double low waters occur at Portland. The predictions are for the first low water. The second low water occus from 3 to 4 hours later and, at springs, may be lower that the first

2020

JANUARY

Date	Day	Time	m
1	W	0232 1010 1517 2232	0.7 1.7 0.6 1.5
2	TH	0258 1045 1549 2310	0.7 1.6 0.7 1.4
3	F ☽	0336 1124 1631 2358	0.8 1.5 0.7 1.4
4	SA	0431 1216 1728	0.9 1.4 0.7
5	SU	0108 0541 1333 1926	1.4 0.9 1.4 0.7
6	M	0228 0704 1452 2016	1.5 0.9 1.4 0.6
7	TU	0333 0829 1559 2102	1.6 0.8 1.6 0.6
8	W	0429 0924 1659 2151	1.8 0.7 1.7 0.5
9	TH	0521 1016 1753 2240	1.9 0.6 1.8 0.4
10	F O	0606 1107 1842 2328	2.1 0.5 1.9 0.4
11	SA	0649 1155 1927	2.2 0.4 2.0
12	SU	0013 0732 1240 2012	0.3 2.2 0.3 2.0
13	M	0057 0815 1325 2055	0.3 2.3 0.2 2.0
14	TU	0141 0859 1410 2137	0.3 2.2 0.2 1.9
15	W	0225 0944 1456 2220	0.3 2.1 0.2 1.8
16	TH	0310 1030 1543 2306	0.4 2.0 0.3 1.7
17	F ☾	0358 1119 1633	0.5 1.8 0.4
18	SA	0002 0451 1220 1729	1.6 0.7 1.6 0.6
19	SU	0116 0553 1337 1835	1.5 0.8 1.5 0.7
20	M	0229 0713 1451 1955	1.5 0.8 1.5 0.7
21	TU	0334 0849 1558 2105	1.6 0.8 1.5 0.7
22	W	0433 0949 1701 2158	1.7 0.7 1.6 0.6
23	TH	0527 1038 1756 2246	1.9 0.6 1.7 0.5
24	F ●	0615 1121 1844 2329	2.0 0.5 1.8 0.4
25	SA	0658 1200 1926	2.1 0.4 1.9
26	SU	0007 0739 1236 2004	0.3 2.1 0.3 1.9
27	M	0044 0815 1313 2035	0.3 2.1 0.3 1.9
28	TU	0119 0848 1348 2105	0.3 2.0 0.3 1.8
29	W	0150 0919 1419 2134	0.4 1.9 0.4 1.7
30	TH	0216 0948 1445 2202	0.4 1.8 0.4 1.6
31	F	0240 1014 1511 2228	0.5 1.7 0.5 1.5

FEBRUARY

Date	Day	Time	m
1	SA	0310 1041 1545 2302	0.5 1.5 0.5 1.5
2	SU ☽	0350 1119 1633 2349	0.6 1.4 0.5 1.4
3	M	0449 1214 1733	0.7 1.4 0.6
4	TU	0057 0601 1335 1843	1.4 0.8 1.3 0.6
5	W	0233 0719 1513 2010	1.5 0.8 1.4 0.6
6	TH	0348 0859 1627 2129	1.6 0.7 1.5 0.5
7	F	0450 1003 1731 2225	1.8 0.6 1.7 0.4
8	SA	0544 1057 1827 2317	2.0 0.4 1.8 0.3
9	SU O	0635 1146 1922	2.2 0.3 2.0
10	M	0003 0724 1230 2016	0.2 2.3 0.1 2.1
11	TU	0047 0812 1313 2101	0.1 2.3 0.0 2.1
12	W	0129 0857 1356 2136	0.1 2.3 0.0 2.1
13	TH	0210 0938 1437 2209	0.1 2.3 0.1 2.0
14	F	0251 1016 1519 2243	0.2 2.1 0.2 1.8
15	SA ☾	0331 1056 1601 2323	0.4 1.9 0.4 1.6
16	SU	0414 1143 1648	0.5 1.6 0.6
17	M	0021 0510 1258 1750	1.5 0.7 1.4 0.7
18	TU	0154 0642 1430 1923	1.4 0.9 1.3 0.8
19	W	0311 0837 1544 2041	1.4 0.8 1.3 0.8
20	TH	0416 0931 1648 2137	1.6 0.7 1.5 0.7
21	F	0510 1018 1741 2226	1.8 0.6 1.6 0.5
22	SA	0558 1101 1827 2311	1.9 0.4 1.8 0.4
23	SU ●	0643 1142 1910 2351	2.0 0.3 1.9 0.3
24	M	0723 1219 1948	2.1 0.2 2.0
25	TU	0027 0800 1254 2020	0.2 2.1 0.1 2.0
26	W	0100 0831 1325 2046	0.2 2.0 0.2 1.9
27	TH	0129 0859 1352 2111	0.2 1.9 0.2 1.8
28	F	0154 0923 1415 2131	0.3 1.8 0.3 1.7
29	SA	0218 0941 1439 2149	0.3 1.7 0.3 1.6

MARCH

Date	Day	Time	m
1	SU	0243 1003 1508 2219	0.4 1.6 0.4 1.6
2	M ☽	0313 1041 1548 2303	0.4 1.5 0.5 1.5
3	TU	0401 1133 1648	0.6 1.4 0.6
4	W	0002 0519 1245 1803	1.4 0.7 1.3 0.6
5	TH	0132 0643 1446 1939	1.4 0.7 1.3 0.7
6	F	0318 0900 1606 2116	1.5 0.6 1.4 0.6
7	SA	0426 0954 1712 2211	1.7 0.5 1.6 0.4
8	SU	0525 1043 1812 2301	1.9 0.3 1.9 0.2
9	M O	0618 1130 1909 2347	2.1 0.1 2.1 0.1
10	TU	0709 1214 2002	2.3 0.0 2.2
11	W	0030 0800 1255 2045	0.0 2.4 -0.1 2.3
12	TH	0111 0846 1335 2120	-0.1 2.4 -0.1 2.2
13	F	0150 0924 1413 2151	0.0 2.3 0.0 2.1
14	SA	0227 0958 1450 2217	0.1 2.1 0.2 1.9
15	SU	0303 1031 1527 2247	0.3 1.8 0.4 1.7
16	M ☾	0341 1110 1605 2328	0.5 1.6 0.6 1.5
17	TU	0430 1210 1659	0.7 1.3 0.8
18	W	0107 0630 1413 1854	1.3 0.9 1.2 0.9
19	TH	0252 0801 1531 2009	1.3 0.8 1.3 0.8
20	F	0359 0858 1631 2106	1.5 0.7 1.4 0.7
21	SA	0451 0945 1720 2157	1.7 0.5 1.6 0.5
22	SU	0537 1031 1804 2244	1.8 0.4 1.8 0.4
23	M	0620 1114 1846 2327	2.0 0.2 1.9 0.3
24	TU ●	0701 1154 1924	2.1 0.1 2.0
25	W	0004 0737 1228 1956	0.2 2.1 0.1 2.0
26	TH	0037 0809 1258 2023	0.2 2.0 0.1 2.0
27	F	0104 0836 1322 2046	0.2 2.0 0.2 1.9
28	SA	0129 0856 1345 2101	0.2 1.8 0.2 1.8
29	SU	0153 0910 1410 2117	0.3 1.7 0.3 1.7
30	M	0219 0936 1438 2149	0.3 1.6 0.3 1.6
31	TU	0247 1016 1511 2234	0.4 1.5 0.4 1.5

APRIL

Date	Day	Time	m
1	W ☽	0327 1110 1610 2333	0.5 1.3 0.6 1.4
2	TH	0448 1226 1735	0.6 1.2 0.7
3	F	0059 0624 1431 1929	1.4 0.7 1.3 0.7
4	SA	0254 0855 1549 2058	1.5 0.6 1.5 0.6
5	SU	0403 0937 1652 2151	1.7 0.4 1.7 0.4
6	M	0503 1023 1750 2240	1.9 0.2 1.9 0.2
7	TU	0557 1109 1844 2327	2.1 0.1 2.1 0.1
8	W O	0649 1152 1934	2.3 0.0 2.3
9	TH	0009 0739 1232 2019	0.0 2.4 -0.1 2.3
10	F	0049 0825 1310 2057	0.0 2.4 0.0 2.3
11	SA	0126 0903 1346 2127	0.0 2.2 0.1 2.1
12	SU	0202 0935 1421 2152	0.2 2.0 0.3 1.9
13	M	0238 1008 1456 2222	0.3 1.8 0.5 1.7
14	TU ☾	0317 1047 1533 2301	0.5 1.5 0.7 1.5
15	W	0411 1140 1621 2356	0.7 1.3 0.9 1.3
16	TH	0604 1352 1818	0.8 1.2 0.9
17	F	0225 0717 1513 1930	1.3 0.8 1.3 0.9
18	SA	0333 0815 1606 2029	1.5 0.7 1.4 0.8
19	SU	0423 0906 1652 2121	1.6 0.5 1.6 0.6
20	M	0508 0954 1735 2209	1.8 0.4 1.8 0.4
21	TU	0550 1039 1814 2255	1.9 0.2 1.9 0.3
22	W	0630 1121 1852 2335	2.0 0.2 2.0 0.3
23	TH ●	0707 1158 1926	2.0 0.2 2.1
24	F	0009 0741 1226 1957	0.2 2.0 0.2 2.0
25	SA	0037 0809 1252 2020	0.2 1.9 0.2 2.0
26	SU	0104 0828 1319 2035	0.3 1.9 0.3 1.9
27	M	0132 0848 1349 2057	0.3 1.7 0.3 1.8
28	TU	0203 0920 1420 2133	0.3 1.6 0.4 1.7
29	W	0236 1005 1457 2221	0.4 1.5 0.5 1.6
30	TH ☽	0324 1103 1558 2322	0.5 1.4 0.6 1.5

MAY

Date	Day	Time	m
1	F	0443 1222 1723	0.6 1.3 0.7
2	SA	0044 0615 1415 1858	1.4 0.6 1.3 0.7
3	SU	0227 0840 1528 2028	1.5 0.5 1.5 0.6
4	M	0337 0914 1627 2125	1.7 0.4 1.7 0.4
5	TU	0437 0958 1722 2215	1.9 0.2 1.9 0.3
6	W	0532 1043 1815 2302	2.1 0.1 2.1 0.2
7	TH O	0624 1127 1903 2346	2.2 0.0 2.3 0.1
8	F	0713 1207 1949	2.3 0.0 2.3
9	SA	0025 0759 1244 2029	0.1 2.2 0.1 2.3
10	SU	0103 0838 1320 2102	0.2 2.1 0.2 2.1
11	M	0140 0914 1356 2132	0.3 1.9 0.4 2.0
12	TU	0219 0950 1433 2206	0.4 1.7 0.5 1.8
13	W	0304 1030 1512 2245	0.6 1.5 0.7 1.6
14	TH ☾	0406 1118 1602 2333	0.7 1.3 0.9 1.4
15	F	0530 1226 1737	0.8 1.2 0.9
16	SA	0045 0636 1434 1849	1.4 0.7 1.3 0.9
17	SU	0243 0734 1529 1949	1.4 0.6 1.4 0.8
18	M	0339 0827 1613 2043	1.5 0.5 1.6 0.7
19	TU	0426 0916 1656 2133	1.6 0.4 1.7 0.6
20	W	0510 1003 1737 2220	1.8 0.3 1.9 0.5
21	TH	0554 1046 1816 2302	1.9 0.3 2.0 0.4
22	F ●	0634 1123 1854 2339	1.9 0.3 2.0 0.4
23	SA	0712 1155 1928	1.9 0.3 2.1
24	SU	0011 0743 1226 1956	0.3 1.9 0.3 2.0
25	M	0043 0807 1300 2019	0.3 1.9 0.3 2.0
26	TU	0119 0837 1336 2051	0.3 1.8 0.3 1.9
27	W	0157 0916 1416 2131	0.3 1.7 0.4 1.8
28	TH	0241 1004 1502 2220	0.4 1.5 0.5 1.7
29	F	0335 1101 1602 2318	0.5 1.4 0.6 1.6
30	SA ☽	0441 1214 1710	0.5 1.4 0.7
31	SU	0029 0553 1348 1824	1.5 0.5 1.4 0.7

JUNE

Date	Day	Time	m
1	M	0155 0718 1459 1944	1.6 0.5 1.5 0.6
2	TU	0305 0837 1557 2053	1.7 0.4 1.7 0.5
3	W	0406 0928 1652 2148	1.8 0.3 1.9 0.4
4	TH	0504 1016 1745 2238	1.9 0.2 2.1 0.4
5	F O	0559 1101 1834 2325	2.0 0.2 2.2 0.3
6	SA	0650 1143 1920	2.1 0.2 2.2
7	SU	0006 0737 1222 2003	0.3 2.1 0.2 2.2
8	M	0046 0820 1301 2042	0.3 2.0 0.3 2.1
9	TU	0126 0858 1339 2117	0.3 1.9 0.4 2.0
10	W	0208 0935 1418 2152	0.4 1.7 0.5 1.9
11	TH	0254 1013 1457 2229	0.5 1.6 0.7 1.7
12	F	0347 1054 1538 2310	0.6 1.4 0.8 1.6
13	SA ☾	0449 1141 1628 2357	0.7 1.3 0.8 1.5
14	SU	0554 1243 1755	0.7 1.3 0.9
15	M	0100 0654 1409 1907	1.4 0.6 1.3 0.8
16	TU	0218 0749 1515 2005	1.4 0.6 1.5 0.8
17	W	0325 0839 1606 2056	1.5 0.5 1.6 0.7
18	TH	0422 0925 1655 2143	1.6 0.4 1.8 0.6
19	F	0514 1008 1740 2229	1.7 0.4 1.9 0.5
20	SA	0601 1050 1823 2311	1.8 0.4 2.0 0.5
21	SU ●	0644 1129 1901 2352	1.9 0.3 2.1 0.4
22	M	0723 1209 1937	1.9 0.3 2.1
23	TU	0032 0758 1249 2012	0.3 1.9 0.3 2.1
24	W	0113 0835 1331 2049	0.3 1.8 0.3 2.0
25	TH	0157 0917 1415 2132	0.3 1.8 0.3 2.0
26	F	0243 1003 1502 2218	0.3 1.7 0.4 1.9
27	SA	0333 1054 1554 2308	0.3 1.6 0.5 1.8
28	SU ☽	0427 1155 1650	0.4 1.5 0.6
29	M	0007 0526 1312 1752	1.6 0.5 1.5 0.7
30	TU	0120 0631 1424 1902	1.6 0.5 1.5 0.7

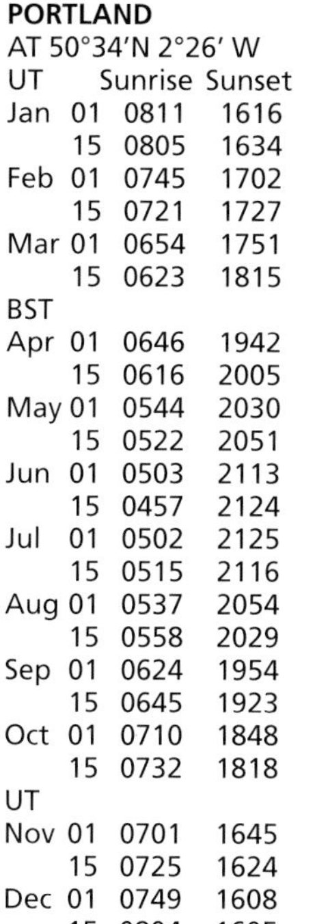

SUNRISE AND SUNSET TIMES
PORTLAND
AT 50°34′N 2°26′ W

UT		Sunrise	Sunset
Jan	01	0811	1616
	15	0805	1634
Feb	01	0745	1702
	15	0721	1727
Mar	01	0654	1751
	15	0623	1815
BST			
Apr	01	0646	1942
	15	0616	2005
May	01	0544	2030
	15	0522	2051
Jun	01	0503	2113
	15	0457	2124
Jul	01	0502	2125
	15	0515	2116
Aug	01	0537	2054
	15	0558	2029
Sep	01	0624	1954
	15	0645	1923
Oct	01	0710	1848
	15	0732	1818
UT			
Nov	01	0701	1645
	15	0725	1624
Dec	01	0749	1608
	15	0804	1605

JULY

m		Time	m		Time	m
1.4 0.6 1.5 0.8	1 W	0233 0747 1526 2019	1.6 0.5 1.6 0.7	16 TH	0210 0755 1506 2014	1.4 0.6 1.5 0.8
1.5 0.5 1.6 0.7	2 TH	0339 0857 1624 2129	1.6 0.5 1.8 0.6	17 F	0326 0846 1608 2111	1.4 0.6 1.6 0.7
1.6 0.4 1.8 0.6	3 F	0442 0952 1720 2226	1.7 0.4 1.9 0.5	18 SA	0434 0934 1703 2204	1.6 0.5 1.8 0.6
1.7 0.4 1.9 0.5	4 SA	0542 1042 1812 2315	1.8 0.4 2.1 0.4	19 SU	0532 1024 1753 2255	1.7 0.4 2.0 0.5
1.8 0.4 2.0 0.5	5 SU O	0635 1127 1859 2358	1.9 0.3 2.1 0.4	20 M ●	0623 1112 1838 2342	1.8 0.4 2.1 0.4
1.9 0.3 2.1 0.4	6 M	0723 1208 1944	1.9 0.3 2.2	21 TU	0710 1158 1922	1.9 0.3 2.2
1.9 0.3 2.1	7 TU	0037 0808 1246 2025	0.3 1.9 0.3 2.1	22 W	0026 0757 1241 2005	0.3 1.9 0.2 2.2
0.3 1.9 0.3 2.1	8 W	0117 0845 1325 2102	0.3 1.9 0.4 2.1	23 TH	0108 0841 1324 2047	0.2 1.9 0.2 2.2
0.3 1.8 0.3 2.0	9 TH	0156 0919 1402 2135	0.3 1.8 0.4 1.9	24 F	0151 0921 1407 2128	0.1 1.9 0.2 2.1
0.3 1.8 0.3 2.0	10 F	0237 0952 1438 2208	0.4 1.7 0.5 1.8	25 SA	0234 0959 1450 2209	0.2 1.8 0.3 2.0
0.3 1.7 0.4 1.9	11 SA	0316 1026 1509 2241	0.5 1.5 0.6 1.7	26 SU	0318 1041 1536 2252	0.2 1.7 0.4 1.9
0.3 1.6 0.5 1.8	12 SU ☾	0352 1102 1538 2316	0.5 1.4 0.7 1.5	27 M ☽	0405 1130 1624 2343	0.3 1.6 0.5 1.7
0.4 1.5 0.6	13 M	0423 1144 1619 2358	0.6 1.4 0.7 1.4	28 TU	0455 1234 1720	0.4 1.5 0.6
1.6 0.5 1.5 0.7	14 TU	0506 1239 1717	0.6 1.3 0.8	29 W	0048 0555 1352 1828	1.5 0.6 1.5 0.8
1.6 0.5 1.5 0.7	15 W	0054 0610 1353 1832	1.4 0.6 1.4 0.8	30 TH	0209 0710 1502 2006	1.4 0.7 1.5 0.8
				31 F	0324 0838 1605 2129	1.5 0.7 1.7 0.7

AUGUST

	Time	m		Time
1 SA	0431 0938 1703 2222	1.6 0.6 1.8 0.6	16 SU	0403 0913 1632 2151
2 SU	0532 1028 1755 2308	1.7 0.5 2.0 0.5	17 M	0509 1007 1728 2242
3 M O	0624 1114 1842 2349	1.8 0.4 2.1 0.3	18 TU	0605 1057 1818 2329
4 TU	0711 1154 1927	1.9 0.3 2.2	19 W ●	0658 1144 1906
5 W	0026 0754 1232 2008	0.2 1.9 0.3 2.2	20 TH	0013 0750 1228 1954
6 TH	0103 0830 1308 2044	0.2 1.9 0.3 2.1	21 F	0055 0840 1310 2039
7 F	0138 0859 1343 2114	0.2 1.9 0.3 2.0	22 SA	0135 0918 1351 2118
8 SA	0212 0927 1414 2143	0.3 1.8 0.4 1.9	23 SU	0216 0949 1431 2154
9 SU	0241 0954 1439 2209	0.4 1.7 0.5 1.7	24 M	0256 1021 1512 2232
10 M	0303 1021 1503 2235	0.4 1.5 0.5 1.6	25 TU ☽	0336 1059 1554 2316
11 TU ☾	0329 1052 1537 2307	0.5 1.5 0.6 1.5	26 W	0420 1151 1646
12 W	0408 1133 1628 2352	0.6 1.4 0.7 1.4	27 TH	0017 0516 1323 1808
13 TH	0504 1232 1735	0.6 1.4 0.8	28 F	0158 0650 1446 2014
14 F	0059 0612 1403 1852	1.3 0.7 1.4 0.8	29 SA	0318 0822 1553 2114
15 SA	0240 0741 1527 2056	1.3 0.7 1.5 0.7	30 SU	0425 0919 1650 2202
			31 M	0520 1009 1739 2246

SEPTEMBER

	Time	m		Time	m
1 TU	0607 1055 1824 2328	1.8 0.4 2.1 0.3	16 W	0547 1038 1757 2310	1.9 0.4 2.1 0.2
2 W O	0651 1136 1907	2.0 0.3 2.2	17 TH ●	0638 1125 1846 2353	2.1 0.2 2.3 0.1
3 TH	0006 0732 1213 1947	0.2 2.0 0.2 2.2	18 F	0729 1209 1934	2.2 0.1 2.4
4 F	0042 0806 1248 2020	0.1 2.0 0.2 2.1	19 SA	0034 0816 1250 2020	0.0 2.3 0.0 2.4
5 SA	0114 0833 1319 2048	0.2 2.0 0.2 2.0	20 SU	0113 0856 1329 2100	0.0 2.3 0.1 2.3
6 SU	0142 0857 1346 2114	0.2 1.9 0.3 1.9	21 M	0151 0927 1407 2134	0.1 2.2 0.2 2.2
7 M	0204 0919 1408 2135	0.3 1.8 0.4 1.7	22 TU	0227 0953 1444 2209	0.3 2.0 0.3 1.9
8 TU	0223 0938 1430 2153	0.4 1.7 0.5 1.6	23 W	0303 1026 1524 2251	0.5 1.8 0.6 1.7
9 W	0246 1003 1457 2222	0.5 1.6 0.6 1.5	24 TH ☽	0341 1109 1617 2351	0.7 1.6 0.8 1.4
10 TH ☾	0318 1042 1537 2309	0.6 1.5 0.7 1.4	25 F	0432 1254 1815	0.9 1.4 0.9
11 F	0413 1138 1654	0.7 1.4 0.8	26 SA	0151 0634 1432 1942	1.3 1.0 1.4 0.9
12 SA	0016 0531 1301 2014	1.3 0.8 1.4 0.8	27 SU	0314 0752 1540 2041	1.4 1.0 1.6 0.7
13 SU	0217 0703 1456 2052	1.3 0.8 1.5 0.7	28 M	0415 0849 1632 2129	1.5 0.8 1.8 0.6
14 M	0345 0858 1606 2137	1.4 0.7 1.7 0.5	29 TU	0501 0940 1718 2214	1.7 0.7 1.9 0.4
15 TU	0450 0949 1704 2224	1.7 0.5 1.9 0.4	30 W	0544 1027 1801 2258	1.9 0.5 2.1 0.3

OCTOBER

	Time	m		Time	m
1 TH O	0625 1109 1842 2338	2.0 0.4 2.2 0.2	16 F ●	0613 1101 1822 2327	2.2 0.3 2.3 0.1
2 F	0703 1148 1920	2.1 0.3 2.2	17 SA	0659 1145 1909	2.3 0.2 2.4
3 SA	0013 0736 1222 1952	0.2 2.1 0.2 2.1	18 SU	0008 0744 1226 1954	0.1 2.4 0.1 2.4
4 SU	0044 0802 1251 2019	0.2 2.1 0.3 2.0	19 M	0047 0823 1304 2034	0.1 2.4 0.2 2.3
5 M	0108 0825 1316 2043	0.3 2.0 0.3 1.9	20 TU	0123 0855 1342 2111	0.2 2.3 0.3 2.1
6 TU	0129 0844 1339 2059	0.4 1.9 0.4 1.8	21 W	0158 0925 1420 2149	0.4 2.1 0.4 1.9
7 W	0149 0858 1401 2117	0.4 1.8 0.5 1.7	22 TH	0233 1001 1502 2233	0.6 1.9 0.6 1.6
8 TH	0211 0923 1425 2150	0.5 1.7 0.5 1.5	23 F ☽	0310 1046 1605 2332	0.8 1.6 0.8 1.4
9 F	0235 1004 1456 2241	0.6 1.6 0.6 1.4	24 SA	0400 1152 1750	1.0 1.5 0.9
10 SA ☾	0308 1102 1617 2355	0.7 1.5 0.8 1.3	25 SU	0135 0559 1409 1858	1.3 1.1 1.4 0.9
11 SU	0457 1226 2016	0.9 1.4 0.8	26 M	0300 0711 1516 1956	1.4 1.1 1.6 0.8
12 M	0204 0643 1429 2040	1.3 0.9 1.5 0.7	27 TU	0352 0810 1606 2048	1.6 0.9 1.7 0.6
13 TU	0328 0837 1541 2116	1.5 0.7 1.7 0.5	28 W	0435 0902 1650 2134	1.8 0.8 1.9 0.5
14 W	0429 0926 1639 2159	1.7 0.6 1.9 0.3	29 TH	0516 0950 1733 2219	1.9 0.6 2.0 0.3
15 TH	0523 1015 1732 2244	2.0 0.4 2.1 0.2	30 F	0554 1035 1812 2302	2.1 0.5 2.1 0.3
			31 SA O	0631 1116 1849 2339	2.1 0.4 2.1 0.3

NOVEMBER

	Time	m		Time	m
1 SU	0702 1153 1922	2.2 0.4 2.1	16 M	0711 1202 1927	2.4 0.3 2.3
2 M	0010 0731 1222 1951	0.3 2.2 0.4 2.0	17 TU	0021 0751 1242 2011	0.2 2.4 0.3 2.2
3 TU	0035 0756 1248 2015	0.4 2.1 0.4 1.9	18 W	0059 0830 1322 2053	0.3 2.3 0.4 2.1
4 W	0059 0814 1315 2033	0.4 2.0 0.4 1.8	19 TH	0136 0907 1404 2135	0.5 2.1 0.5 1.9
5 TH	0125 0833 1343 2058	0.5 1.9 0.5 1.7	20 F	0214 0947 1451 2219	0.6 1.9 0.6 1.7
6 F	0151 0903 1413 2136	0.5 1.8 0.5 1.6	21 SA	0254 1031 1555 2309	0.8 1.7 0.8 1.5
7 SA	0218 0946 1452 2231	0.6 1.7 0.6 1.4	22 SU ☽	0345 1123 1711	1.0 1.6 0.8
8 SU ☾	0253 1046 1609 2344	0.8 1.6 0.7 1.3	23 M	0026 0513 1249 1814	1.3 1.1 1.5 0.8
9 M	0438 1206 2015	0.9 1.5 0.8	24 TU	0218 0626 1431 1912	1.4 1.1 1.5 0.8
10 TU	0141 0614 1353 2031	1.3 0.9 1.5 0.7	25 W	0315 0728 1525 2005	1.5 1.0 1.6 0.6
11 W	0303 0757 1509 2046	1.5 0.8 1.7 0.5	26 TH	0359 0822 1612 2054	1.7 0.9 1.7 0.5
12 TH	0401 0856 1608 2129	1.8 0.7 1.9 0.4	27 F	0440 0912 1656 2140	1.8 0.7 1.8 0.5
13 F	0453 0946 1703 2214	2.0 0.5 2.1 0.3	28 SA	0518 0959 1738 2225	2.0 0.6 1.9 0.4
14 SA	0542 1034 1754 2259	2.2 0.4 2.2 0.2	29 SU	0555 1043 1817 2305	2.1 0.5 2.0 0.4
15 SU ●	0628 1119 1842 2342	2.3 0.3 2.3 0.2	30 M O	0631 1122 1854 2339	2.1 0.5 2.0 0.4

DECEMBER

	Time	m		Time	m
1 TU	0703 1156 1927	2.2 0.5 2.0	16 W	0002 0732 1228 2000	0.3 2.3 0.4 2.1
2 W	0008 0732 1227 1956	0.4 2.1 0.5 1.9	17 TH	0043 0815 1311 2044	0.4 2.3 0.4 2.0
3 TH	0039 0758 1300 2022	0.4 2.1 0.5 1.8	18 F	0122 0857 1354 2125	0.5 2.2 0.4 1.9
4 F	0113 0826 1337 2055	0.5 2.0 0.5 1.7	19 SA	0202 0937 1440 2203	0.6 2.0 0.5 1.7
5 SA	0149 0902 1417 2137	0.5 1.9 0.5 1.6	20 SU	0242 1016 1531 2242	0.7 1.9 0.6 1.6
6 SU	0228 0947 1506 2228	0.6 1.8 0.6 1.5	21 M ☽	0323 1056 1628 2326	0.8 1.7 0.7 1.4
7 M	0318 1041 1607 2330	0.7 1.7 0.6 1.4	22 TU	0409 1142 1728	0.9 1.5 0.7
8 TU ☾	0427 1147 1714	0.8 1.6 0.6	23 W	0020 0521 1241 1828	1.4 1.0 1.4 0.7
9 W	0057 0541 1310 2100	1.4 0.8 1.6 0.7	24 TH	0142 0641 1401 1925	1.4 1.0 1.4 0.7
10 TH	0223 0658 1430 1946	1.5 0.8 1.6 0.6	25 F	0256 0743 1511 2017	1.5 0.9 1.5 0.6
11 F	0324 0814 1533 2051	1.7 0.7 1.8 0.5	26 SA	0349 0837 1608 2105	1.6 0.8 1.6 0.6
12 SA	0419 0915 1632 2144	1.9 0.6 1.9 0.4	27 SU	0435 0926 1700 2151	1.8 0.7 1.7 0.5
13 SU	0511 1008 1729 2233	2.1 0.5 2.0 0.4	28 M	0519 1013 1748 2234	1.9 0.7 1.8 0.5
14 M ●	0600 1059 1822 2319	2.2 0.4 2.1 0.3	29 TU	0601 1058 1831 2314	2.0 0.6 1.8 0.5
15 TU	0647 1145 1912	2.3 0.4 2.1	30 W O	0640 1138 1911 2352	2.1 0.5 1.9 0.4
			31 TH	0716 1217 1948	2.1 0.5 1.9

POOLE HARBOUR
LAT 50°42'N
LONG 1°59'W

TIMES AND HEIGHTS OF HIGH AND LOW WATER (Heights in Metres)

TIME ZONE UT
For Summer Time (area enclosed in shaded box) add 1 hour

Sea level is above mean tide level from 2 hours after LW to 2 hours before the next LW. HW will occur between 5 hours after LW and 3 hours before the next LW. Predictions are for the first identified HW occuring between these times (but lower or higher HWs may occur earlier or later than this).

2020

JANUARY

Day	Time	m	Time	m	Time	m	Time	m
1 W ☽	0759	1.2	1109	1.8	2012	0.9	2328	1.6
2 TH	0841	1.2	1144	1.7	2056	1.0		
3 F ☽	0008	1.6	0930	1.3	1226	1.7	2147	1.1
4 SA	0101	1.5	1027	1.3	1320	1.6	2247	1.1
5 SU	0748	1.9	1133	1.3	1440	1.5	2352	1.1
6 M	0900	1.9	1239	1.2	1827	1.6		
7 TU	0054	1.1	0647	1.8	1334	1.0	1856	1.7
8 W	0149	1.0	0552	1.9	1424	0.9	1934	1.8
9 TH	0240	0.9	0639	2.0	1510	0.7	2019	1.9
10 F ○	0328	0.8	0742	2.1	1556	0.5	2106	2.0
11 SA	0414	0.7	0908	2.2	1640	0.4	2152	2.1
12 SU	0459	0.6	0958	2.3	1724	0.4	2237	2.2
13 M	0544	0.6	1043	2.3	1808	0.4	2321	2.1
14 TU	0630	0.7	1127	2.3	1854	0.4		
15 W	0005	2.0	0718	0.8	1209	2.2	1942	0.5
16 TH	0050	1.9	0808	0.9	1250	2.0	2033	0.6
17 F ☾	0137	1.8	0905	1.0	1330	1.9	2133	0.8
18 SA	0228	1.7	1012	1.1	1414	1.8	2242	0.9
19 SU	0736	2.0	1122	1.1	1507	1.7	2352	0.9
20 M	0834	1.9	1229	1.0	1610	1.6		
21 TU	0056	0.9	0704	1.9	1330	0.9	1922	1.8
22 W	0154	0.9	0741	1.9	1425	0.8	2004	1.8
23 TH	0247	0.8	0817	2.0	1514	0.7	2043	1.9
24 F ●	0335	0.8	0849	2.1	1559	0.6	2116	1.9
25 SA	0420	0.7	0915	2.1	1641	0.5	2145	2.0
26 SU	0501	0.7	0945	2.2	1720	0.5	2216	2.0
27 M	0540	0.8	1020	2.2	1757	0.5	2252	2.0
28 TU	0616	0.8	1057	2.1	1830	0.6	2330	1.9
29 W	0649	0.9	1131	2.0	1902	0.7	2359	1.8
30 TH	0723	0.9	1051	1.8	1937	0.8	2300	1.7
31 F	0801	1.0	1113	1.8	2017	0.9	2326	1.6

FEBRUARY

Day	Time	m	Time	m	Time	m	Time	m
1 SA	0845	1.1	1144	1.7	2103	1.0		
2 SU ☽	0001	1.6	0937	1.1	1223	1.6	2159	1.1
3 M	0050	1.6	1036	1.2	1319	1.6	2301	1.1
4 TU	0213	1.6	1143	1.2	1512	1.5		
5 W	0008	1.1	0417	1.7	1251	1.1	1703	1.6
6 TH	0115	1.1	0518	1.8	1355	0.9	1929	1.7
7 F	0216	0.9	0615	1.9	1450	0.7	2014	1.9
8 SA	0311	0.8	0818	2.1	1540	0.5	2059	2.0
9 SU ○	0400	0.6	0907	2.2	1626	0.3	2143	2.2
10 M	0446	0.5	0952	2.4	1709	0.2	2224	2.3
11 TU	0530	0.4	1034	2.4	1752	0.1	2305	2.3
12 W	0614	0.4	1115	2.4	1836	0.2	2345	2.2
13 TH	0658	0.5	1154	2.3	1920	0.4		
14 F	0025	2.0	0745	0.7	1230	2.1	2008	0.6
15 SA ☾	0104	1.9	0836	0.9	1302	1.9	2101	0.8
16 SU	0141	1.7	0936	1.0	1331	1.7	2210	1.0
17 M	0224	1.6	1052	1.1	1427	1.6	2330	1.1
18 TU	0325	1.6	1208	1.1	1539	1.5		
19 W	0043	1.1	0702	1.8	1316	1.0	1933	1.7
20 TH	0145	1.0	0735	1.8	1412	0.9	2006	1.8
21 F	0237	0.9	0810	1.9	1501	0.7	2040	1.8
22 SA	0324	0.8	0838	1.9	1545	0.6	2108	1.9
23 SU ●	0406	0.7	0854	2.0	1625	0.5	2126	2.0
24 M	0444	0.7	0919	2.1	1701	0.5	2149	2.0
25 TU	0520	0.7	0956	2.2	1734	0.5	2222	2.1
26 W	0551	0.7	1034	2.1	1803	0.6	2259	2.0
27 TH	0620	0.7	1110	2.0	1831	0.6	2333	1.9
28 F	0651	0.8	1125	1.9	1904	0.7	2236	1.8
29 SA	0726	0.8	1043	1.8	1941	0.8	2246	1.8

MARCH

Day	Time	m	Time	m	Time	m	Time	m
1 SU	0806	0.9	1103	1.8	2024	0.9	2316	1.8
2 M ☽	0854	1.0	1140	1.7	2116	1.1	2359	1.7
3 TU	0951	1.1	1229	1.6	2219	1.2		
4 W	0056	1.6	1102	1.1	1344	1.5	2333	1.2
5 TH	0337	1.6	1218	1.1	2107	1.7		
6 F	0050	1.2	0501	1.7	1331	0.9	1924	1.8
7 SA	0159	1.0	0721	1.9	1430	0.6	2005	1.9
8 SU	0255	0.8	0810	2.1	1520	0.4	2047	2.1
9 M ○	0343	0.5	0856	2.3	1607	0.2	2127	2.3
10 TU	0428	0.4	0938	2.4	1649	0.0	2206	2.4
11 W	0511	0.3	1019	2.5	1731	0.0	2245	2.4
12 TH	0553	0.3	1058	2.5	1813	0.1	2323	2.3
13 F	0635	0.4	1136	2.3	1856	0.3		
14 SA	0000	2.1	0720	0.6	1212	2.1	1942	0.6
15 SU	0032	1.9	0808	0.8	1238	1.9	2034	0.9
16 M ☾	0049	1.7	0906	1.0	1245	1.7	2143	1.1
17 TU	0119	1.6	1023	1.1	1350	1.5	2312	1.3
18 W	0241	1.6	1146	1.1	2029	1.9		
19 TH	0029	1.2	0641	1.7	1255	1.0	2154	1.9
20 F	0129	1.1	0500	1.6	1352	0.9	1953	1.8
21 SA	0219	1.0	0546	1.7	1439	0.8	2023	1.8
22 SU	0304	0.9	0642	1.8	1522	0.6	2045	1.9
23 M	0345	0.7	0759	2.0	1601	0.5	2048	2.0
24 TU ●	0422	0.7	0846	2.1	1636	0.5	2114	2.1
25 W	0455	0.6	0928	2.2	1707	0.5	2151	2.2
26 TH	0524	0.6	1008	2.2	1734	0.6	2227	2.1
27 F	0551	0.6	1045	2.1	1802	0.6	2258	2.0
28 SA	0621	0.7	1113	1.9	1834	0.7	2221	1.9
29 SU	0654	0.7	1019	1.8	1909	0.8	2213	1.9
30 M	0732	0.8	1034	1.8	1950	1.0	2245	1.9
31 TU	0816	0.9	1112	1.7	2038	1.1	2330	1.8

APRIL

Day	Time	m	Time	m	Time	m	Time	m
1 W ☽	0911	1.0	1202	1.6	2143	1.2		
2 TH	0025	1.7	1027	1.1	1317	1.5	2307	1.3
3 F	0204	1.6	1151	1.0	2021	1.8		
4 SA	0031	1.2	0616	1.7	1307	0.9	1908	1.8
5 SU	0139	1.0	0702	1.9	1406	0.6	1946	2.0
6 M	0234	0.7	0752	2.1	1457	0.4	2026	2.2
7 TU	0322	0.5	0836	2.3	1543	0.2	2105	2.3
8 W ○	0406	0.3	0919	2.4	1626	0.1	2144	2.4
9 TH	0448	0.2	1000	2.5	1708	0.1	2222	2.4
10 F	0530	0.3	1039	2.4	1750	0.2	2259	2.3
11 SA	0612	0.4	1118	2.3	1833	0.5	2335	2.2
12 SU	0657	0.6	1155	2.1	1920	0.8	2359	2.0
13 M	0745	0.8	1226	1.8	2014	1.0	2351	1.8
14 TU ☾	0841	1.0	1209	1.7	2123	1.2		
15 W	0025	1.7	0955	1.1	1302	1.5	2249	1.3
16 TH	0131	1.6	1115	1.1	2011	2.0		
17 F	0000	1.3	0605	1.7	1222	1.1	2124	2.0
18 SA	0100	1.2	0439	1.6	1319	1.0	1928	1.8
19 SU	0151	1.1	0521	1.7	1408	0.9	1954	1.8
20 M	0236	0.9	0613	1.8	1452	0.8	2002	1.9
21 TU	0317	0.8	0716	1.9	1532	0.7	1955	2.0
22 W	0353	0.7	0814	2.0	1606	0.7	2037	2.1
23 TH ●	0426	0.7	0900	2.1	1637	0.7	2116	2.2
24 F	0454	0.6	0941	2.2	1705	0.7	2153	2.2
25 SA	0524	0.6	1019	2.1	1735	0.7	2222	2.1
26 SU	0555	0.7	1051	2.0	1808	0.8	2219	2.0
27 M	0629	0.7	1057	1.9	1845	0.9	2153	2.0
28 TU	0707	0.8	1017	1.8	1926	1.0	2227	1.9
29 W	0751	0.9	1058	1.7	2016	1.2	2314	1.9
30 TH ☽	0847	1.0	1153	1.6	2124	1.3		

MAY

Day	Time	m	Time	m	Time	m	Time	m
1 F	0014	1.8	1005	1.0	1908	1.9	2251	1.3
2 SA	0316	1.7	1127	1.0	2007	1.9		
3 SU	0008	1.2	0431	1.8	1238	0.8	1844	1.9
4 M	0113	1.0	0638	1.9	1337	0.6	1921	2.1
5 TU	0207	0.8	0729	2.1	1429	0.4	2001	2.2
6 W	0256	0.6	0815	2.2	1516	0.3	2041	2.3
7 TH ○	0342	0.4	0858	2.3	1601	0.2	2120	2.4
8 F	0425	0.3	0939	2.4	1645	0.3	2158	2.4
9 SA	0508	0.3	1020	2.3	1728	0.4	2236	2.3
10 SU	0552	0.4	1100	2.2	1814	0.6	2312	2.2
11 M	0637	0.6	1140	2.0	1902	0.9	2342	2.0
12 TU	0726	0.8	1223	1.8	1957	1.1	2323	1.9
13 W	0820	0.9	1144	1.7	2101	1.3	2355	1.8
14 TH ☾	0922	1.0	1224	1.6	2214	1.3		
15 F	0041	1.7	1034	1.1	1941	2.0	2322	1.3
16 SA	0532	1.7	1141	1.1	2044	2.0		
17 SU	0021	1.3	0607	1.6	1239	1.1	1908	1.8
18 M	0114	1.2	0500	1.7	1331	1.0	1922	1.8
19 TU	0201	1.0	0548	1.7	1416	0.9	1850	1.9
20 W	0243	0.9	0646	1.8	1456	0.9	1916	2.0
21 TH	0320	0.8	0743	2.0	1532	0.8	1957	2.1
22 F ●	0353	0.8	0831	2.0	1605	0.8	2038	2.2
23 SA	0426	0.7	0914	2.1	1638	0.8	2115	2.2
24 SU	0459	0.7	0955	2.1	1713	0.8	2147	2.2
25 M	0535	0.7	1034	2.0	1750	0.9	2212	2.1
26 TU	0612	0.7	1113	1.9	1830	1.0	2209	2.0
27 W	0654	0.8	1157	1.9	1916	1.1	2229	2.0
28 TH	0741	0.8	1113	1.7	2011	1.2	2316	1.9
29 F	0838	0.9	1415	1.7	2117	1.2		
30 SA ☽	0020	1.8	0948	0.9	1859	2.0	2231	1.2
31 SU	0249	1.8	1100	0.9	1956	2.0	2341	1.1

JUNE

Day	Time	m	Time	m	Time	m	Time	m
1 M	0352	1.8	1207	0.8	1820	1.9		
2 TU	0043	1.0	0617	1.9	1307	0.7	1859	2.0
3 W	0139	0.8	0709	2.0	1401	0.6	1939	2.2
4 TH	0230	0.7	0756	2.1	1451	0.5	2020	2.3
5 F ○	0319	0.5	0840	2.2	1539	0.5	2059	2.3
6 SA	0405	0.5	0922	2.2	1626	0.5	2138	2.4
7 SU	0450	0.4	1004	2.2	1711	0.6	2216	2.3
8 M	0535	0.5	1044	2.1	1758	0.8	2252	2.2
9 TU	0620	0.6	1125	2.0	1846	0.9	2327	2.1
10 W	0707	0.7	1209	1.9	1937	1.1	2317	1.9
11 TH	0755	0.8	1305	1.7	2030	1.2	2333	1.8
12 F	0844	1.0	1156	1.7	2127	1.3		
13 SA ☾	0009	1.7	0937	1.1	1239	1.6	2229	1.3
14 SU	0056	1.7	1037	1.2	1953	2.0	2332	1.3
15 M	0159	1.6	1144	1.2	2051	2.0		
16 TU	0029	1.3	0601	1.6	1242	1.2	2148	1.9
17 W	0119	1.2	0600	1.7	1331	1.1	1841	1.9
18 TH	0202	1.1	0631	1.8	1414	1.0	1832	2.0
19 F	0242	0.9	0717	1.8	1454	1.0	1857	2.1
20 SA	0321	0.8	0806	1.9	1535	0.9	1942	2.1
21 SU ●	0400	0.7	0854	2.0	1615	0.9	2035	2.2
22 M	0439	0.7	0940	2.1	1656	0.9	2130	2.2
23 TU	0520	0.6	1025	2.1	1738	0.9	2219	2.2
24 W	0602	0.6	1109	2.1	1822	0.9	2305	2.2
25 TH	0646	0.6	1155	2.0	1910	1.0	2350	2.1
26 F	0733	0.7	1244	1.9	2002	1.1		
27 SA	0037	2.0	0826	0.8	1335	1.9	2101	1.1
28 SU ☽	0126	1.9	0926	0.8	1430	1.8	2205	1.1
29 M	0219	1.9	1031	0.9	1935	2.0	2311	1.1
30 TU	0315	1.8	1137	0.9	1805	1.9		

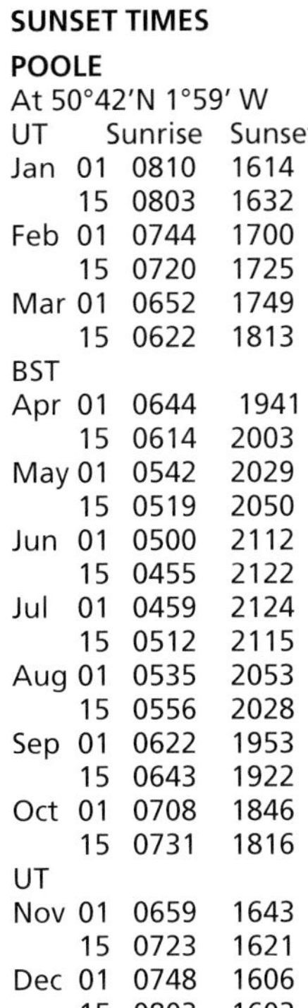

SUNRISE AND SUNSET TIMES

POOLE
At 50°42'N 1°59' W

UT		Sunrise	Sunset
Jan	01	0810	1614
	15	0803	1632
Feb	01	0744	1700
	15	0720	1725
Mar	01	0652	1749
	15	0622	1813
BST			
Apr	01	0644	1941
	15	0614	2003
May	01	0542	2029
	15	0519	2050
Jun	01	0500	2112
	15	0455	2122
Jul	01	0459	2124
	15	0512	2115
Aug	01	0535	2053
	15	0556	2028
Sep	01	0622	1953
	15	0643	1922
Oct	01	0708	1846
	15	0731	1816
UT			
Nov	01	0659	1643
	15	0723	1621
Dec	01	0748	1606
	15	0803	1603

JULY

Day	Time	m	Day	Time	m
1 W	0014 0418 1239 1844	1.0 1.8 0.8 2.0	16 TH	0012 0332 1225 1835	1.3 1.6 1.2 1.8
2 TH	0114 0658 1337 1925	0.9 1.9 0.8 2.1	17 F	0111 0455 1326 1725	1.2 1.7 1.2 1.9
3 F	0209 0745 1432 2005	0.8 2.0 0.8 2.2	18 SA	0204 0600 1421 1813	1.0 1.8 1.1 2.0
4 SA	0301 0830 1523 2044	0.7 2.0 0.7 2.2	19 SU	0252 0758 1510 1907	0.9 1.9 1.0 2.1
5 SU	0350 0911 1612 ○ 2121	0.6 2.1 0.7 2.3	20 M	0339 0847 1557 ● 2034	0.7 2.0 0.9 2.2
6 M	0436 0951 1658 2157	0.5 2.1 0.8 2.3	21 TU	0423 0933 1642 2134	0.6 2.1 0.8 2.3
7 TU	0520 1029 1744 2233	0.5 2.1 0.8 2.3	22 W	0507 1017 1726 2221	0.5 2.2 0.8 2.3
8 W	0604 1106 1828 2308	0.6 2.1 0.9 2.2	23 TH	0550 1100 1811 2305	0.4 2.2 0.8 2.3
9 TH	0646 1144 1911 2341	0.7 2.0 1.0 2.0	24 F	0633 1142 1856 2347	0.4 2.2 0.8 2.3
10 F	0726 1224 1953 2320	0.8 1.8 1.1 1.9	25 SA	0717 1224 1943	0.5 2.1 0.9
11 SA	0804 1133 2034 2341	0.9 1.7 1.2 1.8	26 SU	0028 0805 1307 2035	2.2 0.6 2.0 1.0
12 SU ☾	0844 1202 2119	1.0 1.7 1.3	27 M	0109 0859 1352 ☽ 2135	2.0 0.8 1.9 1.1
13 M	0017 0930 1245 2210	1.7 1.1 1.7 1.3	28 TU	0152 1001 1443 2243	1.9 0.9 1.8 1.1
14 TU	0104 1022 1341 2308	1.7 1.2 1.6 1.3	29 W	0242 1111 2000 2352	1.8 1.0 2.0 1.1
15 W	0204 1122 1511	1.6 1.2 1.7	30 TH	0343 1219 1839	1.7 1.0 2.0
			31 F	0056 0700 1323 1918	1.0 1.8 1.0 2.0

AUGUST

Day	Time	m	Day	Time	m
1 SA	0156 0746 1422 1957	0.9 1.9 1.0 2.1	16 SU	0133 0714 1355 1752	1.1 1.7 1.2 1.9
2 SU	0250 0828 1514 2034	0.8 1.9 0.9 2.1	17 M	0230 0757 1452 1947	0.9 1.9 1.0 2.1
3 M	0339 0906 1602 ○ 2106	0.6 2.0 0.8 2.2	18 TU	0320 0841 1541 2042	0.6 2.0 0.8 2.2
4 TU	0424 0939 1646 2136	0.5 2.1 0.8 2.3	19 W	0406 0923 1627 ● 2128	0.4 2.2 0.7 2.4
5 W	0505 1009 1727 2208	0.5 2.1 0.8 2.3	20 TH	0449 1004 1709 2212	0.3 2.3 0.6 2.5
6 TH	0544 1040 1805 2243	0.5 2.1 0.8 2.3	21 F	0531 1044 1752 2253	0.2 2.4 0.6 2.5
7 F	0620 1113 1841 2318	0.6 2.1 0.9 2.1	22 SA	0613 1123 1834 2333	0.3 2.3 0.6 2.4
8 SA	0653 1148 1914 2345	0.7 2.0 1.0 2.0	23 SU	0655 1203 1919	0.4 2.2 0.7
9 SU	0725 1122 1950 2313	0.8 1.8 1.1 1.9	24 M	0012 0740 1241 2008	2.3 0.6 2.1 0.9
10 M	0802 1127 2030 2339	0.9 1.8 1.1 1.8	25 TU	0050 0830 1321 ☽ 2105	2.1 0.8 1.9 1.1
11 TU ☾	0844 1159 2118	1.1 1.7 1.2	26 W	0128 0932 1405 2218	1.9 1.0 1.8 1.2
12 W	0015 0936 1240 2215	1.7 1.2 1.7 1.3	27 TH	0218 1052 1928 2336	1.7 1.2 2.0 1.2
13 TH	0105 1035 1341 2318	1.6 1.3 1.7 1.3	28 F	0807 1210 1836	1.9 1.2 1.9
14 F	0225 1140 1530	1.6 1.3 1.7	29 SA	0046 0931 1318 1909	1.1 1.9 1.2 2.0
15 SA	0026 0944 1249 1654	1.2 1.8 1.3 1.8	30 SU	0146 0747 1414 1946	0.9 1.9 1.1 2.0
			31 M	0238 0822 1503 2020	0.8 1.9 0.9 2.1

SEPTEMBER

Day	Time	m	Day	Time	m
1 TU	0324 0854 1547 2045	0.6 2.0 0.8 2.2	16 W	0258 0826 1521 2030	0.6 2.1 0.8 2.3
2 W	0406 0920 1628 ○ 2107	0.5 2.1 0.8 2.3	17 TH	0344 0905 1606 ● 2113	0.3 2.3 0.6 2.5
3 TH	0444 0940 1705 2139	0.5 2.2 0.7 2.3	18 F	0427 0945 1648 2155	0.2 2.5 0.4 2.6
4 F	0520 1007 1739 2216	0.5 2.2 0.8 2.3	19 SA	0508 1023 1729 2236	0.1 2.5 0.4 2.6
5 SA	0551 1041 1809 2252	0.6 2.2 0.8 2.2	20 SU	0549 1102 1810 2315	0.2 2.5 0.5 2.5
6 SU	0619 1115 1837 2325	0.7 2.1 0.9 2.0	21 M	0631 1140 1853 2355	0.4 2.3 0.6 2.3
7 M	0649 1129 1910 2248	0.8 1.9 1.0 1.9	22 TU	0715 1216 1941	0.6 2.1 0.8
8 TU	0723 1050 1948 2256	0.9 1.9 1.0 1.8	23 W	0033 0805 1250 2038	2.0 0.9 1.9 1.1
9 W	0803 1107 2034 2321	1.1 1.8 1.1 1.8	24 TH	0114 0911 1325 ☽ 2157	1.8 1.2 1.8 1.2
10 TH ☾	0852 1140 2131	1.2 1.8 1.2	25 F	0640 1042 1900 2321	2.0 1.3 2.0 1.2
11 F	0003 0954 1229 2239	1.7 1.3 1.8 1.3	26 SA	0757 1201 1810	2.0 1.3 1.9
12 SA	0111 1106 1416 2354	1.6 1.4 1.7 1.2	27 SU	0030 0925 1304 1845	1.1 2.0 1.2 1.9
13 SU	0848 1224 1826	1.8 1.4 1.8	28 M	0127 0728 1356 1922	0.9 1.9 1.1 1.9
14 M	0108 0709 1337 1857	1.1 1.8 1.2 1.9	29 TU	0216 0801 1442 1953	0.8 1.9 1.0 2.0
15 TU	0208 0745 1433 1943	0.8 1.9 1.0 2.1	30 W	0300 0829 1524 2006	0.7 2.0 0.8 2.1

OCTOBER

Day	Time	m	Day	Time	m
1 TH	0341 0845 1604 ○ 2027	0.6 2.1 0.7 2.2	16 F	0318 0842 1541 ● 2054	0.3 2.4 0.5 2.5
2 F	0419 0857 1639 2107	0.6 2.2 0.7 2.3	17 SA	0401 0921 1624 2136	0.2 2.5 0.4 2.6
3 SA	0452 0931 1710 2148	0.6 2.3 0.7 2.3	18 SU	0443 1000 1705 2217	0.2 2.5 0.3 2.6
4 SU	0521 1007 1737 2226	0.7 2.3 0.8 2.2	19 M	0525 1039 1747 2258	0.3 2.5 0.4 2.4
5 M	0547 1040 1804 2300	0.8 2.2 0.8 2.1	20 TU	0608 1116 1831 2339	0.5 2.3 0.6 2.2
6 TU	0616 1046 1835 2234	0.9 2.0 0.9 1.9	21 W	0654 1152 1919	0.8 2.2 0.8
7 W	0649 1010 1912 2214	1.0 1.9 1.0 1.8	22 TH	0021 0747 1217 2017	2.0 1.0 2.0 1.0
8 TH	0727 1025 1954 2244	1.1 1.9 1.1 1.8	23 F	0122 0856 1228 ☽ 2133	1.8 1.3 1.8 1.1
9 F	0812 1103 2047 2329	1.2 1.9 1.2 1.7	24 SA	0628 1024 1710 2254	2.1 1.4 1.9 1.1
10 SA ☾	0912 1152 2203	1.4 1.8 1.2	25 SU	0745 1136 1737	2.1 1.3 1.8
11 SU	0032 1039 1308 2327	1.5 1.5 1.7 1.2	26 M	0000 0901 1236 1815	1.1 2.1 1.2 1.8
12 M	0756 1205 1806	1.9 1.4 1.8	27 TU	0056 0700 1328 1851	1.0 1.9 1.1 1.8
13 TU	0042 0649 1315 1840	1.0 1.9 1.2 1.9	28 W	0145 0731 1414 1916	0.9 1.9 1.0 1.9
14 W	0141 0723 1409 1925	0.8 2.0 0.9 2.1	29 TH	0230 0754 1456 1859	0.8 2.0 0.9 2.0
15 TH	0232 0802 1457 2011	0.5 2.2 0.7 2.3	30 F	0312 0736 1536 1951	0.7 2.1 0.8 2.1
			31 SA	0349 0812 1610 ○ 2037	0.7 2.2 0.7 2.2

NOVEMBER

Day	Time	m	Day	Time	m
1 SU	0422 0853 1640 2119	0.7 2.3 0.7 2.2	16 M	0419 0938 1644 2159	0.3 2.5 0.4 2.4
2 M	0450 0931 1708 2159	0.8 2.3 0.8 2.2	17 TU	0503 1017 1727 2242	0.4 2.4 0.4 2.3
3 TU	0518 1002 1737 2235	0.8 2.2 0.8 2.1	18 W	0549 1056 1813 2325	0.6 2.3 0.6 2.1
4 W	0549 1009 1809 2256	0.9 2.1 0.8 1.9	19 TH	0637 1132 1902	0.8 2.2 0.7
5 TH	0624 0945 1846 2152	1.0 2.0 0.9 1.8	20 F	0011 0732 1157 1957	1.9 1.1 2.0 0.9
6 F	0703 1003 1928 2225	1.1 2.0 1.0 1.8	21 SA	0116 0835 1150 2101	1.8 1.3 1.9 1.0
7 SA	0749 1044 2019 2314	1.3 1.9 1.1 1.7	22 SU	0613 0949 1236 ☽ 2213	2.1 1.3 1.7 1.1
8 SU ☾	0849 1137 2133	1.4 1.8 1.1	23 M	0716 1058 1709 2320	2.1 1.3 1.7 1.1
9 M	0025 1017 1255 2258	1.5 1.4 1.7 1.1	24 TU	0821 1159 1750	2.1 1.3 1.7
10 TU	0737 1139 1740	1.9 1.3 1.8	25 W	0018 0641 1253 1826	1.1 1.9 1.2 1.7
11 W	0009 0626 1245 1818	0.9 1.9 1.1 1.9	26 TH	0110 0708 1342 1845	1.0 1.9 1.1 1.8
12 TH	0109 0659 1340 1904	0.7 2.1 0.9 2.1	27 F	0157 0722 1425 1833	0.9 1.9 1.0 1.9
13 F	0201 0738 1429 1950	0.5 2.2 0.7 2.2	28 SA	0239 0655 1504 1923	0.9 2.0 0.9 2.0
14 SA	0249 0818 1515 2034	0.4 2.3 0.5 2.4	29 SU	0317 0730 1540 2009	0.9 2.1 0.8 2.0
15 SU	0335 0858 1600 ● 2117	0.3 2.5 0.4 2.4	30 M	0351 0811 1612 ○ 2053	0.9 2.2 0.8 2.1

DECEMBER

Day	Time	m	Day	Time	m
1 TU	0423 0849 1644 2135	0.9 2.2 0.7 2.1	16 W	0447 1000 1712 2228	0.6 2.4 0.4 2.2
2 W	0456 0921 1717 2216	0.9 2.2 0.7 2.0	17 TH	0535 1039 1758 2310	0.7 2.3 0.5 2.1
3 TH	0532 0946 1753 2256	0.9 2.1 0.7 1.9	18 F	0623 1116 1845 2354	0.8 2.2 0.6 1.9
4 F	0610 0958 1832 2341	1.0 2.0 0.8 1.8	19 SA	0713 1148 1934	1.0 2.0 0.7
5 SA	0652 1003 1916 2227	1.1 2.0 0.9 1.7	20 SU	0042 0805 1131 2024	1.8 1.1 1.9 0.9
6 SU	0741 1042 2008 2314	1.2 1.9 0.9 1.6	21 M	0547 0901 1158 ☽ 2118	2.0 1.2 1.8 1.0
7 M	0838 1135 2110	1.3 1.8 1.0	22 TU	0636 1003 1240 2220	2.0 1.3 1.7 1.1
8 TU	0629 0950 1248 ☾ 2224	2.0 1.3 1.8 1.0	23 W	0729 1110 1339 2329	2.0 1.3 1.6 1.2
9 W	0724 1105 1528 2334	2.0 1.2 1.8 0.9	24 TH	0828 1212 1829	1.9 1.3 1.6
10 TH	0606 1212 1757	1.9 1.1 1.8	25 F	0028 0930 1305 1855	1.1 1.9 1.2 1.6
11 F	0036 0639 1310 1846	0.8 2.0 0.9 2.0	26 SA	0119 0721 1351 1845	1.1 1.8 1.1 1.7
12 SA	0132 0718 1403 1933	0.6 2.1 0.7 2.1	27 SU	0204 0647 1433 1906	1.1 1.9 1.0 1.8
13 SU	0224 0759 1453 2018	0.5 2.2 0.6 2.2	28 M	0243 0641 1510 1948	1.0 2.0 0.9 1.9
14 M	0313 0839 1540 ● 2102	0.5 2.3 0.5 2.2	29 TU	0322 0719 1547 2034	0.9 2.1 0.8 1.9
15 TU	0401 0920 1627 2145	0.5 2.4 0.4 2.2	30 W	0401 0805 1625 ○ 2121	0.9 2.1 0.7 2.0
			31 TH	0440 0857 1703 2206	0.9 2.2 0.6 2.0

SOUTHAMPTON
LAT 50°54′N
LONG 1°24′W

TIMES AND HEIGHTS OF HIGH AND LOW WATER (Heights in Metres)

TIME ZONE UT
For Summer Time (area enclosed in shaded box) add 1 hour

High Waters - important note. Double High Waters occur at Southampton. The predictions are for the first High Water.

2020

JANUARY

Date	Time	m	Time	m	Time	m	Time	m
1 W ☽	0209	4.1	0813	1.7	1417	3.9	2030	1.6
2 TH	0252	4.0	0854	1.9	1459	3.7	2115	1.8
3 F ☽	0336	3.9	0945	2.0	1545	3.6	2212	1.9
4 SA	0424	3.7	1047	2.1	1638	3.5	2316	2.0
5 SU	0519	3.7	1151	2.1	1742	3.5		
6 M	0018	2.0	0626	3.8	1252	1.9	1857	3.6
7 TU	0117	1.8	0737	3.9	1347	1.7	2006	3.8
8 W	0210	1.6	0833	4.1	1437	1.4	2058	4.0
9 TH	0259	1.4	0919	4.3	1524	1.1	2146	4.3
10 F ○	0345	1.1	1002	4.4	1610	0.8	2229	4.4
11 SA	0431	0.9	1047	4.6	1655	0.6	2336	4.6
12 SU	0516	0.8	1131	4.7	1739	0.5		
13 M	0017	4.7	0601	0.7	1233	4.7	1824	0.5
14 TU	0102	4.7	0645	0.8	1319	4.7	1908	0.6
15 W	0150	4.6	0731	0.9	1408	4.5	1954	0.8
16 TH	0244	4.5	0820	1.1	1503	4.4	2044	1.0
17 F ☾	0349	4.4	0914	1.4	1534	4.1	2142	1.3
18 SA	0413	4.1	1018	1.6	1639	3.9	2251	1.5
19 SU	0516	4.0	1134	1.7	1744	3.8		
20 M	0008	1.7	0626	4.0	1250	1.7	1855	3.8
21 TU	0118	1.6	0729	4.1	1352	1.5	1958	3.9
22 W	0216	1.5	0825	4.1	1445	1.3	2147	4.1
23 TH	0307	1.3	0959	4.3	1534	1.1	2235	4.2
24 F ●	0354	1.1	1040	4.4	1618	0.9	2322	4.3
25 SA	0438	1.0	1119	4.4	1701	0.7	2320	4.3
26 SU	0521	0.9	1126	4.3	1742	0.7	2351	4.2
27 M	0602	1.0	1202	4.3	1820	0.8		
28 TU	0029	4.2	0639	1.1	1237	4.2	1854	1.0
29 W	0144	4.3	0709	1.2	1313	4.1	1922	1.1
30 TH	0214	4.2	0736	1.4	1348	4.1	1949	1.3
31 F	0248	4.2	0805	1.5	1421	3.9	2022	1.4

FEBRUARY

Date	Time	m	Time	m	Time	m	Time	m
1 SA	0251	4.0	0845	1.6	1504	3.8	2106	1.6
2 SU ☽	0333	3.9	0935	1.8	1551	3.6	2202	1.8
3 M	0422	3.7	1045	1.9	1658	3.6	2315	2.0
4 TU	0517	3.6	1155	2.0	1747	3.4		
5 W	0029	2.0	0627	3.6	1308	1.8	1908	3.5
6 TH	0139	1.8	0757	3.9	1413	1.5	2038	3.9
7 F	0240	1.5	0859	4.2	1509	1.1	2128	4.2
8 SA	0332	1.1	0950	4.4	1558	0.7	2214	4.4
9 SU ○	0420	0.8	1030	4.6	1644	0.4	2320	4.7
10 M	0505	0.5	1134	4.8	1728	0.2		
11 TU	0000	4.7	0549	0.4	1216	4.8	1811	0.2
12 W	0044	4.8	0631	0.4	1300	4.8	1852	0.2
13 TH	0130	4.7	0714	0.5	1348	4.6	1935	0.4
14 F	0221	4.6	0758	0.7	1441	4.4	2020	0.8
15 SA ☾	0324	4.4	0846	1.1	1548	4.2	2111	1.2
16 SU	0345	4.1	0942	1.4	1610	3.9	2214	1.6
17 M	0448	3.9	1056	1.7	1719	3.7	2339	1.8
18 TU	0557	3.8	1227	1.8	1835	3.7		
19 W	0104	1.9	0702	3.8	1338	1.7	1942	3.7
20 TH	0205	1.7	0806	3.8	1432	1.5	2040	3.8
21 F	0255	1.5	0947	4.1	1519	1.2	2233	4.1
22 SA	0340	1.2	1023	4.2	1602	0.9	2304	4.2
23 SU ●	0423	0.9	1058	4.3	1643	0.7	2339	4.3
24 M	0503	0.8	1104	4.2	1722	0.6	2332	4.2
25 TU	0542	0.8	1144	4.3	1758	0.7		
26 W	0042	4.3	0615	0.9	1216	4.2	1829	0.8
27 TH	0108	4.3	0641	1.0	1312	4.3	1851	1.0
28 F	0133	4.3	0701	1.1	1342	4.3	1914	1.0
29 SA	0203	4.3	0729	1.1	1417	4.2	1945	1.1

MARCH

Date	Time	m	Time	m	Time	m	Time	m
1 SU	0240	4.2	0806	1.2	1434	4.0	2025	1.3
2 M ☽	0259	4.0	0851	1.4	1516	3.8	2114	1.6
3 TU	0345	3.8	0946	1.7	1643	3.7	2218	1.9
4 W	0437	3.6	1105	1.9	1705	3.4	2350	2.1
5 TH	0538	3.4	1238	1.9	1826	3.4		
6 F	0122	1.9	0722	3.7	1359	1.5	2019	3.9
7 SA	0229	1.5	0839	4.1	1456	1.1	2110	4.2
8 SU	0320	1.1	0929	4.4	1543	0.6	2159	4.5
9 M ○	0405	0.6	1015	4.6	1628	0.2	2300	4.7
10 TU	0449	0.3	1114	4.8	1710	0.0	2340	4.8
11 W	0530	0.1	1156	4.9	1751	0.0		
12 TH	0022	4.8	0611	0.1	1240	4.8	1831	0.1
13 F	0108	4.7	0652	0.3	1327	4.7	1913	0.3
14 SA	0157	4.6	0734	0.6	1420	4.5	1955	0.7
15 SU	0300	4.4	0819	0.9	1441	4.1	2044	1.2
16 M ☾	0312	4.0	0912	1.4	1545	3.8	2145	1.7
17 TU	0417	3.8	1023	1.8	1702	3.7	2312	2.0
18 W	0526	3.6	1158	1.9	1807	3.6		
19 TH	0042	2.0	0632	3.5	1314	1.8	1917	3.6
20 F	0146	1.8	0734	3.6	1410	1.6	2018	3.8
21 SA	0235	1.6	0832	3.8	1455	1.3	2108	4.0
22 SU	0318	1.2	1003	4.0	1537	0.9	2149	4.1
23 M	0400	0.9	1033	4.2	1618	0.7	2308	4.3
24 TU ●	0439	0.8	1043	4.2	1656	0.6	2304	4.3
25 W	0515	0.7	1119	4.2	1731	0.7	2339	4.3
26 TH	0547	0.8	1150	4.2	1800	0.8		
27 F	0035	4.4	0610	0.9	1243	4.3	1821	0.9
28 SA	0100	4.4	0631	0.9	1312	4.3	1844	0.9
29 SU	0130	4.4	0700	0.9	1347	4.3	1917	1.0
30 M	0147	4.2	0737	1.0	1404	4.1	1956	1.2
31 TU	0226	4.1	0819	1.2	1452	4.0	2042	1.5

APRIL

Date	Time	m	Time	m	Time	m	Time	m
1 W ☽	0312	3.8	0910	1.6	1615	3.8	2142	1.9
2 TH	0405	3.6	1027	1.9	1737	3.6	2325	2.1
3 F	0511	3.4	1218	1.9	1807	3.5		
4 SA	0109	1.9	0653	3.6	1341	1.5	1951	4.0
5 SU	0213	1.5	0815	4.0	1436	1.0	2047	4.3
6 M	0301	1.0	0906	4.4	1522	0.6	2132	4.6
7 TU	0345	0.6	0952	4.6	1606	0.2	2238	4.8
8 W ○	0428	0.2	1052	4.8	1648	0.0	2318	4.9
9 TH	0508	0.1	1135	4.8	1728	0.0		
10 F	0000	4.8	0549	0.1	1219	4.8	1808	0.2
11 SA	0044	4.7	0630	0.3	1306	4.6	1850	0.4
12 SU	0133	4.6	0711	0.6	1402	4.4	1933	0.8
13 M	0235	4.3	0755	0.9	1418	4.1	2021	1.3
14 TU ☾	0243	3.9	0848	1.4	1524	3.9	2122	1.7
15 W	0343	3.7	0956	1.7	1633	3.7	2242	2.0
16 TH	0454	3.5	1117	1.9	1737	3.6		
17 F	0003	2.1	0638	3.5	1231	1.9	1837	3.6
18 SA	0109	1.9	0656	3.4	1332	1.7	1937	3.7
19 SU	0203	1.7	0757	3.6	1422	1.4	2031	3.9
20 M	0249	1.3	0848	3.8	1506	1.1	2119	4.1
21 TU	0330	1.1	1004	4.1	1547	0.9	2158	4.2
22 W	0409	0.9	1011	4.1	1625	0.8	2236	4.3
23 TH ●	0445	0.8	1047	4.2	1659	0.8	2308	4.3
24 F	0515	0.9	1119	4.2	1728	0.9	2335	4.3
25 SA	0539	0.9	1218	4.3	1752	1.0		
26 SU	0031	4.4	0605	0.9	1248	4.4	1820	1.0
27 M	0103	4.4	0637	0.8	1325	4.4	1855	1.0
28 TU	0122	4.3	0714	0.9	1408	4.3	1935	1.2
29 W	0202	4.1	0758	1.2	1459	4.1	2023	1.5
30 TH ☽	0250	3.9	0851	1.5	1601	3.9	2126	1.9

MAY

Date	Time	m	Time	m	Time	m	Time	m
1 F	0342	3.7	1011	1.8	1631	3.7	2308	2.0
2 SA	0456	3.6	1151	1.7	1752	3.8		
3 SU	0037	1.8	0625	3.7	1309	1.4	1921	4.1
4 M	0143	1.4	0742	4.0	1406	1.1	2022	4.4
5 TU	0234	1.0	0836	4.3	1455	0.7	2108	4.6
6 W	0319	0.6	0924	4.5	1540	0.4	2150	4.7
7 TH ○	0403	0.4	1031	4.7	1622	0.3	2255	4.8
8 F	0445	0.2	1114	4.7	1705	0.3	2338	4.8
9 SA	0527	0.3	1200	4.6	1747	0.4		
10 SU	0023	4.6	0609	0.4	1250	4.5	1830	0.7
11 M	0111	4.5	0652	0.7	1311	4.3	1914	1.0
12 TU	0209	4.3	0737	1.0	1401	4.1	2003	1.4
13 W	0218	3.9	0828	1.3	1501	3.9	2101	1.7
14 TH ☾	0310	3.7	0929	1.6	1604	3.8	2209	1.9
15 F	0416	3.6	1036	1.8	1702	3.7	2318	2.0
16 SA	0555	3.6	1142	1.9	1756	3.7		
17 SU	0024	2.0	0657	3.6	1245	1.8	1857	3.7
18 M	0123	1.8	0801	3.7	1341	1.6	1949	3.9
19 TU	0213	1.5	0853	3.8	1429	1.4	2041	4.1
20 W	0256	1.3	0934	4.0	1511	1.2	2123	4.2
21 TH	0335	1.1	0944	4.1	1550	1.1	2200	4.3
22 F ●	0410	1.0	1022	4.2	1625	1.0	2239	4.3
23 SA	0442	0.9	1057	4.2	1657	1.0	2309	4.3
24 SU	0512	0.9	1158	4.4	1729	1.0		
25 M	0009	4.4	0545	0.9	1231	4.4	1803	1.0
26 TU	0044	4.4	0621	0.9	1310	4.4	1842	1.1
27 W	0100	4.3	0702	1.0	1355	4.3	1926	1.3
28 TH	0147	4.2	0749	1.1	1448	4.2	2017	1.5
29 F	0237	4.0	0845	1.4	1551	4.1	2123	1.7
30 SA ☽	0337	3.8	0959	1.5	1712	4.0	2242	1.8
31 SU	0445	3.8	1117	1.5	1731	4.0	2358	1.7

JUNE

Date	Time	m	Time	m	Time	m	Time	m
1 M	0557	3.8	1229	1.4	1843	4.1		
2 TU	0106	1.4	0709	4.0	1332	1.2	1947	4.3
3 W	0203	1.1	0809	4.2	1425	0.9	2041	4.5
4 TH	0253	0.9	0901	4.4	1514	0.8	2126	4.6
5 F ○	0340	0.6	1015	4.5	1600	0.6	2238	4.7
6 SA	0425	0.5	1101	4.5	1646	0.6	2321	4.6
7 SU	0509	0.5	1150	4.5	1730	0.7		
8 M	0006	4.5	0553	0.6	1245	4.4	1815	0.9
9 TU	0053	4.4	0637	0.8	1254	4.2	1900	1.1
10 W	0142	4.2	0721	1.0	1344	4.1	1946	1.3
11 TH	0155	4.0	0808	1.2	1431	4.0	2037	1.6
12 F	0244	3.8	0858	1.5	1527	3.9	2131	1.8
13 SA ☾	0337	3.7	0954	1.7	1615	3.8	2230	1.9
14 SU	0431	3.5	1052	1.8	1709	3.8	2330	2.0
15 M	0529	3.5	1151	1.8	1805	3.8		
16 TU	0031	1.9	0631	3.5	1250	1.8	1953	4.0
17 W	0127	1.8	0816	3.8	1343	1.7	1959	4.0
18 TH	0214	1.6	0823	3.8	1430	1.5	2049	4.1
19 F	0256	1.4	0914	4.0	1512	1.3	2130	4.2
20 SA	0335	1.2	0955	4.1	1553	1.2	2212	4.3
21 SU ●	0414	1.0	1031	4.2	1633	1.1	2249	4.4
22 M	0453	0.9	1113	4.3	1713	1.1	2328	4.4
23 TU	0533	0.8	1218	4.4	1754	1.0		
24 W	0005	4.4	0615	0.8	1258	4.5	1837	1.1
25 TH	0052	4.4	0658	0.9	1344	4.4	1922	1.1
26 F	0139	4.3	0745	1.0	1435	4.4	2012	1.3
27 SA	0252	4.3	0836	1.1	1534	4.3	2108	1.4
28 SU ☽	0353	4.1	0936	1.3	1645	4.2	2213	1.5
29 M	0422	3.9	1043	1.4	1705	4.1	2322	1.6
30 TU	0530	3.9	1152	1.4	1809	4.1		

SUNRISE AND SUNSET TIMES

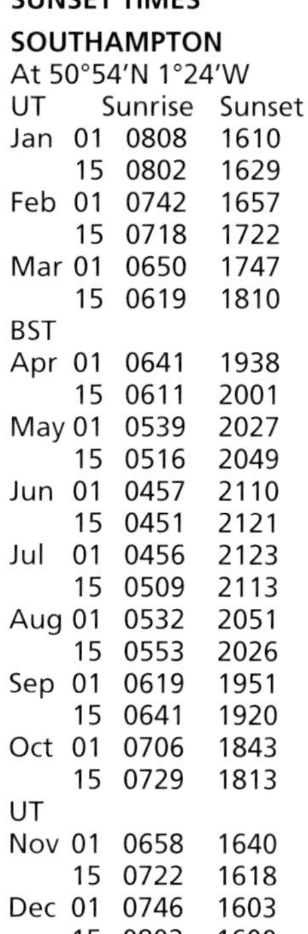

SOUTHAMPTON
At 50°54′N 1°24′W

UT		Sunrise	Sunset
Jan	01	0808	1610
	15	0802	1629
Feb	01	0742	1657
	15	0718	1722
Mar	01	0650	1747
	15	0619	1810
BST			
Apr	01	0641	1938
	15	0611	2001
May	01	0539	2027
	15	0516	2049
Jun	01	0457	2110
	15	0451	2121
Jul	01	0456	2123
	15	0509	2113
Aug	01	0532	2051
	15	0553	2026
Sep	01	0619	1951
	15	0641	1920
Oct	01	0706	1843
	15	0729	1813
UT			
Nov	01	0658	1640
	15	0722	1618
Dec	01	0746	1603
	15	0802	1600

JULY

Date	Day	Time	m	Time	m	Time	m	Time	m
1	W	0031	1.5	0640	4.0	1300	1.4	1918	4.2
2	TH	0136	1.4	0745	4.1	1401	1.3	2016	4.3
3	F	0232	1.1	0843	4.2	1455	1.1	2104	4.4
4	SA	0323	0.9	1011	4.3	1544	1.0	2228	4.5
5	SU ○	0411	0.8	1100	4.4	1632	0.9	2311	4.4
6	M	0456	0.7	1150	4.4	1718	0.9	2354	4.4
7	TU	0540	0.7	1155	4.3	1802	0.9		
8	W	0035	4.3	0623	0.8	1235	4.2	1846	1.1
9	TH	0117	4.2	0704	0.9	1318	4.2	1927	1.2
10	F	0130	4.0	0744	1.1	1403	4.1	2008	1.4
11	SA	0207	3.9	0824	1.3	1444	4.0	2049	1.6
12	SU ☾	0252	3.8	0907	1.6	1525	3.9	2134	1.8
13	M	0333	3.6	0956	1.8	1614	3.8	2227	1.9
14	TU	0423	3.5	1052	1.9	1658	3.7	2325	2.0
15	W	0520	3.4	1151	2.0	1758	3.7		
16	TH	0024	1.9	0625	3.5	1250	1.9	1905	3.8
17	F	0123	1.8	0744	3.7	1348	1.8	2009	3.9
18	SA	0218	1.6	0845	3.9	1441	1.6	2103	4.1
19	SU	0308	1.3	0935	4.1	1530	1.4	2149	4.3
20	M ●	0354	1.0	1017	4.3	1616	1.1	2231	4.4
21	TU	0440	0.8	1058	4.4	1701	1.0	2311	4.5
22	W	0523	0.7	1203	4.6	1745	0.8	2354	4.5
23	TH	0606	0.6	1243	4.6	1828	0.8		
24	F	0057	4.6	0649	0.6	1327	4.6	1911	0.8
25	SA	0142	4.5	0732	0.7	1416	4.5	1956	1.0
26	SU	0232	4.4	0818	0.9	1511	4.4	2046	1.2
27	M ☽	0330	4.3	0909	1.1	1622	4.3	2143	1.4
28	TU	0359	4.0	1010	1.4	1639	4.1	2249	1.6
29	W	0503	3.9	1121	1.6	1744	4.0		
30	TH	0005	1.7	0616	3.8	1237	1.7	1855	4.0
31	F	0119	1.6	0728	3.9	1347	1.6	1959	4.1

AUGUST

Date	Day	Time	m	Time	m	Time	m	Time	m
1	SA	0221	1.4	0834	4.0	1445	1.5	2051	4.2
2	SU	0313	1.2	1013	4.2	1535	1.3	2218	4.3
3	M ○	0400	0.9	1057	4.3	1621	1.1	2257	4.3
4	TU	0444	0.8	1140	4.4	1705	0.9	2337	4.3
5	W	0526	0.7	1223	4.4	1747	0.9	2349	4.2
6	TH	0606	0.7	1216	4.3	1827	1.0		
7	F	0026	4.2	0644	0.8	1250	4.2	1903	1.1
8	SA	0058	4.1	0717	1.0	1410	4.3	1934	1.3
9	SU	0135	4.0	0746	1.2	1443	4.2	2002	1.5
10	M	0209	3.9	0815	1.4	1434	4.0	2035	1.6
11	TU ☾	0246	3.8	0852	1.6	1517	3.9	2119	1.8
12	W	0329	3.6	0943	1.9	1603	3.8	2220	2.0
13	TH	0422	3.5	1052	2.1	1652	3.6	2331	2.1
14	F	0515	3.4	1205	2.1	1752	3.5		
15	SA	0042	2.0	0628	3.4	1315	2.0	1917	3.7
16	SU	0151	1.7	0822	3.9	1420	1.8	2041	4.0
17	M	0250	1.4	0918	4.1	1515	1.4	2129	4.3
18	TU	0340	1.0	1002	4.4	1602	1.1	2211	4.5
19	W ●	0426	0.7	1042	4.6	1647	0.8	2256	4.6
20	TH	0509	0.4	1143	4.7	1730	0.6	2335	4.7
21	F	0550	0.3	1223	4.8	1811	0.5		
22	SA	0037	4.8	0631	0.3	1306	4.8	1852	0.6
23	SU	0121	4.7	0712	0.5	1353	4.7	1935	0.7
24	M	0210	4.5	0755	0.7	1448	4.5	2020	1.0
25	TU ☽	0308	4.3	0843	1.1	1510	4.2	2113	1.4
26	W	0334	4.0	0941	1.5	1616	4.1	2221	1.7
27	TH	0443	3.8	1058	1.9	1726	3.9	2350	1.9
28	F	0559	3.7	1229	2.0	1834	3.9		
29	SA	0110	1.8	0716	3.8	1339	1.9	1938	3.9
30	SU	0210	1.6	0818	3.9	1434	1.6	2128	4.1
31	M	0259	1.3	0914	4.1	1521	1.4	2204	4.2

SEPTEMBER

Date	Day	Time	m	Time	m	Time	m	Time	m
1	TU	0343	1.0	1047	4.3	1605	1.1	2239	4.3
2	W ○	0424	0.8	1121	4.4	1645	0.9	2315	4.3
3	TH	0505	0.7	1157	4.4	1725	0.8	2325	4.3
4	F	0543	0.7	1231	4.4	1802	0.9	2359	4.3
5	SA	0618	0.8	1258	4.4	1835	1.1		
6	SU	0031	4.2	0646	1.0	1323	4.4	1857	1.2
7	M	0127	4.3	0705	1.2	1351	4.3	1917	1.3
8	TU	0200	4.2	0730	1.3	1424	4.3	1948	1.4
9	W	0209	4.0	0805	1.5	1435	4.0	2028	1.6
10	TH ☾	0255	3.9	0850	1.8	1519	3.9	2120	1.9
11	F	0340	3.6	0950	2.1	1608	3.6	2240	2.1
12	SA	0536	3.6	1128	2.3	1709	3.5		
13	SU	0015	2.1	0550	3.4	1257	2.2	1836	3.6
14	M	0136	1.8	0800	3.9	1407	1.8	2020	4.0
15	TU	0234	1.4	0856	4.2	1459	1.4	2110	4.3
16	W	0322	0.9	0937	4.5	1544	0.9	2152	4.6
17	TH ●	0406	0.5	1018	4.7	1627	0.6	2233	4.8
18	F	0448	0.3	1120	4.9	1709	0.4	2332	4.9
19	SA	0529	0.2	1200	4.9	1749	0.3		
20	SU	0014	4.9	0609	0.2	1242	4.9	1830	0.4
21	M	0059	4.8	0649	0.4	1329	4.8	1911	0.7
22	TU	0148	4.6	0731	0.8	1423	4.5	1955	1.0
23	W	0249	4.4	0817	1.2	1440	4.2	2046	1.5
24	TH ☽	0311	4.0	0916	1.7	1548	3.9	2158	1.9
25	F	0430	3.8	1044	2.1	1703	3.8	2335	2.0
26	SA	0544	3.7	1213	2.1	1807	3.7		
27	SU	0048	1.9	0651	3.7	1318	2.0	1909	3.7
28	M	0150	1.7	0754	3.8	1412	1.7	2008	3.8
29	TU	0235	1.4	0847	4.0	1457	1.4	2100	4.0
30	W	0318	1.1	0932	4.2	1540	1.1	2218	4.3

OCTOBER

Date	Day	Time	m	Time	m	Time	m	Time	m
1	TH ○	0359	0.9	1101	4.4	1621	0.9	2250	4.3
2	F	0438	0.8	1047	4.4	1659	0.9	2255	4.3
3	SA	0515	0.8	1122	4.4	1734	0.9	2333	4.3
4	SU	0548	0.9	1223	4.5	1802	1.1		
5	M	0027	4.4	0611	1.1	1247	4.4	1819	1.2
6	TU	0056	4.4	0630	1.2	1314	4.4	1842	1.2
7	W	0128	4.4	0657	1.3	1348	4.4	1915	1.3
8	TH	0207	4.3	0733	1.4	1403	4.2	1955	1.5
9	F	0228	4.0	0816	1.7	1447	3.9	2042	1.8
10	SA ☾	0350	3.9	0911	2.1	1533	3.7	2154	2.1
11	SU	0504	3.7	1100	2.4	1637	3.5	2355	2.1
12	M	0528	3.5	1242	2.2	1806	3.6		
13	TU	0115	1.8	0721	3.9	1346	1.8	1946	4.0
14	W	0210	1.4	0827	4.3	1435	1.3	2039	4.4
15	TH	0257	0.9	0911	4.6	1520	0.9	2126	4.6
16	F ●	0341	0.5	0952	4.8	1603	0.5	2209	4.8
17	SA	0423	0.3	1035	4.9	1644	0.3	2310	5.0
18	SU	0504	0.2	1136	5.0	1725	0.3	2353	4.9
19	M	0544	0.3	1219	4.9	1806	0.4		
20	TU	0038	4.8	0626	0.6	1305	4.8	1848	0.7
21	W	0129	4.6	0708	0.9	1400	4.5	1932	1.1
22	TH	0242	4.4	0756	1.4	1413	4.1	2023	1.5
23	F ☽	0250	4.0	0857	1.8	1519	3.9	2135	1.9
24	SA	0410	3.9	1021	2.1	1629	3.7	2301	2.0
25	SU	0513	3.7	1139	2.2	1817	3.7		
26	M	0010	2.0	0613	3.7	1243	2.1	1834	3.6
27	TU	0109	1.8	0716	3.8	1340	1.8	1934	3.7
28	W	0200	1.6	0810	4.0	1427	1.5	2026	3.9
29	TH	0246	1.3	0856	4.2	1510	1.2	2153	4.2
30	F	0327	1.1	0938	4.3	1551	1.0	2225	4.3
31	SA ○	0407	1.0	1014	4.4	1629	1.0	2230	4.3

NOVEMBER

Date	Day	Time	m	Time	m	Time	m	Time	m
1	SU	0443	1.0	1050	4.4	1702	1.0	2304	4.3
2	M	0515	1.1	1153	4.5	1729	1.1		
3	TU	0003	4.4	0539	1.2	1218	4.5	1750	1.2
4	W	0032	4.4	0603	1.3	1247	4.5	1817	1.2
5	TH	0106	4.4	0634	1.3	1322	4.4	1852	1.2
6	F	0146	4.3	0712	1.5	1339	4.2	1933	1.4
7	SA	0233	4.2	0756	1.7	1424	4.0	2020	1.7
8	SU ☾	0331	4.0	0852	2.1	1511	3.8	2129	2.0
9	M	0445	3.9	1032	2.3	1717	3.8	2320	2.0
10	TU	0511	3.8	1205	2.1	1743	3.7		
11	W	0038	1.8	0637	4.0	1312	1.7	1908	4.0
12	TH	0137	1.4	0750	4.4	1405	1.3	2011	4.3
13	F	0227	1.0	0839	4.6	1452	0.9	2101	4.6
14	SA	0313	0.7	0927	4.8	1537	0.6	2146	4.8
15	SU ●	0356	0.5	1011	4.9	1620	0.4	2249	4.9
16	M	0439	0.5	1113	4.9	1702	0.4	2334	4.8
17	TU	0522	0.5	1158	4.9	1745	0.5		
18	W	0022	4.7	0606	0.7	1245	4.7	1829	0.7
19	TH	0116	4.5	0651	1.1	1338	4.5	1915	1.1
20	F	0136	4.3	0741	1.4	1355	4.1	2006	1.4
21	SA	0232	4.1	0838	1.8	1450	3.9	2108	1.7
22	SU ☽	0339	3.9	0946	2.0	1553	3.7	2217	1.9
23	M	0438	3.8	1057	2.1	1657	3.6	2324	2.0
24	TU	0536	3.8	1202	2.1	1836	3.7		
25	W	0025	1.9	0633	3.8	1301	1.9	1854	3.6
26	TH	0121	1.8	0729	3.9	1352	1.7	1947	3.8
27	F	0210	1.6	0820	4.1	1438	1.4	2126	4.1
28	SA	0253	1.4	0906	4.3	1519	1.3	2202	4.2
29	SU	0334	1.3	0944	4.4	1556	1.1	2206	4.2
30	M ○	0411	1.2	1020	4.4	1630	1.1	2319	4.4

DECEMBER

Date	Day	Time	m	Time	m	Time	m	Time	m
1	TU	0444	1.2	1057	4.4	1700	1.1	2349	4.4
2	W	0514	1.3	1129	4.4	1729	1.1		
3	TH	0018	4.4	0546	1.3	1229	4.5	1802	1.1
4	F	0052	4.4	0621	1.3	1240	4.4	1840	1.2
5	SA	0133	4.4	0702	1.4	1323	4.3	1923	1.3
6	SU	0220	4.3	0748	1.6	1408	4.1	2012	1.5
7	M	0316	4.2	0845	1.8	1502	4.0	2114	1.7
8	TU ☾	0421	4.1	0959	2.0	1604	3.8	2236	1.8
9	W	0448	4.0	1120	1.9	1717	3.8	2354	1.7
10	TH	0559	4.1	1232	1.7	1827	4.0		
11	F	0100	1.5	0709	4.3	1333	1.4	1935	4.2
12	SA	0156	1.2	0811	4.5	1426	1.1	2032	4.4
13	SU	0247	1.0	0858	4.6	1514	0.8	2121	4.5
14	M ●	0334	0.8	0949	4.7	1600	0.7	2236	4.6
15	TU	0421	0.8	1058	4.8	1646	0.6	2324	4.6
16	W	0507	0.8	1144	4.7	1731	0.6		
17	TH	0014	4.6	0553	0.9	1230	4.6	1816	0.7
18	F	0109	4.5	0639	1.1	1318	4.4	1901	0.9
19	SA	0119	4.3	0725	1.3	1409	4.3	1947	1.2
20	SU	0211	4.1	0814	1.5	1425	4.0	2037	1.4
21	M ☽	0304	4.0	0908	1.8	1517	3.8	2132	1.7
22	TU	0354	3.9	1007	2.0	1612	3.7	2232	1.9
23	W	0452	3.9	1111	2.0	1709	3.6	2335	2.0
24	TH	0544	3.8	1216	2.0	1809	3.6		
25	F	0035	1.9	0734	4.0	1313	1.9	1958	3.8
26	SA	0130	1.8	0832	4.1	1403	1.7	2004	3.8
27	SU	0218	1.7	0830	4.1	1446	1.5	2151	4.1
28	M	0301	1.5	0918	4.2	1525	1.3	2145	4.1
29	TU	0341	1.4	0958	4.3	1603	1.2	2224	4.2
30	W ○	0420	1.3	1037	4.4	1641	1.1	2258	4.3
31	TH	0458	1.2	1111	4.4	1718	1.0	2334	4.3

PORTSMOUTH
LAT 50°48'N
LONG 1°07'W

TIMES AND HEIGHTS OF HIGH AND LOW WATER (Heights in Metres)

TIME ZONE UT
For Summer Time (area enclosed in shaded box) add 1 hour

2020

JANUARY

Date	Day	Time	m	Time	m	Time	m	Time	m
1	W	0316	4.3	0820	1.7	1516	4.1	2036	1.6
2	TH	0357	4.2	0902	1.9	1600	3.9	2121	1.7
3	F ☽	0441	4.1	0956	2.0	1650	3.8	2219	1.9
4	SA	0533	4.0	1110	2.1	1751	3.7	2332	1.9
5	SU	0638	3.9	1218	2.0	1909	3.7		
6	M	0036	1.9	0757	4.0	1313	1.8	2028	3.8
7	TU	0130	1.8	0856	4.1	1402	1.6	2123	4.0
8	W	0219	1.6	0942	4.3	1449	1.4	2207	4.2
9	TH	0307	1.4	1021	4.5	1535	1.1	2245	4.4
10	F O	0354	1.2	1058	4.6	1620	0.9	2324	4.6
11	SA	0440	1.0	1137	4.7	1705	0.7		
12	SU	0005	4.7	0524	0.9	1217	4.7	1748	0.6
13	M	0049	4.8	0608	0.8	1300	4.7	1831	0.6
14	TU	0137	4.8	0652	0.9	1346	4.7	1916	0.7
15	W	0231	4.7	0738	1.0	1439	4.6	2003	0.8
16	TH	0329	4.6	0829	1.2	1539	4.4	2055	1.1
17	F ☾	0427	4.5	0927	1.4	1642	4.3	2158	1.3
18	SA	0524	4.4	1038	1.6	1746	4.1	2313	1.5
19	SU	0624	4.3	1154	1.6	1850	4.1		
20	M	0024	1.6	0726	4.3	1302	1.6	1954	4.1
21	TU	0127	1.6	0827	4.3	1401	1.5	2058	4.1
22	W	0224	1.5	0923	4.3	1454	1.3	2158	4.2
23	TH	0316	1.4	1012	4.4	1542	1.1	2248	4.4
24	F ●	0404	1.2	1055	4.5	1627	1.0	2331	4.4
25	SA	0448	1.1	1136	4.5	1710	0.9		
26	SU	0011	4.5	0529	1.0	1217	4.5	1749	0.8
27	M	0052	4.5	0608	1.1	1257	4.5	1826	0.9
28	TU	0132	4.5	0643	1.1	1335	4.4	1858	1.0
29	W	0210	4.4	0714	1.2	1410	4.3	1927	1.1
30	TH	0243	4.4	0743	1.3	1443	4.2	1958	1.2
31	F	0315	4.3	0816	1.5	1520	4.1	2033	1.4

FEBRUARY

Date	Day	Time	m	Time	m	Time	m	Time	m
1	SA	0353	4.2	0856	1.6	1603	3.9	2116	1.6
2	SU ☽	0437	4.0	0945	1.8	1654	3.8	2210	1.8
3	M	0531	3.9	1050	1.9	1756	3.7	2322	1.9
4	TU	0636	3.8	1212	1.9	1915	3.7		
5	W	0045	1.9	0802	3.9	1326	1.7	2050	3.8
6	TH	0152	1.7	0912	4.1	1425	1.5	2144	4.1
7	F	0249	1.5	0958	4.3	1518	1.1	2226	4.4
8	SA	0340	1.2	1039	4.5	1606	0.8	2307	4.6
9	SU O	0427	0.9	1119	4.7	1652	0.5	2349	4.7
10	M	0512	0.7	1200	4.8	1735	0.4		
11	TU	0032	4.8	0555	0.5	1243	4.8	1817	0.3
12	W	0119	4.9	0638	0.5	1329	4.8	1900	0.4
13	TH	0210	4.8	0721	0.6	1420	4.7	1943	0.6
14	F	0305	4.7	0807	0.9	1517	4.5	2030	0.8
15	SA ☾	0400	4.6	0858	1.1	1617	4.3	2125	1.2
16	SU	0454	4.4	1001	1.5	1719	4.1	2237	1.5
17	M	0552	4.2	1121	1.7	1825	3.9	2358	1.7
18	TU	0659	4.0	1238	1.7	1937	3.9		
19	W	0109	1.8	0807	4.0	1345	1.6	2049	3.9
20	TH	0213	1.7	0909	4.1	1441	1.4	2155	4.1
21	F	0306	1.5	0958	4.2	1529	1.2	2238	4.3
22	SA	0351	1.3	1039	4.3	1612	1.0	2313	4.4
23	SU ●	0433	1.1	1118	4.4	1652	0.8	2350	4.5
24	M	0512	0.9	1157	4.4	1730	0.8		
25	TU	0028	4.5	0548	0.9	1236	4.4	1803	0.8
26	W	0106	4.5	0619	1.0	1312	4.4	1832	0.9
27	TH	0140	4.5	0646	1.0	1343	4.4	1858	1.0
28	F	0209	4.4	0711	1.1	1412	4.3	1925	1.0
29	SA	0237	4.3	0741	1.1	1444	4.2	1957	1.1

MARCH

Date	Day	Time	m	Time	m	Time	m	Time	m
1	SU	0311	4.2	0816	1.3	1524	4.1	2035	1.3
2	M ☽	0352	4.1	0859	1.5	1612	3.9	2122	1.6
3	TU	0444	3.9	0955	1.7	1713	3.7	2225	1.9
4	W	0550	3.7	1114	1.9	1833	3.6		
5	TH	0004	2.0	0718	3.7	1301	1.8	2018	3.8
6	F	0136	1.8	0845	3.9	1409	1.5	2119	4.1
7	SA	0236	1.5	0934	4.2	1502	1.1	2204	4.4
8	SU	0326	1.1	1017	4.5	1550	0.7	2245	4.7
9	M O	0412	0.7	1058	4.7	1634	0.4	2327	4.8
10	TU	0456	0.5	1139	4.8	1717	0.2		
11	W	0010	4.9	0537	0.3	1223	4.9	1758	0.1
12	TH	0056	4.9	0619	0.3	1309	4.9	1839	0.2
13	F	0144	4.9	0700	0.4	1359	4.8	1921	0.5
14	SA	0236	4.8	0743	0.7	1455	4.6	2005	0.8
15	SU	0329	4.6	0830	1.0	1554	4.4	2056	1.2
16	M ☾	0421	4.3	0928	1.4	1655	4.1	2208	1.7
17	TU	0520	4.0	1052	1.7	1803	3.9	2335	1.9
18	W	0631	3.8	1213	1.8	1919	3.8		
19	TH	0049	1.9	0746	3.7	1322	1.8	2038	3.9
20	F	0155	1.8	0854	3.9	1420	1.6	2209	4.1
21	SA	0247	1.6	0943	4.0	1507	1.3	2224	4.3
22	SU	0331	1.3	1020	4.2	1549	1.1	2250	4.4
23	M	0411	1.1	1057	4.3	1628	0.9	2325	4.5
24	TU ●	0448	0.9	1135	4.4	1703	0.8		
25	W	0001	4.5	0522	0.9	1212	4.4	1735	0.8
26	TH	0037	4.5	0551	0.9	1247	4.4	1803	0.9
27	F	0108	4.5	0617	0.9	1316	4.4	1829	0.9
28	SA	0135	4.4	0642	1.0	1344	4.4	1856	1.0
29	SU	0202	4.4	0711	1.0	1415	4.3	1928	1.1
30	M	0234	4.3	0745	1.1	1454	4.2	2005	1.3
31	TU	0314	4.1	0827	1.3	1543	4.0	2051	1.5

APRIL

Date	Day	Time	m	Time	m	Time	m	Time	m
1	W ☽	0407	3.9	0920	1.6	1646	3.8	2152	1.9
2	TH	0517	3.7	1036	1.8	1810	3.7	2342	2.0
3	F	0650	3.7	1242	1.8	1950	3.9		
4	SA	0121	1.8	0815	3.9	1349	1.4	2052	4.2
5	SU	0219	1.4	0908	4.2	1441	1.0	2138	4.5
6	M	0307	1.0	0951	4.5	1528	0.7	2220	4.7
7	TU	0351	0.7	1034	4.7	1612	0.4	2303	4.9
8	W O	0434	0.4	1116	4.9	1654	0.2	2345	5.0
9	TH	0516	0.3	1200	4.9	1736	0.2		
10	F	0030	5.0	0557	0.3	1248	4.9	1817	0.4
11	SA	0116	4.9	0638	0.5	1338	4.8	1859	0.6
12	SU	0205	4.8	0721	0.7	1435	4.6	1943	1.0
13	M	0256	4.5	0806	1.1	1535	4.4	2033	1.4
14	TU ☾	0347	4.3	0902	1.4	1633	4.1	2144	1.8
15	W	0444	3.9	1023	1.8	1739	3.9	2308	2.0
16	TH	0557	3.7	1141	1.9	1854	3.8		
17	F	0019	2.0	0716	3.6	1249	1.9	2015	3.9
18	SA	0125	1.9	0830	3.8	1348	1.7	2136	4.1
19	SU	0219	1.7	0920	3.9	1436	1.4	2154	4.3
20	M	0303	1.4	0955	4.1	1518	1.2	2222	4.4
21	TU	0342	1.2	1032	4.3	1556	1.1	2257	4.5
22	W	0418	1.0	1110	4.4	1631	1.0	2332	4.5
23	TH ●	0451	0.9	1147	4.4	1703	1.0		
24	F	0006	4.5	0520	0.9	1221	4.4	1733	1.0
25	SA	0037	4.5	0548	0.9	1251	4.5	1802	1.0
26	SU	0105	4.5	0617	0.9	1321	4.4	1832	1.1
27	M	0133	4.4	0648	1.0	1355	4.4	1906	1.1
28	TU	0207	4.3	0724	1.1	1436	4.3	1945	1.3
29	W	0250	4.2	0807	1.3	1529	4.1	2034	1.6
30	TH ☽	0346	4.0	0902	1.5	1635	4.0	2137	1.8

MAY

Date	Day	Time	m	Time	m	Time	m	Time	m
1	F	0459	3.8	1020	1.7	1755	3.9	2329	1.9
2	SA	0625	3.8	1215	1.7	1918	4.1		
3	SU	0055	1.7	0742	4.0	1321	1.4	2021	4.3
4	M	0152	1.4	0837	4.3	1413	1.1	2109	4.6
5	TU	0241	1.0	0924	4.5	1501	0.8	2153	4.8
6	W	0326	0.7	1008	4.7	1546	0.6	2237	4.9
7	TH O	0410	0.5	1053	4.8	1630	0.5	2320	5.0
8	F	0453	0.4	1140	4.8	1713	0.5		
9	SA	0005	4.9	0535	0.5	1229	4.8	1755	0.6
10	SU	0051	4.8	0617	0.6	1322	4.7	1838	0.8
11	M	0138	4.7	0701	0.8	1421	4.6	1924	1.1
12	TU	0227	4.5	0747	1.1	1519	4.4	2014	1.4
13	W	0318	4.2	0841	1.4	1611	4.2	2118	1.8
14	TH ☾	0411	4.0	0950	1.7	1707	4.0	2232	2.0
15	F	0515	3.7	1101	1.8	1815	3.9	2339	2.0
16	SA	0631	3.6	1205	1.9	1926	3.9		
17	SU	0042	2.0	0743	3.7	1304	1.8	2026	4.1
18	M	0139	1.8	0839	3.9	1355	1.6	2110	4.2
19	TU	0226	1.6	0923	4.0	1439	1.4	2149	4.4
20	W	0305	1.4	1004	4.2	1518	1.3	2226	4.5
21	TH	0342	1.2	1044	4.3	1555	1.2	2303	4.5
22	F ●	0416	1.1	1122	4.4	1630	1.1	2337	4.5
23	SA	0450	1.0	1156	4.4	1705	1.1		
24	SU	0009	4.5	0523	1.0	1230	4.5	1739	1.1
25	M	0040	4.5	0557	1.0	1304	4.5	1815	1.1
26	TU	0113	4.5	0633	1.0	1344	4.5	1853	1.2
27	W	0151	4.4	0713	1.1	1430	4.4	1936	1.3
28	TH	0238	4.3	0759	1.2	1526	4.3	2027	1.5
29	F	0336	4.1	0855	1.4	1629	4.2	2132	1.7
30	SA ☽	0446	4.0	1009	1.5	1737	4.2	2258	1.8
31	SU	0600	4.0	1137	1.5	1846	4.3		

JUNE

Date	Day	Time	m	Time	m	Time	m	Time	m
1	M	0017	1.6	0708	4.1	1246	1.4	1947	4.4
2	TU	0119	1.4	0806	4.3	1342	1.2	2039	4.6
3	W	0212	1.1	0857	4.5	1433	1.0	2127	4.7
4	TH	0300	0.9	0946	4.6	1521	0.8	2213	4.8
5	F O	0347	0.8	1035	4.7	1607	0.8	2259	4.8
6	SA	0432	0.7	1125	4.7	1653	0.8	2345	4.8
7	SU	0517	0.7	1217	4.7	1738	0.9		
8	M	0031	4.7	0601	0.8	1312	4.6	1823	1.0
9	TU	0118	4.6	0645	0.9	1408	4.6	1908	1.2
10	W	0205	4.4	0730	1.1	1458	4.4	1956	1.4
11	TH	0252	4.3	0818	1.3	1544	4.3	2048	1.6
12	F	0341	4.1	0912	1.6	1631	4.2	2148	1.8
13	SA ☾	0434	3.9	1013	1.7	1724	4.0	2250	1.9
14	SU	0535	3.7	1115	1.8	1826	4.0	2352	2.0
15	M	0647	3.7	1213	1.8	1929	4.0		
16	TU	0049	1.9	0752	3.8	1306	1.8	2024	4.1
17	W	0139	1.7	0848	3.9	1353	1.6	2113	4.2
18	TH	0222	1.6	0936	4.1	1437	1.5	2156	4.3
19	F	0303	1.4	1020	4.2	1519	1.4	2235	4.4
20	SA	0343	1.2	1100	4.3	1601	1.3	2311	4.5
21	SU ●	0423	1.1	1136	4.4	1642	1.2	2345	4.5
22	M	0503	1.0	1212	4.5	1723	1.1		
23	TU	0020	4.6	0543	0.9	1252	4.5	1803	1.1
24	W	0058	4.5	0624	0.9	1335	4.6	1845	1.1
25	TH	0140	4.5	0706	0.9	1423	4.5	1930	1.2
26	F	0228	4.4	0753	1.0	1518	4.5	2020	1.3
27	SA	0325	4.3	0845	1.2	1616	4.4	2117	1.4
28	SU ☽	0429	4.2	0947	1.3	1715	4.4	2225	1.5
29	M	0534	4.1	1100	1.4	1815	4.4	2338	1.5
30	TU	0638	4.1	1210	1.4	1916	4.4		

SUNRISE AND SUNSET TIMES

PORTSMOUTH
At 50°48'N 1°07' W

UT		Sunrise	Sunset
Jan	01	0807	1610
	15	0800	1628
Feb	01	0740	1656
	15	0717	1721
Mar	01	0649	1746
	15	0618	1809
BST			
Apr	01	0640	1937
	15	0610	2000
May	01	0538	2026
	15	0515	2047
Jun	01	0457	2109
	15	0451	2120
Jul	01	0455	2121
	15	0508	2112
Aug	01	0531	2050
	15	0552	2025
Sep	01	0618	1950
	15	0640	1918
Oct	01	0705	1842
	15	0628	1812
UT			
Nov	01	0656	1639
	15	0720	1618
Dec	01	0745	1602
	15	0800	1559

PORTSMOUTH
LAT 50°48'N
LONG 1°07'W

TIMES AND HEIGHTS OF HIGH AND LOW WATER (Heights in Metres)

TIME ZONE UT
For Summer Time (area enclosed in shaded box) add 1 hour

2020

JULY

Date	Day	Time	m	Date	Day	Time	m
1	W	0045 0739 1312 2012	1.5 4.2 1.3 4.5	16	TH	0045 0806 1307 2034	1.9 3.8 1.8 4.0
2	TH	0145 0837 1408 2106	1.3 4.3 1.3 4.5	17	F	0139 0910 1400 2127	1.7 3.9 1.7 4.2
3	F	0239 0933 1501 2157	1.2 4.4 1.2 4.6	18	SA	0229 0959 1451 2210	1.5 4.1 1.6 4.3
4	SA	0330 1027 1552 2245	1.0 4.5 1.1 4.6	19	SU	0317 1040 1539 2248	1.3 4.3 1.4 4.4
5	SU ○	0418 1119 1640 2330	0.9 4.5 1.0 4.6	20	M ●	0404 1117 1625 2324	1.1 4.5 1.2 4.6
6	M	0504 1209 1726	0.8 4.6 1.0	21	TU	0448 1155 1709	0.9 4.6 1.0
7	TU	0015 0548 1259 1809	4.6 0.8 4.6 1.1	22	W	0002 0531 1235 1752	4.6 0.7 4.7 0.9
8	W	0059 0630 1346 1852	4.5 0.9 4.5 1.2	23	TH	0042 0613 1319 1834	4.6 0.7 4.7 0.9
9	TH	0143 0711 1431 1934	4.4 1.0 4.5 1.3	24	F	0124 0655 1407 1918	4.6 0.7 4.7 0.9
10	F	0227 0751 1513 2015	4.3 1.2 4.4 1.5	25	SA	0212 0739 1500 2004	4.6 0.8 4.7 1.0
11	SA	0310 0830 1552 2056	4.2 1.4 4.3 1.6	26	SU	0307 0827 1555 2055	4.5 0.9 4.6 1.2
12	SU ☾	0353 0913 1631 2144	4.0 1.6 4.1 1.8	27	M ☽	0407 0921 1650 2155	4.4 1.2 4.5 1.4
13	M	0438 1003 1715 2241	3.9 1.8 4.0 1.9	28	TU	0509 1027 1747 2306	4.2 1.4 4.4 1.5
14	TU	0531 1105 1809 2345	3.7 1.9 3.9 1.9	29	W	0613 1141 1848	4.1 1.5 4.3
15	W	0640 1209 1921	3.7 1.9 3.9	30	TH	0019 0720 1251 1952	1.6 4.1 1.6 4.3
				31	F	0126 0827 1354 2053	1.5 4.1 1.6 4.3

AUGUST

Date	Day	Time	m	Date	Day	Time	m
1	SA	0226 0931 1452 2147	1.4 4.2 1.4 4.4	16	SU	0206 0937 1432 2146	1.7 4.1 1.7 4.2
2	SU	0319 1027 1543 2233	1.2 4.4 1.3 4.5	17	M	0259 1018 1523 2225	1.3 4.3 1.4 4.4
3	M ○	0407 1113 1630 2316	1.0 4.5 1.1 4.5	18	TU	0347 1055 1610 2302	1.0 4.5 1.1 4.6
4	TU	0452 1155 1713 2358	0.9 4.5 1.0 4.5	19	W ●	0432 1133 1654 2341	0.7 4.7 0.8 4.7
5	W	0533 1237 1754	0.8 4.6 1.0	20	TH	0515 1213 1736	0.5 4.8 0.7
6	TH	0039 0612 1319 1832	4.5 0.8 4.5 1.1	21	F	0021 0556 1257 1817	4.8 0.4 4.9 0.6
7	F	0120 0648 1400 1907	4.4 1.0 4.5 1.2	22	SA	0104 0637 1343 1859	4.8 0.4 4.9 0.7
8	SA	0200 0720 1437 1938	4.3 1.1 4.4 1.3	23	SU	0151 0719 1435 1942	4.7 0.6 4.8 0.8
9	SU	0235 0750 1510 2009	4.2 1.3 4.3 1.5	24	M	0244 0803 1529 2030	4.6 0.8 4.7 1.1
10	M	0310 0822 1542 2044	4.1 1.4 4.2 1.6	25	TU ☽	0344 0854 1623 2126	4.5 1.2 4.5 1.4
11	TU ☾	0349 0902 1621 2129	4.0 1.6 4.1 1.8	26	W	0447 0959 1720 2242	4.2 1.5 4.3 1.7
12	W	0436 0952 1708 2228	3.9 1.8 3.9 1.9	27	TH	0554 1124 1825	4.1 1.8 4.1
13	TH	0533 1100 1807 2346	3.7 2.0 3.8 2.0	28	F	0002 0707 1239 1937	1.8 4.0 1.9 4.0
14	F	0648 1224 1932	3.6 2.1 3.8	29	SA	0114 0824 1346 2044	1.7 4.0 1.8 4.1
15	SA	0103 0843 1334 2100	1.9 3.8 1.9 4.0	30	SU	0215 0938 1443 2138	1.6 4.2 1.6 4.2
				31	M	0307 1033 1531 2220	1.3 4.4 1.4 4.4

SEPTEMBER

Date	Day	Time	m	Date	Day	Time	m
1	TU	0352 1101 1614 2259	1.1 4.5 1.2 4.5	16	W	0328 1029 1551 2237	0.9 4.7 1.0 4.7
2	W ○	0434 1135 1655 2338	0.9 4.6 1.0 4.5	17	TH ●	0412 1107 1634 2316	0.6 4.9 0.7 4.9
3	TH	0513 1212 1733	0.8 4.6 0.9	18	F	0454 1148 1716 2357	0.4 5.0 0.5 4.9
4	F	0017 0548 1250 1807	4.5 0.8 4.6 1.0	19	SA	0535 1230 1756	0.3 5.0 0.5
5	SA	0055 0620 1327 1837	4.5 0.9 4.6 1.1	20	SU	0040 0615 1315 1837	5.0 0.4 5.0 0.5
6	SU	0130 0648 1359 1903	4.4 1.1 4.5 1.2	21	M	0127 0656 1404 1919	4.9 0.6 4.9 0.8
7	M	0200 0713 1427 1929	4.3 1.2 4.4 1.3	22	TU	0220 0739 1458 2005	4.7 0.9 4.7 1.1
8	TU	0230 0742 1457 2001	4.3 1.3 4.3 1.4	23	W	0321 0828 1553 2100	4.5 1.3 4.5 1.5
9	W	0308 0817 1535 2040	4.1 1.5 4.1 1.6	24	TH ☽	0428 0937 1653 2223	4.3 1.7 4.2 1.8
10	TH ☾	0354 0901 1623 2132	4.0 1.8 4.0 1.9	25	F	0537 1111 1803 2346	4.0 2.0 4.0 1.9
11	F	0451 1001 1723 2250	3.8 2.1 3.8 2.1	26	SA	0654 1224 1921	3.9 2.1 3.9
12	SA	0605 1152 1843	3.7 2.2 3.7	27	SU	0055 0827 1329 2040	1.9 4.0 2.0 4.0
13	SU	0041 0811 1320 2030	2.0 3.8 2.1 3.9	28	M	0155 1000 1424 2215	1.7 4.3 1.7 4.2
14	M	0149 0910 1418 2119	1.7 4.1 1.7 4.2	29	TU	0245 1047 1510 2206	1.4 4.5 1.4 4.3
15	TU	0241 0951 1507 2159	1.3 4.4 1.3 4.5	30	W	0329 1050 1551 2239	1.2 4.6 1.2 4.4

OCTOBER

Date	Day	Time	m	Date	Day	Time	m
1	TH ○	0409 1111 1630 2315	1.0 4.6 1.0 4.5	16	F ●	0346 1040 1610 2251	0.6 5.0 0.6 4.9
2	F	0446 1145 1706 2353	0.9 4.7 1.0 4.5	17	SA	0429 1120 1652 2333	0.4 5.1 0.5 5.0
3	SA	0520 1220 1739	0.9 4.7 1.0	18	SU	0510 1202 1733	0.4 5.1 0.5
4	SU	0029 0550 1254 1805	4.5 1.0 4.6 1.1	19	M	0017 0551 1247 1814	5.0 0.5 5.1 0.6
5	M	0101 0616 1322 1830	4.5 1.1 4.6 1.2	20	TU	0105 0633 1334 1856	4.9 0.7 4.9 0.8
6	TU	0128 0641 1348 1856	4.5 1.2 4.5 1.2	21	W	0159 0717 1426 1942	4.8 1.0 4.7 1.1
7	W	0157 0709 1417 1926	4.4 1.3 4.4 1.3	22	TH	0303 0807 1523 2038	4.6 1.5 4.4 1.5
8	TH	0234 0743 1455 2004	4.3 1.5 4.2 1.5	23	F ☽	0411 0918 1624 2201	4.3 1.9 4.1 1.8
9	F	0321 0825 1544 2052	4.1 1.8 4.0 1.8	24	SA	0518 1048 1734 2319	4.1 2.1 3.9 2.0
10	SA ☾	0421 0922 1648 2206	3.9 2.1 3.8 2.1	25	SU	0633 1157 1854	4.0 2.1 3.8
11	SU	0540 1140 1813	3.8 2.3 3.7	26	M	0025 0827 1301 2106	2.0 4.1 2.0 3.9
12	M	0024 0729 1304 1953	2.0 3.9 2.1 3.9	27	TU	0124 0935 1356 2159	1.8 4.3 1.8 4.1
13	TU	0127 0837 1357 2048	1.7 4.2 1.7 4.2	28	W	0215 1017 1442 2150	1.6 4.5 1.6 4.3
14	W	0217 0921 1444 2130	1.3 4.5 1.3 4.5	29	TH	0258 1022 1523 2216	1.4 4.6 1.3 4.4
15	TH	0303 1000 1527 2210	0.9 4.8 0.9 4.8	30	F	0338 1043 1601 2252	1.2 4.6 1.2 4.5
				31	SA ○	0414 1116 1636 2329	1.1 4.7 1.1 4.5

NOVEMBER

Date	Day	Time	m	Date	Day	Time	m
1	SU	0448 1151 1707	1.1 4.7 1.1	16	M	0447 1138 1711 2359	0.6 5.1 0.6 5.0
2	M	0004 0518 1223 1735	4.6 1.2 4.6 1.1	17	TU	0530 1223 1754	0.7 5.0 0.7
3	TU	0036 0547 1251 1802	4.6 1.2 4.6 1.2	18	W	0050 0614 1311 1838	4.9 0.9 4.9 0.9
4	W	0104 0615 1318 1831	4.5 1.3 4.5 1.2	19	TH	0146 0700 1402 1925	4.7 1.2 4.7 1.1
5	TH	0135 0646 1348 1903	4.5 1.4 4.4 1.3	20	F	0251 0751 1456 2019	4.6 1.5 4.4 1.5
6	F	0213 0722 1426 1942	4.4 1.5 4.3 1.5	21	SA	0353 0855 1553 2128	4.4 1.8 4.2 1.7
7	SA	0302 0805 1517 2031	4.2 1.8 4.1 1.7	22	SU ☽	0451 1012 1657 2241	4.2 2.0 3.9 1.9
8	SU ☾	0405 0903 1624 2142	4.0 2.0 3.9 1.9	23	M	0555 1120 1809 2346	4.0 2.1 3.8 1.9
9	M	0521 1051 1746 2349	4.0 2.2 3.8 1.9	24	TU	0709 1223 1923	4.0 2.1 3.8
10	TU	0646 1232 1911	4.1 2.0 4.0	25	W	0044 0824 1320 2026	1.9 4.2 1.9 3.9
11	W	0054 0757 1327 2012	1.7 4.3 1.7 4.3	26	TH	0137 0906 1408 2110	1.7 4.3 1.7 4.1
12	TH	0146 0847 1415 2059	1.3 4.6 1.3 4.5	27	F	0222 0938 1450 2150	1.6 4.4 1.5 4.3
13	F	0234 0930 1500 2143	1.0 4.8 1.0 4.8	28	SA	0302 1013 1528 2230	1.4 4.5 1.3 4.4
14	SA	0319 1012 1544 2227	0.8 5.0 0.7 4.9	29	SU	0340 1050 1603 2309	1.3 4.6 1.2 4.5
15	SU ●	0403 1054 1628 2312	0.6 5.1 0.6 5.0	30	M ○	0416 1125 1637 2345	1.3 4.6 1.2 4.5

DECEMBER

Date	Day	Time	m	Date	Day	Time	m
1	TU	0450 1158 1710	1.3 4.6 1.1	16	W	0515 1207 1740	0.9 4.9 0.7
2	W	0018 0524 1228 1742	4.5 1.3 4.6 1.1	17	TH	0043 0600 1254 1825	4.8 1.0 4.8 0.8
3	TH	0050 0557 1258 1816	4.5 1.3 4.5 1.2	18	F	0139 0647 1342 1910	4.7 1.2 4.6 1.0
4	F	0124 0633 1332 1852	4.5 1.4 4.5 1.2	19	SA	0236 0734 1432 1958	4.6 1.4 4.4 1.3
5	SA	0205 0712 1412 1933	4.4 1.5 4.3 1.3	20	SU	0327 0826 1524 2050	4.4 1.6 4.2 1.5
6	SU	0254 0757 1501 2023	4.3 1.6 4.2 1.5	21	M ☽	0416 0925 1617 2150	4.3 1.8 4.0 1.7
7	M	0354 0853 1605 2125	4.2 1.8 4.0 1.6	22	TU	0507 1031 1716 2255	4.1 2.0 3.8 1.9
8	TU ☾	0500 1009 1719 2250	4.2 1.9 4.0 1.7	23	W	0604 1136 1822 2356	4.0 2.0 3.7 1.9
9	W	0609 1142 1831	4.2 1.8 4.1	24	TH	0706 1236 1929	4.0 2.0 3.8
10	TH	0012 0714 1250 1934	1.6 4.4 1.6 4.2	25	F	0051 0805 1329 2029	1.9 4.1 1.8 3.9
11	F	0112 0811 1344 2029	1.4 4.5 1.4 4.4	26	SA	0141 0857 1414 2122	1.8 4.2 1.7 4.0
12	SA	0204 0901 1433 2120	1.2 4.7 1.1 4.6	27	SU	0225 0944 1455 2210	1.7 4.3 1.5 4.2
13	SU	0253 0948 1521 2209	1.0 4.8 0.9 4.7	28	M	0308 1026 1534 2253	1.5 4.4 1.4 4.3
14	M ●	0341 1035 1608 2259	0.9 4.9 0.8 4.8	29	TU	0349 1104 1613 2330	1.4 4.5 1.2 4.4
15	TU	0428 1121 1654 2350	0.9 4.9 0.7 4.8	30	W ○	0429 1138 1651	1.3 4.5 1.1
				31	TH	0004 0507 1211 1729	4.5 1.2 4.6 1.0

IGH WATERS- IMPORTANT NOTE. THE HIGH WATER DURATION AT PORTSMOUTH CAN OCCUR OVER AN EXTENDED TIME PERIOD. I.E. A "HIGH WATER

SHOREHAM
LAT 50°50′N
LONG 0°15′W

TIMES AND HEIGHTS OF HIGH AND LOW WATER (Heights in Metres)

TIME ZONE UT
For Summer Time (area enclosed in shaded box) add 1 hour

2020

JANUARY

Date	Day	Time	m
1	W	0247 0853 1457 2115	5.6 1.6 5.3 1.5
2	TH	0328 0939 1542 2203	5.3 1.8 5.0 1.8
3	F ☽	0417 1032 1641 2257	5.1 2.0 4.8 2.0
4	SA	0517 1132 1748 2359	5.0 2.1 4.7 2.1
5	SU	0621 1238 1853	4.9 2.0 4.8
6	M	0106 0721 1345 1952	2.0 5.1 1.9 5.0
7	TU	0211 0817 1443 2046	1.9 5.3 1.6 5.3
8	W	0306 0907 1532 2135	1.6 5.6 1.3 5.6
9	TH	0353 0952 1616 2221	1.4 5.9 1.1 5.9
10	F O	0436 1036 1659 2305	1.1 6.1 0.9 6.1
11	SA	0519 1119 1742 2349	1.0 6.3 0.7 6.3
12	SU	0602 1203 1826	0.8 6.3 0.6
13	M	0034 0646 1248 1911	6.3 0.8 6.3 0.6
14	TU	0120 0732 1333 1958	6.3 0.8 6.3 0.6
15	W	0206 0821 1421 2047	6.3 0.9 6.1 0.8
16	TH	0255 0913 1512 2140	6.1 1.0 5.9 0.9
17	F ☾	0348 1009 1608 2238	5.9 1.2 5.6 1.2
18	SA	0447 1113 1713 2344	5.6 1.4 5.3 1.4
19	SU	0553 1223 1827	5.4 1.5 5.1
20	M	0055 0707 1333 1946	1.6 5.4 1.5 5.2
21	TU	0204 0819 1437 2056	1.5 5.4 1.4 5.3
22	W	0304 0920 1533 2153	1.4 5.6 1.2 5.6
23	TH	0357 1012 1622 2242	1.2 5.8 1.0 5.8
24	F ●	0443 1058 1706 2326	1.1 6.0 0.9 6.0
25	SA	0526 1139 1747	1.0 6.1 0.8
26	SU	0006 0604 1217 1824	6.1 1.0 6.1 0.8
27	M	0043 0640 1251 1900	6.1 1.0 6.0 0.8
28	TU	0116 0715 1322 1934	6.0 1.0 5.9 0.9
29	W	0145 0748 1350 2007	5.9 1.1 5.7 1.1
30	TH	0212 0823 1419 2042	5.8 1.3 5.5 1.2
31	F	0239 0859 1451 2117	5.6 1.4 5.3 1.5

FEBRUARY

Date	Day	Time	m
1	SA	0313 0939 1530 2157	5.4 1.7 5.1 1.7
2	SU ☽	0356 1028 1622 2250	5.1 1.9 4.8 2.0
3	M	0455 1131 1743	4.9 2.0 4.7
4	TU	0002 0624 1247 1908	2.1 4.8 2.0 4.7
5	W	0121 0738 1402 2014	2.1 5.0 1.8 5.0
6	TH	0233 0839 1505 2112	1.8 5.3 1.5 5.4
7	F	0330 0932 1556 2203	1.4 5.7 1.1 5.8
8	SA	0418 1021 1642 2252	1.1 6.1 0.8 6.2
9	SU O	0503 1107 1727 2338	0.8 6.3 0.5 6.4
10	M	0548 1153 1812	0.6 6.5 0.4
11	TU	0024 0633 1239 1857	6.5 0.5 6.5 0.3
12	W	0109 0719 1323 1943	6.6 0.4 6.5 0.3
13	TH	0153 0805 1408 2029	6.6 0.5 6.4 0.4
14	F	0237 0852 1453 2116	6.4 0.7 6.1 0.7
15	SA ☾	0323 0942 1542 2207	6.1 0.9 5.7 1.1
16	SU	0414 1038 1639 2308	5.7 1.3 5.3 1.5
17	M	0514 1149 1750	5.3 1.6 4.9
18	TU	0026 0629 1310 1920	1.8 5.0 1.8 4.8
19	W	0146 0759 1422 2044	1.8 5.0 1.6 5.0
20	TH	0251 0909 1520 2144	1.7 5.2 1.4 5.4
21	F	0345 1002 1609 2231	1.4 5.5 1.1 5.7
22	SA	0430 1047 1651 2312	1.1 5.8 0.9 5.9
23	SU ●	0509 1126 1728 2349	1.0 5.9 0.8 6.1
24	M	0546 1201 1804	0.9 6.0 0.7
25	TU	0023 0619 1233 1836	6.1 0.9 6.0 0.7
26	W	0052 0651 1258 1909	6.0 0.9 5.9 0.8
27	TH	0115 0722 1321 1939	6.0 0.9 5.9 0.9
28	F	0136 0752 1347 2007	5.9 1.0 5.8 1.0
29	SA	0202 0821 1416 2034	5.8 1.2 5.6 1.2

MARCH

Date	Day	Time	m
1	SU	0233 0851 1451 2107	5.6 1.4 5.4 1.5
2	M ☽	0311 0931 1534 2154	5.3 1.6 5.1 1.8
3	TU	0400 1029 1634 2301	5.0 1.9 4.7 2.1
4	W	0512 1150 1825	4.7 2.1 4.6
5	TH	0037 0704 1325 1948	2.1 4.7 1.9 4.9
6	F	0207 0816 1441 2052	1.9 5.1 1.5 5.4
7	SA	0310 0914 1536 2147	1.4 5.6 1.0 5.9
8	SU	0400 1005 1623 2236	1.0 6.0 0.6 6.3
9	M O	0445 1053 1708 2323	0.6 6.4 0.3 6.6
10	TU	0530 1139 1753	0.4 6.6 0.2
11	W	0008 0614 1225 1837	6.7 0.2 6.7 0.1
12	TH	0052 0659 1308 1922	6.8 0.2 6.7 0.1
13	F	0134 0744 1351 2006	6.7 0.3 6.5 0.3
14	SA	0215 0829 1433 2050	6.5 0.5 6.2 0.6
15	SU	0257 0914 1519 2137	6.1 0.8 5.8 1.1
16	M ☾	0344 1005 1613 2234	5.6 1.3 5.3 1.6
17	TU	0442 1113 1721 2358	5.1 1.7 4.8 2.0
18	W	0557 1247 1855	4.7 1.9 4.6
19	TH	0127 0738 1403 2029	2.0 4.7 1.8 4.9
20	F	0235 0855 1502 2128	1.8 5.0 1.5 5.3
21	SA	0327 0946 1548 2212	1.5 5.3 1.2 5.6
22	SU	0410 1028 1628 2250	1.2 5.6 1.0 5.9
23	M	0447 1105 1703 2325	1.0 5.8 0.8 6.0
24	TU ●	0521 1138 1737 2357	0.9 5.9 0.7 6.1
25	W	0554 1207 1810	0.8 6.0 0.7
26	TH	0022 0625 1231 1841	6.0 0.8 5.9 0.8
27	F	0043 0655 1254 1911	6.0 0.8 5.9 0.9
28	SA	0105 0723 1320 1936	6.0 0.9 5.9 1.0
29	SU	0132 0748 1349 2002	5.9 1.0 5.8 1.1
30	M	0203 0819 1423 2037	5.7 1.2 5.6 1.4
31	TU	0240 0900 1505 2125	5.5 1.5 5.2 1.7

APRIL

Date	Day	Time	m
1	W ☽	0327 0956 1603 2231	5.1 1.8 4.9 2.0
2	TH	0435 1113 1750	4.7 2.0 4.7
3	F	0006 0635 1253 1924	2.1 4.7 1.9 4.9
4	SA	0142 0753 1415 2031	1.8 5.1 1.5 5.4
5	SU	0247 0854 1512 2126	1.3 5.6 1.0 5.9
6	M	0337 0946 1559 2215	0.9 6.0 0.6 6.4
7	TU	0423 1034 1644 2301	0.5 6.4 0.3 6.7
8	W O	0508 1121 1730 2346	0.2 6.6 0.1 6.8
9	TH	0553 1206 1815	0.1 6.7 0.1
10	F	0029 0637 1250 1859	6.8 0.1 6.7 0.2
11	SA	0111 0722 1332 1943	6.7 0.3 6.5 0.4
12	SU	0152 0805 1414 2026	6.4 0.5 6.2 0.8
13	M	0233 0849 1459 2111	6.0 0.9 5.8 1.2
14	TU ☾	0319 0937 1552 2205	5.5 1.3 5.3 1.7
15	W	0416 1039 1657 2325	5.0 1.7 4.9 2.1
16	TH	0526 1217 1819	4.6 2.0 4.7
17	F	0102 0702 1334 1957	2.1 4.5 1.9 4.8
18	SA	0208 0826 1432 2056	1.9 4.8 1.6 5.2
19	SU	0300 0918 1518 2141	1.5 5.2 1.3 5.5
20	M	0341 0959 1557 2219	1.2 5.5 1.1 5.8
21	TU	0418 1035 1633 2253	1.0 5.7 0.9 5.9
22	W	0452 1107 1707 2322	0.9 5.8 0.9 6.0
23	TH ●	0525 1135 1741 2347	0.8 5.9 0.8 6.0
24	F	0558 1201 1814	0.8 5.9 0.9
25	SA	0011 0629 1229 1843	6.0 0.8 5.9 0.9
26	SU	0038 0657 1258 1911	6.0 0.9 5.9 1.0
27	M	0108 0726 1330 1941	5.9 1.0 5.8 1.1
28	TU	0142 0800 1406 2021	5.8 1.1 5.6 1.3
29	W	0221 0844 1451 2111	5.5 1.3 5.4 1.6
30	TH ☽	0310 0941 1552 2217	5.2 1.6 5.0 1.9

MAY

Date	Day	Time	m
1	F	0419 1054 1728 2345	4.8 1.8 4.9 1.9
2	SA	0607 1225 1857	4.8 1.7 5.1
3	SU	0113 0726 1344 2004	1.7 5.1 1.4 5.5
4	M	0219 0829 1443 2100	1.2 5.6 1.0 6.0
5	TU	0311 0922 1533 2150	0.8 6.0 0.6 6.4
6	W	0358 1012 1620 2237	0.5 6.3 0.4 6.6
7	TH O	0445 1100 1706 2323	0.3 6.5 0.3 6.7
8	F	0530 1146 1752	0.2 6.6 0.3
9	SA	0007 0616 1231 1837	6.7 0.3 6.5 0.4
10	SU	0050 0701 1315 1921	6.5 0.4 6.4 0.6
11	M	0131 0745 1358 2005	6.3 0.6 6.1 0.9
12	TU	0213 0828 1443 2050	5.9 1.0 5.8 1.3
13	W	0259 0915 1533 2141	5.5 1.3 5.4 1.7
14	TH ☾	0352 1009 1631 2246	5.0 1.7 5.0 2.0
15	F	0455 1124 1736	4.7 1.9 4.8
16	SA	0017 0606 1249 1854	2.1 4.6 1.9 4.9
17	SU	0128 0731 1350 2007	1.9 4.7 1.7 5.1
18	M	0221 0833 1439 2057	1.7 5.0 1.5 5.3
19	TU	0305 0918 1521 2136	1.4 5.2 1.3 5.6
20	W	0344 0955 1559 2210	1.2 5.5 1.2 5.8
21	TH	0420 1027 1636 2242	1.1 5.7 1.1 5.9
22	F ●	0455 1100 1712 2312	1.0 5.8 1.0 5.9
23	SA	0530 1133 1747 2344	0.9 5.9 1.0 6.0
24	SU	0605 1207 1821	0.9 5.9 1.0
25	M	0016 0637 1242 1854	6.0 0.9 5.9 1.0
26	TU	0052 0712 1318 1930	5.9 1.0 5.9 1.1
27	W	0129 0751 1359 2013	5.8 1.0 5.7 1.3
28	TH	0213 0837 1448 2105	5.6 1.2 5.5 1.4
29	F	0305 0933 1548 2209	5.3 1.4 5.3 1.6
30	SA ☽	0411 1041 1705 2325	5.1 1.5 5.2 1.6
31	SU	0535 1159 1824	5.1 1.5 5.3

JUNE

Date	Day	Time	m
1	M	0042 0653 1312 1932	1.5 5.2 1.3 5.6
2	TU	0148 0759 1414 2031	1.2 5.5 1.0 5.9
3	W	0244 0857 1508 2125	0.9 5.8 0.8 6.2
4	TH	0335 0950 1558 2214	0.7 6.1 0.6 6.4
5	F O	0424 1041 1647 2302	0.5 6.2 0.6 6.4
6	SA	0511 1129 1734 2348	0.5 6.3 0.6 6.4
7	SU	0558 1216 1820	0.5 6.3 0.7
8	M	0031 0643 1301 1904	6.3 0.6 6.2 0.8
9	TU	0114 0727 1344 1947	6.1 0.8 6.0 1.0
10	W	0156 0810 1427 2030	5.8 1.0 5.8 1.3
11	TH	0239 0852 1511 2115	5.5 1.2 5.5 1.5
12	F	0326 0939 1600 2206	5.2 1.5 5.3 1.8
13	SA ☾	0419 1032 1654 2306	4.9 1.7 5.1 1.9
14	SU	0517 1133 1751	4.7 1.9 5.0
15	M	0017 0618 1242 1851	2.0 4.7 1.9 5.0
16	TU	0126 0719 1346 1949	1.9 4.8 1.8 5.1
17	W	0220 0816 1438 2040	1.7 5.0 1.6 5.3
18	TH	0306 0905 1523 2125	1.5 5.3 1.4 5.5
19	F	0347 0948 1605 2205	1.3 5.5 1.3 5.7
20	SA	0427 1029 1645 2243	1.1 5.7 1.2 5.9
21	SU ●	0505 1110 1724 2322	1.0 5.9 1.1 6.0
22	M	0544 1149 1803	0.9 6.0 1.0
23	TU	0000 0622 1230 1841	6.0 0.9 6.0 1.0
24	W	0040 0702 1311 1923	6.0 0.8 6.0 1.0
25	TH	0122 0745 1355 2008	5.9 0.9 5.9 1.1
26	F	0208 0832 1443 2059	5.8 1.0 5.8 1.2
27	SA	0259 0925 1537 2157	5.6 1.1 5.7 1.3
28	SU ☽	0357 1025 1638 2302	5.5 1.2 5.6 1.4
29	M	0503 1131 1746	5.3 1.3 5.5
30	TU	0011 0615 1241 1856	1.4 5.3 1.3 5.5

SUNRISE AND SUNSET TIMES

SHOREHAM
At 50°50′N 0°15′W

		Sunrise	Sunset
UT			
Jan	01	0803	1606
	15	0757	1624
Feb	01	0737	1653
	15	0713	1718
Mar	01	0645	1742
	15	0615	1806
BST			
Apr	01	0637	1934
	15	0607	1957
May	01	0535	2022
	15	0512	2044
Jun	01	0453	2105
	15	0447	2116
Jul	01	0452	2118
	15	0505	2108
Aug	01	0527	2046
	15	0548	2021
Sep	01	0615	1946
	15	0636	1915
Oct	01	0701	1839
	15	0724	1809
UT			
Nov	01	0653	1636
	15	0717	1614
Dec	01	0741	1558
	15	0757	1555

SHOREHAM
LAT 50°50'N
LONG 0°15'W

TIMES AND HEIGHTS OF HIGH AND LOW WATER (Heights in Metres)

TIME ZONE UT
For Summer Time (area enclosed in shaded box) add 1 hour

2020

JULY

Date	Time	m	Date	Time	m
1 W	0119 0728 1347 2003	1.3 5.4 1.2 5.7	16 TH	0116 0726 1344 1953	1.9 4.8 1.9 5.1
2 TH	0221 0834 1447 2103	1.1 5.5 1.1 5.9	17 F	0222 0825 1447 2048	1.7 5.1 1.7 5.3
3 F	0317 0934 1542 2158	1.0 5.8 1.0 6.0	18 SA	0316 0917 1538 2136	1.5 5.4 1.5 5.6
4 SA	0409 1028 1632 2248	0.8 5.9 0.9 6.1	19 SU	0402 1005 1622 2221	1.2 5.6 1.3 5.8
5 SU	0458 1118 1720 O 2334	0.7 6.1 0.8 6.2	20 M	0444 1050 1705 ● 2304	1.0 5.9 1.1 6.0
6 M	0544 1204 1805	0.7 6.1 0.9	21 TU	0526 1134 1747 2347	0.8 6.1 0.9 6.1
7 TU	0018 0628 1248 1848	6.1 0.7 6.1 0.9	22 W	0608 1218 1829	0.7 6.2 0.8
8 W	0100 0709 1328 1928	6.0 0.8 6.1 1.0	23 TH	0030 0651 1301 1912	6.2 0.6 6.3 0.8
9 TH	0139 0749 1407 2007	5.8 1.0 5.9 1.2	24 F	0114 0735 1345 1958	6.2 0.6 6.3 0.8
10 F	0217 0826 1444 2046	5.6 1.1 5.7 1.4	25 SA	0158 0821 1430 2046	6.1 0.7 6.2 0.9
11 SA	0255 0906 1523 2127	5.4 1.3 5.5 1.5	26 SU	0245 0910 1518 2138	6.0 0.8 6.0 1.0
12 SU	0336 0948 1606 ☾ 2214	5.1 1.5 5.3 1.7	27 M	0336 1003 1611 ☽ 2235	5.7 1.0 5.8 1.2
13 M	0425 1036 1655 2308	4.9 1.7 5.1 1.9	28 TU	0434 1103 1712 2341	5.5 1.3 5.5 1.4
14 TU	0522 1132 1753	4.7 1.9 4.9	29 W	0542 1212 1822	5.2 1.5 5.4
15 W	0008 0624 1236 1854	2.0 4.7 2.0 4.9	30 TH	0053 0701 1326 1939	1.5 5.1 1.6 5.3
			31 F	0204 0821 1434 2050	1.4 5.2 1.5 5.5

AUGUST

Date	Time	m	Date	Time	m
1 SA	0306 0927 1532 2149	1.3 5.5 1.3 5.7	16 SU	0250 0853 1515 2114	1.6 5.3 1.6 5.5
2 SU	0359 1021 1622 2239	1.1 5.8 1.1 5.9	17 M	0341 0945 1603 2203	1.3 5.7 1.3 5.9
3 M	0447 1109 1708 O 2324	0.9 6.0 1.0 6.0	18 TU	0425 1033 1646 2248	1.0 6.0 1.0 6.1
4 TU	0530 1152 1750	0.8 6.1 0.9	19 W	0507 1118 1729 ● 2332	0.7 6.3 0.7 6.3
5 W	0006 0610 1232 1829	6.1 0.8 6.1 0.9	20 TH	0550 1202 1812	0.5 6.5 0.6
6 TH	0044 0648 1308 1905	6.0 0.8 6.1 1.0	21 F	0016 0633 1246 1855	6.4 0.4 6.6 0.5
7 F	0118 0723 1341 1939	5.9 0.9 6.0 1.1	22 SA	0100 0717 1329 1940	6.5 0.4 6.6 0.5
8 SA	0148 0756 1410 2013	5.8 1.0 5.8 1.2	23 SU	0143 0802 1411 2026	6.4 0.5 6.5 0.6
9 SU	0216 0830 1437 2049	5.6 1.2 5.7 1.4	24 M	0227 0848 1456 2114	6.2 0.7 6.2 0.9
10 M	0246 0906 1506 2127	5.4 1.4 5.4 1.6	25 TU	0314 0937 1544 ☽ 2207	5.9 1.0 5.9 1.2
11 TU	0320 0945 1543 ☾ 2212	5.1 1.6 5.2 1.8	26 W	0408 1034 1642 2312	5.5 1.4 5.4 1.6
12 W	0406 1033 1636 2309	4.9 1.9 4.9 2.0	27 TH	0515 1147 1754	5.1 1.8 5.1
13 TH	0520 1138 1758	4.7 2.1 4.8	28 F	0034 0642 1312 1924	1.8 4.9 1.9 5.0
14 F	0020 0644 1255 1915	2.1 4.6 2.2 4.8	29 SA	0153 0816 1425 2045	1.7 5.0 1.8 5.2
15 SA	0140 0754 1415 2019	2.0 4.9 2.0 5.1	30 SU	0257 0922 1523 2143	1.5 5.4 1.5 5.5
			31 M	0349 1013 1611 2229	1.2 5.7 1.2 5.8

SEPTEMBER

Date	Time	m	Date	Time	m
1 TU	0432 1055 1652 2310	1.0 6.0 1.0 6.0	16 W	0403 1013 1624 2229	0.9 6.2 0.8 6.3
2 W	0511 1134 1730 O 2348	0.8 6.2 0.9 6.1	17 TH	0445 1057 1707 ● 2314	0.6 6.5 0.6 6.5
3 TH	0548 1210 1805	0.8 6.2 0.9	18 F	0527 1141 1750 2358	0.4 6.7 0.4 6.7
4 F	0022 0621 1242 1838	6.1 0.8 6.2 0.9	19 SA	0611 1224 1834	0.3 6.8 0.4
5 SA	0051 0654 1309 1909	6.0 0.9 6.1 1.0	20 SU	0041 0654 1307 1918	6.7 0.3 6.8 0.4
6 SU	0115 0725 1330 1940	5.9 1.0 5.9 1.1	21 M	0123 0739 1348 2002	6.6 0.4 6.6 0.6
7 M	0138 0755 1352 2010	5.8 1.1 5.8 1.3	22 TU	0206 0823 1431 2049	6.3 0.7 6.2 0.9
8 TU	0204 0824 1420 2041	5.6 1.3 5.6 1.5	23 W	0252 0911 1518 2140	5.9 1.1 5.8 1.3
9 W	0236 0855 1455 2118	5.4 1.6 5.4 1.7	24 TH	0346 1007 1616 ☽ 2245	5.4 1.6 5.3 1.8
10 TH	0315 0938 1540 ☾ 2210	5.1 1.9 5.0 2.0	25 F	0455 1125 1732	5.0 2.0 4.9
11 F	0411 1042 1648 2328	4.7 2.2 4.7 2.2	26 SA	0017 0627 1259 1911	2.0 4.8 2.1 4.8
12 SA	0605 1213 1844	4.6 2.3 4.7	27 SU	0139 0805 1412 2034	1.9 5.0 1.9 5.1
13 SU	0103 0727 1347 1956	2.1 4.8 2.1 5.0	28 M	0242 0907 1508 2128	1.6 5.4 1.6 5.5
14 M	0225 0832 1454 2054	1.8 5.3 1.6 5.5	29 TU	0331 0953 1552 2210	1.3 5.8 1.2 5.8
15 TU	0319 0925 1541 2144	1.3 5.8 1.2 6.0	30 W	0411 1032 1630 2249	1.1 6.0 1.0 6.0

OCTOBER

Date	Time	m	Date	Time	m
1 TH	0447 1108 1705 O 2324	0.9 6.2 0.9 6.1	16 F	0419 1033 1642 ● 2252	0.6 6.7 0.5 6.6
2 F	0521 1141 1738 2354	0.8 6.2 0.9 6.1	17 SA	0502 1117 1725 2336	0.4 6.8 0.3 6.8
3 SA	0553 1210 1810	0.9 6.2 0.9	18 SU	0546 1200 1810	0.3 6.9 0.3
4 SU	0019 0624 1232 1840	6.1 0.9 6.1 1.0	19 M	0020 0631 1242 1854	6.7 0.4 6.8 0.4
5 M	0042 0655 1253 1909	6.0 1.0 6.0 1.1	20 TU	0103 0715 1324 1940	6.6 0.6 6.5 0.6
6 TU	0106 0722 1317 1936	5.9 1.1 5.9 1.2	21 W	0147 0801 1408 2026	6.3 0.9 6.2 1.0
7 W	0133 0749 1346 2005	5.8 1.3 5.7 1.4	22 TH	0234 0849 1456 2117	5.9 1.3 5.7 1.4
8 TH	0204 0821 1420 2042	5.6 1.6 5.5 1.7	23 F	0329 0944 1554 ☽ 2220	5.5 1.7 5.2 1.8
9 F	0242 0905 1503 2134	5.3 1.9 5.1 2.0	24 SA	0436 1101 1708 2352	5.0 2.1 4.8 2.1
10 SA	0336 1008 1606 ☾ 2248	4.9 2.2 4.7 2.2	25 SU	0601 1236 1844	4.8 2.2 4.7
11 SU	0525 1138 1813	4.6 2.3 4.6	26 M	0112 0735 1347 2006	2.0 5.0 2.0 5.0
12 M	0027 0701 1317 1931	2.2 4.9 2.1 5.0	27 TU	0214 0837 1442 2100	1.8 5.3 1.6 5.3
13 TU	0154 0807 1426 2030	1.8 5.4 1.6 5.5	28 W	0302 0922 1525 2142	1.5 5.7 1.3 5.7
14 W	0251 0901 1515 2121	1.3 5.9 1.1 6.0	29 TH	0342 1001 1602 2220	1.2 5.9 1.1 5.9
15 TH	0337 0948 1559 2207	0.9 6.4 0.7 6.4	30 F	0418 1036 1636 2253	1.1 6.1 1.0 6.0
			31 SA	0452 1107 1709 O 2322	1.0 6.1 0.9 6.0

NOVEMBER

Date	Time	m	Date	Time	m
1 SU	0525 1134 1742 2348	1.0 6.1 0.9 6.1	16 M	0525 1136 1749	0.5 6.8 0.4
2 M	0557 1157 1814	1.0 6.1 1.0	17 TU	0001 0610 1221 1835	6.6 0.6 6.7 0.5
3 TU	0014 0628 1223 1843	6.0 1.1 6.0 1.1	18 W	0047 0656 1305 1921	6.5 0.7 6.4 0.7
4 W	0042 0656 1251 1911	6.0 1.2 5.9 1.2	19 TH	0133 0743 1349 2008	6.3 1.0 6.1 1.0
5 TH	0111 0725 1322 1942	5.9 1.4 5.8 1.4	20 F	0221 0830 1438 2057	6.0 1.3 5.7 1.4
6 F	0144 0801 1358 2022	5.7 1.6 5.5 1.6	21 SA	0313 0923 1533 2154	5.6 1.7 5.3 1.7
7 SA	0225 0847 1443 2114	5.4 1.8 5.2 1.9	22 SU	0412 1029 1637 ☽ 2307	5.2 2.0 4.9 2.0
8 SU	0320 0948 1545 ☾ 2223	5.1 2.1 4.9 2.1	23 M	0519 1154 1751	5.0 2.1 4.8
9 M	0448 1110 1734 2351	4.9 2.2 4.8 2.0	24 TU	0028 0637 1307 1914	2.0 5.0 2.0 4.8
10 TU	0628 1239 1859	5.0 2.0 5.1	25 W	0132 0748 1403 2017	1.9 5.2 1.8 5.1
11 W	0114 0735 1350 2000	1.8 5.5 1.6 5.5	26 TH	0224 0840 1450 2104	1.7 5.5 1.5 5.4
12 TH	0217 0831 1444 2054	1.3 5.9 1.1 6.0	27 F	0308 0922 1530 2144	1.5 5.7 1.3 5.6
13 F	0307 0921 1531 2142	0.9 6.3 0.8 6.3	28 SA	0347 0958 1607 2217	1.3 5.9 1.2 5.8
14 SA	0353 1007 1617 2229	0.7 6.6 0.5 6.5	29 SU	0423 1030 1642 2249	1.2 6.0 1.1 5.9
15 SU	0439 1052 1703 ● 2315	0.5 6.8 0.4 6.7	30 M	0458 1059 1717 O 2320	1.2 6.0 1.0 6.0

DECEMBER

Date	Time	m	Date	Time	m
1 TU	0533 1129 1751 2352	1.1 6.0 1.0 6.0	16 W	0556 1206 1821	0.7 6.5 0.6
2 W	0607 1200 1824	1.2 6.0 1.1	17 TH	0036 0642 1251 1907	6.4 0.8 6.3 0.7
3 TH	0024 0638 1233 1856	6.0 1.2 6.0 1.1	18 F	0122 0728 1336 1952	6.2 1.0 6.1 1.0
4 F	0058 0711 1308 1931	5.9 1.3 5.8 1.3	19 SA	0207 0813 1421 2037	6.0 1.3 5.8 1.2
5 SA	0135 0750 1348 2012	5.8 1.4 5.7 1.4	20 SU	0253 0859 1508 2124	5.8 1.5 5.4 1.5
6 SU	0218 0836 1434 2101	5.6 1.6 5.4 1.6	21 M	0342 0949 1600 ☽ 2215	5.5 1.8 5.1 1.7
7 M	0311 0933 1532 2202	5.4 1.8 5.2 1.7	22 TU	0434 1046 1657 2314	5.2 2.0 4.9 1.9
8 TU	0419 1043 1648 ☾ 2316	5.2 1.9 5.1 1.7	23 W	0531 1155 1758	5.1 2.0 4.8
9 W	0542 1201 1814	5.3 1.8 5.2	24 TH	0022 0631 1307 1902	2.0 5.0 2.0 4.8
10 TH	0033 0655 1312 1924	1.6 5.5 1.5 5.4	25 F	0130 0733 1406 2004	2.0 5.1 1.8 5.0
11 F	0140 0757 1412 2024	1.4 5.8 1.2 5.7	26 SA	0226 0828 1455 2056	1.8 5.3 1.6 5.2
12 SA	0238 0852 1506 2119	1.1 6.1 0.9 6.0	27 SU	0314 0914 1538 2140	1.6 5.5 1.4 5.5
13 SU	0331 0943 1557 2211	0.9 6.4 0.7 6.3	28 M	0356 0954 1618 2220	1.5 5.7 1.2 5.7
14 M	0420 1032 1646 ● 2301	0.8 6.5 0.6 6.4	29 TU	0435 1032 1656 2258	1.3 5.9 1.1 5.8
15 TU	0509 1119 1734 2349	0.7 6.5 0.6 6.4	30 W	0513 1108 1733 O 2335	1.2 6.0 1.0 6.0
			31 TH	0550 1144 1810	1.2 6.0 1.0

DOVER

LAT 51°07′N
LONG 1°19′E

TIMES AND HEIGHTS OF HIGH AND LOW WATER (Heights in Metres)

TIME ZONE UT
For Summer Time (area enclosed in shaded box) add 1 hour

2020

JANUARY

Day	Time	m
1 W	0237 0941 1503 2149	6.1 1.7 5.7 1.9
2 TH	0319 1020 1552 2231	5.9 1.9 5.5 2.1
3 F ☽	0407 1108 1650 2324	5.6 2.0 5.3 2.3
4 SA	0506 1211 1756	5.5 2.2 5.2
5 SU	0035 0612 1322 1858	2.4 5.4 2.1 5.3
6 M	0152 0714 1427 1953	2.3 5.5 2.0 5.5
7 TU	0256 0807 1526 2041	2.0 5.7 1.7 5.7
8 W	0353 0854 1619 2125	1.8 6.0 1.5 6.0
9 TH	0444 0939 1709 2207	1.5 6.2 1.3 6.3
10 F O	0532 1023 1757 2249	1.2 6.4 1.1 6.5
11 SA	0618 1106 1843 2332	1.1 6.6 1.0 6.7
12 SU	0705 1150 1928	0.9 6.7 1.0
13 M	0015 0751 1235 2012	6.8 0.9 6.7 1.0
14 TU	0100 0837 1321 2055	6.8 0.8 6.6 1.0
15 W	0147 0922 1410 2138	6.8 0.9 6.5 1.1
16 TH	0238 1008 1504 2224	6.6 1.0 6.3 1.3
17 F ☾	0332 1058 1604 2316	6.4 1.2 6.0 1.5
18 SA	0433 1154 1714	6.1 1.4 5.7
19 SU	0017 0541 1257 1832	1.8 5.9 1.6 5.6
20 M	0125 0659 1404 1945	1.9 5.8 1.7 5.6
21 TU	0236 0812 1515 2049	1.9 5.8 1.7 5.8
22 W	0350 0916 1630 2145	1.7 6.0 1.5 6.0
23 TH	0458 1010 1730 2231	1.5 6.2 1.3 6.2
24 F ●	0552 1055 1817 2311	1.2 6.3 1.2 6.4
25 SA	0637 1133 1857 2349	1.1 6.4 1.2 6.5
26 SU	0717 1209 1931	1.1 6.4 1.2
27 M	0025 0751 1245 2000	6.6 1.1 6.3 1.3
28 TU	0101 0820 1318 2025	6.5 1.2 6.2 1.3
29 W	0134 0847 1349 2051	6.4 1.3 6.1 1.4
30 TH	0202 0914 1417 2121	6.3 1.4 5.9 1.5
31 F	0228 0946 1446 2156	6.1 1.5 5.7 1.7

FEBRUARY

Day	Time	m
1 SA	0300 1023 1522 2236	5.9 1.7 5.5 1.9
2 SU ☽	0344 1108 1615 2327	5.7 2.0 5.3 2.2
3 M	0446 1211 1749	5.4 2.2 5.1
4 TU	0042 0615 1335 1910	2.3 5.3 2.2 5.2
5 W	0210 0730 1449 2011	2.2 5.4 2.0 5.5
6 TH	0319 0830 1551 2104	1.9 5.7 1.7 5.8
7 F	0418 0923 1648 2152	1.6 6.1 1.3 6.2
8 SA	0513 1011 1742 2237	1.2 6.4 1.1 6.5
9 SU O	0606 1057 1834 2321	0.9 6.6 0.9 6.8
10 M	0657 1141 1923	0.7 6.8 0.8
11 TU	0004 0746 1224 2007	7.0 0.5 6.9 0.7
12 W	0048 0831 1308 2047	7.1 0.5 6.8 0.7
13 TH	0132 0912 1353 2126	7.0 0.5 6.7 0.8
14 F	0218 0953 1441 2205	6.9 0.7 6.5 1.0
15 SA ☾	0307 1035 1533 2249	6.6 1.0 6.1 1.3
16 SU	0401 1123 1634 2343	6.2 1.4 5.7 1.7
17 M	0505 1223 1749	5.8 1.8 5.4
18 TU	0051 0624 1333 1915	2.0 5.5 2.0 5.3
19 W	0208 0757 1450 2035	2.1 5.5 2.0 5.5
20 TH	0332 0915 1618 2135	1.9 5.7 1.8 5.8
21 F	0450 1008 1722 2220	1.6 5.9 1.5 6.1
22 SA	0544 1049 1807 2258	1.3 6.2 1.3 6.4
23 SU ●	0627 1123 1844 2333	1.1 6.3 1.2 6.5
24 M	0703 1154 1915	1.0 6.4 1.1
25 TU	0007 0732 1224 1939	6.6 1.0 6.4 1.1
26 W	0039 0757 1253 2001	6.6 1.1 6.3 1.1
27 TH	0106 0820 1317 2026	6.5 1.1 6.2 1.2
28 F	0126 0846 1337 2054	6.4 1.2 6.2 1.2
29 SA	0148 0915 1401 2126	6.3 1.3 6.1 1.4

MARCH

Day	Time	m
1 SU	0218 0947 1435 2200	6.2 1.5 5.9 1.7
2 M ☽	0257 1024 1518 2243	6.0 1.8 5.6 2.0
3 TU	0347 1114 1618 2342	5.6 2.1 5.2 2.3
4 W	0505 1234 1831	5.2 2.3 5.1
5 TH	0123 0704 1415 1947	2.3 5.3 2.2 5.4
6 F	0249 0813 1526 2046	2.0 5.6 1.8 5.8
7 SA	0354 0909 1628 2136	1.6 6.0 1.4 6.2
8 SU	0454 0959 1726 2222	1.2 6.4 1.1 6.6
9 M O	0551 1044 1821 2306	0.8 6.7 0.8 6.9
10 TU	0645 1127 1909 2348	0.5 6.9 0.6 7.1
11 W	0733 1209 1952	0.3 7.0 0.4
12 TH	0030 0816 1250 2030	7.2 0.2 7.0 0.4
13 F	0113 0854 1333 2106	7.2 0.3 6.9 0.6
14 SA	0156 0931 1418 2143	7.0 0.5 6.6 0.9
15 SU	0243 1010 1507 2224	6.7 1.0 6.2 1.3
16 M ☾	0334 1055 1604 2315	6.2 1.5 5.8 1.8
17 TU	0435 1153 1714	5.7 2.0 5.3
18 W	0024 0552 1307 1840	2.2 5.3 2.3 5.1
19 TH	0147 0746 1429 2015	2.3 5.2 2.2 5.3
20 F	0317 0907 1559 2117	2.0 5.5 1.9 5.7
21 SA	0435 0955 1701 2201	1.6 5.8 1.6 6.1
22 SU	0526 1032 1745 2238	1.3 6.1 1.3 6.3
23 M	0607 1103 1820 2311	1.1 6.3 1.2 6.5
24 TU ●	0640 1131 1848 2343	1.0 6.4 1.1 6.5
25 W	0705 1158 1910	1.0 6.4 1.1
26 TH	0011 0727 1225 1933	6.5 1.0 6.4 1.1
27 F	0035 0752 1246 2000	6.5 1.0 6.3 1.1
28 SA	0053 0819 1304 2029	6.4 1.1 6.3 1.1
29 SU	0116 0847 1330 2059	6.4 1.2 6.3 1.3
30 M	0146 0917 1405 2133	6.3 1.4 6.1 1.6
31 TU	0225 0954 1448 2214	6.1 1.7 5.8 1.9

APRIL

Day	Time	m
1 W ☽	0314 1041 1546 2311	5.7 2.0 5.4 2.2
2 TH	0427 1150 1757	5.3 2.3 5.1
3 F	0045 0644 1344 1922	2.3 5.3 2.2 5.4
4 SA	0220 0755 1500 2024	2.0 5.6 1.8 5.8
5 SU	0329 0853 1604 2116	1.5 6.1 1.4 6.3
6 M	0431 0942 1703 2203	1.1 6.5 1.0 6.7
7 TU	0531 1027 1758 2247	0.7 6.8 0.7 7.0
8 W O	0625 1109 1847 2329	0.4 7.0 0.5 7.2
9 TH	0713 1150 1930	0.2 7.0 0.4
10 F	0010 0755 1231 2008	7.2 0.2 7.0 0.4
11 SA	0053 0833 1313 2045	7.2 0.3 6.9 0.6
12 SU	0136 0910 1357 2123	6.9 0.6 6.6 0.9
13 M	0221 0947 1446 2203	6.6 1.1 6.3 1.3
14 TU ☾	0312 1030 1541 2253	6.1 1.6 5.8 1.8
15 W	0412 1127 1645	5.6 2.1 5.4
16 TH	0002 0523 1243 1802	2.2 5.2 2.4 5.2
17 F	0125 0714 1402 1936	2.3 5.1 2.3 5.3
18 SA	0247 0839 1518 2044	2.0 5.4 2.0 5.7
19 SU	0358 0926 1619 2130	1.7 5.7 1.7 6.0
20 M	0450 1002 1705 2208	1.4 6.0 1.4 6.2
21 TU	0530 1033 1742 2241	1.2 6.2 1.3 6.4
22 W	0602 1100 1811 2312	1.1 6.3 1.2 6.4
23 TH ●	0629 1128 1838 2339	1.1 6.3 1.1 6.4
24 F	0656 1154 1906	1.0 6.4 1.1
25 SA	0002 0724 1217 1936	6.4 1.0 6.4 1.1
26 SU	0025 0754 1240 2007	6.4 1.1 6.4 1.1
27 M	0051 0824 1309 2039	6.4 1.2 6.3 1.3
28 TU	0124 0856 1346 2115	6.3 1.4 6.2 1.5
29 W	0206 0934 1434 2158	6.1 1.7 5.9 1.8
30 TH ☽	0258 1023 1537 2256	5.7 1.9 5.5 2.0

MAY

Day	Time	m
1 F	0420 1130 1727	5.4 2.2 5.4
2 SA	0023 0620 1314 1852	2.1 5.4 2.1 5.6
3 SU	0153 0732 1431 1956	1.8 5.7 1.8 5.9
4 M	0300 0830 1534 2051	1.4 6.1 1.4 6.4
5 TU	0403 0920 1634 2139	1.0 6.4 1.1 6.7
6 W	0504 1006 1730 2225	0.7 6.7 0.8 6.9
7 TH O	0601 1049 1821 2309	0.5 6.8 0.6 7.1
8 F	0650 1131 1906 2351	0.4 6.9 0.5 7.1
9 SA	0733 1212 1947	0.4 6.9 0.6
10 SU	0034 0813 1255 2027	7.0 0.6 6.8 0.7
11 M	0118 0851 1340 2106	6.7 0.9 6.6 1.0
12 TU	0204 0929 1428 2148	6.4 1.2 6.3 1.4
13 W	0254 1010 1520 2236	6.0 1.7 5.9 1.8
14 TH ☾	0351 1102 1618 2338	5.6 2.1 5.6 2.1
15 F	0454 1211 1723	5.3 2.3 5.4
16 SA	0051 0612 1323 1839	2.2 5.2 2.3 5.4
17 SU	0201 0743 1428 1953	2.0 5.3 2.1 5.6
18 M	0303 0839 1525 2046	1.8 5.6 1.9 5.8
19 TU	0355 0919 1614 2128	1.6 5.8 1.6 6.0
20 W	0438 0953 1655 2203	1.4 6.0 1.4 6.2
21 TH	0516 1024 1731 2235	1.3 6.1 1.3 6.3
22 F ●	0551 1054 1806 2305	1.2 6.2 1.2 6.3
23 SA	0626 1124 1841 2333	1.1 6.3 1.1 6.3
24 SU	0701 1152 1916	1.1 6.3 1.1
25 M	0003 0735 1223 1951	6.4 1.1 6.4 1.1
26 TU	0036 0809 1259 2028	6.3 1.2 6.4 1.2
27 W	0114 0845 1341 2107	6.3 1.4 6.2 1.4
28 TH	0200 0926 1433 2153	6.1 1.6 6.0 1.6
29 F	0258 1015 1538 2251	5.8 1.8 5.8 1.7
30 SA ☽	0416 1120 1656	5.6 1.9 5.7
31 SU	0007 0548 1244 1815	1.8 5.6 1.9 5.8

JUNE

Day	Time	m
1 M	0123 0701 1356 1923	1.6 5.8 1.7 6.0
2 TU	0229 0802 1500 2022	1.4 6.0 1.4 6.3
3 W	0332 0856 1602 2115	1.1 6.3 1.2 6.5
4 TH	0436 0945 1702 2204	0.9 6.5 1.0 6.7
5 F O	0536 1031 1756 2252	0.8 6.6 0.8 6.8
6 SA	0628 1115 1845 2337	0.7 6.7 0.8 6.8
7 SU	0714 1158 1930	0.7 6.7 0.8
8 M	0021 0756 1242 2012	6.7 0.9 6.7 0.9
9 TU	0105 0835 1325 2054	6.5 1.1 6.5 1.1
10 W	0149 0913 1410 2134	6.3 1.3 6.4 1.4
11 TH	0236 0951 1457 2217	6.0 1.6 6.1 1.6
12 F	0326 1032 1547 2305	5.7 1.9 5.9 1.9
13 SA ☾	0421 1122 1642	5.5 2.1 5.6
14 SU	0002 0522 1225 1743	2.0 5.3 2.2 5.5
15 M	0103 0630 1329 1849	2.0 5.3 2.2 5.5
16 TU	0202 0734 1428 1949	2.0 5.4 2.1 5.6
17 W	0256 0825 1522 2038	1.8 5.6 1.8 5.8
18 TH	0346 0908 1611 2119	1.6 5.8 1.6 5.9
19 F	0433 0946 1656 2157	1.4 6.0 1.4 6.1
20 SA	0518 1023 1738 2234	1.3 6.1 1.3 6.2
21 SU ●	0600 1059 1819 2311	1.2 6.3 1.2 6.3
22 M	0642 1135 1901 2349	1.1 6.4 1.1 6.4
23 TU	0722 1213 1942	1.1 6.4 1.1
24 W	0028 0802 1254 2023	6.4 1.2 6.5 1.1
25 TH	0112 0842 1339 2106	6.3 1.2 6.4 1.2
26 F	0159 0924 1429 2153	6.2 1.3 6.3 1.2
27 SA	0253 1012 1525 2246	6.1 1.5 6.2 1.4
28 SU ☽	0356 1107 1627 2346	5.9 1.6 6.1 1.5
29 M	0508 1212 1735	5.8 1.7 6.0
30 TU	0051 0624 1320 1847	1.5 5.8 1.7 6.0

SUNRISE AND SUNSET TIMES

DOVER
At 51°07′N 1°19′E

UT		Sunrise	Sunset
Jan	01	0759	1558
	15	0752	1617
Feb	01	0732	1646
	15	0708	1711
Mar	01	0639	1736
	15	0609	1800
BST			
Apr	01	0630	1928
	15	0600	1951
May	01	0528	2017
	15	0504	2039
Jun	01	0445	2101
	15	0439	2112
Jul	01	0444	2113
	15	0457	2104
Aug	01	0520	2041
	15	0541	2016
Sep	01	0608	1940
	15	0630	1909
Oct	01	0655	1832
	15	0718	1802
UT			
Nov	01	0647	1629
	15	0711	1607
Dec	01	0736	1551
	15	0752	1548

DOVER
LAT 51°07′N
LONG 1°19′E

TIMES AND HEIGHTS OF HIGH AND LOW WATER (Heights in Metres)

TIME ZONE UT
For Summer Time (area enclosed in shaded box) add 1 hour

2020

JULY

Date	Time	m	Date	Time	m
1 W	0156 0732 1426 1954	1.4 5.8 1.6 6.1	16 TH	0203 0735 1433 1949	2.0 5.4 2.1 5.5
2 TH	0301 0833 1532 2056	1.4 6.0 1.5 6.2	17 F	0304 0827 1533 2041	1.8 5.6 1.9 5.7
3 F	0409 0928 1638 2152	1.2 6.1 1.3 6.4	18 SA	0400 0914 1625 2128	1.6 5.8 1.6 6.0
4 SA	0516 1019 1738 2243	1.1 6.3 1.1 6.5	19 SU	0451 0958 1714 2212	1.4 6.1 1.3 6.2
5 SU	0612 1105 1831 O 2329	1.0 6.5 1.0 6.5	20 M	0539 1039 1801 ● 2255	1.3 6.3 1.2 6.4
6 M	0700 1147 1918	1.0 6.6 1.0	21 TU	0626 1120 1848 2337	1.1 6.5 1.0 6.5
7 TU	0012 0743 1229 2001	6.5 1.1 6.6 1.0	22 W	0712 1201 1934	1.1 6.6 0.9
8 W	0053 0821 1310 2040	6.4 1.2 6.6 1.1	23 TH	0019 0756 1244 2019	6.6 1.0 6.7 0.9
9 TH	0133 0856 1350 2116	6.3 1.3 6.5 1.3	24 F	0102 0838 1328 2102	6.6 1.0 6.8 0.8
10 F	0214 0926 1431 2149	6.1 1.5 6.3 1.4	25 SA	0148 0918 1414 2145	6.5 1.1 6.7 0.9
11 SA	0256 0953 1512 2221	5.9 1.7 6.1 1.6	26 SU	0236 1000 1504 2230	6.4 1.2 6.6 1.1
12 SU	0341 1027 1556 ☾ 2300	5.6 1.9 5.8 1.8	27 M	0330 1046 1559 ☽ 2320	6.2 1.4 6.3 1.3
13 M	0432 1111 1646 2352	5.4 2.1 5.6 2.0	28 TU	0432 1140 1701	5.9 1.6 6.1
14 TU	0531 1210 1746	5.3 2.2 5.4	29 W	0019 0545 1246 1813	1.5 5.7 1.8 5.8
15 W	0056 0634 1325 1849	2.1 5.2 2.2 5.4	30 TH	0126 0705 1357 1933	1.7 5.6 1.9 5.8
			31 F	0237 0817 1511 2047	1.7 5.7 1.8 5.9

AUGUST

Date	Time	m	Date	Time	m
1 SA	0353 0919 1626 2150	1.6 5.9 1.6 6.1	16 SU	0332 0850 1559 2108	1.8 5.7 1.7 5.9
2 SU	0507 1012 1731 2242	1.4 6.2 1.3 6.3	17 M	0428 0937 1653 2155	1.5 6.1 1.4 6.3
3 M	0603 1056 1823 O 2324	1.3 6.4 1.1 6.4	18 TU	0520 1021 1743 2240	1.3 6.4 1.1 6.5
4 TU	0650 1135 1909	1.2 6.5 1.0	19 W	0610 1103 1833 ● 2322	1.1 6.7 0.9 6.7
5 W	0001 0729 1214 1947	6.4 1.2 6.6 1.0	20 TH	0659 1144 1922	0.9 6.9 0.7
6 TH	0037 0802 1251 2021	6.4 1.2 6.6 1.1	21 F	0003 0743 1226 2006	6.8 0.8 7.0 0.6
7 F	0111 0830 1326 2048	6.3 1.3 6.6 1.2	22 SA	0045 0823 1309 2048	6.8 0.8 7.1 0.6
8 SA	0145 0852 1359 2112	6.2 1.4 6.4 1.3	23 SU	0128 0901 1353 2127	6.8 0.8 7.0 0.7
9 SU	0217 0915 1428 2138	6.0 1.5 6.2 1.5	24 M	0213 0939 1440 2207	6.6 1.0 6.8 1.0
10 M	0247 0945 1458 2210	5.8 1.6 6.0 1.7	25 TU	0303 1021 1532 ☽ 2252	6.3 1.3 6.4 1.3
11 TU	0320 1021 1535 ☾ 2250	5.6 1.9 5.7 1.9	26 W	0402 1110 1633 2348	5.9 1.7 6.0 1.8
12 W	0409 1107 1631 2345	5.3 2.2 5.4 2.2	27 TH	0514 1215 1747	5.6 2.0 5.6
13 TH	0535 1213 1756	5.1 2.4 5.3	28 F	0059 0640 1335 1921	2.1 5.4 2.2 5.5
14 F	0109 0653 1347 1912	2.3 5.2 2.4 5.3	29 SA	0220 0805 1501 2050	2.1 5.5 2.0 5.7
15 SA	0228 0756 1500 2014	2.1 5.4 2.1 5.6	30 SU	0353 0913 1627 2151	1.9 5.8 1.7 6.0
			31 M	0504 1002 1726 2236	1.6 6.1 1.3 6.2

SEPTEMBER

Date	Time	m	Date	Time	m
1 TU	0554 1042 1814 2312	1.3 6.4 1.1 6.4	16 W	0500 1000 1723 2221	1.3 6.6 1.0 6.7
2 W	0635 1118 1853 O 2344	1.2 6.6 1.0 6.5	17 TH	0551 1042 1814 ● 2302	1.0 6.9 0.7 6.9
3 TH	0708 1153 1926	1.2 6.7 1.0	18 F	0638 1123 1903 2342	0.8 7.2 0.5 7.0
4 F	0014 0735 1227 1952	6.5 1.2 6.7 1.1	19 SA	0722 1204 1946	0.7 7.3 0.5
5 SA	0044 0756 1258 2013	6.4 1.3 6.6 1.2	20 SU	0022 0801 1246 2026	7.1 0.7 7.3 0.5
6 SU	0112 0815 1323 2034	6.3 1.3 6.5 1.3	21 M	0104 0838 1329 2103	7.0 0.7 7.1 0.7
7 M	0134 0840 1342 2100	6.2 1.4 6.3 1.4	22 TU	0149 0916 1415 2142	6.7 1.0 6.8 1.0
8 TU	0153 0910 1406 2130	6.1 1.5 6.2 1.6	23 W	0238 0957 1508 2225	6.4 1.3 6.4 1.5
9 W	0220 0944 1440 2206	5.9 1.8 5.9 1.9	24 TH	0337 1045 1610 ☽ 2321	5.9 1.8 5.9 2.0
10 TH	0259 1023 1526 ☾ 2251	5.6 2.1 5.6 2.2	25 F	0448 1152 1726	5.5 2.2 5.4
11 F	0355 1117 1647	5.2 2.4 5.2	26 SA	0038 0613 1320 1914	2.4 5.3 2.4 5.3
12 SA	0000 0617 1255 1846	2.5 5.1 2.6 5.2	27 SU	0210 0749 1500 2046	2.4 5.4 2.1 5.6
13 SU	0155 0729 1430 1954	2.4 5.3 2.3 5.5	28 M	0346 0857 1617 2139	2.0 5.8 1.7 6.0
14 M	0307 0827 1534 2049	2.0 5.8 1.8 6.0	29 TU	0446 0942 1709 2218	1.7 6.2 1.3 6.2
15 TU	0406 0916 1630 2137	1.6 6.2 1.4 6.4	30 W	0530 1020 1752 2250	1.4 6.5 1.1 6.4

OCTOBER

Date	Time	m	Date	Time	m
1 TH	0607 1054 1827 O 2318	1.2 6.7 1.1 6.5	16 F	0524 1017 1750 ● 2240	1.0 7.1 0.7 7.0
2 F	0637 1127 1854 2346	1.2 6.7 1.1 6.5	17 SA	0612 1059 1838 2319	0.8 7.3 0.5 7.1
3 SA	0700 1158 1915	1.2 6.7 1.1	18 SU	0656 1140 1922	0.7 7.3 0.5
4 SU	0013 0720 1225 1936	6.5 1.2 6.6 1.2	19 M	0000 0737 1223 2002	7.1 0.7 7.3 0.6
5 M	0037 0743 1245 2000	6.4 1.3 6.5 1.3	20 TU	0043 0816 1307 2040	7.0 0.8 7.1 0.8
6 TU	0054 0811 1303 2028	6.3 1.3 6.4 1.4	21 W	0128 0855 1354 2120	6.8 1.0 6.7 1.2
7 W	0115 0841 1329 2058	6.3 1.5 6.3 1.6	22 TH	0218 0938 1447 2203	6.4 1.4 6.3 1.7
8 TH	0144 0914 1403 2133	6.1 1.7 6.1 1.9	23 F	0316 1027 1550 ☽ 2259	6.0 1.9 5.8 2.2
9 F	0224 0953 1448 2216	5.9 2.0 5.7 2.2	24 SA	0422 1135 1703	5.6 2.3 5.4
10 SA	0317 1044 1555 ☾ 2316	5.4 2.4 5.3 2.5	25 SU	0017 0539 1303 1849	2.5 5.4 2.4 5.3
11 SU	0540 1205 1823	5.1 2.5 5.2	26 M	0147 0713 1435 2019	2.5 5.4 2.1 5.5
12 M	0115 0700 1357 1931	2.6 5.4 2.3 5.6	27 TU	0309 0823 1545 2110	2.2 5.8 1.7 5.9
13 TU	0239 0800 1506 2027	2.2 5.8 1.8 6.0	28 W	0407 0910 1635 2147	1.8 6.1 1.4 6.1
14 W	0340 0850 1603 2115	1.7 6.3 1.3 6.5	29 TH	0452 0949 1716 2218	1.5 6.4 1.2 6.3
15 TH	0434 0935 1657 2159	1.3 6.7 0.9 6.8	30 F	0529 1024 1749 2247	1.4 6.5 1.2 6.4
			31 SA	0559 1056 1815 O 2315	1.3 6.6 1.2 6.5

NOVEMBER

Date	Time	m	Date	Time	m
1 SU	0624 1126 1839 2342	1.3 6.6 1.2 6.5	16 M	0632 1120 1900 2342	0.8 7.2 0.6 7.0
2 M	0649 1151 1905	1.2 6.5 1.2	17 TU	0717 1204 1943	0.8 7.1 0.7
3 TU	0005 0717 1213 1933	6.4 1.3 6.4 1.3	18 W	0026 0759 1249 2023	6.9 0.9 6.9 1.0
4 W	0026 0747 1235 2003	6.4 1.3 6.4 1.4	19 TH	0112 0842 1337 2104	6.7 1.1 6.6 1.3
5 TH	0050 0819 1304 2035	6.4 1.5 6.3 1.6	20 F	0202 0926 1430 2147	6.5 1.4 6.2 1.7
6 F	0123 0854 1341 2110	6.3 1.7 6.1 1.8	21 SA	0256 1016 1529 2239	6.1 1.8 5.8 2.1
7 SA	0205 0934 1428 2154	6.0 1.9 5.8 2.1	22 SU	0355 1117 1634 ☽ 2347	5.8 2.1 5.4 2.4
8 SU	0302 1025 1538 ☾ 2252	5.6 2.2 5.4 2.4	23 M	0500 1230 1753	5.6 2.2 5.3
9 M	0448 1139 1752	5.4 2.3 5.4	24 TU	0102 0616 1344 1923	2.5 5.5 2.1 5.4
10 TU	0027 0622 1320 1902	2.4 5.5 2.1 5.6	25 W	0212 0731 1449 2022	2.3 5.6 1.9 5.6
11 W	0201 0726 1431 2000	2.2 5.9 1.7 6.0	26 TH	0312 0827 1542 2105	2.0 5.9 1.7 5.9
12 TH	0305 0820 1531 2049	1.7 6.3 1.3 6.4	27 F	0402 0911 1626 2140	1.8 6.1 1.5 6.1
13 F	0401 0907 1627 2134	1.4 6.7 1.0 6.7	28 SA	0444 0949 1702 2212	1.6 6.3 1.4 6.2
14 SA	0455 0952 1722 2217	1.1 7.0 0.7 6.9	29 SU	0519 1022 1735 2243	1.4 6.3 1.3 6.3
15 SU	0545 1036 1813 ● 2259	0.9 7.1 0.6 7.0	30 M	0551 1053 1807 O 2313	1.3 6.4 1.3 6.4

DECEMBER

Date	Time	m	Date	Time	m
1 TU	0623 1122 1840 2341	1.3 6.4 1.2 6.4	16 W	0704 1153 1930	0.9 6.8 0.9
2 W	0657 1150 1914	1.3 6.4 1.3	17 TH	0016 0750 1239 2013	6.8 0.9 6.7 1.1
3 TH	0008 0731 1220 1947	6.4 1.3 6.3 1.4	18 F	0101 0834 1325 2054	6.7 1.1 6.5 1.3
4 F	0039 0807 1253 2022	6.4 1.4 6.3 1.5	19 SA	0147 0918 1413 2134	6.5 1.3 6.2 1.6
5 SA	0116 0844 1333 2059	6.3 1.5 6.1 1.7	20 SU	0235 1002 1504 2215	6.3 1.5 5.9 1.9
6 SU	0201 0926 1423 2143	6.2 1.7 5.9 1.9	21 M	0325 1048 1558 ☽ 2301	6.0 1.8 5.6 2.1
7 M	0257 1016 1527 2237	5.9 1.8 5.7 2.1	22 TU	0419 1141 1659 2358	5.8 2.0 5.4 2.3
8 TU	0410 1121 1659 ☾ 2350	5.8 1.9 5.6 2.1	23 W	0520 1239 1807	5.6 2.1 5.3
9 W	0532 1239 1823	5.7 1.9 5.7	24 TH	0103 0626 1340 1915	2.4 5.5 2.1 5.3
10 TH	0113 0645 1351 1926	2.0 5.9 1.6 5.9	25 F	0207 0731 1437 2011	2.3 5.6 2.0 5.5
11 F	0223 0746 1454 2021	1.8 6.2 1.4 6.2	26 SA	0305 0825 1530 2058	2.1 5.7 1.8 5.7
12 SA	0325 0840 1556 2112	1.5 6.5 1.1 6.4	27 SU	0357 0909 1618 2138	1.8 5.9 1.6 5.9
13 SU	0425 0931 1657 2200	1.2 6.7 1.0 6.6	28 M	0442 0948 1701 2214	1.6 6.0 1.4 6.1
14 M	0522 1020 1753 ● 2246	1.0 6.8 0.8 6.7	29 TU	0523 1024 1742 2249	1.4 6.2 1.3 6.3
15 TU	0615 1107 1844 2331	0.9 6.9 0.8 6.8	30 W	0602 1100 1822 O 2323	1.3 6.3 1.2 6.4
			31 TH	0642 1135 1901 2357	1.2 6.3 1.2 6.5

SHEERNESS
LAT 51°27'N
LONG 0°45'E

TIMES AND HEIGHTS OF HIGH AND LOW WATER (Heights in Metres)

TIME ZONE UT
For Summer Time (area enclosed in shaded box) add 1 hour

2020

JANUARY

Date	Day	Time	m	Time	m	Time	m	Time	m
1	W	0354	5.2	1004	1.1	1632	5.1	2207	1.4
2	TH	0433	5.0	1040	1.2	1715	4.9	2250	1.6
3	F ☽	0518	4.9	1125	1.3	1804	4.7	2342	1.7
4	SA	0612	4.7	1222	1.4	1902	4.6		
5	SU	0046	1.8	0718	4.6	1337	1.5	2006	4.7
6	M	0205	1.7	0828	4.7	1453	1.4	2110	4.9
7	TU	0317	1.6	0932	4.9	1554	1.3	2209	5.1
8	W	0416	1.3	1029	5.1	1646	1.1	2301	5.3
9	TH	0509	1.1	1121	5.4	1734	1.0	2348	5.5
10	F ○	0559	0.9	1208	5.6	1820	0.9		
11	SA	0032	5.6	0647	0.8	1253	5.7	1904	0.8
12	SU	0115	5.7	0736	0.6	1338	5.9	1948	0.8
13	M	0157	5.8	0824	0.5	1422	5.9	2032	0.8
14	TU	0240	5.8	0912	0.4	1508	5.9	2115	0.8
15	W	0323	5.7	0957	0.4	1555	5.8	2157	0.9
16	TH	0409	5.6	1042	0.5	1645	5.6	2241	1.1
17	F ☾	0459	5.5	1129	0.7	1740	5.4	2330	1.2
18	SA	0555	5.3	1223	0.9	1841	5.2		
19	SU	0029	1.4	0700	5.2	1328	1.0	1948	5.1
20	M	0141	1.4	0812	5.1	1439	1.1	2057	5.1
21	TU	0258	1.4	0924	5.1	1548	1.1	2203	5.1
22	W	0412	1.3	1031	5.3	1651	1.1	2303	5.3
23	TH	0521	1.1	1130	5.4	1744	1.0	2354	5.4
24	F ●	0616	0.9	1219	5.6	1827	1.0		
25	SA	0038	5.5	0702	0.8	1304	5.6	1905	1.0
26	SU	0118	5.5	0742	0.7	1343	5.7	1940	1.0
27	M	0154	5.5	0817	0.7	1420	5.6	2011	1.0
28	TU	0227	5.5	0848	0.7	1454	5.5	2041	1.0
29	W	0258	5.5	0916	0.8	1527	5.4	2111	1.1
30	TH	0329	5.4	0942	0.9	1600	5.3	2141	1.2
31	F	0402	5.3	1011	1.0	1634	5.1	2214	1.3

FEBRUARY

Date	Day	Time	m	Time	m	Time	m	Time	m
1	SA	0437	5.1	1044	1.1	1713	4.9	2253	1.4
2	SU ☽	0519	4.9	1125	1.3	1801	4.8	2342	1.6
3	M	0613	4.7	1219	1.5	1902	4.6		
4	TU	0049	1.7	0724	4.6	1341	1.6	2015	4.7
5	W	0222	1.7	0844	4.7	1510	1.5	2128	4.9
6	TH	0340	1.4	0957	5.0	1615	1.3	2232	5.1
7	F	0443	1.1	1058	5.3	1711	1.1	2327	5.4
8	SA	0541	0.9	1152	5.6	1803	0.9		
9	SU ○	0016	5.6	0636	0.6	1240	5.8	1852	0.8
10	M	0101	5.8	0728	0.4	1326	6.0	1939	0.7
11	TU	0144	5.9	0816	0.2	1410	6.1	2023	0.6
12	W	0226	6.0	0902	0.1	1454	6.1	2105	0.6
13	TH	0308	6.0	0944	0.2	1539	6.0	2143	0.7
14	F	0351	5.9	1024	0.3	1624	5.8	2221	0.9
15	SA ☾	0436	5.7	1103	0.6	1712	5.5	2302	1.1
16	SU	0527	5.4	1146	0.9	1807	5.2	2353	1.3
17	M	0629	5.2	1244	1.2	1913	4.9		
18	TU	0104	1.4	0745	4.9	1402	1.4	2027	4.8
19	W	0234	1.5	0907	4.9	1522	1.4	2143	4.9
20	TH	0403	1.3	1022	5.1	1634	1.3	2249	5.1
21	F	0516	1.1	1122	5.4	1731	1.2	2341	5.3
22	SA	0609	0.9	1210	5.5	1814	1.1		
23	SU ●	0024	5.4	0650	0.8	1251	5.6	1849	1.0
24	M	0102	5.5	0725	0.7	1326	5.6	1921	0.9
25	TU	0134	5.6	0756	0.7	1359	5.6	1951	0.9
26	W	0204	5.6	0825	0.6	1428	5.6	2021	0.8
27	TH	0233	5.6	0852	0.7	1458	5.6	2050	0.9
28	F	0302	5.5	0918	0.8	1527	5.4	2118	1.0
29	SA	0332	5.4	0943	0.9	1558	5.3	2145	1.1

MARCH

Date	Day	Time	m	Time	m	Time	m	Time	m
1	SU	0404	5.3	1009	1.0	1633	5.1	2215	1.2
2	M ☽	0442	5.1	1039	1.2	1714	4.9	2255	1.4
3	TU	0529	4.9	1124	1.4	1808	4.7	2354	1.6
4	W	0634	4.7	1237	1.6	1923	4.6		
5	TH	0127	1.6	0801	4.7	1429	1.6	2049	4.7
6	F	0308	1.4	0927	4.9	1547	1.4	2205	5.0
7	SA	0420	1.1	1037	5.3	1650	1.1	2305	5.3
8	SU	0525	0.8	1134	5.7	1746	0.9	2356	5.6
9	M ○	0623	0.5	1223	6.0	1837	0.7		
10	TU	0041	5.9	0714	0.3	1309	6.1	1923	0.6
11	W	0124	6.0	0800	0.1	1352	6.2	2007	0.5
12	TH	0205	6.1	0843	0.0	1434	6.2	2048	0.5
13	F	0247	6.1	0923	0.1	1516	6.0	2125	0.6
14	SA	0329	6.0	0959	0.4	1559	5.8	2200	0.8
15	SU	0412	5.8	1033	0.7	1643	5.5	2237	0.9
16	M ☾	0502	5.5	1111	1.0	1734	5.1	2325	1.2
17	TU	0603	5.1	1205	1.3	1837	4.8		
18	W	0034	1.4	0721	4.8	1327	1.6	1957	4.6
19	TH	0217	1.5	0849	4.8	1457	1.6	2121	4.7
20	F	0351	1.3	1007	5.1	1613	1.4	2229	5.0
21	SA	0501	1.0	1105	5.4	1710	1.3	2321	5.2
22	SU	0550	0.8	1151	5.6	1752	1.1		
23	M	0002	5.4	0627	0.8	1229	5.6	1825	1.0
24	TU ●	0038	5.5	0658	0.7	1302	5.6	1857	0.9
25	W	0109	5.6	0727	0.7	1331	5.7	1927	0.8
26	TH	0137	5.6	0756	0.6	1359	5.7	1958	0.8
27	F	0206	5.7	0824	0.6	1427	5.6	2028	0.8
28	SA	0235	5.6	0851	0.7	1456	5.6	2057	0.9
29	SU	0305	5.5	0917	0.9	1527	5.4	2122	1.0
30	M	0338	5.4	0939	1.1	1600	5.3	2149	1.1
31	TU	0416	5.2	1006	1.2	1640	5.1	2226	1.2

APRIL

Date	Day	Time	m	Time	m	Time	m	Time	m
1	W ☽	0503	5.0	1051	1.4	1732	4.8	2325	1.4
2	TH	0605	4.8	1204	1.6	1844	4.6		
3	F	0054	1.5	0730	4.7	1354	1.7	2015	4.7
4	SA	0241	1.3	0900	5.0	1519	1.4	2136	5.0
5	SU	0357	1.0	1013	5.4	1624	1.1	2239	5.3
6	M	0504	0.7	1111	5.8	1723	0.9	2330	5.7
7	TU	0603	0.4	1201	6.0	1815	0.7		
8	W ○	0016	5.9	0653	0.2	1246	6.2	1902	0.5
9	TH	0100	6.1	0738	0.1	1329	6.2	1946	0.5
10	F	0142	6.2	0819	0.1	1411	6.2	2027	0.4
11	SA	0224	6.2	0858	0.2	1452	6.0	2105	0.5
12	SU	0307	6.0	0933	0.5	1533	5.7	2142	0.7
13	M	0352	5.8	1006	0.8	1616	5.4	2219	0.9
14	TU ☾	0442	5.4	1043	1.2	1704	5.1	2304	1.1
15	W	0542	5.1	1134	1.5	1805	4.8		
16	TH	0011	1.4	0657	4.8	1252	1.7	1923	4.6
17	F	0156	1.4	0821	4.8	1424	1.7	2047	4.6
18	SA	0322	1.3	0938	5.0	1537	1.5	2157	4.9
19	SU	0427	1.0	1036	5.3	1635	1.3	2250	5.2
20	M	0515	0.9	1121	5.5	1718	1.1	2331	5.3
21	TU	0552	0.8	1158	5.6	1754	1.0		
22	W	0006	5.5	0624	0.8	1231	5.6	1827	0.9
23	TH ●	0038	5.5	0654	0.7	1300	5.6	1900	0.8
24	F	0108	5.6	0724	0.7	1329	5.7	1934	0.7
25	SA	0139	5.6	0755	0.7	1359	5.7	2007	0.8
26	SU	0210	5.6	0825	0.8	1429	5.6	2038	0.8
27	M	0243	5.6	0854	0.9	1502	5.5	2108	0.9
28	TU	0319	5.5	0920	1.1	1537	5.3	2138	1.0
29	W	0359	5.3	0952	1.2	1618	5.1	2219	1.1
30	TH ☽	0448	5.1	1040	1.4	1710	4.9	2318	1.3

MAY

Date	Day	Time	m	Time	m	Time	m	Time	m
1	F	0551	5.0	1151	1.6	1820	4.7		
2	SA	0043	1.3	0710	4.9	1326	1.6	1945	4.8
3	SU	0217	1.1	0835	5.1	1448	1.4	2104	5.0
4	M	0331	0.8	0946	5.5	1553	1.1	2208	5.4
5	TU	0438	0.6	1045	5.8	1653	0.9	2302	5.7
6	W	0537	0.4	1135	5.9	1748	0.7	2350	5.9
7	TH ○	0627	0.3	1221	6.1	1838	0.6		
8	F	0035	6.0	0712	0.3	1305	6.1	1924	0.5
9	SA	0120	6.1	0753	0.3	1348	6.0	2008	0.5
10	SU	0205	6.1	0832	0.5	1429	5.9	2049	0.5
11	M	0250	5.9	0908	0.7	1511	5.7	2128	0.7
12	TU	0336	5.7	0942	1.0	1553	5.4	2206	0.9
13	W	0426	5.4	1019	1.3	1639	5.1	2250	1.1
14	TH ☾	0522	5.1	1106	1.5	1735	4.8	2349	1.3
15	F	0627	4.8	1211	1.8	1844	4.6		
16	SA	0118	1.4	0740	4.8	1337	1.8	1959	4.6
17	SU	0236	1.3	0852	4.9	1449	1.7	2109	4.8
18	M	0337	1.1	0953	5.1	1547	1.4	2205	5.0
19	TU	0427	1.0	1041	5.3	1636	1.2	2251	5.2
20	W	0508	0.9	1120	5.4	1717	1.1	2329	5.3
21	TH	0545	0.9	1155	5.5	1756	0.9		
22	F ●	0005	5.5	0619	0.8	1228	5.6	1833	0.9
23	SA	0040	5.5	0653	0.8	1301	5.6	1910	0.8
24	SU	0115	5.6	0728	0.8	1334	5.6	1947	0.8
25	M	0150	5.6	0803	0.9	1408	5.6	2025	0.8
26	TU	0227	5.6	0837	1.0	1444	5.5	2102	0.8
27	W	0307	5.5	0911	1.1	1522	5.4	2141	0.9
28	TH	0351	5.4	0950	1.2	1607	5.2	2225	1.0
29	F	0442	5.3	1039	1.3	1659	5.1	2322	1.0
30	SA ☽	0542	5.2	1142	1.5	1804	5.0		
31	SU	0034	1.0	0653	5.1	1259	1.5	1918	5.0

JUNE

Date	Day	Time	m	Time	m	Time	m	Time	m
1	M	0153	0.9	0808	5.2	1414	1.4	2032	5.1
2	TU	0303	0.8	0917	5.4	1520	1.2	2137	5.4
3	W	0408	0.7	1017	5.6	1622	1.0	2234	5.6
4	TH	0508	0.6	1110	5.8	1721	0.9	2326	5.8
5	F ○	0600	0.5	1159	5.8	1816	0.7		
6	SA	0016	5.9	0646	0.5	1245	5.9	1906	0.6
7	SU	0104	5.9	0729	0.6	1329	5.8	1953	0.5
8	M	0151	5.9	0810	0.7	1412	5.7	2037	0.6
9	TU	0237	5.8	0847	0.9	1453	5.6	2118	0.7
10	W	0323	5.6	0922	1.1	1535	5.4	2157	0.9
11	TH	0409	5.4	0957	1.3	1617	5.2	2235	1.1
12	F	0457	5.1	1037	1.5	1704	5.0	2319	1.2
13	SA ☾	0550	4.9	1126	1.7	1758	4.8		
14	SU	0018	1.3	0648	4.8	1231	1.8	1900	4.7
15	M	0132	1.4	0750	4.7	1346	1.8	2006	4.7
16	TU	0237	1.3	0852	4.8	1453	1.6	2108	4.8
17	W	0332	1.2	0948	5.0	1548	1.4	2203	5.0
18	TH	0421	1.1	1036	5.2	1638	1.2	2251	5.2
19	F	0505	1.0	1119	5.4	1724	1.1	2335	5.3
20	SA	0547	1.0	1159	5.5	1808	0.9		
21	SU ●	0016	5.5	0626	0.9	1238	5.6	1850	0.9
22	M	0056	5.6	0706	0.9	1316	5.6	1933	0.8
23	TU	0136	5.6	0746	0.9	1355	5.6	2016	0.7
24	W	0217	5.7	0826	0.9	1434	5.6	2101	0.7
25	TH	0300	5.7	0907	1.0	1515	5.5	2145	0.7
26	F	0345	5.6	0949	1.1	1559	5.4	2231	0.7
27	SA	0435	5.5	1035	1.2	1649	5.3	2321	0.8
28	SU ☽	0530	5.4	1127	1.3	1745	5.2		
29	M	0018	0.8	0632	5.3	1229	1.4	1850	5.2
30	TU	0123	0.9	0740	5.3	1338	1.4	2000	5.2

SUNRISE AND SUNSET TIMES

SHEERNESS
At 51°27'N 0°45'E

UT		Sunrise	Sunset
Jan	01	0802	1559
	15	0756	1618
Feb	01	0735	1647
	15	0711	1712
Mar	01	0642	1738
	15	0611	1802
BST			
Apr	01	0632	1930
	15	0601	1954
May	01	0529	2020
	15	0505	2042
Jun	01	0446	2105
	15	0440	2116
Jul	01	0445	2117
	15	0458	2107
Aug	01	0521	2045
	15	0543	2020
Sep	01	0610	1943
	15	0632	1911
Oct	01	0658	1835
	15	0721	1804
UT			
Nov	01	0651	1630
	15	0715	1608
Dec	01	0740	1552
	15	0756	1548

SHEERNESS
LAT 51°27′N
LONG 0°45′E

TIMES AND HEIGHTS OF HIGH AND LOW WATER (Heights in Metres)

TIME ZONE UT
For Summer Time (area enclosed in shaded box) add 1 hour

2020

JULY

Date	Day	Time	m
1	W	0231 0847 1447 2108	0.9 5.3 1.3 5.3
2	TH	0338 0951 1555 2212	0.9 5.4 1.2 5.4
3	F	0441 1049 1702 2311	0.8 5.5 1.0 5.6
4	SA	0538 1142 1803	0.8 5.6 0.9
5	SU ○	0005 0626 1231 1856	5.7 0.8 5.7 0.7
6	M	0055 0711 1316 1944	5.8 0.8 5.7 0.6
7	TU	0142 0751 1358 2027	5.8 0.9 5.6 0.6
8	W	0226 0828 1438 2107	5.7 1.0 5.6 0.7
9	TH	0308 0902 1516 2142	5.6 1.1 5.5 0.8
10	F	0348 0934 1552 2213	5.4 1.2 5.3 1.0
11	SA	0427 1007 1630 2244	5.3 1.4 5.2 1.1
12	SU ☾	0508 1045 1711 2321	5.1 1.5 5.0 1.2
13	M	0553 1130 1800	4.9 1.6 4.8
14	TU	0010 0644 1228 1858	1.3 4.7 1.7 4.7
15	W	0116 0745 1343 2005	1.4 4.7 1.8 4.7
16	TH	0232 0849 1458 2112	1.4 4.8 1.6 4.8
17	F	0335 0950 1600 2214	1.3 5.0 1.4 5.0
18	SA	0430 1045 1654 2308	1.2 5.2 1.2 5.2
19	SU	0519 1134 1745 2356	1.1 5.4 1.0 5.4
20	M ●	0605 1219 1834	1.0 5.6 0.9
21	TU	0040 0649 1302 1921	5.6 0.9 5.7 0.7
22	W	0124 0733 1343 2009	5.8 0.9 5.7 0.5
23	TH	0207 0817 1423 2056	5.9 0.8 5.8 0.4
24	F	0250 0900 1504 2141	5.9 0.8 5.8 0.4
25	SA	0335 0941 1547 2224	5.9 0.9 5.7 0.5
26	SU	0421 1022 1632 2306	5.7 1.0 5.6 0.6
27	M ☽	0510 1105 1722 2352	5.6 1.2 5.5 0.8
28	TU	0606 1156 1821	5.3 1.3 5.3
29	W	0048 0709 1302 1931	1.0 5.2 1.4 5.2
30	TH	0159 0818 1420 2046	1.1 5.1 1.4 5.1
31	F	0312 0929 1539 2159	1.2 5.1 1.3 5.2

AUGUST

Date	Day	Time	m
1	SA	0422 1035 1655 2305	1.2 5.3 1.1 5.4
2	SU	0524 1132 1759	1.1 5.4 0.9
3	M ○	0001 0614 1222 1850	5.6 1.1 5.5 0.8
4	TU	0049 0656 1305 1934	5.7 1.0 5.6 0.7
5	W	0131 0734 1343 2013	5.8 1.0 5.6 0.7
6	TH	0210 0808 1419 2047	5.7 1.0 5.6 0.7
7	F	0246 0840 1452 2117	5.7 1.1 5.6 0.8
8	SA	0320 0909 1523 2143	5.5 1.1 5.5 0.9
9	SU	0353 0938 1555 2208	5.4 1.2 5.4 1.0
10	M	0426 1008 1629 2238	5.2 1.3 5.2 1.1
11	TU ☾	0502 1044 1708 2315	5.0 1.5 5.0 1.3
12	W	0545 1129 1757	4.9 1.7 4.8
13	TH	0004 0640 1231 1902	1.5 4.7 1.8 4.6
14	F	0120 0751 1402 2022	1.7 4.7 1.8 4.6
15	SA	0251 0906 1524 2139	1.6 4.8 1.6 4.9
16	SU	0358 1014 1627 2243	1.4 5.1 1.3 5.2
17	M	0454 1111 1725 2337	1.2 5.4 1.0 5.5
18	TU	0545 1200 1819	1.1 5.6 0.8
19	W ●	0024 0632 1244 1909	5.8 0.9 5.8 0.6
20	TH	0108 0719 1325 1956	6.0 0.8 5.9 0.4
21	F	0151 0803 1406 2042	6.1 0.7 6.0 0.3
22	SA	0234 0846 1446 2124	6.1 0.7 6.0 0.3
23	SU	0316 0925 1527 2204	6.0 0.8 6.0 0.4
24	M	0359 1002 1610 2242	5.9 1.0 5.8 0.6
25	TU ☽	0445 1040 1657 2321	5.6 1.1 5.6 0.9
26	W	0536 1126 1754	5.3 1.3 5.3
27	TH	0012 0637 1230 1907	1.2 5.0 1.5 5.1
28	F	0127 0751 1401 2031	1.4 4.9 1.5 5.0
29	SA	0251 0911 1534 2153	1.5 4.9 1.4 5.2
30	SU	0409 1023 1655 2300	1.4 5.1 1.1 5.4
31	M	0513 1121 1753 2352	1.3 5.4 0.9 5.7

SEPTEMBER

Date	Day	Time	m
1	TU	0601 1208 1838	1.2 5.5 0.8
2	W ○	0035 0638 1248 1915	5.8 1.1 5.6 0.7
3	TH	0114 0712 1322 1948	5.8 1.0 5.7 0.7
4	F	0147 0743 1353 2018	5.8 1.0 5.7 0.7
5	SA	0218 0813 1423 2045	5.7 1.0 5.7 0.8
6	SU	0248 0842 1452 2110	5.6 1.0 5.6 0.8
7	M	0317 0909 1521 2134	5.5 1.1 5.5 1.0
8	TU	0346 0936 1553 2159	5.4 1.3 5.4 1.2
9	W	0419 1005 1628 2229	5.2 1.4 5.2 1.4
10	TH ☾	0457 1042 1712 2310	5.0 1.6 4.9 1.6
11	F	0546 1137 1812	4.8 1.7 4.7
12	SA	0017 0655 1304 1935	1.8 4.6 1.8 4.6
13	SU	0205 0823 1449 2105	1.8 4.7 1.6 4.8
14	M	0327 0943 1601 2217	1.6 5.0 1.3 5.2
15	TU	0428 1044 1703 2314	1.3 5.3 0.9 5.6
16	W	0523 1135 1759	1.1 5.7 0.7
17	TH ●	0002 0612 1220 1849	5.9 0.9 5.9 0.4
18	F	0047 0659 1301 1936	6.1 0.8 6.0 0.3
19	SA	0129 0743 1342 2020	6.2 0.7 6.2 0.2
20	SU	0211 0825 1422 2100	6.2 0.7 6.2 0.3
21	M	0252 0904 1503 2138	6.1 0.7 6.1 0.5
22	TU	0334 0940 1547 2212	5.9 0.9 5.9 0.7
23	W	0417 1017 1634 2249	5.6 1.1 5.6 1.1
24	TH ☽	0506 1102 1733 2339	5.3 1.3 5.3 1.4
25	F	0607 1207 1849	4.9 1.5 5.0
26	SA	0056 0725 1350 2017	1.7 4.7 1.6 4.9
27	SU	0231 0850 1527 2140	1.8 4.8 1.4 5.2
28	M	0351 1005 1641 2244	1.6 5.1 1.1 5.5
29	TU	0453 1101 1734 2333	1.4 5.4 0.9 5.7
30	W	0537 1145 1814	1.2 5.5 0.8

OCTOBER

Date	Day	Time	m
1	TH ○	0013 0612 1222 1846	5.8 1.1 5.6 0.8
2	F	0048 0643 1254 1915	5.8 1.0 5.7 0.8
3	SA	0118 0714 1324 1943	5.8 1.0 5.7 0.8
4	SU	0147 0744 1352 2010	5.7 0.9 5.7 0.8
5	M	0214 0814 1421 2036	5.7 0.9 5.7 0.9
6	TU	0242 0843 1451 2102	5.6 1.0 5.6 1.0
7	W	0312 0909 1523 2126	5.5 1.2 5.4 1.2
8	TH	0343 0935 1559 2151	5.3 1.3 5.3 1.4
9	F	0420 1009 1642 2231	5.1 1.4 5.0 1.6
10	SA ☾	0507 1103 1740 2336	4.9 1.6 4.8 1.8
11	SU	0612 1225 1859	4.6 1.7 4.7
12	M	0119 0741 1414 2031	1.9 4.6 1.6 4.9
13	TU	0252 0907 1531 2147	1.7 4.9 1.2 5.3
14	W	0357 1012 1635 2245	1.3 5.3 0.8 5.7
15	TH	0453 1104 1733 2335	1.1 5.7 0.6 6.0
16	F ●	0545 1150 1824	0.9 5.9 0.4
17	SA	0020 0633 1234 1910	6.2 0.8 6.1 0.3
18	SU	0104 0718 1316 1953	6.2 0.7 6.2 0.3
19	M	0145 0801 1358 2033	6.2 0.6 6.2 0.4
20	TU	0227 0842 1442 2110	6.1 0.7 6.1 0.6
21	W	0309 0921 1527 2145	5.9 0.8 5.9 0.9
22	TH	0352 1000 1617 2222	5.5 1.0 5.6 1.3
23	F ☽	0440 1046 1716 2311	5.2 1.2 5.2 1.6
24	SA	0540 1151 1830	4.9 1.5 4.9
25	SU	0024 0656 1334 1952	1.9 4.7 1.5 4.9
26	M	0159 0819 1501 2112	1.9 4.7 1.3 5.1
27	TU	0316 0933 1610 2215	1.7 5.0 1.1 5.4
28	W	0416 1029 1700 2303	1.5 5.2 0.9 5.6
29	TH	0501 1113 1738 2342	1.3 5.4 0.9 5.6
30	F	0538 1150 1809	1.1 5.5 0.9
31	SA ○	0016 0611 1223 1838	5.7 1.0 5.6 0.8

NOVEMBER

Date	Day	Time	m
1	SU	0046 0644 1253 1907	5.7 0.9 5.7 0.8
2	M	0114 0716 1323 1936	5.7 0.9 5.7 0.8
3	TU	0143 0749 1355 2005	5.7 0.9 5.7 0.9
4	W	0213 0820 1427 2034	5.6 1.0 5.6 1.1
5	TH	0244 0850 1501 2101	5.5 1.1 5.5 1.2
6	F	0317 0920 1539 2130	5.4 1.2 5.3 1.4
7	SA	0355 0956 1625 2212	5.2 1.3 5.1 1.6
8	SU ☾	0442 1049 1721 2315	5.0 1.4 5.0 1.7
9	M	0544 1204 1834	4.8 1.5 4.9
10	TU	0041 0705 1339 1958	1.8 4.7 1.4 5.0
11	W	0210 0828 1457 2112	1.6 5.0 1.1 5.3
12	TH	0319 0935 1602 2213	1.4 5.3 0.8 5.7
13	F	0418 1031 1701 2306	1.1 5.6 0.6 5.9
14	SA	0513 1120 1755 2353	0.9 5.9 0.5 6.0
15	SU ●	0605 1207 1842	0.8 6.1 0.4
16	M	0038 0654 1253 1926	6.1 0.7 6.2 0.4
17	TU	0122 0741 1339 2007	6.1 0.6 6.2 0.6
18	W	0205 0825 1426 2045	6.0 0.6 6.0 0.8
19	TH	0248 0908 1513 2122	5.8 0.8 5.8 1.0
20	F	0332 0949 1604 2200	5.5 0.9 5.5 1.3
21	SA	0419 1034 1700 2245	5.2 1.2 5.2 1.6
22	SU ☽	0514 1132 1804 2345	4.9 1.4 5.0 1.8
23	M	0621 1256 1914	4.7 1.5 4.8
24	TU	0107 0734 1415 2026	1.9 4.7 1.4 4.9
25	W	0224 0845 1518 2131	1.8 4.8 1.3 5.1
26	TH	0325 0945 1610 2223	1.6 5.0 1.1 5.2
27	F	0416 1033 1652 2305	1.4 5.2 1.0 5.4
28	SA	0459 1114 1728 2341	1.2 5.4 1.0 5.5
29	SU	0538 1150 1802	1.1 5.5 0.9
30	M ○	0014 0615 1226 1834	5.6 1.0 5.5 0.9

DECEMBER

Date	Day	Time	m
1	TU	0046 0651 1300 1907	5.6 0.9 5.6 0.9
2	W	0118 0727 1334 1940	5.6 0.9 5.6 1.0
3	TH	0151 0803 1410 2013	5.6 0.9 5.6 1.0
4	F	0224 0839 1447 2046	5.5 0.9 5.5 1.1
5	SA	0301 0916 1528 2122	5.4 1.0 5.4 1.3
6	SU	0341 0957 1615 2205	5.3 1.1 5.3 1.4
7	M	0428 1047 1709 2300	5.1 1.2 5.2 1.5
8	TU ☾	0524 1149 1813	5.0 1.2 5.1
9	W	0008 0632 1304 1925	1.6 4.9 1.1 5.1
10	TH	0125 0747 1419 2037	1.6 5.0 1.0 5.3
11	F	0237 0857 1526 2141	1.4 5.3 0.9 5.5
12	SA	0341 0959 1628 2238	1.2 5.5 0.7 5.6
13	SU	0442 1055 1726 2330	1.0 5.7 0.7 5.8
14	M ●	0542 1147 1817	0.9 5.9 0.6
15	TU	0018 0637 1238 1903	5.8 0.7 6.0 0.7
16	W	0104 0728 1327 1946	5.8 0.6 6.0 0.7
17	TH	0149 0815 1415 2026	5.8 0.6 5.9 0.9
18	F	0233 0900 1503 2104	5.7 0.7 5.7 1.1
19	SA	0316 0942 1550 2140	5.5 0.8 5.5 1.3
20	SU	0400 1022 1638 2218	5.3 1.0 5.3 1.5
21	M ☽	0446 1104 1729 2303	5.1 1.2 5.0 1.6
22	TU	0537 1156 1825	4.9 1.3 4.8
23	W	0000 0635 1303 1925	1.8 4.7 1.4 4.7
24	TH	0112 0740 1411 2028	1.8 4.7 1.4 4.7
25	F	0225 0845 1510 2127	1.8 4.7 1.3 4.9
26	SA	0326 0944 1602 2219	1.6 4.9 1.2 5.1
27	SU	0419 1036 1648 2304	1.4 5.1 1.1 5.2
28	M	0506 1121 1729 2345	1.2 5.2 1.1 5.4
29	TU	0550 1202 1808	1.0 5.4 1.0
30	W ○	0023 0631 1242 1845	5.5 0.9 5.5 1.0
31	TH	0100 0711 1320 1922	5.5 0.8 5.6 1.0

LONDON BRIDGE
LAT 51°30′N
LONG 0°05′W

TIMES AND HEIGHTS OF HIGH AND LOW WATER

TIME ZONE UT
For Summer Time (area enclosed in shaded box) add 1 hour

2020

JANUARY

Date	Day	Time	m	Time	m	Time	m	Time	m
1	W	0512	6.3	1138	1.0	1742	6.3	2345	1.4
2	TH	0547	6.1	1212	1.1	1820	6.1		
3	F ☽	0023	1.6	0625	6.0	1249	1.2	1904	5.9
4	SA	0106	1.7	0714	5.8	1334	1.4	2004	5.7
5	SU	0158	1.9	0827	5.6	1434	1.5	2116	5.7
6	M	0310	1.9	0949	5.8	1602	1.4	2222	5.9
7	TU	0445	1.7	1052	6.1	1710	1.3	2323	6.2
8	W	0551	1.3	1149	6.4	1809	1.1		
9	TH	0019	6.5	0649	1.0	1241	6.7	1904	1.0
10	F ○	0110	6.7	0745	0.8	1329	7.0	1958	0.9
11	SA	0156	6.8	0839	0.6	1415	7.1	2050	0.9
12	SU	0241	6.9	0930	0.4	1500	7.3	2139	0.8
13	M	0325	7.0	1018	0.3	1545	7.3	2224	0.8
14	TU	0407	7.0	1102	0.2	1630	7.3	2305	0.8
15	W	0449	6.9	1142	0.2	1716	7.1	2345	0.8
16	TH	0533	6.8	1221	0.3	1805	6.9		
17	F ☾	0026	1.0	0620	6.7	1303	0.4	1859	6.7
18	SA	0114	1.2	0715	6.5	1352	0.7	2000	6.5
19	SU	0211	1.3	0821	6.4	1452	0.9	2104	6.3
20	M	0320	1.4	0931	6.4	1558	1.0	2211	6.3
21	TU	0435	1.4	1041	6.4	1708	1.1	2322	6.3
22	W	0554	1.2	1149	6.5	1823	1.0		
23	TH	0026	6.5	0702	0.9	1249	6.7	1922	0.9
24	F ●	0119	6.6	0758	0.7	1339	6.9	2010	0.9
25	SA	0204	6.7	0846	0.6	1423	7.0	2053	0.9
26	SU	0243	6.8	0928	0.5	1503	7.0	2130	1.0
27	M	0318	6.8	1004	0.6	1539	6.9	2202	1.0
28	TU	0350	6.8	1033	0.6	1611	6.8	2229	1.0
29	W	0420	6.7	1055	0.7	1642	6.7	2257	1.0
30	TH	0451	6.6	1119	0.7	1713	6.5	2327	1.1
31	F	0522	6.5	1145	0.8	1745	6.3	2357	1.3

FEBRUARY

Date	Day	Time	m	Time	m	Time	m	Time	m
1	SA	0555	6.3	1212	1.0	1821	6.1		
2	SU ☽	0028	1.5	0633	6.1	1244	1.1	1903	5.9
3	M	0107	1.6	0721	5.9	1327	1.3	2002	5.7
4	TU	0201	1.8	0830	5.7	1429	1.5	2129	5.7
5	W	0327	1.8	1004	5.8	1616	1.5	2245	5.9
6	TH	0510	1.5	1115	6.2	1733	1.3	2352	6.3
7	F	0620	1.1	1216	6.6	1841	1.1		
8	SA	0050	6.6	0727	0.7	1311	7.0	1947	0.9
9	SU ○	0141	6.9	0828	0.4	1401	7.2	2046	0.8
10	M	0227	7.0	0922	0.2	1447	7.4	2136	0.7
11	TU	0311	7.2	1010	-0.1	1532	7.5	2221	0.5
12	W	0353	7.3	1053	-0.2	1617	7.5	2301	0.5
13	TH	0435	7.3	1131	-0.1	1700	7.3	2338	0.6
14	F	0516	7.2	1205	0.1	1745	7.0		
15	SA ☾	0013	0.8	0559	7.0	1238	0.4	1833	6.7
16	SU	0051	1.0	0648	6.7	1318	0.7	1927	6.4
17	M	0138	1.2	0748	6.5	1411	1.1	2030	6.1
18	TU	0242	1.4	0859	6.2	1519	1.3	2141	5.9
19	W	0400	1.5	1017	6.1	1636	1.4	2302	6.0
20	TH	0529	1.3	1135	6.3	1800	1.3		
21	F	0013	6.3	0648	0.9	1239	6.6	1903	1.1
22	SA	0107	6.5	0743	0.7	1328	6.8	1952	0.9
23	SU ●	0150	6.7	0828	0.5	1410	6.9	2034	0.9
24	M	0228	6.8	0907	0.5	1447	6.9	2112	0.9
25	TU	0300	6.8	0940	0.5	1519	6.9	2144	0.9
26	W	0329	6.9	1008	0.5	1547	6.8	2212	0.9
27	TH	0357	6.9	1031	0.5	1614	6.8	2239	0.9
28	F	0426	6.8	1054	0.6	1642	6.6	2307	1.0
29	SA	0455	6.7	1117	0.7	1712	6.4	2333	1.1

MARCH

Date	Day	Time	m	Time	m	Time	m	Time	m
1	SU	0526	6.5	1139	0.9	1745	6.2	2358	1.3
2	M ☽	0601	6.3	1206	1.0	1824	6.0		
3	TU	0030	1.4	0645	6.1	1244	1.2	1914	5.7
4	W	0118	1.6	0742	5.8	1339	1.5	2030	5.5
5	TH	0230	1.7	0915	5.8	1518	1.7	2207	5.7
6	F	0433	1.5	1043	6.1	1703	1.4	2324	6.1
7	SA	0552	1.0	1152	6.6	1819	1.1		
8	SU	0027	6.5	0710	0.6	1251	7.0	1934	0.9
9	M ○	0120	6.9	0813	0.3	1342	7.3	2032	0.7
10	TU	0207	7.2	0906	0.0	1429	7.5	2122	0.5
11	W	0250	7.4	0952	-0.2	1513	7.5	2206	0.4
12	TH	0332	7.5	1034	-0.3	1556	7.5	2246	0.4
13	F	0413	7.5	1109	-0.1	1639	7.3	2321	0.5
14	SA	0454	7.4	1140	0.2	1721	7.0	2353	0.7
15	SU	0536	7.1	1207	0.5	1805	6.6		
16	M ☾	0025	0.9	0623	6.8	1241	0.9	1853	6.2
17	TU	0106	1.2	0719	6.4	1329	1.3	1952	5.9
18	W	0204	1.4	0830	6.0	1442	1.6	2108	5.7
19	TH	0327	1.5	0952	5.9	1605	1.7	2236	5.7
20	F	0459	1.4	1116	6.1	1732	1.4	2351	6.1
21	SA	0627	1.0	1220	6.5	1837	1.1		
22	SU	0044	6.4	0719	0.7	1308	6.8	1926	1.0
23	M	0127	6.6	0800	0.6	1348	6.8	2008	0.9
24	TU ●	0202	6.8	0836	0.6	1422	6.8	2045	0.9
25	W	0234	6.9	0907	0.6	1451	6.8	2118	0.8
26	TH	0302	6.9	0935	0.5	1517	6.8	2149	0.8
27	F	0330	7.0	1001	0.5	1544	6.8	2218	0.8
28	SA	0359	6.9	1025	0.6	1612	6.7	2246	0.9
29	SU	0429	6.8	1047	0.7	1643	6.5	2310	1.0
30	M	0501	6.6	1110	0.9	1716	6.3	2334	1.1
31	TU	0536	6.4	1138	1.0	1754	6.1		

APRIL

Date	Day	Time	m	Time	m	Time	m	Time	m
1	W ☽	0005	1.2	0619	6.2	1216	1.1	1842	5.8
2	TH	0051	1.3	0716	6.0	1309	1.5	1952	5.6
3	F	0159	1.5	0842	5.9	1441	1.7	2131	5.6
4	SA	0401	1.4	1013	6.1	1634	1.5	2253	6.1
5	SU	0523	0.9	1125	6.6	1753	1.1	2359	6.5
6	M	0645	0.5	1226	7.0	1910	0.9		
7	TU	0053	6.9	0750	0.2	1318	7.3	2009	0.7
8	W ○	0141	7.2	0842	0.0	1405	7.4	2059	0.5
9	TH	0224	7.5	0927	-0.1	1449	7.5	2144	0.4
10	F	0307	7.6	1008	-0.1	1532	7.4	2225	0.3
11	SA	0349	7.6	1042	0.1	1614	7.2	2300	0.4
12	SU	0431	7.5	1110	0.4	1656	6.9	2331	0.6
13	M	0514	7.1	1135	0.7	1737	6.5		
14	TU ☾	0000	0.8	0600	6.7	1208	1.1	1822	6.1
15	W	0037	1.1	0653	6.3	1253	1.5	1916	5.7
16	TH	0130	1.4	0802	5.9	1403	1.8	2030	5.5
17	F	0253	1.5	0920	5.8	1531	1.8	2155	5.6
18	SA	0417	1.3	1040	6.0	1650	1.5	2312	5.9
19	SU	0534	1.1	1147	6.3	1756	1.3		
20	M	0009	6.3	0633	0.8	1237	6.6	1848	1.0
21	TU	0053	6.5	0717	0.7	1316	6.7	1933	0.9
22	W	0129	6.7	0755	0.6	1350	6.7	2012	0.9
23	TH ●	0202	6.9	0829	0.6	1419	6.8	2049	0.8
24	F	0232	7.0	0900	0.6	1447	6.8	2122	0.7
25	SA	0302	7.0	0929	0.6	1515	6.8	2155	0.7
26	SU	0332	7.0	0955	0.7	1547	6.7	2225	0.8
27	M	0405	6.9	1020	0.8	1620	6.5	2252	0.9
28	TU	0440	6.7	1047	0.9	1655	6.3	2318	0.9
29	W	0519	6.6	1120	1.0	1734	6.1	2352	1.0
30	TH ☽	0605	6.4	1201	1.2	1825	5.9		

MAY

Date	Day	Time	m	Time	m	Time	m	Time	m
1	F	0038	1.1	0703	6.2	1256	1.5	1932	5.7
2	SA	0147	1.3	0824	6.1	1428	1.7	2102	5.8
3	SU	0335	1.1	0947	6.3	1605	1.4	2221	6.2
4	M	0453	0.8	1056	6.7	1721	1.2	2327	6.6
5	TU	0610	0.5	1158	7.0	1838	0.9		
6	W	0023	7.0	0718	0.3	1252	7.2	1941	0.7
7	TH ○	0113	7.3	0812	0.1	1340	7.3	2033	0.5
8	F	0159	7.5	0858	0.1	1425	7.3	2120	0.4
9	SA	0243	7.6	0939	0.2	1509	7.2	2202	0.4
10	SU	0327	7.6	1015	0.4	1551	7.1	2239	0.4
11	M	0411	7.4	1043	0.7	1633	6.8	2311	0.6
12	TU	0455	7.0	1109	0.9	1714	6.4	2339	0.8
13	W	0541	6.6	1142	1.2	1756	6.1		
14	TH ☾	0014	1.0	0631	6.2	1226	1.5	1844	5.8
15	F	0102	1.2	0731	5.9	1324	1.7	1949	5.6
16	SA	0212	1.4	0840	5.8	1443	1.8	2105	5.6
17	SU	0331	1.3	0950	5.9	1602	1.7	2216	5.8
18	M	0436	1.1	1055	6.1	1707	1.4	2318	6.1
19	TU	0532	0.9	1151	6.3	1802	1.2		
20	W	0008	6.4	0623	0.8	1236	6.5	1851	1.0
21	TH	0051	6.7	0709	0.7	1313	6.6	1936	0.9
22	F ●	0128	6.8	0750	0.7	1347	6.7	2018	0.8
23	SA	0203	6.9	0827	0.7	1420	6.8	2057	0.7
24	SU	0237	7.0	0900	0.8	1454	6.8	2134	0.7
25	M	0312	7.0	0931	0.8	1529	6.7	2209	0.6
26	TU	0348	6.9	1002	0.8	1605	6.6	2242	0.7
27	W	0427	6.8	1036	0.9	1644	6.4	2314	0.7
28	TH	0510	6.7	1115	1.0	1727	6.2	2352	0.8
29	F	0559	6.5	1200	1.2	1817	6.1		
30	SA ☽	0040	0.9	0657	6.4	1258	1.4	1919	6.0
31	SU	0150	1.0	0809	6.3	1417	1.5	2037	6.1

JUNE

Date	Day	Time	m	Time	m	Time	m	Time	m
1	M	0312	0.9	0922	6.4	1538	1.4	2151	6.3
2	TU	0423	0.7	1029	6.6	1652	1.2	2256	6.6
3	W	0532	0.5	1131	6.8	1807	1.0	2355	6.9
4	TH	0644	0.4	1228	6.9	1913	0.8		
5	F ○	0048	7.1	0741	0.4	1319	7.0	2009	0.6
6	SA	0138	7.3	0831	0.4	1406	7.1	2058	0.4
7	SU	0224	7.4	0914	0.5	1450	7.0	2144	0.4
8	M	0310	7.4	0952	0.7	1534	6.9	2224	0.5
9	TU	0355	7.2	1024	0.9	1615	6.7	2259	0.6
10	W	0440	6.9	1052	1.0	1655	6.4	2328	0.8
11	TH	0523	6.6	1125	1.2	1734	6.2	2358	0.9
12	F	0608	6.3	1204	1.4	1816	6.0		
13	SA ☾	0037	1.0	0657	6.0	1250	1.6	1906	5.8
14	SU	0128	1.2	0754	5.8	1346	1.7	2013	5.7
15	M	0234	1.2	0856	5.8	1458	1.7	2122	5.8
16	TU	0342	1.2	0957	5.9	1613	1.6	2224	6.0
17	W	0441	1.1	1056	6.1	1714	1.3	2321	6.3
18	TH	0535	1.0	1150	6.3	1810	1.1		
19	F	0012	6.6	0626	0.9	1238	6.5	1901	0.9
20	SA	0057	6.8	0715	0.8	1320	6.7	1950	0.7
21	SU ●	0138	6.9	0800	0.8	1401	6.8	2036	0.6
22	M	0218	7.0	0842	0.9	1440	6.8	2120	0.5
23	TU	0258	7.0	0922	0.8	1520	6.8	2204	0.5
24	W	0339	7.1	1001	0.8	1600	6.7	2245	0.4
25	TH	0421	7.0	1042	0.8	1640	6.6	2324	0.4
26	F	0505	6.9	1123	0.9	1723	6.5		
27	SA	0004	0.5	0552	6.8	1209	1.0	1809	6.4
28	SU ☽	0049	0.6	0647	6.6	1300	1.2	1904	6.3
29	M	0143	0.7	0750	6.5	1401	1.3	2012	6.3
30	TU	0246	0.7	0857	6.4	1510	1.3	2122	6.4

SUNRISE AND SUNSET TIMES

LONDON BRIDGE
At 51°30′N 0°05′W

UT		Sunrise	Sunset
Jan	01	0806	1602
	15	0759	1621
Feb	01	0738	1650
	15	0714	1716
Mar	01	0645	1741
	15	0614	1805
BST			
Apr	01	0636	1934
	15	0605	1957
May	01	0532	2024
	15	0508	2046
Jun	01	0449	2108
	15	0443	2119
Jul	01	0448	2121
	15	0501	2111
Aug	01	0524	2048
	15	0546	2023
Sep	01	0613	1947
	15	0635	1915
Oct	01	0701	1838
	15	0724	1807
UT			
Nov	01	0654	1633
	15	0718	1611
Dec	01	0744	1555
	15	0800	1551

LONDON BRIDGE
LAT 51°30′N
LONG 0°05′W

TIMES AND HEIGHTS OF HIGH AND LOW WATER

TIME ZONE UT
For Summer Time (area enclosed in shaded box) add 1 hour

2020

JULY

Date	Day	Time	m	Time	m	Time	m	Time	m
1	W	0352	0.7	1002	6.5	1624	1.2	2228	6.6
2	TH	0459	0.7	1107	6.6	1738	1.1	2332	6.7
3	F	0611	0.7	1209	6.7	1850	0.8		
4	SA	0031	6.9	0716	0.7	1305	6.8	1949	0.6
5	SU O	0125	7.1	0809	0.7	1354	6.8	2042	0.4
6	M	0214	7.2	0856	0.8	1440	6.9	2130	0.4
7	TU	0300	7.2	0938	0.8	1522	6.8	2214	0.4
8	W	0344	7.1	1014	0.9	1601	6.7	2251	0.5
9	TH	0425	6.9	1044	1.0	1637	6.6	2319	0.7
10	F	0503	6.7	1112	1.1	1712	6.4	2343	0.8
11	SA	0541	6.4	1144	1.2	1747	6.3		
12	SU ☾	0011	0.8	0618	6.2	1220	1.3	1825	6.1
13	M	0047	1.0	0701	6.0	1300	1.5	1913	5.9
14	TU	0128	1.2	0755	5.8	1348	1.7	2019	5.8
15	W	0222	1.3	0859	5.7	1454	1.8	2131	5.8
16	TH	0340	1.4	1004	5.8	1623	1.6	2235	6.0
17	F	0450	1.3	1107	6.1	1730	1.3	2335	6.3
18	SA	0549	1.1	1206	6.4	1829	1.0		
19	SU	0028	6.6	0646	1.0	1258	6.6	1925	0.7
20	M ●	0117	6.9	0741	0.9	1344	6.8	2020	0.6
21	TU	0202	7.0	0833	0.9	1428	6.9	2111	0.4
22	W	0246	7.2	0922	0.8	1510	6.9	2200	0.2
23	TH	0329	7.3	1008	0.7	1551	7.0	2244	0.1
24	F	0412	7.3	1050	0.7	1631	6.9	2325	0.0
25	SA	0455	7.2	1129	0.7	1711	6.9		
26	SU	0003	0.1	0539	6.9	1208	0.8	1754	6.8
27	M ☽	0040	0.3	0629	6.7	1249	1.0	1843	6.6
28	TU	0122	0.5	0725	6.5	1338	1.2	1942	6.5
29	W	0214	0.8	0829	6.3	1441	1.3	2052	6.4
30	TH	0319	1.0	0935	6.2	1555	1.3	2203	6.4
31	F	0429	1.1	1046	6.2	1714	1.2	2315	6.5

AUGUST

Date	Day	Time	m	Time	m	Time	m	Time	m
1	SA	0547	1.1	1157	6.4	1834	0.9		
2	SU	0022	6.7	0658	1.0	1257	6.6	1937	0.6
3	M O	0119	6.9	0753	0.9	1346	6.7	2030	0.4
4	TU	0207	7.0	0841	0.9	1430	6.8	2117	0.4
5	W	0250	7.1	0923	0.9	1508	6.9	2158	0.4
6	TH	0329	7.0	1000	0.9	1543	6.9	2232	0.5
7	F	0405	6.9	1030	1.0	1615	6.8	2258	0.6
8	SA	0437	6.8	1056	1.0	1646	6.7	2318	0.6
9	SU	0508	6.6	1122	1.1	1716	6.5	2341	0.8
10	M	0538	6.3	1151	1.2	1748	6.3		
11	TU ☾	0006	0.9	0610	6.1	1222	1.4	1824	6.1
12	W	0035	1.1	0649	5.8	1257	1.6	1909	5.9
13	TH	0112	1.4	0743	5.6	1345	1.8	2014	5.7
14	F	0207	1.6	0907	5.5	1507	1.8	2146	5.7
15	SA	0354	1.7	1026	5.8	1651	1.5	2258	6.1
16	SU	0515	1.4	1136	6.1	1759	1.1		
17	M	0001	6.5	0620	1.2	1234	6.5	1904	0.7
18	TU	0055	6.9	0725	1.0	1324	6.8	2005	0.5
19	W ●	0143	7.1	0824	0.9	1409	7.0	2100	0.2
20	TH	0228	7.3	0915	0.7	1452	7.1	2148	0.0
21	F	0312	7.4	1001	0.6	1533	7.2	2232	-0.1
22	SA	0355	7.4	1042	0.6	1612	7.2	2311	-0.1
23	SU	0437	7.3	1120	0.6	1651	7.2	2345	0.1
24	M	0519	7.0	1154	0.8	1733	7.0		
25	TU ☽	0017	0.4	0604	6.7	1230	1.0	1818	6.8
26	W	0051	0.7	0655	6.3	1312	1.2	1913	6.5
27	TH	0138	1.1	0756	6.1	1409	1.4	2024	6.3
28	F	0245	1.4	0908	5.9	1527	1.5	2143	6.2
29	SA	0403	1.5	1028	5.9	1654	1.3	2303	6.3
30	SU	0531	1.4	1145	6.2	1825	0.9		
31	M	0014	6.6	0643	1.1	1245	6.5	1925	0.6

SEPTEMBER

Date	Day	Time	m	Time	m	Time	m	Time	m
1	TU	0109	6.9	0737	0.9	1333	6.7	2014	0.4
2	W O	0153	7.0	0822	0.9	1412	6.8	2056	0.4
3	TH	0233	7.0	0902	0.9	1447	6.9	2132	0.4
4	F	0307	7.0	0937	0.9	1518	6.9	2202	0.5
5	SA	0338	6.9	1007	0.9	1547	6.9	2225	0.6
6	SU	0405	6.8	1032	0.9	1615	6.9	2245	0.7
7	M	0432	6.6	1058	1.0	1644	6.7	2307	0.8
8	TU	0500	6.4	1124	1.2	1714	6.5	2328	1.0
9	W	0530	6.2	1148	1.3	1747	6.3	2351	1.2
10	TH ☾	0605	5.9	1215	1.5	1828	6.0		
11	F	0022	1.4	0649	5.7	1255	1.6	1920	5.7
12	SA	0110	1.7	0755	5.4	1358	1.8	2044	5.6
13	SU	0228	1.9	0940	5.5	1611	1.7	2219	5.9
14	M	0440	1.7	1102	5.9	1728	1.2	2330	6.4
15	TU	0553	1.3	1205	6.4	1840	0.7		
16	W	0028	6.9	0705	1.0	1258	6.8	1945	0.4
17	TH ●	0119	7.2	0805	0.9	1344	7.1	2039	0.1
18	F	0205	7.4	0857	0.7	1426	7.3	2127	0.0
19	SA	0249	7.5	0943	0.6	1507	7.4	2210	-0.1
20	SU	0331	7.4	1024	0.5	1547	7.5	2248	0.0
21	M	0413	7.3	1101	0.6	1628	7.4	2320	0.3
22	TU	0454	7.0	1135	0.7	1709	7.2	2347	0.6
23	W	0537	6.6	1207	0.9	1755	6.8		
24	TH ☽	0018	1.0	0624	6.2	1245	1.2	1848	6.4
25	F	0102	1.4	0722	5.9	1339	1.4	2000	6.1
26	SA	0211	1.8	0840	5.6	1500	1.6	2123	6.0
27	SU	0338	1.8	1006	5.7	1633	1.4	2246	6.2
28	M	0509	1.6	1125	6.0	1806	0.9	2356	6.6
29	TU	0620	1.2	1223	6.4	1903	0.6		
30	W	0048	6.9	0711	1.0	1309	6.7	1947	0.5

OCTOBER

Date	Day	Time	m	Time	m	Time	m	Time	m
1	TH O	0131	7.0	0755	0.9	1347	6.8	2024	0.5
2	F	0207	6.9	0833	0.9	1419	6.9	2056	0.6
3	SA	0238	6.9	0907	0.9	1448	7.0	2123	0.6
4	SU	0305	6.9	0937	0.9	1516	7.0	2147	0.7
5	M	0330	6.8	1005	0.9	1544	7.0	2210	0.7
6	TU	0357	6.7	1032	1.0	1613	6.8	2232	0.9
7	W	0426	6.5	1057	1.1	1644	6.6	2253	1.0
8	TH	0456	6.3	1119	1.2	1718	6.4	2317	1.2
9	F	0530	6.1	1144	1.3	1758	6.2	2350	1.3
10	SA ☾	0613	5.8	1223	1.4	1850	5.9		
11	SU	0036	1.6	0713	5.5	1320	1.6	2003	5.8
12	M	0146	1.9	0848	5.4	1525	1.7	2140	6.0
13	TU	0400	1.8	1021	5.8	1653	1.2	2255	6.5
14	W	0518	1.4	1129	6.3	1805	0.7	2356	6.9
15	TH	0632	1.1	1224	6.8	1915	0.4		
16	F ●	0049	7.2	0737	0.9	1313	7.2	2011	0.2
17	SA	0137	7.4	0831	0.7	1357	7.4	2059	0.1
18	SU	0222	7.5	0918	0.6	1440	7.6	2142	0.1
19	M	0305	7.4	1001	0.5	1522	7.6	2220	0.3
20	TU	0348	7.2	1040	0.6	1605	7.5	2251	0.6
21	W	0430	6.9	1113	0.7	1648	7.2	2317	0.9
22	TH	0512	6.5	1144	0.9	1735	6.8	2349	1.2
23	F ☽	0557	6.1	1220	1.1	1829	6.4		
24	SA	0031	1.6	0651	5.8	1311	1.4	1936	6.0
25	SU	0137	1.9	0805	5.5	1431	1.5	2055	5.9
26	M	0305	2.0	0930	5.5	1558	1.4	2213	6.0
27	TU	0430	1.7	1048	5.8	1720	1.1	2324	6.4
28	W	0540	1.4	1149	6.2	1821	0.8		
29	TH	0017	6.7	0633	1.2	1235	6.5	1904	0.7
30	F	0059	6.8	0718	1.0	1313	6.7	1940	0.7
31	SA O	0135	6.8	0757	0.9	1346	6.9	2013	0.7

NOVEMBER

Date	Day	Time	m	Time	m	Time	m	Time	m
1	SU	0205	6.8	0833	0.9	1416	7.0	2043	0.7
2	M	0232	6.8	0906	0.8	1445	7.0	2111	0.8
3	TU	0259	6.8	0938	0.8	1515	7.0	2137	0.9
4	W	0328	6.8	1007	0.9	1547	6.9	2201	0.9
5	TH	0400	6.6	1034	1.0	1621	6.7	2227	1.0
6	F	0432	6.4	1058	1.1	1658	6.6	2256	1.2
7	SA	0508	6.2	1128	1.1	1740	6.4	2333	1.3
8	SU ☾	0552	5.9	1207	1.2	1832	6.2		
9	M	0020	1.5	0649	5.7	1303	1.4	1940	6.0
10	TU	0128	1.8	0809	5.6	1445	1.4	2107	6.1
11	W	0320	1.8	0941	5.9	1616	1.1	2220	6.5
12	TH	0441	1.5	1051	6.4	1725	0.7	2323	6.9
13	F	0554	1.2	1150	6.8	1836	0.5		
14	SA	0019	7.1	0704	1.0	1242	7.2	1938	0.4
15	SU ●	0110	7.3	0802	0.8	1330	7.4	2029	0.3
16	M	0157	7.3	0853	0.6	1415	7.6	2114	0.4
17	TU	0242	7.2	0939	0.5	1501	7.6	2153	0.6
18	W	0326	7.1	1020	0.5	1546	7.4	2227	0.8
19	TH	0410	6.8	1056	0.7	1632	7.1	2255	1.1
20	F	0453	6.5	1128	0.9	1720	6.8	2328	1.3
21	SA	0536	6.1	1203	1.1	1811	6.4		
22	SU ☽	0009	1.6	0623	5.8	1248	1.3	1910	6.0
23	M	0103	1.9	0725	5.6	1355	1.4	2018	5.9
24	TU	0219	2.0	0842	5.5	1512	1.4	2126	5.9
25	W	0340	1.9	0953	5.7	1617	1.2	2233	6.1
26	TH	0447	1.6	1057	6.0	1715	1.0	2332	6.3
27	F	0545	1.4	1150	6.3	1806	0.9		
28	SA	0019	6.5	0634	1.2	1235	6.6	1851	0.9
29	SU	0058	6.6	0719	1.0	1313	6.8	1932	0.8
30	M O	0133	6.7	0800	0.9	1347	6.9	2009	0.9

DECEMBER

Date	Day	Time	m	Time	m	Time	m	Time	m
1	TU	0205	6.8	0839	0.8	1420	6.9	2042	0.9
2	W	0236	6.8	0915	0.8	1454	6.9	2112	1.0
3	TH	0310	6.7	0950	0.8	1529	6.9	2141	1.0
4	F	0344	6.6	1022	0.8	1606	6.8	2213	1.0
5	SA	0420	6.5	1053	0.8	1646	6.7	2249	1.1
6	SU	0459	6.3	1126	0.9	1731	6.6	2330	1.2
7	M	0544	6.1	1207	1.0	1821	6.4		
8	TU ☾	0019	1.4	0636	6.0	1300	1.1	1922	6.3
9	W	0122	1.6	0742	6.0	1418	1.1	2037	6.3
10	TH	0245	1.7	0903	6.1	1539	1.0	2148	6.5
11	F	0406	1.5	1015	6.4	1648	0.8	2252	6.7
12	SA	0521	1.3	1118	6.7	1758	0.7	2353	6.8
13	SU	0635	1.0	1216	7.0	1906	0.6		
14	M ●	0048	7.0	0738	0.8	1309	7.2	2002	0.6
15	TU	0139	7.0	0832	0.6	1359	7.3	2051	0.7
16	W	0226	7.0	0922	0.5	1447	7.4	2134	0.8
17	TH	0313	7.0	1007	0.5	1535	7.3	2213	0.9
18	F	0357	6.8	1048	0.6	1621	7.1	2246	1.1
19	SA	0439	6.6	1123	0.8	1706	6.8	2317	1.3
20	SU	0519	6.3	1154	0.9	1752	6.4	2352	1.5
21	M ☽	0600	6.1	1228	1.1	1839	6.2		
22	TU	0033	1.6	0645	5.9	1312	1.2	1932	5.9
23	W	0123	1.8	0745	5.7	1410	1.3	2031	5.8
24	TH	0228	1.9	0854	5.7	1518	1.4	2131	5.8
25	F	0348	1.9	0959	5.8	1620	1.3	2232	6.0
26	SA	0453	1.6	1059	6.1	1716	1.2	2330	6.2
27	SU	0550	1.3	1154	6.3	1809	1.1		
28	M	0021	6.4	0642	1.1	1241	6.6	1858	1.0
29	TU	0106	6.6	0731	0.9	1323	6.7	1943	1.0
30	W O	0146	6.7	0817	0.8	1402	6.8	2024	1.0
31	TH	0224	6.7	0901	0.7	1440	6.9	2102	1.0

WALTON-ON-THE-NAZE

LAT 51°51′N
LONG 1°17′E

TIMES AND HEIGHTS OF HIGH AND LOW WATER (Heights in Metres)

TIME ZONE UT
For Summer Time (area enclosed in shaded box) add 1 hour

2020

JANUARY

Date	Day	Time	m	Time	m	Time	m	Time	m
1	W	0304	3.8	0920	0.7	1537	3.7	2119	1.1
2	TH	0346	3.7	1000	0.7	1624	3.6	2204	1.3
3	F ☽	0434	3.6	1049	0.9	1718	3.4	2259	1.4
4	SA	0531	3.5	1153	1.0	1817	3.4		
5	SU	0015	1.4	0633	3.4	1304	1.0	1918	3.4
6	M	0137	1.3	0737	3.5	1407	0.9	2018	3.5
7	TU	0239	1.2	0838	3.6	1502	0.9	2115	3.7
8	W	0332	1.0	0933	3.8	1551	0.8	2207	3.9
9	TH	0420	0.8	1023	3.9	1635	0.8	2254	4.0
10	F O	0506	0.6	1109	4.1	1717	0.7	2340	4.1
11	SA	0551	0.5	1155	4.3	1758	0.7		
12	SU	0025	4.2	0636	0.4	1241	4.4	1840	0.7
13	M	0110	4.3	0722	0.3	1326	4.4	1923	0.7
14	TU	0154	4.3	0808	0.2	1413	4.4	2009	0.7
15	W	0239	4.2	0855	0.2	1501	4.3	2057	0.8
16	TH	0325	4.1	0945	0.3	1551	4.1	2148	0.9
17	F ☾	0414	4.0	1040	0.4	1647	3.9	2246	1.0
18	SA	0509	3.9	1139	0.5	1749	3.8	2351	1.1
19	SU	0614	3.8	1243	0.6	1858	3.7		
20	M	0102	1.1	0727	3.7	1348	0.7	2010	3.7
21	TU	0215	1.0	0838	3.8	1455	0.8	2118	3.8
22	W	0326	0.9	0940	3.9	1557	0.8	2215	3.9
23	TH	0429	0.7	1034	4.0	1649	0.8	2303	4.0
24	F ●	0521	0.6	1120	4.1	1732	0.8	2345	4.1
25	SA	0605	0.4	1202	4.1	1810	0.8		
26	SU	0024	4.1	0645	0.4	1241	4.1	1845	0.8
27	M	0101	4.1	0720	0.4	1319	4.1	1918	0.8
28	TU	0135	4.1	0751	0.4	1355	4.0	1947	0.8
29	W	0207	4.1	0820	0.5	1430	3.9	2016	0.9
30	TH	0240	4.0	0848	0.5	1505	3.8	2049	0.9
31	F	0314	3.9	0919	0.6	1540	3.7	2125	1.0

FEBRUARY

Date	Day	Time	m	Time	m	Time	m	Time	m
1	SA	0350	3.8	0956	0.7	1619	3.5	2208	1.1
2	SU ☽	0433	3.6	1041	0.9	1708	3.4	2303	1.3
3	M	0527	3.5	1144	1.0	1813	3.4		
4	TU	0024	1.3	0637	3.4	1312	1.1	1924	3.4
5	W	0153	1.2	0752	3.4	1424	1.0	2036	3.5
6	TH	0259	1.0	0902	3.6	1524	0.9	2142	3.7
7	F	0356	0.8	1001	3.8	1616	0.8	2236	3.9
8	SA	0448	0.6	1053	4.1	1703	0.7	2325	4.1
9	SU O	0537	0.4	1141	4.3	1747	0.6		
10	M	0011	4.2	0624	0.2	1228	4.4	1831	0.6
11	TU	0056	4.4	0710	0.1	1314	4.5	1914	0.6
12	W	0140	4.4	0755	0.0	1400	4.5	1958	0.6
13	TH	0223	4.4	0839	0.1	1446	4.3	2041	0.7
14	F	0306	4.4	0923	0.2	1532	4.2	2127	0.8
15	SA ☾	0351	4.2	1009	0.3	1622	3.9	2218	0.9
16	SU	0441	4.0	1102	0.5	1718	3.7	2317	1.0
17	M	0541	3.8	1205	0.8	1824	3.5		
18	TU	0029	1.1	0659	3.6	1317	0.9	1944	3.4
19	W	0153	1.0	0821	3.6	1438	1.0	2103	3.5
20	TH	0322	0.9	0930	3.7	1549	1.0	2203	3.7
21	F	0427	0.7	1026	3.9	1640	0.9	2252	3.9
22	SA	0514	0.5	1111	4.0	1719	0.9	2333	4.0
23	SU ●	0553	0.4	1150	4.0	1753	0.8		
24	M	0009	4.1	0626	0.4	1226	4.1	1825	0.8
25	TU	0042	4.1	0656	0.4	1259	4.1	1856	0.7
26	W	0113	4.1	0724	0.4	1332	4.0	1925	0.7
27	TH	0143	4.1	0750	0.4	1403	4.0	1952	0.7
28	F	0213	4.1	0815	0.5	1433	3.9	2022	0.8
29	SA	0243	4.0	0841	0.5	1503	3.8	2054	0.9

MARCH

Date	Day	Time	m	Time	m	Time	m	Time	m
1	SU	0315	3.9	0911	0.7	1538	3.6	2131	1.0
2	M ☽	0352	3.7	0948	0.8	1620	3.5	2216	1.1
3	TU	0439	3.6	1040	1.0	1717	3.4	2324	1.2
4	W	0543	3.4	1207	1.2	1834	3.3		
5	TH	0108	1.2	0706	3.4	1349	1.1	1959	3.3
6	F	0229	1.0	0834	3.5	1458	1.0	2117	3.6
7	SA	0333	0.7	0942	3.8	1555	0.8	2216	3.8
8	SU	0429	0.4	1036	4.1	1645	0.7	2306	4.1
9	M O	0519	0.2	1125	4.3	1730	0.6	2351	4.3
10	TU	0606	0.1	1210	4.5	1815	0.5		
11	W	0035	4.5	0651	0.0	1256	4.5	1857	0.5
12	TH	0118	4.6	0733	-0.1	1340	4.5	1940	0.5
13	F	0200	4.6	0814	0.0	1424	4.4	2022	0.5
14	SA	0242	4.5	0854	0.2	1509	4.2	2105	0.6
15	SU	0325	4.3	0936	0.4	1555	3.9	2152	0.7
16	M ☾	0413	4.0	1025	0.7	1647	3.6	2248	0.9
17	TU	0513	3.7	1127	1.0	1751	3.4	2359	1.0
18	W	0634	3.5	1244	1.2	1915	3.3		
19	TH	0133	1.0	0802	3.5	1417	1.2	2040	3.4
20	F	0312	0.9	0916	3.7	1534	1.1	2144	3.6
21	SA	0413	0.6	1011	3.8	1622	1.0	2231	3.8
22	SU	0456	0.5	1053	3.9	1658	0.9	2311	3.9
23	M	0530	0.4	1129	4.0	1729	0.8	2344	4.0
24	TU ●	0558	0.4	1202	4.0	1801	0.7		
25	W	0015	4.1	0625	0.4	1234	4.1	1831	0.7
26	TH	0045	4.2	0652	0.4	1305	4.1	1900	0.6
27	F	0115	4.2	0717	0.4	1334	4.0	1929	0.6
28	SA	0145	4.1	0741	0.5	1403	3.9	1958	0.7
29	SU	0215	4.0	0807	0.5	1433	3.8	2029	0.7
30	M	0247	3.9	0836	0.7	1507	3.7	2104	0.8
31	TU	0324	3.8	0912	0.8	1548	3.6	2147	0.9

APRIL

Date	Day	Time	m	Time	m	Time	m	Time	m
1	W ☽	0410	3.7	1002	1.0	1641	3.4	2251	1.0
2	TH	0511	3.5	1125	1.2	1755	3.3		
3	F	0033	1.0	0633	3.4	1316	1.2	1926	3.3
4	SA	0200	0.9	0808	3.6	1431	1.0	2049	3.5
5	SU	0307	0.6	0919	3.8	1530	0.8	2150	3.8
6	M	0405	0.3	1015	4.1	1620	0.7	2241	4.1
7	TU	0455	0.1	1103	4.3	1707	0.6	2326	4.3
8	W O	0542	0.0	1148	4.4	1752	0.5		
9	TH	0009	4.5	0625	0.0	1233	4.5	1836	0.4
10	F	0053	4.6	0707	0.0	1317	4.5	1920	0.4
11	SA	0135	4.6	0747	0.1	1400	4.3	2003	0.4
12	SU	0218	4.5	0825	0.4	1444	4.1	2046	0.5
13	M	0301	4.3	0905	0.6	1528	3.9	2131	0.6
14	TU ☾	0349	4.0	0952	0.9	1618	3.6	2224	0.8
15	W	0449	3.7	1051	1.1	1720	3.4	2331	0.9
16	TH	0608	3.5	1207	1.3	1838	3.3		
17	F	0103	1.0	0732	3.5	1338	1.3	2003	3.3
18	SA	0240	0.9	0846	3.6	1459	1.2	2109	3.5
19	SU	0343	0.7	0942	3.8	1550	1.0	2159	3.7
20	M	0424	0.6	1024	3.9	1627	0.9	2238	3.9
21	TU	0455	0.5	1100	4.0	1700	0.8	2312	4.0
22	W	0523	0.5	1133	4.0	1733	0.7	2343	4.1
23	TH ●	0552	0.4	1204	4.0	1805	0.6		
24	F	0014	4.1	0619	0.4	1235	4.1	1836	0.6
25	SA	0046	4.2	0645	0.5	1306	4.0	1906	0.6
26	SU	0118	4.1	0711	0.5	1337	4.0	1937	0.6
27	M	0151	4.1	0739	0.6	1410	3.9	2010	0.6
28	TU	0226	4.0	0812	0.7	1446	3.8	2047	0.7
29	W	0305	3.9	0852	0.9	1528	3.7	2133	0.8
30	TH ☽	0354	3.8	0946	1.0	1622	3.5	2239	0.9

MAY

Date	Day	Time	m	Time	m	Time	m	Time	m
1	F	0455	3.6	1108	1.2	1733	3.4		
2	SA	0012	0.8	0613	3.6	1245	1.2	1858	3.4
3	SU	0134	0.7	0742	3.7	1359	1.0	2017	3.6
4	M	0239	0.5	0852	3.9	1500	0.9	2120	3.9
5	TU	0337	0.3	0949	4.1	1553	0.7	2212	4.1
6	W	0428	0.2	1039	4.3	1642	0.6	2259	4.4
7	TH O	0515	0.1	1125	4.4	1730	0.5	2344	4.5
8	F	0600	0.1	1209	4.4	1817	0.4		
9	SA	0027	4.6	0642	0.2	1254	4.4	1903	0.4
10	SU	0112	4.6	0723	0.4	1338	4.3	1947	0.4
11	M	0156	4.4	0802	0.6	1421	4.1	2031	0.5
12	TU	0241	4.2	0841	0.8	1505	3.9	2115	0.6
13	W	0329	3.9	0925	1.0	1553	3.7	2204	0.7
14	TH ☾	0427	3.7	1019	1.2	1650	3.5	2304	0.8
15	F	0537	3.5	1125	1.3	1756	3.4		
16	SA	0021	0.9	0649	3.5	1246	1.4	1908	3.4
17	SU	0141	0.9	0759	3.5	1403	1.3	2017	3.5
18	M	0248	0.8	0859	3.7	1503	1.1	2112	3.6
19	TU	0336	0.7	0945	3.8	1548	1.0	2156	3.8
20	W	0413	0.6	1024	3.9	1628	0.8	2233	3.9
21	TH	0446	0.6	1100	4.0	1704	0.7	2309	4.0
22	F ●	0519	0.6	1134	4.0	1739	0.7	2344	4.1
23	SA	0550	0.6	1208	4.1	1814	0.6		
24	SU	0020	4.2	0619	0.6	1243	4.1	1848	0.6
25	M	0056	4.2	0648	0.6	1319	4.0	1923	0.6
26	TU	0133	4.1	0721	0.7	1356	4.0	2001	0.6
27	W	0212	4.1	0759	0.8	1436	3.9	2042	0.6
28	TH	0255	4.0	0845	0.9	1520	3.8	2133	0.6
29	F	0346	3.9	0943	1.0	1614	3.7	2238	0.7
30	SA ☽	0446	3.8	1055	1.1	1719	3.6	2355	0.6
31	SU	0558	3.7	1214	1.1	1832	3.6		

JUNE

Date	Day	Time	m	Time	m	Time	m	Time	m
1	M	0107	0.5	0714	3.8	1326	1.0	1945	3.8
2	TU	0210	0.4	0823	3.9	1429	0.9	2049	3.9
3	W	0308	0.3	0924	4.1	1527	0.8	2145	4.1
4	TH	0402	0.3	1016	4.2	1621	0.7	2235	4.3
5	F O	0452	0.3	1104	4.2	1712	0.5	2322	4.4
6	SA	0538	0.4	1150	4.3	1803	0.4		
7	SU	0008	4.5	0623	0.5	1236	4.3	1851	0.4
8	M	0053	4.4	0705	0.6	1319	4.2	1937	0.4
9	TU	0138	4.3	0745	0.7	1403	4.1	2020	0.5
10	W	0224	4.2	0823	0.9	1445	3.9	2101	0.6
11	TH	0311	3.9	0903	1.0	1530	3.8	2144	0.6
12	F	0403	3.7	0947	1.1	1619	3.7	2233	0.7
13	SA ☾	0500	3.6	1041	1.3	1713	3.6	2333	0.8
14	SU	0600	3.5	1148	1.4	1812	3.5		
15	M	0039	0.9	0700	3.5	1304	1.3	1912	3.5
16	TU	0143	0.9	0800	3.5	1409	1.2	2012	3.6
17	W	0238	0.8	0856	3.6	1505	1.1	2107	3.7
18	TH	0328	0.8	0944	3.8	1553	0.9	2154	3.8
19	F	0411	0.7	1026	3.9	1636	0.8	2237	4.0
20	SA	0451	0.7	1106	4.0	1716	0.7	2318	4.1
21	SU ●	0527	0.7	1146	4.0	1755	0.6	2359	4.1
22	M	0601	0.7	1226	4.1	1835	0.5		
23	TU	0039	4.2	0636	0.7	1307	4.1	1915	0.5
24	W	0121	4.2	0714	0.7	1349	4.1	1958	0.4
25	TH	0204	4.2	0756	0.8	1432	4.0	2043	0.4
26	F	0250	4.1	0844	0.9	1516	4.0	2133	0.5
27	SA	0339	4.0	0937	1.0	1606	3.9	2230	0.5
28	SU ☽	0435	3.9	1037	1.0	1701	3.9	2333	0.5
29	M	0538	3.8	1144	1.1	1805	3.8		
30	TU	0038	0.5	0646	3.8	1254	1.1	1913	3.9

SUNRISE AND SUNSET TIMES

WALTON-ON-THE-NAZE
At 51°51′N 1°17′E

		Sunrise	Sunset
UT			
Jan	01	0802	1555
	15	0755	1614
Feb	01	0734	1643
	15	0709	1709
Mar	01	0640	1735
	15	0609	1800
BST			
Apr	01	0630	1929
	15	0558	1952
May	01	0526	2020
	15	0502	2042
Jun	01	0442	2104
	15	0435	2116
Jul	01	0440	2117
	15	0454	2107
Aug	01	0517	2044
	15	0539	2020
Sep	01	0607	1942
	15	0630	1909
Oct	01	0656	1832
	15	0719	1801
UT			
Nov	01	0649	1627
	15	0714	1604
Dec	01	0740	1548
	15	0756	1544

WALTON-ON-THE-NAZE
LAT 51°51′N
LONG 1°17′E

TIMES AND HEIGHTS OF HIGH AND LOW WATER (Heights in Metres)

TIME ZONE UT
For Summer Time (area enclosed in shaded box) add 1 hour

2020

JULY

Date	Day	Time	m
1	W	0141 0755 1401 2021	0.5 3.8 1.0 3.9
2	TH	0242 0901 1505 2123	0.5 3.9 0.9 4.1
3	F	0340 0959 1606 2218	0.6 4.0 0.7 4.2
4	SA	0435 1051 1703 2308	0.6 4.1 0.6 4.3
5	SU	0524 1138 1755 O 2355	0.6 4.1 0.5 4.3
6	M	0610 1222 1844	0.7 4.2 0.4
7	TU	0040 0651 1306 1928	4.3 0.7 4.2 0.4
8	W	0124 0730 1346 2008	4.3 0.8 4.1 0.4
9	TH	0207 0805 1426 2044	4.1 0.9 4.1 0.5
10	F	0250 0839 1504 2118	4.0 1.0 4.0 0.6
11	SA	0333 0915 1544 2155	3.8 1.1 3.9 0.7
12	SU	0418 0956 1629 ☾ 2240	3.7 1.2 3.7 0.8
13	M	0508 1047 1720 2336	3.5 1.3 3.6 0.9
14	TU	0602 1154 1817	3.5 1.4 3.5
15	W	0043 0659 1313 1917	1.0 3.4 1.3 3.5
16	TH	0148 0800 1420 2020	1.0 3.5 1.2 3.6
17	F	0247 0901 1518 2118	1.0 3.6 1.0 3.7
18	SA	0341 0955 1609 2210	0.9 3.8 0.9 3.9
19	SU	0427 1043 1655 2257	0.9 3.9 0.7 4.0
20	M	0509 1128 1739 ● 2342	0.8 4.1 0.6 4.2
21	TU	0548 1212 1823	0.8 4.2 0.5
22	W	0026 0627 1255 1906	4.3 0.7 4.2 0.4
23	TH	0110 0708 1338 1951	4.4 0.7 4.3 0.3
24	F	0155 0751 1421 2035	4.4 0.7 4.3 0.3
25	SA	0240 0835 1504 2121	4.3 0.8 4.2 0.3
26	SU	0327 0922 1549 2210	4.2 0.9 4.2 0.4
27	M	0417 1014 1638 ☽ 2304	4.0 1.0 4.1 0.5
28	TU	0513 1114 1735	3.9 1.1 4.0
29	W	0006 0617 1223 1844	0.6 3.7 1.1 3.9
30	TH	0112 0729 1336 1959	0.7 3.7 1.1 3.8
31	F	0219 0844 1450 2109	0.8 3.7 1.0 3.9

AUGUST

Date	Day	Time	m
1	SA	0328 0949 1602 2209	0.9 3.8 0.8 4.1
2	SU	0427 1043 1702 2301	0.9 4.0 0.6 4.2
3	M	0516 1130 1751 O 2347	0.8 4.1 0.5 4.2
4	TU	0558 1211 1834	0.8 4.1 0.4
5	W	0028 0635 1251 1913	4.2 0.8 4.2 0.4
6	TH	0108 0710 1327 1947	4.2 0.8 4.2 0.4
7	F	0146 0743 1401 2017	4.1 0.9 4.2 0.5
8	SA	0223 0813 1434 2044	4.0 0.9 4.1 0.6
9	SU	0259 0843 1508 2113	3.9 1.0 4.0 0.7
10	M	0334 0917 1544 2146	3.8 1.0 3.9 0.8
11	TU	0412 0958 1625 ☾ 2227	3.6 1.2 3.7 1.0
12	W	0457 1049 1716 2327	3.5 1.3 3.6 1.1
13	TH	0557 1204 1822	3.4 1.4 3.5
14	F	0055 0706 1334 1935	1.2 3.4 1.3 3.5
15	SA	0210 0819 1443 2046	1.2 3.5 1.1 3.6
16	SU	0313 0926 1543 2147	1.1 3.7 0.9 3.8
17	M	0406 1021 1634 2238	1.0 3.9 0.7 4.0
18	TU	0451 1109 1721 2325	0.9 4.1 0.5 4.2
19	W ●	0533 1153 1806	0.8 4.2 0.3
20	TH	0009 0613 1237 1850	4.4 0.7 4.4 0.2
21	F	0054 0655 1319 1933	4.5 0.7 4.5 0.2
22	SA	0138 0736 1401 2015	4.5 0.7 4.5 0.2
23	SU	0222 0818 1442 2057	4.4 0.7 4.4 0.3
24	M	0306 0902 1525 2140	4.3 0.8 4.3 0.4
25	TU	0353 0950 1611 ☽ 2230	4.1 0.9 4.2 0.6
26	W	0445 1046 1707 2331	3.8 1.0 4.0 0.9
27	TH	0548 1155 1820	3.6 1.1 3.8
28	F	0043 0706 1317 1945	1.0 3.5 1.1 3.7
29	SA	0203 0831 1446 2101	1.1 3.6 1.0 3.8
30	SU	0322 0940 1603 2204	1.1 3.8 0.8 4.0
31	M	0421 1033 1656 2253	1.0 3.9 0.6 4.1

SEPTEMBER

Date	Day	Time	m
1	TU	0504 1117 1739 2335	1.0 4.1 0.5 4.2
2	W O	0541 1154 1815	0.9 4.2 0.4
3	TH	0011 0614 1229 1847	4.2 0.8 4.2 0.4
4	F	0046 0646 1301 1916	4.2 0.8 4.2 0.5
5	SA	0120 0717 1331 1942	4.2 0.8 4.2 0.5
6	SU	0152 0746 1401 2007	4.1 0.8 4.2 0.6
7	M	0222 0814 1432 2031	4.0 0.9 4.1 0.7
8	TU	0251 0845 1504 2058	3.8 1.0 4.0 0.8
9	W	0323 0919 1538 2131	3.7 1.1 3.8 1.0
10	TH	0401 1002 1622 ☾ 2216	3.6 1.2 3.6 1.2
11	F	0453 1103 1722 2336	3.4 1.3 3.5 1.4
12	SA	0609 1246 1846	3.3 1.3 3.4
13	SU	0132 0737 1409 2015	1.4 3.3 1.1 3.5
14	M	0244 0855 1514 2122	1.2 3.6 0.9 3.8
15	TU	0340 0955 1609 2216	1.0 3.8 0.6 4.1
16	W	0427 1044 1657 2303	0.9 4.1 0.4 4.3
17	TH	0510 1128 1742 ● 2347	0.8 4.3 0.2 4.5
18	F	0552 1211 1826	0.7 4.5 0.1
19	SA	0031 0633 1253 1908	4.6 0.6 4.6 0.1
20	SU	0115 0715 1335 1948	4.6 0.6 4.6 0.2
21	M	0158 0758 1416 2027	4.5 0.6 4.6 0.3
22	TU	0241 0841 1459 2108	4.3 0.7 4.4 0.6
23	W	0326 0927 1545 2156	4.0 0.8 4.2 0.8
24	TH	0417 1022 1642 ☽ 2258	3.8 0.9 3.9 1.1
25	F	0520 1131 1801	3.5 1.0 3.7
26	SA	0015 0642 1300 1931	1.3 3.4 1.1 3.7
27	SU	0145 0812 1438 2049	1.4 3.5 0.9 3.8
28	M	0309 0921 1550 2149	1.3 3.7 0.7 4.0
29	TU	0404 1012 1638 2235	1.1 3.9 0.6 4.1
30	W	0443 1054 1716 2313	1.0 4.0 0.5 4.2

OCTOBER

Date	Day	Time	m
1	TH	0516 1129 1746 O 2347	0.9 4.1 0.5 4.2
2	F	0548 1200 1814	0.8 4.2 0.5
3	SA	0018 0619 1230 1841	4.2 0.8 4.2 0.5
4	SU	0049 0650 1259 1906	4.2 0.8 4.3 0.6
5	M	0119 0719 1329 1929	4.1 0.8 4.2 0.7
6	TU	0147 0747 1359 1952	4.0 0.8 4.1 0.8
7	W	0216 0817 1430 2019	3.9 0.9 4.0 0.9
8	TH	0247 0849 1505 2051	3.8 0.9 3.9 1.0
9	F	0323 0929 1548 2135	3.7 1.0 3.7 1.2
10	SA	0411 1025 1644 ☾ 2243	3.5 1.2 3.6 1.4
11	SU	0521 1201 1802	3.3 1.2 3.5
12	M	0045 0653 1334 1940	1.5 3.3 1.0 3.6
13	TU	0208 0819 1441 2052	1.3 3.5 0.8 3.9
14	W	0307 0922 1538 2148	1.1 3.8 0.5 4.2
15	TH	0356 1013 1627 2236	0.9 4.1 0.3 4.4
16	F	0442 1058 1713 ● 2321	0.7 4.4 0.2 4.5
17	SA	0526 1142 1757	0.6 4.6 0.1
18	SU	0005 0610 1225 1839	4.6 0.6 4.7 0.2
19	M	0049 0654 1308 1920	4.6 0.5 4.7 0.3
20	TU	0133 0738 1351 1959	4.5 0.5 4.6 0.5
21	W	0217 0823 1435 2041	4.3 0.6 4.4 0.7
22	TH	0301 0910 1523 2128	4.0 0.7 4.2 1.0
23	F	0350 1003 1622 ☽ 2227	3.7 0.8 3.9 1.3
24	SA	0452 1110 1741 2342	3.5 0.9 3.6 1.5
25	SU	0612 1237 1906	3.4 1.0 3.6
26	M	0111 0738 1409 2023	1.5 3.4 0.9 3.8
27	TU	0235 0848 1520 2121	1.4 3.6 0.8 3.9
28	W	0333 0940 1607 2206	1.2 3.8 0.6 4.1
29	TH	0413 1022 1642 2244	1.1 4.0 0.6 4.1
30	F	0447 1056 1710 2317	0.9 4.1 0.6 4.1
31	SA	0519 1127 1738 O 2348	0.8 4.1 0.6 4.2

NOVEMBER

Date	Day	Time	m
1	SU	0552 1157 1807	0.7 4.2 0.6
2	M	0018 0624 1228 1832	4.2 0.7 4.2 0.7
3	TU	0048 0654 1300 1856	4.2 0.7 4.2 0.7
4	W	0118 0724 1332 1921	4.1 0.7 4.1 0.8
5	TH	0149 0755 1406 1951	4.0 0.8 4.1 0.9
6	F	0222 0830 1443 2028	3.9 0.8 3.9 1.0
7	SA	0300 0911 1528 2115	3.8 0.9 3.8 1.2
8	SU	0348 1008 1623 ☾ 2222	3.6 1.0 3.7 1.4
9	M	0453 1132 1735	3.4 1.0 3.6
10	TU	0000 0615 1259 1902	1.4 3.4 0.9 3.7
11	W	0126 0738 1406 2017	1.3 3.6 0.6 3.9
12	TH	0230 0845 1504 2117	1.1 3.8 0.4 4.1
13	F	0324 0940 1556 2208	0.9 4.1 0.3 4.3
14	SA	0413 1029 1644 2256	0.7 4.4 0.2 4.4
15	SU	0502 1115 1730 ● 2341	0.6 4.5 0.3 4.5
16	M	0550 1200 1814	0.5 4.7 0.3
17	TU	0026 0637 1245 1857	4.5 0.5 4.7 0.5
18	W	0111 0724 1331 1939	4.4 0.5 4.6 0.7
19	TH	0156 0810 1417 2022	4.2 0.5 4.4 0.9
20	F	0241 0857 1507 2107	4.0 0.6 4.1 1.1
21	SA	0329 0947 1604 2159	3.8 0.7 3.8 1.3
22	SU	0426 1047 1713 ☽ 2303	3.6 0.8 3.6 1.5
23	M	0533 1200 1826	3.4 0.9 3.6
24	TU	0021 0646 1318 1937	1.5 3.4 0.9 3.6
25	W	0139 0758 1427 2040	1.5 3.5 0.8 3.7
26	TH	0244 0856 1519 2129	1.3 3.6 0.8 3.9
27	F	0333 0941 1558 2209	1.1 3.8 0.7 3.9
28	SA	0414 1019 1632 2245	1.0 3.9 0.7 4.0
29	SU	0451 1054 1705 2318	0.8 4.0 0.7 4.1
30	M	0527 1128 1737 O 2351	0.7 4.1 0.7 4.1

DECEMBER

Date	Day	Time	m
1	TU	0601 1202 1806	0.7 4.2 0.7
2	W	0024 0634 1238 1832	4.1 0.6 4.2 0.8
3	TH	0058 0708 1314 1901	4.1 0.6 4.1 0.8
4	F	0133 0743 1351 1937	4.0 0.6 4.1 0.9
5	SA	0210 0821 1431 2018	3.9 0.6 4.0 1.0
6	SU	0251 0906 1517 2108	3.8 0.7 3.9 1.1
7	M	0338 1001 1611 2210	3.7 0.7 3.8 1.2
8	TU	0435 1110 1714 ☾ 2325	3.6 0.7 3.8 1.3
9	W	0544 1224 1828	3.6 0.7 3.8
10	TH	0042 0658 1331 1941	1.2 3.7 0.6 3.9
11	F	0152 0809 1431 2046	1.1 3.9 0.5 4.0
12	SA	0253 0910 1526 2144	0.9 4.1 0.4 4.1
13	SU	0349 1004 1619 2235	0.8 4.3 0.4 4.2
14	M	0443 1054 1709 ● 2323	0.6 4.4 0.4 4.3
15	TU	0536 1142 1757	0.5 4.5 0.5
16	W	0010 0627 1230 1843	4.3 0.4 4.5 0.6
17	TH	0056 0716 1316 1926	4.3 0.4 4.4 0.8
18	F	0141 0803 1403 2007	4.2 0.4 4.3 0.9
19	SA	0225 0847 1452 2048	4.0 0.5 4.1 1.1
20	SU	0310 0930 1543 2130	3.9 0.6 3.8 1.2
21	M	0357 1017 1638 ☽ 2219	3.7 0.7 3.7 1.3
22	TU	0450 1112 1737 2320	3.6 0.8 3.5 1.4
23	W	0547 1214 1837	3.5 0.9 3.5
24	TH	0034 0649 1317 1939	1.5 3.4 0.9 3.5
25	F	0145 0752 1416 2038	1.4 3.5 0.9 3.6
26	SA	0246 0850 1509 2129	1.2 3.6 0.9 3.7
27	SU	0338 0940 1556 2213	1.0 3.7 0.8 3.8
28	M	0423 1023 1638 2252	0.9 3.9 0.8 3.9
29	TU	0504 1104 1715 2331	0.7 4.0 0.8 4.0
30	W O	0542 1143 1748	0.6 4.0 0.8
31	TH	0008 0619 1222 1820	4.1 0.5 4.1 0.8

LOWESTOFT
LAT 52°28′N
LONG 1°45′E

TIMES AND HEIGHTS OF HIGH AND LOW WATER (Heights in Metres)

TIME ZONE UT
For Summer Time (area enclosed in shaded box) add 1 hour

2020

JANUARY

Date	Day	Time	m
1	W	0047 0725 1349 1903	2.5 0.8 2.1 1.2
2	TH	0129 0809 1445 1945	2.4 0.9 2.1 1.3
3	F	0215 0901 1558 ☽ 2035	2.3 1.0 2.1 1.4
4	SA	0308 1008 1658 2139	2.3 1.0 2.1 1.4
5	SU	0415 1113 1750 2313	2.2 1.0 2.1 1.4
6	M	0525 1204 1837	2.2 1.0 2.2
7	TU	0019 0622 1250 1919	1.2 2.2 0.9 2.3
8	W	0110 0714 1333 1959	1.1 2.3 0.9 2.4
9	TH	0158 0804 1416 2038	1.0 2.3 0.8 2.4
10	F	0245 0852 1501 O 2117	0.8 2.4 0.8 2.5
11	SA	0334 0940 1546 2157	0.7 2.4 0.8 2.6
12	SU	0423 1027 1631 2239	0.6 2.5 0.8 2.6
13	M	0511 1113 1715 2322	0.5 2.5 0.8 2.6
14	TU	0558 1200 1758	0.4 2.5 0.9
15	W	0006 0646 1249 1841	2.6 0.4 2.4 0.9
16	TH	0052 0735 1340 1926	2.6 0.5 2.3 1.0
17	F	0140 0828 1443 ☾ 2016	2.6 0.6 2.2 1.1
18	SA	0234 0929 1612 2118	2.5 0.6 2.2 1.2
19	SU	0341 1037 1717 2244	2.4 0.7 2.2 1.2
20	M	0502 1142 1813	2.4 0.8 2.2
21	TU	0004 0611 1243 1907	1.1 2.4 0.9 2.3
22	W	0113 0720 1341 1956	1.0 2.4 0.9 2.3
23	TH	0215 0824 1432 2040	0.8 2.4 0.9 2.4
24	F	0306 0916 1517 ● 2121	0.7 2.4 0.9 2.5
25	SA	0351 1001 1556 2159	0.6 2.4 0.9 2.5
26	SU	0432 1041 1631 2236	0.6 2.4 0.9 2.5
27	M	0510 1119 1701 2310	0.6 2.3 0.9 2.5
28	TU	0545 1154 1730 2344	0.6 2.3 0.9 2.5
29	W	0618 1226 1759	0.6 2.2 1.0
30	TH	0019 0650 1300 1832	2.5 0.7 2.2 1.0
31	F	0057 0723 1337 1911	2.5 0.8 2.1 1.1

FEBRUARY

Date	Day	Time	m
1	SA	0138 0801 1421 1956	2.4 0.9 2.1 1.2
2	SU	0224 0848 1523 ☽ 2049	2.3 1.0 2.0 1.3
3	M	0321 0952 1649 2201	2.2 1.1 2.1 1.3
4	TU	0440 1114 1749 2336	2.1 1.1 2.1 1.2
5	W	0552 1215 1841	2.2 1.0 2.2
6	TH	0040 0653 1307 1929	1.1 2.2 1.0 2.3
7	F	0135 0750 1356 2014	0.9 2.3 0.9 2.4
8	SA	0228 0843 1445 2057	0.8 2.4 0.8 2.5
9	SU	0320 0930 1533 O 2139	0.6 2.5 0.7 2.6
10	M	0411 1015 1619 2222	0.4 2.5 0.7 2.7
11	TU	0458 1059 1703 2304	0.3 2.5 0.7 2.7
12	W	0544 1143 1744 2347	0.2 2.5 0.7 2.7
13	TH	0628 1227 1824	0.3 2.4 0.8
14	F	0031 0712 1313 1906	2.7 0.4 2.3 0.9
15	SA	0119 0759 1406 ☾ 1952	2.6 0.5 2.2 1.0
16	SU	0212 0853 1518 2049	2.5 0.7 2.1 1.1
17	M	0325 1004 1640 2218	2.4 0.9 2.1 1.1
18	TU	0455 1122 1744 2352	2.3 1.0 2.1 1.0
19	W	0615 1231 1846	2.3 1.0 2.2
20	TH	0107 0734 1335 1942	0.9 2.3 1.0 2.3
21	F	0208 0830 1426 2027	0.8 2.3 1.0 2.3
22	SA	0256 0912 1507 2105	0.7 2.3 1.0 2.4
23	SU	0337 0949 1541 ● 2140	0.6 2.4 0.9 2.5
24	M	0413 1023 1612 2213	0.5 2.3 0.9 2.5
25	TU	0447 1054 1640 2246	0.5 2.3 0.8 2.5
26	W	0518 1122 1706 2319	0.5 2.3 0.8 2.5
27	TH	0547 1151 1734 2352	0.6 2.3 0.8 2.5
28	F	0615 1221 1806	0.7 2.2 0.9
29	SA	0027 0644 1256 1842	2.4 0.7 2.2 0.9

MARCH

Date	Day	Time	m
1	SU	0106 0718 1335 1924	2.4 0.8 2.1 1.0
2	M	0148 0758 1422 ☽ 2014	2.3 1.0 2.1 1.1
3	TU	0240 0851 1526 2117	2.2 1.1 2.0 1.2
4	W	0355 1012 1656 2258	2.1 1.2 2.1 1.1
5	TH	0530 1145 1802	2.1 1.1 2.1
6	F	0015 0639 1245 1857	1.0 2.2 1.1 2.2
7	SA	0114 0740 1339 1947	0.8 2.3 0.9 2.3
8	SU	0210 0831 1430 2033	0.6 2.4 0.8 2.4
9	M	0303 0915 1518 O 2117	0.4 2.5 0.7 2.6
10	TU	0353 0957 1603 2200	0.3 2.5 0.6 2.7
11	W	0439 1039 1645 2243	0.1 2.5 0.6 2.8
12	TH	0522 1120 1726 2327	0.1 2.5 0.6 2.8
13	F	0604 1202 1806	0.2 2.4 0.6
14	SA	0012 0645 1246 1847	2.7 0.4 2.3 0.7
15	SU	0100 0729 1333 1933	2.6 0.6 2.2 0.8
16	M	0157 0819 1431 ☾ 2031	2.4 0.8 2.1 0.9
17	TU	0321 0928 1553 2204	2.3 1.1 2.1 1.0
18	W	0453 1103 1707 2339	2.2 1.2 2.1 0.9
19	TH	0617 1218 1817	2.2 1.2 2.1
20	F	0051 0731 1323 1920	0.8 2.3 1.1 2.2
21	SA	0149 0819 1411 2006	0.7 2.3 1.1 2.3
22	SU	0234 0856 1448 2042	0.6 2.3 1.0 2.3
23	M	0312 0928 1519 2114	0.6 2.3 0.9 2.4
24	TU	0346 0957 1548 ● 2146	0.5 2.3 0.8 2.5
25	W	0417 1024 1615 2219	0.5 2.3 0.8 2.5
26	TH	0446 1050 1642 2252	0.5 2.3 0.7 2.5
27	F	0514 1118 1712 2326	0.6 2.3 0.7 2.4
28	SA	0541 1149 1744	0.7 2.3 0.8
29	SU	0001 0609 1223 1819	2.4 0.7 2.3 0.8
30	M	0038 0642 1301 1859	2.3 0.8 2.2 0.9
31	TU	0120 0722 1346 1947	2.2 1.0 2.2 1.0

APRIL

Date	Day	Time	m
1	W	0213 0813 1442 ☽ 2050	2.1 1.1 2.1 1.0
2	TH	0326 0923 1556 2229	2.1 1.2 2.1 1.0
3	F	0514 1114 1719 2350	2.1 1.2 2.1 0.9
4	SA	0626 1222 1823	2.2 1.1 2.2
5	SU	0050 0724 1317 1916	0.7 2.3 1.0 2.3
6	M	0147 0812 1409 2004	0.5 2.4 0.9 2.5
7	TU	0240 0854 1457 2050	0.3 2.5 0.7 2.6
8	W	0329 0935 1542 O 2136	0.2 2.5 0.6 2.7
9	TH	0415 1015 1625 2221	0.1 2.5 0.5 2.8
10	F	0457 1056 1706 2307	0.2 2.5 0.5 2.7
11	SA	0538 1138 1748 2355	0.3 2.4 0.5 2.6
12	SU	0619 1220 1832	0.5 2.4 0.6
13	M	0047 0701 1306 1920	2.5 0.7 2.3 0.7
14	TU	0150 0747 1358 ☾ 2019	2.3 1.0 2.2 0.8
15	W	0318 0849 1505 2150	2.2 1.2 2.1 0.9
16	TH	0441 1035 1623 2315	2.2 1.3 2.1 0.8
17	F	0600 1152 1733	2.2 1.3 2.1
18	SA	0020 0708 1254 1838	0.8 2.3 1.2 2.1
19	SU	0116 0755 1341 1930	0.7 2.3 1.1 2.2
20	M	0201 0831 1418 2008	0.7 2.3 1.0 2.3
21	TU	0238 0902 1449 2042	0.6 2.3 0.9 2.3
22	W	0312 0928 1519 2116	0.6 2.3 0.8 2.4
23	TH	0342 0953 1548 ● 2151	0.6 2.4 0.7 2.4
24	F	0411 1020 1618 2226	0.6 2.4 0.7 2.4
25	SA	0440 1049 1651 2302	0.6 2.4 0.7 2.4
26	SU	0510 1122 1726 2338	0.7 2.4 0.7 2.3
27	M	0542 1157 1803	0.8 2.3 0.8
28	TU	0017 0616 1236 1843	2.3 0.9 2.3 0.8
29	W	0102 0657 1321 1933	2.2 1.0 2.2 0.9
30	TH	0157 0749 1414 ☽ 2037	2.2 1.1 2.2 0.9

MAY

Date	Day	Time	m
1	F	0312 0855 1519 2208	2.1 1.2 2.1 0.8
2	SA	0459 1035 1635 2324	2.2 1.3 2.2 0.7
3	SU	0606 1151 1745	2.3 1.2 2.2
4	M	0024 0701 1249 1842	0.6 2.3 1.0 2.3
5	TU	0120 0748 1342 1934	0.4 2.4 0.9 2.5
6	W	0214 0830 1432 2024	0.3 2.5 0.8 2.6
7	TH	0303 0911 1520 O 2113	0.3 2.5 0.6 2.7
8	F	0349 0952 1605 2203	0.3 2.5 0.5 2.7
9	SA	0432 1034 1650 2252	0.3 2.5 0.5 2.6
10	SU	0514 1116 1734 2344	0.5 2.5 0.5 2.5
11	M	0554 1159 1820	0.7 2.4 0.5
12	TU	0039 0635 1244 1908	2.4 0.9 2.4 0.6
13	W	0143 0719 1332 2006	2.3 1.1 2.3 0.7
14	TH	0301 0811 1427 ☾ 2124	2.2 1.3 2.2 0.8
15	F	0416 0935 1532 2240	2.2 1.4 2.2 0.8
16	SA	0526 1107 1640 2340	2.2 1.4 2.1 0.8
17	SU	0630 1208 1742	2.2 1.3 2.1
18	M	0033 0721 1258 1836	0.7 2.2 1.2 2.2
19	TU	0119 0759 1339 1923	0.7 2.3 1.1 2.2
20	W	0158 0830 1413 2005	0.7 2.3 1.0 2.3
21	TH	0232 0856 1446 2045	0.7 2.3 0.9 2.3
22	F	0305 0922 1520 ● 2123	0.7 2.4 0.8 2.3
23	SA	0337 0951 1556 2202	0.7 2.4 0.7 2.3
24	SU	0410 1024 1633 2241	0.7 2.4 0.7 2.3
25	M	0445 1059 1712 2321	0.7 2.4 0.7 2.3
26	TU	0521 1136 1753	0.8 2.4 0.7
27	W	0003 0559 1218 1838	2.3 0.9 2.4 0.7
28	TH	0052 0642 1303 1929	2.2 1.0 2.3 0.7
29	F	0147 0733 1355 2031	2.2 1.1 2.3 0.7
30	SA	0258 0833 1452 ☽ 2146	2.2 1.2 2.3 0.7
31	SU	0436 0951 1558 2256	2.2 1.2 2.3 0.6

JUNE

Date	Day	Time	m
1	M	0540 1112 1710 2356	2.3 1.2 2.3 0.5
2	TU	0634 1215 1812	2.3 1.1 2.4
3	W	0053 0722 1313 1908	0.5 2.4 1.0 2.5
4	TH	0147 0806 1409 2002	0.4 2.4 0.8 2.5
5	F	0238 0849 1501 O 2057	0.4 2.5 0.7 2.6
6	SA	0326 0931 1551 2151	0.5 2.5 0.6 2.6
7	SU	0411 1014 1638 2244	0.6 2.5 0.5 2.5
8	M	0453 1057 1724 2336	0.7 2.5 0.5 2.4
9	TU	0533 1140 1809	0.8 2.5 0.5
10	W	0029 0612 1223 1856	2.3 1.0 2.4 0.6
11	TH	0125 0651 1307 1946	2.2 1.1 2.4 0.7
12	F	0229 0733 1352 2045	2.2 1.2 2.3 0.7
13	SA	0338 0820 1442 ☾ 2152	2.1 1.3 2.3 0.8
14	SU	0441 0926 1541 2254	2.1 1.4 2.2 0.8
15	M	0539 1105 1646 2347	2.1 1.4 2.2 0.8
16	TU	0633 1205 1747	2.2 1.3 2.2
17	W	0033 0716 1253 1840	0.8 2.2 1.2 2.2
18	TH	0115 0752 1335 1930	0.8 2.3 1.1 2.2
19	F	0153 0822 1414 2016	0.8 2.3 1.0 2.3
20	SA	0229 0853 1455 2100	0.8 2.4 0.8 2.3
21	SU	0307 0927 1536 ● 2143	0.8 2.4 0.7 2.3
22	M	0346 1003 1619 2226	0.8 2.5 0.7 2.3
23	TU	0426 1041 1703 2310	0.8 2.5 0.6 2.4
24	W	0507 1121 1749 2355	0.8 2.5 0.6 2.3
25	TH	0549 1203 1835	0.9 2.5 0.6
26	F	0042 0632 1248 1924	2.3 1.0 2.5 0.6
27	SA	0134 0719 1335 2019	2.3 1.1 2.5 0.6
28	SU	0234 0811 1427 ☽ 2120	2.2 1.1 2.4 0.6
29	M	0402 0912 1526 2226	2.2 1.2 2.4 0.6
30	TU	0511 1029 1639 2329	2.2 1.2 2.4 0.6

SUNRISE AND SUNSET TIMES

LOWESTOFT
At 52°28′N 1°45′E

		Sunrise	Sunset
UT			
Jan	01	0804	1550
	15	0756	1609
Feb	01	0734	1640
	15	0709	1706
Mar	01	0639	1732
	15	0607	1758
BST			
Apr	01	0627	1927
	15	0555	1952
May	01	0522	2020
	15	0457	2043
Jun	01	0436	2106
	15	0430	2117
Jul	01	0435	2119
	15	0449	2109
Aug	01	0513	2045
	15	0536	2020
Sep	01	0604	1941
	15	0627	1908
Oct	01	0654	1830
	15	0718	1758
UT			
Nov	01	0649	1623
	15	0715	1600
Dec	01	0741	1543
	15	0757	1539

LOWESTOFT
LAT 52°28′N
LONG 1°45′E

TIMES AND HEIGHTS OF HIGH AND LOW WATER (Heights in Metres)

TIME ZONE UT
For Summer Time (area enclosed in shaded box) add 1 hour

2020

JULY

Date	Day	Time	m
1	W	0606 1145 1749	2.3 1.1 2.4
2	TH	0028 0657 1251 1850	0.6 2.3 1.0 2.4
3	F	0125 0745 1354 1951	0.7 2.4 0.9 2.5
4	SA	0219 0830 1451 2052	0.7 2.4 0.7 2.5
5	SU O	0309 0915 1542 2148	0.7 2.5 0.6 2.5
6	M	0354 0958 1629 2238	0.8 2.6 0.5 2.4
7	TU	0436 1041 1714 2325	0.8 2.6 0.5 2.4
8	W	0514 1121 1756	0.9 2.6 0.5
9	TH	0011 0549 1201 1836	2.3 1.0 2.5 0.6
10	F	0055 0622 1239 1917	2.2 1.1 2.5 0.6
11	SA	0141 0656 1318 1959	2.2 1.1 2.5 0.7
12	SU ☾	0232 0735 1401 2046	2.1 1.2 2.4 0.8
13	M	0337 0820 1449 2145	2.1 1.3 2.3 0.9
14	TU	0438 0917 1550 2252	2.1 1.4 2.2 1.0
15	W	0531 1048 1702 2347	2.1 1.4 2.2 1.0
16	TH	0621 1205 1805	2.2 1.3 2.2
17	F	0034 0706 1258 1901	1.0 2.3 1.2 2.2
18	SA	0118 0747 1346 1955	1.0 2.3 1.0 2.2
19	SU	0200 0826 1432 2045	0.9 2.4 0.9 2.3
20	M ●	0243 0904 1519 2131	0.9 2.5 0.7 2.4
21	TU	0328 0943 1607 2215	0.8 2.5 0.6 2.4
22	W	0412 1024 1654 2258	0.8 2.6 0.5 2.5
23	TH	0456 1105 1739 2342	0.8 2.6 0.4 2.4
24	F	0538 1146 1825	0.8 2.7 0.4
25	SA	0026 0619 1229 1909	2.4 0.9 2.7 0.4
26	SU	0113 0701 1314 1957	2.3 1.0 2.6 0.5
27	M ☽	0205 0747 1403 2050	2.3 1.1 2.6 0.6
28	TU	0314 0841 1501 2154	2.2 1.1 2.5 0.7
29	W	0437 0952 1619 2304	2.2 1.2 2.4 0.8
30	TH	0537 1123 1737	2.2 1.1 2.4
31	F	0010 0633 1240 1848	0.9 2.3 1.0 2.4

AUGUST

Date	Day	Time	m
1	SA	0112 0727 1348 2000	0.9 2.4 0.9 2.4
2	SU	0209 0816 1446 2058	0.9 2.4 0.7 2.4
3	M O	0259 0901 1535 2145	0.9 2.5 0.6 2.4
4	TU	0342 0942 1618 2227	0.9 2.6 0.5 2.4
5	W	0420 1021 1658 2307	0.9 2.6 0.5 2.4
6	TH	0454 1058 1735 2344	0.9 2.6 0.5 2.3
7	F	0524 1134 1809	1.0 2.6 0.6
8	SA	0018 0553 1209 1842	2.3 1.0 2.6 0.7
9	SU	0052 0623 1245 1914	2.2 1.0 2.5 0.8
10	M	0127 0659 1324 1949	2.2 1.1 2.4 0.9
11	TU ☾	0208 0741 1409 2030	2.1 1.2 2.3 1.0
12	W	0302 0831 1503 2124	2.1 1.3 2.2 1.1
13	TH	0423 0936 1618 2249	2.1 1.3 2.2 1.2
14	F	0527 1118 1736 2357	2.2 1.3 2.2 1.2
15	SA	0622 1226 1841	2.2 1.2 2.2
16	SU	0049 0712 1321 1941	1.1 2.3 1.0 2.3
17	M	0138 0758 1412 2033	1.0 2.4 0.9 2.3
18	TU	0225 0840 1502 2117	1.0 2.5 0.7 2.4
19	W ●	0312 0921 1551 2159	0.9 2.6 0.5 2.5
20	TH	0357 1002 1637 2240	0.8 2.7 0.4 2.6
21	F	0441 1043 1721 2321	0.8 2.8 0.3 2.5
22	SA	0522 1125 1804	0.8 2.8 0.3
23	SU	0003 0601 1207 1846	2.5 0.8 2.8 0.4
24	M	0047 0642 1252 1930	2.4 0.9 2.7 0.5
25	TU ☽	0134 0726 1342 2019	2.3 1.0 2.6 0.7
26	W	0231 0819 1444 2120	2.2 1.1 2.5 0.9
27	TH	0354 0931 1616 2243	2.2 1.1 2.4 1.1
28	F	0506 1115 1740 2358	2.2 1.1 2.3 1.1
29	SA	0609 1234 1903	2.3 1.0 2.4
30	SU	0105 0710 1343 2008	1.1 2.3 0.8 2.4
31	M	0204 0801 1436 2054	1.1 2.4 0.7 2.4

SEPTEMBER

Date	Day	Time	m
1	TU	0249 0843 1519 2132	1.1 2.5 0.6 2.5
2	W O	0326 0921 1558 2208	1.0 2.6 0.5 2.4
3	TH	0400 0957 1633 2241	0.9 2.6 0.5 2.4
4	F	0430 1031 1706 2311	0.9 2.7 0.6 2.4
5	SA	0457 1105 1736 2340	0.9 2.6 0.6 2.4
6	SU	0525 1138 1804	0.9 2.6 0.7
7	M	0010 0554 1214 1831	2.3 1.0 2.5 0.8
8	TU	0043 0629 1251 1902	2.3 1.0 2.5 0.9
9	W	0121 0709 1333 1940	2.3 1.1 2.3 1.0
10	TH ☾	0206 0757 1424 2027	2.2 1.2 2.2 1.2
11	F	0303 0857 1535 2134	2.2 1.3 2.2 1.3
12	SA	0427 1034 1714 2319	2.2 1.3 2.2 1.3
13	SU	0539 1157 1825	2.2 1.1 2.2
14	M	0024 0635 1255 1925	1.2 2.3 1.0 2.3
15	TU	0116 0725 1348 2014	1.1 2.4 0.8 2.4
16	W	0205 0810 1439 2056	1.0 2.5 0.6 2.5
17	TH ●	0252 0853 1528 2136	0.9 2.7 0.4 2.6
18	F	0337 0935 1614 2216	0.8 2.8 0.3 2.6
19	SA	0420 1018 1657 2256	0.7 2.9 0.2 2.6
20	SU	0501 1101 1739 2337	0.7 2.9 0.3 2.6
21	M	0542 1145 1820	0.7 2.9 0.4
22	TU	0020 0623 1233 1902	2.5 0.8 2.7 0.6
23	W	0105 0709 1327 1948	2.4 0.9 2.6 0.9
24	TH ☽	0158 0804 1440 2047	2.3 1.0 2.4 1.1
25	F	0309 0924 1620 2222	2.2 1.1 2.3 1.3
26	SA	0431 1106 1744 2345	2.2 1.0 2.3 1.3
27	SU	0540 1220 1904	2.3 0.9 2.4
28	M	0053 0645 1324 1958	1.3 2.3 0.8 2.4
29	TU	0147 0738 1413 2038	1.2 2.4 0.7 2.5
30	W	0228 0818 1454 2111	1.1 2.5 0.6 2.5

OCTOBER

Date	Day	Time	m
1	TH O	0302 0854 1529 2142	1.0 2.6 0.6 2.5
2	F	0333 0928 1602 2210	1.0 2.6 0.6 2.5
3	SA	0402 1001 1632 2237	0.9 2.6 0.6 2.5
4	SU	0430 1035 1659 2305	0.9 2.6 0.7 2.4
5	M	0459 1109 1726 2335	0.9 2.6 0.8 2.4
6	TU	0530 1144 1753	0.9 2.5 0.9
7	W	0007 0604 1222 1824	2.4 1.0 2.4 1.0
8	TH	0045 0643 1303 1901	2.4 1.0 2.3 1.1
9	F	0128 0730 1354 1948	2.3 1.1 2.2 1.2
10	SA ☾	0220 0829 1502 2050	2.3 1.2 2.2 1.4
11	SU	0327 0958 1654 2231	2.2 1.2 2.2 1.4
12	M	0449 1127 1806 2353	2.2 1.0 2.3 1.3
13	TU	0556 1226 1903	2.3 0.8 2.4
14	W	0049 0649 1320 1949	1.2 2.4 0.7 2.5
15	TH	0139 0737 1412 2031	1.1 2.6 0.5 2.6
16	F ●	0227 0823 1501 2111	0.9 2.7 0.4 2.6
17	SA	0313 0908 1547 2150	0.8 2.8 0.3 2.7
18	SU	0357 0953 1630 2231	0.7 2.9 0.3 2.6
19	M	0441 1040 1713 2312	0.7 2.9 0.4 2.6
20	TU	0524 1128 1754 2355	0.7 2.8 0.6 2.5
21	W	0609 1219 1836	0.7 2.7 0.8
22	TH	0040 0657 1320 1921	2.5 0.8 2.5 1.0
23	F ☽	0132 0755 1441 2017	2.4 0.9 2.4 1.3
24	SA	0234 0917 1612 2150	2.3 0.9 2.3 1.4
25	SU	0350 1045 1730 2318	2.3 0.9 2.3 1.4
26	M	0501 1152 1842	2.3 0.8 2.4
27	TU	0023 0606 1251 1934	1.4 2.3 0.8 2.4
28	W	0116 0701 1340 2013	1.3 2.4 0.7 2.4
29	TH	0157 0744 1420 2045	1.2 2.4 0.7 2.4
30	F	0231 0821 1454 2113	1.1 2.5 0.7 2.5
31	SA O	0303 0856 1526 2139	1.0 2.5 0.7 2.5

NOVEMBER

Date	Day	Time	m
1	SU	0333 0932 1555 2205	0.9 2.6 0.7 2.5
2	M	0403 1007 1623 2233	0.9 2.5 0.8 2.5
3	TU	0435 1043 1651 2305	0.9 2.5 0.8 2.5
4	W	0509 1120 1721 2339	0.9 2.4 0.9 2.5
5	TH	0545 1158 1755	0.9 2.4 1.0
6	F	0016 0625 1241 1834	2.4 1.0 2.3 1.1
7	SA	0059 0712 1333 1921	2.4 1.0 2.2 1.2
8	SU ☾	0150 0811 1439 2021	2.3 1.0 2.2 1.3
9	M	0250 0932 1628 2141	2.3 1.0 2.2 1.4
10	TU	0359 1055 1739 2312	2.3 0.9 2.3 1.3
11	W	0513 1155 1834	2.4 0.7 2.4
12	TH	0014 0612 1250 1921	1.2 2.5 0.6 2.5
13	F	0108 0704 1342 2004	1.1 2.6 0.5 2.5
14	SA	0159 0754 1432 2044	0.9 2.7 0.4 2.6
15	SU ●	0248 0843 1520 2126	0.8 2.8 0.4 2.6
16	M	0337 0933 1605 2208	0.7 2.8 0.4 2.6
17	TU	0424 1024 1648 2250	0.6 2.8 0.5 2.6
18	W	0511 1116 1731 2334	0.6 2.7 0.7 2.6
19	TH	0558 1212 1813	0.6 2.5 0.9
20	F	0020 0648 1314 1857	2.5 0.7 2.4 1.1
21	SA	0109 0745 1429 1947	2.4 0.8 2.3 1.3
22	SU ☽	0203 0855 1549 2053	2.4 0.8 2.3 1.5
23	M	0305 1011 1659 2229	2.3 0.8 2.3 1.5
24	TU	0413 1115 1805 2338	2.3 0.8 2.3 1.4
25	W	0517 1210 1859	2.3 0.8 2.3
26	TH	0032 0613 1258 1941	1.4 2.3 0.8 2.3
27	F	0118 0702 1340 2015	1.2 2.3 0.8 2.4
28	SA	0156 0746 1416 2042	1.1 2.4 0.8 2.4
29	SU	0231 0826 1448 2108	1.0 2.4 0.8 2.5
30	M O	0305 0905 1519 2135	0.9 2.4 0.8 2.5

DECEMBER

Date	Day	Time	m
1	TU	0339 0944 1550 2206	0.9 2.4 0.8 2.5
2	W	0416 1022 1624 2240	0.8 2.4 0.9 2.5
3	TH	0454 1102 1659 2317	0.8 2.4 0.9 2.5
4	F	0534 1143 1736 2356	0.8 2.3 1.0 2.5
5	SA	0617 1228 1817	0.8 2.3 1.1
6	SU	0039 0704 1318 1903	2.4 0.9 2.2 1.2
7	M	0128 0800 1417 1958	2.4 0.9 2.2 1.3
8	TU ☾	0221 0907 1543 2102	2.4 0.8 2.2 1.3
9	W	0320 1019 1707 2221	2.4 0.8 2.3 1.3
10	TH	0429 1123 1803 2335	2.4 0.7 2.3 1.2
11	F	0538 1220 1852	2.5 0.6 2.4
12	SA	0036 0636 1314 1937	1.1 2.5 0.6 2.5
13	SU	0133 0731 1407 2021	1.0 2.6 0.5 2.5
14	M ●	0229 0826 1457 2104	0.8 2.7 0.6 2.6
15	TU	0323 0921 1545 2148	0.7 2.7 0.6 2.6
16	W	0413 1017 1630 2233	0.6 2.6 0.7 2.6
17	TH	0502 1111 1712 2317	0.5 2.5 0.8 2.6
18	F	0550 1204 1753	0.5 2.5 1.0
19	SA	0001 0637 1259 1833	2.6 0.6 2.3 1.1
20	SU	0046 0727 1358 1914	2.5 0.6 2.2 1.2
21	M ☽	0132 0821 1508 1959	2.5 0.7 2.2 1.3
22	TU	0220 0924 1616 2053	2.4 0.8 2.1 1.4
23	W	0315 1028 1716 2222	2.3 0.9 2.1 1.5
24	TH	0421 1126 1811 2339	2.3 0.9 2.2 1.4
25	F	0525 1215 1900	2.2 0.9 2.2
26	SA	0034 0621 1300 1938	1.3 2.2 0.9 2.3
27	SU	0120 0713 1339 2010	1.2 2.3 0.9 2.3
28	M	0200 0802 1414 2040	1.1 2.3 0.9 2.4
29	TU	0240 0847 1449 2111	0.9 2.3 0.9 2.5
30	W O	0320 0929 1526 2145	0.8 2.3 0.9 2.5
31	TH	0401 1010 1604 2222	0.8 2.4 0.9 2.5

IMMINGHAM
LAT 53°38′N
LONG 0°11′W

TIMES AND HEIGHTS OF HIGH AND LOW WATER (Heights in Metres)

TIME ZONE UT
For Summer Time (area enclosed in shaded box) add 1 hour

2020

JANUARY

Date	Time	m	Date	Time	m
1 W	0334 0943 1537 2140	1.9 6.1 2.3 6.4	16 TH	0359 0959 1601 2201	1.1 6.7 1.7 7.0
2 TH	0414 1028 1620 2228	2.1 5.8 2.6 6.1	17 F ☾	0450 1056 1653 2300	1.4 6.4 2.0 6.7
3 F ☽	0503 1124 1713 2329	2.3 5.7 2.8 5.9	18 SA	0548 1201 1755	1.6 6.2 2.3
4 SA	0600 1230 1817	2.5 5.6 2.9	19 SU	0010 0652 1308 1908	6.4 1.9 6.0 2.5
5 SU	0037 0702 1336 1925	5.8 2.5 5.7 2.9	20 M	0125 0801 1415 2028	6.2 2.0 6.1 2.4
6 M	0145 0806 1436 2033	5.9 2.4 5.9 2.6	21 TU	0238 0907 1518 2138	6.2 2.0 6.2 2.1
7 TU	0245 0907 1529 2134	6.0 2.2 6.1 2.3	22 W	0346 1006 1613 2237	6.4 1.9 6.5 1.8
8 W	0339 1001 1616 2228	6.3 1.9 6.4 2.0	23 TH	0446 1057 1701 2329	6.5 1.7 6.7 1.5
9 TH	0430 1050 1700 2318	6.6 1.7 6.7 1.6	24 F ●	0537 1144 1744	6.7 1.6 6.9
10 F ○	0518 1136 1742	6.8 1.5 7.0	25 SA	0016 0621 1227 1823	1.3 6.8 1.5 7.1
11 SA	0007 0604 1222 1822	1.3 7.0 1.4 7.2	26 SU	0100 0700 1305 1900	1.2 6.8 1.5 7.1
12 SU	0054 0651 1306 1903	1.1 7.1 1.3 7.3	27 M	0138 0736 1340 1935	1.2 6.7 1.5 7.1
13 M	0140 0736 1349 1944	0.9 7.2 1.3 7.4	28 TU	0211 0808 1411 2007	1.3 6.6 1.6 7.0
14 TU	0225 0821 1431 2026	0.9 7.1 1.3 7.3	29 W	0241 0837 1440 2037	1.5 6.5 1.8 6.9
15 W	0311 0908 1515 2111	0.9 6.9 1.5 7.2	30 TH	0310 0907 1510 2109	1.6 6.3 1.9 6.6
			31 F	0340 0940 1542 2145	1.8 6.1 2.1 6.4

FEBRUARY

Date	Time	m	Date	Time	m
1 SA	0415 1020 1622 2227	2.1 5.9 2.4 6.1	16 SU	0512 1119 1718 2339	1.7 6.1 2.2 6.3
2 SU ☽	0500 1111 1715 2322	2.3 5.7 2.7 5.8	17 M	0613 1226 1829	2.2 5.8 2.5
3 M	0600 1219 1824	2.5 5.5 2.8	18 TU	0059 0730 1340 2005	5.9 2.5 5.7 2.6
4 TU	0037 0709 1341 1938	5.7 2.6 5.6 2.8	19 W	0225 0848 1452 2127	5.8 2.5 5.9 2.3
5 W	0201 0820 1451 2052	5.8 2.4 5.8 2.5	20 TH	0345 0951 1554 2227	6.0 2.3 6.2 1.9
6 TH	0313 0927 1549 2200	6.0 2.2 6.2 2.1	21 F	0446 1043 1644 2317	6.3 2.0 6.5 1.6
7 F	0412 1025 1639 2300	6.4 1.9 6.6 1.6	22 SA	0532 1128 1727	6.5 1.7 6.8
8 SA	0506 1118 1725 2354	6.7 1.6 6.9 1.2	23 SU ●	0002 0610 1210 1805	1.3 6.7 1.6 7.0
9 SU ○	0555 1208 1808	7.0 1.3 7.3	24 M	0042 0643 1248 1840	1.2 6.7 1.4 7.1
10 M	0044 0641 1255 1850	0.8 7.3 1.1 7.5	25 TU	0118 0714 1321 1913	1.1 6.7 1.4 7.1
11 TU	0131 0726 1338 1931	0.5 7.4 0.9 7.7	26 W	0150 0741 1351 1943	1.2 6.7 1.4 7.1
12 W	0215 0808 1420 2013	0.4 7.4 0.9 7.7	27 TH	0218 0806 1418 2012	1.3 6.7 1.5 7.0
13 TH	0257 0850 1501 2056	0.5 7.2 1.1 7.5	28 F	0242 0833 1443 2041	1.4 6.6 1.7 6.8
14 F	0340 0934 1542 2142	0.8 6.9 1.4 7.2	29 SA	0306 0901 1511 2110	1.6 6.4 1.8 6.6
15 SA ☾	0423 1022 1626 2234	1.2 6.6 1.8 6.8			

MARCH

Date	Time	m	Date	Time	m
1 SU	0332 0934 1543 2146	1.9 6.2 2.1 6.3	16 M ☾	0437 1039 1648 2315	1.9 6.1 2.1 6.1
2 M ☽	0407 1014 1627 2232	2.1 5.9 2.4 6.0	17 TU	0532 1147 1756	2.5 5.7 2.5
3 TU	0501 1108 1734 2338	2.5 5.6 2.7 5.7	18 W	0042 0656 1309 1949	5.7 2.8 5.5 2.7
4 W	0618 1234 1857	2.7 5.4 2.7	19 TH	0215 0827 1427 2114	5.6 2.8 5.7 2.3
5 TH	0120 0742 1416 2020	5.6 2.7 5.6 2.5	20 F	0338 0933 1532 2210	5.9 2.5 6.0 1.9
6 F	0255 0900 1524 2138	5.9 2.4 6.0 2.0	21 SA	0435 1023 1622 2256	6.2 2.1 6.4 1.5
7 SA	0400 1006 1617 2243	6.3 2.0 6.5 1.4	22 SU	0515 1106 1704 2338	6.5 1.8 6.7 1.3
8 SU	0454 1101 1704 2338	6.8 1.5 7.0 0.9	23 M	0548 1147 1741	6.6 1.5 6.9
9 M ○	0542 1152 1749	7.1 1.2 7.4	24 TU ●	0015 0618 1224 1815	1.1 6.7 1.4 7.0
10 TU	0027 0626 1239 1832	0.5 7.4 0.9 7.7	25 W	0050 0645 1258 1847	1.1 6.8 1.3 7.0
11 W	0113 0708 1322 1914	0.2 7.5 0.7 7.8	26 TH	0122 0710 1328 1917	1.1 6.8 1.3 7.0
12 TH	0156 0748 1404 1955	0.2 7.5 0.7 7.9	27 F	0150 0736 1355 1947	1.2 6.8 1.4 6.9
13 F	0236 0827 1443 2037	0.3 7.4 0.8 7.7	28 SA	0214 0802 1419 2015	1.4 6.7 1.5 6.8
14 SA	0315 0906 1521 2122	0.7 7.1 1.1 7.3	29 SU	0236 0829 1446 2044	1.5 6.6 1.6 6.6
15 SU	0354 0949 1601 2211	1.2 6.6 1.6 6.7	30 M	0300 0859 1517 2118	1.7 6.4 1.9 6.4
			31 TU	0333 0937 1559 2205	2.0 6.1 2.2 6.0

APRIL

Date	Time	m	Date	Time	m
1 W ☽	0422 1028 1705 2310	2.4 5.7 2.5 5.7	16 TH	0028 0616 1237 1923	5.5 3.0 5.5 2.6
2 TH	0540 1144 1831	2.7 5.5 2.5	17 F	0154 0754 1356 2045	5.5 3.0 5.6 2.3
3 F	0058 0711 1339 1957	5.5 2.8 5.6 2.3	18 SA	0308 0903 1500 2140	5.8 2.6 6.0 1.9
4 SA	0239 0835 1455 2117	5.9 2.5 6.0 1.8	19 SU	0403 0954 1552 2224	6.1 2.2 6.3 1.6
5 SU	0343 0943 1551 2221	6.4 2.0 6.6 1.2	20 M	0443 1037 1634 2304	6.4 1.9 6.6 1.4
6 M	0435 1040 1639 2315	6.8 1.5 7.1 0.7	21 TU	0517 1117 1711 2342	6.6 1.6 6.7 1.2
7 TU	0522 1130 1725	7.2 1.1 7.5	22 W	0546 1155 1745	6.7 1.4 6.8
8 W ○	0004 0604 1218 1809	0.4 7.5 0.8 7.7	23 TH ●	0017 0612 1230 1817	1.2 6.8 1.3 6.9
9 TH	0050 0645 1302 1853	0.2 7.6 0.6 7.8	24 F	0050 0639 1302 1850	1.2 6.8 1.3 6.9
10 F	0132 0724 1344 1937	0.2 7.5 0.6 7.8	25 SA	0120 0708 1331 1923	1.3 6.8 1.4 6.9
11 SA	0212 0801 1424 2020	0.4 7.4 0.7 7.5	26 SU	0147 0736 1359 1954	1.4 6.8 1.4 6.8
12 SU	0250 0840 1502 2104	0.8 7.1 1.1 7.1	27 M	0212 0805 1429 2026	1.5 6.7 1.5 6.6
13 M	0327 0920 1542 2154	1.4 6.7 1.5 6.5	28 TU	0241 0836 1504 2105	1.7 6.5 1.7 6.4
14 TU ☾	0407 1006 1628 2259	2.0 6.2 2.0 5.9	29 W	0317 0916 1550 2154	2.0 6.2 2.0 6.0
15 W	0458 1111 1734	2.6 5.7 2.4	30 TH ☽	0408 1008 1656 2303	2.4 5.9 2.2 5.7

MAY

Date	Time	m	Date	Time	m
1 F	0520 1122 1816	2.6 5.7 2.2	16 SA	0116 0657 1314 1955	5.5 3.0 5.7 2.3
2 SA	0047 0646 1302 1936	5.7 2.7 5.8 2.0	17 SU	0222 0815 1418 2054	5.7 2.8 5.9 2.1
3 SU	0215 0807 1422 2051	6.0 2.4 6.2 1.6	18 M	0317 0913 1512 2141	5.9 2.4 6.1 1.8
4 M	0318 0915 1521 2153	6.4 2.0 6.7 1.1	19 TU	0402 1000 1556 2223	6.2 2.1 6.4 1.6
5 TU	0410 1013 1612 2248	6.8 1.5 7.1 0.8	20 W	0438 1042 1635 2303	6.4 1.8 6.5 1.5
6 W	0457 1105 1701 2337	7.2 1.1 7.4 0.5	21 TH	0509 1122 1712 2341	6.6 1.6 6.7 1.4
7 TH ○	0540 1154 1748	7.4 0.8 7.6	22 F ●	0540 1200 1749	6.7 1.5 6.7
8 F	0024 0621 1241 1835	0.4 7.4 0.7 7.6	23 SA	0018 0611 1236 1826	1.3 6.8 1.4 6.8
9 SA	0108 0700 1325 1920	0.5 7.4 0.7 7.5	24 SU	0052 0644 1311 1903	1.4 6.9 1.4 6.8
10 SU	0149 0739 1407 2006	0.7 7.3 0.8 7.3	25 M	0124 0717 1345 1941	1.4 6.8 1.4 6.7
11 M	0227 0818 1448 2051	1.1 7.0 1.1 6.9	26 TU	0155 0750 1421 2019	1.5 6.8 1.4 6.6
12 TU	0304 0857 1529 2142	1.6 6.7 1.5 6.4	27 W	0230 0825 1502 2102	1.7 6.6 1.6 6.4
13 W	0343 0942 1615 2244	2.1 6.3 1.9 5.9	28 TH	0311 0907 1551 2154	1.9 6.4 1.7 6.2
14 TH ☾	0431 1040 1715	2.6 5.9 2.3	29 F	0402 1000 1653 2302	2.2 6.2 1.8 6.0
15 F	0002 0535 1159 1834	5.6 2.9 5.7 2.4	30 SA ☽	0507 1109 1802	2.4 6.1 1.8
			31 SU	0027 0621 1231 1913	5.9 2.4 6.1 1.7

JUNE

Date	Time	m	Date	Time	m
1 M	0144 0736 1346 2021	6.1 2.3 6.4 1.5	16 TU	0221 0811 1420 2045	5.7 2.7 5.9 2.1
2 TU	0247 0844 1450 2124	6.4 2.0 6.7 1.2	17 W	0311 0911 1511 2136	6.0 2.4 6.1 1.9
3 W	0342 0946 1546 2220	6.7 1.6 6.9 1.0	18 TH	0354 1001 1557 2223	6.2 2.1 6.3 1.8
4 TH	0431 1041 1640 2312	6.9 1.3 7.1 0.9	19 F	0433 1047 1641 2306	6.4 1.9 6.5 1.6
5 F ○	0516 1134 1732	7.1 1.1 7.3	20 SA	0510 1130 1724 2348	6.6 1.6 6.6 1.5
6 SA	0000 0559 1224 1821	0.8 7.2 0.9 7.3	21 SU ●	0548 1213 1807	6.8 1.5 6.7
7 SU	0046 0641 1311 1910	0.9 7.2 0.9 7.2	22 M	0028 0625 1255 1850	1.5 6.9 1.3 6.8
8 M	0129 0721 1355 1956	1.1 7.2 1.0 7.0	23 TU	0106 0703 1336 1932	1.4 6.9 1.2 6.8
9 TU	0208 0801 1437 2042	1.3 7.0 1.2 6.7	24 W	0145 0740 1418 2015	1.5 6.9 1.2 6.8
10 W	0246 0840 1518 2128	1.7 6.8 1.4 6.4	25 TH	0224 0819 1502 2101	1.6 6.9 1.2 6.7
11 TH	0324 0921 1601 2220	2.0 6.5 1.7 6.0	26 F	0307 0903 1551 2151	1.7 6.8 1.3 6.5
12 F	0405 1010 1649 2319	2.4 6.2 2.0 5.7	27 SA	0355 0953 1644 2251	1.9 6.6 1.4 6.3
13 SA ☾	0456 1110 1744	2.7 5.9 2.2	28 SU ☽	0450 1053 1743 2358	2.1 6.5 1.5 6.2
14 SU	0022 0555 1218 1844	5.6 2.8 5.8 2.3	29 M	0554 1202 1847	2.2 6.4 1.6
15 M	0124 0703 1322 1947	5.6 2.8 5.8 2.3	30 TU	0107 0703 1314 1952	6.2 2.2 6.4 1.6

SUNRISE AND SUNSET TIMES

IMMINGHAM
At 53°38′N 0°11′W

UT		Sunrise	Sunset
Jan	01	0818	1551
	15	0809	1612
Feb	01	0746	1643
	15	0719	1711
Mar	01	0649	1738
	15	0615	1805
BST			
Apr	01	0634	1936
	15	0601	2002
May	01	0526	2031
	15	0500	2056
Jun	01	0438	2120
	15	0430	2132
Jul	01	0435	2133
	15	0450	2122
Aug	01	0516	2057
	15	0540	2029
Sep	01	0610	1951
	15	0634	1916
Oct	01	0703	1837
	15	0728	1804
UT			
Nov	01	0700	1628
	15	0727	1603
Dec	01	0754	1545
	15	0811	1540

IMMINGHAM
LAT 53°38'N
LONG 0°11'W

TIMES AND HEIGHTS OF HIGH AND LOW WATER (Heights in Metres)

TIME ZONE UT
For Summer Time (area enclosed in shaded box) add 1 hour

2020

JULY

Date	Day	Time	m
1	W	0212 0815 1422 2057	6.3 2.1 6.5 1.5
2	TH	0312 0922 1527 2156	6.4 1.9 6.6 1.5
3	F	0407 1023 1627 2251	6.6 1.6 6.8 1.4
4	SA	0456 1119 1723 2342	6.8 1.4 6.9 1.3
5	SU ○	0542 1211 1816	7.0 1.2 7.0
6	M	0029 0625 1300 1904	1.3 7.1 1.0 6.9
7	TU	0112 0706 1345 1948	1.4 7.1 1.0 6.9
8	W	0152 0745 1426 2028	1.5 7.1 1.1 6.7
9	TH	0228 0822 1503 2107	1.7 6.9 1.3 6.5
10	F	0303 0859 1539 2145	1.9 6.7 1.6 6.2
11	SA	0338 0938 1615 2225	2.1 6.5 1.8 6.0
12	SU	0416 1022 1657 ☾ 2312	2.3 6.2 2.1 5.8
13	M	0502 1115 1745	2.6 6.0 2.3
14	TU	0008 0557 1217 1840	5.6 2.7 5.8 2.4
15	W	0111 0701 1322 1942	5.6 2.8 5.8 2.4
16	TH	0214 0810 1426 2046	5.7 2.7 5.9 2.3
17	F	0310 0916 1524 2144	6.0 2.4 6.1 2.1
18	SA	0400 1014 1617 2236	6.2 2.1 6.3 1.9
19	SU	0445 1106 1706 2324	6.5 1.8 6.5 1.7
20	M ●	0528 1155 1754	6.8 1.5 6.8
21	TU	0009 0609 1243 1839	1.5 7.0 1.2 6.9
22	W	0053 0650 1328 1924	1.4 7.1 1.0 7.0
23	TH	0135 0730 1412 2007	1.3 7.2 0.8 7.1
24	F	0216 0810 1456 2051	1.3 7.3 0.8 7.0
25	SA	0258 0852 1540 2137	1.4 7.2 0.9 6.8
26	SU	0341 0939 1626 2227	1.6 7.1 1.1 6.6
27	M	0429 1032 1718 ☽ 2325	1.8 6.8 1.4 6.3
28	TU	0524 1134 1817	2.1 6.5 1.7
29	W	0030 0630 1246 1924	6.1 2.3 6.3 2.0
30	TH	0139 0749 1403 2035	6.0 2.4 6.2 2.1
31	F	0246 0908 1518 2140	6.1 2.2 6.3 2.0

AUGUST

Date	Day	Time	m
1	SA	0348 1014 1626 2237	6.4 1.9 6.5 1.8
2	SU	0441 1111 1724 2328	6.6 1.5 6.7 1.7
3	M ○	0527 1202 1813	6.9 1.2 6.8
4	TU	0014 0609 1248 1854	1.5 7.0 1.1 6.8
5	W	0056 0648 1330 1932	1.5 7.1 1.0 6.8
6	TH	0134 0725 1408 2006	1.5 7.2 1.1 6.7
7	F	0208 0800 1440 2037	1.6 7.1 1.3 6.6
8	SA	0239 0833 1510 2105	1.7 6.9 1.5 6.4
9	SU	0308 0905 1538 2135	1.9 6.7 1.7 6.2
10	M	0338 0939 1610 2210	2.1 6.5 2.0 6.0
11	TU	0414 1020 1649 ☾ 2256	2.3 6.2 2.3 5.8
12	W	0501 1113 1741	2.6 5.9 2.5
13	TH	0000 0603 1225 1846	5.6 2.8 5.7 2.7
14	F	0120 0717 1346 1959	5.6 2.8 5.7 2.6
15	SA	0233 0834 1458 2110	5.8 2.6 5.9 2.4
16	SU	0333 0947 1559 2211	6.1 2.2 6.2 2.1
17	M	0423 1047 1652 2304	6.5 1.8 6.6 1.8
18	TU	0508 1140 1741 2353	6.8 1.3 6.9 1.5
19	W ●	0551 1228 1826	7.1 0.9 7.1
20	TH	0038 0632 1315 1909	1.3 7.4 0.6 7.3
21	F	0121 0713 1358 1951	1.1 7.6 0.5 7.4
22	SA	0202 0753 1439 2031	1.0 7.7 0.5 7.3
23	SU	0242 0835 1520 2112	1.1 7.6 0.7 7.1
24	M	0322 0919 1601 2157	1.3 7.4 1.1 6.8
25	TU	0404 1008 1647 ☽ 2248	1.7 7.0 1.6 6.4
26	W	0454 1109 1743 2353	2.1 6.5 2.1 6.0
27	TH	0600 1225 1857	2.5 6.0 2.5
28	F	0108 0732 1354 2019	5.8 2.6 5.9 2.6
29	SA	0224 0902 1521 2129	5.9 2.4 6.0 2.4
30	SU	0332 1008 1630 2225	6.2 1.9 6.3 2.1
31	M	0426 1100 1720 2312	6.5 1.5 6.6 1.8

SEPTEMBER

Date	Day	Time	m
1	TU	0510 1146 1800 2355	6.9 1.2 6.8 1.6
2	W ○	0549 1228 1835	7.1 1.1 6.9
3	TH	0035 0626 1307 1906	1.5 7.2 1.0 6.9
4	F	0111 0701 1341 1935	1.4 7.2 1.1 6.8
5	SA	0143 0733 1410 2001	1.5 7.2 1.2 6.8
6	SU	0211 0803 1436 2026	1.6 7.1 1.4 6.7
7	M	0237 0832 1500 2052	1.7 6.9 1.7 6.5
8	TU	0303 0902 1524 2122	1.9 6.6 1.9 6.3
9	W	0333 0936 1555 2159	2.2 6.3 2.2 6.0
10	TH	0414 1019 1642 ☾ 2250	2.5 5.9 2.6 5.7
11	F	0515 1126 1754	2.8 5.6 2.9
12	SA	0018 0636 1312 1918	5.5 2.9 5.5 2.9
13	SU	0159 0800 1439 2041	5.6 2.7 5.8 2.7
14	M	0306 0923 1543 2149	6.0 2.2 6.2 2.2
15	TU	0358 1027 1635 2244	6.5 1.7 6.7 1.8
16	W	0444 1119 1722 2332	7.0 1.1 7.1 1.4
17	TH ●	0527 1207 1806	7.3 0.7 7.4
18	F	0017 0608 1252 1847	1.1 7.7 0.4 7.5
19	SA	0101 0650 1335 1927	0.9 7.9 0.3 7.6
20	SU	0142 0731 1415 2005	0.8 7.9 0.4 7.5
21	M	0221 0814 1454 2043	0.9 7.8 0.7 7.2
22	TU	0300 0858 1532 2125	1.2 7.4 1.2 6.8
23	W	0340 0947 1614 2213	1.6 6.9 1.8 6.4
24	TH	0427 1048 1707 ☽ 2317	2.1 6.3 2.4 5.9
25	F	0535 1212 1828	2.5 5.8 2.9
26	SA	0039 0723 1348 2002	5.7 2.7 5.7 2.9
27	SU	0202 0853 1516 2113	5.8 2.4 6.0 2.6
28	M	0311 0952 1619 2205	6.1 1.9 6.3 2.3
29	TU	0403 1039 1701 2250	6.5 1.5 6.6 1.9
30	W	0446 1121 1735 2330	6.9 1.3 6.8 1.6

OCTOBER

Date	Day	Time	m
1	TH ○	0524 1200 1806	7.1 1.1 6.9
2	F	0009 0559 1236 1834	1.5 7.2 1.1 7.0
3	SA	0044 0632 1308 1901	1.4 7.2 1.2 6.9
4	SU	0115 0703 1337 1926	1.4 7.2 1.3 6.9
5	M	0143 0733 1402 1951	1.5 7.1 1.5 6.8
6	TU	0208 0803 1424 2016	1.6 6.9 1.7 6.7
7	W	0233 0831 1447 2044	1.8 6.7 1.9 6.5
8	TH	0302 0903 1516 2118	2.1 6.4 2.2 6.2
9	F	0341 0946 1600 2204	2.4 6.0 2.6 5.8
10	SA	0441 1050 1710 ☾ 2316	2.7 5.6 2.9 5.5
11	SU	0605 1243 1841	2.8 5.5 3.1
12	M	0118 0732 1416 2009	5.6 2.6 5.8 2.8
13	TU	0233 0855 1520 2120	6.0 2.1 6.3 2.3
14	W	0328 0958 1612 2215	6.5 1.5 6.8 1.8
15	TH	0415 1051 1658 2305	7.0 1.0 7.2 1.4
16	F	0459 1139 1740 ● 2351	7.5 0.6 7.5 1.1
17	SA	0543 1224 1821	7.8 0.4 7.6
18	SU	0036 0626 1308 1900	0.9 7.9 0.4 7.6
19	M	0119 0710 1348 1938	0.8 7.9 0.6 7.5
20	TU	0200 0754 1427 2016	0.9 7.7 0.9 7.3
21	W	0240 0840 1505 2057	1.1 7.3 1.4 6.9
22	TH	0321 0930 1545 2143	1.6 6.8 2.0 6.4
23	F	0409 1033 1635 ☽ 2244	2.1 6.2 2.6 6.0
24	SA	0517 1201 1752	2.5 5.7 3.1
25	SU	0009 0702 1328 1930	5.7 2.6 5.7 3.1
26	M	0131 0825 1446 2042	5.8 2.4 5.9 2.8
27	TU	0238 0922 1545 2135	6.1 2.0 6.2 2.4
28	W	0332 1007 1627 2220	6.4 1.7 6.5 2.0
29	TH	0416 1048 1701 2300	6.7 1.4 6.7 1.7
30	F	0454 1125 1732 2338	6.9 1.3 6.9 1.5
31	SA ○	0529 1200 1801	7.0 1.3 7.0

NOVEMBER

Date	Day	Time	m
1	SU	0013 0602 1233 1827	1.5 7.1 1.3 7.0
2	M	0046 0634 1303 1854	1.5 7.0 1.4 7.0
3	TU	0116 0707 1330 1922	1.5 7.0 1.5 6.9
4	W	0143 0739 1355 1949	1.6 6.8 1.7 6.8
5	TH	0211 0810 1421 2018	1.7 6.6 1.9 6.6
6	F	0243 0845 1454 2053	1.9 6.4 2.2 6.3
7	SA	0324 0931 1538 2139	2.2 6.1 2.5 6.0
8	SU	0424 1034 1643 ☾ 2245	2.4 5.8 2.8 5.8
9	M	0542 1214 1806	2.5 5.7 3.0
10	TU	0023 0703 1344 1930	5.8 2.3 5.9 2.8
11	W	0150 0819 1448 2042	6.1 1.9 6.3 2.4
12	TH	0251 0923 1542 2142	6.6 1.5 6.8 1.9
13	F	0343 1018 1629 2235	7.0 1.1 7.1 1.5
14	SA	0431 1108 1713 2325	7.4 0.8 7.4 1.1
15	SU ●	0519 1155 1755	7.6 0.7 7.5
16	M	0013 0605 1241 1835	0.9 7.7 0.7 7.5
17	TU	0059 0653 1323 1915	0.8 7.7 0.8 7.5
18	W	0143 0740 1404 1955	0.9 7.5 1.1 7.3
19	TH	0226 0827 1443 2036	1.1 7.1 1.6 7.0
20	F	0309 0919 1523 2121	1.5 6.6 2.1 6.6
21	SA	0357 1020 1609 2216	1.9 6.2 2.6 6.2
22	SU	0457 1136 1711 ☽ 2330	2.3 5.8 3.0 5.9
23	M	0617 1250 1831	2.5 5.7 3.1
24	TU	0048 0736 1357 1951	5.8 2.4 5.8 3.0
25	W	0155 0836 1455 2053	6.0 2.2 6.0 2.7
26	TH	0252 0924 1543 2142	6.2 2.0 6.3 2.3
27	F	0339 1006 1622 2225	6.5 1.8 6.5 2.0
28	SA	0420 1045 1656 2305	6.6 1.6 6.7 1.8
29	SU	0457 1123 1727 2343	6.8 1.5 6.8 1.6
30	M ○	0534 1159 1758	6.8 1.5 6.9

DECEMBER

Date	Day	Time	m
1	TU	0018 0610 1233 1829	1.5 6.9 1.5 7.0
2	W	0053 0646 1304 1901	1.5 6.9 1.6 6.9
3	TH	0125 0723 1334 1932	1.5 6.8 1.7 6.9
4	F	0159 0800 1406 2004	1.6 6.7 1.8 6.7
5	SA	0236 0839 1443 2041	1.7 6.5 2.0 6.6
6	SU	0319 0925 1528 2126	1.9 6.2 2.3 6.4
7	M	0414 1024 1624 2225	2.0 6.0 2.5 6.2
8	TU	0520 1141 1734 ☾ 2340	2.1 5.9 2.7 6.1
9	W	0632 1302 1850	2.0 6.0 2.6
10	TH	0101 0741 1409 2003	6.3 1.8 6.3 2.4
11	F	0211 0847 1507 2109	6.5 1.6 6.6 2.0
12	SA	0312 0946 1600 2208	6.9 1.3 6.9 1.7
13	SU	0408 1040 1647 2303	7.1 1.1 7.1 1.3
14	M	0501 1131 1733 ● 2355	7.3 1.0 7.3 1.1
15	TU	0553 1219 1817	7.4 1.0 7.4
16	W	0044 0643 1304 1858	1.0 7.4 1.1 7.4
17	TH	0132 0732 1346 1940	1.0 7.2 1.3 7.3
18	F	0217 0820 1426 2021	1.1 7.0 1.6 7.1
19	SA	0300 0907 1505 2102	1.4 6.6 2.0 6.8
20	SU	0343 0958 1545 2148	1.7 6.3 2.3 6.5
21	M	0429 1055 1631 ☽ 2243	2.0 5.9 2.6 6.2
22	TU	0521 1156 1726 2349	2.2 5.7 2.9 6.0
23	W	0620 1257 1831	2.4 5.6 3.0
24	TH	0056 0723 1356 1943	5.9 2.4 5.7 2.9
25	F	0159 0824 1451 2050	5.9 2.3 5.9 2.7
26	SA	0255 0917 1539 2144	6.1 2.2 6.2 2.4
27	SU	0344 1004 1620 2231	6.2 2.0 6.4 2.1
28	M	0428 1048 1658 2314	6.4 1.8 6.6 1.8
29	TU	0510 1129 1734 2355	6.6 1.7 6.8 1.6
30	W ○	0551 1208 1811	6.7 1.6 6.9
31	TH	0035 0632 1245 1846	1.5 6.8 1.6 7.0

RIVER TYNE (NORTH SHIELDS)

LAT 55°01′N
LONG 1°26′W

TIMES AND HEIGHTS OF HIGH AND LOW WATER (Heights in Metres)

TIME ZONE UT
For Summer Time (area enclosed in shaded box) add 1 hour

2020

JANUARY

Date	Day	Time	m	Time	m	Time	m	Time	m
1	W	0109	1.4	0724	4.3	1311	1.9	1921	4.5
2	TH	0153	1.6	0812	4.1	1357	2.0	2012	4.3
3	F ☽	0244	1.7	0906	4.0	1455	2.2	2109	4.2
4	SA	0345	1.9	1006	3.9	1607	2.3	2211	4.1
5	**SU**	0451	1.9	1110	4.0	1720	2.2	2317	4.1
6	M	0554	1.8	1211	4.1	1824	2.0		
7	TU	0021	4.2	0650	1.7	1305	4.3	1918	1.8
8	W	0116	4.4	0739	1.5	1350	4.5	2005	1.5
9	TH	0204	4.6	0824	1.3	1430	4.7	2050	1.2
10	F O	0248	4.8	0906	1.2	1509	4.9	2133	1.0
11	SA	0331	5.0	0948	1.1	1548	5.1	2217	0.8
12	**SU**	0415	5.1	1031	1.0	1628	5.2	2301	0.6
13	M	0459	5.1	1113	1.0	1710	5.2	2347	0.6
14	TU	0546	5.1	1156	1.1	1755	5.2		
15	W	0034	0.6	0635	4.9	1242	1.3	1842	5.1
16	TH	0124	0.8	0728	4.7	1330	1.4	1936	4.9
17	F ☾	0218	1.0	0826	4.5	1426	1.6	2036	4.7
18	SA	0318	1.2	0929	4.4	1533	1.8	2145	4.6
19	**SU**	0426	1.4	1037	4.3	1650	1.9	2259	4.5
20	M	0537	1.5	1147	4.3	1808	1.8		
21	TU	0014	4.5	0645	1.5	1252	4.4	1917	1.6
22	W	0121	4.6	0744	1.4	1346	4.6	2015	1.3
23	TH	0217	4.7	0834	1.3	1433	4.8	2104	1.1
24	F ●	0304	4.8	0917	1.3	1514	4.9	2146	1.0
25	SA	0346	4.8	0955	1.2	1551	5.0	2225	0.9
26	**SU**	0424	4.8	1029	1.2	1626	5.0	2300	0.9
27	M	0500	4.8	1102	1.2	1700	5.0	2332	0.9
28	TU	0534	4.7	1133	1.3	1733	4.9		
29	W	0004	1.0	0608	4.6	1204	1.4	1808	4.8
30	TH	0037	1.1	0644	4.4	1237	1.5	1845	4.7
31	F	0112	1.3	0723	4.3	1314	1.7	1925	4.5

FEBRUARY

Date	Day	Time	m	Time	m	Time	m	Time	m
1	SA	0152	1.5	0807	4.1	1357	1.9	2012	4.3
2	**SU** ☽	0239	1.7	0859	4.0	1453	2.1	2108	4.1
3	M	0340	1.9	1001	3.9	1608	2.2	2216	4.0
4	TU	0454	2.0	1112	3.9	1731	2.1	2332	4.0
5	W	0607	1.9	1222	4.1	1843	1.9		
6	TH	0045	4.2	0711	1.7	1321	4.3	1941	1.5
7	F	0144	4.5	0804	1.4	1408	4.6	2032	1.2
8	SA	0233	4.7	0852	1.2	1451	4.9	2119	0.8
9	**SU** O	0318	5.0	0936	1.0	1531	5.1	2205	0.5
10	M	0402	5.2	1019	0.8	1612	5.3	2249	0.3
11	TU	0445	5.3	1101	0.8	1654	5.4	2334	0.2
12	W	0530	5.2	1142	0.8	1738	5.4		
13	TH	0018	0.3	0615	5.1	1224	0.9	1823	5.3
14	F	0103	0.5	0703	4.8	1307	1.1	1913	5.1
15	SA ☾	0151	0.8	0755	4.6	1356	1.4	2010	4.8
16	**SU**	0245	1.2	0854	4.3	1458	1.7	2118	4.5
17	M	0351	1.6	1001	4.1	1619	1.8	2237	4.2
18	TU	0510	1.8	1119	4.1	1751	1.8		
19	W	0004	4.2	0630	1.8	1235	4.2	1911	1.6
20	TH	0117	4.3	0736	1.7	1335	4.4	2010	1.4
21	F	0213	4.5	0825	1.5	1423	4.6	2056	1.1
22	SA	0256	4.6	0905	1.4	1502	4.8	2134	0.9
23	**SU** ●	0333	4.7	0939	1.2	1536	4.9	2208	0.8
24	M	0406	4.8	1011	1.1	1607	5.0	2238	0.8
25	TU	0437	4.8	1040	1.1	1638	5.0	2307	0.8
26	W	0507	4.8	1109	1.1	1708	5.0	2336	0.8
27	TH	0537	4.7	1138	1.1	1740	4.9		
28	F	0005	1.0	0608	4.6	1208	1.3	1812	4.8
29	SA	0036	1.1	0641	4.4	1240	1.4	1848	4.6

MARCH

Date	Day	Time	m	Time	m	Time	m	Time	m
1	**SU**	0109	1.4	0718	4.3	1317	1.6	1929	4.4
2	M ☽	0148	1.6	0802	4.1	1403	1.8	2020	4.1
3	TU	0240	1.9	0900	3.9	1510	2.0	2128	3.9
4	W	0357	2.0	1016	3.8	1643	2.1	2253	3.9
5	TH	0529	2.0	1140	3.9	1810	1.8		
6	F	0019	4.1	0646	1.8	1251	4.2	1918	1.5
7	SA	0124	4.4	0746	1.5	1344	4.5	2013	1.0
8	**SU**	0215	4.8	0834	1.1	1429	4.9	2101	0.6
9	M O	0300	5.1	0919	0.9	1511	5.2	2147	0.3
10	TU	0343	5.3	1001	0.6	1552	5.4	2231	0.0
11	W	0425	5.3	1042	0.5	1634	5.6	2314	0.0
12	TH	0508	5.3	1122	0.5	1718	5.5	2356	0.2
13	F	0551	5.1	1203	0.7	1803	5.4		
14	SA	0038	0.5	0635	4.9	1245	0.9	1853	5.1
15	**SU**	0123	0.9	0724	4.6	1333	1.2	1949	4.7
16	M ☾	0213	1.3	0820	4.3	1432	1.5	2058	4.3
17	TU	0318	1.8	0928	4.0	1556	1.8	2220	4.0
18	W	0445	2.0	1049	3.9	1737	1.8	2352	4.0
19	TH	0616	2.0	1213	4.0	1900	1.6		
20	F	0105	4.2	0721	1.8	1317	4.3	1955	1.3
21	SA	0158	4.4	0808	1.6	1404	4.5	2037	1.1
22	**SU**	0238	4.5	0845	1.4	1441	4.7	2111	0.9
23	M	0312	4.7	0917	1.2	1513	4.8	2142	0.8
24	TU ●	0342	4.8	0947	1.1	1543	4.9	2210	0.8
25	W	0410	4.8	1016	1.0	1612	5.0	2238	0.7
26	TH	0438	4.8	1044	0.9	1642	4.9	2306	0.8
27	F	0506	4.7	1113	1.0	1712	4.9	2334	0.9
28	SA	0536	4.7	1142	1.1	1745	4.8		
29	**SU**	0003	1.1	0606	4.5	1214	1.2	1819	4.6
30	M	0035	1.3	0641	4.4	1250	1.4	1900	4.4
31	TU	0111	1.6	0723	4.2	1335	1.6	1951	4.2

APRIL

Date	Day	Time	m	Time	m	Time	m	Time	m
1	W ☽	0201	1.8	0819	4.0	1440	1.8	2101	4.0
2	TH	0318	2.1	0935	3.9	1610	1.9	2228	3.9
3	F	0459	2.1	1103	3.9	1741	1.7	2355	4.1
4	SA	0621	1.8	1218	4.2	1853	1.3		
5	**SU**	0101	4.5	0722	1.5	1316	4.6	1949	0.8
6	M	0153	4.8	0811	1.1	1403	4.9	2038	0.4
7	TU	0238	5.1	0856	0.8	1447	5.3	2123	0.2
8	W O	0320	5.3	0938	0.6	1529	5.5	2207	0.0
9	TH	0401	5.3	1020	0.4	1612	5.6	2250	0.1
10	F	0443	5.3	1101	0.4	1658	5.5	2331	0.3
11	SA	0525	5.1	1143	0.6	1745	5.3		
12	**SU**	0013	0.6	0609	4.9	1227	0.8	1836	4.9
13	M	0056	1.1	0656	4.6	1315	1.1	1933	4.6
14	TU ☾	0145	1.5	0750	4.3	1414	1.4	2041	4.2
15	W	0248	1.9	0856	4.1	1535	1.7	2159	4.0
16	TH	0415	2.2	1015	3.9	1711	1.7	2325	3.9
17	F	0545	2.1	1138	4.0	1830	1.6		
18	SA	0037	4.1	0651	1.9	1245	4.2	1924	1.4
19	**SU**	0129	4.3	0738	1.7	1333	4.4	2005	1.2
20	M	0208	4.5	0815	1.4	1411	4.6	2038	1.0
21	TU	0241	4.6	0848	1.2	1444	4.7	2109	0.9
22	W	0312	4.7	0919	1.1	1515	4.8	2138	0.8
23	TH ●	0340	4.8	0949	1.0	1545	4.9	2207	0.8
24	F	0409	4.8	1019	0.9	1616	4.9	2237	0.8
25	SA	0438	4.8	1050	0.9	1648	4.8	2306	1.0
26	**SU**	0508	4.7	1122	1.0	1722	4.7	2337	1.1
27	M	0540	4.6	1156	1.1	1800	4.6		
28	TU	0010	1.3	0616	4.5	1235	1.3	1844	4.4
29	W	0050	1.6	0700	4.3	1324	1.4	1938	4.2
30	TH ☽	0142	1.8	0757	4.1	1428	1.6	2048	4.1

MAY

Date	Day	Time	m	Time	m	Time	m	Time	m
1	F	0257	2.0	0909	4.0	1550	1.6	2209	4.0
2	SA	0430	2.0	1031	4.1	1714	1.4	2328	4.2
3	**SU**	0550	1.8	1145	4.3	1823	1.1		
4	M	0033	4.5	0651	1.5	1245	4.6	1920	0.7
5	TU	0126	4.8	0743	1.1	1336	5.0	2011	0.4
6	W	0212	5.0	0830	0.8	1422	5.2	2058	0.3
7	TH O	0255	5.2	0915	0.6	1508	5.4	2143	0.2
8	F	0337	5.3	0959	0.5	1554	5.4	2226	0.3
9	SA	0419	5.2	1043	0.5	1641	5.3	2309	0.5
10	**SU**	0502	5.1	1127	0.6	1730	5.1	2350	0.9
11	M	0546	4.9	1213	0.8	1823	4.8		
12	TU	0033	1.2	0632	4.7	1301	1.1	1918	4.5
13	W	0120	1.6	0724	4.4	1357	1.3	2020	4.2
14	TH ☾	0217	1.9	0825	4.2	1506	1.6	2127	4.0
15	F	0331	2.1	0934	4.0	1625	1.7	2241	3.9
16	SA	0453	2.2	1047	4.0	1738	1.6	2350	4.0
17	**SU**	0602	2.0	1155	4.1	1836	1.5		
18	M	0045	4.1	0654	1.8	1250	4.2	1920	1.3
19	TU	0129	4.3	0736	1.6	1333	4.4	1958	1.2
20	W	0206	4.5	0813	1.4	1410	4.6	2032	1.1
21	TH	0239	4.6	0848	1.2	1445	4.7	2105	1.0
22	F ●	0310	4.7	0922	1.1	1519	4.7	2138	1.0
23	SA	0341	4.8	0956	1.0	1554	4.8	2210	1.0
24	**SU**	0413	4.8	1030	0.9	1629	4.8	2243	1.0
25	M	0446	4.8	1107	1.0	1707	4.7	2318	1.2
26	TU	0521	4.7	1145	1.0	1749	4.6	2356	1.3
27	W	0601	4.6	1229	1.1	1836	4.5		
28	TH	0040	1.5	0647	4.5	1320	1.2	1931	4.4
29	F	0133	1.7	0742	4.4	1420	1.3	2036	4.2
30	SA ☽	0240	1.8	0849	4.3	1531	1.3	2147	4.2
31	**SU**	0359	1.8	1001	4.3	1645	1.2	2258	4.3

JUNE

Date	Day	Time	m	Time	m	Time	m	Time	m
1	M	0514	1.7	1111	4.5	1752	1.0		
2	TU	0003	4.5	0618	1.5	1215	4.7	1851	0.8
3	W	0059	4.7	0714	1.2	1311	4.9	1945	0.7
4	TH	0148	4.9	0807	1.0	1403	5.1	2035	0.6
5	F O	0233	5.0	0856	0.8	1452	5.2	2122	0.6
6	SA	0317	5.1	0944	0.6	1541	5.2	2206	0.7
7	**SU**	0400	5.1	1030	0.6	1630	5.1	2249	0.8
8	M	0443	5.0	1115	0.7	1719	4.9	2331	1.1
9	TU	0527	4.9	1200	0.8	1808	4.7		
10	W	0012	1.3	0611	4.8	1246	1.0	1858	4.5
11	TH	0055	1.6	0658	4.6	1334	1.2	1951	4.2
12	F	0142	1.8	0750	4.4	1427	1.4	2046	4.1
13	SA ☾	0237	2.0	0847	4.2	1527	1.6	2146	3.9
14	**SU**	0345	2.1	0949	4.1	1630	1.7	2248	3.9
15	M	0455	2.1	1053	4.1	1732	1.6	2349	4.0
16	TU	0557	2.0	1154	4.1	1826	1.5		
17	W	0041	4.2	0650	1.8	1249	4.2	1913	1.4
18	TH	0126	4.3	0737	1.6	1335	4.4	1955	1.3
19	F	0206	4.5	0818	1.4	1417	4.5	2034	1.2
20	SA	0242	4.6	0857	1.2	1456	4.6	2112	1.1
21	**SU** ●	0317	4.7	0936	1.0	1535	4.7	2149	1.1
22	M	0352	4.8	1015	0.9	1614	4.8	2227	1.1
23	TU	0428	4.9	1055	0.8	1656	4.8	2306	1.1
24	W	0507	4.9	1138	0.8	1740	4.8	2348	1.2
25	TH	0549	4.8	1223	0.8	1827	4.7		
26	F	0032	1.3	0635	4.8	1313	0.9	1919	4.6
27	SA	0122	1.5	0727	4.7	1407	1.0	2018	4.5
28	**SU** ☽	0219	1.6	0826	4.6	1508	1.1	2121	4.4
29	M	0325	1.7	0932	4.5	1614	1.1	2227	4.4
30	TU	0437	1.7	1040	4.5	1721	1.1	2332	4.4

SUNRISE AND SUNSET TIMES

RIVER TYNE
At 55°01′N 1°26′W

		Sunrise	Sunset
UT			
Jan	01	0831	1548
	15	0821	1609
Feb	01	0756	1643
	15	0728	1712
Mar	01	0656	1742
	15	0621	1810
BST			
Apr	01	0637	1943
	15	0602	2010
May	01	0526	2041
	15	0458	2107
Jun	01	0434	2134
	15	0426	2147
Jul	01	0431	2148
	15	0447	2136
Aug	01	0515	2108
	15	0540	2039
Sep	01	0612	1958
	15	0638	1922
Oct	01	0708	1841
	15	0735	1807
UT			
Nov	01	0710	1628
	15	0738	1602
Dec	01	0807	1542
	15	0825	1537

RIVER TYNE (NORTH SHIELDS)
LAT 55°01′N
LONG 1°26′W

TIMES AND HEIGHTS OF HIGH AND LOW WATER (Heights in Metres)

TIME ZONE UT
For Summer Time (area enclosed in shaded box) add 1 hour

2020

JULY

Date	Day	Time	m
1	W	0547 1149 1825	1.6 4.6 1.1
2	TH	0033 0651 1254 1924	4.5 1.4 4.7 1.0
3	F	0129 0751 1352 2018	4.7 1.2 4.8 1.0
4	SA	0218 0845 1445 2107	4.8 1.0 4.9 1.0
5	SU	0303 0935 1534 O 2152	5.0 0.8 4.9 1.0
6	M	0346 1021 1621 2234	5.0 0.7 4.9 1.1
7	TU	0428 1104 1706 2313	5.0 0.7 4.8 1.2
8	W	0508 1145 1749 2350	5.0 0.8 4.7 1.3
9	TH	0548 1224 1832	4.9 0.9 4.5
10	F	0026 0629 1303 1914	1.5 4.7 1.1 4.4
11	SA	0104 0712 1344 1959	1.6 4.6 1.3 4.2
12	SU	0147 0759 1429 ☾ 2049	1.8 4.4 1.5 4.0
13	M	0237 0851 1522 2143	2.0 4.2 1.7 3.9
14	TU	0341 0950 1624 2244	2.1 4.1 1.8 3.9
15	W	0453 1054 1728 2347	2.1 4.0 1.8 4.0
16	TH	0601 1201 1828	2.0 4.1 1.7
17	F	0045 0700 1301 1921	4.2 1.8 4.2 1.6
18	SA	0134 0750 1352 2008	4.4 1.5 4.4 1.4
19	SU	0216 0836 1437 2051	4.6 1.3 4.6 1.3
20	M	0256 0918 1519 ● 2132	4.7 1.0 4.8 1.1
21	TU	0333 1001 1600 2213	4.9 0.8 4.9 1.0
22	W	0412 1044 1642 2255	5.0 0.6 5.0 1.0
23	TH	0452 1127 1726 2336	5.1 0.5 5.0 1.0
24	F	0533 1212 1812	5.1 0.5 4.9
25	SA	0018 0618 1258 1900	1.1 5.1 0.6 4.8
26	SU	0104 0707 1347 1953	1.2 5.0 0.7 4.6
27	M	0153 0802 1441 ☽ 2051	1.4 4.8 1.0 4.5
28	TU	0252 0904 1544 2155	1.6 4.6 1.2 4.3
29	W	0404 1016 1653 2304	1.7 4.5 1.4 4.3
30	TH	0523 1133 1805	1.7 4.4 1.4
31	F	0014 0640 1248 1912	4.4 1.5 4.5 1.4

AUGUST

Date	Day	Time	m
1	SA	0116 0746 1351 2009	4.5 1.3 4.6 1.3
2	SU	0208 0841 1443 2058	4.7 1.1 4.8 1.2
3	M	0253 0929 1529 O 2140	4.9 0.9 4.8 1.2
4	TU	0334 1010 1609 2217	5.0 0.7 4.9 1.1
5	W	0411 1048 1647 2252	5.0 0.7 4.8 1.1
6	TH	0447 1123 1723 2324	5.0 0.7 4.8 1.2
7	F	0522 1155 1758 2355	5.0 0.9 4.6 1.3
8	SA	0557 1227 1834	4.9 1.0 4.5
9	SU	0027 0633 1301 1911	1.4 4.7 1.2 4.4
10	M	0103 0713 1338 1953	1.6 4.6 1.4 4.2
11	TU	0144 0758 1422 ☾ 2042	1.8 4.3 1.6 4.0
12	W	0236 0853 1518 2141	2.0 4.1 1.9 3.9
13	TH	0347 0958 1629 2250	2.1 4.0 2.0 3.9
14	F	0510 1115 1746	2.1 3.9 2.0
15	SA	0002 0625 1231 1852	4.0 1.9 4.1 1.8
16	SU	0103 0725 1330 1947	4.3 1.6 4.3 1.6
17	M	0152 0815 1418 2033	4.5 1.3 4.6 1.3
18	TU	0234 0900 1501 2116	4.8 0.9 4.9 1.1
19	W	0313 0944 1542 ● 2157	5.1 0.6 5.1 0.9
20	TH	0352 1027 1624 2238	5.3 0.4 5.2 0.8
21	F	0431 1110 1706 2318	5.4 0.2 5.2 0.8
22	SA	0513 1152 1750 2359	5.4 0.2 5.2 0.9
23	SU	0557 1236 1835	5.4 0.4 5.0
24	M	0041 0644 1321 1924	1.0 5.2 0.7 4.7
25	TU	0128 0738 1412 ☽ 2020	1.3 4.9 1.1 4.5
26	W	0225 0842 1514 2125	1.5 4.6 1.5 4.3
27	TH	0340 0959 1630 2240	1.7 4.3 1.7 4.2
28	F	0511 1127 1754 2359	1.8 4.2 1.8 4.2
29	SA	0639 1248 1908	1.6 4.3 1.7
30	SU	0107 0744 1350 2003	4.4 1.3 4.5 1.6
31	M	0159 0835 1437 2046	4.7 1.1 4.7 1.4

SEPTEMBER

Date	Day	Time	m
1	TU	0242 0916 1516 2123	4.9 0.9 4.8 1.3
2	W	0318 0952 1551 O 2156	5.0 0.8 4.9 1.2
3	TH	0350 1024 1623 2227	5.1 0.7 4.9 1.1
4	F	0422 1054 1653 2256	5.1 0.7 4.8 1.1
5	SA	0453 1123 1723 2325	5.1 0.8 4.8 1.2
6	SU	0524 1151 1754 2355	5.0 1.0 4.7 1.3
7	M	0558 1221 1827	4.8 1.2 4.5
8	TU	0027 0634 1254 1903	1.4 4.6 1.4 4.4
9	W	0104 0715 1331 1947	1.7 4.4 1.7 4.2
10	TH	0149 0805 1420 ☾ 2042	1.9 4.2 2.0 4.0
11	F	0254 0912 1533 2156	2.1 3.9 2.2 3.9
12	SA	0424 1036 1707 2319	2.2 3.9 2.2 4.0
13	SU	0552 1202 1827	2.0 4.1 2.0
14	M	0031 0700 1307 1925	4.2 1.6 4.4 1.7
15	TU	0125 0752 1356 2012	4.6 1.2 4.7 1.3
16	W	0208 0838 1439 2055	4.9 0.8 5.0 1.0
17	TH	0248 0922 1520 ● 2136	5.2 0.4 5.3 0.8
18	F	0327 1005 1600 2216	5.5 0.2 5.4 0.7
19	SA	0408 1047 1641 2256	5.6 0.1 5.4 0.6
20	SU	0450 1129 1723 2337	5.6 0.2 5.3 0.7
21	M	0535 1211 1808	5.5 0.5 5.1
22	TU	0019 0623 1255 1855	0.9 5.2 0.9 4.8
23	W	0107 0719 1344 1950	1.2 4.9 1.3 4.5
24	TH	0204 0827 1447 ☽ 2056	1.5 4.5 1.8 4.3
25	F	0325 0949 1612 2217	1.8 4.2 2.1 4.1
26	SA	0505 1122 1745 2343	1.8 4.1 2.1 4.2
27	SU	0632 1241 1857	1.6 4.3 1.9
28	M	0052 0732 1338 1947	4.4 1.3 4.5 1.7
29	TU	0142 0817 1420 2027	4.6 1.1 4.7 1.5
30	W	0222 0854 1455 2100	4.8 1.0 4.8 1.3

OCTOBER

Date	Day	Time	m
1	TH	0255 0925 1525 O 2130	5.0 0.9 4.9 1.2
2	F	0325 0954 1554 2200	5.1 0.8 4.9 1.1
3	SA	0354 1022 1622 2228	5.1 0.8 4.9 1.1
4	SU	0424 1049 1650 2257	5.1 0.9 4.9 1.1
5	M	0455 1117 1719 2327	5.0 1.0 4.8 1.2
6	TU	0528 1145 1750 2358	4.9 1.2 4.7 1.4
7	W	0603 1216 1824	4.7 1.4 4.5
8	TH	0034 0643 1251 1905	1.6 4.4 1.7 4.3
9	F	0119 0733 1338 1958	1.8 4.2 2.0 4.1
10	SA	0221 0840 1449 ☾ 2111	2.0 4.0 2.2 4.0
11	SU	0347 1006 1631 2237	2.1 3.9 2.3 4.0
12	M	0519 1132 1757 2354	1.9 4.1 2.1 4.3
13	TU	0630 1239 1858	1.5 4.5 1.7
14	W	0052 0724 1330 1946	4.6 1.1 4.8 1.4
15	TH	0139 0812 1414 2029	5.0 0.7 5.1 1.0
16	F	0221 0856 1455 ● 2111	5.3 0.4 5.4 0.8
17	SA	0302 0939 1535 2152	5.6 0.2 5.5 0.6
18	SU	0344 1022 1616 2234	5.7 0.2 5.5 0.6
19	M	0429 1104 1658 2317	5.7 0.3 5.4 0.7
20	TU	0516 1146 1741	5.5 0.7 5.1
21	W	0002 0607 1231 1828	0.9 5.2 1.1 4.9
22	TH	0051 0705 1320 1923	1.2 4.8 1.6 4.6
23	F	0151 0814 1422 ☽ 2030	1.5 4.4 2.0 4.3
24	SA	0310 0934 1548 2149	1.7 4.1 2.3 4.2
25	SU	0446 1100 1720 2313	1.8 4.1 2.3 4.2
26	M	0607 1216 1830	1.6 4.2 2.1
27	TU	0022 0705 1311 1919	4.4 1.4 4.4 1.8
28	W	0114 0748 1352 1958	4.6 1.3 4.6 1.6
29	TH	0153 0822 1425 2031	4.7 1.1 4.8 1.4
30	F	0227 0853 1456 2102	4.9 1.0 4.9 1.3
31	SA	0258 0922 1524 O 2133	5.0 1.0 4.9 1.2

NOVEMBER

Date	Day	Time	m
1	SU	0329 0950 1553 2203	5.0 1.0 5.0 1.1
2	M	0400 1019 1621 2234	5.0 1.0 4.9 1.1
3	TU	0432 1048 1651 2305	4.9 1.1 4.9 1.2
4	W	0506 1117 1722 2339	4.8 1.3 4.8 1.3
5	TH	0542 1149 1757	4.7 1.5 4.6
6	F	0017 0624 1226 1838	1.5 4.5 1.7 4.5
7	SA	0103 0715 1314 1930	1.6 4.3 2.0 4.3
8	SU	0203 0820 1421 ☾ 2038	1.8 4.1 2.2 4.2
9	M	0320 0939 1553 2158	1.8 4.1 2.3 4.2
10	TU	0444 1058 1718 2313	1.7 4.2 2.1 4.4
11	W	0554 1205 1822	1.4 4.5 1.8
12	TH	0015 0651 1300 1914	4.7 1.0 4.8 1.4
13	F	0108 0742 1346 2001	5.0 0.7 5.1 1.1
14	SA	0155 0829 1429 2047	5.3 0.5 5.3 0.9
15	SU	0240 0915 1511 ● 2132	5.5 0.4 5.4 0.7
16	M	0326 0959 1553 2217	5.6 0.4 5.4 0.6
17	TU	0414 1043 1636 2303	5.5 0.6 5.3 0.7
18	W	0503 1126 1720 2350	5.3 0.9 5.2 0.9
19	TH	0556 1210 1808	5.0 1.3 4.9
20	F	0040 0653 1258 1900	1.1 4.7 1.7 4.7
21	SA	0137 0756 1355 2001	1.4 4.4 2.0 4.4
22	SU	0246 0905 1507 ☽ 2110	1.6 4.2 2.3 4.3
23	M	0404 1018 1629 2224	1.7 4.1 2.3 4.2
24	TU	0518 1130 1741 2334	1.7 4.1 2.2 4.3
25	W	0619 1228 1837	1.6 4.3 2.0
26	TH	0031 0706 1314 1920	4.4 1.5 4.4 1.8
27	F	0117 0744 1352 1959	4.5 1.4 4.6 1.6
28	SA	0156 0818 1425 2034	4.7 1.3 4.7 1.4
29	SU	0232 0850 1457 2108	4.8 1.2 4.8 1.3
30	M	0306 0922 1528 O 2142	4.8 1.2 4.9 1.2

DECEMBER

Date	Day	Time	m
1	TU	0340 0954 1558 2215	4.9 1.2 4.9 1.2
2	W	0415 1026 1630 2250	4.8 1.2 4.9 1.2
3	TH	0451 1059 1703 2327	4.8 1.3 4.8 1.2
4	F	0530 1134 1740	4.7 1.5 4.8
5	SA	0008 0613 1214 1822	1.3 4.6 1.7 4.6
6	SU	0055 0702 1301 1911	1.4 4.4 1.8 4.5
7	M	0149 0801 1359 2011	1.5 4.3 2.0 4.4
8	TU	0254 0910 1512 ☾ 2120	1.5 4.3 2.1 4.4
9	W	0407 1021 1632 2231	1.5 4.3 2.0 4.5
10	TH	0516 1128 1741 2338	1.3 4.5 1.8 4.7
11	F	0618 1228 1842	1.1 4.7 1.6
12	SA	0039 0714 1320 1937	4.9 0.9 4.9 1.3
13	SU	0134 0806 1408 2028	5.1 0.8 5.1 1.0
14	M	0226 0855 1452 ● 2118	5.2 0.8 5.2 0.8
15	TU	0316 0942 1536 2207	5.3 0.8 5.3 0.7
16	W	0405 1027 1620 2254	5.3 0.9 5.2 0.7
17	TH	0456 1111 1704 2341	5.1 1.1 5.1 0.8
18	F	0546 1153 1750	4.9 1.4 5.0
19	SA	0028 0637 1237 1837	1.0 4.7 1.6 4.8
20	SU	0117 0729 1322 1928	1.2 4.4 1.9 4.6
21	M	0208 0824 1414 ☽ 2024	1.4 4.2 2.1 4.4
22	TU	0306 0923 1517 2125	1.6 4.1 2.2 4.3
23	W	0409 1025 1628 2230	1.8 4.0 2.3 4.2
24	TH	0512 1129 1736 2335	1.8 4.0 2.2 4.2
25	F	0610 1226 1835	1.8 4.2 2.0
26	SA	0034 0700 1314 1924	4.3 1.7 4.3 1.8
27	SU	0125 0744 1356 2008	4.4 1.6 4.5 1.6
28	M	0208 0823 1433 2047	4.5 1.4 4.7 1.4
29	TU	0248 0900 1507 2125	4.6 1.4 4.8 1.3
30	W	0325 0936 1541 O 2202	4.7 1.3 4.9 1.1
31	TH	0402 1011 1614 2240	4.8 1.3 4.9 1.0

LEITH
LAT 55°59′N
LONG 3°11′W

TIMES AND HEIGHTS OF HIGH AND LOW WATER (Heights in Metres)

TIME ZONE UT
For Summer Time (area enclosed in shaded box) add 1 hour

2020

JANUARY

Date	Time	m	Date	Time	m
1 W	0633	4.8	16 TH	0016	0.8
	1138	1.9		0631	5.3
	1840	4.8		1222	1.5
				1848	5.3
2 TH	0013	1.7	17 F	0106	1.1
	0718	4.6		0727	5.1
	1226	2.1		1313	1.7
	1927	4.7		☾ 1949	5.1
3 F	0103	1.9	18 SA	0202	1.3
	0808	4.4		0831	4.9
	1329	2.3		1417	1.9
	☽ 2022	4.5		2100	5.0
4 SA	0207	2.0	19 SU	0312	1.6
	0903	4.4		0938	4.8
	1449	2.4		1535	2.0
	2122	4.5		2211	4.9
5 SU	0328	2.1	20 M	0429	1.7
	1003	4.4		1045	4.8
	1609	2.3		1652	1.9
	2224	4.5		2320	4.9
6 M	0442	2.0	21 TU	0539	1.7
	1104	4.5		1151	4.9
	1710	2.1		1803	1.7
	2326	4.6			
7 TU	0538	1.8	22 W	0025	5.0
	1202	4.7		0638	1.6
	1802	1.9		1251	5.0
				1905	1.4
8 W	0023	4.8	23 TH	0123	5.1
	0625	1.7		0726	1.5
	1255	5.0		1341	5.2
	1848	1.6		1957	1.2
9 TH	0115	5.0	24 F	0211	5.3
	0708	1.5		0807	1.3
	1341	5.2		1425	5.3
	1933	1.3		● 2041	1.0
10 F	0200	5.3	25 SA	0254	5.3
	0751	1.3		0844	1.3
	1422	5.4		1506	5.4
	O 2019	1.0		2119	0.9
11 SA	0243	5.5	26 SU	0334	5.3
	0836	1.1		0915	1.2
	1502	5.5		1543	5.4
	2106	0.8		2151	0.9
12 SU	0325	5.6	27 M	0410	5.3
	0921	1.0		0943	1.2
	1542	5.6		1618	5.4
	2154	0.6		2217	1.0
13 M	0408	5.7	28 TU	0445	5.2
	1008	1.0		1010	1.3
	1623	5.7		1652	5.3
	2242	0.6		2240	1.1
14 TU	0453	5.6	29 W	0520	5.1
	1053	1.1		1039	1.4
	1708	5.6		1726	5.2
	2329	0.7		2306	1.2
15 W	0541	5.5	30 TH	0556	4.9
	1137	1.3		1109	1.6
	1755	5.5		1802	5.0
				2337	1.4
			31 F	0636	4.7
				1142	1.8
				1842	4.8

FEBRUARY

Date	Time	m	Date	Time	m
1 SA	0013	1.6	16 SU	0122	1.4
	0718	4.6		0759	4.8
	1222	2.0		1331	1.8
	1926	4.6		2033	4.9
2 SU	0058	1.9	17 M	0226	1.8
	0808	4.4		0906	4.6
	1321	2.2		1459	2.0
	☽ 2021	4.5		2148	4.7
3 M	0159	2.1	18 TU	0400	2.0
	0907	4.3		1018	4.5
	1448	2.4		1640	2.0
	2128	4.4		2305	4.6
4 TU	0326	2.2	19 W	0526	2.0
	1013	4.3		1134	4.6
	1621	2.3		1807	1.8
	2240	4.4			
5 W	0458	2.1	20 TH	0020	4.8
	1121	4.5		0631	1.9
	1732	2.0		1243	4.8
	2350	4.6		1908	1.5
6 TH	0601	1.9	21 F	0119	5.0
	1225	4.8		0718	1.7
	1828	1.7		1335	5.0
				1954	1.2
7 F	0051	4.9	22 SA	0205	5.1
	0652	1.6		0754	1.5
	1319	5.1		1416	5.2
	1919	1.3		2031	1.0
8 SA	0142	5.2	23 SU	0243	5.2
	0740	1.3		0825	1.3
	1404	5.4		1452	5.3
	2009	0.9		● 2103	0.9
9 SU	0227	5.5	24 M	0316	5.3
	0826	1.0		0855	1.1
	1445	5.6		1525	5.4
	O 2058	0.5		2130	0.8
10 M	0309	5.7	25 TU	0348	5.3
	0912	0.8		0923	1.1
	1526	5.8		1556	5.4
	2145	0.3		2154	0.8
11 TU	0352	5.9	26 W	0418	5.2
	0957	0.7		0951	1.1
	1607	5.9		1626	5.3
	2231	0.2		2217	0.9
12 W	0436	5.8	27 TH	0450	5.2
	1040	0.7		1018	1.1
	1651	5.9		1658	5.3
	2314	0.3		2240	1.0
13 TH	0521	5.7	28 F	0523	5.0
	1120	0.9		1041	1.3
	1737	5.8		1731	5.1
	2356	0.5		2302	1.2
14 F	0609	5.4	29 SA	0558	4.9
	1157	1.1		1103	1.5
	1827	5.5		1806	4.9
				2326	1.4
15 SA	0037	0.9			
	0700	5.1			
	1236	1.5			
	☾ 1924	5.2			

MARCH

Date	Time	m	Date	Time	m
1 SU	0636	4.7	16 M	0046	1.5
	1130	1.7		0729	4.8
	1846	4.7		1259	1.7
	2358	1.7		☾ 2011	4.8
2 M	0720	4.5	17 TU	0145	2.0
	1211	2.0		0836	4.5
	1935	4.5		1434	2.0
	☽			2126	4.5
3 TU	0045	2.0	18 W	0335	2.3
	0814	4.3		0951	4.3
	1323	2.2		1639	2.0
	2038	4.3		2247	4.4
4 W	0212	2.3	19 TH	0512	2.2
	0924	4.2		1112	4.4
	1526	2.3		1803	1.8
	2158	4.3			
5 TH	0423	2.3	20 F	0008	4.6
	1043	4.3		0616	2.0
	1705	2.0		1226	4.7
	2319	4.5		1857	1.5
6 F	0542	2.0	21 SA	0106	4.8
	1156	4.6		0659	1.8
	1810	1.6		1317	4.9
				1937	1.2
7 SA	0028	4.9	22 SU	0148	5.0
	0636	1.6		0731	1.5
	1255	5.0		1357	5.1
	1905	1.1		2009	1.1
8 SU	0122	5.3	23 M	0223	5.2
	0725	1.2		0800	1.2
	1342	5.4		1431	5.2
	1955	0.7		2036	0.9
9 M	0207	5.6	24 TU	0253	5.2
	0810	0.9		0830	1.1
	1424	5.7		1501	5.3
	O 2043	0.3		● 2101	0.8
10 TU	0249	5.8	25 W	0321	5.3
	0855	0.6		0900	0.9
	1505	5.9		1530	5.3
	2129	0.0		2126	0.8
11 W	0331	6.0	26 TH	0350	5.3
	0939	0.4		0930	0.9
	1547	6.1		1600	5.3
	2212	0.0		2151	0.8
12 TH	0414	5.9	27 F	0420	5.2
	1021	0.5		0957	1.0
	1631	6.0		1631	5.3
	2254	0.1		2212	1.0
13 F	0458	5.7	28 SA	0452	5.1
	1059	0.6		1016	1.1
	1717	5.9		1703	5.1
	2333	0.5		2229	1.2
14 SA	0544	5.5	29 SU	0526	5.0
	1134	0.9		1033	1.3
	1807	5.5		1739	5.0
				2247	1.4
15 SU	0008	1.0	30 M	0602	4.8
	0633	5.1		1059	1.5
	1208	1.3		1819	4.8
	1903	5.2		2316	1.6
			31 TU	0643	4.6
				1138	1.7
				1907	4.6

APRIL

Date	Time	m	Date	Time	m
1 W	0000	2.0	16 TH	0303	2.4
	0734	4.4		0922	4.3
	1245	2.0		1620	1.9
	☽ 2007	4.4		2218	4.4
2 TH	0128	2.3	17 F	0436	2.3
	0843	4.3		1039	4.4
	1450	2.1		1735	1.7
	2127	4.4		2338	4.5
3 F	0355	2.3	18 SA	0537	2.1
	1008	4.3		1152	4.5
	1641	1.9		1827	1.5
	2251	4.5			
4 SA	0517	2.0	19 SU	0037	4.7
	1125	4.6		0620	1.8
	1749	1.4		1246	4.8
				1904	1.3
5 SU	0001	4.9	20 M	0119	4.9
	0612	1.6		0654	1.6
	1226	5.0		1326	5.0
	1844	1.0		1934	1.2
6 M	0057	5.3	21 TU	0153	5.1
	0700	1.2		0727	1.3
	1315	5.4		1401	5.1
	1934	0.5		2000	1.0
7 TU	0142	5.6	22 W	0223	5.2
	0746	0.8		0801	1.1
	1358	5.8		1432	5.2
	2021	0.2		2027	0.9
8 W	0225	5.8	23 TH	0252	5.2
	0832	0.5		0834	1.0
	1441	6.0		1502	5.3
	O 2106	0.0		● 2055	0.9
9 TH	0307	5.9	24 F	0321	5.3
	0917	0.3		0906	0.9
	1525	6.1		1534	5.3
	2150	0.0		2122	0.9
10 F	0351	5.9	25 SA	0353	5.2
	1000	0.4		0936	1.0
	1611	6.0		1606	5.2
	2231	0.2		2146	1.0
11 SA	0435	5.7	26 SU	0425	5.2
	1040	0.5		1000	1.1
	1659	5.8		1641	5.2
	2309	0.7		2203	1.2
12 SU	0521	5.4	27 M	0459	5.0
	1117	0.9		1020	1.2
	1750	5.5		1718	5.0
	2343	1.2		2224	1.4
13 M	0609	5.1	28 TU	0536	4.9
	1153	1.2		1048	1.4
	1847	5.1		1800	4.9
				2255	1.7
14 TU	0017	1.7	29 W	0618	4.7
	0704	4.8		1133	1.6
	1242	1.6		1850	4.7
	☾ 1951	4.7		2345	2.0
15 W	0113	2.1	30 TH	0710	4.5
	0809	4.5		1252	1.8
	1421	2.0		1950	4.6
	2101	4.4		☽	

MAY

Date	Time	m	Date	Time	m
1 F	0130	2.2	16 SA	0340	2.3
	0816	4.4		0954	4.4
	1435	1.8		1642	1.8
	2105	4.5		2246	4.4
2 SA	0327	2.2	17 SU	0441	2.2
	0938	4.5		1101	4.5
	1613	1.6		1734	1.7
	2223	4.7		2349	4.5
3 SU	0444	1.9	18 M	0529	1.9
	1053	4.7		1159	4.6
	1720	1.2		1814	1.5
	2332	5.0			
4 M	0540	1.5	19 TU	0036	4.7
	1154	5.1		0611	1.7
	1816	0.9		1245	4.8
				1847	1.3
5 TU	0028	5.3	20 W	0115	4.9
	0630	1.2		0651	1.4
	1246	5.4		1324	5.0
	1907	0.5		1919	1.2
6 W	0116	5.6	21 TH	0148	5.1
	0718	0.8		0729	1.2
	1333	5.7		1400	5.1
	1956	0.3		1951	1.1
7 TH	0200	5.7	22 F	0221	5.2
	0807	0.6		0806	1.1
	1418	5.9		1435	5.2
	O 2042	0.2		● 2023	1.0
8 F	0244	5.8	23 SA	0254	5.2
	0855	0.4		0841	1.0
	1505	6.0		1509	5.2
	2126	0.3		2055	1.0
9 SA	0328	5.8	24 SU	0328	5.2
	0941	0.4		0916	1.0
	1554	5.9		1545	5.2
	2208	0.5		2126	1.1
10 SU	0414	5.6	25 M	0402	5.2
	1025	0.6		0951	1.0
	1643	5.6		1622	5.2
	2247	0.9		2156	1.3
11 M	0500	5.4	26 TU	0438	5.1
	1106	0.9		1027	1.1
	1735	5.3		1703	5.1
	2321	1.3		2227	1.4
12 TU	0549	5.1	27 W	0517	5.0
	1145	1.2		1108	1.2
	1829	5.0		1747	5.0
	2354	1.8		2306	1.7
13 W	0643	4.8	28 TH	0602	4.9
	1230	1.5		1159	1.4
	1928	4.7		1838	4.9
14 TH	0043	2.1	29 F	0008	1.9
	0742	4.6		0653	4.8
	1348	1.8		1304	1.5
	☾ 2029	4.5		1936	4.8
15 F	0207	2.4	30 SA	0131	2.0
	0847	4.4		0756	4.7
	1534	1.9		1420	1.5
	2135	4.4		☽ 2044	4.7
			31 SU	0254	2.0
				0910	4.7
				1540	1.4
				2155	4.8

JUNE

Date	Time	m	Date	Time	m
1 M	0407	1.8	16 TU	0438	2.1
	1022	4.9		1059	4.5
	1647	1.2		1715	1.7
	2301	5.0		2337	4.5
2 TU	0506	1.6	17 W	0530	1.9
	1124	5.1		1154	4.6
	1745	0.9		1759	1.6
	2359	5.2			
3 W	0600	1.3	18 TH	0027	4.7
	1220	5.3		0615	1.6
	1839	0.8		1244	4.8
				1839	1.4
4 TH	0050	5.4	19 F	0111	4.9
	0652	1.0		0658	1.4
	1312	5.6		1328	4.9
	1930	0.6		1917	1.3
5 F	0138	5.5	20 SA	0151	5.1
	0746	0.8		0739	1.2
	1401	5.7		1409	5.1
	O 2019	0.6		1955	1.2
6 SA	0224	5.6	21 SU	0229	5.2
	0838	0.6		0819	1.1
	1451	5.7		1448	5.2
	2105	0.7		● 2034	1.2
7 SU	0310	5.6	22 M	0307	5.3
	0927	0.6		0901	1.0
	1540	5.6		1527	5.3
	2148	0.8		2114	1.1
8 M	0356	5.5	23 TU	0344	5.3
	1013	0.7		0944	0.9
	1630	5.5		1607	5.3
	2226	1.1		2155	1.2
9 TU	0443	5.3	24 W	0422	5.3
	1055	0.9		1028	0.9
	1719	5.3		1649	5.3
	2259	1.4		2239	1.3
10 W	0530	5.2	25 TH	0503	5.3
	1132	1.1		1115	0.9
	1808	5.0		1735	5.3
	2330	1.7		2325	1.4
11 TH	0619	4.9	26 F	0548	5.2
	1208	1.4		1203	1.0
	1858	4.8		1824	5.1
12 F	0010	1.9	27 SA	0014	1.6
	0710	4.7		0638	5.1
	1254	1.6		1256	1.1
	1950	4.6		1918	5.0
13 SA	0106	2.2	28 SU	0112	1.7
	0805	4.6		0735	5.0
	1401	1.8		1356	1.2
	☾ 2045	4.4		☽ 2020	4.9
14 SU	0222	2.3	29 M	0217	1.8
	0902	4.5		0843	4.9
	1523	1.9		1504	1.3
	2142	4.4		2127	4.9
15 M	0338	2.2	30 TU	0328	1.8
	1000	4.4		0953	4.9
	1625	1.8		1613	1.3
	2240	4.4		2232	4.9

SUNRISE AND SUNSET TIMES

Leith
At 55°59′N 3°11′W

UT		Sunrise	Sunset
Jan	01	0844	1549
	15	0834	1611
Feb	01	0807	1646
	15	0738	1717
Mar	01	0704	1747
	15	0628	1816
BST			
Apr	01	0643	1951
	15	0607	2020
May	01	0529	2052
	15	0500	2119
Jun	01	0435	2147
	15	0426	2201
Jul	01	0431	2201
	15	0448	2149
Aug	01	0517	2120
	15	0544	2049
Sep	01	0617	2007
	15	0644	1930
Oct	01	0716	1848
	15	0744	1812
UT			
Nov	01	0720	1632
	15	0749	1605
Dec	01	0820	1544
	15	0838	1538

LEITH
LAT 55°59′N
LONG 3°11′W

TIMES AND HEIGHTS OF HIGH AND LOW WATER (Heights in Metres)

TIME ZONE UT
For Summer Time (area enclosed in shaded box) add 1 hour

2020

JULY

Date	Day	Time	m
1	W	0435 1059 1717 2333	1.7 5.0 1.2 5.0
2	TH	0536 1201 1817	1.5 5.2 1.1
3	F	0029 0636 1259 1911	5.2 1.2 5.3 1.1
4	SA	0122 0734 1352 2001	5.3 1.0 5.4 1.0
5	SU O	0211 0828 1442 2047	5.4 0.8 5.5 1.0
6	M	0257 0917 1529 2129	5.5 0.7 5.5 1.1
7	TU	0342 1001 1615 2205	5.4 0.7 5.4 1.2
8	W	0426 1039 1659 2235	5.4 0.9 5.3 1.3
9	TH	0508 1111 1741 2302	5.3 1.0 5.1 1.5
10	F	0549 1137 1823 2335	5.1 1.2 4.9 1.7
11	SA	0632 1209 1907	4.9 1.4 4.7
12	SU ☾	0017 0717 1252 1953	1.9 4.7 1.6 4.5
13	M	0111 0807 1346 2044	2.1 4.6 1.8 4.4
14	TU	0220 0902 1455 2139	2.2 4.5 2.0 4.4
15	W	0339 1001 1613 2238	2.2 4.4 2.0 4.4
16	TH	0447 1103 1716 2338	2.1 4.5 1.9 4.6
17	F	0543 1204 1807	1.9 4.6 1.7
18	SA	0035 0632 1259 1852	4.8 1.6 4.8 1.6
19	SU	0124 0717 1347 1935	5.0 1.4 5.1 1.4
20	M ●	0208 0802 1429 2018	5.2 1.1 5.3 1.2
21	TU	0248 0848 1510 2103	5.4 0.8 5.4 1.1
22	W	0327 0935 1551 2148	5.5 0.6 5.6 1.0
23	TH	0406 1021 1634 2232	5.6 0.5 5.6 1.0
24	F	0448 1107 1718 2316	5.6 0.5 5.5 1.1
25	SA	0532 1152 1806 2358	5.5 0.6 5.4 1.3
26	SU	0620 1237 1856	5.4 0.8 5.2
27	M ☽	0043 0713 1326 1953	1.5 5.2 1.1 5.0
28	TU	0139 0816 1426 2057	1.7 5.0 1.4 4.8
29	W	0250 0929 1542 2205	1.8 4.9 1.6 4.8
30	TH	0411 1041 1658 2312	1.8 4.9 1.6 4.8
31	F	0527 1151 1805	1.7 4.9 1.6

AUGUST

Date	Day	Time	m
1	SA	0017 0635 1255 1902	5.0 1.4 5.1 1.5
2	SU	0114 0735 1349 1949	5.1 1.1 5.2 1.3
3	M O	0203 0824 1435 2031	5.3 0.9 5.4 1.2
4	TU	0247 0907 1517 2108	5.4 0.8 5.4 1.1
5	W	0327 0944 1556 2140	5.5 0.7 5.4 1.1
6	TH	0405 1016 1633 2208	5.4 0.8 5.3 1.2
7	F	0441 1041 1709 2234	5.4 0.9 5.1 1.3
8	SA	0516 1103 1745 2302	5.2 1.1 5.0 1.4
9	SU	0552 1129 1823 2334	5.1 1.3 4.8 1.6
10	M	0631 1201 1905	4.9 1.5 4.6
11	TU ☾	0012 0715 1243 1951	1.9 4.7 1.8 4.5
12	W	0107 0807 1339 2047	2.1 4.5 2.0 4.4
13	TH	0227 0909 1500 2149	2.3 4.3 2.2 4.3
14	F	0402 1018 1637 2256	2.3 4.3 2.2 4.4
15	SA	0516 1128 1743	2.1 4.5 2.0
16	SU	0002 0612 1233 1834	4.7 1.7 4.8 1.7
17	M	0100 0701 1326 1919	5.0 1.4 5.1 1.4
18	TU	0146 0748 1410 2004	5.2 1.0 5.4 1.1
19	W ●	0227 0835 1451 2048	5.5 0.6 5.6 0.9
20	TH	0306 0921 1532 2132	5.7 0.3 5.8 0.7
21	F	0346 1006 1614 2216	5.9 0.2 5.8 0.7
22	SA	0427 1050 1657 2257	5.9 0.2 5.8 0.8
23	SU	0511 1131 1742 2335	5.8 0.4 5.6 1.0
24	M	0558 1212 1831	5.6 0.8 5.3
25	TU ☽	0013 0650 1255 1925	1.3 5.4 1.2 5.0
26	W	0103 0754 1350 2029	1.6 5.0 1.6 4.7
27	TH	0221 0911 1517 2142	1.9 4.8 2.0 4.6
28	F	0405 1029 1651 2257	2.0 4.7 2.0 4.6
29	SA	0535 1148 1803	1.8 4.8 1.9
30	SU	0010 0643 1254 1856	4.8 1.5 5.0 1.7
31	M	0109 0734 1344 1937	5.1 1.2 5.2 1.5

SEPTEMBER

Date	Day	Time	m
1	TU	0154 0815 1424 2011	5.3 1.0 5.3 1.3
2	W O	0232 0849 1500 2042	5.4 0.8 5.4 1.1
3	TH	0307 0919 1533 2112	5.5 0.8 5.4 1.1
4	F	0339 0945 1604 2140	5.5 0.8 5.3 1.1
5	SA	0411 1007 1636 2206	5.4 0.9 5.2 1.1
6	SU	0443 1028 1709 2230	5.3 1.0 5.1 1.3
7	M	0517 1049 1744 2253	5.2 1.2 5.0 1.5
8	TU	0553 1113 1822 2320	5.0 1.5 4.8 1.7
9	W	0633 1143 1905 2358	4.8 1.7 4.6 2.0
10	TH ☾	0722 1227 1957	4.5 2.1 4.4
11	F	0112 0823 1353 2103	2.3 4.4 2.4 4.3
12	SA	0311 0938 1602 2218	2.4 4.3 2.4 4.4
13	SU	0452 1055 1724 2331	2.1 4.5 2.2 4.6
14	M	0555 1206 1816	1.7 4.8 1.8
15	TU	0032 0644 1302 1901	5.0 1.3 5.2 1.4
16	W	0120 0731 1347 1944	5.3 0.8 5.5 1.1
17	TH ●	0202 0816 1428 2027	5.7 0.4 5.8 0.8
18	F	0241 0901 1508 2111	5.9 0.1 6.0 0.6
19	SA	0321 0945 1549 2153	6.1 0.0 6.0 0.5
20	SU	0404 1027 1633 2234	6.1 0.1 5.9 0.7
21	M	0449 1107 1717 2312	6.0 0.4 5.6 0.9
22	TU	0538 1145 1805 2349	5.7 0.9 5.3 1.3
23	W	0632 1224 1859	5.3 1.4 5.0
24	TH ☽	0039 0738 1320 2005	1.6 4.9 2.0 4.7
25	F	0208 0856 1501 2122	2.0 4.7 2.3 4.5
26	SA	0410 1017 1643 2241	2.0 4.6 2.3 4.6
27	SU	0537 1140 1752 2356	1.7 4.7 2.1 4.8
28	M	0636 1243 1839	1.4 5.0 1.8
29	TU	0052 0719 1328 1914	5.1 1.2 5.2 1.6
30	W	0135 0753 1404 1943	5.3 1.0 5.3 1.3

OCTOBER

Date	Day	Time	m
1	TH O	0210 0821 1436 2013	5.4 0.9 5.4 1.2
2	F	0242 0846 1505 2043	5.4 0.8 5.4 1.0
3	SA	0312 0910 1534 2113	5.5 0.8 5.4 1.0
4	SU	0342 0933 1604 2140	5.4 0.9 5.3 1.1
5	M	0413 0954 1635 2202	5.3 1.0 5.2 1.2
6	TU	0447 1011 1709 2221	5.2 1.2 5.1 1.4
7	W	0523 1031 1745 2245	5.0 1.5 4.9 1.6
8	TH	0603 1057 1826 2322	4.8 1.8 4.7 1.9
9	F	0650 1136 1916	4.6 2.1 4.5
10	SA ☾	0025 0749 1253 2021	2.2 4.4 2.5 4.4
11	SU	0228 0904 1526 2141	2.3 4.4 2.5 4.4
12	M	0423 1024 1656 2258	2.1 4.5 2.2 4.6
13	TU	0529 1136 1750	1.6 4.9 1.8
14	W	0000 0620 1233 1834	5.0 1.2 5.3 1.4
15	TH	0050 0706 1319 1917	5.4 0.7 5.6 1.0
16	F ●	0133 0751 1401 2001	5.8 0.4 5.9 0.7
17	SA	0215 0836 1442 2046	6.0 0.2 6.0 0.5
18	SU	0257 0920 1524 2131	6.2 0.1 6.0 0.5
19	M	0343 1003 1608 2214	6.2 0.3 5.9 0.6
20	TU	0430 1044 1654 2255	6.0 0.7 5.6 0.9
21	W	0521 1121 1742 2337	5.7 1.2 5.3 1.3
22	TH	0618 1159 1837	5.3 1.7 5.0
23	F ☽	0029 0723 1255 1944	1.6 4.9 2.2 4.7
24	SA	0202 0837 1436 2059	2.0 4.6 2.5 4.5
25	SU	0357 0954 1613 2215	2.0 4.5 2.4 4.6
26	M	0513 1113 1718 2327	1.8 4.7 2.2 4.7
27	TU	0608 1215 1804	1.5 4.9 2.0
28	W	0022 0648 1300 1838	5.0 1.4 5.1 1.7
29	TH	0106 0719 1336 1910	5.1 1.2 5.2 1.5
30	F	0141 0745 1407 1942	5.3 1.1 5.3 1.3
31	SA O	0214 0810 1436 2015	5.3 1.0 5.4 1.1

NOVEMBER

Date	Day	Time	m
1	SU	0244 0835 1504 2047	5.4 1.0 5.4 1.1
2	M	0316 0901 1535 2117	5.4 1.0 5.4 1.1
3	TU	0349 0925 1607 2143	5.3 1.2 5.3 1.2
4	W	0423 0945 1640 2206	5.2 1.3 5.2 1.4
5	TH	0500 1006 1716 2233	5.1 1.6 5.0 1.6
6	F	0542 1034 1757 2314	4.9 1.8 4.8 1.8
7	SA	0629 1115 1846	4.7 2.1 4.6
8	SU ☾	0023 0726 1236 1947	2.0 4.6 2.4 4.5
9	M	0200 0835 1447 2105	2.1 4.5 2.5 4.5
10	TU	0342 0952 1615 2222	1.9 4.7 2.2 4.7
11	W	0453 1102 1714 2325	1.5 4.9 1.9 5.1
12	TH	0548 1200 1802	1.1 5.3 1.5
13	F	0018 0636 1250 1848	5.4 0.8 5.6 1.1
14	SA	0106 0724 1334 1935	5.7 0.5 5.8 0.8
15	SU ●	0151 0811 1418 2024	6.0 0.4 5.9 0.6
16	M	0238 0857 1502 2113	6.1 0.4 5.9 0.6
17	TU	0326 0941 1547 2200	6.0 0.6 5.8 0.7
18	W	0416 1024 1634 2246	5.8 1.0 5.6 0.9
19	TH	0508 1102 1723 2331	5.6 1.4 5.3 1.2
20	F	0604 1139 1818	5.2 1.8 5.1
21	SA	0021 0704 1227 1920	1.5 4.9 2.2 4.8
22	SU ☽	0136 0809 1344 2027	1.8 4.6 2.5 4.6
23	M	0312 0916 1516 2135	1.9 4.5 2.5 4.6
24	TU	0425 1025 1622 2241	1.9 4.5 2.4 4.6
25	W	0521 1129 1713 2339	1.8 4.7 2.2 4.8
26	TH	0603 1220 1756	1.6 4.8 1.9
27	F	0028 0636 1300 1835	4.9 1.5 5.0 1.7
28	SA	0109 0705 1335 1913	5.0 1.4 5.1 1.4
29	SU	0145 0734 1407 1949	5.2 1.3 5.3 1.3
30	M O	0219 0805 1439 2024	5.2 1.2 5.3 1.2

DECEMBER

Date	Day	Time	m
1	TU	0254 0835 1511 2059	5.3 1.2 5.3 1.2
2	W	0329 0905 1545 2132	5.3 1.3 5.3 1.2
3	TH	0405 0935 1619 2207	5.2 1.4 5.2 1.3
4	F	0444 1004 1656 2245	5.2 1.6 5.1 1.4
5	SA	0526 1038 1737 2330	5.1 1.8 5.0 1.5
6	SU	0613 1122 1825	4.9 2.0 4.9
7	M	0026 0706 1234 1920	1.6 4.8 2.2 4.8
8	TU ☾	0136 0808 1404 2029	1.7 4.7 2.3 4.7
9	W	0256 0919 1527 2143	1.7 4.8 2.1 4.8
10	TH	0410 1027 1633 2250	1.5 4.9 1.9 5.1
11	F	0512 1128 1729 2349	1.2 5.2 1.6 5.3
12	SA	0607 1222 1823	1.0 5.4 1.3
13	SU	0043 0700 1311 1916	5.5 0.9 5.6 1.0
14	M ●	0135 0750 1358 2010	5.7 0.8 5.7 0.8
15	TU	0225 0839 1445 2103	5.8 0.8 5.7 0.7
16	W	0315 0925 1532 2152	5.8 0.9 5.7 0.7
17	TH	0405 1008 1619 2238	5.7 1.1 5.6 0.9
18	F	0455 1046 1707 2322	5.5 1.4 5.4 1.1
19	SA	0546 1118 1757	5.2 1.7 5.2
20	SU	0002 0637 1153 1849	1.3 5.0 2.0 5.0
21	M ☽	0044 0731 1240 1945	1.6 4.7 2.2 4.8
22	TU	0140 0826 1347 2043	1.9 4.5 2.4 4.6
23	W	0256 0924 1507 2142	2.0 4.4 2.4 4.5
24	TH	0406 1023 1616 2242	2.0 4.4 2.3 4.5
25	F	0501 1122 1713 2339	2.0 4.5 2.1 4.6
26	SA	0548 1215 1802	1.8 4.7 1.9
27	SU	0031 0628 1300 1846	4.8 1.7 4.9 1.7
28	M	0117 0705 1340 1927	4.9 1.6 5.1 1.5
29	TU	0158 0741 1417 2006	5.1 1.5 5.2 1.3
30	W O	0236 0817 1453 2044	5.2 1.4 5.3 1.2
31	TH	0313 0854 1529 2124	5.3 1.3 5.3 1.1

ABERDEEN
LAT 57°09'N
LONG 2°05'W

TIMES AND HEIGHTS OF HIGH AND LOW WATER (Heights in Metres)

TIME ZONE UT
For Summer Time (area enclosed in shaded box) add 1 hour

2020

JANUARY

Date	Day	Time	m	Time	m	Time	m	Time	m
1	W	0521	3.6	1051	1.7	1716	3.8	2332	1.4
2	TH	0610	3.5	1139	1.8	1806	3.7		
3	F ☽	0024	1.6	0702	3.4	1239	2.0	1903	3.6
4	SA	0125	1.7	0801	3.4	1349	2.0	2004	3.5
5	SU	0229	1.7	0905	3.4	1459	2.0	2110	3.5
6	M	0333	1.6	1007	3.5	1605	1.8	2215	3.6
7	TU	0430	1.5	1059	3.7	1658	1.6	2310	3.7
8	W	0517	1.4	1143	3.9	1744	1.4	2357	3.9
9	TH	0600	1.3	1223	4.1	1826	1.2		
10	F ○	0041	4.1	0641	1.1	1302	4.2	1908	0.9
11	SA	0125	4.2	0723	1.0	1341	4.3	1951	0.8
12	SU	0209	4.3	0805	1.0	1421	4.4	2036	0.6
13	M	0254	4.3	0848	1.0	1503	4.4	2121	0.6
14	TU	0340	4.3	0931	1.0	1547	4.4	2209	0.6
15	W	0430	4.2	1017	1.2	1636	4.3	2300	0.7
16	TH	0523	4.0	1108	1.3	1730	4.2	2355	0.9
17	F ☾	0621	3.8	1206	1.5	1831	4.0		
18	SA	0056	1.1	0723	3.7	1314	1.6	1938	3.9
19	SU	0202	1.3	0830	3.6	1428	1.7	2052	3.8
20	M	0315	1.4	0941	3.7	1549	1.6	2209	3.8
21	TU	0426	1.4	1046	3.8	1658	1.4	2315	3.9
22	W	0524	1.3	1140	3.9	1753	1.2		
23	TH	0010	4.0	0611	1.3	1226	4.1	1839	1.1
24	F ●	0058	4.0	0652	1.2	1307	4.2	1921	0.9
25	SA	0140	4.1	0730	1.2	1344	4.2	1959	0.9
26	SU	0219	4.1	0805	1.1	1420	4.3	2034	0.8
27	M	0255	4.0	0838	1.1	1453	4.2	2108	0.9
28	TU	0330	4.0	0910	1.2	1527	4.2	2140	0.9
29	W	0404	3.9	0942	1.3	1601	4.1	2213	1.1
30	TH	0440	3.7	1016	1.4	1637	4.0	2249	1.2
31	F	0520	3.6	1053	1.5	1718	3.8	2329	1.4

FEBRUARY

Date	Day	Time	m	Time	m	Time	m	Time	m
1	SA	0605	3.5	1137	1.7	1807	3.6		
2	SU ☽	0017	1.6	0657	3.4	1235	1.9	1905	3.5
3	M	0118	1.7	0758	3.3	1349	1.9	2012	3.4
4	TU	0229	1.8	0907	3.4	1509	1.9	2126	3.4
5	W	0344	1.7	1017	3.5	1623	1.7	2239	3.6
6	TH	0450	1.6	1114	3.7	1720	1.4	2337	3.8
7	F	0541	1.3	1201	3.9	1809	1.1		
8	SA	0026	4.0	0626	1.1	1244	4.2	1853	0.8
9	SU ○	0112	4.2	0710	0.9	1325	4.4	1938	0.5
10	M	0156	4.4	0752	0.8	1406	4.5	2022	0.3
11	TU	0240	4.4	0834	0.7	1448	4.6	2107	0.3
12	W	0324	4.4	0916	0.8	1531	4.6	2152	0.3
13	TH	0409	4.3	0958	0.9	1617	4.5	2238	0.5
14	F	0457	4.1	1044	1.0	1708	4.3	2327	0.8
15	SA ☾	0550	3.9	1136	1.3	1806	4.0		
16	SU	0023	1.1	0648	3.6	1240	1.5	1913	3.8
17	M	0128	1.4	0756	3.5	1357	1.6	2032	3.6
18	TU	0248	1.6	0913	3.5	1534	1.6	2159	3.6
19	W	0413	1.6	1029	3.6	1651	1.5	2312	3.7
20	TH	0514	1.5	1129	3.7	1746	1.2		
21	F	0007	3.8	0600	1.4	1216	3.9	1830	1.0
22	SA	0051	3.9	0639	1.3	1255	4.0	1907	0.9
23	SU ●	0127	4.0	0714	1.1	1329	4.1	1941	0.8
24	M	0200	4.0	0746	1.0	1401	4.2	2013	0.7
25	TU	0231	4.0	0816	1.0	1431	4.2	2042	0.7
26	W	0301	4.0	0845	1.0	1501	4.2	2111	0.8
27	TH	0331	3.9	0914	1.0	1532	4.1	2140	0.9
28	F	0402	3.8	0945	1.1	1605	4.0	2211	1.1
29	SA	0436	3.7	1017	1.3	1642	3.9	2245	1.2

MARCH

Date	Day	Time	m	Time	m	Time	m	Time	m
1	SU	0514	3.6	1055	1.4	1724	3.7	2325	1.4
2	M ☽	0601	3.4	1143	1.6	1818	3.5		
3	TU	0018	1.7	0702	3.3	1252	1.8	1928	3.3
4	W	0134	1.8	0814	3.3	1421	1.8	2048	3.3
5	TH	0305	1.8	0933	3.3	1551	1.6	2212	3.5
6	F	0426	1.6	1044	3.6	1658	1.3	2318	3.7
7	SA	0523	1.4	1137	3.8	1749	0.9		
8	SU	0009	4.0	0610	1.1	1223	4.1	1835	0.6
9	M ○	0055	4.3	0653	0.8	1305	4.4	1919	0.3
10	TU	0137	4.4	0734	0.6	1346	4.6	2003	0.1
11	W	0219	4.5	0815	0.5	1428	4.7	2046	0.1
12	TH	0301	4.5	0856	0.5	1511	4.7	2129	0.2
13	F	0344	4.3	0937	0.6	1557	4.5	2212	0.5
14	SA	0429	4.1	1021	0.8	1647	4.3	2259	0.8
15	SU	0519	3.9	1111	1.1	1746	4.0	2352	1.2
16	M ☾	0616	3.6	1214	1.4	1855	3.6		
17	TU	0057	1.6	0723	3.4	1335	1.6	2016	3.4
18	W	0223	1.8	0844	3.3	1521	1.6	2149	3.4
19	TH	0358	1.8	1007	3.4	1639	1.4	2302	3.5
20	F	0459	1.6	1110	3.6	1730	1.2	2353	3.7
21	SA	0543	1.4	1156	3.8	1811	1.0		
22	SU	0032	3.8	0619	1.3	1234	3.9	1845	0.9
23	M	0106	3.9	0652	1.1	1306	4.0	1916	0.8
24	TU ●	0135	4.0	0723	1.0	1336	4.1	1945	0.7
25	W	0204	4.0	0752	0.9	1406	4.2	2013	0.7
26	TH	0231	4.0	0820	0.9	1435	4.2	2041	0.7
27	F	0300	4.0	0848	0.9	1506	4.1	2108	0.8
28	SA	0329	3.9	0918	1.0	1539	4.0	2137	1.0
29	SU	0401	3.8	0949	1.1	1615	3.8	2209	1.2
30	M	0436	3.7	1026	1.3	1656	3.7	2247	1.4
31	TU	0519	3.5	1112	1.4	1750	3.5	2338	1.6

APRIL

Date	Day	Time	m	Time	m	Time	m	Time	m
1	W ☽	0618	3.3	1219	1.6	1902	3.3		
2	TH	0057	1.8	0734	3.3	1350	1.6	2023	3.3
3	F	0236	1.8	0855	3.3	1522	1.5	2147	3.5
4	SA	0402	1.6	1011	3.5	1633	1.1	2256	3.7
5	SU	0501	1.3	1110	3.8	1726	0.8	2347	4.0
6	M	0548	1.0	1157	4.1	1813	0.4		
7	TU	0032	4.3	0631	0.7	1241	4.4	1857	0.2
8	W ○	0114	4.4	0712	0.5	1324	4.6	1940	0.1
9	TH	0155	4.5	0753	0.4	1407	4.7	2022	0.1
10	F	0236	4.4	0835	0.4	1451	4.6	2104	0.3
11	SA	0318	4.3	0917	0.5	1539	4.4	2147	0.6
12	SU	0402	4.1	1002	0.7	1631	4.1	2233	1.0
13	M	0451	3.9	1053	1.0	1731	3.8	2324	1.4
14	TU ☾	0547	3.6	1155	1.3	1839	3.5		
15	W	0028	1.7	0653	3.4	1314	1.5	1956	3.3
16	TH	0152	1.9	0809	3.3	1454	1.5	2124	3.3
17	F	0328	1.9	0933	3.4	1611	1.4	2236	3.4
18	SA	0431	1.7	1038	3.5	1702	1.2	2325	3.6
19	SU	0515	1.5	1126	3.7	1741	1.1		
20	M	0003	3.7	0551	1.3	1204	3.8	1814	0.9
21	TU	0036	3.8	0624	1.1	1237	3.9	1845	0.8
22	W	0105	3.9	0655	1.0	1308	4.0	1914	0.8
23	TH ●	0134	4.0	0726	0.9	1339	4.1	1943	0.7
24	F	0202	4.0	0755	0.8	1410	4.1	2011	0.8
25	SA	0231	4.0	0825	0.9	1443	4.0	2040	0.9
26	SU	0301	4.0	0857	0.9	1517	3.9	2111	1.0
27	M	0334	3.9	0931	1.0	1555	3.8	2145	1.2
28	TU	0410	3.7	1010	1.1	1640	3.7	2225	1.4
29	W	0454	3.6	1100	1.3	1736	3.5	2320	1.6
30	TH ☽	0552	3.5	1207	1.4	1847	3.4		

MAY

Date	Day	Time	m	Time	m	Time	m	Time	m
1	F	0038	1.8	0707	3.4	1330	1.4	2003	3.4
2	SA	0210	1.8	0823	3.4	1453	1.2	2121	3.5
3	SU	0330	1.6	0937	3.6	1603	1.0	2228	3.8
4	M	0432	1.3	1039	3.9	1659	0.7	2321	4.0
5	TU	0522	1.0	1130	4.1	1748	0.4		
6	W	0007	4.2	0607	0.8	1217	4.4	1833	0.3
7	TH ○	0049	4.3	0650	0.6	1302	4.5	1917	0.2
8	F	0131	4.4	0734	0.5	1348	4.5	2000	0.3
9	SA	0212	4.4	0817	0.5	1435	4.5	2042	0.5
10	SU	0255	4.3	0902	0.5	1525	4.3	2125	0.8
11	M	0339	4.1	0948	0.7	1618	4.0	2210	1.1
12	TU	0427	3.9	1039	0.9	1716	3.8	2300	1.5
13	W	0521	3.7	1137	1.2	1818	3.5	2358	1.7
14	TH ☾	0623	3.5	1245	1.4	1925	3.3		
15	F	0109	1.9	0729	3.4	1404	1.4	2038	3.3
16	SA	0231	1.9	0841	3.3	1523	1.4	2149	3.4
17	SU	0344	1.8	0950	3.4	1619	1.3	2243	3.5
18	M	0435	1.6	1044	3.5	1702	1.2	2324	3.6
19	TU	0516	1.4	1126	3.7	1738	1.1	2359	3.8
20	W	0553	1.2	1204	3.8	1811	1.0		
21	TH	0032	3.9	0626	1.1	1239	3.9	1843	0.9
22	F ●	0104	4.0	0659	1.0	1314	4.0	1914	0.9
23	SA	0135	4.0	0732	0.9	1348	4.0	1946	0.9
24	SU	0206	4.0	0806	0.9	1424	4.0	2019	1.0
25	M	0239	4.0	0842	0.9	1502	3.9	2054	1.1
26	TU	0314	3.9	0921	0.9	1543	3.9	2132	1.2
27	W	0354	3.9	1004	1.0	1631	3.8	2217	1.4
28	TH	0440	3.8	1056	1.1	1728	3.6	2312	1.5
29	F	0537	3.6	1159	1.1	1833	3.6		
30	SA ☽	0022	1.6	0644	3.6	1311	1.1	1941	3.5
31	SU	0140	1.6	0754	3.6	1423	1.1	2051	3.6

JUNE

Date	Day	Time	m	Time	m	Time	m	Time	m
1	M	0254	1.5	0903	3.7	1531	0.9	2157	3.8
2	TU	0359	1.3	1008	3.9	1631	0.8	2253	3.9
3	W	0455	1.1	1106	4.1	1724	0.6	2342	4.1
4	TH	0546	0.9	1157	4.2	1812	0.6		
5	F ○	0027	4.2	0633	0.7	1247	4.3	1857	0.6
6	SA	0111	4.3	0719	0.6	1335	4.3	1941	0.6
7	SU	0153	4.3	0805	0.6	1424	4.3	2024	0.8
8	M	0236	4.2	0850	0.6	1514	4.1	2107	1.0
9	TU	0320	4.1	0936	0.7	1605	4.0	2149	1.2
10	W	0406	4.0	1023	0.9	1657	3.8	2234	1.4
11	TH	0455	3.8	1113	1.1	1749	3.6	2323	1.6
12	F	0547	3.7	1207	1.2	1844	3.4		
13	SA ☾	0020	1.8	0643	3.5	1306	1.4	1941	3.3
14	SU	0126	1.9	0742	3.4	1410	1.4	2044	3.3
15	M	0234	1.8	0846	3.4	1515	1.4	2146	3.4
16	TU	0341	1.7	0949	3.4	1611	1.4	2237	3.5
17	W	0434	1.6	1044	3.5	1657	1.3	2321	3.6
18	TH	0519	1.4	1130	3.7	1736	1.2	2359	3.8
19	F	0558	1.2	1211	3.8	1813	1.1		
20	SA	0035	3.9	0635	1.1	1251	3.9	1849	1.0
21	SU ●	0111	4.0	0713	1.0	1330	4.0	1925	1.0
22	M	0146	4.1	0751	0.8	1409	4.0	2003	1.0
23	TU	0222	4.1	0831	0.8	1451	4.0	2043	1.0
24	W	0300	4.1	0914	0.8	1535	4.0	2124	1.1
25	TH	0342	4.1	0959	0.8	1623	3.9	2209	1.2
26	F	0428	4.0	1049	0.8	1716	3.8	2301	1.3
27	SA	0521	3.9	1145	0.9	1814	3.7		
28	SU ☽	0000	1.4	0621	3.8	1248	0.9	1915	3.7
29	M	0108	1.5	0726	3.8	1352	1.0	2020	3.7
30	TU	0217	1.5	0833	3.8	1459	1.0	2126	3.7

SUNRISE AND SUNSET TIMES

ABERDEEN
At 57°09'N 2°05'W

UT		Sunrise	Sunset
Jan	01	0847	1537
	15	0836	1600
Feb	01	0808	1637
	15	0737	1709
Mar	01	0701	1741
	15	0624	1812
BST			
Apr	01	0637	1948
	15	0600	2020
May	01	0520	2053
	15	0449	2122
Jun	01	0422	2151
	15	0412	2206
Jul	01	0418	2206
	15	0435	2152
Aug	01	0506	2121
	15	0535	2049
Sep	01	0610	2005
	15	0639	1927
Oct	01	0712	1843
	15	0742	1805
UT			
Nov	01	0719	1623
	15	0751	1555
Dec	01	0822	1532
	15	0842	1525

ABERDEEN
LAT 57°09′N
LONG 2°05′W

TIMES AND HEIGHTS OF HIGH AND LOW WATER (Heights in Metres)

TIME ZONE UT
For Summer Time (area enclosed in shaded box) add 1 hour

2020

JULY

Date	Time	m
1 W	0327 0943 1605 2228	1.4 3.8 1.0 3.8
2 TH	0434 1048 1705 2323	1.3 3.9 0.9 3.9
3 F	0532 1146 1757	1.1 4.0 0.9
4 SA	0011 0623 1240 1844	4.1 0.9 4.1 0.9
5 SU O	0057 0711 1329 1928	4.2 0.7 4.2 0.9
6 M	0140 0756 1417 2009	4.2 0.7 4.1 1.0
7 TU	0221 0839 1502 2048	4.2 0.7 4.1 1.1
8 W	0302 0920 1546 2127	4.2 0.7 3.9 1.2
9 TH	0343 1000 1629 2205	4.1 0.8 3.8 1.3
10 F	0424 1041 1712 2245	4.0 1.0 3.7 1.4
11 SA	0507 1123 1757 2329	3.8 1.1 3.5 1.6
12 SU ☾	0554 1210 1846	3.7 1.3 3.4
13 M	0022 0645 1303 1939	1.7 3.5 1.5 3.3
14 TU	0125 0743 1403 2039	1.8 3.4 1.6 3.3
15 W	0234 0848 1508 2143	1.8 3.4 1.6 3.4
16 TH	0344 0956 1611 2240	1.8 3.4 1.5 3.5
17 F	0444 1056 1703 2328	1.6 3.5 1.4 3.7
18 SA	0532 1146 1748	1.4 3.7 1.3
19 SU	0010 0614 1231 1828	3.8 1.2 3.8 1.2
20 M ●	0049 0655 1314 1909	4.0 0.9 4.0 1.0
21 TU	0127 0737 1356 1950	4.1 0.7 4.1 1.0
22 W	0206 0819 1438 2031	4.2 0.6 4.2 0.9
23 TH	0246 0902 1522 2112	4.3 0.5 4.2 0.9
24 F	0327 0947 1607 2155	4.3 0.5 4.1 1.0
25 SA	0412 1034 1656 2241	4.3 0.6 4.0 1.1
26 SU	0501 1124 1749 2334	4.2 0.7 3.9 1.3
27 M ☽	0557 1220 1846	4.1 0.9 3.7
28 TU	0035 0659 1322 1949	1.4 3.9 1.1 3.6
29 W	0145 0810 1431 2058	1.5 3.8 1.2 3.6
30 TH	0304 0927 1547 2208	1.5 3.7 1.3 3.7
31 F	0424 1042 1655 2310	1.4 3.8 1.3 3.8

AUGUST

Date	Time	m
1 SA	0527 1145 1749	1.2 3.9 1.2
2 SU	0002 0618 1239 1834	4.0 1.0 4.0 1.2
3 M O	0047 0704 1324 1915	4.1 0.8 4.1 1.1
4 TU	0128 0745 1405 1952	4.2 0.7 4.1 1.1
5 W	0205 0823 1443 2027	4.2 0.7 4.1 1.1
6 TH	0241 0858 1519 2101	4.2 0.7 4.0 1.1
7 F	0316 0931 1555 2133	4.2 0.8 3.9 1.2
8 SA	0351 1004 1630 2207	4.1 0.9 3.8 1.3
9 SU	0427 1038 1708 2243	4.0 1.1 3.6 1.4
10 M	0507 1116 1750 2325	3.8 1.3 3.5 1.6
11 TU ☾	0554 1201 1840	3.6 1.5 3.4
12 W	0019 0649 1258 1938	1.8 3.5 1.7 3.3
13 TH	0130 0755 1407 2045	1.9 3.4 1.8 3.3
14 F	0251 0909 1524 2156	1.9 3.3 1.8 3.4
15 SA	0410 1024 1634 2257	1.7 3.4 1.6 3.6
16 SU	0508 1124 1726 2345	1.5 3.6 1.5 3.8
17 M	0554 1213 1810	1.2 3.9 1.2
18 TU	0027 0637 1256 1852	4.1 0.8 4.1 1.0
19 W ●	0107 0719 1338 1933	4.3 0.6 4.3 0.9
20 TH	0146 0801 1420 2013	4.4 0.4 4.4 0.8
21 F	0226 0844 1501 2053	4.6 0.2 4.4 0.7
22 SA	0307 0927 1545 2134	4.6 0.3 4.3 0.8
23 SU	0351 1011 1630 2218	4.5 0.4 4.2 1.0
24 M	0439 1058 1720 2307	4.4 0.7 4.0 1.2
25 TU ☽	0534 1151 1816	4.1 1.0 3.8
26 W	0007 0638 1253 1920	1.4 3.9 1.3 3.6
27 TH	0121 0754 1408 2034	1.6 3.7 1.6 3.5
28 F	0253 0922 1538 2154	1.6 3.6 1.6 3.6
29 SA	0422 1044 1648 2301	1.4 3.7 1.6 3.8
30 SU	0523 1145 1740 2353	1.2 3.8 1.4 4.0
31 M	0611 1232 1822	1.0 4.0 1.3

SEPTEMBER

Date	Time	m
1 TU	0035 0651 1311 1858	4.1 0.8 4.0 1.2
2 W O	0111 0726 1346 1931	4.2 0.7 4.1 1.1
3 TH	0144 0759 1418 2003	4.3 0.7 4.1 1.0
4 F	0216 0829 1448 2033	4.3 0.7 4.1 1.0
5 SA	0247 0858 1518 2102	4.3 0.8 4.0 1.1
6 SU	0318 0927 1549 2132	4.2 0.9 3.9 1.2
7 M	0351 0957 1622 2204	4.1 1.1 3.8 1.3
8 TU	0428 1029 1700 2242	3.9 1.3 3.7 1.5
9 W	0510 1108 1745 2329	3.7 1.5 3.5 1.7
10 TH ☾	0604 1158 1844	3.5 1.7 3.4
11 F	0035 0713 1311 1954	1.9 3.4 1.9 3.3
12 SA	0205 0831 1444 2112	1.9 3.3 2.0 3.4
13 SU	0336 0955 1608 2224	1.7 3.4 1.8 3.6
14 M	0442 1102 1705 2318	1.4 3.7 1.5 3.8
15 TU	0531 1151 1750	1.1 4.0 1.2
16 W	0002 0614 1235 1831	4.1 0.7 4.2 1.0
17 TH ●	0043 0657 1315 1911	4.4 0.4 4.4 0.8
18 F	0122 0738 1356 1951	4.6 0.2 4.6 0.6
19 SA	0203 0820 1436 2031	4.8 0.1 4.6 0.6
20 SU	0245 0902 1518 2112	4.8 0.2 4.5 0.7
21 M	0330 0945 1602 2155	4.7 0.5 4.3 0.9
22 TU	0418 1031 1650 2245	4.4 0.8 4.1 1.1
23 W	0515 1123 1746 2346	4.1 1.2 3.8 1.4
24 TH ☽	0625 1227 1854	3.8 1.6 3.6
25 F	0105 0745 1349 2011	1.6 3.6 1.9 3.5
26 SA	0248 0919 1528 2137	1.6 3.5 1.9 3.6
27 SU	0414 1038 1636 2245	1.4 3.7 1.7 3.8
28 M	0510 1133 1723 2335	1.2 3.8 1.6 3.9
29 TU	0553 1215 1802	1.0 4.0 1.4
30 W	0014 0628 1249 1835	4.1 0.9 4.0 1.2

OCTOBER

Date	Time	m
1 TH O	0048 0700 1319 1906	4.2 0.8 4.1 1.1
2 F	0119 0730 1348 1936	4.3 0.8 4.1 1.0
3 SA	0148 0758 1416 2005	4.3 0.8 4.1 1.0
4 SU	0218 0825 1444 2034	4.3 0.8 4.1 1.0
5 M	0249 0852 1513 2103	4.2 1.0 4.0 1.1
6 TU	0322 0921 1544 2135	4.1 1.1 3.9 1.3
7 W	0358 0952 1619 2211	3.9 1.3 3.8 1.4
8 TH	0440 1028 1701 2256	3.8 1.6 3.7 1.6
9 F	0532 1115 1756 2359	3.6 1.8 3.5 1.8
10 SA ☾	0642 1228 1912	3.4 2.0 3.4
11 SU	0128 0802 1408 2031	1.8 3.4 2.1 3.4
12 M	0300 0925 1537 2146	1.7 3.5 1.9 3.6
13 TU	0411 1034 1637 2245	1.4 3.8 1.6 3.9
14 W	0503 1125 1724 2332	1.0 4.1 1.3 4.2
15 TH	0548 1208 1806	0.6 4.3 1.0
16 F ●	0015 0631 1249 1846	4.5 0.4 4.5 0.8
17 SA	0057 0713 1330 1927	4.7 0.2 4.6 0.6
18 SU	0140 0755 1410 2008	4.8 0.2 4.6 0.6
19 M	0224 0837 1452 2051	4.8 0.4 4.5 0.7
20 TU	0311 0920 1535 2137	4.6 0.7 4.4 0.8
21 W	0403 1006 1623 2229	4.4 1.0 4.1 1.1
22 TH	0503 1058 1720 2332	4.1 1.4 3.9 1.3
23 F ☽	0613 1202 1828	3.8 1.8 3.7
24 SA	0050 0731 1324 1944	1.5 3.6 2.0 3.6
25 SU	0227 0859 1500 2106	1.6 3.5 2.0 3.6
26 M	0350 1015 1609 2216	1.5 3.6 1.9 3.7
27 TU	0444 1107 1656 2306	1.3 3.8 1.7 3.9
28 W	0525 1147 1734 2345	1.2 3.9 1.5 4.0
29 TH	0559 1219 1808	1.0 4.0 1.3
30 F	0019 0629 1249 1839	4.1 1.0 4.1 1.2
31 SA O	0051 0659 1318 1910	4.2 0.9 4.2 1.1

NOVEMBER

Date	Time	m
1 SU	0122 0727 1346 1940	4.2 0.9 4.2 1.0
2 M	0153 0755 1414 2010	4.2 1.0 4.2 1.1
3 TU	0226 0823 1444 2041	4.2 1.1 4.1 1.1
4 W	0300 0853 1515 2114	4.1 1.2 4.0 1.2
5 TH	0337 0925 1550 2152	3.9 1.4 3.9 1.4
6 F	0420 1003 1632 2239	3.8 1.6 3.8 1.5
7 SA	0512 1051 1724 2340	3.6 1.8 3.6 1.6
8 SU ☾	0620 1201 1836	3.5 2.0 3.5
9 M	0100 0735 1333 1953	1.6 3.5 2.0 3.6
10 TU	0223 0850 1457 2105	1.5 3.6 1.9 3.7
11 W	0333 0959 1602 2208	1.3 3.8 1.6 3.9
12 TH	0431 1054 1653 2301	1.0 4.1 1.3 4.2
13 F	0520 1140 1740 2349	0.7 4.3 1.1 4.5
14 SA	0606 1223 1824	0.5 4.5 0.8
15 SU ●	0035 0649 1305 1907	4.7 0.4 4.6 0.7
16 M	0121 0733 1347 1951	4.7 0.5 4.6 0.6
17 TU	0208 0816 1429 2037	4.7 0.6 4.5 0.7
18 W	0258 0901 1514 2125	4.5 0.9 4.4 0.8
19 TH	0352 0947 1602 2217	4.3 1.2 4.2 1.0
20 F	0451 1037 1657 2316	4.0 1.6 4.0 1.2
21 SA	0555 1135 1759	3.8 1.8 3.8
22 SU ☽	0024 0702 1245 1906	1.4 3.6 2.0 3.6
23 M	0141 0816 1404 2018	1.6 3.5 2.1 3.6
24 TU	0301 0929 1520 2129	1.5 3.5 2.0 3.6
25 W	0402 1026 1617 2226	1.5 3.6 1.8 3.7
26 TH	0447 1109 1700 2310	1.4 3.8 1.6 3.8
27 F	0524 1145 1738 2349	1.3 3.9 1.5 4.0
28 SA	0558 1218 1813	1.2 4.0 1.3
29 SU	0024 0629 1250 1846	4.0 1.1 4.1 1.2
30 M O	0059 0700 1320 1919	4.1 1.1 4.2 1.1

DECEMBER

Date	Time	m
1 TU	0133 0730 1351 1952	4.1 1.1 4.2 1.1
2 W	0208 0802 1422 2026	4.1 1.2 4.2 1.1
3 TH	0245 0835 1456 2103	4.1 1.3 4.1 1.1
4 F	0324 0911 1532 2144	4.0 1.4 4.0 1.2
5 SA	0408 0951 1614 2231	3.9 1.5 3.9 1.3
6 SU	0459 1039 1704 2326	3.8 1.7 3.8 1.4
7 M	0600 1140 1807	3.7 1.8 3.8
8 TU ☾	0033 0706 1255 1916	1.4 3.6 1.9 3.7
9 W	0145 0814 1411 2024	1.3 3.7 1.8 3.8
10 TH	0253 0921 1520 2131	1.2 3.8 1.7 4.0
11 F	0356 1022 1621 2233	1.0 4.0 1.4 4.1
12 SA	0453 1114 1716 2328	0.9 4.2 1.2 4.3
13 SU	0544 1201 1806	0.8 4.3 1.0
14 M ●	0019 0631 1246 1854	4.5 0.7 4.4 0.8
15 TU	0110 0717 1330 1942	4.5 0.8 4.5 0.7
16 W	0200 0802 1413 2029	4.5 0.9 4.5 0.7
17 TH	0250 0846 1458 2116	4.4 1.1 4.4 0.8
18 F	0342 0929 1544 2204	4.2 1.3 4.3 0.9
19 SA	0434 1014 1633 2254	4.0 1.5 4.1 1.1
20 SU	0528 1101 1725 2347	3.8 1.7 3.9 1.3
21 M ☽	0622 1155 1821	3.6 1.9 3.7
22 TU	0044 0719 1257 1919	1.5 3.5 2.0 3.6
23 W	0146 0822 1405 2023	1.6 3.4 2.0 3.5
24 TH	0252 0926 1517 2130	1.6 3.4 2.0 3.6
25 F	0355 1022 1619 2228	1.6 3.6 1.8 3.6
26 SA	0445 1108 1707 2317	1.5 3.7 1.7 3.7
27 SU	0526 1148 1748	1.4 3.8 1.5
28 M	0000 0602 1225 1825	3.8 1.4 4.0 1.3
29 TU	0040 0637 1259 1901	3.9 1.3 4.1 1.2
30 W O	0118 0712 1333 1938	4.0 1.2 4.2 1.1
31 TH	0155 0747 1407 2016	4.1 1.2 4.2 1.0

WICK
LAT 58°26'N
LONG 3°05'W

TIMES AND HEIGHTS OF HIGH AND LOW WATER (Heights in Metres)

TIME ZONE UT
For Summer Time (area enclosed in shaded box) add 1 hour

2020

JANUARY

Date	Day	Time	m	Time	m	Time	m	Time	m
1	W	0307	2.9	0830	1.5	1506	3.2	2119	1.2
2	TH	0355	2.8	0916	1.6	1553	3.0	2214	1.3
3	F ☽	0449	2.7	1019	1.7	1648	2.9	2317	1.4
4	SA	0550	2.7	1134	1.7	1751	2.9		
5	SU	0023	1.4	0651	2.8	1248	1.7	1854	2.9
6	M	0127	1.4	0750	2.9	1354	1.6	1955	2.9
7	TU	0221	1.3	0843	3.0	1448	1.4	2052	3.0
8	W	0306	1.2	0930	3.2	1533	1.2	2144	3.2
9	TH	0347	1.1	1013	3.3	1614	1.0	2231	3.3
10	F ○	0426	1.0	1054	3.5	1655	0.9	2317	3.4
11	SA	0507	0.9	1136	3.6	1738	0.7		
12	SU	0002	3.5	0548	0.9	1218	3.7	1821	0.6
13	M	0049	3.5	0630	0.9	1301	3.7	1907	0.6
14	TU	0135	3.5	0714	1.0	1346	3.7	1956	0.6
15	W	0223	3.4	0759	1.1	1432	3.6	2047	0.7
16	TH	0314	3.2	0848	1.2	1523	3.5	2145	0.8
17	F ☾	0409	3.1	0945	1.3	1621	3.3	2250	1.0
18	SA	0510	3.0	1056	1.4	1726	3.2	2359	1.1
19	SU	0615	2.9	1217	1.5	1837	3.1		
20	M	0112	1.2	0724	3.0	1341	1.4	1953	3.1
21	TU	0218	1.2	0832	3.1	1448	1.3	2103	3.1
22	W	0312	1.2	0929	3.2	1542	1.1	2201	3.2
23	TH	0357	1.1	1017	3.3	1627	1.0	2249	3.3
24	F ●	0436	1.1	1059	3.4	1707	0.9	2331	3.3
25	SA	0513	1.0	1138	3.5	1744	0.8		
26	SU	0010	3.3	0547	1.0	1215	3.5	1819	0.8
27	M	0047	3.3	0620	1.0	1250	3.5	1853	0.8
28	TU	0121	3.2	0653	1.1	1323	3.5	1926	0.8
29	W	0155	3.1	0725	1.1	1357	3.4	1959	0.9
30	TH	0229	3.0	0757	1.2	1431	3.3	2034	1.0
31	F	0306	2.9	0832	1.3	1509	3.1	2112	1.2

FEBRUARY

Date	Day	Time	m	Time	m	Time	m	Time	m
1	SA	0348	2.8	0914	1.5	1553	3.0	2201	1.3
2	SU ☽	0439	2.7	1013	1.6	1646	2.8	2308	1.4
3	M	0541	2.7	1140	1.6	1754	2.8		
4	TU	0023	1.5	0650	2.7	1303	1.6	1908	2.8
5	W	0137	1.4	0757	2.8	1417	1.4	2020	2.9
6	TH	0240	1.3	0857	3.0	1513	1.2	2122	3.1
7	F	0329	1.2	0948	3.2	1559	1.0	2216	3.2
8	SA	0413	1.0	1035	3.4	1643	0.7	2304	3.4
9	SU ○	0455	0.9	1119	3.6	1726	0.5	2350	3.6
10	M	0536	0.7	1203	3.7	1809	0.3		
11	TU	0035	3.6	0617	0.7	1247	3.8	1853	0.3
12	W	0120	3.6	0659	0.7	1331	3.8	1938	0.3
13	TH	0204	3.5	0740	0.8	1415	3.7	2024	0.5
14	F	0250	3.3	0824	0.9	1503	3.5	2114	0.7
15	SA ☾	0338	3.1	0912	1.1	1556	3.3	2212	1.0
16	SU	0434	2.9	1017	1.3	1700	3.1	2322	1.2
17	M	0538	2.8	1147	1.4	1816	2.9		
18	TU	0046	1.4	0652	2.8	1331	1.4	1943	2.9
19	W	0207	1.4	0811	2.9	1446	1.2	2059	2.9
20	TH	0304	1.3	0914	3.0	1538	1.1	2154	3.1
21	F	0348	1.2	1003	3.2	1619	0.9	2239	3.1
22	SA	0424	1.1	1045	3.3	1654	0.8	2317	3.2
23	SU ●	0457	1.0	1122	3.4	1726	0.7	2352	3.2
24	M	0528	0.9	1156	3.5	1757	0.7		
25	TU	0024	3.2	0559	0.9	1228	3.5	1827	0.7
26	W	0055	3.2	0629	0.9	1259	3.4	1856	0.7
27	TH	0125	3.2	0658	0.9	1329	3.4	1925	0.8
28	F	0155	3.1	0728	1.0	1400	3.3	1955	0.9
29	SA	0226	3.0	0759	1.1	1434	3.1	2026	1.0

MARCH

Date	Day	Time	m	Time	m	Time	m	Time	m
1	SU	0302	2.9	0834	1.2	1513	3.0	2103	1.2
2	M ☽	0344	2.8	0918	1.4	1602	2.8	2154	1.4
3	TU	0439	2.7	1031	1.5	1706	2.7	2322	1.5
4	W	0553	2.6	1218	1.5	1831	2.7		
5	TH	0057	1.5	0713	2.7	1348	1.4	1953	2.8
6	F	0217	1.4	0824	2.9	1452	1.1	2104	3.0
7	SA	0312	1.2	0923	3.1	1541	0.8	2159	3.2
8	SU	0356	1.0	1013	3.4	1624	0.5	2247	3.4
9	M ○	0438	0.7	1059	3.6	1707	0.3	2332	3.6
10	TU	0518	0.6	1144	3.8	1750	0.1		
11	W	0016	3.6	0558	0.5	1228	3.9	1832	0.1
12	TH	0058	3.6	0639	0.5	1311	3.8	1914	0.2
13	F	0140	3.5	0719	0.6	1356	3.7	1957	0.4
14	SA	0223	3.3	0801	0.7	1442	3.5	2042	0.7
15	SU	0307	3.1	0847	1.0	1534	3.2	2135	1.1
16	M ☾	0359	2.9	0950	1.2	1639	2.9	2245	1.4
17	TU	0503	2.7	1128	1.3	1800	2.7		
18	W	0019	1.5	0621	2.7	1322	1.3	1933	2.7
19	TH	0152	1.5	0746	2.8	1434	1.1	2048	2.8
20	F	0250	1.4	0853	2.9	1523	1.0	2139	2.9
21	SA	0331	1.2	0943	3.1	1600	0.9	2220	3.1
22	SU	0404	1.1	1023	3.2	1631	0.7	2255	3.1
23	M	0435	1.0	1058	3.3	1700	0.7	2327	3.2
24	TU ●	0505	0.8	1131	3.4	1729	0.6	2357	3.2
25	W	0534	0.8	1202	3.4	1758	0.6		
26	TH	0026	3.2	0603	0.7	1232	3.4	1825	0.6
27	F	0055	3.2	0633	0.8	1302	3.3	1853	0.7
28	SA	0123	3.1	0702	0.8	1333	3.2	1921	0.8
29	SU	0153	3.0	0733	0.9	1407	3.1	1951	1.0
30	M	0227	2.9	0807	1.1	1446	2.9	2026	1.2
31	TU	0308	2.8	0850	1.2	1535	2.8	2112	1.3

APRIL

Date	Day	Time	m	Time	m	Time	m	Time	m
1	W ☽	0400	2.7	0955	1.3	1639	2.7	2235	1.5
2	TH	0510	2.6	1148	1.3	1805	2.6		
3	F	0027	1.5	0636	2.7	1320	1.2	1931	2.7
4	SA	0152	1.4	0752	2.8	1426	0.9	2042	3.0
5	SU	0249	1.1	0855	3.1	1517	0.6	2138	3.2
6	M	0334	0.9	0948	3.3	1601	0.3	2225	3.4
7	TU	0416	0.7	1036	3.6	1644	0.1	2310	3.5
8	W ○	0456	0.5	1121	3.7	1726	0.1	2352	3.6
9	TH	0537	0.4	1206	3.8	1808	0.1		
10	F	0034	3.6	0618	0.4	1251	3.8	1849	0.3
11	SA	0115	3.5	0659	0.5	1336	3.6	1930	0.5
12	SU	0156	3.3	0742	0.6	1424	3.3	2013	0.9
13	M	0239	3.1	0831	0.9	1517	3.0	2103	1.2
14	TU ☾	0329	2.9	0937	1.1	1622	2.8	2211	1.5
15	W	0432	2.8	1110	1.2	1741	2.6	2342	1.6
16	TH	0548	2.7	1254	1.2	1909	2.6		
17	F	0120	1.6	0708	2.7	1406	1.1	2021	2.7
18	SA	0221	1.4	0819	2.8	1453	1.0	2111	2.8
19	SU	0302	1.3	0911	2.9	1529	0.9	2151	3.0
20	M	0336	1.1	0952	3.1	1600	0.8	2225	3.1
21	TU	0407	1.0	1028	3.2	1629	0.7	2257	3.1
22	W	0438	0.8	1101	3.2	1658	0.6	2327	3.2
23	TH ●	0509	0.8	1134	3.3	1727	0.6	2356	3.2
24	F	0539	0.7	1205	3.3	1756	0.7		
25	SA	0025	3.2	0609	0.7	1238	3.2	1824	0.7
26	SU	0055	3.2	0640	0.8	1311	3.2	1854	0.9
27	M	0127	3.1	0714	0.8	1348	3.1	1927	1.0
28	TU	0202	3.0	0752	0.9	1430	2.9	2005	1.2
29	W	0245	2.9	0839	1.1	1521	2.8	2055	1.3
30	TH ☽	0337	2.8	0950	1.2	1626	2.7	2217	1.5

MAY

Date	Day	Time	m	Time	m	Time	m	Time	m
1	F	0445	2.7	1129	1.1	1748	2.7		
2	SA	0000	1.5	0606	2.7	1250	1.0	1906	2.8
3	SU	0119	1.3	0719	2.9	1356	0.8	2015	3.0
4	M	0219	1.1	0824	3.1	1450	0.5	2111	3.2
5	TU	0307	0.9	0920	3.3	1536	0.3	2200	3.3
6	W	0351	0.7	1011	3.5	1620	0.2	2245	3.5
7	TH ○	0434	0.5	1100	3.6	1702	0.2	2328	3.5
8	F	0517	0.4	1147	3.7	1744	0.3		
9	SA	0010	3.5	0600	0.4	1234	3.6	1826	0.5
10	SU	0051	3.4	0644	0.5	1320	3.4	1907	0.7
11	M	0133	3.3	0730	0.6	1408	3.2	1950	1.0
12	TU	0216	3.2	0821	0.8	1501	3.0	2037	1.3
13	W	0304	3.0	0924	1.0	1602	2.7	2137	1.5
14	TH ☾	0402	2.8	1039	1.1	1711	2.6	2253	1.6
15	F	0511	2.7	1202	1.2	1823	2.6		
16	SA	0018	1.6	0621	2.7	1317	1.1	1933	2.6
17	SU	0132	1.5	0728	2.7	1409	1.0	2029	2.7
18	M	0221	1.3	0826	2.8	1449	0.9	2113	2.9
19	TU	0301	1.2	0912	2.9	1523	0.9	2150	3.0
20	W	0336	1.0	0953	3.0	1556	0.8	2224	3.1
21	TH	0410	0.9	1030	3.1	1627	0.8	2256	3.2
22	F ●	0444	0.8	1105	3.2	1658	0.7	2328	3.2
23	SA	0517	0.8	1141	3.2	1729	0.8		
24	SU	0000	3.2	0550	0.7	1217	3.2	1800	0.8
25	M	0034	3.2	0625	0.7	1255	3.1	1835	0.9
26	TU	0109	3.2	0704	0.8	1336	3.1	1913	1.0
27	W	0148	3.1	0748	0.8	1421	3.0	1956	1.1
28	TH	0232	3.0	0840	0.9	1513	2.9	2049	1.3
29	F	0324	2.9	0949	0.9	1616	2.8	2203	1.4
30	SA ☽	0427	2.9	1107	0.9	1728	2.8	2328	1.4
31	SU	0539	2.9	1219	0.8	1838	2.8		

JUNE

Date	Day	Time	m	Time	m	Time	m	Time	m
1	M	0042	1.3	0649	3.0	1325	0.7	1943	2.9
2	TU	0146	1.1	0753	3.1	1422	0.6	2042	3.1
3	W	0241	1.0	0854	3.3	1512	0.5	2134	3.2
4	TH	0330	0.8	0950	3.4	1558	0.5	2222	3.4
5	F ○	0417	0.6	1043	3.5	1642	0.5	2307	3.4
6	SA	0503	0.5	1132	3.5	1725	0.6	2350	3.5
7	SU	0549	0.5	1220	3.4	1808	0.7		
8	M	0032	3.4	0635	0.5	1307	3.3	1849	0.9
9	TU	0114	3.4	0721	0.6	1354	3.1	1930	1.1
10	W	0157	3.2	0809	0.8	1442	2.9	2013	1.2
11	TH	0242	3.1	0900	0.9	1534	2.8	2100	1.4
12	F	0331	3.0	0956	1.0	1630	2.7	2158	1.5
13	SA ☾	0427	2.8	1058	1.1	1729	2.6	2306	1.5
14	SU	0529	2.8	1203	1.2	1830	2.6		
15	M	0018	1.5	0629	2.7	1307	1.1	1930	2.7
16	TU	0126	1.4	0729	2.7	1400	1.1	2024	2.8
17	W	0220	1.3	0825	2.8	1444	1.0	2109	2.9
18	TH	0304	1.2	0914	2.9	1522	1.0	2149	3.0
19	F	0344	1.0	0959	3.0	1558	0.9	2226	3.1
20	SA	0422	0.9	1040	3.1	1633	0.9	2302	3.2
21	SU ●	0459	0.8	1121	3.2	1708	0.9	2339	3.3
22	M	0537	0.7	1201	3.2	1745	0.9		
23	TU	0016	3.3	0616	0.7	1243	3.2	1824	0.9
24	W	0056	3.3	0659	0.6	1327	3.2	1906	1.0
25	TH	0138	3.3	0745	0.6	1413	3.1	1951	1.0
26	F	0222	3.2	0836	0.7	1504	3.0	2041	1.1
27	SA	0312	3.2	0935	0.7	1600	2.9	2140	1.2
28	SU ☽	0409	3.1	1041	0.8	1702	2.9	2252	1.3
29	M	0513	3.1	1148	0.8	1807	2.9		
30	TU	0005	1.3	0620	3.0	1255	0.8	1911	2.9

SUNRISE AND SUNSET TIMES

WICK
At 58°26'N 3°05'W

		Sunrise	Sunset
UT			
Jan	01	0901	1531
	15	0848	1556
Feb	01	0818	1635
	15	0745	1709
Mar	01	0708	1743
	15	0628	1815
BST			
Apr	01	0640	1954
	15	0600	2026
May	01	0518	2103
	15	0445	2134
Jun	01	0416	2206
	15	0405	2221
Jul	01	0411	2221
	15	0430	2206
Aug	01	0503	2133
	15	0534	2058
Sep	01	0611	2012
	15	0642	1932
Oct	01	0717	1846
	15	0748	1807
UT			
Nov	01	0728	1623
	15	0801	1552
Dec	01	0835	1527
	15	0856	1519

WICK
LAT 58°26′N
LONG 3°05′W

TIMES AND HEIGHTS OF HIGH AND LOW WATER (Heights in Metres)

TIME ZONE UT
For Summer Time (area enclosed in shaded box) add 1 hour

2020

JULY

Date	Day	Time	m
1	W	0116 0728 1358 2014	1.2 3.1 0.8 3.0
2	TH	0221 0836 1454 2112	1.1 3.1 0.8 3.1
3	F	0318 0938 1543 2204	0.9 3.2 0.8 3.3
4	SA	0409 1034 1629 2251	0.8 3.3 0.8 3.4
5	SU O	0457 1123 1711 2335	0.7 3.3 0.8 3.4
6	M	0542 1210 1752	0.6 3.3 0.9
7	TU	0017 0625 1254 1831	3.4 0.6 3.2 0.9
8	W	0057 0706 1336 1908	3.4 0.6 3.1 1.0
9	TH	0137 0746 1417 1945	3.3 0.7 3.0 1.1
10	F	0216 0826 1458 2023	3.2 0.8 2.9 1.2
11	SA	0257 0908 1543 2106	3.1 1.0 2.8 1.3
12	SU ☾	0341 0956 1632 2159	3.0 1.1 2.7 1.4
13	M	0432 1052 1727 2307	2.8 1.2 2.6 1.5
14	TU	0529 1154 1826	2.7 1.3 2.6
15	W	0020 0631 1259 1926	1.5 2.7 1.3 2.7
16	TH	0133 0735 1400 2023	1.4 2.7 1.2 2.8
17	F	0234 0837 1451 2113	1.3 2.8 1.2 2.9
18	SA	0322 0931 1534 2158	1.2 2.9 1.1 3.1
19	SU	0404 1019 1614 2239	1.0 3.1 1.0 3.2
20	M ●	0444 1104 1653 2320	0.8 3.2 0.9 3.4
21	TU	0524 1147 1732	0.7 3.3 0.9
22	W	0001 0605 1232 1813	3.5 0.5 3.3 0.8
23	TH	0043 0648 1316 1855	3.5 0.4 3.3 0.8
24	F	0125 0733 1401 1937	3.5 0.4 3.3 0.9
25	SA	0209 0820 1447 2022	3.5 0.5 3.2 1.0
26	SU	0256 0912 1537 2113	3.4 0.6 3.1 1.1
27	M ☽	0348 1010 1633 2215	3.3 0.8 3.0 1.2
28	TU	0448 1116 1735 2332	3.1 0.9 2.9 1.3
29	W	0557 1227 1842	3.0 1.0 2.9
30	TH	0056 0711 1341 1951	1.3 3.0 1.1 2.9
31	F	0216 0830 1444 2057	1.2 3.0 1.1 3.1

AUGUST

Date	Day	Time	m
1	SA	0318 0936 1536 2152	1.0 3.1 1.1 3.2
2	SU	0408 1029 1620 2239	0.8 3.2 1.0 3.3
3	M O	0452 1116 1659 2321	0.7 3.2 1.0 3.4
4	TU	0531 1157 1735	0.6 3.3 0.9
5	W	0001 0608 1236 1809	3.5 0.6 3.2 0.9
6	TH	0038 0642 1312 1843	3.5 0.6 3.2 0.9
7	F	0113 0716 1346 1915	3.4 0.7 3.1 1.0
8	SA	0147 0749 1420 1948	3.3 0.8 3.0 1.1
9	SU	0221 0822 1456 2022	3.2 0.9 2.9 1.2
10	M	0258 0858 1535 2102	3.1 1.1 2.8 1.3
11	TU ☾	0340 0942 1622 2156	2.9 1.2 2.7 1.5
12	W	0430 1043 1720 2319	2.8 1.4 2.6 1.6
13	TH	0535 1158 1827	2.7 1.5 2.7
14	F	0046 0650 1316 1935	1.5 2.7 1.4 2.7
15	SA	0205 0804 1424 2038	1.4 2.7 1.4 2.9
16	SU	0301 0908 1515 2130	1.2 2.9 1.2 3.1
17	M	0346 1000 1557 2216	1.0 3.1 1.1 3.3
18	TU	0427 1047 1637 2259	0.7 3.3 0.9 3.5
19	W ●	0508 1131 1716 2342	0.5 3.4 0.8 3.6
20	TH	0549 1214 1756	0.3 3.5 0.7
21	F	0024 0630 1258 1836	3.7 0.2 3.5 0.7
22	SA	0107 0713 1340 1917	3.8 0.3 3.5 0.7
23	SU	0150 0757 1424 1959	3.7 0.4 3.3 0.8
24	M	0236 0843 1510 2045	3.6 0.6 3.2 1.0
25	TU ☽	0326 0937 1602 2144	3.4 0.9 3.0 1.2
26	W	0426 1044 1703 2309	3.1 1.1 2.9 1.3
27	TH	0540 1205 1815	2.9 1.3 2.8
28	F	0052 0706 1333 1934	1.3 2.9 1.4 2.9
29	SA	0219 0832 1440 2046	1.2 2.9 1.3 3.0
30	SU	0317 0933 1529 2140	1.0 3.1 1.2 3.2
31	M	0402 1021 1607 2225	0.9 3.2 1.1 3.3

SEPTEMBER

Date	Day	Time	m
1	TU	0439 1101 1641 2304	0.7 3.2 1.0 3.5
2	W O	0512 1138 1713 2340	0.6 3.3 0.9 3.5
3	TH	0543 1211 1745	0.6 3.3 0.9
4	F	0013 0613 1243 1815	3.5 0.6 3.3 0.9
5	SA	0045 0643 1313 1845	3.5 0.7 3.2 0.9
6	SU	0116 0712 1342 1915	3.4 0.8 3.1 1.0
7	M	0147 0741 1413 1946	3.3 0.9 3.0 1.1
8	TU	0221 0811 1448 2021	3.2 1.1 2.9 1.3
9	W	0259 0846 1529 2104	3.0 1.3 2.8 1.4
10	TH ☾	0346 0932 1621 2216	2.8 1.4 2.7 1.6
11	F	0448 1056 1731	2.7 1.6 2.7
12	SA	0005 0611 1237 1851	1.6 2.6 1.6 2.7
13	SU	0135 0735 1359 2002	1.4 2.7 1.5 2.9
14	M	0237 0846 1454 2101	1.2 2.9 1.3 3.1
15	TU	0323 0939 1537 2150	0.9 3.2 1.1 3.4
16	W	0405 1026 1616 2235	0.6 3.4 0.9 3.6
17	TH ●	0445 1109 1655 2319	0.4 3.6 0.7 3.8
18	F	0526 1152 1735	0.2 3.7 0.6
19	SA	0002 0606 1234 1814	3.9 0.1 3.7 0.6
20	SU	0045 0648 1316 1855	3.9 0.2 3.6 0.6
21	M	0129 0730 1357 1937	3.8 0.4 3.5 0.8
22	TU	0215 0814 1442 2023	3.6 0.7 3.3 1.0
23	W	0307 0905 1531 2123	3.3 1.1 3.1 1.2
24	TH ☽	0410 1013 1633 2259	3.1 1.4 2.9 1.4
25	F	0530 1145 1750	2.9 1.6 2.8
26	SA	0051 0703 1324 1914	1.3 2.8 1.6 2.9
27	SU	0211 0825 1428 2027	1.2 2.9 1.5 3.0
28	M	0304 0920 1513 2120	1.0 3.1 1.4 3.2
29	TU	0344 1002 1547 2203	0.9 3.2 1.2 3.3
30	W	0416 1038 1618 2240	0.8 3.3 1.1 3.4

OCTOBER

Date	Day	Time	m
1	TH O	0444 1111 1648 2313	0.7 3.3 1.0 3.5
2	F	0513 1142 1718 2345	0.7 3.3 0.9 3.5
3	SA	0541 1211 1748	0.7 3.3 0.9
4	SU	0015 0609 1240 1817	3.5 0.7 3.3 0.9
5	M	0046 0637 1308 1847	3.4 0.8 3.3 1.0
6	TU	0117 0705 1338 1918	3.3 1.0 3.2 1.1
7	W	0151 0734 1411 1952	3.2 1.1 3.1 1.2
8	TH	0229 0807 1450 2034	3.0 1.3 3.0 1.4
9	F	0317 0850 1540 2137	2.9 1.5 2.9 1.5
10	SA ☾	0418 1001 1646 2331	2.7 1.7 2.8 1.5
11	SU	0542 1202 1811	2.7 1.7 2.8
12	M	0101 0708 1328 1926	1.4 2.8 1.6 2.9
13	TU	0206 0818 1426 2028	1.1 3.0 1.4 3.2
14	W	0255 0913 1511 2121	0.8 3.3 1.1 3.4
15	TH	0338 1000 1551 2208	0.6 3.5 0.9 3.7
16	F ●	0419 1044 1631 2254	0.3 3.6 0.7 3.9
17	SA	0500 1126 1711 2339	0.2 3.7 0.6 4.0
18	SU	0541 1208 1753	0.2 3.8 0.6
19	M	0024 0623 1250 1835	3.9 0.4 3.7 0.6
20	TU	0110 0705 1332 1919	3.8 0.6 3.5 0.8
21	W	0158 0748 1416 2008	3.6 1.0 3.4 1.0
22	TH	0252 0837 1505 2113	3.3 1.3 3.2 1.2
23	F ☽	0357 0944 1607 2247	3.0 1.6 3.0 1.3
24	SA	0516 1115 1723	2.8 1.8 2.9
25	SU	0030 0643 1255 1842	1.3 2.8 1.7 2.9
26	M	0147 0800 1401 1954	1.2 2.9 1.6 3.0
27	TU	0237 0853 1445 2050	1.1 3.0 1.5 3.2
28	W	0314 0934 1520 2133	1.0 3.1 1.3 3.3
29	TH	0345 1009 1551 2210	0.9 3.2 1.2 3.4
30	F	0414 1041 1621 2244	0.8 3.3 1.0 3.4
31	SA O	0442 1111 1652 2317	0.8 3.4 1.0 3.5

NOVEMBER

Date	Day	Time	m
1	SU	0511 1141 1723 2348	0.8 3.4 0.9 3.4
2	M	0539 1209 1754	0.9 3.4 0.9
3	TU	0020 0607 1239 1825	3.4 0.9 3.4 1.0
4	W	0054 0636 1310 1858	3.3 1.1 3.3 1.1
5	TH	0130 0707 1344 1935	3.2 1.2 3.2 1.2
6	F	0210 0743 1424 2019	3.1 1.4 3.1 1.3
7	SA	0258 0828 1513 2123	2.9 1.5 3.0 1.4
8	SU ☾	0359 0934 1616 2301	2.8 1.7 2.9 1.4
9	M	0517 1124 1734	2.8 1.7 2.9
10	TU	0023 0636 1247 1848	1.3 2.9 1.6 3.0
11	W	0130 0745 1350 1952	1.1 3.1 1.4 3.2
12	TH	0223 0842 1440 2049	0.8 3.3 1.2 3.4
13	F	0310 0932 1525 2141	0.6 3.5 1.0 3.7
14	SA	0354 1018 1608 2230	0.5 3.6 0.8 3.8
15	SU ●	0436 1101 1651 2319	0.4 3.7 0.7 3.9
16	M	0519 1144 1736	0.5 3.8 0.6
17	TU	0007 0601 1227 1821	3.8 0.6 3.7 0.7
18	W	0055 0644 1310 1908	3.7 0.9 3.6 0.8
19	TH	0145 0728 1355 2001	3.5 1.1 3.5 0.9
20	F	0239 0815 1443 2103	3.2 1.4 3.3 1.1
21	SA	0340 0913 1540 2218	3.0 1.6 3.1 1.3
22	SU ☽	0448 1027 1648 2341	2.8 1.8 3.0 1.3
23	M	0600 1151 1758	2.8 1.8 3.0
24	TU	0059 0711 1310 1905	1.3 2.8 1.7 3.0
25	W	0155 0810 1404 2005	1.2 2.9 1.6 3.1
26	TH	0236 0856 1446 2055	1.2 3.0 1.4 3.1
27	F	0310 0935 1522 2137	1.1 3.2 1.3 3.2
28	SA	0342 1009 1557 2215	1.0 3.3 1.2 3.3
29	SU	0413 1042 1630 2251	1.0 3.4 1.1 3.3
30	M O	0443 1113 1704 2326	1.0 3.4 1.0 3.4

DECEMBER

Date	Day	Time	m
1	TU	0514 1145 1737	1.0 3.5 1.0
2	W	0001 0544 1217 1811	3.4 1.1 3.4 1.0
3	TH	0038 0617 1251 1847	3.3 1.1 3.4 1.0
4	F	0116 0652 1327 1928	3.2 1.2 3.3 1.1
5	SA	0158 0732 1408 2015	3.1 1.3 3.3 1.1
6	SU	0246 0818 1456 2114	3.0 1.5 3.2 1.2
7	M	0343 0917 1553 2229	2.9 1.6 3.1 1.2
8	TU ☾	0450 1040 1700 2343	2.9 1.6 3.1 1.1
9	W	0601 1200 1811	2.9 1.6 3.1
10	TH	0050 0707 1309 1917	1.0 3.0 1.5 3.2
11	F	0151 0809 1409 2020	0.9 3.2 1.3 3.4
12	SA	0244 0904 1502 2119	0.8 3.4 1.1 3.5
13	SU	0332 0954 1551 2214	0.7 3.5 0.9 3.6
14	M ●	0418 1041 1639 2306	0.7 3.6 0.8 3.7
15	TU	0502 1126 1727 2356	0.7 3.7 0.7 3.7
16	W	0546 1210 1814	0.9 3.7 0.7
17	TH	0045 0629 1254 1902	3.6 1.0 3.6 0.7
18	F	0134 0711 1338 1950	3.4 1.2 3.5 0.9
19	SA	0222 0754 1423 2041	3.2 1.3 3.4 1.0
20	SU	0313 0839 1512 2135	3.0 1.5 3.3 1.1
21	M ☽	0408 0931 1606 2235	2.9 1.6 3.1 1.3
22	TU	0506 1035 1706 2340	2.8 1.7 3.0 1.4
23	W	0607 1147 1808	2.7 1.7 2.9
24	TH	0048 0709 1303 1909	1.4 2.8 1.7 2.9
25	F	0146 0807 1405 2009	1.3 2.9 1.6 3.0
26	SA	0232 0856 1453 2102	1.3 3.0 1.4 3.0
27	SU	0312 0937 1535 2147	1.2 3.1 1.3 3.1
28	M	0348 1015 1613 2229	1.2 3.3 1.2 3.2
29	TU	0422 1050 1649 2308	1.1 3.4 1.1 3.3
30	W O	0456 1125 1725 2346	1.1 3.4 1.0 3.3
31	TH	0530 1201 1802	1.1 3.5 0.9

LERWICK

LAT 60°09′N
LONG 1°08′W

TIMES AND HEIGHTS OF HIGH AND LOW WATER (Heights in Metres)

TIME ZONE UT
For Summer Time (area enclosed in shaded box) add 1 hour

2020

JANUARY

Date	Day	Time	m	Time	m	Time	m	Time	m
1	W	0247	1.8	0825	1.0	1442	2.0	2111	0.9
2	TH	0330	1.8	0911	1.1	1526	1.9	2204	0.9
3	F ☽	0420	1.7	1012	1.2	1618	1.8	2306	1.0
4	SA	0520	1.7	1130	1.2	1718	1.8		
5	SU	0011	1.0	0633	1.7	1241	1.1	1834	1.8
6	M	0109	1.0	0733	1.8	1339	1.1	1942	1.8
7	TU	0200	0.9	0821	1.9	1429	1.0	2034	1.9
8	W	0245	0.9	0904	2.0	1513	0.8	2122	2.0
9	TH	0328	0.8	0945	2.1	1556	0.7	2208	2.1
10	F O	0411	0.8	1027	2.2	1639	0.6	2254	2.2
11	SA	0453	0.7	1109	2.3	1723	0.5	2341	2.2
12	SU	0535	0.7	1152	2.3	1807	0.4		
13	M	0028	2.2	0618	0.7	1237	2.3	1852	0.4
14	TU	0117	2.2	0702	0.7	1323	2.3	1939	0.4
15	W	0206	2.1	0748	0.8	1411	2.2	2028	0.5
16	TH	0256	2.0	0836	0.8	1503	2.2	2123	0.6
17	F ☾	0350	1.9	0931	0.9	1600	2.1	2225	0.7
18	SA	0449	1.8	1040	1.0	1706	2.0	2341	0.8
19	SU	0557	1.8	1210	1.0	1822	1.9		
20	M	0055	0.8	0707	1.8	1329	0.9	1937	1.9
21	TU	0159	0.8	0810	1.9	1433	0.8	2044	1.9
22	W	0253	0.8	0906	2.0	1526	0.7	2142	2.0
23	TH	0340	0.8	0954	2.1	1611	0.7	2231	2.0
24	F ●	0421	0.8	1038	2.2	1652	0.6	2314	2.1
25	SA	0500	0.8	1117	2.2	1731	0.5	2352	2.1
26	SU	0537	0.7	1153	2.2	1807	0.5		
27	M	0028	2.0	0611	0.8	1228	2.2	1841	0.5
28	TU	0103	2.0	0644	0.8	1301	2.2	1915	0.6
29	W	0136	1.9	0716	0.8	1334	2.1	1949	0.7
30	TH	0210	1.9	0748	0.9	1407	2.0	2024	0.7
31	F	0245	1.8	0824	0.9	1445	1.9	2103	0.8

FEBRUARY

Date	Day	Time	m	Time	m	Time	m	Time	m
1	SA	0326	1.7	0908	1.0	1530	1.8	2151	0.9
2	SU ☽	0414	1.7	1006	1.1	1623	1.8	2255	1.0
3	M	0512	1.7	1135	1.1	1727	1.7		
4	TU	0015	1.0	0625	1.7	1256	1.1	1848	1.7
5	W	0122	1.0	0739	1.8	1359	1.0	2004	1.8
6	TH	0220	0.9	0834	1.9	1452	0.8	2101	1.9
7	F	0310	0.8	0923	2.0	1540	0.6	2153	2.0
8	SA	0356	0.7	1009	2.2	1625	0.5	2241	2.1
9	SU O	0440	0.6	1054	2.3	1709	0.3	2329	2.2
10	M	0522	0.6	1139	2.4	1752	0.2		
11	TU	0015	2.2	0603	0.5	1224	2.4	1835	0.2
12	W	0101	2.2	0645	0.5	1308	2.4	1919	0.2
13	TH	0146	2.1	0728	0.6	1354	2.3	2005	0.3
14	F	0231	2.0	0813	0.6	1442	2.2	2054	0.5
15	SA ☾	0319	1.9	0904	0.8	1536	2.0	2149	0.7
16	SU	0412	1.8	1006	0.9	1639	1.9	2302	0.9
17	M	0516	1.7	1144	0.9	1800	1.8		
18	TU	0032	0.9	0636	1.7	1319	0.9	1929	1.7
19	W	0147	1.0	0752	1.8	1428	0.8	2042	1.8
20	TH	0245	0.9	0853	1.9	1521	0.7	2136	1.9
21	F	0331	0.9	0942	2.0	1603	0.6	2220	1.9
22	SA	0410	0.8	1024	2.1	1639	0.5	2258	2.0
23	SU ●	0445	0.7	1101	2.1	1712	0.5	2332	2.0
24	M	0517	0.6	1134	2.2	1744	0.4		
25	TU	0004	2.0	0548	0.6	1206	2.2	1814	0.4
26	W	0035	2.0	0617	0.6	1236	2.1	1843	0.5
27	TH	0104	1.9	0647	0.6	1305	2.1	1913	0.5
28	F	0132	1.9	0717	0.7	1335	2.0	1944	0.6
29	SA	0203	1.8	0751	0.8	1409	1.9	2019	0.7

MARCH

Date	Day	Time	m	Time	m	Time	m	Time	m
1	SU	0239	1.8	0829	0.8	1450	1.8	2058	0.8
2	M ☽	0323	1.7	0918	0.9	1541	1.7	2149	0.9
3	TU	0418	1.6	1027	1.0	1645	1.6	2307	1.0
4	W	0526	1.6	1213	1.0	1806	1.6		
5	TH	0049	1.0	0652	1.6	1331	0.9	1939	1.7
6	F	0159	0.9	0806	1.8	1430	0.7	2044	1.8
7	SA	0254	0.8	0901	1.9	1521	0.5	2136	2.0
8	SU	0340	0.7	0949	2.1	1606	0.3	2224	2.1
9	M O	0423	0.5	1035	2.2	1650	0.1	2310	2.2
10	TU	0504	0.4	1120	2.3	1732	0.1	2355	2.2
11	W	0544	0.3	1204	2.4	1814	0.0		
12	TH	0037	2.2	0625	0.3	1249	2.4	1856	0.1
13	F	0120	2.1	0707	0.4	1334	2.3	1939	0.3
14	SA	0202	2.0	0752	0.5	1422	2.1	2025	0.5
15	SU	0246	1.9	0841	0.6	1515	1.9	2117	0.7
16	M ☾	0335	1.8	0944	0.8	1617	1.7	2227	0.9
17	TU	0436	1.7	1128	0.8	1743	1.6		
18	W	0009	1.0	0602	1.6	1305	0.8	1921	1.6
19	TH	0130	1.0	0730	1.7	1414	0.7	2030	1.7
20	F	0229	0.9	0833	1.8	1504	0.6	2119	1.8
21	SA	0313	0.8	0921	1.9	1543	0.5	2158	1.8
22	SU	0350	0.7	1001	2.0	1616	0.5	2232	1.9
23	M	0423	0.6	1036	2.0	1646	0.4	2304	1.9
24	TU ●	0453	0.6	1109	2.1	1715	0.4	2334	2.0
25	W	0522	0.5	1139	2.1	1743	0.4		
26	TH	0003	2.0	0550	0.5	1208	2.0	1810	0.4
27	F	0030	1.9	0620	0.5	1236	2.0	1839	0.5
28	SA	0057	1.9	0651	0.6	1306	2.0	1910	0.6
29	SU	0126	1.9	0725	0.6	1341	1.9	1943	0.7
30	M	0200	1.8	0804	0.7	1422	1.8	2021	0.8
31	TU	0242	1.7	0852	0.8	1513	1.7	2110	0.9

APRIL

Date	Day	Time	m	Time	m	Time	m	Time	m
1	W ☽	0335	1.6	0956	0.9	1619	1.6	2222	1.0
2	TH	0445	1.6	1134	0.9	1741	1.5		
3	F	0019	1.0	0610	1.6	1302	0.7	1917	1.6
4	SA	0136	0.9	0736	1.7	1405	0.6	2023	1.8
5	SU	0231	0.7	0835	1.9	1457	0.4	2114	1.9
6	M	0318	0.6	0925	2.0	1543	0.2	2201	2.0
7	TU	0400	0.4	1012	2.2	1626	0.1	2246	2.1
8	W O	0441	0.3	1058	2.3	1708	0.0	2329	2.2
9	TH	0523	0.2	1143	2.3	1750	0.0		
10	F	0010	2.2	0604	0.2	1229	2.3	1832	0.2
11	SA	0052	2.1	0647	0.3	1315	2.2	1914	0.4
12	SU	0132	2.0	0733	0.4	1404	2.0	1959	0.6
13	M	0216	1.9	0825	0.5	1458	1.8	2050	0.8
14	TU ☾	0304	1.8	0930	0.7	1559	1.6	2158	1.0
15	W	0402	1.7	1107	0.8	1722	1.5	2336	1.0
16	TH	0523	1.6	1236	0.7	1856	1.5		
17	F	0059	1.0	0655	1.6	1344	0.7	2001	1.6
18	SA	0200	0.9	0759	1.7	1434	0.6	2047	1.7
19	SU	0245	0.8	0848	1.8	1512	0.5	2125	1.8
20	M	0322	0.7	0928	1.8	1544	0.5	2159	1.8
21	TU	0354	0.6	1004	1.9	1614	0.4	2231	1.9
22	W	0424	0.5	1038	1.9	1642	0.4	2301	1.9
23	TH ●	0454	0.5	1109	2.0	1710	0.4	2330	2.0
24	F	0524	0.5	1140	2.0	1740	0.4	2358	2.0
25	SA	0556	0.5	1210	1.9	1810	0.5		
26	SU	0026	1.9	0629	0.5	1244	1.9	1842	0.6
27	M	0058	1.9	0706	0.5	1321	1.8	1917	0.7
28	TU	0133	1.8	0748	0.6	1405	1.7	1958	0.8
29	W	0215	1.8	0838	0.7	1459	1.6	2050	0.9
30	TH ☽	0309	1.7	0942	0.7	1606	1.6	2202	1.0

MAY

Date	Day	Time	m	Time	m	Time	m	Time	m
1	F	0419	1.6	1108	0.7	1725	1.6	2346	0.9
2	SA	0541	1.6	1231	0.6	1851	1.6		
3	SU	0105	0.8	0703	1.7	1335	0.5	1956	1.7
4	M	0203	0.7	0806	1.8	1429	0.3	2048	1.9
5	TU	0251	0.6	0859	2.0	1517	0.2	2135	2.0
6	W	0336	0.4	0948	2.1	1601	0.1	2219	2.1
7	TH O	0419	0.3	1036	2.2	1644	0.1	2302	2.1
8	F	0502	0.2	1123	2.2	1727	0.2	2344	2.1
9	SA	0546	0.2	1211	2.2	1810	0.3		
10	SU	0025	2.1	0631	0.3	1301	2.1	1852	0.5
11	M	0108	2.0	0719	0.4	1350	1.9	1938	0.7
12	TU	0152	1.9	0812	0.5	1442	1.8	2028	0.8
13	W	0239	1.8	0914	0.6	1539	1.6	2129	1.0
14	TH ☾	0333	1.7	1030	0.7	1646	1.5	2248	1.0
15	F	0438	1.6	1148	0.7	1807	1.5		
16	SA	0008	1.0	0603	1.6	1257	0.7	1912	1.5
17	SU	0115	0.9	0713	1.6	1350	0.7	2002	1.6
18	M	0206	0.8	0806	1.7	1432	0.6	2043	1.7
19	TU	0246	0.7	0850	1.7	1506	0.6	2120	1.8
20	W	0321	0.6	0929	1.8	1537	0.5	2155	1.9
21	TH	0354	0.6	1005	1.9	1608	0.5	2227	1.9
22	F ●	0426	0.5	1040	1.9	1640	0.5	2259	2.0
23	SA	0500	0.5	1115	1.9	1712	0.5	2330	2.0
24	SU	0535	0.5	1150	1.9	1746	0.6		
25	M	0003	2.0	0612	0.5	1229	1.9	1822	0.6
26	TU	0038	2.0	0653	0.5	1310	1.8	1902	0.7
27	W	0117	1.9	0738	0.5	1358	1.8	1947	0.8
28	TH	0202	1.8	0830	0.5	1454	1.7	2041	0.8
29	F	0257	1.8	0931	0.6	1556	1.6	2146	0.9
30	SA ☽	0403	1.7	1043	0.6	1705	1.6	2307	0.9
31	SU	0515	1.7	1159	0.5	1820	1.6		

JUNE

Date	Day	Time	m	Time	m	Time	m	Time	m
1	M	0028	0.8	0631	1.7	1305	0.5	1924	1.7
2	TU	0131	0.7	0737	1.8	1402	0.4	2019	1.8
3	W	0225	0.6	0834	2.0	1452	0.3	2108	1.9
4	TH	0314	0.5	0927	2.0	1539	0.3	2155	2.0
5	F O	0401	0.4	1019	2.1	1624	0.3	2239	2.1
6	SA	0447	0.3	1110	2.1	1708	0.4	2323	2.1
7	SU	0533	0.3	1200	2.1	1751	0.5		
8	M	0006	2.1	0619	0.3	1249	2.0	1834	0.6
9	TU	0049	2.0	0707	0.4	1336	1.9	1919	0.7
10	W	0133	2.0	0756	0.5	1423	1.8	2005	0.8
11	TH	0218	1.9	0848	0.6	1511	1.7	2055	0.9
12	F	0305	1.8	0944	0.7	1602	1.6	2153	1.0
13	SA ☾	0356	1.7	1045	0.7	1702	1.5	2300	1.0
14	SU	0456	1.6	1148	0.7	1811	1.5		
15	M	0009	1.0	0611	1.6	1248	0.7	1909	1.6
16	TU	0112	0.9	0716	1.6	1339	0.7	1958	1.6
17	W	0202	0.8	0808	1.7	1421	0.7	2041	1.7
18	TH	0245	0.7	0853	1.7	1500	0.7	2119	1.8
19	F	0324	0.7	0934	1.8	1537	0.6	2156	1.9
20	SA	0402	0.6	1015	1.9	1614	0.6	2232	2.0
21	SU ●	0440	0.5	1055	1.9	1651	0.6	2309	2.0
22	M	0519	0.5	1136	1.9	1730	0.6	2347	2.0
23	TU	0600	0.4	1219	1.9	1810	0.6		
24	W	0026	2.0	0643	0.4	1305	1.9	1852	0.7
25	TH	0109	2.0	0730	0.4	1353	1.9	1938	0.7
26	F	0156	2.0	0819	0.4	1445	1.8	2028	0.8
27	SA	0248	1.9	0914	0.5	1541	1.7	2124	0.8
28	SU ☽	0347	1.9	1015	0.5	1641	1.7	2230	0.8
29	M	0451	1.8	1125	0.5	1746	1.7	2348	0.8
30	TU	0601	1.8	1235	0.5	1853	1.7		

SUNRISE AND SUNSET TIMES

LERWICK
At 60°09′N 1°08′W

UT		Sunrise	Sunset
Jan	01	0908	1509
	15	0853	1535
Feb	01	0819	1618
	15	0743	1655
Mar	01	0703	1732
	15	0621	1807
BST			
Apr	01	0629	1949
	15	0547	2023
May	01	0502	2103
	15	0426	2138
Jun	01	0352	2214
	15	0339	2231
Jul	01	0345	2231
	15	0407	2213
Aug	01	0444	2136
	15	0518	2058
Sep	01	0559	2008
	15	0632	1926
Oct	01	0710	1837
	15	0744	1755
UT			
Nov	01	0728	1608
	15	0804	1534
Dec	01	0841	1506
	15	0903	1456

LERWICK
LAT 60°09′N
LONG 1°08′W

TIMES AND HEIGHTS OF HIGH AND LOW WATER (Heights in Metres)

TIME ZONE UT
For Summer Time (area enclosed in shaded box) add 1 hour

2020

JULY

Date	Day	Time	m	Time	m	Time	m	Time	m
1	W	0102	0.8	0712	1.8	1338	0.5	1952	1.8
2	TH	0205	0.7	0816	1.9	1433	0.5	2046	1.9
3	F	0301	0.6	0916	1.9	1523	0.6	2137	2.0
4	SA	0351	0.5	1012	2.0	1610	0.6	2225	2.1
5	SU O	0439	0.4	1104	2.0	1654	0.6	2310	2.1
6	M	0524	0.4	1151	2.0	1737	0.6	2352	2.1
7	TU	0608	0.4	1235	2.0	1818	0.7		
8	W	0034	2.1	0651	0.4	1317	1.9	1858	0.7
9	TH	0114	2.0	0732	0.5	1357	1.8	1937	0.8
10	F	0153	2.0	0814	0.5	1437	1.7	2017	0.8
11	SA	0233	1.9	0857	0.6	1517	1.7	2059	0.9
12	SU ☾	0315	1.8	0943	0.7	1602	1.6	2151	0.9
13	M	0402	1.7	1038	0.8	1654	1.6	2259	1.0
14	TU	0456	1.6	1140	0.8	1800	1.6		
15	W	0012	1.0	0606	1.6	1242	0.9	1907	1.6
16	TH	0117	0.9	0721	1.6	1337	0.8	2000	1.7
17	F	0211	0.9	0819	1.7	1426	0.8	2046	1.8
18	SA	0258	0.8	0908	1.8	1511	0.8	2128	1.9
19	SU	0342	0.7	0954	1.9	1554	0.7	2210	2.0
20	M ●	0424	0.5	1039	1.9	1636	0.7	2251	2.1
21	TU	0506	0.4	1124	2.0	1717	0.6	2333	2.1
22	W	0548	0.3	1209	2.0	1759	0.6		
23	TH	0016	2.2	0631	0.3	1255	2.0	1840	0.6
24	F	0100	2.2	0715	0.3	1341	2.0	1924	0.6
25	SA	0145	2.1	0801	0.3	1428	1.9	2009	0.7
26	SU	0233	2.1	0851	0.4	1518	1.8	2059	0.7
27	M ☽	0326	2.0	0946	0.5	1611	1.8	2158	0.8
28	TU	0426	1.9	1051	0.6	1712	1.7	2315	0.9
29	W	0537	1.8	1209	0.7	1822	1.7		
30	TH	0045	0.8	0656	1.8	1321	0.8	1931	1.8
31	F	0158	0.8	0810	1.8	1423	0.8	2033	1.9

AUGUST

Date	Day	Time	m	Time	m	Time	m	Time	m
1	SA	0258	0.7	0915	1.9	1516	0.8	2127	2.0
2	SU	0349	0.6	1010	1.9	1602	0.7	2216	2.1
3	M O	0433	0.5	1056	2.0	1643	0.7	2259	2.1
4	TU	0513	0.4	1138	2.0	1721	0.7	2338	2.2
5	W	0551	0.4	1216	2.0	1758	0.6		
6	TH	0015	2.2	0627	0.4	1252	2.0	1832	0.7
7	F	0050	2.1	0702	0.5	1325	1.9	1906	0.7
8	SA	0124	2.1	0736	0.5	1359	1.8	1939	0.8
9	SU	0158	2.0	0811	0.6	1433	1.8	2014	0.8
10	M	0234	1.9	0848	0.7	1511	1.7	2055	0.9
11	TU ☾	0316	1.8	0931	0.8	1555	1.7	2149	1.0
12	W	0406	1.7	1029	0.9	1648	1.6	2312	1.0
13	TH	0506	1.6	1148	1.0	1756	1.6		
14	F	0036	1.0	0625	1.6	1300	1.0	1915	1.7
15	SA	0141	0.9	0748	1.7	1400	0.9	2015	1.8
16	SU	0236	0.8	0846	1.8	1452	0.9	2104	1.9
17	M	0323	0.7	0936	1.9	1538	0.8	2149	2.0
18	TU	0407	0.5	1022	2.0	1621	0.7	2233	2.2
19	W ●	0449	0.3	1107	2.1	1701	0.6	2316	2.3
20	TH	0530	0.2	1152	2.2	1742	0.5	2359	2.3
21	F	0612	0.2	1235	2.2	1822	0.5		
22	SA	0042	2.3	0654	0.2	1319	2.1	1904	0.5
23	SU	0127	2.3	0738	0.3	1403	2.0	1947	0.6
24	M	0213	2.2	0824	0.4	1449	1.9	2035	0.7
25	TU ☽	0305	2.1	0916	0.6	1540	1.8	2132	0.8
26	W	0405	1.9	1020	0.8	1639	1.8	2255	0.9
27	TH	0520	1.8	1150	0.9	1754	1.7		
28	F	0041	0.9	0653	1.7	1313	1.0	1917	1.8
29	SA	0158	0.8	0813	1.8	1418	0.9	2024	1.9
30	SU	0256	0.7	0913	1.9	1508	0.9	2118	2.0
31	M	0342	0.6	1000	1.9	1550	0.8	2203	2.1

SEPTEMBER

Date	Day	Time	m	Time	m	Time	m	Time	m
1	TU	0420	0.5	1040	2.0	1626	0.7	2242	2.2
2	W O	0455	0.4	1116	2.0	1700	0.7	2317	2.2
3	TH	0527	0.4	1149	2.0	1733	0.6	2350	2.2
4	F	0559	0.4	1220	2.0	1804	0.6		
5	SA	0021	2.2	0628	0.5	1250	2.0	1833	0.6
6	SU	0051	2.1	0658	0.6	1319	1.9	1904	0.7
7	M	0122	2.0	0729	0.7	1349	1.9	1937	0.8
8	TU	0156	2.0	0801	0.8	1423	1.8	2015	0.9
9	W	0235	1.9	0839	0.9	1505	1.8	2103	1.0
10	TH ☾	0325	1.7	0927	1.0	1557	1.7	2212	1.1
11	F	0426	1.7	1042	1.1	1701	1.7	2359	1.0
12	SA	0543	1.6	1230	1.1	1824	1.7		
13	SU	0114	1.0	0722	1.7	1339	1.0	1945	1.8
14	M	0212	0.8	0826	1.8	1433	0.9	2040	1.9
15	TU	0301	0.6	0916	2.0	1519	0.8	2126	2.1
16	W	0345	0.4	1001	2.1	1600	0.6	2211	2.2
17	TH ●	0427	0.3	1045	2.2	1640	0.5	2254	2.4
18	F	0508	0.2	1128	2.3	1720	0.4	2337	2.4
19	SA	0549	0.1	1210	2.3	1800	0.4		
20	SU	0020	2.4	0630	0.2	1252	2.2	1842	0.4
21	M	0106	2.4	0713	0.3	1335	2.1	1926	0.5
22	TU	0154	2.2	0758	0.5	1419	2.0	2015	0.7
23	W	0247	2.1	0848	0.8	1509	1.9	2115	0.8
24	TH ☽	0350	1.9	0953	1.0	1608	1.8	2251	0.9
25	F	0510	1.7	1136	1.1	1728	1.8		
26	SA	0035	0.9	0652	1.7	1302	1.1	1900	1.8
27	SU	0149	0.8	0807	1.8	1405	1.0	2008	1.9
28	M	0242	0.7	0858	1.9	1452	0.9	2058	2.0
29	TU	0323	0.6	0939	2.0	1530	0.8	2140	2.1
30	W	0358	0.6	1014	2.0	1604	0.7	2217	2.1

OCTOBER

Date	Day	Time	m	Time	m	Time	m	Time	m
1	TH O	0429	0.5	1047	2.1	1635	0.7	2251	2.2
2	F	0458	0.5	1118	2.1	1705	0.6	2322	2.2
3	SA	0527	0.5	1147	2.1	1735	0.6	2351	2.2
4	SU	0555	0.5	1214	2.1	1804	0.6		
5	M	0020	2.1	0623	0.6	1242	2.0	1835	0.7
6	TU	0051	2.1	0652	0.7	1310	2.0	1909	0.8
7	W	0124	2.0	0724	0.8	1343	1.9	1947	0.9
8	TH	0204	1.9	0800	1.0	1423	1.9	2034	1.0
9	F	0254	1.8	0846	1.1	1514	1.8	2138	1.0
10	SA ☾	0358	1.7	0955	1.2	1621	1.7	2320	1.0
11	SU	0516	1.6	1158	1.2	1742	1.7		
12	M	0044	0.9	0653	1.7	1314	1.1	1911	1.8
13	TU	0144	0.8	0801	1.9	1408	0.9	2011	2.0
14	W	0234	0.6	0850	2.0	1454	0.8	2100	2.1
15	TH	0319	0.4	0935	2.2	1535	0.6	2145	2.3
16	F ●	0401	0.3	1019	2.3	1616	0.5	2229	2.4
17	SA	0443	0.2	1101	2.3	1657	0.4	2314	2.5
18	SU	0525	0.2	1143	2.3	1739	0.4	2359	2.5
19	M	0607	0.3	1224	2.3	1823	0.4		
20	TU	0047	2.4	0649	0.5	1307	2.2	1908	0.5
21	W	0138	2.2	0735	0.7	1351	2.1	2000	0.7
22	TH	0234	2.0	0825	0.9	1442	2.0	2104	0.8
23	F ☽	0337	1.9	0930	1.1	1541	1.9	2239	0.9
24	SA	0455	1.7	1108	1.2	1658	1.8		
25	SU	0013	0.9	0632	1.7	1234	1.2	1830	1.8
26	M	0123	0.8	0740	1.8	1337	1.1	1937	1.9
27	TU	0215	0.8	0828	1.9	1425	1.0	2028	2.0
28	W	0255	0.7	0907	1.9	1504	0.9	2110	2.0
29	TH	0329	0.6	0942	2.0	1537	0.8	2147	2.1
30	F	0359	0.6	1014	2.1	1609	0.7	2221	2.1
31	SA O	0427	0.6	1045	2.1	1638	0.7	2253	2.2

NOVEMBER

Date	Day	Time	m	Time	m	Time	m	Time	m
1	SU	0455	0.6	1114	2.1	1708	0.7	2324	2.2
2	M	0523	0.6	1142	2.1	1740	0.7	2355	2.1
3	TU	0553	0.7	1210	2.1	1813	0.7		
4	W	0027	2.1	0623	0.8	1241	2.1	1848	0.8
5	TH	0103	2.0	0657	0.9	1314	2.0	1929	0.8
6	F	0145	1.9	0734	1.0	1355	2.0	2017	0.9
7	SA	0236	1.8	0822	1.1	1445	1.9	2119	0.9
8	SU ☾	0340	1.7	0929	1.2	1552	1.8	2241	0.9
9	M	0454	1.7	1110	1.2	1709	1.8		
10	TU	0007	0.9	0618	1.8	1238	1.1	1831	1.9
11	W	0110	0.7	0728	1.9	1336	1.0	1937	2.0
12	TH	0204	0.6	0821	2.0	1425	0.8	2031	2.2
13	F	0251	0.5	0907	2.2	1510	0.7	2119	2.3
14	SA	0336	0.4	0952	2.3	1554	0.6	2207	2.4
15	SU ●	0419	0.3	1035	2.3	1637	0.5	2255	2.4
16	M	0502	0.4	1118	2.4	1722	0.4	2344	2.4
17	TU	0546	0.5	1200	2.3	1808	0.5		
18	W	0035	2.3	0630	0.7	1245	2.3	1856	0.5
19	TH	0128	2.2	0716	0.8	1331	2.2	1950	0.6
20	F	0222	2.0	0806	1.0	1421	2.1	2051	0.8
21	SA	0319	1.9	0905	1.1	1516	2.0	2206	0.9
22	SU ☽	0424	1.8	1020	1.2	1620	1.9	2328	0.9
23	M	0542	1.7	1142	1.2	1740	1.8		
24	TU	0039	0.9	0651	1.7	1253	1.1	1852	1.9
25	W	0135	0.9	0744	1.8	1348	1.1	1948	1.9
26	TH	0219	0.8	0828	1.9	1432	1.0	2034	2.0
27	F	0255	0.8	0906	2.0	1509	0.9	2114	2.0
28	SA	0326	0.8	0941	2.1	1542	0.8	2151	2.1
29	SU	0356	0.7	1014	2.1	1614	0.8	2227	2.1
30	M O	0426	0.7	1046	2.2	1647	0.7	2301	2.1

DECEMBER

Date	Day	Time	m	Time	m	Time	m	Time	m
1	TU	0457	0.8	1117	2.2	1721	0.7	2336	2.1
2	W	0530	0.8	1148	2.2	1757	0.7		
3	TH	0012	2.1	0604	0.8	1222	2.2	1835	0.7
4	F	0052	2.0	0640	0.9	1258	2.1	1918	0.7
5	SA	0136	2.0	0722	1.0	1340	2.1	2007	0.8
6	SU	0227	1.9	0810	1.0	1430	2.0	2102	0.8
7	M	0325	1.8	0909	1.1	1530	1.9	2208	0.8
8	TU ☾	0430	1.8	1021	1.1	1638	1.9	2323	0.8
9	W	0541	1.8	1146	1.1	1752	1.9		
10	TH	0033	0.7	0651	1.9	1258	1.0	1902	2.0
11	F	0133	0.6	0749	2.0	1356	0.9	2003	2.1
12	SA	0225	0.6	0841	2.1	1448	0.8	2058	2.2
13	SU	0314	0.5	0929	2.2	1537	0.6	2151	2.3
14	M ●	0400	0.5	1015	2.3	1624	0.5	2244	2.3
15	TU	0446	0.6	1100	2.3	1712	0.5	2337	2.3
16	W	0530	0.7	1145	2.3	1759	0.5		
17	TH	0028	2.2	0615	0.8	1231	2.3	1847	0.5
18	F	0117	2.1	0700	0.9	1316	2.3	1937	0.6
19	SA	0205	2.0	0745	1.0	1402	2.2	2028	0.7
20	SU	0253	1.9	0833	1.1	1449	2.1	2123	0.8
21	M ☽	0343	1.8	0927	1.1	1539	1.9	2223	0.9
22	TU	0440	1.7	1030	1.2	1636	1.9	2329	0.9
23	W	0546	1.7	1144	1.2	1747	1.8		
24	TH	0034	0.9	0650	1.7	1256	1.1	1857	1.8
25	F	0130	0.9	0743	1.8	1353	1.1	1954	1.8
26	SA	0214	0.9	0829	1.9	1438	1.0	2042	1.9
27	SU	0253	0.9	0909	2.0	1518	0.9	2125	2.0
28	M	0328	0.9	0946	2.1	1555	0.8	2205	2.0
29	TU	0404	0.8	1022	2.1	1631	0.8	2244	2.1
30	W O	0439	0.8	1058	2.2	1708	0.7	2324	2.1
31	TH	0515	0.8	1133	2.2	1747	0.6		

ULLAPOOL
LAT 57°54′N
LONG 5°10′W

TIMES AND HEIGHTS OF HIGH AND LOW WATER (Heights in Metres)

TIME ZONE UT
For Summer Time (area enclosed in shaded box) add 1 hour

2020

JANUARY

Date	Day	Time	m
1	W	0444 1042 1715 2319	1.9 4.5 1.8 4.1
2	TH	0529 1136 1803	2.2 4.3 2.0
3	F ☽	0023 0623 1243 1859	3.9 2.4 4.2 2.2
4	SA	0137 0732 1354 2007	3.9 2.5 4.1 2.2
5	SU	0248 0848 1459 2116	3.9 2.5 4.1 2.2
6	M	0348 0954 1556 2214	4.1 2.3 4.3 2.0
7	TU	0435 1047 1645 2303	4.3 2.1 4.4 1.8
8	W	0515 1133 1729 2346	4.6 1.8 4.6 1.5
9	TH	0552 1215 1810	4.8 1.5 4.9
10	F O	0028 0628 1258 1852	1.3 5.1 1.2 5.0
11	SA	0109 0706 1340 1934	1.1 5.3 1.0 5.2
12	SU	0151 0746 1423 2018	1.0 5.4 0.9 5.2
13	M	0232 0829 1507 2105	1.0 5.4 0.8 5.1
14	TU	0315 0914 1552 2154	1.0 5.3 0.9 5.0
15	W	0400 1003 1640 2248	1.2 5.2 1.0 4.8
16	TH	0449 1100 1732 2350	1.4 4.9 1.3 4.5
17	F ☾	0543 1205 1831	1.7 4.7 1.5
18	SA	0057 0646 1319 1939	4.4 1.9 4.5 1.8
19	SU	0209 0801 1436 2055	4.3 2.1 4.4 1.9
20	M	0321 0922 1552 2209	4.3 2.0 4.4 1.8
21	TU	0425 1035 1655 2309	4.5 1.9 4.5 1.7
22	W	0518 1134 1746 2359	4.7 1.7 4.7 1.5
23	TH	0601 1224 1830	4.9 1.4 4.8
24	F ●	0042 0640 1307 1907	1.4 5.1 1.3 4.9
25	SA	0122 0715 1346 1941	1.3 5.2 1.1 4.9
26	SU	0158 0748 1421 2013	1.2 5.2 1.1 4.9
27	M	0232 0820 1455 2044	1.2 5.2 1.1 4.8
28	TU	0306 0852 1528 2114	1.3 5.1 1.2 4.6
29	W	0339 0924 1602 2147	1.4 4.9 1.3 4.5
30	TH	0412 1000 1636 2223	1.6 4.7 1.5 4.3
31	F	0448 1040 1714 2307	1.8 4.5 1.7 4.1

FEBRUARY

Date	Day	Time	m
1	SA	0529 1130 1757	2.1 4.3 2.0
2	SU ☽	0008 0619 1238 1851	3.9 2.3 4.1 2.2
3	M	0130 0728 1358 2002	3.8 2.5 4.0 2.3
4	TU	0248 0856 1512 2124	3.9 2.5 4.0 2.2
5	W	0356 1012 1617 2232	4.1 2.2 4.2 2.0
6	TH	0449 1110 1711 2326	4.4 1.9 4.5 1.7
7	F	0533 1159 1758	4.7 1.5 4.8
8	SA	0012 0613 1244 1840	1.4 5.0 1.1 5.1
9	SU O	0056 0652 1328 1921	1.0 5.3 0.7 5.3
10	M	0138 0732 1410 2003	0.8 5.6 0.5 5.4
11	TU	0220 0813 1452 2046	0.6 5.6 0.4 5.4
12	W	0301 0856 1535 2130	0.6 5.6 0.5 5.2
13	TH	0344 0941 1618 2219	0.8 5.4 0.7 4.9
14	F	0428 1032 1704 2314	1.0 5.1 1.0 4.6
15	SA ☾	0516 1133 1756	1.4 4.7 1.5
16	SU	0020 0613 1250 1858	4.3 1.8 4.3 1.8
17	M	0137 0726 1418 2021	4.1 2.1 4.1 2.1
18	TU	0259 0901 1546 2153	4.1 2.2 4.1 2.1
19	W	0412 1030 1653 2301	4.3 2.0 4.2 1.9
20	TH	0508 1131 1743 2350	4.5 1.7 4.4 1.7
21	F	0551 1216 1821	4.7 1.5 4.6
22	SA	0031 0626 1255 1853	1.4 4.9 1.2 4.7
23	SU ●	0108 0658 1330 1922	1.2 5.1 1.1 4.8
24	M	0141 0728 1401 1949	1.1 5.2 0.9 4.9
25	TU	0212 0756 1431 2016	1.0 5.2 0.9 4.9
26	W	0242 0824 1500 2042	1.1 5.1 1.0 4.8
27	TH	0312 0853 1530 2110	1.1 5.0 1.1 4.6
28	F	0342 0924 1600 2141	1.3 4.8 1.2 4.5
29	SA	0413 0959 1633 2216	1.5 4.6 1.5 4.3

MARCH

Date	Day	Time	m
1	SU	0449 1041 1711 2301	1.8 4.3 1.7 4.0
2	M ☽	0531 1138 1756	2.0 4.0 2.0
3	TU	0010 0628 1305 1859	3.8 2.3 3.9 2.3
4	W	0151 0758 1435 2035	3.8 2.4 3.8 2.3
5	TH	0316 0941 1553 2206	3.9 2.2 4.0 2.1
6	F	0422 1050 1654 2307	4.2 1.8 4.3 1.7
7	SA	0512 1141 1741 2355	4.6 1.3 4.7 1.3
8	SU	0554 1226 1823	5.0 0.9 5.1
9	M O	0038 0633 1309 1902	0.9 5.4 0.4 5.4
10	TU	0120 0712 1351 1942	0.5 5.7 0.2 5.5
11	W	0201 0752 1431 2022	0.3 5.8 0.1 5.5
12	TH	0242 0834 1512 2104	0.3 5.7 0.2 5.3
13	F	0323 0918 1553 2149	0.5 5.4 0.5 5.0
14	SA	0406 1008 1636 2241	0.8 5.0 0.9 4.6
15	SU	0452 1109 1724 2347	1.2 4.5 1.5 4.3
16	M ☾	0546 1230 1823	1.7 4.1 1.9
17	TU	0108 0659 1404 1951	4.0 2.1 3.9 2.3
18	W	0236 0846 1536 2137	4.0 2.2 3.9 2.2
19	TH	0353 1020 1642 2246	4.1 2.0 4.0 2.0
20	F	0449 1116 1728 2332	4.3 1.7 4.3 1.7
21	SA	0531 1157 1803	4.5 1.4 4.5
22	SU	0011 0604 1233 1831	1.4 4.7 1.2 4.6
23	M	0046 0634 1305 1857	1.2 4.9 1.0 4.8
24	TU ●	0118 0702 1334 1922	1.0 5.0 0.9 4.9
25	W	0147 0729 1403 1946	0.9 5.1 0.8 4.9
26	TH	0216 0756 1430 2011	0.9 5.0 0.8 4.8
27	F	0244 0824 1458 2038	1.0 4.9 0.9 4.7
28	SA	0313 0855 1528 2107	1.1 4.8 1.1 4.6
29	SU	0344 0930 1600 2141	1.3 4.5 1.3 4.4
30	M	0419 1011 1636 2223	1.5 4.3 1.6 4.2
31	TU	0500 1108 1719 2325	1.8 4.0 1.9 3.9

APRIL

Date	Day	Time	m
1	W ☽	0555 1236 1820	2.1 3.8 2.2
2	TH	0108 0722 1409 1958	3.8 2.2 3.8 2.3
3	F	0240 0913 1529 2140	3.9 2.1 4.0 2.1
4	SA	0351 1026 1631 2243	4.2 1.6 4.3 1.7
5	SU	0445 1118 1718 2332	4.6 1.1 4.7 1.2
6	M	0529 1203 1800	5.0 0.7 5.1
7	TU	0016 0609 1246 1838	0.8 5.4 0.3 5.4
8	W O	0058 0649 1327 1917	0.4 5.6 0.1 5.5
9	TH	0139 0730 1407 1957	0.2 5.7 0.0 5.5
10	F	0220 0812 1447 2039	0.2 5.5 0.2 5.3
11	SA	0302 0858 1528 2123	0.4 5.2 0.6 5.0
12	SU	0346 0950 1611 2215	0.7 4.8 1.0 4.6
13	M	0432 1054 1658 2321	1.2 4.3 1.5 4.3
14	TU ☾	0527 1215 1755	1.6 4.0 2.0
15	W	0040 0638 1344 1919	4.0 2.0 3.7 2.3
16	TH	0204 0819 1511 2104	3.9 2.1 3.8 2.3
17	F	0321 0950 1616 2215	4.0 2.0 3.9 2.1
18	SA	0418 1045 1701 2303	4.2 1.7 4.1 1.8
19	SU	0500 1126 1735 2342	4.4 1.5 4.3 1.5
20	M	0535 1201 1803	4.5 1.2 4.5
21	TU	0017 0605 1233 1829	1.3 4.7 1.0 4.7
22	W	0049 0634 1303 1854	1.1 4.8 0.9 4.8
23	TH ●	0120 0701 1332 1918	1.0 4.9 0.8 4.8
24	F	0149 0730 1400 1944	0.9 4.9 0.8 4.8
25	SA	0219 0800 1429 2011	1.0 4.8 0.9 4.8
26	SU	0249 0833 1500 2043	1.1 4.7 1.1 4.6
27	M	0322 0911 1534 2119	1.2 4.5 1.3 4.5
28	TU	0359 0958 1612 2205	1.4 4.2 1.5 4.2
29	W	0443 1102 1658 2311	1.7 4.0 1.8 4.0
30	TH ☽	0541 1225 1801	1.9 3.9 2.1

MAY

Date	Day	Time	m
1	F	0043 0705 1347 1934	3.9 2.0 3.9 2.2
2	SA	0208 0843 1501 2108	4.0 1.8 4.0 2.0
3	SU	0318 0954 1602 2213	4.2 1.5 4.3 1.6
4	M	0414 1049 1652 2304	4.6 1.0 4.7 1.2
5	TU	0502 1136 1735 2350	4.9 0.7 5.0 0.8
6	W	0545 1220 1815	5.2 0.4 5.3
7	TH O	0034 0628 1303 1855	0.5 5.4 0.2 5.4
8	F	0118 0711 1344 1936	0.4 5.4 0.3 5.4
9	SA	0201 0756 1425 2018	0.4 5.2 0.5 5.2
10	SU	0245 0844 1507 2104	0.5 5.0 0.8 5.0
11	M	0330 0938 1550 2155	0.8 4.6 1.2 4.6
12	TU	0417 1041 1637 2256	1.2 4.2 1.6 4.3
13	W	0510 1151 1732	1.5 3.9 2.0
14	TH ☾	0006 0614 1307 1843	4.1 1.8 3.7 2.2
15	F	0120 0733 1425 2011	4.0 2.0 3.7 2.3
16	SA	0232 0855 1532 2126	3.9 1.9 3.8 2.1
17	SU	0333 0957 1621 2221	4.0 1.8 4.0 1.9
18	M	0421 1043 1659 2305	4.2 1.6 4.2 1.7
19	TU	0500 1122 1731 2343	4.3 1.4 4.4 1.5
20	W	0534 1157 1759	4.5 1.2 4.5
21	TH	0017 0605 1230 1826	1.3 4.6 1.1 4.7
22	F ●	0051 0636 1302 1853	1.2 4.7 1.0 4.8
23	SA	0124 0708 1333 1921	1.1 4.7 1.0 4.8
24	SU	0157 0742 1406 1953	1.0 4.7 1.0 4.8
25	M	0231 0820 1440 2029	1.1 4.6 1.1 4.7
26	TU	0308 0904 1517 2110	1.2 4.5 1.3 4.6
27	W	0349 0956 1559 2201	1.3 4.3 1.5 4.4
28	TH	0437 1059 1648 2305	1.5 4.1 1.7 4.2
29	F	0535 1210 1750	1.6 4.0 1.9
30	SA ☽	0022 0648 1321 1909	4.2 1.7 4.0 2.0
31	SU	0137 0808 1430 2030	4.2 1.6 4.1 1.9

JUNE

Date	Day	Time	m
1	M	0245 0918 1532 2138	4.3 1.4 4.4 1.6
2	TU	0345 1018 1625 2235	4.5 1.1 4.6 1.3
3	W	0438 1109 1712 2327	4.8 0.9 4.9 1.0
4	TH	0527 1157 1756	5.0 0.7 5.1
5	F O	0015 0613 1243 1838	0.8 5.1 0.6 5.2
6	SA	0102 0700 1326 1920	0.7 5.1 0.7 5.2
7	SU	0148 0747 1409 2004	0.7 5.0 0.8 5.1
8	M	0233 0835 1451 2048	0.7 4.8 1.0 5.0
9	TU	0317 0925 1534 2135	0.9 4.5 1.2 4.7
10	W	0403 1017 1618 2226	1.2 4.3 1.5 4.5
11	TH	0450 1112 1706 2322	1.4 4.0 1.8 4.2
12	F	0542 1212 1802	1.7 3.8 2.0
13	SA ☾	0024 0639 1319 1907	4.1 1.8 3.7 2.2
14	SU	0130 0745 1427 2020	4.0 1.9 3.7 2.2
15	M	0235 0852 1528 2127	3.9 1.9 3.8 2.1
16	TU	0332 0950 1616 2221	4.0 1.8 4.0 1.9
17	W	0420 1038 1655 2306	4.1 1.7 4.2 1.7
18	TH	0502 1120 1729 2346	4.3 1.5 4.4 1.6
19	F	0540 1158 1801	4.4 1.4 4.6
20	SA	0024 0616 1235 1832	1.4 4.5 1.2 4.7
21	SU ●	0102 0653 1312 1905	1.2 4.6 1.1 4.8
22	M	0140 0732 1349 1941	1.1 4.7 1.1 4.9
23	TU	0219 0813 1427 2021	1.0 4.7 1.1 4.9
24	W	0300 0859 1507 2105	1.0 4.6 1.2 4.8
25	TH	0343 0949 1551 2154	1.1 4.5 1.3 4.7
26	F	0431 1045 1640 2251	1.2 4.4 1.4 4.6
27	SA	0524 1146 1736 2357	1.3 4.3 1.6 4.4
28	SU ☽	0624 1251 1841	1.4 4.2 1.7
29	M	0106 0732 1358 1952	4.4 1.5 4.2 1.8
30	TU	0215 0842 1502 2104	4.4 1.5 4.3 1.7

SUNRISE AND SUNSET TIMES

ULLAPOOL
At 57°54′N 5°10′W

UT		Sunrise	Sunset
Jan	01	0905	1544
	15	0853	1608
Feb	01	0824	1646
	15	0751	1719
Mar	01	0715	1752
	15	0637	1824
BST			
Apr	01	0649	2002
	15	0610	2033
May	01	0529	2108
	15	0457	2139
Jun	01	0429	2210
	15	0418	2225
Jul	01	0424	2225
	15	0442	2210
Aug	01	0515	2138
	15	0544	2104
Sep	01	0621	2020
	15	0651	1940
Oct	01	0725	1854
	15	0756	1816
UT			
Nov	01	0735	1633
	15	0807	1603
Dec	01	0840	1539
	15	0900	1532

ULLAPOOL
LAT 57°54'N
LONG 5°10'W

TIMES AND HEIGHTS OF HIGH AND LOW WATER (Heights in Metres)

TIME ZONE UT
For Summer Time (area enclosed in shaded box) add 1 hour

2020

JULY

Day	Time	m	Day	Time	m
1 W	0321 0948 1602 2211	4.4 1.4 4.5 1.5	16 TH	0337 0950 1617 2229	4.0 2.0 4.0 2.0
2 TH	0424 1048 1656 2310	4.5 1.3 4.7 1.3	17 F	0431 1044 1701 2319	4.1 1.8 4.2 1.8
3 F	0520 1141 1744	4.7 1.1 4.9	18 SA	0518 1131 1739	4.3 1.6 4.5
4 SA	0004 0610 1230 1828	1.1 4.8 1.0 5.0	19 SU	0003 0600 1214 1815	1.5 4.5 1.4 4.7
5 SU O	0054 0657 1315 1910	1.0 4.8 1.0 5.1	20 M ●	0045 0640 1255 1851	1.3 4.7 1.2 4.9
6 M	0140 0741 1357 1951	0.9 4.8 1.0 5.1	21 TU	0126 0720 1335 1929	1.0 4.8 1.0 5.1
7 TU	0223 0823 1437 2030	0.9 4.7 1.1 5.0	22 W	0207 0801 1416 2009	0.8 4.9 0.9 5.2
8 W	0304 0903 1517 2110	0.9 4.6 1.2 4.9	23 TH	0249 0845 1457 2051	0.7 4.9 0.9 5.1
9 TH	0343 0943 1556 2150	1.1 4.4 1.4 4.7	24 F	0331 0930 1539 2137	0.7 4.9 1.0 5.1
10 F	0423 1024 1636 2232	1.2 4.2 1.6 4.4	25 SA	0415 1020 1624 2228	0.8 4.7 1.1 4.9
11 SA	0504 1109 1719 2322	1.5 4.0 1.8 4.2	26 SU	0503 1116 1714 2327	1.0 4.5 1.4 4.7
12 SU ☾	0547 1204 1808	1.7 3.9 2.0	27 M ☽	0555 1219 1811	1.2 4.3 1.6
13 M	0021 0637 1311 1907	4.0 1.9 3.8 2.2	28 TU	0037 0656 1328 1918	4.4 1.5 4.2 1.8
14 TU	0129 0736 1420 2018	3.9 2.0 3.8 2.3	29 W	0152 0807 1439 2037	4.3 1.7 4.2 1.9
15 W	0235 0844 1524 2130	3.9 2.0 3.9 2.2	30 TH	0310 0926 1548 2158	4.2 1.7 4.3 1.8
			31 F	0423 1037 1648 2306	4.3 1.7 4.5 1.6

AUGUST

Day	Time	m	Day	Time	m
1 SA	0522 1134 1738	4.4 1.5 4.7	16 SU	0459 1109 1718 2344	4.2 1.8 4.5 1.6
2 SU	0001 0610 1223 1820	1.3 4.6 1.3 4.9	17 M	0544 1155 1757	4.5 1.5 4.8
3 M O	0049 0651 1305 1858	1.1 4.7 1.2 5.1	18 TU	0028 0624 1238 1833	1.2 4.8 1.2 5.1
4 TU	0131 0728 1344 1933	1.0 4.8 1.1 5.1	19 W ●	0110 0703 1319 1911	0.8 5.1 0.9 5.3
5 W	0208 0802 1420 2007	0.9 4.8 1.1 5.1	20 TH	0150 0742 1359 1950	0.5 5.2 0.7 5.5
6 TH	0243 0834 1455 2039	0.9 4.7 1.1 5.0	21 F	0231 0822 1439 2030	0.4 5.3 0.6 5.5
7 F	0317 0905 1528 2112	1.0 4.6 1.2 4.8	22 SA	0311 0904 1520 2113	0.4 5.2 0.7 5.4
8 SA	0350 0936 1602 2147	1.1 4.4 1.4 4.6	23 SU	0353 0950 1603 2201	0.5 5.0 0.9 5.1
9 SU	0424 1011 1638 2225	1.3 4.3 1.6 4.4	24 M	0436 1043 1649 2259	0.8 4.7 1.2 4.7
10 M	0500 1052 1717 2313	1.5 4.1 1.9 4.2	25 TU ☽	0525 1147 1743	1.2 4.4 1.6
11 TU ☾	0540 1149 1804	1.8 3.9 2.1	26 W	0014 0622 1302 1850	4.4 1.7 4.2 1.9
12 W	0020 0629 1309 1907	3.9 2.0 3.8 2.3	27 TH	0140 0738 1422 2021	4.1 2.0 4.1 2.1
13 TH	0140 0734 1428 2033	3.8 2.2 3.8 2.4	28 F	0311 0914 1540 2158	4.1 2.1 4.2 2.0
14 F	0257 0858 1539 2156	3.8 2.2 3.9 2.2	29 SA	0427 1033 1642 2307	4.2 1.9 4.5 1.7
15 SA	0405 1013 1634 2256	4.0 2.1 4.2 1.9	30 SU	0522 1128 1729 2356	4.4 1.7 4.7 1.4
			31 M	0604 1211 1807	4.6 1.4 4.9

SEPTEMBER

Day	Time	m	Day	Time	m
1 TU	0037 0637 1250 1840	1.2 4.7 1.2 5.1	16 W	0006 0602 1217 1810	1.0 5.0 1.1 5.3
2 W O	0113 0707 1325 1911	1.0 4.8 1.1 5.2	17 TH ●	0047 0640 1258 1847	0.6 5.3 0.7 5.6
3 TH	0146 0735 1357 1940	0.9 4.9 1.0 5.2	18 F	0127 0717 1337 1926	0.3 5.5 0.5 5.7
4 F	0217 0801 1428 2008	0.8 4.9 1.0 5.1	19 SA	0207 0756 1417 2006	0.2 5.5 0.4 5.7
5 SA	0246 0828 1458 2037	0.9 4.8 1.1 5.0	20 SU	0246 0837 1458 2049	0.2 5.4 0.5 5.5
6 SU	0316 0855 1529 2108	1.0 4.7 1.3 4.8	21 M	0327 0921 1540 2137	0.5 5.2 0.8 5.1
7 M	0346 0925 1601 2142	1.2 4.5 1.5 4.5	22 TU	0410 1011 1626 2237	0.9 4.8 1.2 4.7
8 TU	0418 0959 1635 2223	1.5 4.3 1.8 4.3	23 W	0457 1117 1720	1.4 4.5 1.6
9 W	0454 1042 1717 2320	1.7 4.1 2.1 4.0	24 TH ☽	0000 0553 1240 1830	4.3 1.9 4.2 2.0
10 TH ☾	0537 1151 1812	2.1 3.9 2.3	25 F	0135 0715 1407 2013	4.0 2.3 4.1 2.2
11 F	0051 0635 1336 1938	3.8 2.3 3.8 2.5	26 SA	0309 0905 1527 2155	4.0 2.3 4.2 2.0
12 SA	0223 0808 1501 2126	3.8 2.4 3.9 2.3	27 SU	0420 1022 1627 2255	4.1 2.1 4.4 1.7
13 SU	0340 0947 1606 2235	3.9 2.3 4.1 2.0	28 M	0510 1111 1711 2338	4.4 1.8 4.7 1.5
14 M	0438 1048 1654 2323	4.2 1.9 4.5 1.5	29 TU	0546 1152 1746	4.6 1.5 4.9
15 TU	0523 1135 1734	4.6 1.5 4.9	30 W	0015 0615 1228 1816	1.2 4.7 1.3 5.0

OCTOBER

Day	Time	m	Day	Time	m
1 TH O	0048 0641 1300 1844	1.0 4.9 1.1 5.1	16 F ●	0020 0614 1233 1823	0.6 5.4 0.7 5.7
2 F	0118 0706 1331 1912	0.9 5.0 1.1 5.2	17 SA	0101 0652 1313 1903	0.3 5.6 0.5 5.8
3 SA	0146 0730 1400 1939	0.9 5.0 1.1 5.1	18 SU	0141 0731 1355 1945	0.2 5.7 0.4 5.7
4 SU	0214 0755 1429 2006	0.9 4.9 1.1 5.0	19 M	0222 0812 1437 2029	0.3 5.5 0.5 5.5
5 M	0242 0821 1458 2036	1.0 4.8 1.3 4.8	20 TU	0303 0856 1521 2120	0.6 5.3 0.8 5.1
6 TU	0311 0849 1529 2110	1.2 4.7 1.5 4.6	21 W	0346 0947 1609 2224	1.1 4.9 1.2 4.6
7 W	0343 0921 1603 2150	1.5 4.5 1.7 4.3	22 TH	0433 1053 1704 2349	1.6 4.6 1.7 4.2
8 TH	0417 1001 1643 2246	1.8 4.3 2.0 4.1	23 F ☽	0531 1215 1815	2.1 4.3 2.1
9 F	0459 1100 1736	2.1 4.0 2.3	24 SA	0119 0652 1341 1954	4.0 2.4 4.2 2.2
10 SA ☾	0018 0554 1249 1859	3.8 2.4 3.9 2.4	25 SU	0249 0836 1500 2128	4.0 2.4 4.2 2.1
11 SU	0153 0728 1423 2054	3.8 2.5 3.9 2.3	26 M	0358 0953 1600 2226	4.1 2.2 4.4 1.8
12 M	0311 0917 1532 2206	4.0 2.3 4.2 1.9	27 TU	0445 1043 1644 2308	4.3 1.9 4.6 1.6
13 TU	0411 1021 1624 2256	4.3 1.9 4.6 1.4	28 W	0520 1123 1719 2344	4.5 1.7 4.8 1.4
14 W	0457 1109 1706 2339	4.7 1.5 5.0 1.0	29 TH	0549 1159 1750	4.7 1.5 4.9
15 TH	0537 1151 1745	5.1 1.1 5.4	30 F	0016 0614 1232 1818	1.2 4.9 1.3 5.0
			31 SA O	0047 0639 1303 1846	1.1 5.0 1.2 5.1

NOVEMBER

Day	Time	m	Day	Time	m
1 SU	0116 0704 1333 1914	1.1 5.0 1.2 5.1	16 M	0119 0711 1336 1930	0.5 5.6 0.6 5.6
2 M	0144 0728 1403 1943	1.1 5.0 1.2 5.0	17 TU	0201 0753 1421 2018	0.6 5.5 0.7 5.3
3 TU	0213 0755 1434 2015	1.2 5.0 1.3 4.8	18 W	0244 0839 1507 2112	0.9 5.3 0.9 5.0
4 W	0243 0824 1506 2051	1.3 4.8 1.5 4.6	19 TH	0328 0930 1556 2213	1.3 5.0 1.3 4.6
5 TH	0316 0858 1542 2135	1.5 4.7 1.7 4.4	20 F	0416 1030 1650 2325	1.7 4.7 1.6 4.2
6 F	0352 0940 1624 2233	1.8 4.4 1.9 4.2	21 SA	0510 1141 1753	2.1 4.4 2.0
7 SA	0435 1040 1717 2355	2.0 4.2 2.1 4.0	22 SU ☽	0042 0618 1258 1910	4.0 2.4 4.3 2.1
8 SU ☾	0531 1211 1835	2.3 4.1 2.3	23 M	0204 0742 1413 2032	3.9 2.5 4.2 2.1
9 M	0120 0656 1341 2013	4.0 2.5 4.1 2.2	24 TU	0315 0902 1517 2138	4.0 2.4 4.3 2.0
10 TU	0235 0835 1452 2128	4.1 2.3 4.3 1.8	25 W	0408 1001 1607 2227	4.2 2.2 4.4 1.8
11 W	0338 0944 1549 2223	4.4 2.0 4.7 1.4	26 TH	0447 1048 1647 2308	4.4 2.0 4.6 1.7
12 TH	0428 1037 1636 2310	4.8 1.6 5.0 1.0	27 F	0520 1127 1722 2343	4.6 1.8 4.7 1.5
13 F	0511 1123 1720 2354	5.1 1.2 5.3 0.7	28 SA	0549 1203 1754	4.7 1.6 4.8
14 SA	0551 1208 1802	5.4 0.9 5.6	29 SU	0016 0616 1238 1825	1.4 4.9 1.5 4.9
15 SU ●	0036 0630 1252 1845	0.5 5.6 0.7 5.7	30 M O	0048 0642 1310 1856	1.3 5.0 1.4 4.9

DECEMBER

Day	Time	m	Day	Time	m
1 TU	0119 0710 1343 1929	1.3 5.0 1.4 4.9	16 W	0147 0743 1412 2013	0.9 5.5 0.9 5.2
2 W	0151 0739 1417 2004	1.3 5.0 1.4 4.8	17 TH	0231 0828 1458 2102	1.1 5.4 1.0 4.9
3 TH	0224 0812 1452 2044	1.4 4.9 1.4 4.7	18 F	0314 0914 1544 2153	1.3 5.2 1.2 4.6
4 F	0259 0849 1530 2130	1.5 4.8 1.6 4.5	19 SA	0359 1003 1632 2246	1.6 4.9 1.5 4.4
5 SA	0337 0934 1614 2225	1.7 4.7 1.7 4.4	20 SU	0446 1057 1722 2344	1.9 4.6 1.7 4.1
6 SU	0422 1029 1706 2331	1.9 4.5 1.9 4.2	21 M ☽	0538 1157 1817	2.1 4.4 2.0
7 M	0516 1139 1811	2.1 4.4 2.0	22 TU	0051 0639 1305 1919	4.0 2.3 4.2 2.1
8 TU ☾	0044 0626 1258 1928	4.2 2.2 4.4 1.9	23 W	0205 0750 1414 2027	3.9 2.4 4.2 2.2
9 W	0155 0747 1409 2042	4.2 2.2 4.5 1.8	24 TH	0313 0902 1517 2132	4.0 2.4 4.2 2.1
10 TH	0300 0901 1513 2146	4.4 2.0 4.6 1.5	25 F	0406 1004 1610 2225	4.1 2.3 4.3 2.0
11 F	0357 1003 1609 2241	4.7 1.7 4.9 1.3	26 SA	0449 1054 1654 2309	4.3 2.1 4.4 1.8
12 SA	0447 1058 1700 2330	5.0 1.4 5.1 1.0	27 SU	0525 1136 1734 2348	4.5 1.9 4.6 1.7
13 SU	0532 1148 1749	5.2 1.2 5.3	28 M	0557 1215 1810	4.7 1.7 4.7
14 M ●	0017 0615 1237 1837	0.9 5.4 1.0 5.4	29 TU	0024 0627 1253 1845	1.5 4.9 1.5 4.8
15 TU	0103 0659 1325 1925	0.9 5.5 0.9 5.3	30 W O	0100 0658 1329 1921	1.4 5.0 1.4 4.9
			31 TH	0135 0730 1406 1958	1.3 5.1 1.3 4.9

STORNOWAY
LAT 58°12′N
LONG 6°23′W

TIMES AND HEIGHTS OF HIGH AND LOW WATER (Heights in Metres)

TIME ZONE UT
For Summer Time (area enclosed in shaded box) add 1 hour

2020

JANUARY

Date	Day	Time	m	Time	m	Time	m	Time	m
1	W	0435	1.8	1037	4.3	1710	1.7	2314	3.7
2	TH	0520	2.0	1131	4.1	1759	1.9		
3	F ☽	0019	3.6	0614	2.2	1238	3.9	1855	2.0
4	SA	0136	3.6	0722	2.3	1348	3.9	2003	2.1
5	SU	0247	3.6	0839	2.3	1452	3.9	2111	2.0
6	M	0346	3.8	0946	2.2	1549	4.0	2209	1.8
7	TU	0432	4.0	1040	2.0	1638	4.1	2257	1.6
8	W	0511	4.2	1127	1.7	1722	4.3	2340	1.4
9	TH	0547	4.5	1210	1.4	1803	4.5		
10	F O	0020	1.2	0623	4.7	1252	1.2	1844	4.7
11	SA	0101	1.1	0700	4.9	1334	1.0	1927	4.8
12	SU	0142	0.9	0740	5.0	1417	0.8	2011	4.8
13	M	0224	0.9	0823	5.1	1501	0.8	2058	4.7
14	TU	0307	1.0	0908	5.0	1546	0.8	2147	4.6
15	W	0351	1.1	0957	4.9	1635	1.0	2242	4.4
16	TH	0440	1.3	1053	4.7	1727	1.2	2344	4.2
17	F ☾	0534	1.6	1159	4.4	1826	1.4		
18	SA	0053	4.0	0636	1.8	1314	4.2	1934	1.6
19	SU	0206	3.9	0751	2.0	1431	4.1	2051	1.7
20	M	0317	4.0	0914	1.9	1545	4.1	2204	1.7
21	TU	0420	4.2	1028	1.8	1648	4.2	2303	1.5
22	W	0512	4.4	1128	1.6	1740	4.3	2352	1.4
23	TH	0555	4.6	1218	1.4	1823	4.4		
24	F ●	0035	1.3	0633	4.8	1301	1.2	1900	4.5
25	SA	0114	1.2	0709	4.9	1340	1.1	1934	4.5
26	SU	0150	1.1	0742	4.9	1415	1.0	2006	4.5
27	M	0224	1.1	0814	4.9	1449	1.0	2037	4.4
28	TU	0257	1.2	0846	4.8	1523	1.1	2107	4.3
29	W	0330	1.3	0918	4.6	1557	1.2	2139	4.1
30	TH	0404	1.5	0954	4.4	1631	1.4	2216	3.9
31	F	0440	1.7	1035	4.2	1709	1.6	2300	3.7

FEBRUARY

Date	Day	Time	m	Time	m	Time	m	Time	m
1	SA	0520	1.9	1125	4.0	1752	1.8		
2	SU ☽	0003	3.6	0610	2.2	1233	3.8	1846	2.0
3	M	0129	3.5	0720	2.3	1352	3.7	1957	2.1
4	TU	0248	3.6	0848	2.3	1506	3.7	2118	2.1
5	W	0354	3.8	1007	2.1	1611	3.9	2226	1.9
6	TH	0446	4.0	1105	1.8	1705	4.1	2319	1.6
7	F	0529	4.4	1154	1.4	1751	4.4		
8	SA	0005	1.3	0608	4.7	1239	1.0	1833	4.7
9	SU O	0048	1.0	0646	5.0	1322	0.7	1914	4.9
10	M	0130	0.7	0726	5.2	1404	0.5	1956	5.0
11	TU	0211	0.6	0807	5.3	1446	0.3	2039	4.9
12	W	0253	0.6	0849	5.2	1529	0.4	2123	4.8
13	TH	0335	0.7	0935	5.1	1612	0.6	2212	4.5
14	F	0419	1.0	1026	4.8	1659	1.0	2307	4.2
15	SA ☾	0507	1.3	1127	4.4	1750	1.3		
16	SU	0015	4.0	0603	1.7	1246	4.0	1852	1.7
17	M	0134	3.8	0717	2.0	1414	3.8	2016	2.0
18	TU	0254	3.8	0855	2.1	1539	3.8	2148	1.9
19	W	0406	4.0	1026	1.9	1647	3.9	2254	1.8
20	TH	0501	4.2	1126	1.6	1737	4.1	2343	1.5
21	F	0544	4.4	1211	1.4	1815	4.2		
22	SA	0023	1.3	0619	4.6	1250	1.2	1847	4.4
23	SU ●	0059	1.2	0651	4.8	1324	1.0	1915	4.5
24	M	0133	1.0	0721	4.8	1355	0.9	1942	4.5
25	TU	0204	1.0	0749	4.8	1425	0.9	2008	4.5
26	W	0234	1.0	0817	4.8	1455	0.9	2035	4.4
27	TH	0304	1.1	0847	4.7	1524	1.0	2103	4.3
28	F	0334	1.2	0918	4.5	1555	1.2	2133	4.1
29	SA	0406	1.4	0953	4.3	1628	1.4	2209	3.9

MARCH

Date	Day	Time	m	Time	m	Time	m	Time	m
1	SU	0441	1.6	1036	4.0	1704	1.6	2255	3.7
2	M ☽	0523	1.9	1133	3.8	1749	1.9		
3	TU	0007	3.5	0619	2.2	1259	3.6	1850	2.1
4	W	0150	3.5	0751	2.3	1431	3.6	2026	2.2
5	TH	0314	3.6	0937	2.1	1548	3.7	2159	2.0
6	F	0418	3.9	1046	1.7	1647	4.0	2259	1.6
7	SA	0506	4.3	1136	1.3	1735	4.4	2347	1.2
8	SU	0547	4.7	1221	0.8	1816	4.7		
9	M O	0030	0.8	0626	5.0	1304	0.4	1855	5.0
10	TU	0112	0.5	0705	5.3	1345	0.1	1935	5.1
11	W	0153	0.3	0745	5.4	1425	0.1	2015	5.1
12	TH	0234	0.3	0827	5.3	1506	0.2	2057	4.9
13	F	0315	0.4	0911	5.0	1547	0.5	2142	4.6
14	SA	0357	0.7	1001	4.7	1630	0.9	2234	4.3
15	SU	0444	1.1	1102	4.2	1717	1.4	2341	4.0
16	M ☾	0538	1.6	1228	3.8	1815	1.8		
17	TU	0105	3.7	0651	1.9	1402	3.6	1942	2.1
18	W	0230	3.7	0843	2.1	1530	3.6	2131	2.1
19	TH	0345	3.8	1018	1.9	1638	3.7	2238	1.9
20	F	0442	4.0	1112	1.6	1724	3.9	2325	1.6
21	SA	0524	4.3	1153	1.3	1758	4.1		
22	SU	0003	1.4	0557	4.5	1228	1.1	1825	4.3
23	M	0038	1.1	0627	4.6	1259	0.9	1851	4.4
24	TU ●	0109	1.0	0654	4.7	1328	0.8	1915	4.5
25	W	0139	0.9	0721	4.7	1356	0.7	1939	4.5
26	TH	0209	0.9	0749	4.7	1424	0.8	2004	4.5
27	F	0237	0.9	0817	4.6	1452	0.9	2031	4.4
28	SA	0307	1.0	0848	4.4	1522	1.0	2100	4.2
29	SU	0338	1.2	0923	4.2	1553	1.2	2133	4.1
30	M	0412	1.4	1005	4.0	1628	1.5	2216	3.8
31	TU	0453	1.7	1103	3.7	1710	1.8	2320	3.6

APRIL

Date	Day	Time	m	Time	m	Time	m	Time	m
1	W ☽	0547	2.0	1231	3.5	1808	2.0		
2	TH	0104	3.5	0716	2.1	1406	3.5	1947	2.2
3	F	0236	3.6	0909	1.9	1524	3.7	2131	2.0
4	SA	0345	3.9	1021	1.5	1625	4.0	2235	1.6
5	SU	0438	4.3	1113	1.0	1712	4.4	2324	1.2
6	M	0522	4.7	1157	0.6	1754	4.7		
7	TU	0008	0.7	0602	5.0	1240	0.2	1832	5.0
8	W O	0050	0.4	0642	5.3	1321	0.0	1911	5.1
9	TH	0131	0.3	0723	5.3	1401	0.0	1951	5.1
10	F	0213	0.2	0805	5.2	1441	0.2	2032	4.9
11	SA	0254	0.4	0851	4.9	1521	0.5	2116	4.6
12	SU	0338	0.7	0943	4.4	1603	1.0	2207	4.3
13	M	0425	1.1	1049	4.0	1649	1.4	2314	4.0
14	TU ☾	0519	1.5	1215	3.6	1745	1.9		
15	W	0036	3.8	0631	1.9	1342	3.5	1908	2.2
16	TH	0158	3.7	0818	2.0	1506	3.5	2055	2.2
17	F	0311	3.8	0949	1.8	1613	3.6	2207	2.0
18	SA	0409	3.9	1042	1.6	1658	3.8	2255	1.7
19	SU	0452	4.1	1121	1.3	1731	4.0	2334	1.4
20	M	0527	4.3	1156	1.1	1758	4.2		
21	TU	0009	1.2	0557	4.4	1227	1.0	1823	4.3
22	W	0041	1.1	0626	4.5	1257	0.8	1847	4.4
23	TH ●	0112	0.9	0654	4.6	1325	0.8	1912	4.5
24	F	0142	0.9	0722	4.6	1354	0.8	1937	4.5
25	SA	0212	0.9	0752	4.5	1423	0.9	2004	4.4
26	SU	0243	1.0	0825	4.3	1453	1.0	2035	4.3
27	M	0316	1.1	0904	4.1	1526	1.2	2112	4.2
28	TU	0353	1.3	0952	3.9	1603	1.4	2159	4.0
29	W	0437	1.6	1057	3.7	1647	1.7	2306	3.8
30	TH ☽	0534	1.8	1220	3.5	1748	2.0		

MAY

Date	Day	Time	m	Time	m	Time	m	Time	m
1	F	0038	3.7	0700	1.9	1343	3.6	1921	2.1
2	SA	0203	3.7	0838	1.7	1456	3.7	2057	1.9
3	SU	0311	4.0	0950	1.3	1557	4.0	2204	1.6
4	M	0407	4.3	1043	0.9	1646	4.3	2256	1.2
5	TU	0455	4.6	1130	0.6	1729	4.7	2342	0.8
6	W	0538	4.9	1214	0.3	1809	4.9		
7	TH O	0027	0.5	0620	5.1	1256	0.2	1849	5.0
8	F	0110	0.4	0704	5.1	1338	0.2	1929	5.0
9	SA	0154	0.4	0749	4.9	1418	0.4	2011	4.9
10	SU	0237	0.5	0837	4.6	1459	0.7	2056	4.6
11	M	0323	0.8	0931	4.2	1542	1.1	2148	4.4
12	TU	0410	1.1	1036	3.9	1627	1.5	2249	4.1
13	W	0504	1.4	1150	3.6	1721	1.9		
14	TH ☾	0001	3.9	0608	1.7	1305	3.4	1830	2.1
15	F	0114	3.8	0729	1.9	1420	3.4	1958	2.2
16	SA	0223	3.7	0852	1.8	1528	3.5	2116	2.1
17	SU	0323	3.8	0954	1.7	1618	3.7	2212	1.9
18	M	0411	3.9	1039	1.5	1655	3.9	2257	1.6
19	TU	0451	4.1	1117	1.3	1726	4.0	2335	1.4
20	W	0526	4.2	1151	1.1	1754	4.2		
21	TH	0010	1.2	0557	4.3	1224	1.0	1820	4.3
22	F ●	0044	1.1	0628	4.4	1255	0.9	1847	4.4
23	SA	0117	1.0	0700	4.4	1326	0.9	1915	4.5
24	SU	0150	1.0	0734	4.4	1358	0.9	1946	4.5
25	M	0225	1.0	0813	4.3	1432	1.0	2022	4.4
26	TU	0302	1.1	0857	4.1	1508	1.2	2104	4.3
27	W	0343	1.2	0950	4.0	1549	1.4	2155	4.1
28	TH	0431	1.4	1053	3.8	1637	1.6	2259	4.0
29	F	0530	1.5	1204	3.7	1739	1.8		
30	SA ☽	0015	3.9	0644	1.6	1317	3.7	1858	1.9
31	SU	0130	3.9	0804	1.5	1425	3.8	2020	1.8

JUNE

Date	Day	Time	m	Time	m	Time	m	Time	m
1	M	0238	4.1	0913	1.3	1527	4.0	2128	1.6
2	TU	0338	4.3	1012	1.0	1620	4.3	2227	1.3
3	W	0431	4.5	1104	0.8	1707	4.5	2319	1.0
4	TH	0520	4.7	1151	0.6	1750	4.7		
5	F O	0007	0.8	0606	4.7	1236	0.6	1831	4.8
6	SA	0055	0.7	0653	4.7	1319	0.6	1913	4.9
7	SU	0141	0.6	0740	4.6	1401	0.7	1956	4.8
8	M	0226	0.7	0828	4.4	1443	0.9	2041	4.7
9	TU	0311	0.9	0918	4.2	1525	1.2	2128	4.5
10	W	0357	1.1	1011	3.9	1608	1.5	2219	4.2
11	TH	0445	1.3	1109	3.7	1656	1.7	2316	4.0
12	F	0536	1.6	1211	3.5	1750	1.9		
13	SA ☾	0018	3.9	0634	1.7	1317	3.4	1855	2.1
14	SU	0124	3.8	0740	1.8	1424	3.4	2008	2.1
15	M	0226	3.7	0846	1.8	1524	3.5	2117	2.0
16	TU	0322	3.8	0945	1.7	1612	3.7	2213	1.9
17	W	0411	3.9	1033	1.5	1651	3.9	2259	1.7
18	TH	0453	4.0	1114	1.4	1725	4.1	2340	1.5
19	F	0532	4.1	1151	1.3	1756	4.3		
20	SA	0018	1.3	0608	4.2	1228	1.1	1827	4.4
21	SU ●	0056	1.2	0645	4.3	1304	1.1	1859	4.5
22	M	0134	1.1	0724	4.4	1340	1.0	1935	4.6
23	TU	0213	1.0	0806	4.4	1418	1.0	2014	4.6
24	W	0253	1.0	0851	4.3	1458	1.1	2058	4.5
25	TH	0337	1.0	0942	4.2	1541	1.2	2148	4.4
26	F	0425	1.1	1038	4.1	1630	1.4	2244	4.3
27	SA	0519	1.2	1140	3.9	1725	1.5	2349	4.2
28	SU ☽	0620	1.3	1246	3.9	1830	1.7		
29	M	0058	4.1	0727	1.4	1354	3.9	1942	1.7
30	TU	0208	4.1	0837	1.3	1458	4.0	2055	1.7

SUNRISE AND SUNSET TIMES

STORNOWAY
At 58°12′N 6°23′W

UT		Sunrise	Sunset
Jan	01	0912	1546
	15	0900	1610
Feb	01	0830	1649
	15	0757	1723
Mar	01	0720	1756
	15	0641	1829
BST			
Apr	01	0653	2007
	15	0614	2038
May	01	0532	2115
	15	0500	2145
Jun	01	0431	2217
	15	0420	2232
Jul	01	0426	2232
	15	0445	2217
Aug	01	0518	2145
	15	0548	2110
Sep	01	0625	2024
	15	0655	1945
Oct	01	0730	1859
	15	0801	1820
UT			
Nov	01	0741	1637
	15	0813	1606
Dec	01	0847	1542
	15	0907	1534

STORNOWAY
LAT 58°12′N
LONG 6°23′W

TIMES AND HEIGHTS OF HIGH AND LOW WATER (Heights in Metres)

TIME ZONE UT
For Summer Time (area enclosed in shaded box) add 1 hour

2020

JULY

Date	Day	Time	m
1	W	0315 0943 1558 2203	4.2 1.3 4.1 1.5
2	TH	0417 1043 1651 2303	4.3 1.2 4.4 1.3
3	F	0512 1135 1738 2357	4.4 1.1 4.6 1.1
4	SA	0603 1222 1822	4.4 1.0 4.7
5	SU O	0047 0649 1307 1903	0.9 4.5 0.9 4.8
6	M	0133 0734 1348 1944	0.8 4.4 1.0 4.8
7	TU	0216 0816 1428 2023	0.8 4.4 1.0 4.7
8	W	0258 0856 1507 2103	0.9 4.2 1.2 4.6
9	TH	0338 0936 1546 2143	1.0 4.0 1.3 4.4
10	F	0418 1017 1626 2226	1.2 3.9 1.5 4.2
11	SA	0459 1104 1709 2315	1.4 3.7 1.7 4.0
12	SU ☾	0543 1201 1758	1.6 3.5 1.9
13	M	0015 0632 1310 1857	3.8 1.8 3.5 2.1
14	TU	0123 0731 1420 2009	3.7 1.9 3.5 2.2
15	W	0229 0839 1522 2122	3.7 1.9 3.6 2.1
16	TH	0330 0944 1615 2224	3.7 1.8 3.8 1.9
17	F	0424 1038 1658 2314	3.8 1.7 4.0 1.7
18	SA	0511 1124 1735 2358	4.0 1.5 4.2 1.5
19	SU	0553 1206 1810	4.2 1.3 4.4
20	M ●	0039 0633 1247 1845	1.2 4.3 1.1 4.6
21	TU	0121 0713 1326 1923	1.0 4.5 1.0 4.8
22	W	0201 0754 1407 2002	0.8 4.6 0.9 4.9
23	TH	0243 0837 1448 2045	0.7 4.6 0.9 4.9
24	F	0325 0923 1530 2130	0.7 4.5 0.9 4.8
25	SA	0410 1013 1615 2221	0.7 4.3 1.1 4.6
26	SU	0457 1109 1704 2320	0.9 4.2 1.3 4.4
27	M ☽	0550 1214 1801	1.2 4.0 1.5
28	TU	0029 0651 1324 1908	4.2 1.4 3.9 1.7
29	W	0146 0803 1435 2028	4.0 1.6 3.9 1.8
30	TH	0304 0921 1543 2151	4.0 1.6 4.0 1.7
31	F	0416 1031 1642 2301	4.0 1.5 4.2 1.5

AUGUST

Date	Day	Time	m
1	SA	0516 1127 1731 2356	4.1 1.4 4.5 1.3
2	SU	0604 1214 1814	4.3 1.3 4.6
3	M O	0043 0645 1257 1851	1.1 4.4 1.1 4.8
4	TU	0125 0721 1335 1926	0.9 4.4 1.0 4.8
5	W	0203 0755 1411 2000	0.8 4.4 1.0 4.8
6	TH	0238 0827 1446 2033	0.8 4.3 1.1 4.7
7	F	0312 0858 1520 2106	0.9 4.2 1.2 4.6
8	SA	0345 0929 1554 2140	1.0 4.1 1.3 4.4
9	SU	0419 1004 1630 2219	1.2 3.9 1.6 4.2
10	M	0455 1046 1709 2307	1.5 3.7 1.8 3.9
11	TU ☾	0535 1145 1756	1.7 3.6 2.0
12	W	0013 0623 1309 1859	3.7 1.9 3.5 2.2
13	TH	0135 0727 1430 2027	3.6 2.1 3.5 2.3
14	F	0252 0851 1538 2152	3.6 2.1 3.7 2.1
15	SA	0358 1006 1631 2253	3.7 2.0 3.9 1.8
16	SU	0453 1102 1714 2340	3.9 1.7 4.2 1.5
17	M	0537 1148 1752	4.2 1.4 4.5
18	TU	0023 0617 1230 1827	1.1 4.4 1.1 4.8
19	W ●	0104 0656 1311 1904	0.8 4.7 0.9 5.0
20	TH	0145 0735 1351 1943	0.5 4.8 0.7 5.2
21	F	0225 0815 1431 2023	0.4 4.9 0.6 5.2
22	SA	0305 0858 1512 2107	0.3 4.8 0.7 5.1
23	SU	0347 0944 1555 2154	0.5 4.6 0.8 4.8
24	M	0431 1036 1641 2251	0.8 4.3 1.1 4.4
25	TU ☽	0519 1141 1734	1.2 4.1 1.5
26	W	0007 0616 1259 1841	4.1 1.6 3.9 1.8
27	TH	0137 0732 1419 2014	3.9 1.9 3.9 2.0
28	F	0305 0909 1534 2155	3.8 2.0 4.0 1.9
29	SA	0421 1026 1635 2303	3.9 1.8 4.2 1.6
30	SU	0516 1120 1722 2352	4.0 1.6 4.4 1.3
31	M	0558 1203 1800	4.2 1.4 4.6

SEPTEMBER

Date	Day	Time	m
1	TU	0032 0631 1242 1833	1.1 4.4 1.2 4.8
2	W O	0108 0701 1317 1903	0.9 4.5 1.1 4.9
3	TH	0140 0728 1349 1932	0.8 4.5 1.0 4.9
4	F	0211 0755 1420 2001	0.8 4.5 1.0 4.8
5	SA	0241 0821 1451 2030	0.8 4.4 1.1 4.7
6	SU	0310 0848 1522 2101	1.0 4.3 1.2 4.5
7	M	0341 0917 1554 2135	1.1 4.1 1.4 4.3
8	TU	0413 0952 1629 2217	1.4 4.0 1.7 4.0
9	W	0448 1037 1709 2315	1.7 3.8 2.0 3.7
10	TH ☾	0529 1150 1804	1.9 3.6 2.2
11	F	0047 0625 1338 1933	3.5 2.2 3.5 2.4
12	SA	0220 0759 1500 2125	3.5 2.3 3.7 2.2
13	SU	0335 0939 1602 2232	3.7 2.1 3.9 1.8
14	M	0432 1041 1649 2319	3.9 1.8 4.2 1.4
15	TU	0518 1127 1728	4.3 1.4 4.6
16	W	0001 0556 1209 1804	1.0 4.6 1.1 5.0
17	TH ●	0042 0634 1250 1841	0.6 4.9 0.7 5.3
18	F	0121 0711 1329 1919	0.3 5.1 0.5 5.4
19	SA	0201 0750 1409 1959	0.2 5.1 0.4 5.4
20	SU	0241 0830 1450 2042	0.2 5.0 0.5 5.2
21	M	0321 0914 1533 2130	0.4 4.8 0.7 4.8
22	TU	0403 1005 1619 2230	0.8 4.5 1.1 4.4
23	W	0450 1111 1712 2357	1.3 4.1 1.5 4.0
24	TH ☽	0546 1237 1823	1.8 3.9 1.9
25	F	0133 0707 1402 2011	3.7 2.2 3.9 2.1
26	SA	0303 0859 1519 2154	3.7 2.2 4.0 1.9
27	SU	0416 1014 1619 2252	3.8 2.0 4.2 1.6
28	M	0506 1104 1704 2334	4.0 1.7 4.4 1.4
29	TU	0542 1143 1739	4.2 1.5 4.6
30	W	0010 0610 1219 1809	1.1 4.4 1.3 4.8

OCTOBER

Date	Day	Time	m
1	TH O	0042 0635 1252 1837	1.0 4.5 1.1 4.8
2	F	0112 0700 1323 1904	0.9 4.6 1.0 4.9
3	SA	0140 0724 1353 1931	0.8 4.6 1.0 4.8
4	SU	0208 0748 1422 1959	0.9 4.6 1.1 4.7
5	M	0236 0814 1452 2029	1.0 4.5 1.2 4.5
6	TU	0305 0842 1523 2103	1.2 4.4 1.4 4.3
7	W	0336 0914 1557 2144	1.4 4.2 1.6 4.0
8	TH	0410 0954 1637 2241	1.7 4.0 1.9 3.8
9	F	0450 1057 1729	1.9 3.7 2.2
10	SA ☾	0015 0543 1249 1855	3.6 2.2 3.6 2.3
11	SU	0151 0716 1420 2053	3.5 2.4 3.7 2.2
12	M	0307 0907 1527 2203	3.7 2.2 4.0 1.8
13	TU	0406 1013 1617 2252	4.0 1.9 4.3 1.3
14	W	0452 1101 1659 2334	4.4 1.4 4.7 0.9
15	TH	0532 1143 1738	4.7 1.0 5.1
16	F ●	0015 0609 1225 1816	0.5 5.0 0.7 5.3
17	SA	0056 0646 1306 1856	0.3 5.2 0.5 5.5
18	SU	0135 0725 1347 1938	0.2 5.3 0.4 5.4
19	M	0216 0806 1429 2023	0.3 5.2 0.5 5.1
20	TU	0256 0850 1514 2114	0.6 4.9 0.8 4.7
21	W	0339 0940 1601 2219	1.0 4.6 1.2 4.3
22	TH	0425 1046 1656 2348	1.5 4.3 1.6 3.9
23	F ☽	0521 1212 1809	2.0 4.0 1.9
24	SA	0118 0640 1336 1952	3.7 2.3 3.9 2.1
25	SU	0244 0827 1451 2128	3.7 2.3 4.0 1.9
26	M	0355 0944 1551 2223	3.8 2.1 4.2 1.7
27	TU	0442 1035 1636 2304	4.0 1.9 4.3 1.5
28	W	0516 1115 1711 2339	4.2 1.6 4.5 1.3
29	TH	0544 1151 1742	4.4 1.4 4.6
30	F	0010 0609 1225 1810	1.1 4.5 1.3 4.7
31	SA O	0041 0633 1256 1838	1.0 4.6 1.2 4.8

NOVEMBER

Date	Day	Time	m
1	SU	0109 0657 1326 1906	1.0 4.7 1.1 4.7
2	M	0138 0722 1357 1936	1.0 4.7 1.2 4.7
3	TU	0206 0748 1428 2008	1.1 4.6 1.3 4.5
4	W	0236 0817 1500 2044	1.2 4.5 1.4 4.3
5	TH	0308 0851 1536 2129	1.4 4.4 1.6 4.1
6	F	0343 0934 1618 2230	1.7 4.2 1.8 3.8
7	SA	0425 1036 1712 2352	1.9 4.0 2.0 3.7
8	SU ☾	0520 1208 1832	2.2 3.8 2.1
9	M	0117 0644 1337 2010	3.7 2.3 3.9 2.0
10	TU	0231 0825 1446 2124	3.8 2.2 4.1 1.7
11	W	0333 0935 1542 2218	4.1 1.9 4.4 1.3
12	TH	0423 1029 1630 2305	4.4 1.5 4.7 0.9
13	F	0506 1116 1713 2348	4.8 1.2 5.0 0.6
14	SA	0546 1200 1756	5.0 0.9 5.2
15	SU ●	0030 0625 1245 1838	0.5 5.2 0.7 5.3
16	M	0113 0705 1329 1923	0.4 5.3 0.6 5.2
17	TU	0154 0747 1414 2012	0.6 5.2 0.7 4.9
18	W	0236 0833 1500 2105	0.8 5.0 0.9 4.6
19	TH	0320 0923 1549 2208	1.2 4.7 1.2 4.2
20	F	0406 1024 1644 2323	1.6 4.4 1.5 3.9
21	SA	0500 1137 1748	2.0 4.2 1.8
22	SU ☽	0042 0606 1253 1906	3.7 2.2 4.1 2.0
23	M	0200 0730 1404 2030	3.6 2.4 4.0 2.0
24	TU	0311 0851 1507 2135	3.7 2.3 4.1 1.9
25	W	0405 0952 1558 2223	3.9 2.1 4.2 1.7
26	TH	0444 1039 1639 2302	4.0 1.9 4.3 1.5
27	F	0516 1120 1714 2337	4.2 1.7 4.4 1.4
28	SA	0544 1156 1746	4.4 1.5 4.5
29	SU	0010 0610 1231 1817	1.3 4.5 1.4 4.6
30	M O	0041 0637 1304 1849	1.2 4.6 1.3 4.6

DECEMBER

Date	Day	Time	m
1	TU	0112 0704 1337 1921	1.2 4.7 1.3 4.6
2	W	0143 0733 1411 1957	1.2 4.7 1.3 4.5
3	TH	0215 0805 1446 2037	1.3 4.6 1.4 4.3
4	F	0250 0843 1525 2124	1.4 4.5 1.5 4.2
5	SA	0328 0929 1609 2220	1.6 4.4 1.6 4.0
6	SU	0412 1025 1702 2326	1.8 4.2 1.8 3.9
7	M	0506 1135 1808	2.0 4.1 1.8
8	TU ☾	0040 0616 1252 1925	3.8 2.1 4.1 1.8
9	W	0151 0738 1403 2038	3.9 2.1 4.2 1.6
10	TH	0256 0852 1506 2141	4.1 1.9 4.4 1.4
11	F	0353 0955 1603 2236	4.3 1.7 4.6 1.1
12	SA	0442 1050 1654 2325	4.6 1.4 4.8 0.9
13	SU	0527 1141 1743	4.9 1.1 4.9
14	M ●	0011 0610 1231 1830	0.8 5.0 0.9 5.0
15	TU	0056 0653 1318 1918	0.8 5.1 0.8 4.9
16	W	0140 0736 1405 2007	0.9 5.1 0.8 4.8
17	TH	0223 0821 1452 2056	1.0 5.0 0.9 4.5
18	F	0306 0908 1538 2147	1.2 4.9 1.1 4.3
19	SA	0350 0957 1626 2241	1.5 4.6 1.4 4.0
20	SU	0436 1051 1717 2341	1.8 4.4 1.6 3.8
21	M ☽	0527 1152 1812	2.0 4.2 1.8
22	TU	0049 0627 1300 1914	3.6 2.2 4.0 2.0
23	W	0202 0738 1406 2022	3.6 2.3 3.9 2.0
24	TH	0309 0852 1508 2127	3.7 2.3 4.0 2.0
25	F	0403 0955 1601 2220	3.8 2.2 4.0 1.8
26	SA	0445 1047 1646 2304	4.0 2.0 4.1 1.7
27	SU	0521 1130 1726 2342	4.2 1.8 4.3 1.5
28	M	0553 1209 1802	4.4 1.6 4.4
29	TU	0018 0622 1247 1837	1.4 4.5 1.5 4.4
30	W O	0053 0652 1323 1913	1.3 4.7 1.3 4.5
31	TH	0127 0724 1400 1950	1.3 4.7 1.2 4.5

OBAN
LAT 56°25′N
LONG 5°29′W

TIMES AND HEIGHTS OF HIGH AND LOW WATER (Heights in Metres)

TIME ZONE UT
For Summer Time (area enclosed in shaded box) add 1 hour

2020

JANUARY

Date	Day	Time	m
1	W	0331 0922 1603 2127	1.5 3.5 1.8 3.2
2	TH	0415 1009 1653 2213	1.7 3.4 2.0 3.1
3	F ☽	0504 1106 1749 2313	1.9 3.2 2.0 3.0
4	SA	0559 1226 1850	1.9 3.2 2.0
5	SU	0040 0659 1353 1951	2.9 2.0 3.2 1.9
6	M	0205 0804 1454 2048	3.0 1.9 3.3 1.8
7	TU	0303 0908 1542 2137	3.2 1.8 3.5 1.6
8	W	0350 1002 1624 2221	3.4 1.6 3.7 1.3
9	TH	0432 1050 1705 2303	3.6 1.4 3.8 1.1
10	F ○	0512 1135 1743 2344	3.8 1.2 3.9 0.9
11	SA	0551 1219 1821	3.9 1.0 3.9
12	SU	0026 0630 1303 1858	0.7 4.0 0.9 3.9
13	M	0110 0710 1348 1938	0.6 4.0 0.9 3.8
14	TU	0154 0753 1434 2021	0.6 4.0 1.0 3.7
15	W	0241 0838 1523 2107	0.7 3.9 1.1 3.5
16	TH	0330 0927 1617 2159	0.8 3.7 1.3 3.3
17	F ☾	0425 1023 1718 2302	1.0 3.5 1.5 3.1
18	SA	0526 1134 1827	1.2 3.3 1.6
19	SU	0029 0634 1312 1942	3.0 1.4 3.2 1.6
20	M	0200 0748 1437 2055	3.1 1.4 3.2 1.6
21	TU	0309 0902 1543 2154	3.2 1.4 3.3 1.5
22	W	0400 1007 1630 2242	3.4 1.3 3.4 1.3
23	TH	0442 1100 1707 2323	3.6 1.2 3.6 1.2
24	F ●	0521 1146 1741	3.8 1.2 3.7
25	SA	0001 0558 1227 1814	1.1 4.0 1.1 3.7
26	SU	0039 0634 1305 1847	1.0 4.0 1.1 3.8
27	M	0116 0710 1341 1919	1.0 4.0 1.2 3.8
28	TU	0151 0744 1415 1951	1.0 4.0 1.3 3.7
29	W	0225 0818 1449 2022	1.2 3.8 1.4 3.6
30	TH	0258 0851 1524 2054	1.3 3.7 1.6 3.5
31	F	0331 0926 1602 2128	1.5 3.5 1.7 3.3

FEBRUARY

Date	Day	Time	m
1	SA	0407 1004 1647 2208	1.7 3.3 1.9 3.1
2	SU ☽	0452 1052 1744 2300	1.9 3.1 2.0 3.0
3	M	0552 1211 1850	2.0 3.0 2.0
4	TU	0019 0704 1418 1957	2.9 2.0 3.0 1.9
5	W	0224 0824 1526 2101	3.0 1.9 3.2 1.6
6	TH	0331 0943 1614 2156	3.2 1.6 3.4 1.4
7	F	0420 1042 1656 2244	3.5 1.3 3.6 1.0
8	SA	0503 1130 1735 2329	3.7 1.0 3.8 0.7
9	SU ○	0543 1213 1812	4.0 0.8 3.9
10	M	0012 0622 1255 1848	0.5 4.1 0.6 4.0
11	TU	0056 0701 1337 1925	0.3 4.2 0.6 4.0
12	W	0140 0741 1418 2004	0.3 4.1 0.6 3.8
13	TH	0224 0822 1501 2045	0.3 4.0 0.8 3.6
14	F	0311 0905 1548 2130	0.5 3.7 1.0 3.4
15	SA ☾	0401 0952 1640 2222	0.8 3.4 1.3 3.1
16	SU	0457 1050 1743 2337	1.1 3.1 1.5 2.9
17	M	0603 1226 1858	1.4 2.9 1.7
18	TU	0124 0720 1440 2030	2.9 1.6 2.8 1.7
19	W	0256 0853 1618 2144	3.0 1.6 3.0 1.5
20	TH	0357 1009 1653 2234	3.2 1.5 3.2 1.4
21	F	0434 1059 1707 2314	3.5 1.3 3.4 1.2
22	SA	0509 1138 1732 2350	3.7 1.2 3.5 1.0
23	SU ●	0544 1213 1802	3.9 1.1 3.7
24	M	0024 0618 1246 1831	0.9 4.0 1.0 3.8
25	TU	0057 0651 1318 1900	0.8 4.0 1.0 3.8
26	W	0129 0722 1348 1928	0.9 4.0 1.1 3.8
27	TH	0158 0751 1417 1955	1.0 3.9 1.2 3.7
28	F	0224 0820 1445 2021	1.2 3.7 1.3 3.6
29	SA	0248 0847 1512 2051	1.3 3.6 1.5 3.4

MARCH

Date	Day	Time	m
1	SU	0313 0918 1549 2125	1.5 3.3 1.7 3.2
2	M ☽	0347 0957 1642 2209	1.7 3.1 1.8 3.0
3	TU	0443 1055 1757 2313	1.9 2.9 1.9 2.9
4	W	0622 1347 1916	2.0 2.8 1.9
5	TH	0144 0802 1514 2029	2.8 1.9 3.0 1.6
6	F	0315 0937 1604 2133	3.1 1.6 3.3 1.3
7	SA	0406 1034 1644 2226	3.5 1.2 3.6 0.9
8	SU	0449 1119 1721 2312	3.8 0.8 3.8 0.5
9	M ○	0528 1200 1756 2356	4.1 0.5 4.0 0.2
10	TU	0607 1239 1830	4.2 0.4 4.1
11	W	0039 0645 1318 1905	0.1 4.3 0.3 4.0
12	TH	0123 0723 1357 1942	0.0 4.2 0.4 3.9
13	F	0206 0801 1437 2021	0.2 4.0 0.6 3.7
14	SA	0251 0840 1520 2102	0.4 3.7 0.9 3.5
15	SU	0340 0922 1609 2150	0.7 3.3 1.2 3.2
16	M ☾	0434 1013 1708 2257	1.1 3.0 1.5 2.9
17	TU	0538 1142 1821	1.5 2.6 1.7
18	W	0057 0659 1513 2002	2.8 1.7 2.6 1.7
19	TH	0246 0854 1617 2125	2.9 1.7 2.8 1.6
20	F	0347 1004 1649 2216	3.1 1.5 3.0 1.3
21	SA	0417 1046 1650 2255	3.4 1.3 3.2 1.1
22	SU	0448 1120 1710 2329	3.6 1.1 3.5 0.9
23	M	0522 1150 1738	3.8 1.0 3.7
24	TU ●	0002 0554 1220 1807	0.8 3.9 0.9 3.8
25	W	0033 0626 1249 1834	0.8 4.0 0.9 3.9
26	TH	0102 0656 1318 1900	0.8 4.0 0.9 3.8
27	F	0129 0723 1345 1926	0.9 3.9 1.0 3.8
28	SA	0152 0749 1408 1951	1.1 3.7 1.1 3.7
29	SU	0211 0815 1434 2020	1.3 3.6 1.3 3.5
30	M	0236 0845 1509 2054	1.4 3.3 1.5 3.3
31	TU	0311 0924 1559 2138	1.6 3.1 1.7 3.1

APRIL

Date	Day	Time	m
1	W ☽	0405 1022 1715 2242	1.8 2.8 1.8 2.9
2	TH	0601 1320 1841	1.9 2.7 1.8
3	F	0102 0753 1452 1959	2.9 1.8 2.9 1.6
4	SA	0251 0919 1542 2107	3.2 1.5 3.2 1.2
5	SU	0343 1013 1623 2203	3.5 1.1 3.5 0.8
6	M	0426 1057 1658 2251	3.8 0.7 3.8 0.5
7	TU	0506 1137 1732 2336	4.1 0.5 4.0 0.2
8	W ○	0545 1216 1807	4.3 0.3 4.1
9	TH	0020 0623 1255 1843	0.0 4.3 0.3 4.1
10	F	0104 0701 1333 1920	0.1 4.2 0.4 4.0
11	SA	0148 0739 1413 1959	0.2 3.9 0.6 3.8
12	SU	0233 0817 1455 2040	0.5 3.6 0.9 3.5
13	M	0321 0857 1543 2126	0.8 3.2 1.2 3.2
14	TU ☾	0414 0945 1639 2228	1.2 2.9 1.5 3.0
15	W	0517 1103 1749	1.6 2.6 1.7
16	TH	0025 0639 1436 1921	2.8 1.7 2.6 1.7
17	F	0213 0833 1545 2051	2.9 1.7 2.7 1.6
18	SA	0311 0937 1609 2145	3.1 1.5 2.9 1.4
19	SU	0346 1017 1613 2226	3.3 1.4 3.2 1.2
20	M	0419 1049 1638 2301	3.5 1.2 3.4 1.0
21	TU	0452 1118 1707 2332	3.7 1.0 3.6 0.9
22	W	0526 1146 1737	3.8 0.9 3.7
23	TH ●	0002 0557 1216 1805	0.9 3.9 0.9 3.8
24	F	0031 0628 1246 1832	0.9 3.9 0.9 3.8
25	SA	0059 0656 1314 1859	1.0 3.8 0.9 3.8
26	SU	0124 0724 1340 1927	1.1 3.7 1.0 3.7
27	M	0148 0753 1411 1959	1.2 3.5 1.2 3.5
28	TU	0218 0828 1450 2036	1.4 3.3 1.3 3.4
29	W	0300 0912 1541 2124	1.6 3.1 1.5 3.2
30	TH ☽	0406 1017 1650 2233	1.7 2.8 1.6 3.0

MAY

Date	Day	Time	m
1	F	0555 1220 1810	1.8 2.7 1.6
2	SA	0025 0734 1418 1927	3.0 1.7 2.9 1.4
3	SU	0214 0850 1512 2036	3.2 1.4 3.2 1.2
4	M	0312 0945 1554 2135	3.5 1.1 3.5 0.8
5	TU	0359 1030 1631 2227	3.8 0.8 3.7 0.5
6	W	0441 1112 1707 2315	4.0 0.6 3.9 0.3
7	TH ○	0522 1152 1744	4.2 0.4 4.0
8	F	0001 0601 1231 1822	0.2 4.1 0.4 4.1
9	SA	0046 0640 1310 1901	0.3 4.0 0.5 4.0
10	SU	0131 0719 1351 1941	0.4 3.8 0.7 3.8
11	M	0217 0758 1434 2023	0.7 3.5 0.9 3.6
12	TU	0304 0839 1521 2109	1.0 3.2 1.2 3.4
13	W	0356 0926 1614 2205	1.3 2.9 1.4 3.1
14	TH ☾	0455 1030 1715 2329	1.6 2.7 1.6 2.9
15	F	0608 1308 1829	1.8 2.6 1.7
16	SA	0120 0738 1422 1954	2.9 1.8 2.7 1.7
17	SU	0224 0849 1500 2100	3.1 1.7 2.9 1.5
18	M	0308 0934 1529 2146	3.2 1.5 3.1 1.4
19	TU	0344 1009 1600 2224	3.4 1.3 3.3 1.3
20	W	0420 1040 1633 2256	3.6 1.2 3.5 1.1
21	TH	0455 1111 1706 2328	3.7 1.0 3.6 1.1
22	F ●	0530 1142 1737	3.8 1.0 3.7
23	SA	0000 0603 1215 1807	1.0 3.8 0.9 3.8
24	SU	0033 0635 1248 1838	1.1 3.7 0.9 3.7
25	M	0106 0707 1321 1911	1.1 3.6 1.0 3.7
26	TU	0141 0742 1358 1949	1.2 3.5 1.1 3.6
27	W	0220 0823 1441 2031	1.3 3.3 1.2 3.5
28	TH	0310 0912 1531 2123	1.4 3.1 1.3 3.3
29	F	0417 1014 1632 2229	1.6 3.0 1.4 3.2
30	SA ☽	0541 1139 1742 2353	1.6 2.9 1.4 3.2
31	SU	0704 1329 1855	1.5 3.0 1.3

JUNE

Date	Day	Time	m
1	M	0129 0815 1434 2004	3.3 1.4 3.2 1.2
2	TU	0238 0914 1523 2107	3.5 1.1 3.4 0.9
3	W	0332 1003 1606 2203	3.7 0.9 3.6 0.8
4	TH	0419 1048 1645 2255	3.8 0.8 3.8 0.6
5	F ○	0502 1130 1725 2344	3.9 0.7 3.9 0.6
6	SA	0544 1211 1806	3.9 0.7 4.0
7	SU	0031 0625 1252 1846	0.6 3.8 0.7 4.0
8	M	0117 0705 1334 1927	0.7 3.7 0.8 3.9
9	TU	0202 0744 1416 2009	0.9 3.5 1.0 3.7
10	W	0248 0825 1500 2053	1.2 3.3 1.2 3.5
11	TH	0336 0907 1547 2140	1.4 3.1 1.4 3.3
12	F	0427 0956 1638 2236	1.6 2.9 1.5 3.1
13	SA ☾	0523 1100 1734 2348	1.8 2.8 1.7 3.0
14	SU	0626 1232 1835	1.8 2.7 1.7
15	M	0112 0732 1348 1941	3.0 1.8 2.8 1.7
16	TU	0216 0831 1437 2043	3.1 1.7 3.0 1.7
17	W	0304 0918 1520 2134	3.2 1.5 3.1 1.5
18	TH	0347 0958 1600 2216	3.4 1.4 3.3 1.4
19	F	0428 1036 1638 2255	3.5 1.2 3.5 1.3
20	SA	0508 1113 1715 2335	3.6 1.1 3.6 1.2
21	SU ●	0546 1150 1751	3.7 1.0 3.7
22	M	0015 0622 1228 1827	1.1 3.7 0.9 3.8
23	TU	0056 0658 1307 1904	1.1 3.7 0.8 3.8
24	W	0138 0736 1347 1944	1.1 3.6 0.8 3.7
25	TH	0223 0818 1431 2028	1.1 3.4 0.9 3.6
26	F	0313 0905 1520 2118	1.2 3.3 1.0 3.5
27	SA	0409 0959 1614 2214	1.3 3.1 1.1 3.4
28	SU ☽	0515 1104 1715 2323	1.4 3.0 1.2 3.3
29	M	0626 1229 1823	1.4 3.0 1.2
30	TU	0046 0738 1354 1933	3.3 1.4 3.1 1.2

SUNRISE AND SUNSET TIMES

OBAN
At 56°25′N 5°29′W

		Sunrise	Sunset
UT			
Jan	01	0856	1556
	15	0845	1618
Feb	01	0818	1654
	15	0748	1725
Mar	01	0714	1756
	15	0637	1825
BST			
Apr	01	0652	2001
	15	0615	2030
May	01	0536	2103
	15	0507	2131
Jun	01	0441	2200
	15	0432	2213
Jul	01	0437	2214
	15	0454	2201
Aug	01	0524	2131
	15	0551	2100
Sep	01	0625	2017
	15	0653	1940
Oct	01	0725	1857
	15	0754	1820
UT			
Nov	01	0731	1640
	15	0801	1612
Dec	01	0831	1550
	15	0850	1544

OBAN
LAT 56°25′N
LONG 5°29′W

TIMES AND HEIGHTS OF HIGH AND LOW WATER (Heights in Metres)

TIME ZONE UT
For Summer Time (area enclosed in shaded box) add 1 hour

2020

JULY

Date	Day	Time	m
1	W	0208 0843 1457 2041	3.3 1.3 3.2 1.2
2	TH	0313 0940 1549 2144	3.4 1.2 3.4 1.1
3	F	0407 1030 1634 2241	3.5 1.1 3.6 1.0
4	SA	0454 1115 1716 2333	3.6 0.9 3.8 0.9
5	SU ○	0537 1158 1756	3.7 0.9 3.9
6	M	0020 0617 1239 1836	0.9 3.7 0.8 4.0
7	TU	0105 0655 1320 1915	0.9 3.6 0.9 3.9
8	W	0148 0732 1359 1954	1.0 3.5 1.0 3.8
9	TH	0229 0807 1439 2032	1.2 3.4 1.1 3.7
10	F	0310 0843 1518 2111	1.3 3.3 1.3 3.5
11	SA	0351 0921 1559 2153	1.5 3.2 1.4 3.3
12	SU ☾	0436 1003 1643 2241	1.7 3.0 1.6 3.2
13	M	0526 1054 1733 2341	1.8 2.9 1.8 3.1
14	TU	0623 1205 1828	1.8 2.8 1.8
15	W	0101 0723 1333 1930	3.0 1.8 2.9 1.9
16	TH	0220 0824 1441 2036	3.1 1.7 3.0 1.8
17	F	0320 0920 1534 2140	3.2 1.5 3.2 1.6
18	SA	0409 1007 1620 2234	3.4 1.3 3.4 1.4
19	SU	0454 1050 1702 2321	3.5 1.1 3.6 1.2
20	M ●	0535 1131 1742	3.6 0.9 3.7
21	TU	0006 0614 1212 1820	1.0 3.7 0.7 3.9
22	W	0049 0650 1252 1858	0.9 3.8 0.6 3.9
23	TH	0131 0727 1334 1937	0.8 3.7 0.6 3.9
24	F	0215 0805 1418 2018	0.8 3.6 0.6 3.9
25	SA	0300 0847 1504 2102	0.9 3.5 0.7 3.7
26	SU	0348 0934 1554 2152	1.1 3.3 0.8 3.5
27	M ☽	0444 1030 1650 2251	1.2 3.1 1.0 3.3
28	TU	0548 1144 1755	1.4 3.0 1.2
29	W	0009 0700 1321 1906	3.1 1.5 3.0 1.4
30	TH	0149 0817 1443 2022	3.1 1.5 3.1 1.4
31	F	0312 0927 1545 2136	3.1 1.4 3.3 1.3

AUGUST

Date	Day	Time	m
1	SA	0416 1022 1632 2238	3.3 1.2 3.5 1.2
2	SU	0500 1107 1711 2328	3.4 1.1 3.7 1.1
3	M ○	0536 1148 1748	3.5 0.9 3.9
4	TU	0011 0610 1227 1824	1.0 3.6 0.9 4.0
5	W	0052 0642 1304 1859	1.0 3.7 0.8 4.0
6	TH	0129 0714 1340 1933	1.0 3.7 0.9 4.0
7	F	0204 0744 1414 2006	1.1 3.6 1.0 3.9
8	SA	0239 0814 1446 2039	1.2 3.5 1.2 3.7
9	SU	0313 0845 1520 2112	1.4 3.4 1.4 3.5
10	M	0350 0918 1556 2148	1.5 3.3 1.6 3.3
11	TU ☾	0434 0956 1638 2230	1.7 3.1 1.8 3.1
12	W	0528 1046 1733 2334	1.8 2.9 1.9 2.9
13	TH	0631 1205 1842	1.9 2.8 2.0
14	F	0144 0740 1414 2000	2.9 1.9 2.9 2.0
15	SA	0308 0847 1522 2126	3.1 1.7 3.1 1.8
16	SU	0401 0945 1609 2229	3.3 1.4 3.4 1.5
17	M	0444 1032 1651 2315	3.5 1.1 3.6 1.2
18	TU	0524 1114 1730 2357	3.7 0.8 3.9 0.9
19	W ●	0601 1155 1808	3.8 0.6 4.1
20	TH	0037 0635 1236 1844	0.7 3.9 0.4 4.2
21	F	0116 0708 1317 1921	0.6 3.9 0.3 4.2
22	SA	0156 0744 1400 1959	0.6 3.8 0.3 4.0
23	SU	0237 0823 1445 2040	0.7 3.7 0.5 3.8
24	M	0322 0906 1533 2125	0.9 3.5 0.7 3.5
25	TU ☽	0413 0957 1628 2217	1.1 3.2 1.0 3.2
26	W	0513 1107 1732 2336	1.4 3.0 1.3 2.9
27	TH	0627 1303 1847	1.6 2.9 1.6
28	F	0150 0757 1442 2016	2.8 1.6 3.0 1.6
29	SA	0348 0919 1549 2145	2.9 1.5 3.3 1.5
30	SU	0439 1014 1628 2240	3.1 1.3 3.5 1.3
31	M	0504 1057 1659 2321	3.3 1.1 3.7 1.2

SEPTEMBER

Date	Day	Time	m
1	TU	0524 1134 1731 2356	3.5 0.9 3.9 1.0
2	W ○	0551 1209 1804	3.7 0.8 4.1
3	TH	0030 0620 1243 1835	1.0 3.8 0.8 4.1
4	F	0102 0648 1315 1906	1.0 3.8 0.8 4.1
5	SA	0134 0715 1345 1936	1.0 3.8 1.0 4.0
6	SU	0204 0742 1413 2005	1.1 3.7 1.1 3.8
7	M	0235 0809 1440 2033	1.3 3.6 1.4 3.6
8	TU	0306 0839 1508 2102	1.5 3.5 1.6 3.4
9	W	0342 0913 1541 2137	1.7 3.3 1.8 3.2
10	TH ☾	0433 0955 1636 2227	1.8 3.1 2.0 2.9
11	F	0545 1058 1809	2.0 2.9 2.2
12	SA	0131 0702 1402 1947	2.8 1.9 2.9 2.1
13	SU	0300 0818 1512 2126	3.0 1.8 3.1 1.8
14	M	0348 0921 1555 2218	3.2 1.4 3.5 1.4
15	TU	0429 1011 1633 2300	3.5 1.1 3.8 1.0
16	W	0505 1054 1710 2338	3.7 0.7 4.1 0.7
17	TH ●	0539 1135 1746	3.9 0.4 4.3
18	F	0016 0611 1216 1822	0.5 4.0 0.2 4.4
19	SA	0054 0644 1258 1858	0.4 4.1 0.2 4.3
20	SU	0132 0719 1341 1936	0.4 4.0 0.2 4.2
21	M	0211 0758 1426 2015	0.6 3.8 0.4 3.9
22	TU	0255 0839 1514 2056	0.8 3.6 0.8 3.5
23	W	0344 0928 1609 2145	1.1 3.3 1.1 3.1
24	TH ☽	0443 1036 1713 2303	1.4 3.0 1.5 2.8
25	F	0557 1253 1833	1.7 2.9 1.7
26	SA	0227 0735 1439 2026	2.7 1.7 3.1 1.7
27	SU	0351 0901 1540 2144	2.9 1.6 3.3 1.6
28	M	0433 0955 1609 2227	3.1 1.3 3.5 1.4
29	TU	0445 1036 1635 2301	3.3 1.1 3.8 1.2
30	W	0457 1112 1705 2331	3.5 1.0 3.9 1.1

OCTOBER

Date	Day	Time	m
1	TH ○	0523 1145 1736	3.7 0.9 4.1
2	F	0001 0551 1217 1807	1.0 3.9 0.8 4.1
3	SA	0031 0618 1247 1836	0.9 3.9 0.9 4.1
4	SU	0101 0645 1315 1905	1.0 4.0 1.0 4.0
5	M	0131 0711 1341 1933	1.1 3.9 1.2 3.9
6	TU	0159 0738 1404 1959	1.2 3.8 1.4 3.7
7	W	0226 0806 1427 2027	1.4 3.6 1.7 3.5
8	TH	0258 0839 1457 2101	1.6 3.4 1.9 3.2
9	F	0344 0921 1548 2152	1.8 3.2 2.1 2.9
10	SA ☾	0458 1023 1749	2.0 3.0 2.2
11	SU	0116 0623 1334 1939	2.8 2.0 3.0 2.1
12	M	0236 0742 1446 2104	3.0 1.8 3.3 1.7
13	TU	0325 0849 1529 2153	3.2 1.5 3.6 1.4
14	W	0404 0942 1607 2234	3.5 1.1 3.9 1.0
15	TH	0439 1028 1644 2313	3.8 0.7 4.2 0.7
16	F ●	0511 1112 1720 2350	4.0 0.4 4.4 0.5
17	SA	0544 1154 1757	4.1 0.3 4.4
18	SU	0027 0618 1238 1834	0.4 4.2 0.2 4.4
19	M	0106 0656 1322 1912	0.5 4.1 0.4 4.2
20	TU	0147 0735 1408 1951	0.6 4.0 0.6 3.8
21	W	0230 0817 1457 2033	0.9 3.7 0.9 3.5
22	TH	0319 0906 1552 2120	1.2 3.4 1.3 3.1
23	F ☽	0417 1012 1656 2232	1.5 3.2 1.7 2.7
24	SA	0527 1231 1818	1.7 3.0 1.9
25	SU	0205 0659 1410 2010	2.7 1.8 3.1 1.8
26	M	0323 0828 1507 2119	2.9 1.7 3.3 1.7
27	TU	0400 0924 1538 2158	3.1 1.5 3.5 1.5
28	W	0404 1007 1605 2230	3.3 1.3 3.7 1.3
29	TH	0423 1044 1635 2259	3.5 1.1 3.9 1.2
30	F	0450 1117 1707 2328	3.7 1.1 4.0 1.1
31	SA ○	0520 1148 1738 2357	3.9 1.0 4.1 1.0

NOVEMBER

Date	Day	Time	m
1	SU	0549 1217 1809	4.0 1.1 4.1
2	M	0028 0616 1246 1838	1.0 4.0 1.2 4.0
3	TU	0100 0644 1314 1907	1.1 3.9 1.3 3.9
4	W	0129 0713 1339 1936	1.2 3.8 1.5 3.7
5	TH	0158 0743 1405 2007	1.4 3.7 1.7 3.5
6	F	0233 0819 1442 2046	1.5 3.5 1.9 3.2
7	SA	0319 0903 1541 2142	1.7 3.3 2.1 3.0
8	SU ☾	0423 1007 1730 2319	1.8 3.2 2.1 2.8
9	M	0542 1156 1910	1.9 3.1 2.0
10	TU	0157 0700 1400 2026	3.0 1.7 3.4 1.7
11	W	0251 0810 1453 2120	3.2 1.5 3.6 1.4
12	TH	0333 0909 1536 2204	3.5 1.1 3.9 1.1
13	F	0409 1000 1616 2245	3.8 0.8 4.2 0.8
14	SA	0443 1048 1655 2324	4.0 0.6 4.3 0.7
15	SU ●	0519 1134 1735	4.1 0.5 4.4
16	M	0003 0557 1220 1814	0.6 4.2 0.5 4.3
17	TU	0044 0637 1306 1853	0.6 4.2 0.6 4.1
18	W	0126 0719 1353 1934	0.8 4.1 0.8 3.8
19	TH	0210 0802 1442 2016	1.0 3.9 1.1 3.5
20	F	0258 0851 1535 2102	1.2 3.6 1.4 3.1
21	SA	0352 0949 1635 2201	1.5 3.4 1.7 2.9
22	SU ☽	0454 1120 1746	1.7 3.2 1.9
23	M	0032 0607 1316 1913	2.7 1.8 3.2 1.9
24	TU	0208 0732 1418 2027	2.8 1.8 3.3 1.9
25	W	0251 0841 1459 2115	3.0 1.6 3.4 1.7
26	TH	0316 0931 1532 2151	3.2 1.5 3.6 1.6
27	F	0345 1012 1605 2223	3.4 1.4 3.7 1.4
28	SA	0417 1047 1638 2254	3.6 1.3 3.9 1.3
29	SU	0450 1118 1712 2327	3.8 1.3 3.9 1.2
30	M ○	0523 1149 1746	3.9 1.3 4.0

DECEMBER

Date	Day	Time	m
1	TU	0000 0554 1223 1819	1.1 3.9 1.3 3.9
2	W	0035 0626 1256 1851	1.1 3.9 1.4 3.8
3	TH	0108 0658 1328 1924	1.2 3.8 1.5 3.7
4	F	0142 0732 1403 2000	1.3 3.8 1.6 3.5
5	SA	0220 0811 1445 2042	1.4 3.6 1.7 3.3
6	SU	0305 0857 1542 2135	1.5 3.5 1.8 3.2
7	M	0359 0955 1659 2244	1.6 3.4 1.9 3.0
8	TU ☾	0504 1110 1824	1.6 3.3 1.9
9	W	0021 0616 1248 1938	3.0 1.6 3.4 1.7
10	TH	0200 0728 1408 2040	3.2 1.5 3.6 1.5
11	F	0255 0834 1505 2132	3.4 1.3 3.8 1.3
12	SA	0339 0934 1552 2219	3.6 1.0 3.9 1.1
13	SU	0421 1028 1637 2303	3.9 0.9 4.1 0.9
14	M ●	0502 1119 1720 2346	4.0 0.8 4.1 0.8
15	TU	0544 1207 1801	4.1 0.7 4.1
16	W	0028 0625 1255 1842	0.8 4.2 0.8 3.9
17	TH	0112 0708 1342 1923	0.9 4.1 1.0 3.7
18	F	0155 0751 1428 2004	1.0 4.0 1.2 3.5
19	SA	0240 0836 1516 2045	1.1 3.8 1.4 3.3
20	SU	0327 0923 1606 2130	1.3 3.6 1.7 3.1
21	M ☽	0417 1017 1659 2223	1.5 3.4 1.8 3.0
22	TU	0512 1126 1759 2338	1.7 3.2 2.0 2.9
23	W	0614 1258 1904	1.8 3.2 2.0
24	TH	0115 0723 1407 2007	2.9 1.8 3.2 1.9
25	F	0218 0836 1455 2059	3.0 1.8 3.3 1.8
26	SA	0304 0933 1536 2143	3.2 1.7 3.5 1.6
27	SU	0346 1016 1615 2223	3.4 1.6 3.6 1.5
28	M	0425 1053 1654 2301	3.5 1.5 3.7 1.3
29	TU	0504 1130 1733 2338	3.7 1.4 3.8 1.2
30	W ○	0541 1207 1809	3.8 1.4 3.8
31	TH	0015 0616 1245 1844	1.1 3.9 1.3 3.8

GREENOCK

LAT 55°57′N
LONG 4°46′W

TIMES AND HEIGHTS OF HIGH AND LOW WATER (Heights in Metres)

TIME ZONE UT
For Summer Time (area enclosed in shaded box) add 1 hour

2020

JANUARY

Date	Day	Time	m	Time	m	Time	m	Time	m
1	W	0405	3.1	0929	1.0	1616	3.4	2207	0.7
2	TH	0450	3.1	1015	1.1	1659	3.3	2302	0.9
3	F ☽	0538	3.0	1107	1.2	1748	3.1		
4	SA	0003	0.9	0630	2.9	1208	1.3	1845	3.0
5	SU	0107	1.0	0731	2.9	1315	1.3	1950	3.0
6	M	0208	0.9	0838	3.0	1422	1.2	2100	3.0
7	TU	0301	0.8	0942	3.1	1518	1.1	2202	3.1
8	W	0348	0.7	1034	3.2	1605	0.9	2256	3.2
9	TH	0431	0.6	1119	3.4	1647	0.7	2344	3.3
10	F ○	0511	0.6	1159	3.5	1728	0.5		
11	SA	0031	3.3	0552	0.5	1239	3.6	1809	0.4
12	SU	0117	3.4	0635	0.5	1320	3.7	1853	0.3
13	M	0203	3.4	0720	0.4	1402	3.8	1939	0.3
14	TU	0248	3.4	0808	0.4	1445	3.9	2027	0.2
15	W	0334	3.4	0857	0.5	1530	3.8	2118	0.3
16	TH	0422	3.3	0950	0.6	1616	3.7	2213	0.4
17	F ☾	0511	3.2	1046	0.7	1706	3.6	2312	0.5
18	SA	0606	3.1	1148	0.8	1802	3.4		
19	SU	0019	0.6	0712	3.0	1300	0.9	1908	3.2
20	M	0131	0.7	0831	3.0	1412	0.8	2032	3.1
21	TU	0239	0.8	0944	3.1	1517	0.7	2154	3.1
22	W	0339	0.7	1042	3.2	1613	0.5	2258	3.2
23	TH	0430	0.7	1131	3.4	1701	0.4	2351	3.2
24	F ●	0516	0.6	1215	3.5	1744	0.3		
25	SA	0037	3.3	0556	0.6	1255	3.6	1822	0.3
26	SU	0118	3.2	0633	0.6	1332	3.6	1858	0.3
27	M	0154	3.2	0708	0.6	1406	3.6	1932	0.4
28	TU	0228	3.2	0743	0.6	1440	3.6	2008	0.4
29	W	0303	3.2	0818	0.7	1514	3.5	2046	0.5
30	TH	0339	3.2	0855	0.7	1549	3.5	2126	0.6
31	F	0416	3.2	0934	0.8	1626	3.3	2209	0.7

FEBRUARY

Date	Day	Time	m	Time	m	Time	m	Time	m
1	SA	0455	3.1	1017	0.9	1707	3.2	2258	0.8
2	SU ☽	0537	3.0	1106	1.0	1755	3.0	2356	1.0
3	M	0627	2.9	1205	1.2	1853	2.9		
4	TU	0102	1.0	0728	2.8	1316	1.2	2004	2.8
5	W	0213	1.0	0846	2.9	1432	1.1	2125	2.9
6	TH	0316	0.9	0959	3.0	1536	0.9	2235	3.0
7	F	0408	0.7	1053	3.2	1627	0.6	2331	3.2
8	SA	0454	0.5	1140	3.4	1712	0.4		
9	SU ○	0020	3.3	0536	0.4	1223	3.6	1754	0.2
10	M	0107	3.3	0620	0.3	1307	3.7	1838	0.0
11	TU	0153	3.4	0704	0.2	1350	3.8	1922	0.0
12	W	0237	3.4	0750	0.2	1434	3.9	2008	0.0
13	TH	0320	3.4	0837	0.2	1518	3.9	2056	0.1
14	F	0401	3.4	0926	0.3	1602	3.8	2146	0.2
15	SA ☾	0443	3.3	1018	0.4	1646	3.6	2241	0.4
16	SU	0527	3.1	1118	0.6	1734	3.4	2345	0.7
17	M	0620	2.9	1231	0.7	1829	3.1		
18	TU	0103	0.9	0738	2.8	1352	0.8	1952	2.8
19	W	0222	0.9	0921	2.9	1502	0.7	2153	2.8
20	TH	0327	0.9	1027	3.1	1559	0.5	2257	3.0
21	F	0419	0.7	1117	3.3	1647	0.3	2347	3.1
22	SA	0504	0.6	1201	3.4	1729	0.3		
23	SU ●	0029	3.1	0543	0.6	1241	3.5	1805	0.2
24	M	0105	3.2	0617	0.5	1317	3.5	1838	0.3
25	TU	0136	3.2	0648	0.5	1349	3.5	1908	0.3
26	W	0206	3.2	0717	0.5	1419	3.5	1939	0.4
27	TH	0237	3.2	0747	0.5	1450	3.5	2012	0.4
28	F	0308	3.3	0820	0.5	1522	3.4	2046	0.4
29	SA	0341	3.3	0856	0.5	1556	3.3	2124	0.5

MARCH

Date	Day	Time	m	Time	m	Time	m	Time	m
1	SU	0414	3.2	0937	0.6	1633	3.2	2208	0.7
2	M ☽	0451	3.1	1023	0.8	1716	3.0	2300	0.9
3	TU	0533	2.9	1119	1.0	1810	2.8		
4	W	0004	1.0	0627	2.8	1227	1.1	1921	2.7
5	TH	0123	1.1	0745	2.7	1349	1.0	2056	2.7
6	F	0245	0.9	0920	2.9	1508	0.8	2221	2.9
7	SA	0346	0.7	1028	3.1	1605	0.4	2318	3.1
8	SU	0435	0.5	1118	3.3	1652	0.2		
9	M ○	0006	3.3	0518	0.2	1205	3.5	1735	-0.1
10	TU	0052	3.3	0601	0.1	1250	3.7	1817	-0.2
11	W	0136	3.4	0644	0.0	1335	3.8	1900	-0.2
12	TH	0217	3.4	0728	0.0	1419	3.8	1945	-0.1
13	F	0257	3.5	0813	0.0	1502	3.8	2030	0.0
14	SA	0335	3.4	0900	0.1	1544	3.7	2118	0.2
15	SU	0413	3.3	0951	0.2	1626	3.5	2210	0.5
16	M ☾	0453	3.2	1050	0.5	1710	3.2	2313	0.8
17	TU	0539	2.9	1208	0.7	1801	2.9		
18	W	0038	1.0	0643	2.7	1333	0.7	1914	2.6
19	TH	0202	1.1	0853	2.7	1443	0.6	2148	2.7
20	F	0308	1.0	1005	3.0	1539	0.5	2245	2.9
21	SA	0401	0.8	1055	3.2	1626	0.3	2329	3.0
22	SU	0445	0.6	1138	3.3	1706	0.2		
23	M	0007	3.1	0522	0.5	1218	3.4	1741	0.2
24	TU ●	0041	3.1	0554	0.5	1253	3.4	1812	0.2
25	W	0110	3.2	0622	0.5	1325	3.4	1840	0.3
26	TH	0138	3.2	0647	0.4	1354	3.4	1908	0.3
27	F	0207	3.3	0715	0.4	1423	3.4	1938	0.4
28	SA	0236	3.3	0748	0.4	1455	3.3	2012	0.4
29	SU	0307	3.4	0824	0.4	1529	3.3	2050	0.5
30	M	0339	3.3	0906	0.5	1606	3.2	2135	0.6
31	TU	0413	3.2	0953	0.6	1648	3.0	2228	0.8

APRIL

Date	Day	Time	m	Time	m	Time	m	Time	m
1	W ☽	0452	3.0	1050	0.8	1740	2.8	2331	1.0
2	TH	0543	2.9	1158	0.9	1852	2.6		
3	F	0048	1.1	0656	2.8	1319	0.8	2035	2.7
4	SA	0214	1.0	0841	2.8	1440	0.6	2203	2.9
5	SU	0321	0.7	0959	3.1	1540	0.3	2258	3.1
6	M	0412	0.4	1053	3.3	1628	0.0	2345	3.3
7	TU	0457	0.2	1141	3.5	1712	-0.2		
8	W ○	0029	3.4	0539	0.0	1229	3.6	1754	-0.2
9	TH	0112	3.4	0622	-0.1	1315	3.7	1837	-0.2
10	F	0153	3.5	0705	-0.1	1400	3.7	1921	-0.1
11	SA	0231	3.5	0749	-0.1	1443	3.7	2006	0.1
12	SU	0308	3.5	0836	0.0	1525	3.6	2053	0.3
13	M	0346	3.4	0926	0.2	1607	3.4	2145	0.6
14	TU ☾	0425	3.2	1026	0.4	1652	3.1	2246	0.9
15	W	0511	3.0	1145	0.6	1743	2.8		
16	TH	0007	1.1	0610	2.8	1307	0.7	1858	2.5
17	F	0131	1.2	0808	2.7	1414	0.6	2119	2.6
18	SA	0238	1.0	0931	2.9	1509	0.4	2214	2.8
19	SU	0332	0.9	1023	3.1	1556	0.3	2256	3.0
20	M	0417	0.7	1107	3.2	1636	0.2	2333	3.1
21	TU	0455	0.5	1146	3.3	1711	0.2		
22	W	0006	3.2	0526	0.5	1223	3.3	1741	0.3
23	TH ●	0038	3.2	0553	0.5	1255	3.3	1810	0.3
24	F	0108	3.3	0619	0.4	1325	3.3	1839	0.4
25	SA	0137	3.4	0647	0.4	1356	3.3	1910	0.4
26	SU	0206	3.4	0721	0.4	1429	3.3	1946	0.4
27	M	0237	3.5	0800	0.4	1506	3.2	2028	0.5
28	TU	0310	3.4	0843	0.4	1545	3.1	2116	0.6
29	W	0346	3.3	0934	0.5	1629	3.0	2210	0.8
30	TH ☽	0426	3.2	1032	0.6	1723	2.8	2313	0.9

MAY

Date	Day	Time	m	Time	m	Time	m	Time	m
1	F	0516	3.0	1141	0.7	1835	2.7		
2	SA	0026	1.0	0626	2.9	1258	0.6	2012	2.7
3	SU	0144	0.9	0807	2.9	1411	0.4	2135	2.9
4	M	0252	0.7	0927	3.1	1511	0.2	2230	3.1
5	TU	0346	0.4	1025	3.3	1601	0.0	2318	3.3
6	W	0434	0.2	1116	3.5	1647	-0.1		
7	TH ○	0003	3.4	0518	0.0	1206	3.6	1731	-0.1
8	F	0046	3.4	0601	-0.1	1254	3.6	1815	-0.1
9	SA	0127	3.5	0645	-0.1	1340	3.6	1859	0.1
10	SU	0206	3.5	0729	-0.1	1425	3.5	1945	0.2
11	M	0244	3.5	0815	0.1	1508	3.4	2033	0.4
12	TU	0323	3.4	0905	0.2	1551	3.2	2124	0.7
13	W	0403	3.3	1003	0.4	1638	3.0	2220	0.9
14	TH ☾	0449	3.1	1113	0.5	1730	2.8	2327	1.1
15	F	0546	2.9	1228	0.6	1838	2.6		
16	SA	0043	1.2	0709	2.8	1334	0.6	2009	2.6
17	SU	0153	1.1	0840	2.8	1429	0.5	2120	2.7
18	M	0252	1.0	0940	3.0	1517	0.4	2208	2.9
19	TU	0340	0.8	1027	3.1	1559	0.3	2250	3.0
20	W	0420	0.7	1109	3.2	1636	0.3	2328	3.2
21	TH	0454	0.6	1146	3.2	1710	0.3		
22	F ●	0003	3.2	0524	0.5	1221	3.2	1741	0.4
23	SA	0036	3.3	0554	0.5	1255	3.2	1813	0.4
24	SU	0107	3.4	0625	0.4	1330	3.2	1848	0.4
25	M	0139	3.5	0702	0.4	1408	3.2	1928	0.5
26	TU	0213	3.5	0743	0.4	1448	3.2	2014	0.5
27	W	0249	3.5	0829	0.4	1531	3.1	2104	0.6
28	TH	0328	3.5	0921	0.4	1619	3.0	2158	0.7
29	F	0411	3.3	1020	0.5	1714	2.9	2258	0.8
30	SA ☽	0502	3.2	1125	0.5	1822	2.8		
31	SU	0004	0.8	0608	3.1	1235	0.5	1942	2.9

JUNE

Date	Day	Time	m	Time	m	Time	m	Time	m
1	M	0113	0.8	0734	3.1	1342	0.4	2058	3.0
2	TU	0221	0.7	0854	3.2	1443	0.2	2158	3.1
3	W	0320	0.5	0957	3.3	1536	0.1	2250	3.2
4	TH	0412	0.3	1052	3.4	1625	0.1	2338	3.3
5	F ○	0500	0.1	1144	3.5	1712	0.1		
6	SA	0022	3.4	0545	0.0	1234	3.4	1757	0.2
7	SU	0105	3.5	0629	0.0	1322	3.4	1842	0.3
8	M	0145	3.5	0713	0.0	1408	3.3	1928	0.4
9	TU	0224	3.5	0757	0.1	1453	3.2	2015	0.5
10	W	0303	3.5	0844	0.2	1537	3.1	2102	0.7
11	TH	0344	3.3	0936	0.4	1622	2.9	2152	0.8
12	F	0427	3.2	1033	0.5	1711	2.8	2245	0.9
13	SA ☾	0517	3.0	1137	0.6	1804	2.8	2344	1.0
14	SU	0616	2.9	1241	0.6	1902	2.7		
15	M	0048	1.1	0727	2.8	1340	0.6	2004	2.8
16	TU	0155	1.1	0838	2.9	1432	0.5	2106	2.9
17	W	0253	1.0	0937	2.9	1518	0.5	2200	3.0
18	TH	0341	0.8	1025	3.0	1601	0.5	2247	3.1
19	F	0422	0.7	1108	3.1	1640	0.5	2329	3.2
20	SA	0459	0.6	1148	3.1	1717	0.5		
21	SU ●	0006	3.3	0533	0.5	1228	3.1	1753	0.5
22	M	0042	3.4	0609	0.4	1309	3.2	1832	0.5
23	TU	0117	3.5	0648	0.3	1352	3.2	1915	0.5
24	W	0155	3.6	0731	0.3	1436	3.2	2002	0.5
25	TH	0234	3.6	0818	0.3	1522	3.1	2052	0.5
26	F	0316	3.6	0909	0.3	1610	3.1	2144	0.5
27	SA	0400	3.5	1004	0.3	1703	3.0	2239	0.6
28	SU ☽	0450	3.4	1104	0.4	1801	3.0	2338	0.7
29	M	0548	3.3	1208	0.4	1906	2.9		
30	TU	0043	0.7	0700	3.2	1314	0.4	2017	2.9

SUNRISE AND SUNSET TIMES

GREENOCK
At 55°57′N 4°46′W

		Sunrise	Sunset
UT			
Jan	01	0850	1556
	15	0840	1618
Feb	01	0813	1653
	15	0744	1723
Mar	01	0710	1754
	15	0634	1823
BST			
Apr	01	0650	1958
	15	0614	2026
May	01	0535	2058
	15	0506	2126
Jun	01	0441	2153
	15	0433	2207
Jul	01	0438	2208
	15	0454	2155
Aug	01	0523	2126
	15	0550	2055
Sep	01	0624	2013
	15	0651	1936
Oct	01	0722	1854
	15	0750	1818
UT			
Nov	01	0726	1638
	15	0756	1611
Dec	01	0826	1550
	15	0844	1544

GREENOCK
LAT 55°57′N
LONG 4°46′W

TIMES AND HEIGHTS OF HIGH AND LOW WATER (Heights in Metres)

TIME ZONE UT
For Summer Time (area enclosed in shaded box) add 1 hour

2020

JULY

Date	Time	m
1 W	0151 0820 1417 2126	0.7 3.1 0.4 3.0
2 TH	0257 0932 1515 2225	0.6 3.2 0.4 3.1
3 F	0355 1034 1609 2318	0.4 3.2 0.3 3.3
4 SA	0447 1130 1658	0.2 3.3 0.4
5 SU O	0005 0533 1223 1745	3.4 0.1 3.3 0.4
6 M	0050 0617 1311 1829	3.4 0.1 3.2 0.5
7 TU	0130 0659 1356 1912	3.5 0.1 3.1 0.5
8 W	0209 0740 1438 1954	3.5 0.1 3.1 0.6
9 TH	0246 0821 1518 2036	3.5 0.2 3.0 0.6
10 F	0324 0905 1559 2119	3.4 0.3 3.0 0.7
11 SA	0402 0952 1640 2203	3.3 0.4 3.0 0.8
12 SU ☾	0443 1044 1724 2251	3.2 0.6 2.9 0.9
13 M	0528 1141 1811 2344	3.0 0.7 2.9 1.0
14 TU	0621 1241 1902	2.9 0.7 2.8
15 W	0045 0722 1342 2000	1.1 2.8 0.7 2.8
16 TH	0153 0831 1437 2105	1.1 2.8 0.7 2.9
17 F	0258 0939 1528 2206	1.0 2.9 0.7 3.0
18 SA	0352 1035 1614 2256	0.8 3.0 0.6 3.2
19 SU	0437 1124 1656 2340	0.7 3.0 0.5 3.3
20 M ●	0517 1210 1736	0.5 3.1 0.5
21 TU	0019 0555 1255 1817	3.4 0.3 3.1 0.4
22 W	0059 0635 1340 1900	3.5 0.2 3.2 0.4
23 TH	0140 0717 1425 1946	3.6 0.1 3.2 0.4
24 F	0221 0802 1511 2033	3.7 0.1 3.2 0.3
25 SA	0304 0850 1556 2123	3.7 0.1 3.2 0.4
26 SU	0348 0942 1642 2215	3.7 0.2 3.2 0.4
27 M ☽	0434 1038 1731 2311	3.6 0.3 3.1 0.5
28 TU	0525 1139 1826	3.4 0.4 3.0
29 W	0015 0624 1247 1933	0.7 3.2 0.6 2.9
30 TH	0127 0742 1357 2056	0.7 3.0 0.6 2.9
31 F	0240 0914 1503 2209	0.7 3.0 0.6 3.0

AUGUST

Date	Time	m
1 SA	0344 1030 1600 2306	0.5 3.0 0.6 3.2
2 SU	0438 1129 1651 2354	0.3 3.1 0.6 3.4
3 M O	0525 1219 1736	0.2 3.1 0.5
4 TU	0037 0606 1305 1817	3.5 0.1 3.1 0.5
5 W	0117 0644 1344 1854	3.5 0.1 3.1 0.5
6 TH	0153 0719 1419 1930	3.5 0.2 3.1 0.6
7 F	0227 0754 1452 2006	3.5 0.3 3.1 0.6
8 SA	0300 0831 1527 2042	3.5 0.3 3.1 0.6
9 SU	0334 0910 1603 2121	3.4 0.4 3.1 0.7
10 M	0409 0953 1641 2202	3.3 0.6 3.1 0.8
11 TU ☾	0447 1041 1722 2248	3.1 0.7 3.0 0.9
12 W	0533 1138 1808 2342	3.0 0.9 2.9 1.1
13 TH	0629 1245 1903	2.8 1.0 2.9
14 F	0050 0737 1355 2009	1.2 2.7 1.0 2.8
15 SA	0212 0858 1459 2124	1.1 2.7 0.9 2.9
16 SU	0324 1014 1551 2227	0.9 2.9 0.7 3.1
17 M	0416 1110 1636 2315	0.7 3.0 0.6 3.3
18 TU	0459 1157 1717 2359	0.4 3.1 0.4 3.5
19 W ●	0538 1242 1758	0.2 3.2 0.3
20 TH	0041 0617 1327 1840	3.6 0.1 3.2 0.3
21 F	0124 0658 1410 1924	3.7 0.0 3.3 0.2
22 SA	0207 0741 1452 2010	3.8 0.0 3.3 0.2
23 SU	0250 0826 1533 2058	3.8 0.0 3.3 0.3
24 M	0332 0915 1615 2148	3.8 0.2 3.3 0.4
25 TU ☽	0416 1008 1657 2244	3.6 0.4 3.2 0.5
26 W	0502 1109 1745 2351	3.4 0.6 3.0 0.7
27 TH	0554 1224 1847	3.1 0.8 2.9
28 F	0111 0704 1346 2032	0.8 2.8 0.9 2.8
29 SA	0230 0921 1456 2157	0.8 2.8 0.9 3.0
30 SU	0335 1035 1553 2253	0.6 2.9 0.8 3.2
31 M	0427 1126 1641 2340	0.4 3.1 0.7 3.4

SEPTEMBER

Date	Time	m
1 TU	0511 1211 1723	0.2 3.1 0.6
2 W O	0021 0549 1250 1800	3.5 0.2 3.1 0.6
3 TH	0059 0623 1322 1832	3.5 0.2 3.1 0.6
4 F	0133 0654 1350 1902	3.5 0.3 3.1 0.6
5 SA	0204 0724 1420 1932	3.5 0.3 3.2 0.6
6 SU	0233 0755 1451 2005	3.5 0.4 3.2 0.6
7 M	0305 0829 1525 2040	3.5 0.5 3.3 0.6
8 TU	0338 0906 1559 2119	3.4 0.6 3.3 0.7
9 W	0414 0947 1637 2203	3.2 0.8 3.2 0.9
10 TH ☾	0455 1038 1720 2256	3.0 1.0 3.0 1.0
11 F	0548 1144 1813	2.8 1.1 2.9
12 SA	0002 0658 1309 1921	1.2 2.7 1.2 2.8
13 SU	0128 0829 1431 2044	1.2 2.7 1.1 2.9
14 M	0256 1001 1529 2157	1.0 2.9 0.9 3.1
15 TU	0352 1056 1614 2250	0.6 3.1 0.6 3.4
16 W	0435 1141 1656 2336	0.3 3.3 0.4 3.5
17 TH ●	0515 1224 1736	0.1 3.3 0.3
18 F	0020 0554 1306 1817	3.7 0.0 3.4 0.2
19 SA	0105 0635 1347 1900	3.8 -0.1 3.4 0.1
20 SU	0150 0717 1427 1945	3.9 -0.1 3.5 0.1
21 M	0233 0801 1506 2032	3.9 0.1 3.5 0.2
22 TU	0315 0848 1545 2122	3.8 0.3 3.4 0.4
23 W	0357 0939 1626 2219	3.6 0.5 3.3 0.6
24 TH ☽	0441 1041 1712 2333	3.4 0.8 3.1 0.8
25 F	0532 1207 1811	3.0 1.1 2.9
26 SA	0101 0642 1334 2009	0.9 2.7 1.2 2.9
27 SU	0216 0926 1442 2138	0.8 2.8 1.1 3.1
28 M	0317 1025 1537 2232	0.6 3.0 0.9 3.3
29 TU	0407 1110 1623 2317	0.4 3.1 0.7 3.5
30 W	0449 1148 1703 2357	0.3 3.2 0.6 3.6

OCTOBER

Date	Time	m
1 TH O	0526 1222 1737	0.2 3.3 0.6
2 F	0034 0557 1251 1806	3.6 0.3 3.3 0.6
3 SA	0107 0625 1318 1832	3.5 0.4 3.3 0.6
4 SU	0136 0653 1347 1859	3.5 0.4 3.4 0.6
5 M	0205 0722 1418 1931	3.5 0.5 3.4 0.6
6 TU	0237 0754 1450 2006	3.5 0.6 3.5 0.6
7 W	0310 0830 1523 2046	3.4 0.7 3.5 0.7
8 TH	0347 0911 1558 2131	3.3 0.8 3.4 0.9
9 F	0427 1002 1639 2225	3.1 1.1 3.2 1.0
10 SA ☾	0518 1105 1729 2331	2.9 1.3 3.0 1.2
11 SU	0629 1227 1838	2.7 1.3 2.9
12 M	0054 0807 1357 2005	1.1 2.7 1.2 3.0
13 TU	0222 0941 1500 2124	0.9 3.0 1.0 3.2
14 W	0321 1034 1549 2222	0.6 3.2 0.7 3.4
15 TH	0407 1118 1632 2311	0.3 3.4 0.4 3.6
16 F ●	0449 1159 1713 2357	0.1 3.5 0.2 3.8
17 SA	0530 1241 1755	0.0 3.5 0.1
18 SU	0044 0611 1322 1838	3.9 0.0 3.6 0.1
19 M	0130 0654 1401 1922	3.9 0.0 3.6 0.1
20 TU	0215 0738 1441 2009	3.9 0.2 3.6 0.2
21 W	0258 0825 1520 2100	3.8 0.5 3.6 0.4
22 TH	0341 0917 1601 2159	3.6 0.7 3.4 0.6
23 F ☽	0426 1018 1648 2317	3.3 1.0 3.2 0.8
24 SA	0519 1143 1747	3.0 1.3 3.0
25 SU	0042 0640 1308 1930	0.9 2.7 1.3 2.9
26 M	0151 0901 1416 2103	0.8 2.8 1.2 3.1
27 TU	0249 0957 1511 2200	0.6 3.0 1.0 3.3
28 W	0338 1039 1557 2245	0.5 3.2 0.9 3.5
29 TH	0420 1115 1637 2326	0.4 3.3 0.7 3.5
30 F	0456 1147 1711	0.4 3.4 0.7
31 SA O	0003 0528 1218 1739	3.5 0.4 3.4 0.7

NOVEMBER

Date	Time	m
1 SU	0037 0557 1248 1805	3.5 0.5 3.5 0.7
2 M	0108 0625 1318 1833	3.5 0.6 3.6 0.7
3 TU	0139 0655 1348 1904	3.5 0.6 3.6 0.7
4 W	0212 0728 1420 1941	3.5 0.7 3.6 0.7
5 TH	0248 0806 1454 2022	3.4 0.8 3.6 0.7
6 F	0326 0850 1530 2109	3.3 0.9 3.5 0.8
7 SA	0408 0942 1611 2204	3.1 1.1 3.4 1.0
8 SU ☾	0459 1043 1659 2309	3.0 1.3 3.2 1.0
9 M	0607 1156 1803	2.8 1.3 3.1
10 TU	0025 0738 1316 1926	1.0 2.9 1.2 3.1
11 W	0143 0906 1425 2048	0.8 3.0 1.0 3.3
12 TH	0246 1003 1519 2151	0.6 3.3 0.7 3.5
13 F	0337 1050 1607 2244	0.3 3.4 0.5 3.7
14 SA	0423 1133 1652 2335	0.2 3.5 0.3 3.8
15 SU ●	0507 1216 1735	0.1 3.6 0.2
16 M	0024 0550 1258 1819	3.8 0.1 3.7 0.2
17 TU	0112 0635 1339 1904	3.8 0.2 3.7 0.2
18 W	0159 0720 1420 1951	3.8 0.4 3.7 0.3
19 TH	0244 0808 1501 2042	3.6 0.6 3.7 0.4
20 F	0329 0859 1543 2140	3.4 0.9 3.5 0.6
21 SA	0416 0956 1631 2249	3.2 1.1 3.4 0.8
22 SU ☽	0511 1105 1727	3.0 1.3 3.2
23 M	0005 0620 1224 1843	0.8 2.8 1.4 3.1
24 TU	0114 0754 1335 2009	0.8 2.8 1.3 3.1
25 W	0212 0904 1434 2115	0.7 2.9 1.2 3.2
26 TH	0302 0953 1524 2206	0.6 3.1 1.0 3.3
27 F	0346 1033 1606 2250	0.6 3.3 0.9 3.4
28 SA	0424 1111 1642 2330	0.5 3.4 0.8 3.4
29 SU	0500 1146 1714	0.5 3.5 0.8
30 M O	0006 0532 1220 1743	3.4 0.6 3.6 0.7

DECEMBER

Date	Time	m
1 TU	0041 0603 1252 1813	3.4 0.7 3.6 0.7
2 W	0116 0635 1324 1847	3.4 0.7 3.7 0.7
3 TH	0152 0711 1358 1925	3.4 0.7 3.7 0.7
4 F	0231 0752 1434 2007	3.4 0.8 3.7 0.7
5 SA	0312 0837 1512 2055	3.3 0.9 3.7 0.7
6 SU	0356 0928 1553 2149	3.2 1.0 3.6 0.8
7 M	0445 1025 1640 2249	3.1 1.1 3.4 0.8
8 TU ☾	0545 1128 1737 2356	3.0 1.2 3.3 0.8
9 W	0700 1237 1849	3.0 1.1 3.3
10 TH	0105 0820 1347 2008	0.7 3.0 1.0 3.3
11 F	0211 0927 1449 2119	0.6 3.2 0.8 3.4
12 SA	0309 1021 1544 2220	0.5 3.3 0.6 3.6
13 SU	0400 1110 1633 2315	0.4 3.5 0.4 3.6
14 M ●	0448 1156 1720	0.3 3.6 0.3
15 TU	0008 0535 1240 1806	3.7 0.3 3.7 0.2
16 W	0059 0621 1323 1851	3.6 0.4 3.7 0.2
17 TH	0147 0707 1405 1938	3.6 0.5 3.7 0.3
18 F	0234 0754 1447 2025	3.5 0.7 3.7 0.4
19 SA	0319 0841 1529 2116	3.3 0.8 3.6 0.5
20 SU	0404 0930 1614 2211	3.2 1.0 3.5 0.6
21 M ☽	0452 1023 1702 2312	3.0 1.1 3.3 0.8
22 TU	0544 1122 1757	2.9 1.2 3.2
23 W	0019 0640 1230 1859	0.8 2.9 1.3 3.1
24 TH	0122 0743 1340 2009	0.8 2.9 1.3 3.1
25 F	0219 0847 1441 2114	0.8 3.0 1.2 3.1
26 SA	0308 0944 1531 2210	0.8 3.1 1.1 3.2
27 SU	0353 1034 1614 2258	0.7 3.3 0.9 3.2
28 M	0433 1117 1652 2341	0.7 3.4 0.8 3.3
29 TU	0511 1156 1726	0.7 3.5 0.8
30 W O	0021 0546 1231 1759	3.3 0.7 3.6 0.7
31 TH	0100 0622 1305 1834	3.3 0.7 3.7 0.6

LIVERPOOL (GLADSTONE DOCK)

LAT 53°24'N
LONG 3°01'W

TIMES AND HEIGHTS OF HIGH AND LOW WATER (Heights in Metres)

TIME ZONE UT
For Summer Time (area enclosed in shaded box) add 1 hour

2020

JANUARY

Date	Day	Time	m	Time	m	Time	m	Time	m
1	W	0236	8.0	0908	2.9	1455	8.3	2141	2.7
2	TH	0321	7.7	0949	3.2	1544	7.9	2225	3.0
3	F	0413	7.3	1040	3.5	1640	7.6	☽ 2321	3.2
4	SA	0514	7.1	1145	3.6	1744	7.5		
5	SU	0028	3.2	0623	7.2	1300	3.5	1849	7.5
6	M	0138	3.1	0729	7.4	1409	3.2	1950	7.7
7	TU	0238	2.8	0825	7.8	1507	2.8	2044	8.1
8	W	0331	2.4	0913	8.2	1559	2.4	2132	8.4
9	TH	0419	2.0	0956	8.6	1648	2.0	2217	8.8
10	F	0505	1.7	1038	9.0	1735	1.6	O 2300	9.1
11	SA	0550	1.5	1120	9.3	1821	1.3	2344	9.3
12	SU	0634	1.3	1203	9.5	1907	1.1		
13	M	0029	9.4	0717	1.3	1248	9.5	1952	1.1
14	TU	0116	9.3	0800	1.4	1334	9.5	2037	1.1
15	W	0203	9.2	0844	1.6	1423	9.3	2124	1.4
16	TH	0253	8.9	0930	1.9	1514	9.0	2213	1.7
17	F	0346	8.5	1021	2.2	1611	8.7	☾ 2308	2.1
18	SA	0446	8.2	1120	2.5	1715	8.3		
19	SU	0012	2.4	0554	7.9	1230	2.8	1826	8.1
20	M	0124	2.5	0707	7.9	1347	2.7	1939	8.1
21	TU	0234	2.4	0816	8.1	1501	2.5	2046	8.2
22	W	0337	2.2	0915	8.4	1605	2.2	2143	8.5
23	TH	0431	2.0	1005	8.7	1659	1.9	2232	8.7
24	F	0518	1.8	1049	9.0	1746	1.7	● 2315	8.8
25	SA	0559	1.7	1128	9.1	1827	1.6	2353	8.9
26	SU	0636	1.7	1205	9.2	1903	1.5		
27	M	0027	8.8	0708	1.8	1239	9.2	1935	1.6
28	TU	0100	8.7	0739	1.9	1312	9.0	2005	1.8
29	W	0132	8.6	0808	2.1	1346	8.8	2033	2.0
30	TH	0205	8.3	0838	2.3	1421	8.6	2103	2.2
31	F	0239	8.1	0913	2.6	1457	8.2	2138	2.6

FEBRUARY

Date	Day	Time	m	Time	m	Time	m	Time	m
1	SA	0318	7.7	0952	3.0	1539	7.9	2221	2.9
2	SU	0404	7.4	1042	3.3	1632	7.5	☽ 2316	3.2
3	M	0505	7.1	1150	3.5	1741	7.3		
4	TU	0031	3.3	0622	7.1	1315	3.5	1858	7.3
5	W	0152	3.2	0739	7.4	1430	3.1	2009	7.6
6	TH	0258	2.7	0842	7.9	1533	2.5	2108	8.1
7	F	0355	2.3	0934	8.4	1629	1.9	2200	8.6
8	SA	0447	1.8	1021	9.0	1721	1.4	2247	9.1
9	SU	0536	1.3	1106	9.4	1810	0.9	O 2332	9.5
10	M	0623	1.0	1150	9.7	1857	0.6		
11	TU	0016	9.7	0707	0.8	1235	9.9	1941	0.4
12	W	0101	9.7	0749	0.8	1319	9.9	2023	0.5
13	TH	0145	9.5	0831	1.0	1404	9.7	2105	0.9
14	F	0230	9.2	0912	1.4	1450	9.3	2147	1.4
15	SA	0318	8.7	0957	1.9	1541	8.8	☾ 2235	2.0
16	SU	0411	8.2	1049	2.4	1641	8.2	2335	2.6
17	M	0517	7.8	1158	2.8	1756	7.7		
18	TU	0051	2.9	0637	7.5	1325	3.0	1921	7.6
19	W	0213	2.9	0757	7.7	1449	2.8	2038	7.8
20	TH	0324	2.6	0903	8.1	1559	2.4	2137	8.1
21	F	0421	2.3	0954	8.5	1652	2.0	2224	8.5
22	SA	0507	2.0	1036	8.8	1735	1.7	2302	8.7
23	SU	0545	1.8	1113	9.0	1811	1.5	● 2336	8.8
24	M	0618	1.6	1146	9.2	1842	1.4		
25	TU	0007	8.9	0647	1.6	1218	9.2	1910	1.4
26	W	0036	8.9	0715	1.6	1248	9.1	1936	1.5
27	TH	0105	8.8	0743	1.7	1318	9.0	2003	1.6
28	F	0134	8.6	0812	1.9	1348	8.8	2032	1.9
29	SA	0203	8.4	0843	2.2	1419	8.5	2103	2.2

MARCH

Date	Day	Time	m	Time	m	Time	m	Time	m
1	SU	0235	8.1	0918	2.6	1454	8.1	2138	2.6
2	M	0313	7.7	0958	3.0	1538	7.7	☽ 2223	3.1
3	TU	0404	7.3	1056	3.3	1642	7.3	2331	3.4
4	W	0523	7.1	1223	3.5	1811	7.1		
5	TH	0105	3.4	0655	7.2	1356	3.1	1938	7.4
6	F	0227	3.0	0812	7.7	1508	2.5	2047	8.0
7	SA	0332	2.3	0912	8.4	1610	1.8	2142	8.7
8	SU	0429	1.7	1002	9.0	1704	1.1	2230	9.2
9	M	0520	1.1	1047	9.6	1753	0.5	O 2314	9.7
10	TU	0607	0.7	1131	10.0	1839	0.2	2358	9.9
11	W	0651	0.5	1215	10.1	1922	0.1		
12	TH	0040	9.9	0731	0.4	1258	10.1	2002	0.2
13	F	0123	9.7	0811	0.6	1341	9.8	2041	0.7
14	SA	0205	9.3	0851	1.1	1425	9.3	2120	1.3
15	SU	0249	8.8	0933	1.7	1513	8.7	2204	2.1
16	M	0340	8.2	1024	2.3	1612	8.0	☾ 2300	2.8
17	TU	0445	7.7	1132	2.9	1730	7.4		
18	W	0021	3.3	0608	7.3	1306	3.1	1903	7.2
19	TH	0153	3.2	0734	7.5	1435	2.8	2025	7.5
20	F	0308	2.9	0844	7.9	1543	2.4	2123	7.9
21	SA	0404	2.4	0934	8.3	1633	2.0	2206	8.3
22	SU	0448	2.1	1014	8.7	1712	1.7	2241	8.6
23	M	0523	1.8	1049	8.9	1745	1.5	2312	8.8
24	TU	0553	1.6	1120	9.1	1813	1.4	● 2340	8.9
25	W	0622	1.4	1151	9.1	1840	1.3		
26	TH	0008	8.9	0649	1.4	1221	9.1	1906	1.3
27	F	0036	8.9	0718	1.4	1250	9.0	1934	1.4
28	SA	0104	8.8	0748	1.6	1319	8.8	2003	1.7
29	SU	0132	8.5	0819	1.9	1349	8.5	2034	2.1
30	M	0203	8.3	0852	2.3	1424	8.2	2107	2.5
31	TU	0240	8.0	0930	2.7	1509	7.8	2149	2.9

APRIL

Date	Day	Time	m	Time	m	Time	m	Time	m
1	W	0330	7.6	1024	3.1	1611	7.4	☽ 2252	3.3
2	TH	0446	7.2	1147	3.3	1739	7.2		
3	F	0026	3.4	0622	7.3	1325	3.0	1910	7.4
4	SA	0156	3.0	0743	7.8	1442	2.3	2023	8.1
5	SU	0306	2.3	0845	8.4	1546	1.6	2119	8.7
6	M	0405	1.7	0937	9.1	1641	0.9	2207	9.3
7	TU	0457	1.1	1024	9.6	1730	0.4	2252	9.7
8	W	0545	0.6	1108	10.0	1815	0.1	O 2334	9.9
9	TH	0629	0.4	1152	10.1	1858	0.1		
10	F	0016	9.9	0710	0.3	1236	10.0	1937	0.3
11	SA	0058	9.7	0751	0.6	1319	9.7	2016	0.8
12	SU	0140	9.3	0831	1.0	1403	9.1	2055	1.5
13	M	0224	8.8	0914	1.6	1451	8.5	2137	2.2
14	TU	0313	8.2	1004	2.3	1548	7.8	☾ 2231	2.9
15	W	0417	7.7	1112	2.9	1704	7.2	2350	3.4
16	TH	0537	7.3	1241	3.1	1835	7.1		
17	F	0122	3.4	0700	7.4	1405	2.9	1956	7.3
18	SA	0236	3.1	0809	7.7	1509	2.5	2053	7.8
19	SU	0331	2.6	0901	8.1	1558	2.1	2135	8.2
20	M	0414	2.2	0942	8.5	1636	1.8	2210	8.5
21	TU	0450	1.9	1017	8.7	1709	1.6	2241	8.7
22	W	0521	1.7	1050	8.9	1739	1.4	2310	8.8
23	TH	0552	1.5	1121	9.0	1808	1.4	● 2339	8.9
24	F	0622	1.4	1152	9.0	1837	1.3		
25	SA	0008	8.9	0654	1.4	1224	8.9	1908	1.4
26	SU	0037	8.8	0726	1.5	1255	8.7	1939	1.7
27	M	0108	8.7	0759	1.8	1329	8.5	2011	2.0
28	TU	0142	8.4	0835	2.1	1407	8.2	2047	2.4
29	W	0222	8.1	0915	2.5	1455	7.9	2131	2.8
30	TH	0316	7.8	1010	2.8	1558	7.5	☽ 2233	3.1

MAY

Date	Day	Time	m	Time	m	Time	m	Time	m
1	F	0430	7.5	1128	2.9	1720	7.4	2357	3.2
2	SA	0556	7.6	1256	2.6	1843	7.7		
3	SU	0122	2.8	0712	8.0	1412	2.1	1954	8.2
4	M	0234	2.3	0816	8.6	1516	1.5	2052	8.8
5	TU	0336	1.7	0910	9.1	1613	1.0	2141	9.2
6	W	0430	1.2	0958	9.5	1703	0.6	2227	9.6
7	TH	0519	0.8	1045	9.8	1749	0.4	O 2310	9.7
8	F	0605	0.6	1130	9.8	1832	0.4	2353	9.7
9	SA	0649	0.6	1215	9.7	1913	0.7		
10	SU	0036	9.6	0732	0.8	1300	9.3	1953	1.1
11	M	0119	9.2	0815	1.2	1345	8.9	2033	1.7
12	TU	0203	8.8	0859	1.7	1432	8.3	2115	2.4
13	W	0251	8.3	0948	2.3	1526	7.7	2205	3.0
14	TH	0350	7.8	1049	2.7	1633	7.3	☾ 2312	3.4
15	F	0500	7.5	1203	3.0	1749	7.1		
16	SA	0033	3.5	0612	7.4	1316	2.9	1905	7.2
17	SU	0145	3.3	0720	7.6	1418	2.7	2007	7.5
18	M	0243	2.9	0816	7.9	1509	2.4	2053	7.9
19	TU	0329	2.6	0902	8.2	1551	2.1	2132	8.2
20	W	0409	2.2	0941	8.5	1628	1.9	2206	8.5
21	TH	0445	1.9	1017	8.6	1702	1.7	2238	8.7
22	F	0521	1.7	1052	8.8	1736	1.5	● 2310	8.8
23	SA	0556	1.5	1126	8.8	1810	1.5	2342	8.8
24	SU	0632	1.5	1200	8.8	1845	1.5		
25	M	0015	8.8	0709	1.6	1237	8.7	1920	1.7
26	TU	0051	8.8	0746	1.7	1315	8.6	1956	1.9
27	W	0130	8.6	0826	1.9	1359	8.4	2036	2.2
28	TH	0216	8.4	0911	2.1	1449	8.1	2123	2.5
29	F	0310	8.1	1006	2.3	1550	7.9	2222	2.7
30	SA	0418	8.0	1113	2.4	1701	7.8	☽ 2334	2.8
31	SU	0531	8.0	1227	2.3	1814	7.9		

JUNE

Date	Day	Time	m	Time	m	Time	m	Time	m
1	M	0048	2.6	0641	8.2	1339	2.0	1922	8.2
2	TU	0159	2.3	0745	8.6	1444	1.6	2022	8.6
3	W	0303	1.9	0843	8.9	1543	1.3	2115	9.0
4	TH	0402	1.5	0935	9.2	1636	1.0	2204	9.3
5	F	0456	1.2	1025	9.4	1725	0.9	O 2250	9.4
6	SA	0545	1.0	1113	9.4	1810	0.9	2334	9.4
7	SU	0632	0.9	1159	9.3	1853	1.1		
8	M	0018	9.3	0717	1.1	1245	9.0	1934	1.4
9	TU	0101	9.1	0801	1.4	1329	8.7	2014	1.9
10	W	0144	8.8	0844	1.7	1413	8.3	2054	2.3
11	TH	0229	8.5	0929	2.2	1500	7.9	2137	2.8
12	F	0319	8.1	1017	2.5	1553	7.5	2228	3.1
13	SA	0416	7.8	1111	2.8	1653	7.2	☾ 2329	3.4
14	SU	0518	7.6	1212	3.0	1759	7.2		
15	M	0036	3.4	0622	7.5	1314	2.9	1904	7.3
16	TU	0141	3.2	0722	7.6	1411	2.7	2001	7.5
17	W	0236	2.9	0816	7.9	1501	2.5	2048	7.9
18	TH	0325	2.6	0903	8.1	1546	2.2	2129	8.2
19	F	0410	2.2	0945	8.3	1627	2.0	2207	8.5
20	SA	0452	1.9	1024	8.5	1708	1.8	2244	8.7
21	SU	0534	1.7	1103	8.7	1747	1.6	● 2321	8.8
22	M	0615	1.6	1142	8.8	1827	1.6	2359	8.9
23	TU	0657	1.5	1223	8.8	1907	1.6		
24	W	0039	9.0	0739	1.5	1306	8.8	1948	1.7
25	TH	0123	8.9	0822	1.5	1352	8.7	2030	1.9
26	F	0210	8.8	0908	1.7	1442	8.5	2117	2.1
27	SA	0302	8.6	0958	1.8	1536	8.3	2209	2.3
28	SU	0400	8.4	1055	2.0	1637	8.1	☽ 2309	2.4
29	M	0504	8.3	1158	2.1	1743	8.0		
30	TU	0015	2.5	0610	8.3	1306	2.1	1851	8.1

SUNRISE AND SUNSET TIMES

LIVERPOOL
At 53°24'N 3°01'N

UT		Sunrise	Sunset
Jan	01	0828	1604
	15	0820	1624
Feb	01	0757	1655
	15	0730	1723
Mar	01	0700	1750
	15	0627	1816
BST			
Apr	01	0645	1948
	15	0612	2013
May	01	0538	2042
	15	0512	2106
Jun	01	0450	2130
	15	0443	2142
Jul	01	0448	2143
	15	0503	2133
Aug	01	0528	2107
	15	0552	2040
Sep	01	0621	2001
	15	0646	1928
Oct	01	0714	1849
	15	0739	1816
UT			
Nov	01	0711	1640
	15	0738	1615
Dec	01	0805	1557
	15	0821	1553

LIVERPOOL (GLADSTONE DOCK)
LAT 53°24'N
LONG 3°01'W

TIMES AND HEIGHTS OF HIGH AND LOW WATER (Heights in Metres)

TIME ZONE UT
For Summer Time (area enclosed in shaded box) add 1 hour

2020

JULY

Day	Time	m	Time	m	Time	m	Time	m
1 W	0126	2.4	0718	8.4	1414	2.0	1956	8.3
2 TH	0236	2.2	0821	8.5	1517	1.8	2054	8.6
3 F	0341	1.9	0920	8.7	1614	1.6	2147	8.9
4 SA	0439	1.6	1013	8.9	1706	1.5	2236	9.1
5 SU	0532	1.4	1103	9.0	1753	1.4	○ 2321	9.2
6 M	0621	1.3	1149	8.9	1837	1.5		
7 TU	0004	9.2	0706	1.3	1232	8.8	1917	1.6
8 W	0045	9.1	0747	1.4	1312	8.6	1955	1.9
9 TH	0125	8.9	0825	1.7	1350	8.4	2031	2.2
10 F	0204	8.7	0901	2.0	1428	8.1	2105	2.5
11 SA	0245	8.4	0936	2.3	1510	7.8	2142	2.8
12 SU	0330	8.1	1014	2.6	1557	7.5	☾ 2226	3.1
13 M	0421	7.7	1100	2.9	1652	7.3	2321	3.3
14 TU	0520	7.5	1159	3.1	1755	7.1		
15 W	0029	3.4	0623	7.4	1307	3.1	1902	7.2
16 TH	0141	3.3	0727	7.5	1411	2.9	2003	7.5
17 F	0243	2.9	0826	7.7	1507	2.6	2055	7.9
18 SA	0338	2.5	0916	8.0	1557	2.3	2140	8.3
19 SU	0428	2.1	1002	8.4	1644	2.0	2222	8.7
20 M	0516	1.8	1045	8.7	1729	1.7	● 2303	9.0
21 TU	0602	1.4	1127	8.9	1813	1.5	2344	9.2
22 W	0647	1.2	1210	9.1	1857	1.4		
23 TH	0027	9.3	0731	1.0	1254	9.2	1939	1.3
24 F	0111	9.4	0815	1.0	1339	9.1	2022	1.4
25 SA	0157	9.3	0858	1.2	1426	8.9	2105	1.6
26 SU	0244	9.1	0942	1.4	1515	8.7	2151	1.9
27 M	0336	8.8	1031	1.8	1609	8.3	☽ 2243	2.2
28 TU	0434	8.5	1127	2.1	1712	8.0	2345	2.5
29 W	0542	8.1	1235	2.4	1823	7.9		
30 TH	0059	2.6	0656	8.0	1350	2.5	1935	8.0
31 F	0219	2.5	0809	8.1	1500	2.3	2041	8.3

AUGUST

Day	Time	m	Time	m	Time	m	Time	m
1 SA	0331	2.2	0914	8.3	1602	2.1	2138	8.6
2 SU	0434	1.9	1009	8.5	1656	1.9	2227	8.9
3 M	0527	1.6	1056	8.7	1742	1.7	○ 2310	9.1
4 TU	0612	1.4	1138	8.8	1823	1.6	2349	9.2
5 W	0652	1.3	1215	8.8	1900	1.7		
6 TH	0026	9.2	0727	1.4	1249	8.7	1932	1.8
7 F	0100	9.1	0758	1.6	1322	8.6	2002	1.9
8 SA	0134	8.9	0827	1.8	1354	8.4	2032	2.2
9 SU	0208	8.6	0855	2.1	1428	8.1	2103	2.5
10 M	0245	8.3	0926	2.4	1505	7.8	2139	2.8
11 TU	0325	7.9	1003	2.8	1549	7.5	☾ 2224	3.2
12 W	0415	7.5	1053	3.1	1645	7.2	2325	3.5
13 TH	0520	7.2	1201	3.4	1800	7.0		
14 F	0046	3.5	0637	7.1	1323	3.3	1918	7.2
15 SA	0206	3.2	0751	7.4	1433	3.0	2024	7.7
16 SU	0311	2.7	0852	7.8	1531	2.5	2117	8.2
17 M	0407	2.2	0943	8.3	1624	2.1	2203	8.7
18 TU	0459	1.6	1028	8.8	1713	1.6	2245	9.2
19 W	0548	1.1	1111	9.2	1759	1.3	● 2327	9.6
20 TH	0634	0.8	1153	9.5	1844	1.0		
21 F	0009	9.8	0717	0.6	1237	9.6	1926	0.9
22 SA	0053	9.8	0759	0.6	1320	9.5	2007	1.0
23 SU	0136	9.7	0839	0.8	1403	9.3	2047	1.3
24 M	0221	9.4	0920	1.2	1449	8.9	2130	1.7
25 TU	0309	8.9	1004	1.8	1540	8.4	☽ 2219	2.2
26 W	0405	8.4	1058	2.4	1641	7.9	2321	2.7
27 TH	0517	7.8	1209	2.9	1759	7.6		
28 F	0044	2.9	0643	7.6	1335	3.0	1921	7.7
29 SA	0214	2.8	0807	7.7	1452	2.8	2034	8.1
30 SU	0330	2.4	0913	8.1	1556	2.4	2131	8.5
31 M	0429	1.9	1004	8.4	1647	2.1	2216	8.9

SEPTEMBER

Day	Time	m	Time	m	Time	m	Time	m
1 TU	0517	1.6	1045	8.7	1729	1.8	2255	9.1
2 W	0556	1.4	1120	8.9	1805	1.7	○ 2329	9.2
3 TH	0630	1.4	1152	8.9	1836	1.6		
4 F	0001	9.2	0659	1.4	1222	8.9	1904	1.6
5 SA	0032	9.2	0725	1.5	1251	8.8	1932	1.8
6 SU	0103	9.0	0751	1.7	1320	8.6	2000	2.0
7 M	0133	8.8	0818	1.9	1349	8.4	2030	2.3
8 TU	0205	8.5	0847	2.3	1421	8.1	2103	2.6
9 W	0239	8.1	0921	2.7	1457	7.7	2143	3.1
10 TH	0321	7.6	1003	3.1	1545	7.3	☾ 2237	3.5
11 F	0421	7.2	1105	3.5	1700	7.0	2359	3.6
12 SA	0549	7.0	1236	3.6	1835	7.1		
13 SU	0132	3.4	0719	7.2	1401	3.3	1953	7.6
14 M	0245	2.7	0829	7.8	1507	2.7	2052	8.3
15 TU	0345	2.0	0922	8.5	1603	2.0	2140	8.9
16 W	0439	1.4	1008	9.1	1653	1.5	2223	9.5
17 TH	0528	0.8	1050	9.5	1740	1.0	● 2305	9.9
18 F	0613	0.5	1132	9.8	1825	0.8	2347	10.1
19 SA	0656	0.3	1213	9.9	1907	0.7		
20 SU	0029	10.1	0736	0.4	1256	9.8	1947	0.8
21 M	0113	9.9	0816	0.7	1338	9.5	2027	1.1
22 TU	0157	9.5	0855	1.3	1422	9.0	2109	1.7
23 W	0245	8.9	0938	2.0	1512	8.4	2159	2.3
24 TH	0342	8.2	1031	2.7	1615	7.9	☽ 2305	2.9
25 F	0459	7.5	1148	3.3	1738	7.5		
26 SA	0036	3.1	0633	7.3	1322	3.3	1906	7.6
27 SU	0207	2.9	0800	7.6	1441	3.0	2019	8.0
28 M	0318	2.4	0902	8.0	1542	2.5	2114	8.5
29 TU	0412	1.9	0947	8.4	1628	2.2	2156	8.8
30 W	0455	1.7	1024	8.7	1706	1.9	2231	9.1

OCTOBER

Day	Time	m	Time	m	Time	m	Time	m
1 TH	0529	1.5	1056	8.9	1738	1.7	○ 2303	9.2
2 F	0559	1.4	1124	9.0	1807	1.6	2333	9.3
3 SA	0626	1.4	1152	9.0	1835	1.6		
4 SU	0003	9.2	0651	1.5	1220	9.0	1902	1.7
5 M	0033	9.1	0718	1.6	1248	8.8	1931	1.9
6 TU	0103	8.8	0746	1.9	1316	8.6	2002	2.2
7 W	0133	8.5	0816	2.2	1346	8.3	2035	2.5
8 TH	0206	8.2	0849	2.7	1421	8.0	2113	3.0
9 F	0248	7.7	0929	3.2	1508	7.6	2204	3.3
10 SA	0346	7.3	1027	3.6	1619	7.2	☾ 2323	3.5
11 SU	0512	7.0	1156	3.7	1756	7.2		
12 M	0100	3.3	0646	7.3	1328	3.3	1919	7.7
13 TU	0216	2.7	0800	7.9	1438	2.7	2021	8.4
14 W	0318	1.9	0856	8.6	1536	2.0	2112	9.1
15 TH	0413	1.3	0942	9.2	1628	1.4	2157	9.6
16 F	0502	0.7	1025	9.7	1716	1.0	● 2240	10.0
17 SA	0548	0.4	1107	10.0	1801	0.7	2323	10.2
18 SU	0631	0.3	1149	10.0	1844	0.6		
19 M	0007	10.1	0711	0.5	1232	9.9	1926	0.8
20 TU	0051	9.8	0751	0.9	1314	9.5	2008	1.2
21 W	0136	9.3	0832	1.5	1359	9.1	2053	1.7
22 TH	0225	8.7	0915	2.3	1450	8.5	2145	2.4
23 F	0324	8.0	1009	3.0	1553	7.9	☽ 2253	2.9
24 SA	0440	7.4	1126	3.5	1714	7.6		
25 SU	0020	3.1	0610	7.2	1258	3.5	1837	7.6
26 M	0143	2.9	0735	7.5	1413	3.2	1949	7.9
27 TU	0249	2.5	0835	7.9	1512	2.8	2043	8.3
28 W	0340	2.1	0920	8.3	1557	2.4	2125	8.7
29 TH	0420	1.9	0955	8.6	1634	2.1	2201	8.9
30 F	0454	1.7	1026	8.8	1706	1.9	2234	9.1
31 SA	0523	1.6	1055	9.0	1736	1.8	○ 2305	9.1

NOVEMBER

Day	Time	m	Time	m	Time	m	Time	m
1 SU	0551	1.6	1123	9.0	1806	1.7	2336	9.1
2 M	0620	1.6	1152	9.0	1837	1.7		
3 TU	0007	9.0	0649	1.7	1221	8.9	1908	1.9
4 W	0038	8.8	0720	1.9	1251	8.7	1941	2.1
5 TH	0111	8.6	0752	2.2	1323	8.5	2017	2.4
6 F	0147	8.2	0827	2.6	1401	8.2	2056	2.8
7 SA	0231	7.9	0908	3.0	1449	7.9	2148	3.1
8 SU	0329	7.5	1005	3.4	1557	7.6	☾ 2300	3.2
9 M	0446	7.3	1124	3.5	1723	7.5		
10 TU	0026	3.0	0611	7.5	1250	3.3	1842	7.9
11 W	0142	2.5	0725	8.0	1402	2.7	1947	8.5
12 TH	0246	1.9	0824	8.6	1504	2.1	2041	9.1
13 F	0342	1.3	0914	9.2	1559	1.6	2130	9.5
14 SA	0434	0.9	1000	9.6	1650	1.2	2217	9.9
15 SU	0521	0.7	1044	9.8	1738	0.9	● 2302	10.0
16 M	0606	0.6	1127	9.9	1824	0.8	2348	9.9
17 TU	0649	0.8	1211	9.8	1909	0.9		
18 W	0034	9.6	0731	1.2	1256	9.5	1954	1.3
19 TH	0122	9.1	0813	1.8	1342	9.1	2041	1.8
20 F	0211	8.6	0858	2.4	1432	8.6	2133	2.3
21 SA	0306	8.0	0950	3.0	1530	8.1	2235	2.8
22 SU	0412	7.5	1055	3.4	1639	7.8	☽ 2347	3.0
23 M	0527	7.2	1213	3.6	1752	7.7		
24 TU	0058	3.0	0645	7.3	1325	3.4	1900	7.8
25 W	0201	2.8	0751	7.6	1425	3.1	1959	8.0
26 TH	0254	2.5	0840	8.0	1514	2.8	2047	8.3
27 F	0337	2.3	0919	8.3	1555	2.5	2127	8.6
28 SA	0414	2.1	0954	8.6	1632	2.2	2204	8.7
29 SU	0447	1.9	1026	8.8	1706	2.0	2239	8.9
30 M	0520	1.8	1057	8.9	1740	1.9	○ 2312	8.9

DECEMBER

Day	Time	m	Time	m	Time	m	Time	m
1 TU	0553	1.8	1129	8.9	1815	1.8	2346	8.9
2 W	0626	1.8	1201	8.9	1851	1.9		
3 TH	0020	8.8	0700	1.9	1235	8.8	1928	2.0
4 F	0057	8.6	0736	2.1	1311	8.7	2007	2.2
5 SA	0137	8.4	0814	2.4	1352	8.5	2049	2.4
6 SU	0223	8.2	0858	2.7	1440	8.3	2139	2.6
7 M	0317	7.9	0951	3.0	1540	8.1	2240	2.7
8 TU	0422	7.8	1056	3.1	1651	8.0	☾ 2351	2.7
9 W	0535	7.8	1209	3.0	1803	8.1		
10 TH	0103	2.4	0646	8.1	1322	2.7	1910	8.5
11 F	0210	2.1	0750	8.5	1429	2.3	2011	8.8
12 SA	0311	1.7	0846	8.9	1531	1.9	2107	9.2
13 SU	0407	1.4	0937	9.2	1627	1.5	2158	9.4
14 M	0458	1.2	1025	9.5	1720	1.2	● 2248	9.5
15 TU	0546	1.1	1112	9.6	1810	1.1	2337	9.5
16 W	0631	1.2	1157	9.6	1858	1.1		
17 TH	0024	9.3	0715	1.4	1243	9.4	1944	1.3
18 F	0111	9.0	0758	1.8	1328	9.2	2030	1.6
19 SA	0157	8.6	0841	2.2	1413	8.8	2117	2.1
20 SU	0243	8.2	0925	2.7	1502	8.4	2205	2.5
21 M	0334	7.8	1014	3.1	1555	8.1	☽ 2257	2.8
22 TU	0431	7.4	1111	3.4	1655	7.8	2355	3.1
23 W	0535	7.2	1216	3.6	1759	7.6		
24 TH	0057	3.1	0643	7.3	1323	3.5	1903	7.6
25 F	0156	3.0	0746	7.5	1422	3.2	2001	7.8
26 SA	0248	2.8	0838	7.8	1513	2.9	2052	8.1
27 SU	0333	2.5	0921	8.1	1558	2.6	2136	8.3
28 M	0414	2.3	1000	8.4	1640	2.3	2216	8.5
29 TU	0453	2.1	1036	8.7	1720	2.0	2254	8.7
30 W	0531	1.9	1111	8.9	1800	1.8	○ 2330	8.8
31 TH	0610	1.8	1146	9.0	1840	1.7		

HOLYHEAD
LAT 53°19′N
LONG 4°37′W

TIMES AND HEIGHTS OF HIGH AND LOW WATER (Heights in Metres)

TIME ZONE UT
For Summer Time (area enclosed in shaded box) add 1 hour

2020

JANUARY

Date	Day	Time	m	Time	m	Time	m	Time	m
1	W	0157	4.8	0758	1.9	1409	5.1	2031	1.7
2	TH	0243	4.6	0845	2.1	1457	4.9	2122	1.9
3	F ☽	0338	4.4	0940	2.3	1553	4.7	2220	2.0
4	SA	0444	4.3	1045	2.4	1658	4.6	2324	2.1
5	SU	0554	4.4	1155	2.3	1806	4.6		
6	M	0027	2.0	0657	4.6	1257	2.2	1908	4.7
7	TU	0122	1.8	0749	4.8	1351	1.9	2001	4.9
8	W	0211	1.6	0834	5.0	1438	1.6	2048	5.1
9	TH	0254	1.4	0914	5.3	1521	1.3	2132	5.3
10	F ○	0335	1.2	0953	5.5	1604	1.1	2214	5.5
11	SA	0417	1.0	1033	5.7	1646	0.9	2257	5.6
12	SU	0459	0.9	1115	5.8	1730	0.7	2341	5.6
13	M	0542	0.9	1159	5.9	1816	0.7		
14	TU	0027	5.6	0627	0.9	1245	5.8	1903	0.7
15	W	0116	5.4	0715	1.0	1333	5.7	1954	0.9
16	TH	0207	5.2	0806	1.2	1425	5.5	2049	1.1
17	F ☾	0303	5.0	0904	1.5	1523	5.3	2151	1.3
18	SA	0407	4.8	1009	1.7	1630	5.1	2259	1.5
19	SU	0520	4.7	1122	1.8	1746	5.0		
20	M	0009	1.6	0632	4.8	1236	1.8	1900	4.9
21	TU	0117	1.6	0738	4.9	1344	1.6	2006	5.0
22	W	0217	1.5	0833	5.1	1443	1.4	2101	5.1
23	TH	0307	1.3	0920	5.3	1533	1.2	2148	5.2
24	F ●	0351	1.2	1002	5.5	1616	1.1	2229	5.3
25	SA	0430	1.1	1040	5.6	1655	1.0	2307	5.3
26	SU	0506	1.1	1117	5.6	1731	1.0	2341	5.3
27	M	0540	1.1	1151	5.6	1805	1.0		
28	TU	0014	5.2	0613	1.2	1225	5.5	1838	1.1
29	W	0047	5.1	0647	1.3	1259	5.4	1912	1.3
30	TH	0121	5.0	0722	1.5	1334	5.2	1949	1.4
31	F	0157	4.8	0801	1.7	1412	5.0	2029	1.6

FEBRUARY

Date	Day	Time	m	Time	m	Time	m	Time	m
1	SA	0238	4.6	0844	2.0	1457	4.8	2116	1.9
2	SU ☽	0329	4.4	0938	2.2	1552	4.6	2213	2.1
3	M	0436	4.3	1047	2.3	1703	4.5	2324	2.1
4	TU	0556	4.3	1205	2.3	1822	4.5		
5	W	0037	2.0	0708	4.5	1316	2.0	1932	4.7
6	TH	0140	1.8	0806	4.8	1414	1.7	2029	4.9
7	F	0233	1.5	0854	5.1	1503	1.3	2117	5.2
8	SA	0319	1.2	0936	5.4	1549	0.9	2201	5.5
9	SU ○	0402	0.9	1018	5.7	1632	0.6	2243	5.7
10	M	0445	0.6	1100	6.0	1715	0.4	2327	5.8
11	TU	0527	0.5	1143	6.1	1759	0.3		
12	W	0010	5.8	0610	0.5	1228	6.1	1844	0.3
13	TH	0056	5.6	0655	0.6	1313	5.9	1931	0.6
14	F	0142	5.4	0743	0.9	1401	5.7	2021	0.9
15	SA ☾	0232	5.1	0835	1.2	1455	5.3	2118	1.3
16	SU	0330	4.8	0937	1.5	1600	5.0	2226	1.6
17	M	0441	4.6	1054	1.8	1721	4.7	2343	1.8
18	TU	0605	4.6	1218	1.9	1851	4.6		
19	W	0101	1.9	0723	4.7	1337	1.7	2005	4.7
20	TH	0208	1.7	0824	4.9	1439	1.5	2100	4.9
21	F	0259	1.5	0911	5.2	1526	1.2	2142	5.1
22	SA	0341	1.3	0950	5.4	1605	1.1	2217	5.2
23	SU ●	0416	1.1	1024	5.5	1638	0.9	2249	5.3
24	M	0448	1.0	1056	5.6	1709	0.9	2319	5.3
25	TU	0518	1.0	1127	5.6	1739	0.9	2347	5.3
26	W	0548	1.0	1158	5.5	1808	0.9		
27	TH	0017	5.2	0618	1.1	1230	5.5	1839	1.1
28	F	0048	5.1	0650	1.2	1302	5.3	1911	1.2
29	SA	0120	5.0	0724	1.4	1337	5.1	1946	1.4

MARCH

Date	Day	Time	m	Time	m	Time	m	Time	m
1	SU	0155	4.8	0802	1.7	1415	4.9	2026	1.7
2	M ☽	0236	4.6	0849	1.9	1502	4.6	2117	2.0
3	TU	0332	4.4	0953	2.1	1608	4.4	2228	2.2
4	W	0454	4.3	1118	2.2	1741	4.3	2355	2.2
5	TH	0627	4.4	1243	2.0	1907	4.5		
6	F	0112	1.9	0738	4.7	1350	1.6	2010	4.8
7	SA	0212	1.5	0831	5.1	1443	1.1	2100	5.2
8	SU	0300	1.1	0916	5.5	1529	0.7	2143	5.5
9	M ○	0344	0.7	0958	5.8	1612	0.3	2225	5.8
10	TU	0425	0.4	1040	6.1	1654	0.1	2306	5.9
11	W	0507	0.2	1122	6.2	1737	0.0	2349	5.9
12	TH	0550	0.2	1206	6.2	1821	0.2		
13	F	0032	5.8	0633	0.4	1252	6.0	1905	0.4
14	SA	0116	5.5	0720	0.7	1339	5.6	1953	0.9
15	SU	0203	5.2	0811	1.0	1431	5.2	2047	1.3
16	M ☾	0258	4.9	0912	1.5	1535	4.8	2154	1.8
17	TU	0407	4.6	1030	1.8	1703	4.4	2317	2.1
18	W	0537	4.4	1200	1.9	1842	4.4		
19	TH	0042	2.1	0704	4.6	1324	1.8	1956	4.6
20	F	0152	1.9	0807	4.8	1424	1.5	2047	4.8
21	SA	0243	1.6	0853	5.0	1508	1.3	2125	5.0
22	SU	0321	1.4	0929	5.2	1543	1.1	2156	5.1
23	M	0354	1.1	1001	5.4	1613	0.9	2224	5.2
24	TU ●	0424	1.0	1031	5.5	1641	0.8	2252	5.3
25	W	0452	0.9	1100	5.5	1709	0.8	2319	5.3
26	TH	0521	0.9	1130	5.5	1738	0.9	2347	5.3
27	F	0551	0.9	1201	5.4	1807	1.0		
28	SA	0017	5.2	0622	1.1	1234	5.3	1838	1.1
29	SU	0049	5.1	0655	1.2	1307	5.1	1911	1.3
30	M	0122	5.0	0732	1.5	1345	4.9	1950	1.6
31	TU	0202	4.7	0818	1.7	1431	4.6	2040	1.9

APRIL

Date	Day	Time	m	Time	m	Time	m	Time	m
1	W ☽	0254	4.5	0920	2.0	1536	4.4	2150	2.1
2	TH	0411	4.3	1045	2.0	1711	4.3	2321	2.2
3	F	0550	4.4	1214	1.8	1843	4.5		
4	SA	0044	1.9	0706	4.7	1324	1.4	1947	4.8
5	SU	0146	1.5	0803	5.1	1418	0.9	2037	5.2
6	M	0236	1.1	0850	5.5	1505	0.5	2120	5.5
7	TU	0320	0.7	0933	5.8	1548	0.2	2202	5.8
8	W ○	0402	0.3	1016	6.1	1630	0.0	2243	5.9
9	TH	0445	0.2	1100	6.2	1713	0.0	2325	5.9
10	F	0528	0.2	1145	6.1	1757	0.2		
11	SA	0008	5.8	0613	0.3	1232	5.8	1841	0.6
12	SU	0053	5.6	0700	0.6	1320	5.5	1928	1.0
13	M	0140	5.3	0752	1.0	1412	5.0	2021	1.5
14	TU ☾	0232	4.9	0853	1.4	1517	4.6	2126	1.9
15	W	0338	4.6	1009	1.8	1642	4.3	2247	2.2
16	TH	0503	4.4	1135	1.9	1817	4.3		
17	F	0011	2.2	0629	4.5	1253	1.8	1929	4.5
18	SA	0121	2.0	0734	4.7	1353	1.6	2019	4.7
19	SU	0213	1.7	0821	4.9	1437	1.3	2056	4.9
20	M	0252	1.5	0858	5.1	1512	1.1	2127	5.0
21	TU	0325	1.3	0930	5.2	1542	1.0	2155	5.2
22	W	0355	1.1	1001	5.3	1610	0.9	2222	5.3
23	TH ●	0424	1.0	1032	5.4	1638	0.9	2250	5.3
24	F	0454	0.9	1103	5.4	1708	0.9	2320	5.3
25	SA	0525	1.0	1135	5.3	1738	1.0	2351	5.3
26	SU	0558	1.0	1209	5.2	1811	1.1		
27	M	0024	5.2	0633	1.2	1246	5.1	1846	1.3
28	TU	0101	5.1	0713	1.4	1326	4.9	1928	1.6
29	W	0143	4.9	0802	1.6	1416	4.6	2020	1.8
30	TH ☽	0237	4.7	0904	1.7	1522	4.4	2129	2.0

MAY

Date	Day	Time	m	Time	m	Time	m	Time	m
1	F	0350	4.5	1024	1.8	1650	4.4	2254	2.1
2	SA	0517	4.6	1145	1.6	1815	4.6		
3	SU	0013	1.8	0632	4.8	1254	1.2	1918	4.9
4	M	0116	1.5	0731	5.2	1349	0.9	2010	5.2
5	TU	0208	1.1	0822	5.5	1438	0.5	2055	5.5
6	W	0255	0.7	0908	5.8	1523	0.3	2137	5.7
7	TH ○	0339	0.4	0954	5.9	1607	0.2	2220	5.8
8	F	0424	0.3	1040	6.0	1651	0.3	2303	5.8
9	SA	0510	0.3	1127	5.9	1735	0.5	2348	5.7
10	SU	0556	0.5	1214	5.6	1821	0.8		
11	M	0033	5.6	0645	0.7	1304	5.3	1908	1.1
12	TU	0120	5.3	0736	1.1	1356	4.9	1959	1.5
13	W	0211	5.0	0834	1.4	1456	4.6	2058	1.9
14	TH ☾	0310	4.7	0941	1.7	1609	4.3	2208	2.2
15	F	0420	4.5	1055	1.8	1730	4.3	2325	2.2
16	SA	0536	4.5	1206	1.8	1842	4.4		
17	SU	0034	2.1	0643	4.6	1306	1.7	1936	4.5
18	M	0129	1.9	0736	4.7	1354	1.5	2017	4.7
19	TU	0213	1.7	0819	4.9	1433	1.3	2051	4.9
20	W	0250	1.5	0856	5.1	1506	1.2	2122	5.1
21	TH	0324	1.3	0930	5.2	1538	1.1	2152	5.2
22	F ●	0356	1.1	1004	5.2	1609	1.0	2223	5.3
23	SA	0429	1.1	1038	5.3	1641	1.0	2255	5.3
24	SU	0504	1.0	1113	5.3	1715	1.1	2330	5.3
25	M	0540	1.0	1151	5.2	1751	1.1		
26	TU	0007	5.3	0619	1.1	1232	5.1	1830	1.3
27	W	0048	5.2	0703	1.2	1317	4.9	1916	1.5
28	TH	0134	5.1	0754	1.4	1409	4.8	2010	1.7
29	F	0228	4.9	0854	1.5	1512	4.6	2114	1.8
30	SA ☽	0334	4.8	1004	1.5	1627	4.6	2228	1.8
31	SU	0448	4.8	1116	1.4	1742	4.7	2341	1.7

JUNE

Date	Day	Time	m	Time	m	Time	m	Time	m
1	M	0558	5.0	1222	1.2	1847	4.9		
2	TU	0044	1.5	0700	5.2	1321	0.9	1941	5.1
3	W	0141	1.2	0756	5.4	1413	0.7	2030	5.4
4	TH	0232	0.9	0847	5.6	1501	0.6	2116	5.5
5	F ○	0321	0.7	0937	5.7	1548	0.6	2201	5.7
6	SA	0409	0.6	1025	5.7	1634	0.6	2246	5.7
7	SU	0456	0.6	1113	5.6	1719	0.8	2331	5.7
8	M	0544	0.7	1201	5.4	1804	1.0		
9	TU	0016	5.5	0631	0.8	1249	5.1	1848	1.2
10	W	0102	5.4	0719	1.1	1337	4.9	1935	1.5
11	TH	0148	5.1	0809	1.3	1427	4.6	2025	1.8
12	F	0237	4.9	0903	1.6	1523	4.4	2121	2.0
13	SA ☾	0332	4.7	1003	1.8	1627	4.3	2225	2.2
14	SU	0434	4.6	1106	1.8	1734	4.3	2332	2.2
15	M	0539	4.5	1207	1.8	1836	4.4		
16	TU	0034	2.1	0639	4.6	1301	1.7	1928	4.6
17	W	0127	1.9	0733	4.7	1348	1.6	2011	4.7
18	TH	0212	1.7	0819	4.9	1429	1.5	2049	4.9
19	F	0252	1.5	0900	5.0	1506	1.3	2125	5.1
20	SA	0331	1.3	0939	5.1	1542	1.2	2159	5.2
21	SU ●	0408	1.2	1017	5.2	1619	1.1	2235	5.3
22	M	0447	1.0	1056	5.2	1657	1.1	2313	5.4
23	TU	0527	1.0	1137	5.2	1737	1.1	2354	5.4
24	W	0610	1.0	1221	5.2	1820	1.1		
25	TH	0037	5.4	0655	1.0	1308	5.1	1906	1.2
26	F	0124	5.3	0744	1.0	1358	5.0	1957	1.4
27	SA	0216	5.2	0839	1.1	1455	4.9	2055	1.5
28	SU ☽	0313	5.1	0940	1.2	1559	4.8	2159	1.6
29	M	0418	5.0	1046	1.3	1708	4.8	2308	1.6
30	TU	0527	5.0	1153	1.2	1815	4.8		

SUNRISE AND SUNSET TIMES

HOLYHEAD
At 53°19′N 4°37′W

		Sunrise	Sunset
UT			
Jan	01	0834	1611
	15	0826	1631
Feb	01	0803	1702
	15	0736	1730
Mar	01	0706	1757
	15	0633	1823
BST			
Apr	01	0652	1954
	15	0619	2020
May	01	0544	2048
	15	0519	2112
Jun	01	0457	2136
	15	0450	2148
Jul	01	0455	2149
	15	0510	2139
Aug	01	0535	2114
	15	0559	2046
Sep	01	0628	2008
	15	0652	1934
Oct	01	0720	1855
	15	0745	1822
UT			
Nov	01	0717	1646
	15	0744	1622
Dec	01	0811	1604
	15	0827	1600

HOLYHEAD
LAT 53°19'N
LONG 4°37'W

TIMES AND HEIGHTS OF HIGH AND LOW WATER (Heights in Metres)

TIME ZONE UT
For Summer Time (area enclosed in shaded box) add 1 hour

2020

JULY

Day	Time	m	Time	m	Time	m	Time	m
1 W	0015	1.5	0634	5.1	1256	1.2	1916	5.0
2 TH	0119	1.4	0737	5.2	1354	1.1	2012	5.2
3 F	0217	1.2	0835	5.3	1447	1.0	2102	5.3
4 SA	0311	1.0	0928	5.3	1536	0.9	2149	5.5
5 SU O	0401	0.8	1017	5.4	1622	0.9	2234	5.6
6 M	0448	0.8	1104	5.3	1705	1.0	2317	5.6
7 TU	0533	0.8	1148	5.3	1747	1.1	2359	5.5
8 W	0615	0.9	1230	5.1	1827	1.2		
9 TH	0039	5.4	0656	1.0	1310	4.9	1907	1.4
10 F	0120	5.3	0737	1.2	1351	4.8	1948	1.6
11 SA	0200	5.1	0820	1.4	1433	4.6	2033	1.8
12 SU ☾	0244	4.9	0906	1.6	1521	4.4	2123	2.0
13 M	0334	4.7	0958	1.8	1619	4.3	2222	2.2
14 TU	0433	4.5	1058	1.9	1724	4.3	2329	2.2
15 W	0539	4.5	1201	2.0	1830	4.4		
16 TH	0035	2.1	0645	4.5	1301	1.9	1929	4.6
17 F	0134	1.9	0744	4.6	1353	1.7	2017	4.8
18 SA	0224	1.7	0834	4.8	1439	1.5	2100	5.0
19 SU	0309	1.4	0919	5.0	1521	1.3	2139	5.2
20 M ●	0351	1.2	1000	5.2	1601	1.1	2218	5.4
21 TU	0432	0.9	1041	5.3	1642	1.0	2258	5.6
22 W	0513	0.8	1123	5.4	1723	0.9	2339	5.7
23 TH	0556	0.7	1207	5.4	1806	0.9		
24 F	0023	5.7	0640	0.6	1252	5.4	1851	0.9
25 SA	0108	5.6	0727	0.7	1340	5.2	1938	1.1
26 SU	0156	5.5	0817	0.9	1430	5.1	2030	1.3
27 M ☽	0248	5.3	0912	1.1	1528	4.9	2130	1.5
28 TU	0349	5.1	1016	1.3	1634	4.8	2238	1.6
29 W	0500	4.9	1126	1.5	1747	4.7	2353	1.7
30 TH	0617	4.8	1237	1.5	1859	4.8		
31 F	0106	1.6	0731	4.9	1343	1.5	2001	5.0

AUGUST

Day	Time	m	Time	m	Time	m	Time	m
1 SA	0213	1.4	0834	5.0	1441	1.4	2055	5.2
2 SU	0309	1.2	0927	5.1	1529	1.2	2141	5.4
3 M O	0357	1.0	1012	5.2	1612	1.1	2222	5.5
4 TU	0439	0.9	1052	5.3	1651	1.0	2301	5.6
5 W	0517	0.8	1129	5.2	1727	1.0	2338	5.6
6 TH	0553	0.9	1204	5.2	1802	1.1		
7 F	0013	5.5	0627	1.0	1238	5.1	1835	1.2
8 SA	0047	5.4	0701	1.1	1311	5.0	1911	1.4
9 SU	0122	5.2	0736	1.3	1346	4.8	1949	1.6
10 M	0159	5.0	0815	1.5	1425	4.6	2031	1.9
11 TU ☾	0241	4.8	0859	1.8	1512	4.5	2121	2.1
12 W	0333	4.6	0952	2.0	1613	4.3	2226	2.3
13 TH	0440	4.4	1059	2.2	1731	4.3	2344	2.3
14 F	0600	4.3	1214	2.2	1847	4.4		
15 SA	0058	2.1	0714	4.5	1321	2.0	1948	4.7
16 SU	0159	1.8	0814	4.7	1415	1.7	2037	5.0
17 M	0248	1.4	0901	5.0	1501	1.4	2119	5.3
18 TU	0332	1.1	0944	5.3	1543	1.1	2158	5.6
19 W ●	0413	0.7	1024	5.5	1624	0.8	2238	5.8
20 TH	0454	0.5	1105	5.6	1704	0.6	2319	6.0
21 F	0536	0.3	1147	5.7	1746	0.6		
22 SA	0002	6.0	0618	0.4	1230	5.6	1829	0.6
23 SU	0046	5.9	0702	0.5	1315	5.5	1915	0.8
24 M	0133	5.7	0750	0.8	1403	5.3	2005	1.1
25 TU ☽	0223	5.4	0843	1.1	1457	5.0	2103	1.4
26 W	0323	5.1	0947	1.5	1603	4.7	2215	1.7
27 TH	0441	4.7	1103	1.8	1725	4.6	2340	1.9
28 F	0613	4.6	1224	1.9	1848	4.7		
29 SA	0103	1.8	0735	4.7	1338	1.8	1956	4.9
30 SU	0213	1.5	0836	4.9	1435	1.6	2048	5.2
31 M	0305	1.2	0923	5.1	1520	1.4	2130	5.4

SEPTEMBER

Day	Time	m	Time	m	Time	m	Time	m
1 TU	0346	1.0	1000	5.2	1557	1.2	2206	5.5
2 W O	0422	0.9	1033	5.3	1631	1.1	2239	5.6
3 TH	0454	0.9	1104	5.3	1702	1.0	2311	5.6
4 F	0524	0.9	1134	5.3	1733	1.0	2343	5.6
5 SA	0554	1.0	1203	5.2	1804	1.1		
6 SU	0014	5.5	0624	1.1	1234	5.1	1836	1.3
7 M	0047	5.3	0656	1.3	1306	5.0	1910	1.5
8 TU	0121	5.1	0730	1.5	1341	4.8	1948	1.8
9 W	0159	4.9	0809	1.8	1421	4.6	2034	2.0
10 TH ☾	0245	4.6	0858	2.1	1514	4.4	2135	2.3
11 F	0348	4.4	1004	2.3	1633	4.3	2258	2.4
12 SA	0520	4.3	1130	2.4	1806	4.4		
13 SU	0025	2.2	0648	4.4	1251	2.1	1918	4.7
14 M	0133	1.8	0753	4.7	1351	1.8	2011	5.0
15 TU	0225	1.3	0841	5.1	1439	1.4	2054	5.4
16 W	0309	0.9	0923	5.4	1521	1.0	2134	5.8
17 TH ●	0350	0.5	1002	5.7	1601	0.7	2214	6.0
18 F	0430	0.3	1042	5.9	1641	0.5	2255	6.2
19 SA	0511	0.2	1122	5.9	1723	0.4	2338	6.2
20 SU	0553	0.2	1205	5.8	1806	0.5		
21 M	0023	6.1	0637	0.5	1249	5.7	1852	0.7
22 TU	0110	5.8	0724	0.9	1336	5.4	1942	1.1
23 W	0202	5.4	0817	1.3	1430	5.1	2043	1.5
24 TH ☽	0305	4.9	0922	1.8	1537	4.8	2200	1.8
25 F	0430	4.6	1044	2.1	1705	4.6	2331	2.0
26 SA	0611	4.5	1211	2.2	1835	4.7		
27 SU	0056	1.8	0731	4.7	1325	2.0	1942	5.0
28 M	0201	1.5	0827	4.9	1420	1.7	2031	5.2
29 TU	0248	1.3	0907	5.1	1502	1.5	2110	5.4
30 W	0325	1.1	0940	5.2	1536	1.3	2142	5.5

OCTOBER

Day	Time	m	Time	m	Time	m	Time	m
1 TH O	0357	1.0	1008	5.3	1607	1.1	2213	5.6
2 F	0426	0.9	1036	5.4	1635	1.1	2243	5.6
3 SA	0453	0.9	1103	5.4	1704	1.1	2313	5.6
4 SU	0521	1.0	1131	5.4	1734	1.1	2344	5.5
5 M	0550	1.1	1201	5.3	1806	1.3		
6 TU	0015	5.4	0620	1.3	1233	5.2	1838	1.5
7 W	0049	5.2	0653	1.5	1306	5.0	1915	1.7
8 TH	0126	4.9	0731	1.8	1345	4.8	2000	2.0
9 F	0212	4.7	0818	2.1	1435	4.6	2100	2.2
10 SA ☾	0314	4.4	0924	2.4	1549	4.4	2223	2.3
11 SU	0447	4.3	1053	2.4	1726	4.5	2353	2.1
12 M	0621	4.5	1219	2.2	1844	4.8		
13 TU	0102	1.7	0726	4.8	1322	1.8	1939	5.1
14 W	0156	1.2	0815	5.2	1412	1.4	2025	5.5
15 TH	0241	0.8	0857	5.6	1455	1.0	2107	5.9
16 F ●	0323	0.4	0937	5.8	1536	0.6	2149	6.1
17 SA	0404	0.2	1017	6.0	1617	0.4	2232	6.3
18 SU	0445	0.2	1058	6.0	1700	0.4	2316	6.2
19 M	0529	0.3	1141	6.0	1745	0.5		
20 TU	0003	6.0	0613	0.6	1226	5.8	1833	0.7
21 W	0052	5.7	0701	1.0	1314	5.5	1926	1.1
22 TH	0146	5.3	0755	1.5	1408	5.2	2028	1.5
23 F ☽	0251	4.8	0859	2.0	1515	4.9	2144	1.8
24 SA	0417	4.5	1020	2.3	1639	4.7	2311	2.0
25 SU	0552	4.5	1145	2.3	1805	4.7		
26 M	0030	1.9	0708	4.6	1258	2.1	1913	4.9
27 TU	0133	1.7	0801	4.8	1352	1.9	2002	5.1
28 W	0219	1.4	0840	5.0	1434	1.7	2041	5.3
29 TH	0256	1.3	0911	5.2	1508	1.4	2114	5.4
30 F	0327	1.2	0940	5.3	1539	1.3	2145	5.5
31 SA O	0355	1.1	1007	5.4	1609	1.2	2215	5.6

NOVEMBER

Day	Time	m	Time	m	Time	m	Time	m
1 SU	0423	1.1	1035	5.5	1638	1.2	2246	5.5
2 M	0451	1.1	1104	5.5	1709	1.2	2318	5.5
3 TU	0521	1.2	1134	5.4	1742	1.3	2351	5.3
4 W	0553	1.4	1207	5.3	1817	1.5		
5 TH	0026	5.2	0627	1.6	1242	5.2	1855	1.6
6 F	0106	5.0	0706	1.8	1323	5.0	1941	1.8
7 SA	0153	4.7	0755	2.0	1413	4.8	2040	2.0
8 SU ☾	0255	4.5	0859	2.3	1521	4.7	2156	2.1
9 M	0419	4.4	1020	2.3	1647	4.7	2317	1.9
10 TU	0546	4.6	1142	2.2	1804	4.9		
11 W	0026	1.6	0652	4.9	1248	1.8	1904	5.2
12 TH	0123	1.2	0744	5.2	1341	1.4	1954	5.6
13 F	0211	0.8	0829	5.6	1427	1.0	2041	5.9
14 SA	0256	0.6	0912	5.8	1512	0.7	2126	6.1
15 SU ●	0340	0.4	0954	6.0	1557	0.5	2212	6.1
16 M	0424	0.4	1037	6.0	1643	0.5	2259	6.1
17 TU	0509	0.6	1122	6.0	1730	0.6	2348	5.9
18 W	0555	0.8	1208	5.8	1821	0.8		
19 TH	0039	5.5	0643	1.2	1257	5.6	1913	1.1
20 F	0133	5.2	0736	1.6	1350	5.3	2012	1.5
21 SA	0234	4.8	0835	2.0	1450	5.0	2119	1.8
22 SU ☽	0347	4.5	0944	2.3	1600	4.8	2234	1.9
23 M	0508	4.4	1101	2.4	1716	4.7	2346	1.9
24 TU	0623	4.5	1211	2.3	1825	4.8		
25 W	0048	1.8	0719	4.7	1311	2.1	1920	4.9
26 TH	0139	1.7	0803	4.9	1358	1.9	2004	5.1
27 F	0219	1.5	0839	5.1	1437	1.7	2042	5.2
28 SA	0254	1.4	0910	5.2	1511	1.5	2117	5.3
29 SU	0325	1.3	0941	5.3	1544	1.4	2150	5.4
30 M O	0356	1.3	1010	5.4	1616	1.3	2223	5.4

DECEMBER

Day	Time	m	Time	m	Time	m	Time	m
1 TU	0427	1.3	1041	5.5	1650	1.3	2258	5.4
2 W	0459	1.3	1114	5.5	1725	1.3	2333	5.3
3 TH	0534	1.4	1149	5.4	1803	1.4		
4 F	0012	5.2	0611	1.5	1228	5.3	1843	1.5
5 SA	0054	5.1	0652	1.6	1311	5.2	1930	1.6
6 SU	0142	4.9	0741	1.8	1400	5.1	2024	1.7
7 M	0239	4.7	0839	2.0	1459	5.0	2129	1.7
8 TU ☾	0348	4.7	0948	2.1	1609	4.9	2240	1.7
9 W	0504	4.7	1102	2.0	1721	5.0	2348	1.5
10 TH	0613	4.9	1210	1.8	1827	5.2		
11 F	0049	1.3	0712	5.1	1310	1.5	1925	5.4
12 SA	0144	1.0	0803	5.4	1403	1.2	2019	5.6
13 SU	0234	0.8	0851	5.6	1454	1.0	2110	5.8
14 M ●	0322	0.7	0937	5.8	1543	0.8	2200	5.9
15 TU	0409	0.7	1023	5.9	1632	0.7	2249	5.8
16 W	0456	0.8	1109	5.9	1722	0.7	2338	5.7
17 TH	0542	1.0	1155	5.8	1811	0.8		
18 F	0027	5.4	0628	1.2	1242	5.7	1900	1.1
19 SA	0117	5.2	0715	1.5	1329	5.5	1950	1.3
20 SU	0207	4.9	0804	1.8	1418	5.2	2043	1.6
21 M ☽	0302	4.6	0858	2.0	1512	5.0	2141	1.8
22 TU	0403	4.5	1000	2.3	1612	4.8	2244	2.0
23 W	0511	4.4	1108	2.4	1717	4.7	2348	2.0
24 TH	0618	4.4	1214	2.3	1822	4.7		
25 F	0046	2.0	0715	4.6	1312	2.2	1919	4.8
26 SA	0137	1.8	0801	4.8	1401	2.0	2009	4.9
27 SU	0220	1.7	0841	5.0	1444	1.8	2051	5.0
28 M	0258	1.6	0917	5.2	1523	1.6	2130	5.2
29 TU	0333	1.4	0951	5.3	1559	1.4	2206	5.2
30 W O	0408	1.3	1024	5.4	1636	1.3	2243	5.3
31 TH	0444	1.3	1100	5.5	1713	1.2	2321	5.3

MILFORD HAVEN
LAT 51°42'N
LONG 5°03'W

TIMES AND HEIGHTS OF HIGH AND LOW WATER (Heights in Metres)

TIME ZONE UT
For Summer Time (area enclosed in shaded box) add 1 hour

2020

JANUARY

Date	Day	Time	m	Time	m	Time	m	Time	m
1	W	0344	2.0	0956	6.0	1613	2.1	2215	5.6
2	TH	0424	2.3	1039	5.8	1658	2.3	2301	5.4
3	F ☽	0513	2.5	1130	5.5	1754	2.5	2357	5.2
4	SA	0618	2.7	1232	5.3	1901	2.6		
5	SU	0107	5.1	0732	2.7	1344	5.3	2010	2.5
6	M	0220	5.3	0842	2.5	1449	5.5	2112	2.3
7	TU	0319	5.6	0942	2.2	1544	5.8	2206	1.9
8	W	0410	6.0	1032	1.9	1633	6.2	2253	1.6
9	TH	0456	6.4	1119	1.5	1719	6.5	2337	1.3
10	F ○	0540	6.7	1203	1.2	1804	6.7		
11	SA	0021	1.1	0623	7.0	1247	1.0	1848	6.9
12	SU	0105	0.9	0707	7.1	1332	0.8	1933	7.0
13	M	0148	0.8	0752	7.2	1416	0.8	2018	7.0
14	TU	0232	0.9	0837	7.1	1502	0.8	2104	6.8
15	W	0317	1.0	0924	7.0	1548	1.0	2151	6.6
16	TH	0405	1.3	1013	6.7	1637	1.3	2242	6.3
17	F ☾	0456	1.5	1107	6.4	1733	1.6	2339	5.9
18	SA	0556	1.8	1208	6.1	1838	1.9		
19	SU	0045	5.7	0706	2.1	1317	5.8	1952	2.1
20	M	0158	5.7	0824	2.1	1431	5.8	2105	2.0
21	TU	0310	5.8	0936	1.9	1542	5.9	2209	1.8
22	W	0414	6.1	1037	1.7	1642	6.1	2303	1.6
23	TH	0508	6.4	1128	1.4	1733	6.4	2349	1.4
24	F ●	0554	6.6	1213	1.3	1816	6.5		
25	SA	0030	1.2	0634	6.8	1253	1.1	1854	6.6
26	SU	0108	1.2	0711	6.8	1329	1.1	1930	6.6
27	M	0142	1.2	0746	6.8	1403	1.1	2003	6.5
28	TU	0215	1.3	0819	6.7	1435	1.2	2035	6.4
29	W	0245	1.4	0852	6.5	1506	1.4	2106	6.2
30	TH	0315	1.6	0924	6.3	1538	1.6	2138	6.0
31	F	0347	1.8	0959	6.0	1612	1.9	[illegible]	5.7

FEBRUARY

Date	Day	Time	m	Time	m	Time	m	Time	m
1	SA	0423	2.1	1037	5.7	1652	2.2	2255	5.4
2	SU ☽	0508	2.4	1125	5.4	1743	2.5	2350	5.2
3	M	0610	2.7	1228	5.2	1856	2.6		
4	TU	0104	5.1	0738	2.7	1348	5.2	2020	2.5
5	W	0228	5.2	0900	2.5	1505	5.4	2131	2.2
6	TH	0337	5.6	1005	2.0	1608	5.8	2229	1.8
7	F	0433	6.1	1059	1.6	1701	6.3	2319	1.3
8	SA	0523	6.6	1148	1.1	1750	6.7		
9	SU ○	0006	0.9	0609	7.0	1235	0.7	1835	7.1
10	M	0052	0.6	0655	7.4	1320	0.4	1920	7.3
11	TU	0136	0.4	0739	7.5	1404	0.3	2004	7.3
12	W	0220	0.4	0823	7.5	1447	0.4	2048	7.2
13	TH	0302	0.5	0907	7.3	1530	0.6	2131	6.9
14	F	0345	0.8	0952	7.0	1613	1.0	2216	6.5
15	SA ☾	0430	1.2	1039	6.5	1700	1.5	2306	6.0
16	SU	0521	1.7	1133	6.0	1756	2.0		
17	M	0007	5.6	0628	2.1	1242	5.5	1913	2.3
18	TU	0124	5.4	0756	2.3	1406	5.3	2043	2.4
19	W	0250	5.4	0921	2.2	1530	5.5	2157	2.1
20	TH	0403	5.8	1028	1.9	1634	5.8	2253	1.8
21	F	0457	6.2	1119	1.6	1722	6.1	2338	1.5
22	SA	0541	6.5	1200	1.3	1802	6.4		
23	SU ●	0016	1.2	0618	6.7	1237	1.1	1837	6.6
24	M	0050	1.1	0652	6.8	1309	1.0	1909	6.6
25	TU	0122	1.0	0724	6.9	1340	1.0	1939	6.6
26	W	0151	1.0	0754	6.8	1409	1.0	2007	6.6
27	TH	0219	1.1	0823	6.7	1437	1.1	2035	6.4
28	F	0247	1.3	0852	6.5	1505	1.3	2104	6.2
29	SA	0316	1.5	0922	6.3	1535	1.6	2134	6.0

MARCH

Date	Day	Time	m	Time	m	Time	m	Time	m
1	SU	0347	1.8	0955	5.9	1608	1.9	2209	5.7
2	M ☽	0424	2.1	1035	5.6	1649	2.3	2255	5.4
3	TU	0513	2.5	1131	5.2	1748	2.6		
4	W	0003	5.1	0633	2.7	1254	5.0	1926	2.7
5	TH	0139	5.1	0821	2.6	1430	5.2	2059	2.4
6	F	0307	5.5	0940	2.1	1545	5.7	2206	1.8
7	SA	0411	6.1	1039	1.5	1642	6.3	2300	1.3
8	SU	0504	6.7	1130	0.9	1732	6.8	2348	0.8
9	M ○	0552	7.2	1217	0.4	1818	7.2		
10	TU	0034	0.4	0637	7.5	1302	0.1	1901	7.5
11	W	0118	0.1	0720	7.7	1345	0.0	1944	7.5
12	TH	0201	0.1	0803	7.7	1426	0.1	2025	7.4
13	F	0242	0.3	0845	7.4	1506	0.5	2107	7.1
14	SA	0323	0.6	0927	7.0	1546	0.9	2149	6.6
15	SU	0405	1.1	1012	6.4	1628	1.5	2235	6.1
16	M ☾	0452	1.7	1102	5.8	1720	2.1	2333	5.6
17	TU	0556	2.2	1209	5.3	1837	2.6		
18	W	0053	5.2	0731	2.5	1342	5.0	2021	2.6
19	TH	0229	5.3	0905	2.4	1515	5.2	2140	2.3
20	F	0345	5.6	1012	2.0	1618	5.6	2236	1.9
21	SA	0438	6.1	1100	1.6	1702	6.0	2318	1.5
22	SU	0519	6.4	1138	1.3	1739	6.3	2353	1.3
23	M	0555	6.6	1211	1.1	1812	6.5		
24	TU ●	0025	1.1	0626	6.8	1243	0.9	1842	6.7
25	W	0056	1.0	0657	6.8	1312	0.9	1911	6.7
26	TH	0124	0.9	0726	6.8	1340	0.9	1938	6.7
27	F	0152	1.0	0754	6.7	1407	1.0	2005	6.6
28	SA	0220	1.1	0822	6.6	1435	1.2	2033	6.4
29	SU	0248	1.3	0852	6.3	1505	1.5	2103	6.2
30	M	0319	1.6	0924	6.0	1536	1.8	2137	5.9
31	TU	0355	2.0	1003	5.7	1616	2.2	2221	5.6

APRIL

Date	Day	Time	m	Time	m	Time	m	Time	m
1	W ☽	0443	2.3	1057	5.3	1712	2.5	2327	5.2
2	TH	0558	2.6	1220	5.0	1846	2.7		
3	F	0103	5.1	0750	2.5	1401	5.2	2029	2.4
4	SA	0237	5.5	0913	2.0	1520	5.7	2140	1.8
5	SU	0345	6.1	1014	1.4	1619	6.3	2236	1.2
6	M	0440	6.7	1106	0.8	1709	6.9	2325	0.7
7	TU	0528	7.2	1153	0.3	1754	7.3		
8	W ○	0011	0.3	0613	7.6	1239	0.1	1838	7.5
9	TH	0056	0.1	0657	7.7	1321	0.0	1920	7.6
10	F	0138	0.1	0740	7.6	1402	0.2	2001	7.4
11	SA	0220	0.3	0822	7.3	1442	0.6	2042	7.1
12	SU	0301	0.7	0904	6.9	1521	1.1	2124	6.6
13	M	0343	1.2	0947	6.3	1603	1.6	2210	6.1
14	TU ☾	0430	1.8	1037	5.7	1652	2.2	2306	5.6
15	W	0532	2.3	1141	5.2	1805	2.6		
16	TH	0023	5.2	0702	2.6	1312	4.9	1947	2.7
17	F	0156	5.2	0834	2.4	1443	5.1	2108	2.4
18	SA	0311	5.5	0939	2.1	1546	5.5	2203	2.0
19	SU	0404	5.9	1026	1.7	1631	5.9	2245	1.7
20	M	0446	6.2	1105	1.4	1708	6.2	2321	1.4
21	TU	0522	6.5	1139	1.2	1741	6.4	2354	1.2
22	W	0555	6.6	1210	1.1	1811	6.6		
23	TH ●	0025	1.1	0626	6.7	1241	1.0	1840	6.7
24	F	0056	1.0	0656	6.7	1310	1.0	1909	6.7
25	SA	0125	1.0	0726	6.7	1340	1.1	1938	6.7
26	SU	0155	1.1	0756	6.6	1410	1.2	2008	6.5
27	M	0227	1.3	0828	6.4	1442	1.4	2041	6.3
28	TU	0301	1.6	0904	6.1	1517	1.7	2119	6.1
29	W	0341	1.9	0946	5.8	1600	2.1	2206	5.7
30	TH ☽	0433	2.2	1044	5.4	1659	2.3	2313	5.5

MAY

Date	Day	Time	m	Time	m	Time	m	Time	m
1	F	0546	2.3	1203	5.2	1825	2.5		
2	SA	0040	5.4	0723	2.2	1334	5.4	1958	2.2
3	SU	0207	5.7	0842	1.8	1450	5.8	2109	1.8
4	M	0315	6.2	0945	1.3	1550	6.3	2207	1.2
5	TU	0412	6.7	1039	0.8	1641	6.8	2259	0.8
6	W	0502	7.1	1127	0.5	1728	7.2	2346	0.5
7	TH ○	0549	7.4	1213	0.3	1813	7.4		
8	F	0032	0.3	0634	7.4	1257	0.3	1856	7.4
9	SA	0117	0.3	0718	7.3	1339	0.5	1939	7.3
10	SU	0200	0.5	0801	7.0	1420	0.8	2021	7.0
11	M	0242	0.9	0844	6.6	1500	1.2	2104	6.6
12	TU	0325	1.3	0928	6.1	1542	1.7	2150	6.1
13	W	0412	1.8	1016	5.7	1630	2.2	2243	5.7
14	TH ☾	0509	2.2	1114	5.2	1732	2.5	2348	5.4
15	F	0622	2.5	1229	5.0	1856	2.7		
16	SA	0107	5.3	0742	2.4	1351	5.1	2015	2.5
17	SU	0220	5.4	0849	2.2	1457	5.3	2115	2.2
18	M	0318	5.7	0941	1.9	1547	5.7	2203	1.9
19	TU	0404	6.0	1023	1.7	1628	6.0	2243	1.7
20	W	0444	6.2	1101	1.4	1704	6.2	2319	1.4
21	TH	0520	6.4	1136	1.3	1738	6.4	2354	1.3
22	F ●	0555	6.5	1209	1.2	1810	6.6		
23	SA	0027	1.2	0628	6.6	1243	1.1	1842	6.7
24	SU	0102	1.2	0702	6.6	1317	1.1	1916	6.7
25	M	0136	1.2	0737	6.5	1351	1.2	1951	6.6
26	TU	0213	1.3	0814	6.4	1428	1.4	2029	6.4
27	W	0252	1.5	0854	6.2	1509	1.6	2112	6.2
28	TH	0337	1.7	0942	5.9	1556	1.9	2203	6.0
29	F	0430	1.9	1040	5.7	1654	2.1	2307	5.8
30	SA ☽	0537	2.0	1149	5.5	1807	2.1		
31	SU	0020	5.8	0655	1.9	1305	5.6	1926	2.0

JUNE

Date	Day	Time	m	Time	m	Time	m	Time	m
1	M	0136	5.9	0809	1.7	1417	5.9	2036	1.7
2	TU	0243	6.2	0914	1.4	1519	6.2	2138	1.4
3	W	0343	6.5	1010	1.1	1614	6.6	2233	1.1
4	TH	0437	6.8	1102	0.9	1704	6.9	2324	0.8
5	F ○	0527	7.0	1150	0.7	1752	7.0		
6	SA	0012	0.7	0615	7.0	1236	0.7	1837	7.1
7	SU	0059	0.7	0701	6.9	1320	0.8	1922	7.0
8	M	0143	0.8	0745	6.8	1402	1.0	2005	6.8
9	TU	0227	1.1	0828	6.5	1443	1.3	2048	6.6
10	W	0309	1.4	0911	6.1	1524	1.7	2131	6.2
11	TH	0353	1.7	0954	5.8	1607	2.0	2217	5.9
12	F	0440	2.0	1042	5.4	1656	2.3	2309	5.6
13	SA ☾	0534	2.3	1137	5.2	1756	2.5		
14	SU	0009	5.4	0636	2.4	1245	5.1	1904	2.6
15	M	0118	5.4	0742	2.3	1354	5.2	2012	2.4
16	TU	0221	5.5	0843	2.2	1453	5.4	2110	2.2
17	W	0315	5.7	0935	2.0	1543	5.7	2200	2.0
18	TH	0403	5.9	1021	1.8	1626	6.0	2244	1.7
19	F	0445	6.1	1102	1.5	1705	6.2	2324	1.5
20	SA	0525	6.3	1141	1.4	1744	6.5		
21	SU ●	0003	1.4	0604	6.5	1220	1.2	1821	6.6
22	M	0043	1.2	0643	6.6	1259	1.2	1900	6.7
23	TU	0123	1.2	0724	6.6	1339	1.2	1940	6.7
24	W	0204	1.1	0805	6.5	1420	1.2	2023	6.7
25	TH	0247	1.2	0850	6.4	1503	1.3	2109	6.5
26	F	0333	1.3	0938	6.2	1550	1.5	2159	6.4
27	SA	0424	1.5	1030	6.0	1643	1.7	2254	6.2
28	SU ☽	0521	1.6	1129	5.9	1744	1.8	2356	6.1
29	M	0626	1.7	1234	5.8	1853	1.9		
30	TU	0104	6.0	0735	1.8	1343	5.8	2003	1.8

SUNRISE AND SUNSET TIMES

MILFORD HAVEN
At 51°42'N 5°03'W

UT		Sunrise	Sunset
Jan	01	0827	1621
	15	0820	1640
Feb	01	0759	1709
	15	0734	1735
Mar	01	0705	1800
	15	0634	1825
BST			
Apr	01	0655	1954
	15	0624	2017
May	01	0551	2044
	15	0528	2107
Jun	01	0508	2129
	15	0501	2140
Jul	01	0506	2142
	15	0520	2132
Aug	01	0543	2109
	15	0605	2043
Sep	01	0633	2007
	15	0655	1935
Oct	01	0721	1858
	15	0745	1826
UT			
Nov	01	0714	1652
	15	0739	1630
Dec	01	0805	1614
	15	0820	1610

MILFORD HAVEN
LAT 51°42′N
LONG 5°03′W

TIMES AND HEIGHTS OF HIGH AND LOW WATER (Heights in Metres)

TIME ZONE UT
For Summer Time (area enclosed in shaded box) add 1 hour

2020

JULY

Date	Day	Time	m	Time	m	Time	m	Time	m
1	W	0212	6.1	0843	1.7	1449	6.0	2111	1.6
2	TH	0317	6.2	0946	1.5	1551	6.2	2213	1.4
3	F	0418	6.4	1043	1.3	1647	6.5	2308	1.2
4	SA	0513	6.5	1134	1.2	1738	6.7	2359	1.1
5	SU ○	0603	6.6	1221	1.1	1825	6.8		
6	M	0046	1.0	0649	6.7	1305	1.1	1909	6.9
7	TU	0130	1.0	0731	6.6	1346	1.1	1950	6.8
8	W	0211	1.1	0812	6.4	1425	1.3	2030	6.6
9	TH	0250	1.3	0850	6.2	1502	1.5	2108	6.4
10	F	0327	1.5	0927	6.0	1538	1.8	2147	6.2
11	SA	0405	1.8	1005	5.7	1616	2.0	2227	5.9
12	SU ☾	0445	2.0	1047	5.5	1659	2.3	2313	5.6
13	M	0532	2.2	1136	5.3	1752	2.5		
14	TU	0007	5.4	0630	2.4	1237	5.1	1859	2.6
15	W	0112	5.3	0736	2.4	1349	5.1	2010	2.5
16	TH	0221	5.3	0843	2.3	1454	5.4	2116	2.3
17	F	0321	5.5	0941	2.1	1549	5.7	2211	2.0
18	SA	0414	5.8	1032	1.8	1637	6.0	2259	1.7
19	SU	0501	6.1	1117	1.5	1722	6.4	2344	1.4
20	M ●	0546	6.4	1201	1.3	1805	6.7		
21	TU	0027	1.1	0629	6.6	1244	1.1	1847	6.9
22	W	0111	0.9	0712	6.8	1327	0.9	1930	7.0
23	TH	0154	0.8	0756	6.8	1410	0.9	2014	7.0
24	F	0238	0.8	0840	6.8	1453	0.9	2058	7.0
25	SA	0322	0.9	0925	6.6	1538	1.1	2145	6.8
26	SU	0408	1.1	1012	6.4	1625	1.3	2234	6.5
27	M ☽	0457	1.4	1103	6.1	1717	1.6	2329	6.2
28	TU	0553	1.7	1203	5.8	1820	1.9		
29	W	0032	5.9	0701	2.0	1312	5.7	1935	2.0
30	TH	0146	5.7	0819	2.0	1426	5.7	2053	2.0
31	F	0301	5.8	0931	1.9	1537	5.9	2203	1.8

AUGUST

Date	Day	Time	m	Time	m	Time	m	Time	m
1	SA	0410	6.0	1033	1.7	1639	6.2	2301	1.5
2	SU	0507	6.2	1125	1.4	1731	6.5	2351	1.3
3	M ○	0555	6.4	1210	1.2	1815	6.7		
4	TU	0035	1.1	0637	6.6	1251	1.1	1855	6.8
5	W	0115	1.0	0715	6.6	1328	1.1	1932	6.8
6	TH	0151	1.0	0750	6.5	1403	1.2	2007	6.8
7	F	0224	1.1	0823	6.4	1435	1.3	2040	6.6
8	SA	0256	1.3	0855	6.3	1505	1.5	2112	6.4
9	SU	0327	1.5	0927	6.0	1536	1.7	2146	6.1
10	M	0359	1.8	1000	5.8	1610	2.0	2222	5.8
11	TU ☾	0435	2.1	1039	5.5	1651	2.3	2306	5.5
12	W	0521	2.4	1128	5.2	1747	2.6		
13	TH	0003	5.2	0626	2.6	1237	5.0	1909	2.8
14	F	0120	5.1	0751	2.7	1402	5.1	2036	2.6
15	SA	0243	5.2	0907	2.4	1517	5.5	2144	2.2
16	SU	0348	5.6	1007	2.0	1614	5.9	2239	1.8
17	M	0441	6.1	1057	1.6	1703	6.4	2326	1.3
18	TU	0529	6.5	1143	1.2	1748	6.8		
19	W ●	0011	0.9	0613	6.9	1228	0.8	1831	7.2
20	TH	0055	0.6	0656	7.1	1311	0.6	1914	7.4
21	F	0139	0.4	0739	7.2	1354	0.5	1957	7.5
22	SA	0221	0.4	0821	7.2	1436	0.6	2040	7.3
23	SU	0303	0.6	0904	7.0	1518	0.8	2124	7.1
24	M	0345	0.9	0948	6.6	1602	1.2	2209	6.6
25	TU ☽	0429	1.4	1035	6.2	1650	1.6	2300	6.1
26	W	0521	1.9	1132	5.8	1751	2.1		
27	TH	0004	5.7	0631	2.3	1245	5.5	1915	2.3
28	F	0126	5.4	0803	2.4	1412	5.5	2047	2.3
29	SA	0255	5.4	0925	2.2	1532	5.8	2200	2.0
30	SU	0408	5.8	1028	1.9	1633	6.2	2256	1.6
31	M	0500	6.1	1116	1.5	1720	6.5	2341	1.3

SEPTEMBER

Date	Day	Time	m	Time	m	Time	m	Time	m
1	TU	0543	6.4	1157	1.3	1800	6.8		
2	W ○	0019	1.1	0619	6.6	1233	1.1	1835	6.9
3	TH	0053	1.0	0653	6.7	1305	1.1	1908	6.9
4	F	0125	1.0	0724	6.7	1336	1.1	1939	6.9
5	SA	0154	1.0	0753	6.6	1404	1.2	2008	6.8
6	SU	0222	1.2	0821	6.5	1432	1.3	2037	6.6
7	M	0250	1.4	0849	6.3	1500	1.6	2107	6.3
8	TU	0319	1.7	0919	6.0	1531	1.9	2139	6.0
9	W	0351	2.0	0952	5.7	1606	2.3	2216	5.6
10	TH ☾	0429	2.4	1034	5.4	1653	2.6	2307	5.2
11	F	0524	2.7	1137	5.1	1808	2.9		
12	SA	0026	5.0	0659	2.9	1312	5.0	2001	2.8
13	SU	0207	5.1	0836	2.6	1447	5.4	2120	2.3
14	M	0325	5.5	0943	2.1	1551	5.9	2217	1.8
15	TU	0421	6.1	1036	1.6	1641	6.5	2306	1.2
16	W	0508	6.7	1123	1.0	1727	7.1	2351	0.7
17	TH ●	0552	7.1	1207	0.6	1811	7.5		
18	F	0034	0.4	0635	7.4	1251	0.4	1853	7.7
19	SA	0117	0.2	0717	7.5	1333	0.3	1935	7.7
20	SU	0159	0.3	0758	7.5	1415	0.4	2018	7.5
21	M	0239	0.5	0840	7.2	1456	0.7	2100	7.2
22	TU	0320	1.0	0922	6.8	1539	1.2	2145	6.6
23	W	0403	1.5	1009	6.3	1626	1.7	2235	6.0
24	TH ☽	0453	2.1	1105	5.8	1729	2.3	2340	5.4
25	F	0606	2.6	1223	5.4	1903	2.6		
26	SA	0111	5.1	0752	2.7	1400	5.4	2041	2.5
27	SU	0249	5.3	0917	2.4	1521	5.7	2151	2.1
28	M	0356	5.7	1015	2.0	1617	6.2	2241	1.7
29	TU	0443	6.1	1059	1.6	1700	6.6	2321	1.4
30	W	0522	6.5	1135	1.3	1737	6.8	2354	1.2

OCTOBER

Date	Day	Time	m	Time	m	Time	m	Time	m
1	TH ○	0555	6.7	1208	1.2	1810	6.9		
2	F	0025	1.0	0625	6.8	1238	1.1	1840	7.0
3	SA	0055	1.0	0654	6.8	1307	1.1	1909	6.9
4	SU	0123	1.1	0722	6.8	1335	1.2	1937	6.8
5	M	0150	1.2	0749	6.7	1402	1.3	2005	6.7
6	TU	0218	1.4	0816	6.5	1430	1.6	2034	6.4
7	W	0246	1.7	0845	6.3	1501	1.9	2105	6.1
8	TH	0317	2.0	0918	5.9	1535	2.2	2141	5.7
9	F	0354	2.4	0959	5.6	1621	2.6	2231	5.3
10	SA ☾	0447	2.7	1059	5.3	1732	2.9	2350	5.0
11	SU	0616	2.9	1234	5.1	1928	2.8		
12	M	0134	5.1	0805	2.7	1414	5.5	2051	2.3
13	TU	0257	5.6	0916	2.2	1522	6.0	2151	1.7
14	W	0355	6.2	1010	1.5	1614	6.7	2241	1.1
15	TH	0443	6.8	1058	1.0	1701	7.2	2326	0.6
16	F ●	0528	7.3	1143	0.6	1746	7.6		
17	SA	0010	0.3	0610	7.6	1228	0.3	1829	7.8
18	SU	0054	0.2	0653	7.7	1311	0.3	1913	7.8
19	M	0135	0.3	0735	7.6	1353	0.4	1956	7.5
20	TU	0217	0.7	0817	7.3	1436	0.8	2039	7.1
21	W	0258	1.1	0900	6.8	1520	1.3	2124	6.5
22	TH	0341	1.7	0948	6.3	1609	1.9	2215	5.9
23	F ☽	0432	2.3	1045	5.8	1713	2.4	2320	5.3
24	SA	0545	2.7	1201	5.4	1844	2.7		
25	SU	0049	5.1	0727	2.8	1334	5.4	2017	2.5
26	M	0222	5.2	0850	2.5	1452	5.7	2124	2.2
27	TU	0328	5.6	0947	2.2	1547	6.1	2212	1.8
28	W	0414	6.0	1030	1.8	1630	6.4	2250	1.5
29	TH	0452	6.4	1106	1.5	1707	6.7	2323	1.3
30	F	0525	6.6	1138	1.3	1740	6.8	2355	1.2
31	SA ○	0556	6.7	1209	1.2	1811	6.9		

NOVEMBER

Date	Day	Time	m	Time	m	Time	m	Time	m
1	SU	0024	1.2	0625	6.8	1239	1.2	1840	6.9
2	M	0054	1.2	0653	6.8	1308	1.3	1910	6.8
3	TU	0123	1.3	0722	6.7	1338	1.4	1939	6.6
4	W	0152	1.4	0751	6.6	1409	1.6	2010	6.4
5	TH	0223	1.7	0823	6.4	1442	1.8	2044	6.1
6	F	0257	2.0	0858	6.1	1520	2.1	2123	5.8
7	SA	0337	2.3	0942	5.8	1608	2.4	2215	5.5
8	SU ☾	0431	2.6	1043	5.5	1716	2.6	2330	5.2
9	M	0550	2.7	1207	5.4	1853	2.6		
10	TU	0101	5.3	0728	2.6	1336	5.6	2015	2.2
11	W	0221	5.7	0841	2.1	1447	6.1	2118	1.7
12	TH	0322	6.2	0940	1.6	1544	6.7	2212	1.2
13	F	0414	6.7	1031	1.1	1634	7.1	2300	0.8
14	SA	0501	7.2	1119	0.7	1722	7.4	2346	0.5
15	SU ●	0547	7.4	1205	0.5	1808	7.6		
16	M	0031	0.5	0631	7.5	1251	0.5	1853	7.5
17	TU	0115	0.6	0715	7.5	1336	0.6	1938	7.3
18	W	0158	0.9	0759	7.2	1421	0.9	2023	6.9
19	TH	0241	1.3	0845	6.9	1507	1.4	2109	6.4
20	F	0325	1.7	0932	6.4	1556	1.8	2159	5.9
21	SA	0414	2.2	1026	6.0	1654	2.3	2257	5.5
22	SU ☽	0517	2.6	1130	5.6	1807	2.5		
23	M	0009	5.2	0638	2.8	1247	5.5	1926	2.6
24	TU	0130	5.2	0759	2.7	1401	5.6	2035	2.4
25	W	0239	5.4	0901	2.4	1502	5.8	2128	2.1
26	TH	0332	5.7	0950	2.1	1550	6.1	2211	1.8
27	F	0415	6.1	1031	1.8	1631	6.3	2249	1.6
28	SA	0452	6.3	1107	1.6	1708	6.5	2324	1.5
29	SU	0526	6.5	1142	1.5	1743	6.6	2357	1.4
30	M ○	0559	6.7	1215	1.4	1816	6.7		

DECEMBER

Date	Day	Time	m	Time	m	Time	m	Time	m
1	TU	0029	1.3	0630	6.7	1248	1.4	1848	6.7
2	W	0102	1.3	0702	6.7	1321	1.4	1922	6.6
3	TH	0135	1.4	0735	6.7	1356	1.5	1957	6.5
4	F	0210	1.6	0811	6.5	1433	1.7	2035	6.3
5	SA	0248	1.8	0851	6.3	1515	1.9	2118	6.0
6	SU	0331	2.0	0937	6.1	1603	2.1	2209	5.8
7	M	0423	2.2	1034	5.9	1703	2.2	2313	5.6
8	TU ☾	0528	2.4	1143	5.8	1817	2.2		
9	W	0026	5.5	0647	2.3	1258	5.9	1934	2.1
10	TH	0141	5.7	0802	2.1	1409	6.1	2042	1.8
11	F	0247	6.1	0907	1.7	1512	6.4	2142	1.4
12	SA	0345	6.5	1005	1.4	1609	6.8	2236	1.1
13	SU	0438	6.8	1058	1.1	1702	7.0	2326	0.9
14	M ●	0528	7.1	1149	0.9	1752	7.1		
15	TU	0014	0.8	0616	7.2	1238	0.8	1840	7.1
16	W	0100	0.9	0702	7.2	1325	0.8	1927	7.0
17	TH	0144	1.0	0748	7.1	1410	1.0	2012	6.8
18	F	0228	1.3	0832	6.9	1455	1.3	2056	6.4
19	SA	0310	1.6	0917	6.6	1540	1.6	2140	6.1
20	SU	0354	1.9	1003	6.2	1626	2.0	2226	5.7
21	M ☽	0441	2.3	1052	5.9	1718	2.3	2319	5.4
22	TU	0537	2.5	1149	5.6	1817	2.5		
23	W	0021	5.2	0643	2.7	1255	5.5	1923	2.5
24	TH	0132	5.2	0754	2.6	1402	5.5	2028	2.4
25	F	0237	5.4	0858	2.5	1501	5.6	2124	2.2
26	SA	0331	5.6	0951	2.2	1552	5.8	2212	2.0
27	SU	0418	5.9	1036	2.0	1637	6.1	2254	1.8
28	M	0458	6.2	1117	1.7	1718	6.3	2333	1.6
29	TU	0536	6.4	1155	1.6	1756	6.4		
30	W ○	0010	1.4	0612	6.6	1233	1.4	1833	6.5
31	TH	0047	1.3	0649	6.7	1310	1.3	1910	6.6

BRISTOL (AVONMOUTH)

LAT 51°30'N
LONG 2°44'W

TIMES AND HEIGHTS OF HIGH AND LOW WATER (Heights in Metres)

TIME ZONE UT
For Summer Time (area enclosed in shaded box) add 1 hour

2020

JANUARY

Date	Day	Time	m	Time	m	Time	m	Time	m
1	W	0440	2.8	1043	11.2	1707	2.8	2300	10.8
2	TH	0513	3.1	1120	10.7	1745	3.1	2339	10.4
3	F ☽	0554	3.4	1206	10.3	1833	3.4		
4	SA	0030	10.0	0648	3.8	1308	9.9	1934	3.7
5	SU	0137	9.8	0759	4.0	1422	10.0	2045	3.7
6	M	0254	10.0	0919	3.8	1533	10.4	2159	3.4
7	TU	0403	10.6	1032	3.3	1634	11.0	2306	2.8
8	W	0501	11.3	1135	2.7	1728	11.7		
9	TH	0004	2.2	0551	12.1	1231	2.1	1817	12.3
10	F O	0057	1.8	0638	12.7	1323	1.8	1905	12.7
11	SA	0147	1.5	0724	13.1	1414	1.6	1951	13.0
12	SU	0235	1.3	0809	13.4	1502	1.4	2037	13.2
13	M	0320	1.3	0853	13.4	1546	1.4	2121	13.2
14	TU	0402	1.3	0938	13.4	1627	1.4	2205	13.0
15	W	0440	1.4	1022	13.1	1704	1.6	2248	12.7
16	TH	0518	1.7	1107	12.7	1742	1.9	2334	12.1
17	F ☾	0558	2.1	1156	12.1	1825	2.3		
18	SA	0025	11.4	0645	2.6	1255	11.4	1915	2.9
19	SU	0130	10.8	0746	3.1	1408	10.9	2026	3.3
20	M	0247	10.6	0912	3.4	1523	10.8	2158	3.4
21	TU	0359	10.8	1034	3.1	1631	11.1	2309	2.9
22	W	0502	11.3	1137	2.6	1730	11.6		
23	TH	0008	2.4	0556	12.0	1233	2.0	1821	12.1
24	F ●	0101	1.9	0644	12.5	1325	1.7	1908	12.5
25	SA	0150	1.6	0728	12.8	1413	1.5	1952	12.6
26	SU	0235	1.5	0809	12.9	1457	1.5	2031	12.6
27	M	0315	1.6	0846	12.8	1534	1.7	2106	12.4
28	TU	0346	1.9	0920	12.5	1602	2.0	2136	12.1
29	W	0407	2.2	0950	12.2	1622	2.2	2204	11.8
30	TH	0424	2.3	1018	11.8	1644	2.3	2232	11.5
31	F	0448	2.4	1047	11.4	1712	2.5	[illegible]	[illegible]

FEBRUARY

Date	Day	Time	m	Time	m	Time	m	Time	m
1	SA	0520	2.6	1121	10.9	1747	2.8	2340	10.6
2	SU ☽	0600	3.1	1205	10.4	1833	3.3		
3	M	0030	10.2	0651	3.6	1305	10.0	1934	3.7
4	TU	0137	9.8	0807	4.0	1425	9.8	2102	3.8
5	W	0305	10.0	0944	3.8	1551	10.3	2226	3.3
6	TH	0426	10.7	1102	3.1	1701	11.1	2335	2.6
7	F	0528	11.6	1207	2.3	1759	12.0		
8	SA	0035	1.9	0620	12.6	1307	1.7	1850	12.8
9	SU O	0133	1.4	0709	13.3	1404	1.3	1938	13.3
10	M	0226	1.0	0756	13.8	1455	0.9	2025	13.7
11	TU	0314	0.7	0842	14.1	1541	0.7	2109	13.9
12	W	0356	0.6	0925	14.1	1620	0.7	2151	13.7
13	TH	0433	0.7	1007	13.9	1654	0.9	2231	13.3
14	F	0505	1.0	1048	13.3	1724	1.4	2310	12.6
15	SA ☾	0537	1.6	1130	12.4	1755	2.0	2353	11.7
16	SU	0613	2.3	1218	11.4	1834	2.8		
17	M	0046	10.7	0659	3.2	1325	10.4	1927	3.6
18	TU	0207	10.0	0811	3.8	1454	10.0	2108	4.1
19	W	0333	10.0	1005	3.8	1610	10.2	2246	3.6
20	TH	0443	10.6	1118	3.1	1714	10.9	2348	2.8
21	F	0540	11.4	1214	2.3	1807	11.7		
22	SA	0041	2.0	0628	12.2	1306	1.7	1853	12.3
23	SU ●	0130	1.5	0712	12.7	1354	1.3	1934	12.6
24	M	0216	1.3	0751	13.0	1438	1.2	2011	12.7
25	TU	0257	1.3	0826	12.9	1516	1.3	2044	12.6
26	W	0331	1.5	0858	12.7	1546	1.6	2113	12.4
27	TH	0354	1.9	0926	12.4	1605	1.9	2138	12.1
28	F	0405	2.0	0951	12.1	1618	2.0	2202	11.9
29	SA	0422	2.1	1016	11.8	1640	2.1	2229	11.6

MARCH

Date	Day	Time	m	Time	m	Time	m	Time	m
1	SU	0450	2.2	1046	11.4	1710	2.3	2302	11.1
2	M ☽	0523	2.6	1125	10.8	1748	2.9	2346	10.5
3	TU	0606	3.2	1217	10.1	1839	3.5		
4	W	0046	9.9	0707	3.8	1331	9.7	1958	4.0
5	TH	0210	9.7	0852	4.0	1512	9.8	2151	3.8
6	F	0353	10.3	1037	3.4	1639	10.8	2313	2.9
7	SA	0507	11.4	1151	2.4	1742	11.9		
8	SU	0019	2.0	0603	12.5	1254	1.6	1834	12.9
9	M O	0118	1.2	0653	13.5	1350	0.9	1922	13.7
10	TU	0212	0.6	0740	14.2	1441	0.4	2007	14.2
11	W	0300	0.2	0824	14.5	1525	0.2	2050	14.3
12	TH	0341	0.1	0907	14.5	1603	0.3	2130	14.2
13	F	0416	0.3	0947	14.2	1634	0.7	2208	13.6
14	SA	0445	0.8	1025	13.4	1659	1.3	2244	12.8
15	SU	0512	1.5	1103	12.4	1724	2.1	2322	11.7
16	M ☾	0542	2.3	1145	11.2	1757	2.9		
17	TU	0008	10.5	0623	3.2	1244	10.0	1845	3.9
18	W	0128	9.6	0729	4.1	1429	9.4	2011	4.5
19	TH	0310	9.5	0937	4.2	1550	9.7	2224	4.0
20	F	0421	10.2	1057	3.3	1653	10.5	2326	3.0
21	SA	0518	11.2	1151	2.3	1745	11.5		
22	SU	0017	2.1	0606	12.0	1241	1.6	1829	12.2
23	M	0105	1.4	0648	12.6	1327	1.2	1908	12.6
24	TU ●	0150	1.1	0725	12.9	1411	1.0	1944	12.8
25	W	0232	1.1	0800	12.9	1450	1.2	2016	12.7
26	TH	0307	1.4	0831	12.7	1522	1.5	2044	12.5
27	F	0333	1.7	0859	12.4	1542	1.8	2110	12.3
28	SA	0344	2.0	0924	12.2	1552	1.9	2133	12.1
29	SU	0358	1.9	0949	11.9	1612	2.0	2200	11.8
30	M	0424	2.0	1019	11.6	1641	2.1	2234	11.4
31	TU	0456	2.3	1058	11.0	1717	2.6	[illegible]	[illegible]

APRIL

Date	Day	Time	m	Time	m	Time	m	Time	m
1	W ☽	0537	2.9	1149	10.3	1804	3.3		
2	TH	0015	10.1	0633	3.6	1300	9.7	1915	4.0
3	F	0137	9.7	0807	4.0	1441	9.7	2120	3.9
4	SA	0325	10.2	1014	3.4	1617	10.7	2252	2.9
5	SU	0443	11.4	1132	2.3	1721	11.9	2359	1.9
6	M	0542	12.6	1233	1.4	1813	13.1		
7	TU	0056	1.1	0631	13.6	1328	0.7	1900	13.9
8	W O	0149	0.5	0718	14.3	1417	0.2	1944	14.3
9	TH	0237	0.1	0802	14.5	1502	0.1	2026	14.4
10	F	0318	0.0	0845	14.5	1539	0.3	2106	14.2
11	SA	0354	0.3	0925	14.0	1610	0.8	2144	13.6
12	SU	0423	0.9	1003	13.2	1634	1.5	2220	12.7
13	M	0448	1.6	1040	12.1	1657	2.2	2256	11.6
14	TU ☾	0517	2.4	1119	10.9	1729	3.1	2339	10.4
15	W	0558	3.3	1213	9.8	1815	4.0		
16	TH	0055	9.5	0701	4.1	1359	9.1	1935	4.6
17	F	0241	9.4	0842	4.2	1519	9.5	2148	4.2
18	SA	0349	10.1	1022	3.5	1621	10.3	2253	3.2
19	SU	0445	10.9	1118	2.5	1712	11.2	2344	2.3
20	M	0533	11.8	1207	1.8	1756	12.0		
21	TU	0031	1.6	0615	12.3	1253	1.3	1835	12.4
22	W	0117	1.3	0652	12.6	1337	1.2	1910	12.6
23	TH ●	0159	1.3	0728	12.7	1417	1.3	1944	12.6
24	F	0236	1.5	0801	12.5	1451	1.5	2014	12.5
25	SA	0305	1.7	0831	12.4	1515	1.8	2042	12.3
26	SU	0323	1.9	0859	12.2	1531	1.9	2109	12.2
27	M	0340	2.0	0928	12.0	1553	1.9	2140	12.0
28	TU	0407	2.0	1002	11.6	1623	2.1	2216	11.6
29	W	0441	2.2	1044	11.1	1700	2.5	2302	11.0
30	TH ☽	0523	2.7	1136	10.5	1748	3.1		

MAY

Date	Day	Time	m	Time	m	Time	m	Time	m
1	F	0000	10.4	0620	3.3	1245	10.0	1858	3.7
2	SA	0120	10.1	0748	3.6	1417	10.1	2051	3.6
3	SU	0257	10.5	0944	3.2	1548	10.9	2224	2.8
4	M	0414	11.5	1102	2.3	1653	11.9	2330	1.9
5	TU	0515	12.5	1204	1.4	1747	13.0		
6	W	0027	1.1	0606	13.4	1259	0.8	1834	13.7
7	TH O	0120	0.6	0654	14.0	1349	0.5	1919	14.1
8	F	0209	0.3	0739	14.1	1434	0.4	2002	14.1
9	SA	0253	0.3	0822	14.0	1514	0.6	2043	13.8
10	SU	0331	0.7	0904	13.5	1547	1.1	2122	13.2
11	M	0404	1.2	0944	12.8	1614	1.8	2200	12.4
12	TU	0431	1.9	1022	11.8	1639	2.4	2237	11.5
13	W	0501	2.5	1101	10.9	1710	3.1	2320	10.5
14	TH ☾	0541	3.2	1150	9.9	1754	3.8		
15	F	0023	9.8	0637	3.8	1309	9.4	1901	4.3
16	SA	0158	9.6	0751	4.0	1434	9.5	2028	4.2
17	SU	0306	10.0	0911	3.6	1536	10.0	2156	3.6
18	M	0402	10.6	1024	2.9	1628	10.8	2258	2.8
19	TU	0451	11.3	1121	2.3	1715	11.5	2349	2.2
20	W	0535	11.8	1211	1.8	1756	12.0		
21	TH	0035	1.8	0615	12.2	1257	1.6	1835	12.3
22	F ●	0120	1.6	0654	12.3	1339	1.5	1911	12.5
23	SA	0200	1.6	0731	12.4	1418	1.6	1946	12.5
24	SU	0236	1.8	0806	12.3	1450	1.7	2020	12.4
25	M	0305	1.9	0841	12.2	1517	1.8	2053	12.3
26	TU	0331	2.0	0917	12.0	1545	1.9	2129	12.1
27	W	0401	2.0	0956	11.8	1617	2.1	2210	11.8
28	TH	0438	2.2	1040	11.4	1657	2.4	2257	11.4
29	F	0523	2.5	1131	11.0	1747	2.8	2354	11.0
30	SA ☽	0620	2.9	1234	10.6	1852	3.2		
31	SU	0105	10.7	0735	3.1	1352	10.6	[illegible]	[illegible]

JUNE

Date	Day	Time	m	Time	m	Time	m	Time	m
1	M	0227	11.0	0906	2.9	1512	11.0	2147	2.7
2	TU	0342	11.5	1026	2.4	1620	11.7	2257	2.1
3	W	0445	12.2	1131	1.8	1718	12.5	2357	1.5
4	TH	0540	12.9	1228	1.3	1809	13.1		
5	F O	0051	1.1	0630	13.3	1320	1.0	1855	13.5
6	SA	0142	0.9	0717	13.4	1408	0.9	1940	13.5
7	SU	0230	0.9	0803	13.3	1452	1.1	2023	13.3
8	M	0312	1.1	0847	12.9	1530	1.5	2105	12.9
9	TU	0350	1.5	0929	12.4	1601	2.0	2144	12.3
10	W	0421	2.0	1008	11.8	1628	2.5	2222	11.6
11	TH	0450	2.5	1045	11.1	1657	2.9	2302	10.9
12	F	0526	2.9	1125	10.5	1735	3.3	2349	10.3
13	SA ☾	0611	3.2	1215	10.0	1825	3.7		
14	SU	0052	9.9	0705	3.5	1321	9.7	1928	3.9
15	M	0204	9.9	0808	3.5	1431	9.8	2038	3.8
16	TU	0306	10.2	0913	3.2	1532	10.3	2149	3.4
17	W	0401	10.7	1020	2.9	1627	10.9	2254	2.8
18	TH	0452	11.2	1121	2.4	1716	11.5	2350	2.3
19	F	0538	11.7	1214	2.0	1800	12.0		
20	SA	0040	2.0	0622	12.0	1303	1.7	1842	12.3
21	SU ●	0127	1.8	0705	12.2	1348	1.6	1923	12.5
22	M	0211	1.8	0747	12.3	1430	1.6	2003	12.6
23	TU	0252	1.8	0829	12.4	1509	1.7	2044	12.6
24	W	0331	1.8	0911	12.3	1545	1.8	2125	12.5
25	TH	0408	1.9	0953	12.2	1622	1.9	2208	12.3
26	F	0446	2.0	1037	12.0	1701	2.1	2254	12.0
27	SA	0528	2.1	1124	11.7	1746	2.3	2345	11.7
28	SU ☽	0616	2.3	1218	11.3	1840	2.6		
29	M	0045	11.4	0713	2.6	1323	11.0	1946	2.9
30	TU	0156	11.2	0824	2.8	1436	11.0	2107	2.9

SUNRISE AND SUNSET TIMES

BRISTOL (AVONMOUTH)
At 51°30'N 2°44'W

UT		Sunrise	Sunset
Jan	01	0817	1613
	15	0810	1632
Feb	01	0749	1701
	15	0725	1726
Mar	01	0656	1751
	15	0625	1816
BST			
Apr	01	0646	1944
	15	0615	2008
May	01	0543	2034
	15	0519	2056
Jun	01	0459	2119
	15	0453	2130
Jul	01	0458	2131
	15	0511	2122
Aug	01	0535	2059
	15	0557	2033
Sep	01	0624	1957
	15	0646	1925
Oct	01	0712	1848
	15	0735	1817
UT			
Nov	01	0705	1644
	15	0729	1621
Dec	01	0754	1605
	15	0810	1602

BRISTOL (AVONMOUTH)
LAT 51°30'N
LONG 2°44'W

TIMES AND HEIGHTS OF HIGH AND LOW WATER (Heights in Metres)

TIME ZONE UT
For Summer Time (area enclosed in shaded box) add 1 hour

2020

JULY

Date	Day	Time	m	Time	m	Time	m	Time	m
1	W	0309	11.3	0947	2.8	1547	11.3	2225	2.6
2	TH	0416	11.6	1100	2.4	1650	11.8	2330	2.1
3	F	0516	12.0	1201	2.0	1746	12.3		
4	SA	0027	1.7	0610	12.4	1256	1.7	1836	12.7
5	SU	0121	1.4	0701	12.7	1348	1.5	O 1923	13.0
6	M	0212	1.3	0748	12.7	1435	1.4	2008	13.0
7	TU	0258	1.4	0833	12.6	1518	1.6	2051	12.8
8	W	0339	1.6	0915	12.3	1553	2.0	2130	12.4
9	TH	0413	2.0	0952	11.9	1620	2.3	2205	12.0
10	F	0440	2.3	1025	11.5	1643	2.6	2239	11.5
11	SA	0506	2.5	1057	11.1	1712	2.8	2314	11.0
12	SU	0539	2.7	1132	10.6	1747	3.1	☾ 2355	10.5
13	M	0620	3.0	1216	10.2	1833	3.4		
14	TU	0047	10.1	0711	3.3	1313	9.9	1933	3.7
15	W	0153	9.9	0814	3.5	1423	9.9	2047	3.8
16	TH	0303	10.1	0925	3.4	1534	10.3	2202	3.4
17	F	0407	10.5	1035	2.9	1636	10.9	2309	2.8
18	SA	0504	11.1	1137	2.4	1730	11.6		
19	SU	0007	2.3	0556	11.7	1233	2.0	1818	12.2
20	M	0101	1.9	0644	12.2	1325	1.7	● 1904	12.6
21	TU	0154	1.7	0731	12.5	1416	1.6	1950	12.9
22	W	0244	1.6	0817	12.7	1503	1.5	2034	13.1
23	TH	0330	1.5	0902	12.9	1546	1.4	2117	13.2
24	F	0412	1.4	0945	12.9	1624	1.4	2200	13.1
25	SA	0448	1.5	1027	12.7	1700	1.5	2243	12.8
26	SU	0523	1.6	1110	12.3	1737	1.8	2328	12.3
27	M ☽	0600	2.0	1156	11.8	1818	2.3		
28	TU	0019	11.7	0644	2.5	1251	11.2	1909	2.8
29	W	0123	11.1	0740	3.0	1402	10.7	2023	3.3
30	TH	0240	10.7	0907	3.4	1520	10.6	2157	3.3
31	F	0354	10.8	1035	3.2	1630	11.0	2310	2.8

AUGUST

Date	Day	Time	m	Time	m	Time	m	Time	m
1	SA	0500	11.2	1141	2.7	1730	11.6		
2	SU	0010	2.2	0557	11.8	1239	2.1	1823	12.3
3	M	0105	1.7	0648	12.2	1331	1.7	O 1910	12.7
4	TU	0156	1.4	0735	12.5	1420	1.5	1954	12.9
5	W	0244	1.3	0818	12.6	1505	1.5	2035	12.9
6	TH	0326	1.4	0856	12.5	1542	1.7	2111	12.7
7	F	0400	1.7	0930	12.2	1609	2.1	2142	12.3
8	SA	0424	2.1	0958	11.9	1626	2.3	2211	11.9
9	SU	0442	2.3	1025	11.5	1644	2.5	2238	11.4
10	M	0505	2.4	1053	11.1	1710	2.7	2309	10.9
11	TU	0535	2.7	1126	10.7	1744	3.1	☾ 2347	10.4
12	W	0614	3.1	1210	10.2	1830	3.6		
13	TH	0041	9.9	0709	3.6	1312	9.7	1939	4.1
14	F	0159	9.6	0831	3.9	1439	9.7	2116	4.0
15	SA	0327	9.9	0956	3.6	1602	10.3	2238	3.4
16	SU	0438	10.7	1108	2.9	1706	11.3	2345	2.6
17	M	0536	11.5	1210	2.2	1759	12.2		
18	TU	0044	1.9	0627	12.3	1309	1.7	1848	12.9
19	W	0141	1.5	0716	12.9	1404	1.4	● 1934	13.4
20	TH	0234	1.2	0802	13.3	1454	1.1	2019	13.8
21	F	0322	0.9	0847	13.5	1538	0.9	2103	13.9
22	SA	0403	0.9	0928	13.5	1615	0.9	2144	13.7
23	SU	0437	1.0	1008	13.3	1648	1.2	2224	13.3
24	M	0507	1.4	1048	12.8	1718	1.6	2305	12.6
25	TU	0535	2.0	1129	12.0	1751	2.3	☽ 2350	11.6
26	W	0610	2.7	1218	11.0	1833	3.1		
27	TH	0049	10.6	0657	3.5	1330	10.2	1938	3.9
28	F	0218	10.0	0822	4.2	1501	10.0	2140	4.0
29	SA	0341	10.1	1021	3.8	1616	10.5	2257	3.3
30	SU	0449	10.7	1127	3.0	1718	11.3	2355	2.4
31	M	0545	11.5	1221	2.2	1809	12.2		

SEPTEMBER

Date	Day	Time	m	Time	m	Time	m	Time	m
1	TU	0047	1.7	0634	12.2	1312	1.6	1854	12.8
2	W	0137	1.2	0717	12.7	1400	1.3	O 1935	13.1
3	TH	0223	1.1	0756	12.8	1444	1.2	2012	13.1
4	F	0304	1.2	0831	12.7	1521	1.4	2046	12.9
5	SA	0338	1.5	0901	12.5	1550	1.9	2114	12.5
6	SU	0401	1.9	0927	12.2	1604	2.3	2140	12.1
7	M	0414	2.2	0951	11.8	1613	2.4	2203	11.7
8	TU	0429	2.3	1015	11.5	1635	2.5	2229	11.2
9	W	0454	2.5	1044	11.0	1705	2.8	2303	10.7
10	TH	0527	3.0	1123	10.4	1742	3.4	☾ 2350	10.0
11	F	0612	3.7	1219	9.8	1837	4.1		
12	SA	0101	9.4	0724	4.3	1343	9.5	2024	4.5
13	SU	0248	9.5	0922	4.1	1532	10.0	2215	3.8
14	M	0417	10.4	1047	3.3	1644	11.1	2329	2.7
15	TU	0518	11.5	1154	2.4	1740	12.3		
16	W	0029	1.9	0609	12.6	1252	1.6	1829	13.2
17	TH	0125	1.2	0657	13.4	1347	1.1	● 1915	13.9
18	F	0217	0.8	0742	13.9	1436	0.7	1959	14.3
19	SA	0303	0.5	0825	14.1	1519	0.6	2042	14.4
20	SU	0343	0.6	0906	14.0	1557	0.7	2123	14.1
21	M	0416	0.9	0945	13.6	1628	1.1	2202	13.5
22	TU	0443	1.5	1023	12.9	1655	1.7	2241	12.6
23	W	0507	2.2	1101	11.9	1723	2.5	2323	11.4
24	TH ☽	0537	3.0	1147	10.8	1802	3.4		
25	F	0018	10.1	0620	4.0	1303	9.8	1904	4.3
26	SA	0203	9.4	0745	4.7	1447	9.6	2128	4.4
27	SU	0327	9.7	1008	4.2	1559	10.3	2241	3.5
28	M	0431	10.5	1108	3.1	1658	11.3	2335	2.4
29	TU	0525	11.5	1159	2.2	1747	12.2		
30	W	0023	1.6	0610	12.3	1247	1.5	1830	12.9

OCTOBER

Date	Day	Time	m	Time	m	Time	m	Time	m
1	TH	0110	1.1	0651	12.8	1332	1.2	O 1909	13.2
2	F	0154	1.0	0727	12.9	1415	1.1	1944	13.2
3	SA	0235	1.1	0800	12.9	1453	1.4	2016	12.9
4	SU	0309	1.4	0830	12.6	1522	1.8	2045	12.6
5	M	0333	1.9	0856	12.3	1537	2.3	2109	12.2
6	TU	0344	2.2	0919	12.0	1546	2.4	2132	11.8
7	W	0358	2.3	0943	11.7	1607	2.5	2159	11.4
8	TH	0423	2.5	1013	11.3	1636	2.7	2234	10.9
9	F	0455	2.9	1052	10.7	1712	3.2	2320	10.2
10	SA ☾	0536	3.6	1146	10.0	1802	4.0		
11	SU	0027	9.5	0639	4.3	1305	9.5	1929	4.5
12	M	0210	9.4	0843	4.4	1500	10.0	2149	4.0
13	TU	0352	10.3	1024	3.5	1619	11.1	2308	2.8
14	W	0455	11.6	1131	2.4	1716	12.4		
15	TH	0007	1.8	0546	12.7	1229	1.6	1805	13.4
16	F	0101	1.1	0633	13.6	1321	1.0	● 1852	14.1
17	SA	0151	0.6	0717	14.1	1410	0.6	1936	14.5
18	SU	0237	0.5	0800	14.3	1454	0.5	2019	14.5
19	M	0317	0.6	0841	14.2	1533	0.7	2101	14.1
20	TU	0351	1.0	0921	13.7	1605	1.2	2141	13.4
21	W	0419	1.7	1000	12.9	1634	1.9	2220	12.4
22	TH	0443	2.4	1039	11.8	1703	2.7	2301	11.2
23	F	0513	3.3	1124	10.7	1741	3.6	☽ 2356	10.0
24	SA	0556	4.2	1240	9.7	1843	4.4		
25	SU	0140	9.3	0714	4.8	1424	9.6	2052	4.5
26	M	0301	9.6	0938	4.4	1531	10.2	2210	3.7
27	TU	0402	10.4	1038	3.4	1627	11.1	2303	2.7
28	W	0454	11.3	1127	2.5	1716	12.0	2351	1.9
29	TH	0539	12.1	1213	1.8	1759	12.6		
30	F	0036	1.4	0618	12.6	1258	1.4	1837	12.9
31	SA	0119	1.2	0654	12.8	1340	1.4	O 1912	13.0

NOVEMBER

Date	Day	Time	m	Time	m	Time	m	Time	m
1	SU	0200	1.2	0728	12.8	1419	1.6	1945	12.8
2	M	0235	1.5	0759	12.7	1450	1.9	2016	12.5
3	TU	0302	1.9	0827	12.4	1511	2.2	2044	12.2
4	W	0320	2.2	0853	12.1	1526	2.4	2110	11.9
5	TH	0337	2.3	0921	11.9	1549	2.5	2141	11.5
6	F	0404	2.5	0954	11.5	1620	2.7	2219	11.1
7	SA	0438	2.8	1036	11.0	1658	3.1	2306	10.5
8	SU ☾	0521	3.4	1130	10.4	1749	3.7		
9	M	0009	9.9	0621	4.0	1243	10.0	1905	4.1
10	TU	0136	9.8	0759	4.2	1420	10.3	2105	3.8
11	W	0315	10.5	0947	3.5	1544	11.2	2232	2.9
12	TH	0423	11.5	1059	2.6	1646	12.3	2335	2.0
13	F	0518	12.6	1158	1.7	1739	13.2		
14	SA	0030	1.3	0607	13.4	1252	1.1	1827	13.9
15	SU	0121	0.9	0652	14.0	1342	0.8	● 1913	14.2
16	M	0208	0.7	0736	14.2	1428	0.7	1958	14.2
17	TU	0251	0.8	0819	14.0	1510	0.9	2042	13.8
18	W	0329	1.2	0901	13.5	1547	1.4	2124	13.1
19	TH	0401	1.8	0942	12.8	1620	2.0	2205	12.2
20	F	0429	2.5	1023	11.9	1651	2.7	2248	11.2
21	SA	0500	3.2	1108	11.0	1730	3.4	2337	10.3
22	SU ☽	0541	3.9	1211	10.1	1822	4.0		
23	M	0053	9.6	0642	4.4	1341	9.8	1934	4.3
24	TU	0217	9.6	0809	4.5	1450	10.1	2101	4.0
25	W	0319	10.1	0943	3.9	1546	10.7	2212	3.3
26	TH	0412	10.8	1043	3.2	1636	11.4	2306	2.6
27	F	0459	11.5	1132	2.5	1721	11.9	2354	2.0
28	SA	0542	12.1	1218	2.0	1802	12.3		
29	SU	0039	1.7	0620	12.4	1302	1.8	1840	12.5
30	M	0122	1.5	0656	12.6	1342	1.8	O 1917	12.5

DECEMBER

Date	Day	Time	m	Time	m	Time	m	Time	m
1	TU	0200	1.6	0731	12.6	1419	1.9	1952	12.4
2	W	0234	1.8	0805	12.5	1450	2.1	2026	12.2
3	TH	0303	2.0	0838	12.3	1516	2.3	2059	12.0
4	F	0328	2.2	0911	12.1	1544	2.4	2135	11.7
5	SA	0358	2.4	0948	11.8	1617	2.6	2215	11.4
6	SU	0434	2.6	1031	11.5	1657	2.8	2301	11.0
7	M	0518	3.0	1122	11.1	1747	3.1	2357	10.7
8	TU ☾	0614	3.4	1225	10.8	1850	3.4		
9	W	0106	10.4	0725	3.6	1341	10.8	2012	3.4
10	TH	0228	10.6	0857	3.4	1502	11.2	2145	3.1
11	F	0344	11.3	1020	2.8	1612	11.9	2259	2.5
12	SA	0447	12.1	1125	2.2	1711	12.6	2359	1.8
13	SU	0541	12.8	1223	1.6	1805	13.1		
14	M	0053	1.4	0630	13.4	1316	1.2	● 1854	13.5
15	TU	0144	1.1	0717	13.6	1406	1.1	1941	13.5
16	W	0231	1.1	0802	13.6	1453	1.2	2027	13.3
17	TH	0313	1.4	0847	13.3	1535	1.5	2112	12.9
18	F	0351	1.8	0929	12.9	1612	1.9	2154	12.3
19	SA	0422	2.3	1011	12.2	1644	2.4	2234	11.6
20	SU	0451	2.8	1051	11.5	1717	2.9	2313	10.9
21	M	0524	3.3	1136	10.8	1756	3.3	☽ 2358	10.3
22	TU	0607	3.7	1231	10.3	1845	3.6		
23	W	0056	9.9	0702	4.0	1341	10.0	1942	3.8
24	TH	0209	9.8	0808	4.1	1448	10.2	2048	3.7
25	F	0314	10.1	0921	3.8	1546	10.5	2157	3.3
26	SA	0411	10.6	1032	3.3	1638	11.0	2302	2.8
27	SU	0501	11.2	1131	2.7	1726	11.5	2356	2.3
28	M	0547	11.8	1222	2.3	1810	11.9		
29	TU	0045	1.9	0629	12.2	1309	2.0	1852	12.2
30	W	0130	1.7	0709	12.5	1353	1.9	O 1933	12.3
31	TH	0213	1.7	0749	12.6	1435	2.0	2013	12.4

COBH
LAT 51°51′N
LONG 8°18′W

TIMES AND HEIGHTS OF HIGH AND LOW WATER (Heights in Metres)

TIME ZONE UT
For Summer Time (area enclosed in shaded box) add 1 hour

2020

JANUARY

Date	Time	m	Time	m	Time	m	Time	m
1 W	0319	1.1	0913	3.7	1540	1.2	2122	3.5
2 TH	0405	1.2	0958	3.6	1627	1.3	2209	3.4
3 F ☽	0457	1.3	1048	3.5	1721	1.4	2304	3.4
4 SA	0556	1.4	1145	3.4	1823	1.4		
5 SU	0008	3.3	0659	1.4	1250	3.4	1925	1.4
6 M	0116	3.4	0759	1.3	1353	3.5	2024	1.3
7 TU	0219	3.5	0857	1.2	1450	3.6	2120	1.1
8 W	0316	3.7	0950	1.0	1543	3.8	2211	0.9
9 TH	0408	3.9	1040	0.8	1631	3.9	2258	0.8
10 F ○	0456	4.0	1126	0.7	1716	4.0	2342	0.6
11 SA	0540	4.1	1209	0.6	1759	4.1		
12 SU	0024	0.5	0623	4.2	1253	0.5	1842	4.1
13 M	0108	0.5	0707	4.2	1336	0.5	1926	4.1
14 TU	0153	0.5	0753	4.2	1422	0.6	2012	4.0
15 W	0239	0.5	0840	4.1	1509	0.7	2100	3.9
16 TH	0329	0.6	0930	4.0	1559	0.8	2150	3.8
17 F ☾	0421	0.8	1022	3.8	1653	0.9	2244	3.7
18 SA	0519	0.9	1120	3.7	1755	1.1	2346	3.6
19 SU	0626	1.0	1225	3.5	1905	1.1		
20 M	0055	3.5	0739	1.1	1337	3.5	2017	1.1
21 TU	0208	3.5	0852	1.0	1446	3.6	2124	1.0
22 W	0316	3.7	0958	0.9	1547	3.7	2223	0.8
23 TH	0414	3.8	1053	0.8	1639	3.8	2312	0.7
24 F ●	0503	4.0	1138	0.7	1724	3.9	2354	0.6
25 SA	0545	4.1	1216	0.7	1802	4.0		
26 SU	0030	0.6	0623	4.1	1251	0.7	1836	4.0
27 M	0105	0.6	0658	4.1	1322	0.7	1909	3.9
28 TU	0137	0.7	0732	4.0	1353	0.8	1940	3.9
29 W	0209	0.8	0806	3.9	1426	0.9	2014	3.8
30 TH	0243	0.9	0841	3.8	1501	1.0	2050	3.7
31 F	0320	1.0	0918	3.7	1540	1.1	2129	3.6

FEBRUARY

Date	Time	m	Time	m	Time	m	Time	m
1 SA	0402	1.2	0959	3.6	1624	1.3	2214	3.5
2 SU ☽	0452	1.3	1046	3.5	1719	1.4	2309	3.4
3 M	0556	1.4	1144	3.4	1827	1.5		
4 TU	0014	3.3	0707	1.4	1254	3.3	1939	1.4
5 W	0129	3.4	0817	1.3	1407	3.4	2046	1.2
6 TH	0241	3.5	0922	1.1	1514	3.6	2147	1.0
7 F	0344	3.7	1020	0.8	1612	3.8	2240	0.7
8 SA	0438	4.0	1111	0.6	1701	4.0	2327	0.5
9 SU ○	0525	4.1	1156	0.4	1746	4.1		
10 M	0011	0.3	0609	4.3	1239	0.3	1829	4.2
11 TU	0054	0.2	0653	4.3	1322	0.2	1912	4.2
12 W	0137	0.2	0736	4.3	1405	0.3	1955	4.1
13 TH	0221	0.3	0821	4.2	1449	0.4	2039	4.0
14 F	0307	0.4	0906	4.0	1534	0.5	2125	3.9
15 SA ☾	0355	0.6	0953	3.8	1622	0.8	2213	3.7
16 SU	0447	0.8	1045	3.6	1718	1.0	2310	3.5
17 M	0549	1.0	1148	3.4	1826	1.2		
18 TU	0020	3.3	0704	1.2	1307	3.2	1946	1.2
19 W	0144	3.3	0832	1.2	1426	3.3	2108	1.1
20 TH	0300	3.5	0947	1.0	1533	3.5	2212	0.9
21 F	0400	3.7	1043	0.8	1626	3.7	2301	0.7
22 SA	0448	3.9	1126	0.7	1709	3.8	2341	0.6
23 SU ●	0529	4.0	1202	0.6	1746	3.9		
24 M	0014	0.5	0604	4.1	1232	0.6	1819	4.0
25 TU	0044	0.5	0637	4.1	1259	0.6	1848	3.9
26 W	0111	0.6	0707	4.0	1325	0.7	1916	3.9
27 TH	0139	0.7	0737	3.9	1354	0.7	1946	3.9
28 F	0209	0.8	0807	3.9	1426	0.9	2017	3.8
29 SA	0242	0.9	0840	3.8	1500	1.0	2052	3.7

MARCH

Date	Time	m	Time	m	Time	m	Time	m
1 SU	0320	1.0	0916	3.7	1538	1.1	2132	3.6
2 M ☽	0404	1.2	1000	3.5	1625	1.3	2222	3.4
3 TU	0502	1.3	1055	3.3	1731	1.4	2326	3.3
4 W	0619	1.4	1206	3.2	1854	1.5		
5 TH	0045	3.2	0740	1.4	1328	3.2	2012	1.3
6 F	0209	3.4	0854	1.1	1448	3.4	2120	1.0
7 SA	0320	3.6	0957	0.8	1550	3.7	2217	0.7
8 SU	0416	3.9	1050	0.5	1642	3.9	2307	0.4
9 M ○	0504	4.1	1136	0.2	1727	4.1	2351	0.1
10 TU	0549	4.3	1219	0.1	1810	4.3		
11 W	0034	0.0	0632	4.3	1302	0.0	1852	4.3
12 TH	0117	0.0	0714	4.3	1344	0.1	1933	4.2
13 F	0200	0.1	0757	4.2	1426	0.2	2015	4.1
14 SA	0244	0.2	0840	4.0	1509	0.4	2059	3.9
15 SU	0330	0.5	0925	3.8	1556	0.6	2145	3.7
16 M ☾	0420	0.7	1014	3.5	1648	0.9	2239	3.4
17 TU	0519	1.0	1115	3.2	1754	1.2	2350	3.2
18 W	0634	1.2	1239	3.0	1919	1.3		
19 TH	0122	3.1	0810	1.2	1407	3.1	2049	1.1
20 F	0241	3.3	0930	1.0	1515	3.3	2155	0.9
21 SA	0339	3.6	1024	0.8	1606	3.6	2243	0.7
22 SU	0426	3.8	1106	0.6	1648	3.8	2321	0.5
23 M	0505	3.9	1140	0.5	1724	3.9	2352	0.5
24 TU ●	0540	4.0	1207	0.5	1756	3.9		
25 W	0019	0.5	0611	4.0	1231	0.5	1823	3.9
26 TH	0043	0.5	0639	4.0	1255	0.6	1850	3.9
27 F	0109	0.6	0706	3.9	1324	0.7	1917	3.9
28 SA	0138	0.7	0735	3.9	1355	0.8	1948	3.8
29 SU	0211	0.8	0806	3.8	1429	0.9	2021	3.8
30 M	0249	0.9	0842	3.7	1506	1.0	2100	3.6
31 TU	0332	1.1	0926	3.5	1551	1.2	2140	3.5

APRIL

Date	Time	m	Time	m	Time	m	Time	m
1 W ☽	0428	1.3	1022	3.3	1654	1.3	2252	3.3
2 TH	0543	1.4	1133	3.2	1818	1.4		
3 F	0013	3.2	0707	1.3	1258	3.2	1940	1.2
4 SA	0140	3.3	0823	1.0	1419	3.4	2050	0.9
5 SU	0252	3.6	0929	0.7	1524	3.7	2150	0.6
6 M	0350	3.9	1024	0.4	1616	4.0	2242	0.3
7 TU	0440	4.1	1112	0.1	1703	4.2	2329	0.1
8 W ○	0525	4.3	1156	0.0	1747	4.3		
9 TH	0013	-0.1	0609	4.3	1240	-0.1	1829	4.3
10 F	0057	-0.1	0651	4.3	1322	0.0	1911	4.3
11 SA	0140	0.0	0734	4.1	1405	0.2	1953	4.1
12 SU	0224	0.2	0817	3.9	1449	0.4	2036	3.9
13 M	0310	0.5	0901	3.7	1536	0.6	2122	3.7
14 TU ☾	0400	0.7	0949	3.4	1628	0.9	2215	3.4
15 W	0457	1.0	1048	3.1	1732	1.1	2326	3.2
16 TH	0609	1.2	1211	3.0	1852	1.2		
17 F	0056	3.1	0737	1.2	1339	3.0	2016	1.1
18 SA	0212	3.3	0855	1.0	1445	3.2	2122	0.9
19 SU	0308	3.5	0949	0.8	1535	3.5	2210	0.7
20 M	0354	3.7	1032	0.7	1618	3.7	2249	0.6
21 TU	0434	3.8	1106	0.6	1654	3.8	2321	0.5
22 W	0510	3.9	1135	0.6	1727	3.9	2348	0.5
23 TH ●	0542	3.9	1200	0.6	1756	3.9		
24 F	0013	0.6	0610	3.9	1227	0.6	1823	3.9
25 SA	0041	0.6	0638	3.9	1257	0.6	1852	3.9
26 SU	0113	0.7	0707	3.8	1331	0.7	1924	3.8
27 M	0149	0.8	0742	3.8	1407	0.8	2000	3.8
28 TU	0229	0.9	0821	3.7	1448	1.0	2041	3.7
29 W	0315	1.0	0907	3.5	1537	1.1	2132	3.5
30 TH ☽	0412	1.1	1004	3.4	1639	1.2	2235	3.4

MAY

Date	Time	m	Time	m	Time	m	Time	m
1 F	0522	1.2	1113	3.3	1754	1.2	2351	3.3
2 SA	0640	1.2	1232	3.3	1912	1.1		
3 SU	0112	3.4	0754	0.9	1349	3.5	2021	0.8
4 M	0223	3.7	0858	0.7	1453	3.7	2122	0.5
5 TU	0321	3.9	0955	0.4	1548	4.0	2216	0.3
6 W	0414	4.1	1046	0.2	1638	4.1	2306	0.1
7 TH ○	0502	4.2	1134	0.1	1725	4.2	2353	0.0
8 F	0548	4.2	1219	0.1	1809	4.3		
9 SA	0038	0.1	0631	4.2	1304	0.1	1851	4.2
10 SU	0123	0.2	0714	4.0	1348	0.2	1934	4.1
11 M	0208	0.3	0757	3.9	1433	0.4	2018	3.9
12 TU	0254	0.6	0841	3.6	1520	0.7	2104	3.7
13 W	0342	0.8	0928	3.4	1611	0.9	2156	3.4
14 TH ☾	0437	1.0	1022	3.2	1710	1.1	2259	3.2
15 F	0541	1.2	1132	3.0	1819	1.2		
16 SA	0017	3.2	0653	1.2	1253	3.1	1930	1.1
17 SU	0129	3.2	0801	1.1	1359	3.2	2032	1.0
18 M	0226	3.4	0857	1.0	1452	3.4	2122	0.9
19 TU	0314	3.6	0943	0.8	1537	3.6	2205	0.8
20 W	0357	3.7	1023	0.7	1617	3.7	2241	0.7
21 TH	0435	3.8	1057	0.7	1653	3.8	2314	0.6
22 F ●	0510	3.8	1129	0.7	1726	3.8	2346	0.6
23 SA	0543	3.9	1202	0.6	1759	3.9		
24 SU	0019	0.6	0614	3.9	1237	0.7	1832	3.9
25 M	0055	0.7	0648	3.8	1314	0.7	1908	3.9
26 TU	0135	0.7	0727	3.8	1355	0.8	1948	3.8
27 W	0218	0.8	0810	3.7	1440	0.8	2033	3.8
28 TH	0307	0.9	0859	3.6	1530	0.9	2125	3.7
29 F	0402	1.0	0955	3.5	1628	1.0	2224	3.6
30 SA ☽	0505	1.0	1058	3.4	1734	1.0	2332	3.5
31 SU	0615	1.0	1207	3.4	1845	0.9		

JUNE

Date	Time	m	Time	m	Time	m	Time	m
1 M	0044	3.6	0725	0.9	1317	3.6	1952	0.8
2 TU	0152	3.7	0829	0.7	1421	3.7	2054	0.6
3 W	0253	3.8	0928	0.5	1520	3.9	2152	0.4
4 TH	0348	4.0	1023	0.4	1614	4.0	2246	0.3
5 F ○	0441	4.1	1114	0.3	1705	4.1	2336	0.3
6 SA	0529	4.1	1202	0.3	1752	4.1		
7 SU	0022	0.3	0614	4.0	1248	0.3	1835	4.1
8 M	0108	0.3	0658	3.9	1332	0.4	1919	4.0
9 TU	0152	0.5	0740	3.8	1416	0.5	2001	3.9
10 W	0236	0.6	0822	3.7	1502	0.7	2046	3.7
11 TH	0322	0.8	0906	3.5	1549	0.9	2133	3.5
12 F	0410	1.0	0953	3.3	1640	1.0	2225	3.4
13 SA ☾	0504	1.1	1046	3.2	1736	1.1	2324	3.3
14 SU	0602	1.2	1149	3.2	1836	1.1		
15 M	0029	3.3	0702	1.2	1255	3.2	1934	1.1
16 TU	0131	3.3	0757	1.1	1355	3.3	2027	1.0
17 W	0225	3.4	0849	1.0	1447	3.4	2115	0.9
18 TH	0313	3.6	0936	0.9	1534	3.6	2201	0.8
19 F	0358	3.7	1021	0.8	1618	3.7	2243	0.8
20 SA	0439	3.8	1102	0.7	1659	3.8	2323	0.7
21 SU ●	0519	3.8	1142	0.7	1739	3.9		
22 M	0002	0.6	0557	3.9	1222	0.6	1817	3.9
23 TU	0043	0.6	0636	3.9	1303	0.6	1857	3.9
24 W	0125	0.6	0718	3.8	1345	0.6	1940	3.9
25 TH	0210	0.7	0803	3.8	1431	0.7	2026	3.9
26 F	0258	0.7	0851	3.7	1520	0.7	2116	3.8
27 SA	0349	0.8	0944	3.7	1613	0.8	2211	3.7
28 SU ☽	0445	0.9	1039	3.6	1711	0.8	2310	3.7
29 M	0547	0.9	1140	3.6	1815	0.9		
30 TU	0014	3.6	0653	0.9	1245	3.6	1922	0.8

SUNRISE AND SUNSET TIMES

COBH
At 51°51′N 8°18′W

		Sunrise	Sunset
UT			
Jan	01	0841	1633
	15	0834	1652
Feb	01	0812	1722
	15	0748	1748
Mar	01	0719	1813
	15	0647	1838
BST			
Apr	01	0708	2007
	15	0637	2031
May	01	0604	2058
	15	0540	2120
Jun	01	0520	2143
	15	0513	2154
Jul	01	0518	2155
	15	0532	2146
Aug	01	0556	2122
	15	0618	2056
Sep	01	0645	2020
	15	0708	1948
Oct	01	0734	1911
	15	0758	1839
UT			
Nov	01	0728	1705
	15	0753	1642
Dec	01	0818	1626
	15	0834	1622

COBH
LAT 51°51′N
LONG 8°18′W

TIMES AND HEIGHTS OF HIGH AND LOW WATER (Heights in Metres)

TIME ZONE UT
For Summer Time (area enclosed in shaded box) add 1 hour

2020

JULY

Date	Day	Time	m	Time	m	Time	m	Time	m
1	W	0121	3.6	0800	0.8	1351	3.6	2028	0.8
2	TH	0226	3.7	0903	0.7	1455	3.7	2132	0.7
3	F	0327	3.8	1004	0.6	1555	3.9	2231	0.6
4	SA	0424	3.9	1059	0.5	1650	4.0	2323	0.5
5	SU O	0515	3.9	1148	0.4	1738	4.0		
6	M	0009	0.5	0600	3.9	1233	0.4	1822	4.0
7	TU	0053	0.5	0642	3.9	1315	0.5	1903	4.0
8	W	0133	0.6	0722	3.8	1356	0.6	1943	3.9
9	TH	0213	0.7	0800	3.7	1437	0.7	2022	3.8
10	F	0253	0.8	0838	3.6	1517	0.8	2103	3.7
11	SA	0333	1.0	0918	3.5	1559	0.9	2145	3.5
12	SU ☾	0417	1.1	1001	3.4	1644	1.1	2231	3.4
13	M	0505	1.2	1050	3.3	1736	1.2	2322	3.4
14	TU	0600	1.2	1146	3.3	1833	1.2		
15	W	0022	3.3	0659	1.3	1250	3.3	1932	1.2
16	TH	0126	3.3	0759	1.2	1354	3.3	2030	1.1
17	F	0227	3.4	0856	1.1	1454	3.5	2125	1.0
18	SA	0322	3.6	0950	1.0	1548	3.6	2217	0.9
19	SU	0413	3.7	1039	0.8	1637	3.8	2304	0.7
20	M ●	0459	3.8	1124	0.6	1722	3.9	2347	0.6
21	TU	0542	3.9	1206	0.5	1804	4.0		
22	W	0029	0.5	0624	3.9	1249	0.5	1845	4.1
23	TH	0112	0.5	0706	3.9	1331	0.4	1928	4.1
24	F	0156	0.5	0751	3.9	1416	0.4	2013	4.0
25	SA	0241	0.5	0837	3.9	1502	0.5	2100	3.9
26	SU	0329	0.6	0924	3.8	1551	0.6	2149	3.8
27	M ☽	0419	0.7	1015	3.7	1643	0.7	2242	3.7
28	TU	0516	0.9	1110	3.6	1742	0.9	2343	3.6
29	W	0620	1.0	1214	3.5	1850	1.0		
30	TH	0051	3.5	0731	1.0	1325	3.5	2005	1.0
31	F	0204	3.5	0844	1.0	1438	3.5	2118	0.9

AUGUST

Date	Day	Time	m	Time	m	Time	m	Time	m
1	SA	0312	3.5	0951	0.8	1543	3.7	2222	0.7
2	SU	0412	3.7	1049	0.7	1639	3.9	2314	0.6
3	M O	0503	3.8	1136	0.5	1726	4.0	2358	0.5
4	TU	0546	3.9	1218	0.5	1807	4.0		
5	W	0036	0.5	0624	3.9	1256	0.5	1844	4.0
6	TH	0111	0.6	0700	3.8	1330	0.5	1919	3.9
7	F	0143	0.7	0733	3.8	1404	0.6	1953	3.9
8	SA	0216	0.8	0806	3.7	1437	0.8	2028	3.8
9	SU	0250	0.9	0841	3.6	1511	0.9	2103	3.7
10	M	0327	1.0	0919	3.5	1548	1.0	2142	3.6
11	TU ☾	0408	1.1	1001	3.4	1632	1.2	2225	3.4
12	W	0457	1.3	1051	3.3	1729	1.3	2319	3.3
13	TH	0600	1.4	1151	3.2	1838	1.4		
14	F	0025	3.3	0712	1.4	1304	3.2	1949	1.3
15	SA	0141	3.3	0820	1.3	1419	3.4	2054	1.1
16	SU	0251	3.4	0922	1.0	1523	3.6	2153	0.9
17	M	0350	3.6	1017	0.8	1616	3.8	2244	0.7
18	TU	0439	3.8	1104	0.6	1702	4.0	2329	0.5
19	W ●	0524	4.0	1147	0.4	1746	4.1		
20	TH	0011	0.3	0606	4.1	1229	0.3	1827	4.2
21	F	0053	0.3	0648	4.1	1311	0.2	1909	4.2
22	SA	0135	0.3	0730	4.1	1354	0.2	1952	4.1
23	SU	0219	0.3	0814	4.0	1439	0.3	2036	4.0
24	M	0304	0.5	0859	3.9	1525	0.5	2122	3.9
25	TU ☽	0352	0.7	0947	3.7	1615	0.7	2213	3.7
26	W	0445	0.9	1041	3.5	1712	0.9	2311	3.4
27	TH	0549	1.1	1146	3.4	1822	1.1		
28	F	0026	3.3	0707	1.2	1308	3.3	1948	1.2
29	SA	0150	3.3	0833	1.1	1429	3.4	2113	1.0
30	SU	0303	3.4	0945	0.9	1535	3.6	2216	0.8
31	M	0401	3.6	1040	0.7	1626	3.8	2304	0.7

SEPTEMBER

Date	Day	Time	m	Time	m	Time	m	Time	m
1	TU	0448	3.8	1124	0.5	1709	4.0	2343	0.6
2	W O	0528	3.9	1200	0.5	1747	4.1		
3	TH	0015	0.5	0603	3.9	1232	0.5	1820	4.1
4	F	0044	0.6	0634	3.9	1301	0.5	1851	4.0
5	SA	0109	0.7	0704	3.9	1328	0.6	1921	3.9
6	SU	0137	0.8	0733	3.8	1356	0.8	1951	3.8
7	M	0208	0.9	0804	3.7	1426	0.9	2022	3.8
8	TU	0242	1.0	0839	3.6	1501	1.0	2057	3.7
9	W	0320	1.1	0918	3.5	1542	1.2	2138	3.5
10	TH ☾	0405	1.3	1005	3.4	1635	1.4	2230	3.4
11	F	0507	1.4	1105	3.2	1748	1.5	2336	3.2
12	SA	0628	1.5	1221	3.2	1911	1.4		
13	SU	0059	3.2	0746	1.4	1347	3.3	2025	1.2
14	M	0222	3.4	0854	1.1	1458	3.6	2127	0.9
15	TU	0325	3.6	0951	0.8	1552	3.8	2220	0.6
16	W	0416	3.9	1040	0.5	1639	4.1	2306	0.4
17	TH ●	0501	4.1	1124	0.3	1722	4.3	2349	0.2
18	F	0543	4.2	1206	0.1	1804	4.3		
19	SA	0030	0.1	0624	4.3	1249	0.1	1845	4.3
20	SU	0112	0.2	0707	4.2	1331	0.1	1928	4.2
21	M	0155	0.3	0750	4.1	1416	0.3	2011	4.1
22	TU	0240	0.4	0834	4.0	1502	0.5	2056	3.9
23	W	0328	0.7	0922	3.7	1551	0.8	2145	3.6
24	TH ☽	0421	0.9	1016	3.5	1648	1.0	2244	3.3
25	F	0526	1.2	1125	3.3	1801	1.3		
26	SA	0005	3.1	0650	1.3	1257	3.2	1938	1.3
27	SU	0139	3.1	0823	1.1	1419	3.4	2104	1.1
28	M	0250	3.4	0932	0.9	1519	3.6	2201	0.9
29	TU	0344	3.6	1023	0.7	1607	3.8	2245	0.7
30	W	0428	3.8	1103	0.5	1647	4.0	2320	0.6

OCTOBER

Date	Day	Time	m	Time	m	Time	m	Time	m
1	TH O	0506	3.9	1137	0.5	1722	4.1	2349	0.6
2	F	0539	4.0	1205	0.5	1754	4.1		
3	SA	0013	0.6	0607	4.0	1229	0.6	1822	4.0
4	SU	0036	0.7	0634	3.9	1253	0.7	1849	4.0
5	M	0102	0.8	0701	3.9	1320	0.8	1916	3.9
6	TU	0133	0.9	0731	3.8	1351	0.9	1946	3.8
7	W	0206	1.0	0805	3.7	1427	1.1	2020	3.7
8	TH	0244	1.1	0843	3.6	1508	1.2	2102	3.6
9	F	0330	1.3	0930	3.5	1601	1.4	2154	3.4
10	SA ☾	0431	1.5	1031	3.3	1713	1.5	2302	3.2
11	SU	0552	1.5	1148	3.2	1838	1.5		
12	M	0025	3.2	0714	1.4	1315	3.4	1955	1.3
13	TU	0150	3.4	0824	1.1	1428	3.6	2059	0.9
14	W	0256	3.7	0923	0.8	1524	3.9	2153	0.6
15	TH	0348	4.0	1014	0.5	1612	4.2	2241	0.4
16	F ●	0434	4.2	1100	0.2	1657	4.3	2325	0.2
17	SA	0519	4.3	1144	0.1	1741	4.4		
18	SU	0008	0.1	0601	4.4	1228	0.1	1823	4.4
19	M	0051	0.2	0644	4.3	1312	0.2	1906	4.3
20	TU	0135	0.3	0728	4.2	1357	0.3	1949	4.1
21	W	0221	0.5	0813	4.0	1444	0.6	2034	3.8
22	TH	0310	0.7	0902	3.8	1534	0.9	2123	3.6
23	F ☽	0404	1.0	0957	3.5	1632	1.1	2222	3.3
24	SA	0509	1.2	1108	3.3	1744	1.3	2343	3.1
25	SU	0632	1.3	1236	3.2	1917	1.3		
26	M	0115	3.1	0759	1.2	1354	3.4	2036	1.2
27	TU	0225	3.3	0903	1.0	1451	3.6	2130	1.0
28	W	0316	3.6	0952	0.8	1537	3.8	2213	0.8
29	TH	0359	3.8	1033	0.7	1617	4.0	2249	0.7
30	F	0437	3.9	1106	0.6	1653	4.0	2318	0.7
31	SA O	0510	4.0	1135	0.7	1725	4.1	2342	0.7

NOVEMBER

Date	Day	Time	m	Time	m	Time	m	Time	m
1	SU	0539	4.0	1159	0.7	1754	4.0		
2	M	0006	0.7	0607	4.0	1226	0.8	1820	4.0
3	TU	0035	0.8	0635	4.0	1255	0.9	1848	4.0
4	W	0107	0.9	0706	3.9	1328	1.0	1920	3.9
5	TH	0143	1.0	0741	3.8	1406	1.1	1956	3.8
6	F	0223	1.1	0822	3.7	1450	1.2	2040	3.7
7	SA	0311	1.3	0911	3.6	1544	1.4	2133	3.5
8	SU ☾	0412	1.4	1011	3.5	1651	1.5	2240	3.4
9	M	0525	1.4	1123	3.4	1808	1.4	2357	3.4
10	TU	0642	1.3	1242	3.5	1924	1.2		
11	W	0115	3.5	0752	1.1	1354	3.7	2028	1.0
12	TH	0222	3.8	0853	0.8	1452	4.0	2125	0.7
13	F	0318	4.0	0947	0.5	1545	4.2	2216	0.5
14	SA	0408	4.2	1038	0.4	1633	4.3	2304	0.3
15	SU ●	0456	4.3	1126	0.3	1720	4.4	2350	0.2
16	M	0542	4.4	1212	0.2	1805	4.3		
17	TU	0034	0.3	0627	4.3	1258	0.3	1848	4.2
18	W	0120	0.4	0712	4.2	1344	0.5	1932	4.0
19	TH	0206	0.6	0758	4.0	1431	0.7	2017	3.8
20	F	0255	0.8	0847	3.8	1521	0.9	2106	3.6
21	SA	0349	1.0	0941	3.6	1616	1.2	2200	3.3
22	SU ☽	0449	1.2	1043	3.4	1720	1.3	2307	3.2
23	M	0600	1.3	1157	3.3	1835	1.4		
24	TU	0028	3.2	0713	1.3	1310	3.4	1946	1.3
25	W	0140	3.3	0817	1.1	1409	3.5	2043	1.2
26	TH	0235	3.5	0908	1.0	1458	3.7	2129	1.0
27	F	0321	3.7	0952	0.9	1541	3.8	2209	0.9
28	SA	0401	3.8	1030	0.9	1620	3.9	2243	0.9
29	SU	0438	3.9	1104	0.8	1656	4.0	2314	0.8
30	M O	0513	4.0	1135	0.8	1728	4.0	2344	0.8

DECEMBER

Date	Day	Time	m	Time	m	Time	m	Time	m
1	TU	0545	4.0	1206	0.8	1759	4.0		
2	W	0016	0.8	0617	4.0	1240	0.9	1830	4.0
3	TH	0052	0.9	0652	4.0	1316	0.9	1905	3.9
4	F	0131	0.9	0729	3.9	1357	1.0	1944	3.9
5	SA	0213	1.0	0812	3.9	1442	1.1	2029	3.7
6	SU	0302	1.1	0901	3.8	1533	1.2	2121	3.6
7	M	0357	1.2	0957	3.7	1632	1.3	2221	3.5
8	TU ☾	0500	1.2	1100	3.6	1739	1.3	2328	3.5
9	W	0609	1.2	1209	3.6	1849	1.2		
10	TH	0038	3.6	0718	1.1	1317	3.7	1956	1.0
11	F	0146	3.7	0823	0.9	1420	3.9	2057	0.8
12	SA	0247	3.9	0923	0.7	1518	4.0	2153	0.7
13	SU	0345	4.1	1020	0.6	1613	4.1	2246	0.5
14	M ●	0438	4.2	1112	0.5	1704	4.2	2335	0.4
15	TU	0528	4.3	1201	0.4	1751	4.2		
16	W	0022	0.4	0615	4.3	1248	0.5	1836	4.1
17	TH	0108	0.5	0701	4.2	1333	0.6	1919	4.0
18	F	0153	0.6	0745	4.1	1418	0.7	2002	3.9
19	SA	0239	0.7	0831	3.9	1504	0.9	2046	3.7
20	SU	0327	0.9	0918	3.7	1552	1.1	2132	3.5
21	M ☽	0418	1.1	1009	3.6	1643	1.2	2222	3.4
22	TU	0514	1.2	1105	3.4	1741	1.4	2321	3.3
23	W	0615	1.3	1207	3.4	1842	1.4		
24	TH	0029	3.3	0716	1.3	1310	3.4	1941	1.3
25	F	0135	3.3	0812	1.2	1408	3.5	2035	1.3
26	SA	0232	3.5	0904	1.2	1459	3.6	2124	1.1
27	SU	0322	3.6	0952	1.1	1546	3.7	2209	1.0
28	M	0408	3.8	1035	1.0	1629	3.9	2250	0.9
29	TU	0450	3.9	1115	0.9	1709	3.9	2328	0.8
30	W O	0529	4.0	1153	0.8	1745	4.0		
31	TH	0004	0.8	0606	4.0	1230	0.8	1820	4.0

DUBLIN (NORTH WALL)

LAT 53°21′N
LONG 6°13′W

TIMES AND HEIGHTS OF HIGH AND LOW WATER (Heights in Metres)

TIME ZONE UT
For Summer Time (area enclosed in shaded box) add 1 hour

2020

JANUARY

Day	Time	m	Time	m	Time	m	Time	m
1 W	0331	3.5	0906	1.3	1537	3.7	2142	1.2
2 TH	0424	3.4	1000	1.5	1628	3.6	2234	1.3
3 F ☽	0525	3.3	1058	1.6	1726	3.5	2331	1.4
4 SA	0628	3.3	1159	1.7	1831	3.4		
5 SU	0030	1.4	0728	3.3	1300	1.6	1933	3.4
6 M	0128	1.4	0821	3.5	1356	1.5	2029	3.5
7 TU	0221	1.3	0908	3.6	1445	1.4	2119	3.6
8 W	0305	1.2	0950	3.7	1528	1.2	2204	3.7
9 TH	0345	1.1	1028	3.9	1609	1.0	2246	3.8
10 F O	0423	0.9	1105	4.0	1649	0.8	2327	3.9
11 SA	0502	0.8	1144	4.1	1730	0.6		
12 SU	0009	4.0	0542	0.7	1227	4.2	1814	0.5
13 M	0055	4.0	0625	0.7	1312	4.3	1901	0.5
14 TU	0143	4.0	0712	0.8	1400	4.2	1952	0.5
15 W	0234	3.9	0803	0.9	1452	4.2	2047	0.6
16 TH	0328	3.9	0900	1.0	1547	4.1	2145	0.7
17 F ☾	0427	3.7	1001	1.2	1647	4.0	2247	0.9
18 SA	0532	3.6	1108	1.3	1754	3.8	2353	1.0
19 SU	0642	3.6	1220	1.4	1906	3.7		
20 M	0103	1.1	0750	3.6	1334	1.4	2018	3.7
21 TU	0213	1.1	0854	3.7	1443	1.3	2125	3.7
22 W	0314	1.1	0952	3.8	1541	1.1	2224	3.8
23 TH	0404	1.0	1042	3.9	1630	1.0	2313	3.8
24 F ●	0447	0.9	1124	4.0	1713	0.8	2354	3.8
25 SA	0525	0.9	1159	4.0	1751	0.8		
26 SU	0027	3.8	0559	0.9	1231	4.0	1827	0.7
27 M	0058	3.7	0633	0.9	1304	4.0	1903	0.8
28 TU	0131	3.7	0707	0.9	1339	4.0	1938	0.8
29 W	0207	3.6	0744	1.0	1417	3.9	2014	0.9
30 TH	0245	3.5	0822	1.1	1457	3.8	2051	1.0
31 F	0327	3.5	0904	1.2	1539	3.7	[illegible]	1.1

FEBRUARY

Day	Time	m	Time	m	Time	m	Time	m
1 SA	0413	3.4	0952	1.4	1627	3.5	2218	1.3
2 SU ☽	0508	3.3	1050	1.5	1722	3.3	2316	1.4
3 M	0615	3.2	1158	1.6	1829	3.3		
4 TU	0026	1.5	0727	3.2	1306	1.6	1944	3.3
5 W	0134	1.5	0828	3.4	1408	1.4	2048	3.4
6 TH	0234	1.3	0920	3.6	1502	1.2	2142	3.6
7 F	0324	1.1	1005	3.8	1549	0.9	2228	3.8
8 SA	0407	0.9	1046	4.0	1632	0.6	2311	4.0
9 SU O	0447	0.7	1127	4.2	1715	0.3	2354	4.1
10 M	0528	0.5	1209	4.3	1758	0.2		
11 TU	0036	4.1	0609	0.5	1253	4.4	1843	0.2
12 W	0121	4.1	0653	0.5	1340	4.3	1931	0.2
13 TH	0209	4.0	0741	0.6	1429	4.3	2022	0.4
14 F	0259	3.9	0834	0.7	1522	4.1	2116	0.6
15 SA ☾	0353	3.7	0932	0.9	1620	3.9	2214	0.9
16 SU	0456	3.6	1036	1.2	1729	3.7	2318	1.1
17 M	0608	3.5	1150	1.3	1846	3.5		
18 TU	0033	1.3	0722	3.5	1314	1.4	2003	3.5
19 W	0155	1.4	0833	3.5	1433	1.3	2116	3.5
20 TH	0303	1.3	0937	3.7	1534	1.1	2217	3.6
21 F	0353	1.1	1029	3.8	1620	0.9	2305	3.7
22 SA	0434	1.0	1111	3.9	1659	0.8	2342	3.7
23 SU ●	0509	0.9	1144	3.9	1734	0.7		
24 M	0009	3.7	0540	0.8	1211	4.0	1805	0.7
25 TU	0033	3.7	0611	0.8	1239	3.9	1835	0.7
26 W	0100	3.7	0640	0.8	1311	3.9	1904	0.7
27 TH	0131	3.7	0710	0.8	1345	3.9	1932	0.8
28 F	0205	3.6	0743	0.9	1422	3.8	2004	0.9
29 SA	0243	3.6	0820	1.0	1503	3.7	2041	1.0

MARCH

Day	Time	m	Time	m	Time	m	Time	m
1 SU	0325	3.5	0902	1.1	1548	3.5	2124	1.2
2 M ☽	0413	3.3	0951	1.3	1639	3.3	2215	1.4
3 TU	0512	3.2	1056	1.4	1742	3.2	2325	1.5
4 W	0628	3.1	1220	1.5	1904	3.2		
5 TH	0053	1.5	0748	3.2	1336	1.3	2021	3.3
6 F	0207	1.4	0850	3.5	1439	1.0	2121	3.5
7 SA	0305	1.1	0941	3.7	1530	0.7	2210	3.8
8 SU	0350	0.8	1026	4.0	1615	0.3	2253	4.0
9 M O	0431	0.5	1108	4.2	1657	0.1	2334	4.1
10 TU	0510	0.3	1149	4.3	1739	0.0		
11 W	0014	4.2	0550	0.2	1233	4.4	1822	0.0
12 TH	0057	4.1	0633	0.3	1318	4.4	1907	0.1
13 F	0141	4.1	0719	0.4	1407	4.2	1956	0.3
14 SA	0229	3.9	0810	0.6	1459	4.0	2047	0.6
15 SU	0321	3.7	0908	0.8	1557	3.8	2144	0.9
16 M ☾	0420	3.6	1012	1.0	1708	3.5	2246	1.2
17 TU	0535	3.4	1124	1.2	1828	3.4		
18 W	0000	1.5	0654	3.4	1253	1.3	1948	3.3
19 TH	0132	1.5	0809	3.4	1417	1.2	2103	3.4
20 F	0244	1.4	0916	3.6	1516	1.0	2203	3.5
21 SA	0334	1.2	1009	3.7	1600	0.9	2247	3.6
22 SU	0413	1.0	1050	3.8	1637	0.7	2320	3.6
23 M	0447	0.9	1121	3.9	1709	0.7	2345	3.6
24 TU ●	0518	0.8	1148	3.9	1738	0.7		
25 W	0006	3.7	0546	0.7	1214	3.9	1804	0.7
26 TH	0030	3.7	0613	0.7	1243	3.9	1828	0.7
27 F	0058	3.7	0639	0.7	1316	3.8	1855	0.7
28 SA	0131	3.7	0711	0.7	1354	3.8	1928	0.8
29 SU	0209	3.7	0748	0.8	1435	3.7	2006	0.9
30 M	0252	3.6	0830	1.0	1520	3.5	2050	1.1
31 TU	0339	3.4	0921	1.1	1611	3.4	2142	1.3

APRIL

Day	Time	m	Time	m	Time	m	Time	m
1 W ☽	0434	3.3	1025	1.3	1713	3.2	2251	1.5
2 TH	0546	3.2	1149	1.3	1835	3.2		
3 F	0021	1.5	0710	3.2	1309	1.2	1955	3.3
4 SA	0141	1.4	0819	3.5	1415	0.9	2057	3.5
5 SU	0241	1.1	0915	3.7	1509	0.5	2148	3.8
6 M	0329	0.8	1003	4.0	1555	0.2	2232	4.0
7 TU	0411	0.5	1047	4.2	1637	0.0	2312	4.1
8 W O	0451	0.3	1130	4.3	1719	-0.1	2352	4.2
9 TH	0532	0.2	1213	4.4	1801	0.0		
10 F	0033	4.1	0614	0.2	1259	4.3	1845	0.1
11 SA	0117	4.1	0700	0.3	1348	4.1	1932	0.4
12 SU	0203	3.9	0752	0.5	1441	3.9	2022	0.7
13 M	0254	3.8	0850	0.7	1540	3.7	2117	1.0
14 TU ☾	0352	3.6	0952	1.0	1649	3.4	2218	1.3
15 W	0505	3.4	1102	1.1	1805	3.3	2327	1.5
16 TH	0623	3.4	1224	1.2	1924	3.3		
17 F	0052	1.6	0737	3.4	1346	1.2	2037	3.3
18 SA	0210	1.5	0843	3.5	1445	1.0	2134	3.5
19 SU	0303	1.3	0937	3.7	1530	0.9	2216	3.6
20 M	0344	1.1	1018	3.7	1607	0.8	2248	3.6
21 TU	0418	0.9	1052	3.8	1639	0.7	2314	3.7
22 W	0450	0.8	1121	3.8	1707	0.7	2338	3.7
23 TH ●	0519	0.7	1148	3.8	1732	0.7		
24 F	0001	3.7	0544	0.7	1217	3.8	1755	0.7
25 SA	0029	3.8	0612	0.7	1251	3.8	1824	0.8
26 SU	0104	3.8	0645	0.7	1330	3.7	1900	0.8
27 M	0144	3.7	0725	0.8	1413	3.7	1941	1.0
28 TU	0228	3.7	0811	0.9	1500	3.6	2028	1.1
29 W	0316	3.5	0906	1.0	1553	3.4	2124	1.3
30 TH ☽	0413	3.4	1012	1.1	1656	3.3	2233	1.4

MAY

Day	Time	m	Time	m	Time	m	Time	m
1 F	0520	3.4	1129	1.1	1812	3.3	2354	1.5
2 SA	0637	3.4	1243	1.0	1927	3.4		
3 SU	0109	1.3	0747	3.6	1349	0.8	2029	3.6
4 M	0211	1.1	0846	3.8	1444	0.5	2122	3.8
5 TU	0303	0.8	0938	4.0	1533	0.3	2209	4.0
6 W	0349	0.6	1026	4.2	1617	0.1	2251	4.1
7 TH O	0432	0.4	1112	4.3	1700	0.1	2332	4.1
8 F	0515	0.3	1158	4.3	1743	0.2		
9 SA	0014	4.1	0559	0.3	1245	4.2	1826	0.4
10 SU	0057	4.1	0647	0.4	1334	4.0	1912	0.6
11 M	0144	4.0	0739	0.6	1427	3.8	2001	0.8
12 TU	0234	3.8	0835	0.7	1524	3.6	2054	1.1
13 W	0330	3.7	0934	0.9	1627	3.4	2151	1.3
14 TH ☾	0435	3.5	1037	1.1	1735	3.3	2254	1.5
15 F	0547	3.5	1146	1.2	1846	3.2		
16 SA	0003	1.6	0656	3.4	1300	1.2	1952	3.3
17 SU	0118	1.5	0759	3.5	1402	1.1	2048	3.4
18 M	0219	1.4	0853	3.6	1451	1.0	2132	3.5
19 TU	0305	1.2	0938	3.7	1531	0.9	2208	3.6
20 W	0344	1.1	1017	3.7	1604	0.9	2240	3.7
21 TH	0418	1.0	1051	3.7	1634	0.8	2308	3.7
22 F ●	0449	0.9	1122	3.7	1700	0.8	2334	3.8
23 SA	0518	0.8	1153	3.8	1728	0.8		
24 SU	0004	3.8	0548	0.8	1230	3.8	1800	0.8
25 M	0042	3.8	0625	0.8	1311	3.7	1838	0.9
26 TU	0124	3.8	0709	0.8	1356	3.7	1923	1.0
27 W	0210	3.8	0759	0.9	1446	3.6	2013	1.1
28 TH	0301	3.7	0857	0.9	1540	3.6	2111	1.2
29 F	0357	3.7	1001	0.9	1641	3.5	2216	1.3
30 SA ☽	0500	3.6	1109	0.9	1748	3.5	2326	1.3
31 SU	0608	3.7	1216	0.9	1856	3.5		

JUNE

Day	Time	m	Time	m	Time	m	Time	m
1 M	0036	1.3	0715	3.7	1320	0.7	1959	3.6
2 TU	0140	1.1	0818	3.9	1418	0.6	2056	3.8
3 W	0237	0.9	0916	4.0	1511	0.5	2147	3.9
4 TH	0329	0.8	1010	4.1	1559	0.4	2233	4.0
5 F O	0417	0.6	1100	4.1	1645	0.4	2317	4.1
6 SA	0504	0.5	1148	4.1	1728	0.5	2359	4.1
7 SU	0550	0.5	1234	4.0	1811	0.6		
8 M	0042	4.1	0637	0.6	1322	3.9	1854	0.8
9 TU	0126	4.0	0726	0.6	1410	3.8	1940	0.9
10 W	0213	3.9	0818	0.8	1501	3.6	2029	1.1
11 TH	0304	3.8	0912	0.9	1556	3.4	2122	1.3
12 F	0401	3.7	1007	1.0	1655	3.3	2218	1.4
13 SA ☾	0503	3.6	1105	1.1	1757	3.3	2318	1.5
14 SU	0608	3.5	1205	1.2	1858	3.3		
15 M	0021	1.5	0710	3.5	1306	1.2	1954	3.3
16 TU	0123	1.5	0806	3.5	1401	1.2	2043	3.4
17 W	0218	1.4	0856	3.5	1447	1.1	2127	3.6
18 TH	0304	1.3	0940	3.6	1526	1.1	2205	3.7
19 F	0344	1.1	1020	3.7	1600	1.0	2238	3.7
20 SA	0419	1.0	1057	3.7	1632	1.0	2310	3.8
21 SU ●	0453	0.9	1133	3.8	1705	0.9	2344	3.9
22 M	0530	0.8	1212	3.8	1742	0.9		
23 TU	0023	4.0	0610	0.8	1255	3.8	1822	0.9
24 W	0106	4.0	0656	0.7	1341	3.8	1907	0.9
25 TH	0153	4.0	0747	0.7	1431	3.8	1957	1.0
26 F	0244	4.0	0843	0.7	1523	3.7	2053	1.1
27 SA	0339	3.9	0942	0.8	1620	3.7	2153	1.2
28 SU ☽	0437	3.9	1044	0.8	1721	3.6	2256	1.2
29 M	0541	3.8	1148	0.8	1826	3.6		
30 TU	0003	1.2	0648	3.8	1252	0.8	1930	3.6

SUNRISE AND SUNSET TIMES

DUBLIN
At 53°21′N 6°13′W

UT		Sunrise	Sunset
Jan	01	0840	1617
	15	0832	1637
Feb	01	0809	1708
	15	0743	1736
Mar	01	0712	1803
	15	0639	1829
BST			
Apr	01	0658	2000
	15	0625	2026
May	01	0551	2054
	15	0525	2118
Jun	01	0503	2143
	15	0456	2155
Jul	01	0501	2156
	15	0516	2145
Aug	01	0541	2120
	15	0605	2053
Sep	01	0634	2014
	15	0659	1940
Oct	01	0727	1901
	15	0752	1829
UT			
Nov	01	0724	1652
	15	0750	1628
Dec	01	0817	1610
	15	0834	1606

DUBLIN (NORTH WALL)
LAT 53°21′N
LONG 6°13′W

TIMES AND HEIGHTS OF HIGH AND LOW WATER (Heights in Metres)

TIME ZONE UT
For Summer Time (area enclosed in shaded box) add 1 hour

2020

JULY

Date	Time	m
1 W	0111	1.2
	0755	3.8
	1354	0.8
	2032	3.7
2 TH	0215	1.1
	0900	3.9
	1452	0.8
	2129	3.8
3 F	0315	1.0
	1000	3.9
	1545	0.8
	2221	3.9
4 SA	0409	0.9
	1053	4.0
	1633	0.7
	2306	4.0
5 SU	0458	0.8
	1141	3.9
	1716	0.8
	O 2347	4.0
6 M	0543	0.7
	1225	3.9
	1757	0.8
7 TU	0026	4.0
	0626	0.7
	1307	3.8
	1836	0.9
8 W	0106	4.0
	0710	0.7
	1348	3.7
	1916	0.9
9 TH	0148	4.0
	0755	0.8
	1431	3.6
	2000	1.0
10 F	0232	3.9
	0842	0.9
	1516	3.5
	2047	1.2
11 SA	0318	3.8
	0930	1.0
	1605	3.4
	2137	1.3
12 SU	0409	3.6
	1020	1.1
	1659	3.3
	☾ 2232	1.4
13 M	0506	3.5
	1112	1.3
	1759	3.2
	2330	1.5
14 TU	0611	3.4
	1208	1.4
	1859	3.3
15 W	0029	1.6
	0715	3.4
	1305	1.4
	1956	3.3
16 TH	0129	1.5
	0814	3.4
	1400	1.4
	2047	3.5
17 F	0224	1.4
	0907	3.5
	1449	1.3
	2132	3.6
18 SA	0312	1.3
	0953	3.6
	1531	1.2
	2212	3.7
19 SU	0354	1.1
	1035	3.7
	1609	1.0
	2248	3.9
20 M	0433	0.9
	1115	3.8
	1646	0.9
	● 2325	4.0
21 TU	0512	0.7
	1155	3.9
	1725	0.8
22 W	0004	4.1
	0554	0.6
	1237	3.9
	1805	0.7
23 TH	0047	4.2
	0639	0.5
	1322	3.9
	1849	0.7
24 F	0133	4.2
	0727	0.5
	1409	3.9
	1936	0.8
25 SA	0222	4.2
	0820	0.5
	1459	3.9
	2028	0.9
26 SU	0314	4.1
	0917	0.6
	1553	3.8
	2125	1.0
27 M	0411	4.0
	1016	0.7
	1650	3.7
	☽ 2226	1.1
28 TU	0514	3.9
	1118	0.9
	1756	3.6
	2334	1.3
29 W	0626	3.7
	1224	1.0
	1906	3.6
30 TH	0047	1.3
	0741	3.7
	1333	1.1
	2014	3.6
31 F	0202	1.3
	0852	3.7
	1439	1.1
	2117	3.7

AUGUST

Date	Time	m
1 SA	0309	1.1
	0956	3.8
	1536	1.0
	2211	3.9
2 SU	0405	1.0
	1050	3.8
	1623	1.0
	2258	4.0
3 M	0452	0.8
	1136	3.8
	1704	0.9
	O 2336	4.0
4 TU	0533	0.7
	1214	3.8
	1741	0.9
5 W	0009	4.0
	0611	0.7
	1247	3.7
	1815	0.9
6 TH	0042	4.0
	0648	0.7
	1319	3.7
	1850	0.9
7 F	0118	4.0
	0725	0.8
	1354	3.6
	1927	0.9
8 SA	0156	3.9
	0803	0.9
	1432	3.6
	2007	1.0
9 SU	0236	3.8
	0843	1.0
	1512	3.5
	2049	1.2
10 M	0320	3.7
	0925	1.1
	1556	3.4
	2137	1.3
11 TU	0407	3.5
	1013	1.3
	1647	3.3
	☾ 2232	1.5
12 W	0504	3.4
	1108	1.4
	1752	3.2
	2337	1.6
13 TH	0616	3.2
	1211	1.5
	1905	3.2
14 F	0044	1.6
	0734	3.2
	1317	1.5
	2009	3.3
15 SA	0150	1.5
	0838	3.4
	1418	1.4
	2102	3.5
16 SU	0246	1.3
	0931	3.5
	1508	1.3
	2147	3.7
17 M	0333	1.0
	1016	3.7
	1550	1.0
	2227	3.9
18 TU	0415	0.7
	1057	3.9
	1629	0.8
	2305	4.1
19 W	0454	0.5
	1136	4.0
	1707	0.6
	● 2344	4.3
20 TH	0535	0.3
	1216	4.1
	1746	0.5
21 F	0024	4.3
	0617	0.2
	1258	4.1
	1827	0.5
22 SA	0108	4.4
	0703	0.3
	1343	4.0
	1912	0.6
23 SU	0156	4.3
	0753	0.4
	1431	4.0
	2002	0.7
24 M	0247	4.2
	0847	0.6
	1522	3.8
	2057	0.9
25 TU	0343	4.0
	0945	0.8
	1619	3.7
	☽ 2159	1.1
26 W	0449	3.8
	1048	1.1
	1726	3.6
	2310	1.3
27 TH	0610	3.6
	1158	1.3
	1844	3.5
28 F	0031	1.4
	0732	3.5
	1316	1.4
	1958	3.6
29 SA	0157	1.3
	0848	3.6
	1429	1.3
	2105	3.7
30 SU	0307	1.2
	0952	3.7
	1525	1.2
	2201	3.9
31 M	0358	1.0
	1044	3.7
	1610	1.1
	2247	4.0

SEPTEMBER

Date	Time	m
1 TU	0440	0.8
	1126	3.8
	1648	0.9
	2322	4.0
2 W	0516	0.7
	1159	3.8
	1722	0.9
	O 2349	4.0
3 TH	0550	0.7
	1223	3.7
	1753	0.8
4 F	0017	4.0
	0620	0.7
	1249	3.7
	1823	0.8
5 SA	0049	4.0
	0650	0.7
	1319	3.7
	1855	0.8
6 SU	0123	3.9
	0720	0.8
	1352	3.7
	1928	0.9
7 M	0201	3.8
	0752	0.9
	1429	3.6
	2005	1.1
8 TU	0242	3.7
	0829	1.1
	1510	3.5
	2046	1.2
9 W	0327	3.5
	0911	1.3
	1557	3.4
	2136	1.4
10 TH	0419	3.3
	1004	1.5
	1653	3.3
	☾ 2241	1.6
11 F	0525	3.2
	1118	1.7
	1808	3.2
12 SA	0004	1.6
	0656	3.2
	1241	1.7
	1930	3.3
13 SU	0120	1.5
	0812	3.3
	1352	1.5
	2032	3.5
14 M	0224	1.2
	0910	3.5
	1447	1.3
	2122	3.7
15 TU	0313	0.9
	0956	3.8
	1530	1.0
	2204	4.0
16 W	0355	0.5
	1036	4.0
	1609	0.7
	2243	4.2
17 TH	0434	0.2
	1114	4.1
	1646	0.5
	● 2322	4.4
18 F	0514	0.1
	1153	4.2
	1725	0.4
19 SA	0001	4.5
	0555	0.0
	1233	4.2
	1805	0.4
20 SU	0045	4.4
	0638	0.1
	1316	4.1
	1849	0.4
21 M	0131	4.3
	0726	0.4
	1402	4.0
	1938	0.6
22 TU	0223	4.2
	0818	0.6
	1453	3.9
	2034	0.8
23 W	0321	3.9
	0916	1.0
	1550	3.7
	2138	1.1
24 TH	0432	3.7
	1020	1.3
	1700	3.6
	☽ 2251	1.3
25 F	0558	3.5
	1133	1.5
	1821	3.5
26 SA	0018	1.4
	0722	3.4
	1258	1.6
	1938	3.6
27 SU	0149	1.3
	0840	3.5
	1413	1.5
	2048	3.7
28 M	0253	1.1
	0941	3.7
	1507	1.3
	2144	3.9
29 TU	0341	0.9
	1029	3.8
	1550	1.1
	2228	4.0
30 W	0419	0.8
	1107	3.8
	1626	1.0
	2302	4.0

OCTOBER

Date	Time	m
1 TH	0453	0.7
	1135	3.8
	1659	0.9
	O 2328	4.0
2 F	0523	0.7
	1157	3.8
	1730	0.8
	2354	4.0
3 SA	0551	0.7
	1220	3.8
	1758	0.8
4 SU	0022	4.0
	0616	0.8
	1248	3.8
	1826	0.8
5 M	0055	3.9
	0641	0.9
	1320	3.8
	1857	0.9
6 TU	0132	3.8
	0712	1.0
	1356	3.7
	1932	1.0
7 W	0213	3.7
	0749	1.1
	1437	3.6
	2013	1.2
8 TH	0258	3.6
	0832	1.3
	1523	3.5
	2102	1.3
9 F	0350	3.4
	0924	1.5
	1617	3.4
	2206	1.5
10 SA	0454	3.2
	1036	1.7
	1724	3.3
	☾ 2330	1.5
11 SU	0622	3.2
	1207	1.7
	1848	3.3
12 M	0050	1.4
	0743	3.3
	1323	1.6
	1957	3.5
13 TU	0157	1.1
	0843	3.6
	1421	1.3
	2051	3.8
14 W	0248	0.7
	0931	3.8
	1506	1.0
	2137	4.1
15 TH	0332	0.4
	1012	4.0
	1546	0.7
	2219	4.3
16 F	0413	0.2
	1051	4.2
	1625	0.5
	● 2300	4.4
17 SA	0453	0.0
	1129	4.3
	1705	0.3
	2341	4.5
18 SU	0534	0.1
	1209	4.3
	1747	0.3
19 M	0025	4.4
	0616	0.2
	1253	4.2
	1831	0.4
20 TU	0114	4.3
	0702	0.5
	1339	4.1
	1922	0.6
21 W	0207	4.1
	0753	0.8
	1430	4.0
	2018	0.8
22 TH	0307	3.8
	0851	1.1
	1528	3.8
	2122	1.1
23 F	0420	3.6
	0954	1.4
	1637	3.7
	☽ 2233	1.3
24 SA	0540	3.4
	1105	1.6
	1754	3.6
	2355	1.3
25 SU	0702	3.4
	1227	1.7
	1910	3.6
26 M	0121	1.3
	0817	3.5
	1343	1.6
	2018	3.7
27 TU	0226	1.1
	0916	3.6
	1439	1.4
	2115	3.8
28 W	0313	1.0
	1002	3.7
	1523	1.2
	2159	3.9
29 TH	0352	0.9
	1037	3.8
	1601	1.1
	2235	4.0
30 F	0425	0.8
	1106	3.8
	1635	1.0
	2304	4.0
31 SA	0455	0.8
	1131	3.9
	1706	0.9
	O 2332	3.9

NOVEMBER

Date	Time	m
1 SU	0522	0.8
	1155	3.9
	1735	0.9
2 M	0000	3.9
	0545	0.9
	1222	3.9
	1803	0.9
3 TU	0032	3.9
	0611	0.9
	1253	3.9
	1833	1.0
4 W	0109	3.8
	0643	1.0
	1331	3.8
	1910	1.0
5 TH	0151	3.7
	0721	1.2
	1413	3.8
	1952	1.1
6 F	0238	3.6
	0806	1.3
	1500	3.6
	2043	1.3
7 SA	0330	3.5
	0900	1.5
	1553	3.5
	2145	1.4
8 SU	0433	3.3
	1009	1.7
	1655	3.5
	☾ 2300	1.4
9 M	0549	3.3
	1131	1.7
	1806	3.5
10 TU	0016	1.3
	0704	3.4
	1246	1.6
	1916	3.6
11 W	0123	1.0
	0807	3.6
	1347	1.3
	2015	3.8
12 TH	0218	0.7
	0859	3.9
	1437	1.1
	2107	4.1
13 F	0307	0.5
	0945	4.1
	1523	0.8
	2155	4.3
14 SA	0351	0.3
	1028	4.2
	1606	0.6
	2242	4.4
15 SU	0434	0.2
	1109	4.3
	1649	0.5
	● 2327	4.4
16 M	0516	0.3
	1151	4.3
	1734	0.4
17 TU	0014	4.3
	0559	0.4
	1236	4.3
	1820	0.5
18 W	0104	4.2
	0644	0.6
	1322	4.2
	1911	0.6
19 TH	0157	4.0
	0734	0.9
	1413	4.1
	2006	0.8
20 F	0256	3.8
	0828	1.2
	1509	3.9
	2106	1.0
21 SA	0402	3.6
	0928	1.4
	1612	3.8
	2210	1.2
22 SU	0513	3.4
	1033	1.6
	1721	3.7
	☽ 2320	1.3
23 M	0625	3.4
	1143	1.7
	1830	3.6
24 TU	0036	1.3
	0734	3.4
	1258	1.7
	1935	3.7
25 W	0144	1.2
	0834	3.6
	1401	1.5
	2032	3.7
26 TH	0237	1.1
	0921	3.7
	1451	1.4
	2121	3.8
27 F	0320	1.1
	0959	3.8
	1532	1.2
	2202	3.8
28 SA	0355	1.0
	1032	3.8
	1609	1.1
	2238	3.8
29 SU	0427	1.0
	1103	3.9
	1643	1.1
	2310	3.8
30 M	0455	1.0
	1132	3.9
	1714	1.0
	O 2341	3.8

DECEMBER

Date	Time	m
1 TU	0520	1.0
	1200	3.9
	1744	1.0
2 W	0014	3.8
	0548	1.0
	1232	3.9
	1816	1.0
3 TH	0052	3.8
	0622	1.1
	1311	3.9
	1854	1.0
4 F	0135	3.7
	0702	1.2
	1354	3.9
	1938	1.0
5 SA	0222	3.7
	0748	1.3
	1441	3.8
	2029	1.1
6 SU	0314	3.6
	0841	1.4
	1532	3.8
	2127	1.1
7 M	0412	3.5
	0943	1.5
	1629	3.7
	2231	1.1
8 TU	0516	3.5
	1052	1.5
	1731	3.7
	☾ 2339	1.1
9 W	0624	3.5
	1203	1.5
	1836	3.8
10 TH	0045	1.0
	0728	3.7
	1309	1.4
	1939	3.9
11 F	0147	0.8
	0826	3.8
	1408	1.2
	2040	4.0
12 SA	0242	0.7
	0919	4.0
	1502	1.0
	2136	4.1
13 SU	0333	0.6
	1008	4.1
	1552	0.8
	2229	4.2
14 M	0419	0.5
	1055	4.2
	1640	0.7
	● 2320	4.2
15 TU	0504	0.5
	1139	4.3
	1727	0.6
16 W	0008	4.2
	0547	0.6
	1224	4.3
	1813	0.6
17 TH	0057	4.1
	0631	0.8
	1309	4.2
	1902	0.6
18 F	0146	3.9
	0716	0.9
	1356	4.1
	1952	0.7
19 SA	0239	3.8
	0805	1.1
	1447	4.0
	2044	0.9
20 SU	0334	3.6
	0858	1.3
	1540	3.9
	2139	1.0
21 M	0433	3.5
	0956	1.5
	1639	3.7
	☽ 2237	1.2
22 TU	0536	3.4
	1056	1.6
	1741	3.6
	2338	1.3
23 W	0638	3.4
	1201	1.7
	1844	3.5
24 TH	0044	1.4
	0737	3.4
	1308	1.6
	1944	3.5
25 F	0148	1.4
	0830	3.5
	1409	1.5
	2038	3.6
26 SA	0241	1.3
	0916	3.6
	1500	1.4
	2127	3.6
27 SU	0323	1.3
	0958	3.7
	1543	1.3
	2210	3.7
28 M	0359	1.2
	1035	3.8
	1619	1.2
	2249	3.7
29 TU	0430	1.1
	1108	3.9
	1653	1.1
	2324	3.7
30 W	0500	1.1
	1140	4.0
	1725	1.0
	O 2358	3.8
31 TH	0531	1.0
	1214	4.0
	1800	0.9

BELFAST
LAT 54°36′N
LONG 5°55′W

TIMES AND HEIGHTS OF HIGH AND LOW WATER (Heights in Metres)

TIME ZONE UT
For Summer Time (area enclosed in shaded box) add 1 hour

2020

JANUARY

Day		Time	m
1	W	0259 0839 1511 2119	3.1 1.0 3.4 0.9
2	TH	0348 0925 1557 2208	3.0 1.1 3.3 0.9
3	F ☽	0439 1016 1649 2308	3.0 1.2 3.2 1.0
4	SA	0534 1116 1747	2.9 1.3 3.1
5	SU	0019 0632 1228 1848	1.1 2.9 1.3 3.0
6	M	0123 0731 1337 1950	1.0 3.0 1.2 3.1
7	TU	0215 0827 1432 2046	0.9 3.1 1.1 3.1
8	W	0301 0916 1520 2134	0.8 3.3 0.9 3.2
9	TH	0343 1000 1603 2217	0.7 3.4 0.8 3.3
10	F ○	0424 1039 1646 2257	0.7 3.5 0.6 3.4
11	SA	0505 1118 1728 2338	0.7 3.6 0.5 3.4
12	SU	0547 1159 1811	0.6 3.7 0.4
13	M	0023 0631 1244 1856	3.4 0.7 3.7 0.4
14	TU	0112 0718 1332 1943	3.3 0.7 3.7 0.3
15	W	0204 0807 1422 2033	3.3 0.7 3.7 0.4
16	TH	0259 0859 1515 2127	3.2 0.8 3.7 0.5
17	F ☾	0357 0955 1611 2227	3.1 0.8 3.5 0.6
18	SA	0500 1059 1715 2335	3.0 0.9 3.4 0.7
19	SU	0610 1211 1828	3.0 1.0 3.3
20	M	0046 0720 1324 1941	0.8 3.0 1.0 3.3
21	TU	0151 0824 1430 2046	0.8 3.1 0.9 3.3
22	W	0249 0920 1528 2142	0.8 3.3 0.7 3.3
23	TH	0340 1011 1619 2232	0.8 3.4 0.6 3.3
24	F ●	0425 1056 1704 2317	0.8 3.5 0.6 3.3
25	SA	0505 1138 1743 2358	0.8 3.6 0.5 3.3
26	SU	0543 1215 1820	0.8 3.6 0.6
27	M	0035 0618 1251 1853	3.2 0.8 3.6 0.6
28	TU	0111 0652 1325 1926	3.2 0.8 3.5 0.6
29	W	0148 0727 1401 2000	3.1 0.8 3.5 0.6
30	TH	0227 0805 1437 2037	3.1 0.8 3.4 0.7
31	F	0310 0846 1515 2118	3.1 0.8 3.3 0.8

FEBRUARY

Day		Time	m
1	SA	0355 0931 1556 2205	3.0 0.9 3.2 0.9
2	SU ☽	0445 1022 1648 2303	2.9 1.1 3.0 1.0
3	M	0541 1124 1754	2.9 1.2 2.9
4	TU	0024 0641 1247 1902	1.1 2.9 1.2 2.9
5	W	0141 0743 1403 2008	1.0 2.9 1.1 3.0
6	TH	0237 0842 1459 2108	0.9 3.1 0.9 3.1
7	F	0325 0933 1547 2158	0.8 3.3 0.6 3.2
8	SA	0409 1018 1631 2243	0.6 3.4 0.4 3.3
9	SU ○	0451 1100 1714 2326	0.5 3.6 0.3 3.3
10	M	0533 1143 1756	0.5 3.7 0.2
11	TU	0010 0615 1229 1839	3.3 0.4 3.8 0.1
12	W	0058 0659 1316 1924	3.3 0.4 3.8 0.1
13	TH	0147 0745 1406 2011	3.3 0.4 3.8 0.2
14	F	0237 0834 1457 2101	3.2 0.5 3.7 0.3
15	SA ☾	0330 0927 1551 2156	3.2 0.6 3.5 0.5
16	SU	0426 1029 1650 2304	3.1 0.8 3.3 0.8
17	M	0531 1146 1801	3.0 0.9 3.1
18	TU	0021 0650 1305 1924	0.9 2.9 0.9 3.0
19	W	0134 0805 1416 2035	1.0 3.0 0.8 3.0
20	TH	0237 0905 1520 2132	0.9 3.2 0.7 3.1
21	F	0331 0956 1612 2220	0.8 3.3 0.6 3.2
22	SA	0415 1041 1653 2303	0.8 3.4 0.5 3.2
23	SU ●	0451 1121 1726 2340	0.7 3.5 0.5 3.2
24	M	0523 1157 1756	0.7 3.5 0.5
25	TU	0014 0554 1230 1825	3.1 0.7 3.4 0.5
26	W	0046 0626 1259 1855	3.1 0.6 3.4 0.5
27	TH	0118 0659 1328 1927	3.1 0.6 3.4 0.5
28	F	0151 0734 1358 2001	3.1 0.6 3.3 0.6
29	SA	0226 0812 1431 2038	3.1 0.6 3.3 0.6

MARCH

Day		Time	m
1	SU	0303 0853 1509 2120	3.1 0.7 3.2 0.8
2	M ☽	0348 0939 1558 2211	3.0 0.9 3.0 1.0
3	TU	0445 1035 1705 2318	2.9 1.0 2.8 1.1
4	W	0552 1154 1822	2.8 1.1 2.8
5	TH	0109 0700 1338 1935	1.1 2.8 1.0 2.8
6	F	0215 0806 1439 2044	1.0 3.0 0.8 3.0
7	SA	0307 0905 1529 2139	0.8 3.2 0.5 3.1
8	SU	0352 0954 1613 2225	0.6 3.4 0.2 3.3
9	M ○	0434 1039 1655 2308	0.4 3.6 0.1 3.4
10	TU	0515 1124 1735 2352	0.3 3.7 0.0 3.4
11	W	0555 1210 1817	0.3 3.8 0.0
12	TH	0038 0637 1258 1900	3.4 0.3 3.8 0.0
13	F	0126 0721 1348 1945	3.4 0.3 3.7 0.2
14	SA	0214 0809 1439 2033	3.3 0.4 3.6 0.4
15	SU	0304 0901 1532 2127	3.2 0.5 3.4 0.6
16	M ☾	0356 1004 1629 2234	3.1 0.7 3.2 0.9
17	TU	0456 1125 1738 2356	3.0 0.8 3.0 1.1
18	W	0615 1245 1908	2.9 0.9 2.9
19	TH	0111 0741 1359 2020	1.1 2.9 0.8 2.9
20	F	0220 0845 1505 2116	1.0 3.1 0.6 3.0
21	SA	0318 0935 1555 2201	0.9 3.2 0.5 3.1
22	SU	0400 1018 1632 2241	0.8 3.3 0.4 3.1
23	M	0431 1057 1700 2316	0.7 3.4 0.4 3.1
24	TU ●	0459 1131 1727 2348	0.7 3.4 0.5 3.1
25	W	0529 1202 1755	0.6 3.3 0.5
26	TH	0017 0600 1228 1825	3.1 0.6 3.3 0.5
27	F	0044 0632 1251 1855	3.2 0.5 3.3 0.5
28	SA	0113 0705 1320 1928	3.2 0.5 3.3 0.6
29	SU	0146 0741 1356 2004	3.2 0.5 3.2 0.6
30	M	0223 0821 1438 2046	3.2 0.6 3.1 0.8
31	TU	0306 0906 1529 2135	3.1 0.8 3.0 1.0

APRIL

Day		Time	m
1	W ☽	0400 1002 1636 2240	3.0 0.9 2.8 1.1
2	TH	0509 1117 1753	2.8 1.0 2.7
3	F	0031 0622 1309 1909	1.2 2.8 0.9 2.8
4	SA	0149 0734 1414 2021	1.0 3.0 0.6 2.9
5	SU	0244 0837 1505 2117	0.8 3.2 0.4 3.1
6	M	0331 0930 1550 2203	0.6 3.4 0.1 3.3
7	TU	0413 1016 1631 2246	0.4 3.6 0.0 3.4
8	W ○	0453 1102 1711 2331	0.3 3.7 0.0 3.5
9	TH	0534 1149 1752	0.2 3.8 0.0
10	F	0016 0615 1238 1835	3.5 0.2 3.8 0.1
11	SA	0104 0700 1329 1921	3.4 0.2 3.7 0.3
12	SU	0152 0748 1420 2009	3.4 0.3 3.5 0.5
13	M	0240 0841 1513 2103	3.3 0.5 3.3 0.8
14	TU ☾	0330 0945 1609 2207	3.2 0.6 3.1 1.0
15	W	0425 1103 1715 2325	3.1 0.8 2.9 1.2
16	TH	0533 1218 1844	2.9 0.8 2.8
17	F	0038 0706 1330 1956	1.2 2.9 0.8 2.8
18	SA	0147 0814 1433 2050	1.1 3.0 0.7 2.9
19	SU	0246 0906 1522 2134	1.0 3.1 0.5 3.0
20	M	0330 0949 1558 2212	0.9 3.2 0.5 3.1
21	TU	0402 1027 1626 2246	0.8 3.3 0.5 3.2
22	W	0432 1100 1655 2317	0.7 3.3 0.5 3.2
23	TH ●	0503 1129 1725 2345	0.6 3.3 0.5 3.2
24	F	0535 1153 1756	0.6 3.3 0.6
25	SA	0012 0606 1217 1827	3.3 0.6 3.3 0.6
26	SU	0041 0640 1251 1901	3.3 0.5 3.3 0.6
27	M	0116 0716 1331 1938	3.3 0.5 3.2 0.7
28	TU	0157 0757 1418 2022	3.3 0.6 3.1 0.8
29	W	0242 0844 1513 2114	3.2 0.7 3.0 1.0
30	TH ☽	0335 0942 1618 2219	3.1 0.8 2.9 1.1

MAY

Day		Time	m
1	F	0439 1056 1731 2347	3.0 0.9 2.8 1.2
2	SA	0551 1232 1847	3.0 0.8 2.8
3	SU	0113 0704 1342 1956	1.0 3.1 0.5 3.0
4	M	0214 0810 1436 2052	0.8 3.3 0.3 3.2
5	TU	0304 0905 1522 2139	0.6 3.5 0.2 3.3
6	W	0349 0955 1605 2225	0.5 3.7 0.1 3.4
7	TH ○	0432 1042 1647 2310	0.4 3.7 0.1 3.5
8	F	0515 1130 1730 2356	0.3 3.7 0.2 3.5
9	SA	0559 1219 1814	0.3 3.7 0.3
10	SU	0043 0644 1310 1900	3.5 0.3 3.6 0.5
11	M	0131 0733 1401 1949	3.5 0.4 3.4 0.7
12	TU	0218 0826 1453 2042	3.4 0.5 3.2 0.9
13	W	0306 0927 1546 2141	3.4 0.6 3.1 1.0
14	TH ☾	0356 1035 1645 2248	3.2 0.7 2.9 1.2
15	F	0453 1143 1758 2356	3.1 0.8 2.8 1.2
16	SA	0604 1247 1914	3.0 0.8 2.8
17	SU	0100 0726 1347 2011	1.2 3.0 0.7 2.9
18	M	0158 0826 1436 2056	1.1 3.1 0.7 3.0
19	TU	0248 0912 1517 2134	1.0 3.1 0.6 3.1
20	W	0328 0950 1551 2209	0.9 3.2 0.6 3.2
21	TH	0403 1025 1623 2243	0.8 3.2 0.6 3.3
22	F ●	0437 1056 1656 2315	0.7 3.2 0.6 3.3
23	SA	0511 1123 1730 2344	0.7 3.3 0.6 3.4
24	SU	0546 1151 1805	0.6 3.3 0.7
25	M	0016 0622 1229 1842	3.4 0.6 3.2 0.7
26	TU	0055 0700 1313 1923	3.4 0.6 3.2 0.8
27	W	0138 0743 1403 2010	3.4 0.6 3.1 0.9
28	TH	0226 0833 1459 2104	3.4 0.6 3.0 1.0
29	F	0318 0931 1602 2207	3.3 0.7 2.9 1.0
30	SA ☽	0417 1039 1711 2317	3.2 0.7 2.9 1.1
31	SU	0523 1155 1822	3.2 0.6 2.9

JUNE

Day		Time	m
1	M	0030 0635 1305 1929	1.0 3.2 0.5 3.0
2	TU	0137 0744 1404 2026	0.9 3.4 0.4 3.2
3	W	0235 0843 1455 2117	0.7 3.5 0.3 3.3
4	TH	0326 0935 1542 2205	0.6 3.6 0.3 3.4
5	F ○	0415 1025 1627 2252	0.5 3.6 0.3 3.5
6	SA	0502 1114 1712 2339	0.4 3.6 0.4 3.5
7	SU	0548 1203 1758	0.4 3.5 0.6
8	M	0026 0634 1252 1844	3.6 0.4 3.4 0.7
9	TU	0112 0722 1341 1931	3.6 0.4 3.3 0.8
10	W	0157 0811 1430 2019	3.5 0.5 3.2 0.9
11	TH	0241 0903 1519 2109	3.5 0.6 3.0 1.0
12	F	0327 0959 1610 2202	3.3 0.7 2.9 1.1
13	SA ☾	0416 1059 1704 2301	3.2 0.8 2.8 1.2
14	SU	0511 1200 1803	3.1 0.8 2.8
15	M	0005 0613 1259 1904	1.2 3.0 0.8 2.9
16	TU	0107 0719 1351 2000	1.2 3.0 0.8 3.0
17	W	0203 0820 1436 2047	1.1 3.0 0.7 3.1
18	TH	0251 0909 1517 2130	1.0 3.1 0.7 3.2
19	F	0333 0950 1554 2210	0.9 3.2 0.7 3.3
20	SA	0412 1027 1631 2247	0.8 3.2 0.7 3.4
21	SU ●	0450 1100 1708 2321	0.7 3.2 0.7 3.4
22	M	0529 1134 1747 2356	0.6 3.3 0.7 3.5
23	TU	0609 1213 1829	0.5 3.2 0.7
24	W	0037 0650 1259 1913	3.5 0.5 3.2 0.8
25	TH	0122 0735 1349 2001	3.5 0.5 3.2 0.8
26	F	0210 0824 1444 2052	3.5 0.5 3.1 0.8
27	SA	0301 0917 1543 2148	3.5 0.5 3.0 0.9
28	SU ☽	0356 1017 1646 2249	3.4 0.5 3.0 0.9
29	M	0457 1123 1753 2355	3.4 0.6 3.0 0.9
30	TU	0606 1232 1900	3.3 0.6 3.1

SUNRISE AND SUNSET TIMES

BELFAST
At 54°36′N 5°55′ W

		Sunrise	Sunset
UT			
Jan	01	0846	1609
	15	0837	1630
Feb	01	0813	1703
	15	0745	1732
Mar	01	0713	1800
	15	0638	1828
BST			
Apr	01	0656	2000
	15	0621	2027
May	01	0545	2058
	15	0518	2123
Jun	01	0455	2149
	15	0447	2202
Jul	01	0452	2203
	15	0507	2151
Aug	01	0535	2124
	15	0600	2055
Sep	01	0631	2015
	15	0656	1940
Oct	01	0726	1900
	15	0753	1825
UT			
Nov	01	0726	1647
	15	0754	1622
Dec	01	0823	1603
	15	0840	1558

BELFAST
LAT 54°36′N
LONG 5°55′W

TIMES AND HEIGHTS OF HIGH AND LOW WATER (Heights in Metres)

TIME ZONE UT
For Summer Time (area enclosed in shaded box) add 1 hour

2020

JULY

Date	Time	m	Time	m	Time	m	Time	m
1 W	0105	0.9	0718	3.3	1336	0.5	2002	3.1
2 TH	0211	0.8	0824	3.4	1433	0.5	2058	3.3
3 F	0310	0.7	0922	3.4	1525	0.5	2151	3.4
4 SA	0403	0.6	1014	3.5	1614	0.6	2240	3.5
5 SU ○	0453	0.5	1103	3.4	1700	0.6	2326	3.5
6 M	0540	0.4	1150	3.4	1744	0.7		
7 TU	0010	3.6	0624	0.4	1236	3.3	1827	0.8
8 W	0053	3.6	0707	0.5	1320	3.2	1909	0.8
9 TH	0134	3.5	0748	0.5	1403	3.1	1949	0.9
10 F	0215	3.5	0827	0.6	1447	3.0	2030	0.9
11 SA	0257	3.4	0908	0.7	1533	3.0	2113	1.0
12 SU ☾	0341	3.3	0954	0.8	1622	2.9	2200	1.0
13 M	0428	3.1	1048	0.9	1713	2.9	2253	1.1
14 TU	0522	3.0	1157	1.0	1808	2.9		
15 W	0000	1.2	0621	2.9	1303	1.0	1904	2.9
16 TH	0114	1.2	0725	2.9	1358	0.9	2000	3.0
17 F	0215	1.1	0826	3.0	1445	0.8	2053	3.2
18 SA	0306	0.9	0919	3.1	1529	0.8	2140	3.3
19 SU	0351	0.8	1004	3.2	1610	0.7	2221	3.4
20 M ●	0433	0.6	1043	3.2	1650	0.7	2259	3.5
21 TU	0513	0.5	1119	3.3	1731	0.7	2337	3.5
22 W	0554	0.4	1159	3.3	1813	0.7		
23 TH	0018	3.6	0636	0.3	1244	3.2	1856	0.7
24 F	0104	3.6	0719	0.3	1332	3.2	1943	0.7
25 SA	0151	3.7	0805	0.3	1424	3.2	2031	0.7
26 SU	0241	3.6	0855	0.3	1519	3.1	2123	0.7
27 M ☽	0334	3.5	0949	0.4	1618	3.1	2220	0.8
28 TU	0433	3.4	1051	0.6	1721	3.0	2327	0.9
29 W	0539	3.3	1204	0.7	1831	3.0		
30 TH	0043	0.9	0656	3.2	1316	0.8	1942	3.1
31 F	0156	0.9	0811	3.2	1419	0.8	2045	3.2

AUGUST

Date	Time	m	Time	m	Time	m	Time	m
1 SA	0300	0.7	0914	3.2	1515	0.8	2141	3.3
2 SU	0357	0.6	1008	3.3	1604	0.7	2230	3.5
3 M ○	0446	0.5	1055	3.3	1648	0.8	2314	3.5
4 TU	0530	0.5	1139	3.3	1728	0.8	2355	3.5
5 W	0608	0.5	1218	3.2	1806	0.8		
6 TH	0033	3.5	0643	0.5	1256	3.1	1840	0.8
7 F	0109	3.5	0715	0.5	1334	3.1	1914	0.8
8 SA	0145	3.5	0746	0.6	1413	3.1	1951	0.8
9 SU	0222	3.4	0820	0.7	1455	3.1	2030	0.8
10 M	0301	3.3	0859	0.7	1540	3.0	2113	0.9
11 TU ☾	0342	3.2	0943	0.9	1628	3.0	2201	1.0
12 W	0430	3.0	1036	1.0	1721	2.9	2259	1.2
13 TH	0531	2.9	1152	1.1	1818	2.9		
14 F	0018	1.2	0637	2.8	1321	1.1	1917	3.0
15 SA	0144	1.1	0746	2.9	1419	1.0	2016	3.1
16 SU	0242	0.9	0851	3.0	1507	0.9	2110	3.2
17 M	0331	0.7	0943	3.1	1551	0.7	2155	3.4
18 TU	0414	0.5	1025	3.2	1632	0.6	2235	3.5
19 W ●	0455	0.4	1103	3.3	1712	0.6	2315	3.6
20 TH	0535	0.2	1143	3.3	1752	0.5	2358	3.7
21 F	0615	0.2	1225	3.3	1834	0.5		
22 SA	0043	3.8	0656	0.2	1312	3.3	1918	0.5
23 SU	0132	3.8	0740	0.2	1402	3.3	2004	0.6
24 M	0222	3.7	0828	0.3	1454	3.2	2055	0.6
25 TU ☽	0315	3.6	0919	0.5	1550	3.2	2152	0.8
26 W	0413	3.4	1020	0.8	1652	3.1	2305	0.9
27 TH	0519	3.2	1139	1.0	1804	3.0		
28 F	0030	1.0	0642	3.0	1300	1.0	1925	3.1
29 SA	0147	0.9	0804	3.0	1409	1.0	2033	3.2
30 SU	0256	0.7	0907	3.1	1508	0.9	2128	3.3
31 M	0353	0.6	0958	3.2	1556	0.9	2215	3.5

SEPTEMBER

Date	Time	m	Time	m	Time	m	Time	m
1 TU	0438	0.5	1042	3.2	1635	0.8	2257	3.5
2 W ○	0515	0.5	1121	3.2	1708	0.8	2335	3.5
3 TH	0545	0.5	1157	3.2	1739	0.8		
4 F	0009	3.5	0611	0.6	1229	3.2	1809	0.8
5 SA	0040	3.4	0639	0.6	1301	3.2	1841	0.8
6 SU	0111	3.4	0708	0.6	1335	3.2	1915	0.8
7 M	0143	3.4	0741	0.7	1413	3.2	1953	0.8
8 TU	0215	3.3	0816	0.8	1453	3.2	2034	0.9
9 W	0252	3.2	0857	0.9	1537	3.1	2119	1.0
10 TH ☾	0337	3.1	0945	1.1	1631	3.0	2213	1.1
11 F	0441	2.9	1047	1.2	1732	2.9	2325	1.3
12 SA	0557	2.8	1242	1.3	1836	2.9		
13 SU	0114	1.2	0711	2.8	1353	1.2	1940	3.1
14 M	0218	0.9	0824	3.0	1446	1.0	2039	3.2
15 TU	0309	0.7	0921	3.1	1530	0.8	2128	3.5
16 W	0352	0.4	1003	3.3	1611	0.6	2211	3.6
17 TH ●	0431	0.2	1042	3.4	1649	0.5	2253	3.8
18 F	0510	0.1	1122	3.5	1727	0.5	2337	3.8
19 SA	0549	0.1	1205	3.5	1808	0.4		
20 SU	0023	3.9	0630	0.1	1251	3.5	1851	0.5
21 M	0113	3.8	0714	0.3	1339	3.4	1938	0.5
22 TU	0204	3.7	0801	0.5	1431	3.4	2030	0.6
23 W	0259	3.6	0852	0.7	1526	3.3	2129	0.8
24 TH ☽	0357	3.3	0953	1.0	1626	3.2	2248	0.9
25 F	0505	3.1	1117	1.2	1739	3.1		
26 SA	0016	1.0	0631	2.9	1243	1.3	1905	3.1
27 SU	0135	0.9	0753	3.0	1356	1.2	2015	3.2
28 M	0245	0.8	0853	3.1	1457	1.1	2109	3.4
29 TU	0338	0.6	0940	3.2	1543	1.0	2154	3.5
30 W	0420	0.5	1021	3.2	1616	0.9	2235	3.5

OCTOBER

Date	Time	m	Time	m	Time	m	Time	m
1 TH ○	0450	0.6	1058	3.3	1643	0.9	2311	3.5
2 F	0513	0.6	1130	3.3	1711	0.8	2342	3.5
3 SA	0539	0.7	1159	3.3	1741	0.8		
4 SU	0009	3.4	0606	0.7	1228	3.3	1811	0.8
5 M	0034	3.4	0635	0.7	1258	3.4	1845	0.8
6 TU	0103	3.4	0706	0.8	1332	3.4	1921	0.8
7 W	0137	3.3	0741	0.8	1409	3.3	2001	0.8
8 TH	0217	3.2	0821	1.0	1451	3.3	2045	1.0
9 F	0304	3.1	0909	1.1	1543	3.1	2139	1.1
10 SA ☾	0408	2.9	1010	1.3	1648	3.0	2248	1.2
11 SU	0525	2.8	1144	1.4	1758	3.0		
12 M	0037	1.2	0642	2.8	1323	1.3	1906	3.1
13 TU	0149	0.9	0756	3.0	1419	1.1	2009	3.3
14 W	0240	0.6	0853	3.2	1505	0.9	2101	3.5
15 TH	0324	0.4	0938	3.4	1546	0.7	2147	3.7
16 F ●	0404	0.2	1019	3.5	1624	0.5	2232	3.9
17 SA	0442	0.2	1101	3.6	1703	0.5	2318	3.9
18 SU	0522	0.2	1145	3.6	1745	0.4		
19 M	0005	3.9	0604	0.3	1231	3.6	1829	0.5
20 TU	0057	3.8	0650	0.4	1320	3.6	1918	0.5
21 W	0150	3.7	0738	0.7	1411	3.5	2011	0.7
22 TH	0245	3.5	0831	0.9	1505	3.4	2113	0.8
23 F ☽	0343	3.3	0932	1.2	1603	3.3	2232	0.9
24 SA	0449	3.1	1051	1.3	1710	3.2	2353	1.0
25 SU	0612	2.9	1213	1.4	1834	3.1		
26 M	0107	0.9	0730	3.0	1326	1.4	1946	3.2
27 TU	0216	0.8	0828	3.1	1428	1.2	2041	3.3
28 W	0308	0.7	0914	3.2	1515	1.1	2127	3.4
29 TH	0347	0.7	0954	3.3	1548	1.0	2207	3.5
30 F	0415	0.7	1029	3.3	1616	0.9	2242	3.5
31 SA ○	0440	0.7	1100	3.4	1645	0.9	2313	3.4

NOVEMBER

Date	Time	m	Time	m	Time	m	Time	m
1 SU	0508	0.7	1129	3.4	1716	0.8	2339	3.4
2 M	0537	0.8	1158	3.5	1748	0.8		
3 TU	0004	3.4	0607	0.8	1228	3.5	1821	0.8
4 W	0034	3.4	0640	0.9	1301	3.5	1857	0.8
5 TH	0112	3.3	0716	0.9	1339	3.5	1937	0.8
6 F	0155	3.3	0757	1.0	1423	3.4	2022	0.9
7 SA	0245	3.1	0847	1.2	1513	3.3	2117	1.0
8 SU ☾	0347	3.0	0948	1.3	1613	3.2	2224	1.1
9 M	0459	2.9	1105	1.4	1722	3.2	2348	1.0
10 TU	0614	2.9	1236	1.3	1833	3.2		
11 W	0107	0.8	0725	3.1	1342	1.1	1938	3.4
12 TH	0204	0.6	0824	3.3	1433	0.9	2035	3.6
13 F	0252	0.4	0912	3.4	1518	0.7	2125	3.8
14 SA	0335	0.3	0957	3.6	1601	0.6	2213	3.9
15 SU ●	0417	0.3	1041	3.7	1644	0.5	2301	3.9
16 M	0500	0.4	1127	3.7	1728	0.5	2351	3.8
17 TU	0545	0.5	1214	3.7	1815	0.5		
18 W	0042	3.7	0631	0.6	1304	3.7	1905	0.6
19 TH	0136	3.6	0721	0.8	1354	3.7	1959	0.6
20 F	0230	3.4	0814	1.0	1445	3.6	2059	0.8
21 SA	0325	3.2	0912	1.2	1538	3.4	2208	0.9
22 SU ☽	0425	3.1	1019	1.3	1636	3.3	2318	0.9
23 M	0535	2.9	1130	1.4	1745	3.2		
24 TU	0025	1.0	0649	2.9	1237	1.4	1901	3.2
25 W	0127	0.9	0750	3.0	1339	1.3	2003	3.2
26 TH	0221	0.9	0838	3.1	1431	1.2	2053	3.3
27 F	0303	0.8	0920	3.2	1513	1.1	2135	3.4
28 SA	0337	0.8	0956	3.4	1548	1.0	2212	3.4
29 SU	0409	0.8	1030	3.4	1622	0.9	2246	3.4
30 M ○	0441	0.8	1104	3.5	1655	0.9	2316	3.4

DECEMBER

Date	Time	m	Time	m	Time	m	Time	m
1 TU	0514	0.8	1135	3.6	1730	0.8	2343	3.4
2 W	0548	0.9	1206	3.6	1806	0.8		
3 TH	0015	3.3	0623	0.9	1241	3.6	1843	0.8
4 F	0054	3.3	0702	1.0	1320	3.6	1924	0.8
5 SA	0139	3.2	0745	1.0	1404	3.5	2010	0.8
6 SU	0230	3.2	0835	1.1	1452	3.5	2103	0.8
7 M	0327	3.1	0932	1.2	1547	3.4	2204	0.9
8 TU ☾	0431	3.0	1036	1.2	1648	3.3	2311	0.8
9 W	0541	3.0	1147	1.2	1757	3.3		
10 TH	0022	0.8	0651	3.1	1258	1.1	1906	3.4
11 F	0127	0.7	0754	3.2	1400	1.0	2009	3.5
12 SA	0222	0.6	0848	3.4	1454	0.8	2106	3.7
13 SU	0312	0.5	0938	3.5	1545	0.7	2158	3.7
14 M ●	0359	0.5	1026	3.6	1633	0.6	2249	3.7
15 TU	0446	0.5	1114	3.7	1720	0.5	2339	3.7
16 W	0532	0.6	1202	3.7	1809	0.5		
17 TH	0030	3.6	0619	0.8	1250	3.7	1857	0.5
18 F	0121	3.5	0707	0.9	1338	3.7	1948	0.6
19 SA	0211	3.3	0755	1.0	1424	3.6	2040	0.7
20 SU	0301	3.2	0845	1.1	1511	3.5	2135	0.8
21 M ☽	0352	3.1	0937	1.2	1600	3.4	2234	0.9
22 TU	0445	3.0	1035	1.3	1654	3.3	2335	1.0
23 W	0543	2.9	1139	1.3	1754	3.1		
24 TH	0035	1.0	0645	2.9	1246	1.3	1900	3.1
25 F	0131	1.0	0745	3.0	1345	1.2	2005	3.1
26 SA	0220	1.0	0837	3.1	1437	1.1	2058	3.2
27 SU	0303	0.9	0922	3.3	1521	1.0	2143	3.2
28 M	0342	0.9	1003	3.4	1600	0.9	2223	3.3
29 TU	0419	0.8	1042	3.5	1638	0.8	2259	3.3
30 W ○	0456	0.8	1118	3.5	1716	0.7	2331	3.3
31 TH	0534	0.8	1150	3.6	1755	0.7		

GALWAY

LAT 53°16′N
LONG 9°03′W

TIMES AND HEIGHTS OF HIGH AND LOW WATER (Heights in Metres)

TIME ZONE UT
For Summer Time (area enclosed in shaded box) add 1 hour

2020

JANUARY

Date	Day	Time	m	Time	m	Time	m	Time	m
1	W	0227	1.9	0859	4.5	1458	1.7	2132	4.2
2	TH	0317	2.1	0946	4.3	1552	1.9	2221	4.1
3	F ☽	0425	2.3	1037	4.1	1701	2.0	2314	4.0
4	SA	0547	2.3	1133	4.0	1814	2.1		
5	SU	0014	4.0	0651	2.2	1238	4.0	1914	2.0
6	M	0123	4.1	0746	2.1	1349	4.1	2006	1.8
7	TU	0221	4.3	0835	1.8	1445	4.4	2052	1.6
8	W	0308	4.5	0918	1.6	1532	4.6	2133	1.4
9	TH	0350	4.8	0958	1.3	1616	4.8	2212	1.2
10	F O	0432	5.0	1037	1.1	1700	5.0	2250	1.1
11	SA	0515	5.2	1117	0.9	1744	5.1	2331	1.0
12	SU	0558	5.3	1158	0.7	1829	5.2		
13	M	0013	0.9	0642	5.4	1242	0.7	1914	5.2
14	TU	0058	0.9	0728	5.3	1327	0.7	2001	5.0
15	W	0145	1.1	0816	5.2	1415	0.9	2051	4.9
16	TH	0236	1.3	0907	4.9	1507	1.1	2144	4.6
17	F ☾	0332	1.5	1004	4.7	1604	1.4	2244	4.4
18	SA	0435	1.7	1108	4.4	1711	1.6	2353	4.3
19	SU	0549	1.8	1227	4.3	1833	1.7		
20	M	0109	4.3	0714	1.8	1344	4.3	1955	1.7
21	TU	0215	4.5	0827	1.6	1447	4.4	2056	1.6
22	W	0311	4.7	0923	1.4	1540	4.6	2143	1.5
23	TH	0359	4.9	1008	1.2	1627	4.8	2223	1.4
24	F ●	0443	5.0	1047	1.1	1711	4.9	2258	1.3
25	SA	0523	5.2	1120	1.0	1751	5.0	2331	1.2
26	SU	0602	5.2	1152	0.9	1829	5.0		
27	M	0004	1.2	0638	5.2	1227	1.0	1905	4.9
28	TU	0040	1.2	0715	5.1	1302	1.1	1941	4.8
29	W	0115	1.4	0751	4.9	1337	1.2	2017	4.6
30	TH	0150	1.5	0829	4.7	1413	1.4	2056	4.4
31	F	0227	1.7	0910	4.5	1450	1.6	2138	4.3

FEBRUARY

Date	Day	Time	m	Time	m	Time	m	Time	m
1	SA	0307	1.9	0955	4.3	1533	1.9	2225	4.1
2	SU ☽	0355	2.1	1046	4.1	1623	2.1	2318	4.0
3	M	0457	2.3	1144	4.0	1732	2.2		
4	TU	0018	4.0	0709	2.3	1250	4.0	1934	2.1
5	W	0125	4.1	0810	2.0	1402	4.1	2031	1.9
6	TH	0231	4.3	0901	1.7	1504	4.4	2118	1.6
7	F	0325	4.7	0946	1.3	1555	4.8	2201	1.3
8	SA	0412	5.0	1027	0.9	1642	5.1	2241	1.0
9	SU O	0458	5.3	1107	0.6	1727	5.3	2320	0.7
10	M	0542	5.5	1146	0.4	1811	5.4		
11	TU	0001	0.6	0626	5.6	1227	0.3	1855	5.4
12	W	0043	0.6	0711	5.6	1309	0.4	1940	5.3
13	TH	0127	0.7	0757	5.4	1353	0.6	2027	5.1
14	F	0213	0.9	0845	5.1	1440	0.9	2116	4.8
15	SA ☾	0304	1.2	0937	4.7	1534	1.3	2209	4.5
16	SU	0404	1.6	1038	4.4	1638	1.7	2314	4.2
17	M	0519	1.8	1159	4.1	1801	2.0		
18	TU	0042	4.1	0649	1.9	1331	4.0	1934	2.0
19	W	0202	4.2	0816	1.8	1440	4.2	2046	1.9
20	TH	0301	4.4	0918	1.5	1533	4.4	2136	1.6
21	F	0349	4.7	1002	1.3	1618	4.6	2214	1.4
22	SA	0431	4.9	1036	1.1	1657	4.8	2245	1.2
23	SU ●	0509	5.0	1103	0.9	1734	4.9	2312	1.1
24	M	0545	5.1	1130	0.8	1809	5.0	2342	1.0
25	TU	0620	5.1	1200	0.8	1842	5.0		
26	W	0014	1.0	0653	5.1	1232	0.8	1914	4.9
27	TH	0047	1.0	0726	4.9	1305	1.0	1946	4.7
28	F	0119	1.2	0759	4.8	1338	1.1	2020	4.6
29	SA	0154	1.4	0835	4.5	1413	1.4	2056	4.4

MARCH

Date	Day	Time	m	Time	m	Time	m	Time	m
1	SU	0232	1.6	0915	4.3	1453	1.6	2140	4.1
2	M ☽	0316	1.9	1006	4.1	1539	1.9	2233	4.0
3	TU	0408	2.1	1105	3.9	1635	2.1	2335	3.9
4	W	0515	2.2	1211	3.8	1757	2.3		
5	TH	0043	3.9	0749	2.0	1327	4.0	2012	2.0
6	F	0158	4.2	0844	1.6	1443	4.3	2102	1.6
7	SA	0303	4.6	0930	1.1	1538	4.7	2146	1.1
8	SU	0354	5.0	1011	0.7	1624	5.1	2225	0.7
9	M O	0439	5.4	1050	0.3	1707	5.4	2304	0.4
10	TU	0523	5.6	1128	0.1	1750	5.6	2343	0.3
11	W	0607	5.8	1206	0.1	1833	5.6		
12	TH	0022	0.3	0651	5.7	1246	0.2	1916	5.5
13	F	0105	0.4	0736	5.5	1328	0.5	2000	5.2
14	SA	0149	0.7	0823	5.1	1413	0.9	2047	4.9
15	SU	0238	1.1	0913	4.7	1504	1.4	2137	4.5
16	M ☾	0338	1.5	1011	4.2	1610	1.8	2236	4.1
17	TU	0457	1.8	1135	3.9	1739	2.1		
18	W	0015	3.9	0625	1.9	1321	3.8	1907	2.1
19	TH	0147	4.0	0755	1.8	1429	4.0	2028	1.9
20	F	0246	4.2	0903	1.5	1519	4.3	2118	1.7
21	SA	0333	4.5	0942	1.3	1601	4.5	2153	1.4
22	SU	0413	4.7	1011	1.1	1637	4.7	2221	1.2
23	M	0449	4.9	1036	0.9	1711	4.9	2248	1.0
24	TU ●	0523	5.0	1103	0.8	1743	4.9	2317	0.9
25	W	0556	5.0	1132	0.7	1815	4.9	2347	0.8
26	TH	0629	5.0	1203	0.7	1846	4.9		
27	F	0019	0.9	0701	4.9	1234	0.8	1916	4.8
28	SA	0052	1.0	0731	4.7	1308	1.0	1945	4.6
29	SU	0127	1.1	0803	4.5	1344	1.2	2018	4.4
30	M	0205	1.4	0842	4.3	1423	1.5	2100	4.2
31	TU	0248	1.6	0933	4.1	1509	1.8	2155	4.0

APRIL

Date	Day	Time	m	Time	m	Time	m	Time	m
1	W ☽	0339	1.9	1034	3.9	1604	2.1	2259	3.9
2	TH	0444	2.0	1142	3.8	1720	2.2		
3	F	0010	3.9	0724	1.9	1300	3.9	1950	2.0
4	SA	0129	4.1	0822	1.5	1421	4.3	2041	1.5
5	SU	0240	4.5	0908	1.0	1517	4.7	2124	1.0
6	M	0332	5.0	0949	0.5	1602	5.1	2204	0.6
7	TU	0418	5.4	1027	0.2	1644	5.4	2242	0.3
8	W O	0502	5.6	1104	0.0	1726	5.6	2320	0.1
9	TH	0546	5.7	1142	0.1	1809	5.6		
10	F	0000	0.2	0630	5.6	1221	0.2	1851	5.5
11	SA	0042	0.3	0715	5.3	1303	0.6	1935	5.2
12	SU	0127	0.7	0802	5.0	1348	1.0	2021	4.9
13	M	0217	1.1	0852	4.5	1440	1.5	2110	4.5
14	TU ☾	0318	1.5	0949	4.1	1550	1.9	2206	4.1
15	W	0438	1.8	1110	3.8	1716	2.2	2328	3.9
16	TH	0556	1.9	1300	3.8	1833	2.2		
17	F	0121	3.9	0710	1.8	1405	4.0	1944	2.0
18	SA	0221	4.1	0817	1.6	1454	4.2	2039	1.7
19	SU	0307	4.3	0901	1.4	1535	4.4	2118	1.5
20	M	0347	4.5	0934	1.1	1610	4.6	2150	1.2
21	TU	0422	4.7	1003	1.0	1643	4.7	2220	1.0
22	W	0456	4.8	1033	0.8	1714	4.8	2250	0.9
23	TH ●	0529	4.8	1103	0.8	1745	4.9	2321	0.8
24	F	0603	4.8	1134	0.8	1817	4.9	2353	0.8
25	SA	0635	4.8	1206	0.9	1846	4.8		
26	SU	0027	0.9	0706	4.7	1241	1.0	1915	4.7
27	M	0104	1.0	0739	4.5	1319	1.2	1949	4.5
28	TU	0144	1.2	0820	4.3	1400	1.5	2032	4.3
29	W	0229	1.4	0911	4.1	1447	1.7	2127	4.1
30	TH ☽	0321	1.7	1012	3.9	1546	2.0	2232	4.0

MAY

Date	Day	Time	m	Time	m	Time	m	Time	m
1	F	0428	1.8	1120	3.9	1704	2.1	2342	4.0
2	SA	0628	1.7	1235	4.0	1914	1.9		
3	SU	0059	4.2	0752	1.4	1353	4.3	2012	1.4
4	M	0213	4.5	0841	0.9	1450	4.7	2057	1.0
5	TU	0308	4.9	0922	0.6	1536	5.1	2138	0.6
6	W	0355	5.3	1001	0.3	1620	5.4	2218	0.4
7	TH O	0441	5.5	1039	0.2	1703	5.5	2259	0.3
8	F	0526	5.5	1118	0.3	1746	5.5	2340	0.3
9	SA	0612	5.4	1159	0.5	1830	5.4		
10	SU	0023	0.5	0657	5.2	1242	0.8	1913	5.2
11	M	0110	0.8	0745	4.8	1328	1.2	1959	4.9
12	TU	0200	1.1	0835	4.5	1422	1.6	2048	4.5
13	W	0300	1.4	0929	4.2	1529	1.9	2141	4.2
14	TH ☾	0411	1.7	1035	3.9	1647	2.1	2242	4.0
15	F	0521	1.8	1216	3.8	1755	2.1		
16	SA	0032	3.9	0624	1.8	1327	3.9	1857	2.0
17	SU	0142	4.0	0722	1.7	1418	4.1	1952	1.8
18	M	0232	4.1	0812	1.5	1500	4.3	2037	1.6
19	TU	0313	4.3	0853	1.3	1536	4.4	2116	1.4
20	W	0349	4.5	0930	1.2	1609	4.6	2151	1.2
21	TH	0424	4.6	1004	1.1	1641	4.7	2224	1.1
22	F ●	0500	4.7	1036	1.0	1714	4.8	2256	1.0
23	SA	0535	4.7	1108	1.0	1747	4.8	2330	0.9
24	SU	0610	4.7	1142	1.0	1820	4.8		
25	M	0007	0.9	0646	4.7	1220	1.1	1853	4.8
26	TU	0047	1.0	0723	4.6	1301	1.2	1931	4.7
27	W	0130	1.1	0807	4.4	1345	1.4	2017	4.5
28	TH	0217	1.3	0857	4.3	1436	1.6	2110	4.3
29	F	0311	1.4	0955	4.1	1536	1.8	2211	4.2
30	SA ☽	0415	1.5	1059	4.1	1647	1.9	2318	4.2
31	SU	0530	1.5	1209	4.2	1812	1.7		

JUNE

Date	Day	Time	m	Time	m	Time	m	Time	m
1	M	0031	4.3	0700	1.3	1322	4.4	1931	1.5
2	TU	0144	4.5	0806	1.1	1422	4.7	2027	1.1
3	W	0244	4.8	0854	0.9	1512	5.0	2114	0.8
4	TH	0335	5.0	0938	0.7	1558	5.2	2158	0.6
5	F O	0424	5.2	1019	0.7	1643	5.4	2242	0.5
6	SA	0511	5.2	1101	0.7	1728	5.4	2325	0.6
7	SU	0557	5.2	1143	0.9	1812	5.3		
8	M	0009	0.7	0643	5.0	1226	1.1	1856	5.1
9	TU	0055	0.9	0729	4.8	1312	1.3	1941	4.9
10	W	0143	1.1	0816	4.5	1401	1.6	2027	4.7
11	TH	0235	1.4	0905	4.3	1457	1.9	2115	4.4
12	F	0333	1.6	0957	4.1	1603	2.0	2207	4.2
13	SA ☾	0435	1.7	1055	3.9	1711	2.1	2304	4.0
14	SU	0537	1.8	1210	3.9	1812	2.1		
15	M	0018	3.9	0634	1.8	1322	3.9	1908	2.0
16	TU	0136	4.0	0728	1.7	1413	4.1	1958	1.8
17	W	0228	4.1	0816	1.6	1454	4.3	2043	1.6
18	TH	0311	4.3	0859	1.5	1530	4.5	2123	1.4
19	F	0350	4.4	0937	1.3	1607	4.6	2201	1.3
20	SA	0429	4.6	1013	1.2	1643	4.8	2237	1.1
21	SU ●	0508	4.7	1048	1.1	1720	4.9	2314	1.0
22	M	0548	4.8	1125	1.1	1758	4.9	2353	0.9
23	TU	0628	4.8	1205	1.1	1837	4.9		
24	W	0034	0.9	0709	4.8	1249	1.1	1919	4.9
25	TH	0119	0.9	0754	4.7	1335	1.2	2005	4.8
26	F	0207	1.0	0843	4.5	1425	1.4	2056	4.7
27	SA	0259	1.1	0936	4.4	1522	1.5	2152	4.5
28	SU ☽	0356	1.3	1035	4.3	1624	1.6	2254	4.4
29	M	0459	1.4	1140	4.3	1734	1.6		
30	TU	0004	4.3	0610	1.4	1252	4.4	1849	1.6

SUNRISE AND SUNSET TIMES

GALWAY
At 53°16′N 9°03′W

		Sunrise	Sunset
UT			
Jan	01	0851	1629
	15	0843	1649
Feb	01	0820	1720
	15	0754	1747
Mar	01	0723	1814
	15	0651	1841
BST			
Apr	01	0710	2012
	15	0637	2037
May	01	0602	2106
	15	0537	2129
Jun	01	0515	2154
	15	0508	2206
Jul	01	0513	2207
	15	0528	2156
Aug	01	0553	2131
	15	0616	2104
Sep	01	0646	2025
	15	0710	1952
Oct	01	0738	1913
	15	0803	1840
UT			
Nov	01	0735	1704
	15	0801	1640
Dec	01	0828	1622
	15	0845	1618

GALWAY
LAT 53°16′N
LONG 9°03′W

TIMES AND HEIGHTS OF HIGH AND LOW WATER (Heights in Metres)

TIME ZONE UT
For Summer Time (area enclosed in shaded box) add 1 hour

2020

JULY

Date	Day	Time	m
1	W	0119 0728 1357 2000	4.4 1.4 4.6 1.4
2	TH	0225 0832 1453 2057	4.5 1.2 4.8 1.1
3	F	0321 0923 1543 2147	4.7 1.1 5.0 1.0
4	SA	0412 1008 1630 2232	4.9 1.1 5.1 0.8
5	SU O	0500 1050 1716 2315	5.0 1.0 5.2 0.8
6	M	0546 1131 1759 2357	5.0 1.1 5.2 0.8
7	TU	0631 1211 1842	4.9 1.2 5.1
8	W	0037 0713 1251 1922	0.9 4.8 1.3 5.0
9	TH	0118 0754 1332 2004	1.0 4.7 1.5 4.8
10	F	0200 0836 1416 2046	1.2 4.5 1.7 4.6
11	SA	0244 0919 1503 2131	1.4 4.3 1.9 4.3
12	SU ☾	0333 1004 1601 2219	1.7 4.1 2.1 4.1
13	M	0430 1054 1714 2311	1.8 4.0 2.2 4.0
14	TU	0538 1149 1823	2.0 3.9 2.2
15	W	0010 0644 1253 1921	3.9 2.0 4.0 2.1
16	TH	0120 0741 1358 2013	3.9 1.9 4.1 1.9
17	F	0225 0832 1450 2100	4.1 1.7 4.3 1.6
18	SA	0316 0917 1534 2143	4.3 1.6 4.5 1.4
19	SU	0401 0957 1616 2224	4.5 1.4 4.8 1.1
20	M ●	0445 1036 1657 2302	4.7 1.2 5.0 0.9
21	TU	0527 1114 1739 2342	4.9 1.0 5.1 0.7
22	W	0610 1154 1822	5.0 0.9 5.2
23	TH	0022 0653 1237 1904	0.6 5.0 0.9 5.2
24	F	0106 0737 1321 1950	0.6 5.0 0.9 5.1
25	SA	0151 0823 1409 2038	0.7 4.8 1.0 5.0
26	SU	0239 0913 1500 2130	0.9 4.7 1.2 4.7
27	M ☽	0331 1008 1558 2229	1.1 4.5 1.5 4.5
28	TU	0430 1110 1704 2338	1.4 4.3 1.6 4.3
29	W	0538 1224 1822	1.6 4.3 1.7
30	TH	0101 0702 1339 1946	4.2 1.7 4.3 1.6
31	F	0215 0822 1442 2054	4.3 1.6 4.5 1.4

AUGUST

Date	Day	Time	m
1	SA	0314 0920 1535 2146	4.4 1.5 4.8 1.2
2	SU	0406 1005 1622 2229	4.6 1.3 5.0 1.0
3	M O	0452 1044 1705 2306	4.8 1.2 5.1 0.9
4	TU	0534 1118 1746 2340	4.9 1.1 5.2 0.8
5	W	0614 1151 1825	4.9 1.1 5.1
6	TH	0013 0651 1226 1901	0.8 4.9 1.1 5.0
7	F	0048 0727 1301 1937	0.9 4.8 1.2 4.9
8	SA	0123 0803 1336 2015	1.0 4.6 1.4 4.7
9	SU	0159 0841 1413 2055	1.2 4.4 1.6 4.5
10	M	0236 0922 1452 2139	1.5 4.2 1.8 4.2
11	TU ☾	0316 1007 1537 2228	1.7 4.1 2.1 4.0
12	W	0403 1058 1637 2323	2.0 3.9 2.2 3.9
13	TH	0504 1155 1848	2.1 3.9 2.2
14	F	0025 0711 1300 1950	3.8 2.1 3.9 2.0
15	SA	0137 0811 1410 2042	3.9 1.9 4.2 1.7
16	SU	0247 0900 1507 2128	4.2 1.7 4.5 1.4
17	M	0339 0944 1554 2210	4.5 1.4 4.8 1.0
18	TU	0424 1023 1637 2249	4.8 1.1 5.1 0.7
19	W ●	0507 1101 1720 2326	5.0 0.8 5.3 0.4
20	TH	0549 1139 1802	5.2 0.6 5.5
21	F	0005 0631 1220 1845	0.3 5.3 0.5 5.5
22	SA	0046 0714 1302 1930	0.3 5.2 0.6 5.4
23	SU	0128 0759 1346 2017	0.4 5.1 0.8 5.1
24	M	0213 0846 1435 2107	0.7 4.8 1.0 4.8
25	TU ☽	0304 0938 1531 2205	1.1 4.6 1.4 4.4
26	W	0402 1038 1640 2317	1.5 4.3 1.7 4.1
27	TH	0516 1200 1808	1.8 4.1 1.8
28	F	0053 0651 1329 1944	3.9 2.0 4.1 1.7
29	SA	0212 0820 1435 2055	4.1 1.8 4.4 1.5
30	SU	0310 0916 1527 2143	4.3 1.6 4.6 1.2
31	M	0358 0958 1611 2220	4.5 1.4 4.9 1.0

SEPTEMBER

Date	Day	Time	m
1	TU	0439 1031 1651 2250	4.7 1.2 5.0 0.8
2	W O	0517 1058 1728 2315	4.9 1.0 5.1 0.7
3	TH	0552 1126 1803 2344	4.9 1.0 5.1 0.7
4	F	0626 1157 1837	4.9 1.0 5.0
5	SA	0015 0658 1230 1910	0.8 4.8 1.0 4.9
6	SU	0048 0730 1303 1944	0.9 4.7 1.2 4.7
7	M	0121 0804 1337 2020	1.1 4.5 1.4 4.5
8	TU	0156 0841 1414 2101	1.3 4.3 1.6 4.2
9	W	0234 0924 1456 2150	1.6 4.1 1.9 4.0
10	TH ☾	0318 1015 1546 2246	1.9 3.9 2.1 3.8
11	F	0410 1114 1653 2349	2.2 3.8 2.3 3.7
12	SA	0526 1219 1929	2.3 3.8 2.1
13	SU	0101 0752 1333 2023	3.8 2.1 4.0 1.7
14	M	0224 0842 1443 2109	4.1 1.7 4.4 1.2
15	TU	0320 0926 1532 2150	4.5 1.3 4.8 0.8
16	W	0403 1005 1615 2228	4.9 0.9 5.2 0.4
17	TH ●	0444 1041 1658 2305	5.2 0.6 5.5 0.2
18	F	0525 1119 1740 2342	5.4 0.3 5.7 0.1
19	SA	0607 1157 1824	5.5 0.3 5.6
20	SU	0021 0649 1239 1908	0.1 5.4 0.4 5.5
21	M	0102 0733 1323 1955	0.4 5.2 0.6 5.1
22	TU	0147 0819 1411 2046	0.8 4.9 1.0 4.7
23	W	0237 0910 1508 2144	1.2 4.6 1.4 4.3
24	TH ☽	0338 1009 1624 2302	1.7 4.2 1.7 3.9
25	F	0503 1137 1757	2.1 4.0 1.9
26	SA	0050 0638 1319 1934	3.8 2.1 4.0 1.8
27	SU	0205 0808 1422 2045	4.0 2.0 4.3 1.5
28	M	0258 0901 1511 2126	4.3 1.7 4.5 1.2
29	TU	0341 0938 1553 2157	4.5 1.4 4.8 1.0
30	W	0419 1008 1630 2222	4.7 1.2 4.9 0.9

OCTOBER

Date	Day	Time	m
1	TH O	0454 1033 1705 2246	4.8 1.0 5.0 0.8
2	F	0526 1100 1738 2314	4.9 0.9 5.0 0.7
3	SA	0557 1129 1810 2344	4.9 0.9 5.0 0.8
4	SU	0628 1201 1843	4.9 0.9 4.9
5	M	0016 0658 1234 1915	0.9 4.8 1.0 4.7
6	TU	0049 0730 1308 1949	1.1 4.6 1.2 4.5
7	W	0124 0803 1345 2028	1.3 4.4 1.5 4.3
8	TH	0202 0844 1427 2116	1.6 4.2 1.7 4.0
9	F	0246 0936 1516 2214	1.9 4.0 2.0 3.8
10	SA ☾	0338 1037 1619 2319	2.2 3.9 2.2 3.7
11	SU	0450 1144 1904	2.3 3.8 2.0
12	M	0032 0728 1259 2000	3.8 2.1 4.0 1.6
13	TU	0158 0820 1414 2046	4.1 1.7 4.4 1.1
14	W	0255 0902 1507 2126	4.6 1.2 4.9 0.7
15	TH	0338 0941 1551 2203	5.0 0.8 5.3 0.3
16	F ●	0419 1018 1634 2239	5.3 0.5 5.6 0.1
17	SA	0500 1055 1718 2316	5.6 0.3 5.7 0.1
18	SU	0542 1135 1803 2356	5.6 0.2 5.6 0.2
19	M	0625 1216 1849	5.5 0.4 5.4
20	TU	0037 0709 1302 1936	0.5 5.3 0.6 5.1
21	W	0123 0756 1351 2028	1.0 5.0 1.0 4.7
22	TH	0215 0846 1451 2127	1.4 4.6 1.4 4.2
23	F ☽	0321 0944 1610 2245	1.9 4.3 1.7 3.9
24	SA	0448 1105 1735	2.2 4.0 1.9
25	SU	0033 0610 1255 1854	3.9 2.2 4.0 1.8
26	M	0143 0727 1358 2005	4.0 2.0 4.2 1.6
27	TU	0234 0826 1447 2049	4.2 1.8 4.4 1.4
28	W	0316 0906 1528 2121	4.5 1.5 4.6 1.2
29	TH	0353 0937 1604 2148	4.6 1.3 4.7 1.0
30	F	0425 1005 1637 2216	4.8 1.1 4.8 0.9
31	SA O	0456 1034 1710 2246	4.9 1.0 4.9 0.9

NOVEMBER

Date	Day	Time	m
1	SU	0527 1104 1744 2317	4.9 1.0 4.9 0.9
2	M	0559 1136 1818 2349	4.9 1.0 4.8 1.0
3	TU	0630 1209 1852	4.9 1.1 4.7
4	W	0022 0701 1245 1925	1.1 4.7 1.2 4.5
5	TH	0059 0733 1324 2004	1.4 4.6 1.4 4.3
6	F	0138 0813 1406 2051	1.6 4.4 1.6 4.1
7	SA	0223 0904 1457 2148	1.9 4.2 1.8 3.9
8	SU ☾	0318 1006 1600 2253	2.1 4.0 2.0 3.9
9	M	0430 1113 1807	2.3 4.0 1.9
10	TU	0003 0646 1225 1927	3.9 2.1 4.1 1.6
11	W	0121 0747 1339 2015	4.2 1.7 4.5 1.2
12	TH	0223 0833 1438 2057	4.6 1.3 4.9 0.8
13	F	0310 0914 1527 2136	5.0 0.9 5.2 0.5
14	SA	0353 0953 1613 2214	5.3 0.6 5.5 0.4
15	SU ●	0436 1034 1659 2254	5.6 0.4 5.6 0.4
16	M	0520 1116 1745 2335	5.6 0.4 5.5 0.5
17	TU	0605 1200 1833	5.5 0.5 5.3
18	W	0019 0650 1247 1921	0.8 5.4 0.8 5.0
19	TH	0106 0737 1337 2013	1.2 5.1 1.1 4.7
20	F	0159 0827 1436 2109	1.6 4.8 1.4 4.3
21	SA	0302 0921 1546 2215	1.9 4.4 1.7 4.1
22	SU ☽	0419 1024 1659 2347	2.2 4.2 1.8 3.9
23	M	0532 1203 1806	2.2 4.0 1.8
24	TU	0102 0637 1318 1906	4.0 2.1 4.1 1.8
25	W	0158 0735 1412 1957	4.1 2.0 4.2 1.6
26	TH	0243 0823 1455 2039	4.3 1.8 4.4 1.5
27	F	0320 0902 1533 2115	4.5 1.6 4.5 1.3
28	SA	0353 0937 1608 2149	4.7 1.4 4.7 1.2
29	SU	0426 1011 1643 2222	4.8 1.2 4.8 1.2
30	M O	0459 1044 1719 2254	4.9 1.2 4.8 1.1

DECEMBER

Date	Day	Time	m
1	TU	0533 1117 1756 2328	4.9 1.1 4.8 1.2
2	W	0606 1152 1832	4.9 1.1 4.8
3	TH	0003 0639 1229 1908	1.3 4.9 1.2 4.6
4	F	0042 0714 1310 1947	1.4 4.8 1.3 4.5
5	SA	0124 0754 1354 2033	1.5 4.6 1.4 4.3
6	SU	0210 0843 1444 2126	1.7 4.5 1.6 4.2
7	M	0305 0940 1543 2226	1.9 4.3 1.7 4.1
8	TU ☾	0410 1043 1653 2331	2.0 4.3 1.7 4.1
9	W	0527 1151 1816	2.0 4.3 1.6
10	TH	0042 0651 1304 1932	4.3 1.8 4.5 1.4
11	F	0149 0756 1411 2026	4.6 1.4 4.7 1.1
12	SA	0244 0847 1506 2112	4.9 1.1 5.0 0.9
13	SU	0332 0934 1557 2156	5.2 0.9 5.2 0.8
14	M ●	0419 1019 1645 2239	5.4 0.7 5.3 0.8
15	TU	0504 1104 1733 2323	5.5 0.7 5.3 0.9
16	W	0550 1149 1821	5.5 0.7 5.2
17	TH	0007 0636 1236 1909	1.0 5.4 0.9 5.0
18	F	0053 0721 1323 1957	1.3 5.2 1.1 4.8
19	SA	0141 0808 1413 2046	1.5 4.9 1.3 4.5
20	SU	0233 0856 1508 2137	1.8 4.7 1.6 4.3
21	M ☽	0334 0946 1609 2234	2.0 4.4 1.8 4.1
22	TU	0442 1043 1713 2342	2.2 4.2 1.9 4.0
23	W	0548 1152 1814	2.2 4.0 2.0
24	TH	0057 0647 1314 1909	4.0 2.2 4.0 1.9
25	F	0155 0741 1412 2000	4.1 2.0 4.1 1.8
26	SA	0241 0829 1458 2045	4.3 1.8 4.3 1.7
27	SU	0320 0912 1539 2126	4.5 1.7 4.5 1.6
28	M	0356 0952 1618 2204	4.6 1.5 4.6 1.4
29	TU	0433 1029 1657 2240	4.8 1.3 4.7 1.3
30	W O	0510 1105 1736 2315	4.9 1.2 4.8 1.3
31	TH	0547 1141 1815 2352	5.0 1.1 4.9 1.2

ESBJERG
LAT 55°28′N
LONG 8°27′E

TIMES AND HEIGHTS OF HIGH AND LOW WATER (Heights in Metres)

TIME ZONE –0100 (Danish Standard Time). **Subtract 1 hour for UT. For Danish Summer Time (area enclosed in shaded box) add 1 hour**

2020

SUNRISE AND SUNSET TIMES

ESBJERG
At 55°28′N 8°27′E

	Sunrise	Sunset
European Standard Time (UT-1)		
Jan 01	0854	1606
15	0844	1627
Feb 01	0819	1702
15	0750	1732
Mar 01	0717	1801
15	0641	1830
European Summer Time (UT-2)		
Apr 01	0657	2004
15	0622	2032
May 01	0544	2104
15	0516	2130
Jun 01	0452	2157
15	0443	2210
Jul 01	0449	2211
15	0505	2159
Aug 01	0533	2131
15	0559	2101
Sep 01	0632	2020
15	0658	1943
Oct 01	0729	1902
15	0757	1826
European Standard Time (UT-1)		
Nov 01	0732	1647
15	0800	1621
Dec 01	0830	1600

JANUARY

Date	Time	m	Time	m	Time	m	Time	m
1 W	0005	0.7	0614	2.2	1241	0.7	1843	1.9
2 TH	0043	0.7	0652	2.1	1323	0.7	1924	1.9
3 F ☽	0126	0.8	0737	2.1	1408	0.7	2014	1.9
4 SA	0214	0.8	0829	2.1	1500	0.8	2112	1.9
5 SU	0311	0.8	0929	2.1	1559	0.8	2219	1.9
6 M	0417	0.8	1037	2.0	1702	0.7	2328	1.9
7 TU	0524	0.8	1148	2.0	1802	0.7		
8 W	0032	2.0	0627	0.7	1252	2.0	1857	0.7
9 TH	0128	2.0	0722	0.7	1350	2.1	1946	0.6
10 F ○	0217	2.1	0811	0.6	1441	2.1	2031	0.6
11 SA	0302	2.1	0858	0.5	1529	2.1	2115	0.5
12 SU	0344	2.2	0943	0.4	1613	2.1	2158	0.5
13 M	0424	2.2	1027	0.4	1655	2.0	2241	0.5
14 TU	0504	2.2	1113	0.3	1738	2.0	2325	0.5
15 W	0546	2.3	1159	0.3	1823	2.0		
16 TH	0011	0.5	0632	2.3	1248	0.4	1911	2.0
17 F ☾	0100	0.5	0723	2.2	1340	0.4	2004	1.9
18 SA	0153	0.5	0820	2.2	1436	0.5	2105	1.9
19 SU	0253	0.6	0927	2.2	1539	0.5	2214	1.9
20 M	0359	0.6	1042	2.1	1645	0.6	2323	1.9
21 TU	0509	0.6	1154	2.1	1751	0.6		
22 W	0028	2.0	0617	0.5	1300	2.1	1850	0.5
23 TH	0126	2.1	0718	0.5	1358	2.1	1943	0.5
24 F ●	0219	2.1	0812	0.4	1450	2.1	2031	0.5
25 SA	0307	2.2	0901	0.4	1537	2.0	2114	0.5
26 SU	0349	2.2	0945	0.4	1616	2.0	2154	0.5
27 M	0425	2.2	1025	0.4	1649	1.9	2231	0.5
28 TU	0454	2.1	1101	0.5	1716	1.9	2305	0.5
29 W	0520	2.1	1135	0.5	1740	1.8	2338	0.5
30 TH	0546	2.1	1208	0.5	1807	1.9		
31 F	0012	0.5	0619	2.1	1242	0.6	1842	1.9

FEBRUARY

Date	Time	m	Time	m	Time	m	Time	m
1 SA	0049	0.6	0658	2.1	1320	0.6	1925	1.9
2 SU ☽	0131	0.6	0744	2.0	1404	0.6	2015	1.9
3 M	0220	0.6	0838	2.0	1456	0.6	2113	1.8
4 TU	0318	0.7	0940	1.9	1559	0.7	2220	1.8
5 W	0429	0.7	1054	1.9	1711	0.7	2338	1.9
6 TH	0546	0.7	1215	1.9	1820	0.6		
7 F	0050	1.9	0654	0.6	1325	1.9	1919	0.6
8 SA	0150	2.0	0750	0.5	1423	2.0	2010	0.5
9 SU ○	0241	2.1	0840	0.3	1514	2.0	2057	0.4
10 M	0327	2.1	0927	0.3	1600	2.0	2141	0.3
11 TU	0410	2.2	1011	0.2	1643	2.0	2224	0.3
12 W	0452	2.2	1056	0.2	1724	2.0	2308	0.3
13 TH	0533	2.2	1140	0.2	1804	2.0	2352	0.3
14 F	0617	2.2	1226	0.2	1848	1.9		
15 SA ☾	0039	0.3	0705	2.2	1314	0.3	1935	1.9
16 SU	0129	0.3	0759	2.1	1407	0.4	2030	1.9
17 M	0226	0.4	0904	2.0	1507	0.5	2138	1.8
18 TU	0332	0.5	1021	1.9	1616	0.6	2253	1.8
19 W	0449	0.5	1137	1.9	1728	0.6		
20 TH	0004	1.9	0603	0.5	1244	1.9	1832	0.6
21 F	0106	2.0	0706	0.4	1343	1.9	1927	0.5
22 SA	0201	2.0	0759	0.3	1434	1.9	2014	0.4
23 SU ●	0249	2.1	0846	0.3	1519	1.9	2057	0.4
24 M	0331	2.1	0927	0.3	1557	1.9	2134	0.4
25 TU	0407	2.1	1003	0.3	1628	1.9	2209	0.4
26 W	0434	2.0	1036	0.4	1651	1.8	2240	0.4
27 TH	0457	2.0	1106	0.4	1712	1.8	2311	0.4
28 F	0519	2.0	1135	0.4	1736	1.8	2342	0.4
29 SA	0548	2.0	1206	0.4	1807	1.9		

MARCH

Date	Time	m	Time	m	Time	m	Time	m
1 SU	0017	0.4	0625	2.0	1241	0.4	1846	1.9
2 M ☽	0056	0.4	0708	2.0	1323	0.5	1932	1.9
3 TU	0143	0.4	0759	1.9	1411	0.5	2026	1.8
4 W	0238	0.5	0900	1.8	1511	0.6	2129	1.8
5 TH	0348	0.6	1014	1.8	1626	0.6	2248	1.8
6 F	0513	0.6	1145	1.8	1747	0.6		
7 SA	0013	1.8	0629	0.5	1302	1.8	1853	0.5
8 SU	0121	1.9	0729	0.3	1403	1.9	1947	0.4
9 M ○	0217	2.0	0820	0.2	1455	1.9	2035	0.3
10 TU	0306	2.1	0906	0.1	1541	2.0	2120	0.2
11 W	0351	2.2	0951	0.1	1622	2.0	2204	0.1
12 TH	0434	2.2	1034	0.1	1702	2.0	2247	0.1
13 F	0515	2.2	1117	0.1	1740	1.9	2331	0.1
14 SA	0558	2.1	1201	0.2	1820	1.9		
15 SU	0016	0.2	0644	2.0	1247	0.3	1904	1.8
16 M ☾	0105	0.2	0737	1.9	1336	0.4	1956	1.8
17 TU	0201	0.3	0840	1.8	1434	0.5	2101	1.8
18 W	0309	0.4	1000	1.8	1546	0.6	2222	1.8
19 TH	0431	0.5	1117	1.7	1704	0.6	2338	1.8
20 F	0547	0.4	1223	1.8	1811	0.5		
21 SA	0041	1.9	0649	0.3	1321	1.8	1905	0.4
22 SU	0137	2.0	0740	0.3	1411	1.8	1952	0.4
23 M	0225	2.0	0824	0.2	1454	1.9	2034	0.3
24 TU ●	0307	2.0	0903	0.2	1532	1.9	2111	0.3
25 W	0342	2.0	0937	0.3	1602	1.8	2144	0.3
26 TH	0409	2.0	1007	0.3	1625	1.8	2214	0.3
27 F	0432	1.9	1035	0.3	1645	1.8	2244	0.3
28 SA	0454	1.9	1103	0.3	1708	1.8	2315	0.3
29 SU	0522	1.9	1134	0.3	1738	1.9	2350	0.3
30 M	0558	1.9	1210	0.3	1815	1.9		
31 TU	0030	0.3	0641	1.9	1251	0.4	1900	1.8

APRIL

Date	Time	m	Time	m	Time	m	Time	m
1 W ☽	0116	0.3	0732	1.8	1339	0.4	1952	1.8
2 TH	0211	0.4	0832	1.7	1438	0.5	2054	1.8
3 F	0322	0.4	0948	1.7	1554	0.6	2210	1.8
4 SA	0447	0.4	1121	1.7	1717	0.6	2339	1.8
5 SU	0604	0.3	1239	1.7	1826	0.4		
6 M	0053	1.9	0704	0.2	1339	1.8	1922	0.3
7 TU	0151	2.0	0755	0.1	1431	1.9	2011	0.2
8 W ○	0243	2.1	0842	0.0	1516	1.9	2057	0.1
9 TH	0329	2.1	0927	0.0	1558	1.9	2142	0.0
10 F	0413	2.1	1010	0.0	1637	1.9	2225	0.0
11 SA	0456	2.1	1052	0.1	1715	1.9	2309	0.0
12 SU	0538	2.0	1135	0.2	1753	1.9	2355	0.1
13 M	0623	1.9	1219	0.3	1835	1.8		
14 TU ☾	0044	0.2	0714	1.8	1307	0.4	1924	1.8
15 W	0140	0.3	0816	1.7	1403	0.5	2026	1.8
16 TH	0248	0.4	0934	1.6	1513	0.6	2147	1.7
17 F	0409	0.4	1050	1.6	1632	0.6	2304	1.8
18 SA	0523	0.4	1154	1.7	1741	0.5		
19 SU	0009	1.8	0623	0.3	1250	1.7	1836	0.4
20 M	0105	1.9	0712	0.2	1339	1.8	1924	0.4
21 TU	0154	1.9	0755	0.2	1423	1.8	2005	0.3
22 W	0236	2.0	0833	0.2	1501	1.8	2043	0.3
23 TH ●	0313	1.9	0906	0.2	1533	1.8	2116	0.3
24 F	0342	1.9	0936	0.3	1559	1.8	2148	0.3
25 SA	0407	1.9	1005	0.3	1621	1.8	2219	0.2
26 SU	0432	1.8	1036	0.3	1646	1.8	2252	0.2
27 M	0502	1.8	1109	0.3	1716	1.9	2329	0.2
28 TU	0538	1.8	1146	0.3	1753	1.9		
29 W	0011	0.2	0622	1.8	1229	0.3	1836	1.9
30 TH ☽	0059	0.3	0713	1.7	1318	0.4	1928	1.8

MAY

Date	Time	m	Time	m	Time	m	Time	m
1 F	0156	0.3	0814	1.7	1417	0.5	2029	1.8
2 SA	0305	0.4	0930	1.6	1529	0.5	2144	1.8
3 SU	0424	0.3	1058	1.6	1647	0.5	2310	1.8
4 M	0536	0.3	1212	1.7	1756	0.4		
5 TU	0024	1.9	0637	0.2	1312	1.8	1854	0.3
6 W	0125	2.0	0729	0.1	1404	1.9	1946	0.2
7 TH ○	0219	2.1	0817	0.0	1451	1.9	2034	0.1
8 F	0308	2.1	0903	0.0	1534	1.9	2120	0.0
9 SA	0354	2.0	0946	0.1	1614	1.9	2206	0.0
10 SU	0438	2.0	1029	0.2	1652	1.9	2251	0.1
11 M	0521	1.9	1112	0.2	1731	1.9	2337	0.1
12 TU	0605	1.8	1155	0.4	1811	1.9		
13 W	0026	0.2	0652	1.7	1241	0.5	1857	1.8
14 TH ☾	0120	0.3	0748	1.6	1333	0.5	1952	1.8
15 F	0222	0.4	0856	1.6	1435	0.6	2103	1.8
16 SA	0335	0.5	1008	1.6	1548	0.6	2219	1.8
17 SU	0445	0.4	1113	1.6	1658	0.6	2326	1.8
18 M	0545	0.4	1210	1.7	1757	0.5		
19 TU	0024	1.8	0636	0.3	1301	1.7	1848	0.4
20 W	0115	1.9	0719	0.3	1347	1.8	1932	0.4
21 TH	0200	1.9	0759	0.3	1428	1.8	2012	0.3
22 F ●	0240	1.9	0834	0.3	1503	1.9	2049	0.3
23 SA	0314	1.9	0907	0.3	1534	1.9	2123	0.3
24 SU	0345	1.8	0939	0.3	1601	1.9	2158	0.3
25 M	0416	1.8	1013	0.3	1629	1.9	2235	0.2
26 TU	0449	1.8	1049	0.3	1701	1.9	2315	0.2
27 W	0528	1.8	1129	0.3	1739	1.9	2359	0.2
28 TH	0612	1.7	1214	0.3	1823	1.9		
29 F	0049	0.2	0703	1.7	1304	0.4	1914	1.9
30 SA ☽	0145	0.3	0803	1.7	1401	0.4	2014	1.9
31 SU	0249	0.3	0913	1.7	1507	0.5	2124	1.9

JUNE

Date	Time	m	Time	m	Time	m	Time	m
1 M	0358	0.3	1030	1.7	1617	0.5	2242	1.9
2 TU	0506	0.3	1142	1.7	1725	0.4	2356	2.0
3 W	0608	0.2	1244	1.8	1827	0.3		
4 TH	0101	2.0	0703	0.2	1338	1.9	1922	0.2
5 F ○	0158	2.0	0754	0.2	1428	1.9	2014	0.1
6 SA	0251	2.0	0841	0.2	1514	1.9	2103	0.1
7 SU	0339	2.0	0926	0.2	1556	2.0	2150	0.1
8 M	0425	1.9	1009	0.3	1636	2.0	2236	0.2
9 TU	0507	1.8	1052	0.3	1714	1.9	2322	0.2
10 W	0548	1.7	1134	0.4	1752	1.9		
11 TH	0009	0.3	0629	1.7	1217	0.5	1833	1.9
12 F	0057	0.4	0714	1.6	1303	0.5	1919	1.9
13 SA ☾	0150	0.5	0806	1.6	1354	0.6	2013	1.8
14 SU	0247	0.5	0907	1.6	1453	0.6	2116	1.8
15 M	0350	0.5	1012	1.6	1559	0.6	2225	1.8
16 TU	0451	0.5	1115	1.7	1704	0.6	2329	1.8
17 W	0547	0.5	1212	1.7	1802	0.5		
18 TH	0027	1.8	0637	0.4	1304	1.8	1854	0.5
19 F	0119	1.9	0721	0.4	1351	1.8	1940	0.4
20 SA	0206	1.9	0802	0.4	1433	1.9	2022	0.4
21 SU ●	0249	1.9	0840	0.4	1510	1.9	2102	0.4
22 M	0328	1.9	0917	0.4	1544	1.9	2142	0.3
23 TU	0406	1.8	0956	0.4	1618	2.0	2222	0.3
24 W	0443	1.8	1035	0.3	1653	2.0	2304	0.2
25 TH	0523	1.8	1117	0.3	1731	2.0	2349	0.2
26 F	0607	1.8	1202	0.4	1815	2.0		
27 SA	0038	0.2	0655	1.8	1250	0.4	1904	2.0
28 SU ☽	0130	0.3	0749	1.8	1343	0.4	2000	2.0
29 M	0227	0.3	0850	1.7	1442	0.4	2104	2.0
30 TU	0330	0.3	0959	1.7	1548	0.4	2217	2.0

ESBJERG
LAT 55°28′N
LONG 8°27′E

TIMES AND HEIGHTS OF HIGH AND LOW WATER (Heights in Metres)

TIME ZONE –0100 (Danish Standard Time). **Subtract 1 hour for UT. For Danish Summer Time (area enclosed in shaded box) add 1 hour**

2020

JULY

Date	Day	Time	m
1	W	0436 1110 1656 2332	0.4 1.8 0.4 2.0
2	TH	0540 1216 1802	0.4 1.8 0.4
3	F	0041 0639 1315 1903	2.0 0.3 1.9 0.3
4	SA	0143 0734 1409 1959	2.0 0.3 2.0 0.3
5	SU	0239 0823 1458 O 2050	2.0 0.3 2.0 0.2
6	M	0329 0910 1543 2138	1.9 0.4 2.0 0.2
7	TU	0415 0953 1624 2224	1.9 0.4 2.0 0.3
8	W	0455 1034 1701 2307	1.8 0.4 2.0 0.3
9	TH	0531 1114 1735 2349	1.8 0.4 2.0 0.4
10	F	0604 1153 1808	1.7 0.5 2.0
11	SA	0030 0637 1232 1844	0.4 1.7 0.5 2.0
12	SU	0111 0714 1314 1926	0.5 1.7 0.6 2.0
13	M	0154 0759 1400 ☾ 2015	0.6 1.7 0.6 1.9
14	TU	0243 0853 1453 2112	0.6 1.7 0.6 1.9
15	W	0339 0957 1555 2217	0.6 1.7 0.7 1.9
16	TH	0441 1106 1704 2329	0.6 1.8 0.7 1.8
17	F	0544 1213 1810	0.6 1.8 0.6
18	SA	0036 0640 1311 1907	1.9 0.6 1.9 0.6
19	SU	0134 0730 1402 1957	1.9 0.5 1.9 0.5
20	M	0226 0816 1447 ● 2043	1.9 0.5 2.0 0.4
21	TU	0313 0858 1528 2126	1.9 0.4 2.0 0.4
22	W	0356 0940 1606 2209	1.9 0.4 2.1 0.3
23	TH	0436 1021 1644 2252	1.9 0.4 2.1 0.3
24	F	0516 1103 1723 2335	1.9 0.3 2.2 0.2
25	SA	0557 1147 1806	1.9 0.3 2.2
26	SU	0021 0640 1233 1852	0.3 1.9 0.3 2.2
27	M	0110 0728 1323 ☽ 1944	0.3 1.9 0.4 2.2
28	TU	0202 0822 1417 2044	0.4 1.9 0.4 2.1
29	W	0300 0925 1519 2155	0.5 1.8 0.5 2.0
30	TH	0405 1038 1630 2314	0.5 1.8 0.5 2.0
31	F	0514 1151 1743	0.6 1.9 0.5

AUGUST

Date	Day	Time	m
1	SA	0028 0619 1256 1849	2.0 0.6 2.0 0.4
2	SU	0132 0717 1354 1948	2.0 0.5 2.0 0.4
3	M	0229 0809 1445 O 2040	2.0 0.5 2.1 0.3
4	TU	0319 0855 1531 2126	2.0 0.5 2.1 0.3
5	W	0402 0937 1611 2209	2.0 0.5 2.2 0.4
6	TH	0439 1016 1646 2247	1.9 0.5 2.1 0.4
7	F	0509 1052 1714 2323	1.9 0.5 2.1 0.5
8	SA	0535 1127 1741 2357	1.9 0.5 2.1 0.5
9	SU	0600 1201 1810	1.9 0.5 2.1
10	M	0031 0630 1236 1846	0.6 1.9 0.5 2.1
11	TU	0106 0709 1315 ☾ 1928	0.6 1.9 0.6 2.0
12	W	0146 0755 1401 2018	0.6 1.9 0.6 2.0
13	TH	0233 0849 1454 2117	0.7 1.9 0.7 1.9
14	F	0331 0953 1602 2229	0.8 1.9 0.8 1.9
15	SA	0443 1110 1723 2352	0.8 1.9 0.8 1.9
16	SU	0558 1227 1835	0.8 1.9 0.7
17	M	0104 0700 1329 1933	1.9 0.7 2.0 0.6
18	TU	0204 0752 1422 2022	2.0 0.6 2.1 0.5
19	W	0255 0838 1508 ● 2108	2.0 0.5 2.2 0.4
20	TH	0340 0921 1550 2151	2.1 0.4 2.3 0.3
21	F	0421 1003 1630 2233	2.1 0.4 2.3 0.3
22	SA	0500 1045 1710 2316	2.1 0.3 2.3 0.3
23	SU	0539 1128 1751	2.1 0.3 2.3
24	M	0000 0619 1213 1836	0.3 2.0 0.3 2.3
25	TU	0045 0703 1300 ☽ 1926	0.4 2.0 0.4 2.2
26	W	0134 0752 1353 2024	0.5 2.0 0.5 2.1
27	TH	0230 0852 1455 2138	0.6 1.9 0.6 2.0
28	F	0335 1008 1609 2302	0.7 1.9 0.6 2.0
29	SA	0451 1129 1730	0.8 2.0 0.6
30	SU	0016 0602 1238 1839	2.0 0.8 2.1 0.6
31	M	0119 0702 1337 1936	2.0 0.7 2.2 0.5

SEPTEMBER

Date	Day	Time	m
1	TU	0214 0753 1429 2025	2.1 0.6 2.2 0.4
2	W	0302 0837 1514 O 2109	2.1 0.6 2.3 0.4
3	TH	0343 0918 1553 2148	2.1 0.5 2.3 0.4
4	F	0417 0954 1625 2222	2.0 0.5 2.2 0.5
5	SA	0444 1028 1651 2254	2.0 0.5 2.2 0.6
6	SU	0505 1100 1713 2323	2.0 0.5 2.2 0.6
7	M	0526 1131 1738 2353	2.0 0.6 2.2 0.6
8	TU	0554 1203 1811	2.0 0.6 2.2
9	W	0025 0629 1240 1851	0.6 2.1 0.6 2.1
10	TH	0102 0712 1322 ☾ 1939	0.7 2.1 0.6 2.1
11	F	0147 0802 1413 2035	0.7 2.0 0.7 2.0
12	SA	0241 0902 1518 2145	0.8 2.0 0.8 2.0
13	SU	0352 1014 1643 2314	0.9 2.0 0.8 2.0
14	M	0517 1141 1804	0.9 2.0 0.7
15	TU	0036 0629 1254 1907	2.0 0.8 2.1 0.6
16	W	0139 0725 1353 1958	2.1 0.7 2.2 0.5
17	TH	0231 0813 1443 ● 2044	2.2 0.6 2.3 0.4
18	F	0317 0858 1528 2128	2.2 0.5 2.4 0.3
19	SA	0359 0941 1610 2210	2.2 0.4 2.4 0.3
20	SU	0438 1024 1651 2253	2.2 0.3 2.4 0.3
21	M	0516 1107 1733 2335	2.2 0.3 2.4 0.4
22	TU	0554 1151 1818	2.2 0.4 2.3
23	W	0020 0636 1239 1907	0.5 2.1 0.5 2.2
24	TH	0107 0724 1332 ☽ 2006	0.6 2.1 0.6 2.1
25	F	0202 0823 1435 2124	0.8 2.1 0.7 2.0
26	SA	0308 0942 1554 2248	0.9 2.0 0.7 2.0
27	SU	0428 1106 1717 2359	0.9 2.1 0.7 2.0
28	M	0542 1215 1823	0.9 2.2 0.6
29	TU	0059 0641 1314 1918	2.1 0.8 2.2 0.5
30	W	0152 0731 1406 2004	2.1 0.7 2.3 0.5

OCTOBER

Date	Day	Time	m
1	TH	0238 0815 1451 O 2045	2.2 0.6 2.3 0.5
2	F	0317 0854 1529 2122	2.2 0.6 2.3 0.5
3	SA	0350 0930 1600 2154	2.2 0.6 2.3 0.6
4	SU	0416 1002 1624 2223	2.1 0.6 2.2 0.6
5	M	0437 1032 1646 2251	2.1 0.6 2.2 0.6
6	TU	0457 1103 1710 2319	2.1 0.6 2.2 0.7
7	W	0523 1135 1742 2352	2.2 0.6 2.2 0.7
8	TH	0557 1212 1822	2.2 0.6 2.2
9	F	0030 0639 1255 1909	0.7 2.2 0.7 2.1
10	SA	0114 0728 1346 ☾ 2006	0.8 2.2 0.7 2.1
11	SU	0208 0825 1450 2115	0.8 2.1 0.8 2.0
12	M	0317 0935 1612 2242	0.9 2.1 0.8 2.0
13	TU	0441 1100 1733	0.9 2.1 0.7
14	W	0006 0555 1219 1837	2.0 0.8 2.2 0.6
15	TH	0110 0655 1322 1930	2.1 0.7 2.3 0.5
16	F	0204 0746 1415 ● 2018	2.2 0.6 2.4 0.4
17	SA	0251 0833 1503 2103	2.3 0.5 2.4 0.4
18	SU	0334 0918 1549 2146	2.3 0.4 2.5 0.4
19	M	0414 1002 1632 2229	2.3 0.4 2.4 0.4
20	TU	0452 1046 1715 2311	2.3 0.4 2.4 0.5
21	W	0531 1132 1801 2356	2.2 0.4 2.3 0.6
22	TH	0612 1221 1850	2.2 0.5 2.1
23	F	0043 0659 1314 ☽ 1950	0.8 2.2 0.6 2.0
24	SA	0136 0758 1419 2106	0.9 2.1 0.7 2.0
25	SU	0241 0915 1537 2225	1.0 2.1 0.8 2.0
26	M	0359 1036 1654 2332	1.0 2.1 0.8 2.0
27	TU	0512 1145 1758	0.9 2.2 0.7
28	W	0030 0612 1243 1851	2.1 0.8 2.3 0.6
29	TH	0121 0703 1335 1936	2.1 0.7 2.3 0.6
30	F	0207 0747 1420 2017	2.2 0.7 2.3 0.6
31	SA	0247 0828 1500 O 2052	2.2 0.6 2.3 0.6

NOVEMBER

Date	Day	Time	m
1	SU	0321 0904 1533 2124	2.2 0.6 2.3 0.6
2	M	0349 0936 1559 2153	2.2 0.6 2.2 0.7
3	TU	0412 1008 1622 2222	2.2 0.6 2.2 0.7
4	W	0434 1039 1649 2253	2.2 0.6 2.2 0.7
5	TH	0501 1114 1722 2327	2.2 0.6 2.1 0.7
6	F	0534 1152 1801	2.2 0.6 2.1
7	SA	0007 0615 1237 1849	0.7 2.3 0.6 2.1
8	SU	0053 0704 1330 ☾ 1946	0.8 2.2 0.7 2.0
9	M	0147 0800 1433 2053	0.8 2.2 0.7 2.0
10	TU	0253 0907 1547 2213	0.9 2.2 0.7 2.0
11	W	0408 1025 1701 2333	0.9 2.2 0.7 2.1
12	TH	0521 1144 1805	0.8 2.3 0.6
13	F	0038 0623 1250 1901	2.1 0.7 2.3 0.5
14	SA	0134 0718 1348 1951	2.2 0.6 2.4 0.4
15	SU	0224 0808 1441 ● 2038	2.2 0.5 2.4 0.4
16	M	0309 0856 1529 2123	2.3 0.4 2.4 0.5
17	TU	0351 0943 1616 2207	2.3 0.4 2.3 0.5
18	W	0432 1029 1701 2250	2.3 0.4 2.2 0.6
19	TH	0512 1117 1747 2334	2.3 0.5 2.1 0.7
20	F	0554 1206 1836	2.2 0.6 2.1
21	SA	0021 0640 1259 1931	0.8 2.2 0.6 2.0
22	SU	0112 0734 1359 ☽ 2037	0.9 2.2 0.7 1.9
23	M	0211 0841 1508 2147	0.9 2.2 0.8 1.9
24	TU	0319 0956 1618 2251	1.0 2.2 0.8 1.9
25	W	0430 1104 1721 2349	0.9 2.2 0.7 2.0
26	TH	0533 1204 1815	0.8 2.2 0.7
27	F	0042 0627 1257 1902	2.1 0.8 2.2 0.6
28	SA	0129 0716 1345 1944	2.1 0.7 2.2 0.6
29	SU	0213 0758 1428 2021	2.2 0.7 2.2 0.6
30	M	0251 0837 1505 O 2055	2.2 0.7 2.2 0.7

DECEMBER

Date	Day	Time	m
1	TU	0324 0913 1537 2127	2.2 0.7 2.1 0.7
2	W	0351 0947 1606 2159	2.2 0.7 2.1 0.7
3	TH	0417 1022 1636 2233	2.2 0.6 2.1 0.7
4	F	0446 1059 1710 2310	2.2 0.6 2.1 0.7
5	SA	0520 1140 1751 2352	2.2 0.6 2.1 0.7
6	SU	0601 1226 1837	2.3 0.6 2.0
7	M	0038 0648 1317 1931	0.7 2.3 0.6 2.0
8	TU	0131 0742 1415 ☾ 2033	0.7 2.3 0.6 2.0
9	W	0231 0845 1520 2143	0.8 2.3 0.6 2.0
10	TH	0338 0956 1628 2257	0.8 2.2 0.6 2.0
11	F	0447 1112 1733	0.7 2.3 0.6
12	SA	0005 0552 1223 1832	2.1 0.7 2.3 0.5
13	SU	0105 0652 1326 1926	2.1 0.6 2.3 0.5
14	M	0159 0747 1423 ● 2016	2.2 0.5 2.3 0.5
15	TU	0248 0839 1516 2103	2.2 0.4 2.2 0.5
16	W	0334 0928 1605 2148	2.2 0.4 2.2 0.6
17	TH	0417 1016 1651 2233	2.2 0.4 2.1 0.6
18	F	0459 1104 1735 2316	2.2 0.5 2.0 0.7
19	SA	0539 1152 1819	2.2 0.5 2.0
20	SU	0001 0622 1240 1904	0.7 2.2 0.6 1.9
21	M	0047 0708 1332 1954	0.8 2.2 0.7 1.9
22	TU	0137 0800 1427 ☽ 2050	0.8 2.2 0.7 1.9
23	W	0233 0900 1527 2153	0.8 2.1 0.8 1.9
24	TH	0335 1007 1629 2255	0.9 2.1 0.8 1.9
25	F	0441 1111 1728 2353	0.8 2.1 0.7 2.0
26	SA	0543 1211 1820	0.8 2.1 0.7
27	SU	0047 0639 1305 1907	2.0 0.8 2.1 0.7
28	M	0136 0728 1354 1950	2.1 0.7 2.1 0.7
29	TU	0220 0811 1438 2028	2.1 0.7 2.1 0.6
30	W	0259 0851 1517 O 2105	2.1 0.6 2.1 0.6
31	TH	0333 0930 1554 2141	2.1 0.6 2.0 0.6

HELGOLAND
LAT 54°11′N
LONG 7°53′E

TIMES AND HEIGHTS OF HIGH AND LOW WATER (Heights in Metres)

TIME ZONE –0100 (German Standard Time). **Subtract 1 hour for UT. For German Summer Time (area enclosed in shaded box) add 1 hour**

2020

SUNRISE AND SUNSET TIMES

HELGOLAND
At 54°11′N 7°53′E

		Sunrise	Sunset
European Standard Time (UT-1)			
Jan	01	0848	1616
	15	0840	1637
Feb	01	0816	1709
	15	0749	1737
Mar	01	0717	1805
	15	0643	1833
European Summer Time (UT-2)			
Apr	01	0701	2005
	15	0627	2031
May	01	0551	2101
	15	0525	2126
Jun	01	0502	2151
	15	0455	2204
Jul	01	0500	2205
	15	0515	2153
Aug	01	0541	2127
	15	0606	2059
Sep	01	0636	2020
	15	0702	1945
Oct	01	0731	1905
	15	0757	1831
European Standard Time (UT-1)			
Nov	01	0730	1654
	15	0757	1629
Dec	01	0825	1610

JANUARY

Day	Time	m	Day	Time	m
1 W	0322 1009 1548 2215	3.2 0.7 2.9 0.8	16 TH	0330 1031 1607 2243	3.3 0.5 2.9 0.6
2 TH	0401 1048 1630 2257	3.2 0.8 2.8 0.9	17 F ☾	0420 1120 1659 2334	3.2 0.5 2.9 0.6
3 F ☽	0444 1131 1716 2344	3.1 0.9 2.8 1.0	18 SA	0514 1212 1754	3.2 0.6 2.8
4 SA	0532 1219 1808	3.0 0.9 2.8	19 SU	0030 0614 1311 1856	0.7 3.1 0.7 2.8
5 SU	0041 0630 1318 1910	1.0 2.9 0.9 2.8	20 M	0138 0726 1423 2007	0.8 3.0 0.7 2.8
6 M	0149 0738 1424 2016	1.0 2.9 0.9 2.8	21 TU	0256 0843 1536 2119	0.8 3.0 0.8 2.9
7 TU	0259 0846 1530 2119	0.9 3.0 0.9 2.9	22 W	0409 0953 1641 2220	0.7 3.0 0.7 3.0
8 W	0403 0947 1629 2214	0.8 3.0 0.8 3.0	23 TH	0512 1052 1735 2312	0.6 3.0 0.7 3.1
9 TH	0500 1040 1722 2303	0.7 3.1 0.7 3.1	24 F ●	0604 1142 1822 2359	0.5 3.0 0.6 3.1
10 F ○	0549 1129 1808 2347	0.7 3.1 0.7 3.1	25 SA	0649 1226 1904	0.5 3.0 0.6
11 SA	0635 1214 1852	0.6 3.2 0.7	26 SU	0041 0731 1306 1943	3.2 0.4 3.0 0.5
12 SU	0030 0721 1300 1938	3.2 0.6 3.2 0.6	27 M	0119 0809 1342 2017	3.2 0.4 3.0 0.5
13 M	0115 0810 1347 2024	3.3 0.5 3.1 0.6	28 TU	0153 0842 1415 2047	3.2 0.5 2.9 0.5
14 TU	0200 0857 1432 2109	3.3 0.5 3.1 0.6	29 W	0224 0912 1446 2117	3.2 0.5 2.9 0.5
15 W	0244 0943 1518 2154	3.3 0.4 3.0 0.6	30 TH	0255 0944 1519 2151	3.2 0.5 2.9 0.6
			31 F	0331 1018 1555 [illegible]	3.1 0.6 2.8 [illegible]

FEBRUARY

Day	Time	m	Day	Time	m
1 SA	0406 1048 1628 2257	3.1 0.7 2.8 0.7	16 SU	0450 1141 1721 2359	3.1 0.5 2.8 0.6
2 SU ☽	0440 1119 1703 2335	3.0 0.7 2.8 0.8	17 M	0543 1232 1817	3.0 0.7 2.8
3 M	0523 1204 1754	2.9 0.8 2.7	18 TU	0103 0652 1344 1930	0.7 2.8 0.8 2.8
4 TU	0036 0628 1312 1905	0.9 2.8 0.9 2.7	19 W	0226 0816 1508 2052	0.7 2.8 0.8 2.8
5 W	0156 0749 1434 2025	0.9 2.8 0.9 2.7	20 TH	0352 0938 1625 2205	0.7 2.8 0.8 2.9
6 TH	0319 0908 1552 2139	0.8 2.8 0.8 2.8	21 F	0503 1043 1724 2301	0.6 2.9 0.7 3.0
7 F	0432 1016 1658 2240	0.7 2.9 0.7 3.0	22 SA	0556 1132 1810 2346	0.5 2.9 0.6 3.1
8 SA	0533 1113 1753 2331	0.6 3.0 0.6 3.1	23 SU ●	0638 1212 1850	0.4 2.9 0.5
9 SU ○	0625 1203 1843	0.5 3.1 0.6	24 M	0025 0716 1248 1926	3.1 0.3 2.9 0.4
10 M	0017 0713 1249 1930	3.2 0.4 3.1 0.5	25 TU	0059 0750 1320 1958	3.1 0.3 2.9 0.3
11 TU	0103 0802 1335 2017	3.3 0.3 3.1 0.4	26 W	0130 0819 1350 2026	3.1 0.3 2.9 0.3
12 W	0149 0849 1420 2101	3.3 0.3 3.1 0.4	27 TH	0159 0847 1419 2054	3.1 0.3 2.9 0.4
13 TH	0233 0934 1504 2143	3.3 0.3 3.0 0.4	28 F	0229 0916 1450 2126	3.1 0.4 2.9 0.4
14 F	0318 1017 1548 2227	3.3 0.3 3.0 0.4	29 SA	0302 0947 1521 2156	3.0 0.4 2.9 0.4
15 SA ☾	0403 1059 1634 2311	3.2 0.4 2.9 0.4			

MARCH

Day	Time	m	Day	Time	m
1 SU	0333 1012 1548 2220	3.0 0.5 2.8 0.5	16 M ☾	0425 1109 1648 2331	2.9 0.5 2.8 0.4
2 M ☽	0400 1033 1614 2248	2.9 0.6 2.8 0.6	17 TU	0515 1156 1742	2.8 0.6 2.8
3 TU	0434 1108 1656 2340	2.8 0.8 2.7 0.8	18 W	0033 0623 1307 1856	0.6 2.6 0.8 2.7
4 W	0534 1215 1808	2.7 0.9 2.6	19 TH	0158 0750 1437 2025	0.7 2.6 0.8 2.8
5 TH	0105 0701 1347 1939	0.8 2.6 0.9 2.7	20 F	0331 0919 1604 2146	0.6 2.6 0.8 2.9
6 F	0242 0835 1521 2107	0.7 2.7 0.8 2.8	21 SA	0448 1028 1707 2243	0.5 2.7 0.6 3.0
7 SA	0409 0955 1638 2218	0.5 2.8 0.7 3.0	22 SU	0539 1115 1750 2324	0.4 2.8 0.5 3.0
8 SU	0517 1057 1739 2314	0.4 2.9 0.6 3.1	23 M	0616 1150 1827	0.3 2.8 0.4
9 M ○	0612 1148 1830	0.3 3.0 0.4	24 TU ●	0000 0651 1224 1903	3.1 0.3 2.9 0.3
10 TU	0001 0700 1233 1916	3.2 0.2 3.1 0.3	25 W	0034 0724 1255 1935	3.1 0.3 2.9 0.3
11 W	0046 0746 1316 2001	3.3 0.2 3.1 0.2	26 TH	0104 0752 1324 2003	3.1 0.2 2.9 0.3
12 TH	0131 0831 1400 2045	3.3 0.2 3.0 0.2	27 F	0133 0818 1351 2030	3.1 0.3 2.9 0.3
13 F	0216 0914 1443 2127	3.2 0.2 3.0 0.2	28 SA	0202 0846 1420 2059	3.0 0.3 2.9 0.3
14 SA	0300 0954 1524 2207	3.2 0.2 3.0 0.2	29 SU	0233 0914 1450 2129	3.0 0.4 2.9 0.3
15 SU	0342 1032 1605 2247	3.1 0.3 2.9 0.3	30 M	0304 0940 1517 2154	2.9 0.5 2.9 0.4
			31 TU	0333 1003 1544 [illegible]	2.9 0.6 2.8 [illegible]

APRIL

Day	Time	m	Day	Time	m
1 W ☽	0408 1038 1624 2312	2.7 0.7 2.7 0.6	16 TH	0008 0558 1234 1826	0.6 2.6 0.9 2.8
2 TH	0504 1142 1733	2.6 0.8 2.7	17 F	0128 0719 1400 1951	0.7 2.5 0.9 2.8
3 F	0034 0630 1315 1905	0.7 2.6 0.8 2.7	18 SA	0258 0846 1528 2112	0.7 2.6 0.8 2.9
4 SA	0214 0807 1454 2037	0.6 2.6 0.8 2.8	19 SU	0415 0957 1634 2212	0.6 2.7 0.7 3.0
5 SU	0345 0931 1615 2151	0.4 2.8 0.6 3.0	20 M	0506 1044 1718 2252	0.5 2.8 0.6 3.0
6 M	0456 1035 1718 2250	0.3 2.9 0.5 3.1	21 TU	0542 1119 1755 2327	0.4 2.9 0.5 3.1
7 TU	0552 1126 1810 2339	0.1 3.0 0.3 3.2	22 W	0617 1153 1832	0.3 2.9 0.4
8 W ○	0639 1210 1856	0.1 3.0 0.2	23 TH ●	0003 0651 1226 1907	3.1 0.3 2.9 0.3
9 TH	0024 0722 1252 1940	3.2 0.1 3.1 0.2	24 F	0036 0722 1255 1936	3.1 0.3 3.0 0.3
10 F	0108 0805 1334 2023	3.2 0.1 3.1 0.1	25 SA	0105 0749 1322 2004	3.0 0.3 3.0 0.3
11 SA	0153 0847 1417 2106	3.2 0.2 3.1 0.1	26 SU	0135 0816 1351 2034	3.0 0.3 3.0 0.3
12 SU	0238 0927 1458 2146	3.1 0.3 3.0 0.2	27 M	0207 0846 1422 2105	3.0 0.4 3.0 0.3
13 M	0321 1004 1538 2225	3.0 0.4 3.0 0.3	28 TU	0241 0916 1454 2139	2.9 0.4 3.0 0.3
14 TU ☾	0404 1041 1622 2309	2.8 0.5 2.9 0.4	29 W	0318 0949 1530 2216	2.8 0.5 2.9 0.4
15 W	0454 1127 1715	2.7 0.7 2.8	30 TH ☽	0400 1030 1614 2306	2.7 0.7 2.8 0.5

MAY

Day	Time	m	Day	Time	m
1 F	0456 1131 1717	2.6 0.8 2.8	16 SA	0052 0641 1315 1906	0.8 2.6 0.9 2.9
2 SA	0020 0612 1255 1840	0.5 2.6 0.8 2.8	17 SU	0209 0757 1435 2020	0.7 2.6 0.9 3.0
3 SU	0151 0741 1427 2007	0.5 2.6 0.7 2.9	18 M	0321 0906 1543 2123	0.6 2.7 0.7 3.0
4 M	0317 0902 1546 2121	0.3 2.7 0.6 3.0	19 TU	0416 0958 1633 2209	0.5 2.8 0.6 3.0
5 TU	0426 1005 1650 2222	0.2 2.9 0.4 3.1	20 W	0457 1038 1715 2249	0.5 2.9 0.5 3.0
6 W	0522 1058 1743 2314	0.2 3.0 0.3 3.2	21 TH	0536 1116 1756 2328	0.4 2.9 0.5 3.0
7 TH ○	0611 1144 1831	0.1 3.0 0.2	22 F ●	0615 1152 1835	0.3 3.0 0.4
8 F	0002 0655 1227 1915	3.2 0.2 3.1 0.2	23 SA	0005 0649 1224 1907	3.0 0.3 3.0 0.3
9 SA	0046 0737 1309 1959	3.2 0.2 3.1 0.2	24 SU	0038 0720 1255 1939	3.0 0.3 3.0 0.3
10 SU	0132 0820 1353 2044	3.1 0.3 3.1 0.2	25 M	0112 0752 1327 2014	3.0 0.4 3.0 0.3
11 M	0219 0902 1436 2127	3.0 0.4 3.1 0.3	26 TU	0148 0826 1403 2051	2.9 0.4 3.0 0.3
12 TU	0304 0940 1518 2207	2.9 0.5 3.1 0.4	27 W	0228 0903 1441 2132	2.9 0.5 3.0 0.3
13 W	0348 1018 1601 2251	2.8 0.6 3.1 0.5	28 TH	0311 0944 1524 2217	2.8 0.5 3.0 0.4
14 TH ☾	0435 1103 1652 2344	2.7 0.8 3.0 0.7	29 F	0400 1032 1613 2310	2.8 0.6 3.0 0.4
15 F	0532 1201 1753	2.6 0.9 3.0	30 SA ☽	0456 1130 1711	2.7 0.7 2.9
			31 SU	0014 0601 1240 [illegible]	0.4 2.7 0.7 [illegible]

JUNE

Day	Time	m	Day	Time	m
1 M	0129 0716 1359 1938	0.4 2.7 0.6 3.0	16 TU	0212 0759 1437 2021	0.7 2.7 0.8 3.0
2 TU	0246 0830 1513 2051	0.4 2.8 0.6 3.1	17 W	0312 0858 1537 2117	0.6 2.8 0.7 3.0
3 W	0353 0934 1618 2154	0.4 2.9 0.5 3.2	18 TH	0405 0949 1630 2207	0.6 2.9 0.6 3.0
4 TH	0450 1028 1715 2250	0.4 3.0 0.5 3.2	19 F	0453 1035 1718 2253	0.5 2.9 0.5 3.0
5 F ○	0542 1118 1807 2341	0.3 3.1 0.4 3.2	20 SA	0538 1117 1802 2336	0.4 3.0 0.4 3.0
6 SA	0630 1205 1854	0.4 3.2 0.3	21 SU ●	0619 1156 1842	0.4 3.0 0.4
7 SU	0029 0715 1249 1940	3.2 0.4 3.2 0.3	22 M	0016 0657 1232 1921	3.0 0.4 3.1 0.3
8 M	0116 0759 1335 2027	3.1 0.5 3.3 0.4	23 TU	0055 0735 1311 2002	3.0 0.4 3.1 0.3
9 TU	0203 0842 1419 2111	3.1 0.6 3.3 0.4	24 W	0137 0815 1351 2044	3.0 0.4 3.1 0.3
10 W	0248 0920 1500 2151	3.0 0.6 3.3 0.5	25 TH	0220 0856 1432 2128	2.9 0.5 3.1 0.3
11 TH	0329 0957 1541 2232	2.9 0.7 3.2 0.6	26 F	0305 0940 1518 2217	2.9 0.5 3.1 0.3
12 F	0412 1038 1626 2317	2.8 0.8 3.2 0.7	27 SA	0356 1030 1608 2309	2.8 0.6 3.1 0.4
13 SA ☾	0500 1127 1717	2.8 0.9 3.1	28 SU ☽	0450 1124 1703	2.8 0.6 3.1
14 SU	0010 0555 1225 1814	0.8 2.7 0.9 3.0	29 M	0004 0547 1223 1803	0.4 2.8 0.7 3.1
15 M	0109 0656 1330 1917	0.8 2.7 0.9 3.0	30 TU	0105 0649 1330 1912	0.5 2.8 0.7 3.1

HELGOLAND
LAT 54°11′N
LONG 7°53′E

TIMES AND HEIGHTS OF HIGH AND LOW WATER (Heights in Metres)

TIME ZONE –0100 (German Standard Time). **Subtract 1 hour for UT. For German Summer Time (area enclosed in shaded box) add 1 hour**

2020

JULY

Date	Day	Time	m
1	W	0213 0757 1442 2023	0.5 2.9 0.7 3.1
2	TH	0321 0904 1550 2131	0.6 3.0 0.7 3.2
3	F	0423 1003 1653 2231	0.6 3.1 0.6 3.2
4	SA	0520 1057 1749 2327	0.6 3.2 0.5 3.2
5	SU ○	0612 1149 1841	0.6 3.2 0.5
6	M	0018 0700 1237 1928	3.1 0.6 3.3 0.5
7	TU	0105 0744 1321 2014	3.1 0.6 3.3 0.5
8	W	0149 0825 1403 2055	3.1 0.6 3.4 0.5
9	TH	0229 0900 1440 2131	3.0 0.7 3.4 0.6
10	F	0305 0934 1516 2207	3.0 0.7 3.3 0.6
11	SA	0342 1011 1555 2245	2.9 0.7 3.2 0.7
12	SU	0424 1052 1638 2325	2.8 0.8 3.2 0.7
13	M ☾	0507 1135 1721	2.8 0.8 3.1
14	TU	0006 0552 1223 1811	0.8 2.8 0.9 3.0
15	W	0056 0646 1324 1912	0.8 2.8 0.9 2.9
16	TH	0159 0749 1433 2020	0.8 2.7 0.8 2.9
17	F	0306 0855 1542 2125	0.7 2.8 0.7 2.9
18	SA	0410 0955 1643 2222	0.7 2.9 0.6 2.9
19	SU	0505 1047 1736 2313	0.6 3.0 0.5 3.0
20	M ●	0554 1133 1822 2359	0.5 3.0 0.5 3.0
21	TU	0639 1215 1907	0.5 3.1 0.4
22	W	0043 0723 1257 1953	3.1 0.5 3.2 0.3
23	TH	0127 0807 1340 2037	3.0 0.5 3.2 0.3
24	F	0211 0849 1422 2121	3.0 0.4 3.2 0.3
25	SA	0254 0932 1506 2207	2.9 0.5 3.2 0.3
26	SU	0342 1019 1555 2256	2.9 0.5 3.2 0.4
27	M ☽	0433 1109 1647 2344	2.9 0.5 3.2 0.5
28	TU	0524 1200 1741	2.9 0.6 3.1
29	W	0036 0619 1300 1845	0.6 2.9 0.7 3.1
30	TH	0140 0725 1414 2000	0.7 2.9 0.8 3.0
31	F	0254 0839 1532 2116	0.8 3.0 0.8 3.1

AUGUST

Date	Day	Time	m
1	SA	0406 0947 1642 2223	0.8 3.1 0.7 3.1
2	SU	0507 1046 1741 2320	0.8 3.2 0.6 3.1
3	M ○	0601 1139 1833	0.7 3.2 0.5
4	TU	0009 0648 1226 1918	3.1 0.7 3.3 0.5
5	W	0053 0730 1307 1959	3.1 0.6 3.4 0.5
6	TH	0131 0807 1343 2034	3.1 0.6 3.4 0.6
7	F	0205 0838 1415 2104	3.1 0.6 3.4 0.6
8	SA	0236 0907 1447 2135	3.0 0.6 3.3 0.6
9	SU	0309 0941 1522 2209	3.0 0.7 3.2 0.7
10	M	0346 1017 1559 2241	2.9 0.7 3.2 0.7
11	TU ☾	0421 1049 1633 2309	2.9 0.8 3.1 0.8
12	W	0453 1123 1710 2346	2.9 0.9 3.0 0.9
13	TH	0537 1215 1807	2.8 1.0 2.8
14	F	0047 0642 1331 1924	1.0 2.7 1.0 2.8
15	SA	0209 0802 1457 2046	0.9 2.7 0.9 2.8
16	SU	0331 0918 1613 2157	0.9 2.8 0.7 2.9
17	M	0439 1021 1715 2255	0.7 3.0 0.6 3.0
18	TU	0535 1113 1807 2343	0.6 3.1 0.5 3.0
19	W ●	0624 1158 1854	0.6 3.2 0.4
20	TH	0028 0709 1241 1940	3.1 0.5 3.3 0.3
21	F	0111 0754 1324 2024	3.1 0.4 3.3 0.2
22	SA	0154 0836 1406 2107	3.0 0.4 3.3 0.2
23	SU	0237 0918 1449 2148	3.0 0.4 3.3 0.3
24	M	0320 1001 1535 2231	3.0 0.4 3.2 0.4
25	TU ☽	0406 1045 1623 2314	2.9 0.5 3.1 0.5
26	W	0454 1133 1715	2.9 0.6 3.0
27	TH	0002 0547 1231 1819	0.7 2.9 0.7 2.9
28	F	0107 0656 1350 1941	0.8 2.9 0.8 2.8
29	SA	0231 0819 1519 2108	0.9 2.9 0.9 2.9
30	SU	0354 0938 1638 2221	0.9 3.1 0.8 3.0
31	M	0501 1041 1737 2315	0.9 3.2 0.7 3.0

SEPTEMBER

Date	Day	Time	m
1	TU	0551 1128 1822 2357	0.8 3.3 0.6 3.0
2	W ○	0633 1210 1901	0.7 3.3 0.6
3	TH	0035 0711 1246 1936	3.0 0.6 3.3 0.6
4	F	0108 0744 1318 2006	3.1 0.6 3.4 0.6
5	SA	0138 0813 1347 2033	3.1 0.6 3.3 0.6
6	SU	0206 0840 1417 2101	3.1 0.7 3.3 0.7
7	M	0236 0910 1448 2131	3.1 0.7 3.2 0.7
8	TU	0308 0942 1521 2158	3.0 0.7 3.2 0.8
9	W	0337 1009 1551 2220	3.0 0.8 3.1 0.9
10	TH ☾	0405 1036 1624 2251	3.0 0.9 2.9 1.0
11	F	0443 1122 1716 2351	2.9 1.0 2.8 1.1
12	SA	0547 1240 1837	2.8 1.0 2.7
13	SU	0120 0716 1417 2011	1.1 2.7 0.9 2.7
14	M	0256 0845 1547 2133	1.0 2.8 0.7 2.8
15	TU	0416 0956 1656 2235	0.8 3.0 0.5 2.9
16	W	0516 1051 1749 2324	0.7 3.1 0.4 3.0
17	TH ●	0605 1137 1835	0.5 3.2 0.3
18	F	0007 0650 1220 1919	3.0 0.4 3.3 0.2
19	SA	0048 0733 1302 2002	3.1 0.3 3.3 0.2
20	SU	0131 0816 1346 2044	3.0 0.3 3.3 0.2
21	M	0213 0858 1429 2123	3.0 0.3 3.2 0.3
22	TU	0254 0938 1512 2201	3.0 0.4 3.1 0.4
23	W	0336 1019 1558 2241	3.0 0.5 3.0 0.6
24	TH ☽	0422 1106 1650 2329	2.9 0.6 2.9 0.8
25	F	0517 1205 1756	2.9 0.8 2.8
26	SA	0036 0629 1327 1921	1.0 2.9 0.9 2.7
27	SU	0205 0757 1502 2054	1.1 2.9 1.0 2.8
28	M	0337 0924 1626 2211	1.1 3.1 0.9 2.9
29	TU	0448 1028 1723 2302	1.0 3.2 0.8 3.0
30	W	0534 1110 1801 2337	0.9 3.3 0.7 3.0

OCTOBER

Date	Day	Time	m
1	TH ○	0609 1145 1834	0.8 3.3 0.7
2	F	0009 0645 1219 1906	3.1 0.7 3.3 0.6
3	SA	0041 0718 1250 1935	3.1 0.7 3.3 0.6
4	SU	0110 0746 1319 2001	3.2 0.7 3.3 0.7
5	M	0136 0812 1347 2027	3.2 0.7 3.2 0.7
6	TU	0203 0840 1417 2054	3.1 0.7 3.2 0.8
7	W	0232 0909 1447 2120	3.1 0.7 3.1 0.8
8	TH	0301 0937 1519 2146	3.1 0.8 3.0 0.9
9	F	0330 1007 1554 2219	3.0 0.9 2.9 1.0
10	SA ☾	0409 1052 1646 2317	2.9 1.0 2.7 1.1
11	SU	0511 1207 1805	2.8 1.0 2.7
12	M	0045 0638 1344 1939	1.1 2.8 0.9 2.7
13	TU	0223 0810 1518 2105	1.0 2.9 0.7 2.8
14	W	0347 0926 1629 2209	0.8 3.0 0.5 2.9
15	TH	0450 1024 1723 2258	0.7 3.1 0.3 3.0
16	F ●	0540 1112 1809 2341	0.5 3.2 0.2 3.0
17	SA	0625 1156 1852	0.4 3.2 0.2
18	SU	0022 0708 1238 1934	3.1 0.3 3.3 0.2
19	M	0104 0751 1323 2016	3.1 0.3 3.2 0.3
20	TU	0147 0835 1408 2057	3.1 0.4 3.2 0.4
21	W	0229 0917 1453 2135	3.1 0.4 3.1 0.5
22	TH	0311 0958 1538 2214	3.1 0.5 3.0 0.7
23	F ☽	0357 1044 1630 2302	3.0 0.7 2.8 0.9
24	SA	0452 1143 1734	3.0 0.9 2.7
25	SU	0007 0602 1300 1854	1.1 3.0 1.0 2.7
26	M	0131 0726 1431 2023	1.2 3.0 1.1 2.7
27	TU	0302 0851 1553 2140	1.2 3.1 1.0 2.8
28	W	0415 0957 1651 2232	1.0 3.2 0.9 3.0
29	TH	0503 1040 1728 2306	0.9 3.3 0.8 3.1
30	F	0538 1113 1759 2338	0.9 3.3 0.7 3.1
31	SA ○	0613 1147 1832	0.8 3.3 0.7

NOVEMBER

Date	Day	Time	m
1	SU	0010 0648 1221 1903	3.1 0.7 3.2 0.7
2	M	0040 0718 1251 1930	3.2 0.7 3.2 0.7
3	TU	0107 0746 1320 1956	3.2 0.7 3.2 0.7
4	W	0135 0814 1350 2024	3.2 0.7 3.1 0.8
5	TH	0204 0844 1423 2054	3.1 0.7 3.0 0.8
6	F	0236 0917 1459 2126	3.1 0.8 3.0 0.9
7	SA	0310 0953 1541 2206	3.1 0.8 2.9 1.0
8	SU ☾	0353 1041 1633 2302	3.0 0.9 2.8 1.1
9	M	0451 1149 1743	2.9 0.9 2.7
10	TU	0019 0609 1315 1907	1.1 2.9 0.8 2.7
11	W	0149 0734 1442 2030	1.0 2.9 0.7 2.8
12	TH	0311 0851 1555 2136	0.9 3.0 0.5 2.9
13	F	0416 0952 1651 2227	0.7 3.2 0.4 3.0
14	SA	0510 1044 1739 2313	0.6 3.2 0.4 3.0
15	SU ●	0558 1132 1824 2356	0.5 3.2 0.4 3.1
16	M	0643 1217 1907	0.4 3.2 0.4
17	TU	0039 0728 1303 1951	3.2 0.4 3.2 0.5
18	W	0124 0814 1352 2035	3.2 0.4 3.1 0.6
19	TH	0210 0901 1439 2116	3.2 0.5 3.1 0.7
20	F	0254 0945 1524 2156	3.2 0.6 3.0 0.8
21	SA	0339 1029 1612 2240	3.2 0.7 2.9 1.0
22	SU ☽	0430 1122 1708 2337	3.1 0.9 2.8 1.1
23	M	0530 1227 1815	3.1 1.0 2.7
24	TU	0047 0641 1341 1931	1.2 3.0 1.0 2.7
25	W	0207 0757 1456 2044	1.1 3.0 1.0 2.8
26	TH	0320 0905 1557 2142	1.0 3.1 0.9 2.9
27	F	0417 0957 1642 2225	0.9 3.1 0.8 3.0
28	SA	0500 1037 1720 2302	0.9 3.2 0.8 3.1
29	SU	0539 1115 1757 2337	0.8 3.2 0.7 3.1
30	M ○	0617 1152 1832	0.7 3.2 0.7

DECEMBER

Date	Day	Time	m
1	TU	0011 0650 1225 1902	3.1 0.7 3.1 0.7
2	W	0041 0722 1258 1933	3.2 0.7 3.1 0.7
3	TH	0113 0756 1334 2006	3.2 0.7 3.1 0.7
4	F	0147 0831 1410 2040	3.2 0.7 3.0 0.8
5	SA	0222 0908 1450 2118	3.2 0.7 3.0 0.8
6	SU	0301 0950 1535 2202	3.2 0.8 2.9 0.9
7	M	0346 1039 1626 2254	3.1 0.8 2.8 0.9
8	TU ☾	0439 1137 1725 2358	3.1 0.8 2.8 0.9
9	W	0543 1247 1835	3.0 0.7 2.7
10	TH	0113 0658 1403 1949	0.9 3.0 0.7 2.8
11	F	0230 0813 1514 2057	0.9 3.1 0.6 2.9
12	SA	0339 0920 1616 2155	0.8 3.2 0.6 3.0
13	SU	0440 1018 1710 2246	0.7 3.2 0.5 3.1
14	M ●	0535 1112 1801 2335	0.5 3.2 0.5 3.1
15	TU	0625 1202 1848	0.5 3.2 0.5
16	W	0022 0713 1251 1934	3.2 0.4 3.2 0.6
17	TH	0109 0802 1340 2021	3.2 0.5 3.1 0.6
18	F	0157 0850 1428 2102	3.3 0.5 3.0 0.7
19	SA	0241 0934 1510 2140	3.3 0.6 3.0 0.7
20	SU	0322 1014 1552 2219	3.3 0.7 2.9 0.8
21	M	0405 1058 1637 2305	3.2 0.8 2.8 0.9
22	TU ☽	0454 1147 1729 2358	3.1 0.9 2.8 1.0
23	W	0549 1241 1827	3.0 0.9 2.7
24	TH	0059 0650 1342 1930	1.0 3.0 0.9 2.8
25	F	0208 0757 1446 2035	1.0 3.0 0.9 2.8
26	SA	0314 0900 1545 2133	0.9 3.0 0.9 2.9
27	SU	0413 0955 1637 2222	0.9 3.0 0.9 3.0
28	M	0504 1043 1723 2306	0.8 3.0 0.8 3.0
29	TU	0548 1126 1804 2345	0.8 3.1 0.7 3.1
30	W ○	0628 1205 1841	0.7 3.1 0.7
31	TH	0021 0705 1243 1918	3.2 0.7 3.1 0.7

CUXHAVEN
LAT 53°52′N
LONG 8°43′E

TIMES AND HEIGHTS OF HIGH AND LOW WATER (Heights in Metres)

TIME ZONE –0100 (German Standard Time). **Subtract 1 hour for UT. For German Summer Time (area enclosed in shaded box) add 1 hour**

2020

SUNRISE AND SUNSET TIMES

CUXHAVEN
At 53°52′N 8°43′E
European Standard Time (UT-1)

		Sunrise	Sunset
Jan	01	0843	1614
	15	0835	1635
Feb	01	0811	1707
	15	0745	1735
Mar	01	0713	1802
	15	0640	1829
European Summer Time (UT-2)			
Apr	01	0658	2001
	15	0625	2027
May	01	0549	2056
	15	0523	2121
Jun	01	0501	2146
	15	0453	2158
Jul	01	0458	2159
	15	0513	2148
Aug	01	0539	2123
	15	0603	2055
Sep	01	0634	2015
	15	0658	1941
Oct	01	0727	1901
	15	0753	1828
European Standard Time (UT-1)			
Nov	01	0725	1651
	15	0752	1626
Dec	01	0820	1608
	15	0837	1603

JANUARY

Day	Time	m	Time	m	Time	m	Time	m
1 W	0434	3.8	1128	0.7	1701	3.4	2330	0.8
2 TH	0512	3.7	1205	0.8	1741	3.3		
3 F ☽	0009	0.9	0554	3.6	1246	0.8	1826	3.3
4 SA	0054	0.9	0642	3.5	1332	0.9	1917	3.3
5 SU	0150	0.9	0740	3.4	1430	0.9	2017	3.3
6 M	0258	0.9	0846	3.4	1537	0.9	2123	3.3
7 TU	0411	0.9	0953	3.5	1645	0.8	2227	3.4
8 W	0519	0.8	1054	3.6	1746	0.8	2325	3.5
9 TH	0618	0.7	1148	3.6	1841	0.7		
10 F ○	0015	3.6	0709	0.6	1238	3.7	1928	0.6
11 SA	0100	3.7	0756	0.6	1326	3.7	2013	0.6
12 SU	0143	3.8	0844	0.6	1413	3.7	2100	0.6
13 M	0228	3.9	0933	0.5	1501	3.7	2147	0.6
14 TU	0314	3.9	1020	0.4	1548	3.6	2231	0.6
15 W	0358	3.9	1105	0.4	1634	3.6	2314	0.6
16 TH	0443	3.9	1151	0.5	1722	3.5		
17 F ☾	0000	0.6	0531	3.8	1238	0.5	1812	3.4
18 SA	0048	0.6	0623	3.7	1327	0.6	1906	3.3
19 SU	0142	0.7	0723	3.6	1425	0.6	2007	3.3
20 M	0248	0.7	0834	3.5	1535	0.7	2118	3.4
21 TU	0406	0.8	0951	3.5	1651	0.8	2228	3.5
22 W	0523	0.7	1102	3.6	1758	0.7	2330	3.6
23 TH	0629	0.6	1203	3.6	1854	0.6		
24 F ●	0023	3.6	0723	0.5	1254	3.5	1942	0.6
25 SA	0110	3.7	0810	0.4	1340	3.5	2024	0.5
26 SU	0153	3.7	0851	0.4	1420	3.5	2103	0.5
27 M	0230	3.8	0929	0.4	1457	3.5	2137	0.5
28 TU	0304	3.8	1003	0.4	1528	3.5	2207	0.5
29 W	0335	3.8	1033	0.5	1558	3.4	2235	0.5
30 TH	0407	3.7	1104	0.5	1631	3.4	2307	0.5
31 F	0442	3.7	1137	0.6	1706	3.4		

FEBRUARY

Day	Time	m	Time	m	Time	m	Time	m
1 SA	0517	3.6	1206	0.6	1738	3.3		
2 SU ☽	0009	0.6	0550	3.5	1234	0.7	1812	3.3
3 M	0044	0.7	0632	3.4	1314	0.8	1902	3.2
4 TU	0140	0.8	0734	3.3	1419	0.8	2012	3.2
5 W	0300	0.8	0852	3.3	1542	0.8	2131	3.3
6 TH	0428	0.7	1013	3.4	1704	0.8	2246	3.4
7 F	0546	0.6	1123	3.5	1814	0.7	2350	3.6
8 SA	0651	0.5	1223	3.6	1912	0.6		
9 SU ○	0043	3.7	0745	0.5	1315	3.7	2003	0.5
10 M	0130	3.8	0835	0.4	1403	3.7	2052	0.5
11 TU	0215	3.9	0925	0.3	1450	3.7	2140	0.4
12 W	0301	3.9	1012	0.3	1536	3.7	2223	0.4
13 TH	0346	3.9	1056	0.3	1620	3.6	2304	0.4
14 F	0430	3.9	1138	0.3	1703	3.5	2346	0.4
15 SA ☾	0515	3.8	1218	0.4	1747	3.5		
16 SU	0027	0.4	0600	3.7	1257	0.5	1832	3.4
17 M	0110	0.5	0652	3.5	1343	0.6	1927	3.3
18 TU	0209	0.6	0800	3.4	1451	0.7	2038	3.3
19 W	0331	0.7	0923	3.3	1615	0.8	2159	3.4
20 TH	0500	0.7	1046	3.4	1736	0.7	2313	3.5
21 F	0616	0.6	1152	3.4	1839	0.6		
22 SA	0010	3.6	0713	0.4	1243	3.4	1927	0.5
23 SU ●	0056	3.7	0757	0.4	1325	3.4	2009	0.4
24 M	0135	3.7	0835	0.3	1402	3.4	2046	0.4
25 TU	0210	3.7	0910	0.3	1435	3.5	2118	0.3
26 W	0241	3.7	0940	0.3	1503	3.5	2145	0.3
27 TH	0310	3.7	1007	0.3	1531	3.5	2213	0.3
28 F	0341	3.6	1035	0.4	1601	3.4	2244	0.4
29 SA	0414	3.6	1106	0.4	1632	3.4	2314	0.4

MARCH

Day	Time	m	Time	m	Time	m	Time	m
1 SU	0444	3.6	1131	0.5	1659	3.4	2335	0.5
2 M ☽	0510	3.5	1148	0.6	1723	3.3	2357	0.6
3 TU	0542	3.3	1216	0.7	1804	3.2		
4 W	0043	0.7	0639	3.2	1317	0.8	1915	3.2
5 TH	0205	0.7	0804	3.2	1450	0.8	2045	3.2
6 F	0346	0.7	0939	3.2	1628	0.8	2213	3.4
7 SA	0519	0.5	1102	3.4	1752	0.7	2326	3.5
8 SU	0634	0.4	1208	3.5	1857	0.5		
9 M ○	0024	3.7	0733	0.3	1301	3.6	1951	0.4
10 TU	0113	3.8	0822	0.2	1347	3.7	2039	0.3
11 W	0158	3.9	0908	0.2	1431	3.7	2124	0.2
12 TH	0243	3.9	0953	0.2	1515	3.7	2207	0.2
13 F	0328	3.9	1036	0.2	1558	3.6	2247	0.2
14 SA	0412	3.8	1115	0.2	1638	3.6	2326	0.2
15 SU	0455	3.7	1150	0.3	1718	3.5		
16 M ☾	0003	0.3	0537	3.5	1223	0.4	1759	3.4
17 TU	0042	0.4	0625	3.3	1304	0.6	1851	3.3
18 W	0136	0.5	0731	3.2	1410	0.7	2004	3.2
19 TH	0258	0.6	0857	3.1	1540	0.8	2132	3.3
20 F	0434	0.6	1026	3.2	1711	0.7	2253	3.5
21 SA	0558	0.5	1137	3.3	1820	0.6	2353	3.6
22 SU	0655	0.4	1225	3.4	1906	0.5		
23 M	0034	3.6	0735	0.3	1302	3.4	1945	0.4
24 TU ●	0110	3.6	0810	0.3	1337	3.4	2022	0.3
25 W	0145	3.6	0843	0.2	1409	3.5	2055	0.2
26 TH	0216	3.6	0912	0.2	1436	3.5	2123	0.2
27 F	0244	3.6	0938	0.3	1503	3.5	2149	0.3
28 SA	0314	3.6	1005	0.3	1531	3.5	2218	0.3
29 SU	0345	3.5	1033	0.4	1600	3.5	2247	0.3
30 M	0415	3.5	1058	0.4	1627	3.5	2310	0.4
31 TU	0443	3.4	1118	0.5	1653	3.4		

APRIL

Day	Time	m	Time	m	Time	m	Time	m
1 W ☽	0517	3.3	1145	0.7	1733	3.3		
2 TH	0016	0.6	0612	3.2	1243	0.8	1841	3.2
3 F	0134	0.6	0736	3.1	1416	0.8	2012	3.2
4 SA	0316	0.6	0913	3.2	1559	0.7	2144	3.4
5 SU	0454	0.4	1040	3.3	1727	0.6	2300	3.5
6 M	0611	0.2	1147	3.5	1835	0.4		
7 TU	0000	3.7	0711	0.1	1240	3.6	1930	0.3
8 W ○	0051	3.8	0801	0.1	1325	3.6	2018	0.2
9 TH	0137	3.8	0844	0.1	1407	3.7	2102	0.1
10 F	0221	3.8	0926	0.1	1449	3.7	2144	0.1
11 SA	0306	3.8	1008	0.2	1531	3.7	2226	0.1
12 SU	0352	3.7	1047	0.3	1612	3.6	2304	0.2
13 M	0435	3.5	1122	0.3	1651	3.5	2341	0.3
14 TU ☾	0517	3.4	1154	0.5	1732	3.5		
15 W	0020	0.4	0605	3.2	1234	0.7	1824	3.4
16 TH	0112	0.5	0707	3.1	1336	0.8	1933	3.3
17 F	0228	0.7	0828	3.1	1502	0.9	2058	3.4
18 SA	0400	0.6	0955	3.1	1634	0.8	2221	3.5
19 SU	0525	0.5	1106	3.2	1746	0.6	2322	3.6
20 M	0622	0.4	1154	3.3	1834	0.5		
21 TU	0003	3.6	0700	0.3	1230	3.4	1912	0.4
22 W	0038	3.6	0735	0.3	1304	3.5	1951	0.4
23 TH ●	0114	3.6	0810	0.2	1338	3.5	2027	0.3
24 F	0148	3.6	0841	0.2	1407	3.5	2056	0.3
25 SA	0217	3.6	0907	0.3	1434	3.6	2124	0.3
26 SU	0247	3.5	0934	0.3	1502	3.5	2152	0.3
27 M	0318	3.5	1002	0.3	1533	3.5	2223	0.3
28 TU	0353	3.4	1032	0.4	1605	3.5	2255	0.3
29 W	0430	3.4	1102	0.5	1640	3.5	2328	0.4
30 TH ☽	0512	3.3	1138	0.6	1724	3.4		

MAY

Day	Time	m	Time	m	Time	m	Time	m
1 F	0014	0.5	0608	3.2	1235	0.7	1827	3.4
2 SA	0125	0.5	0724	3.1	1358	0.7	1950	3.3
3 SU	0255	0.4	0852	3.2	1533	0.6	2117	3.4
4 M	0426	0.3	1014	3.3	1658	0.5	2231	3.6
5 TU	0541	0.2	1120	3.4	1806	0.4	2333	3.7
6 W	0641	0.1	1213	3.6	1903	0.3		
7 TH ○	0026	3.8	0733	0.1	1300	3.6	1953	0.2
8 F	0115	3.8	0817	0.1	1343	3.7	2038	0.2
9 SA	0200	3.8	0858	0.2	1424	3.7	2121	0.2
10 SU	0246	3.7	0939	0.3	1506	3.7	2203	0.2
11 M	0333	3.6	1020	0.4	1549	3.7	2245	0.3
12 TU	0418	3.5	1057	0.5	1630	3.7	2324	0.4
13 W	0501	3.4	1132	0.6	1712	3.6		
14 TH ☾	0004	0.5	0547	3.2	1212	0.8	1801	3.6
15 F	0053	0.6	0643	3.1	1306	0.9	1902	3.5
16 SA	0156	0.7	0751	3.1	1419	0.9	2015	3.5
17 SU	0314	0.7	0908	3.1	1541	0.8	2131	3.5
18 M	0431	0.6	1016	3.2	1654	0.7	2234	3.5
19 TU	0530	0.5	1108	3.3	1748	0.6	2321	3.6
20 W	0614	0.4	1149	3.4	1832	0.5		
21 TH	0000	3.6	0654	0.4	1227	3.5	1914	0.4
22 F ●	0039	3.6	0733	0.3	1303	3.5	1954	0.4
23 SA	0116	3.6	0807	0.3	1336	3.6	2027	0.3
24 SU	0150	3.6	0838	0.3	1406	3.6	2059	0.3
25 M	0224	3.5	0908	0.3	1439	3.6	2132	0.3
26 TU	0300	3.5	0941	0.3	1515	3.6	2209	0.3
27 W	0340	3.4	1018	0.4	1553	3.6	2248	0.3
28 TH	0425	3.4	1058	0.5	1635	3.6	2332	0.4
29 F	0514	3.3	1143	0.6	1724	3.6		
30 SA ☽	0023	0.4	0611	3.3	1238	0.6	1823	3.5
31 SU	0125	0.4	0717	3.2	1347	0.6		

JUNE

Day	Time	m	Time	m	Time	m	Time	m
1 M	0239	0.4	0831	3.2	1507	0.6	2051	3.5
2 TU	0357	0.4	0946	3.3	1625	0.6	2203	3.6
3 W	0508	0.3	1050	3.5	1733	0.5	2306	3.8
4 TH	0609	0.3	1145	3.6	1833	0.5		
5 F ○	0002	3.8	0704	0.3	1234	3.7	1928	0.4
6 SA	0055	3.8	0752	0.3	1320	3.8	2017	0.3
7 SU	0143	3.7	0835	0.4	1404	3.8	2101	0.4
8 M	0230	3.7	0918	0.5	1447	3.9	2146	0.4
9 TU	0317	3.6	0959	0.6	1530	3.9	2229	0.4
10 W	0401	3.6	1037	0.6	1611	3.9	2308	0.5
11 TH	0442	3.5	1112	0.7	1652	3.9	2348	0.6
12 F	0525	3.3	1150	0.8	1736	3.8		
13 SA ☾	0031	0.7	0613	3.3	1236	0.9	1826	3.7
14 SU	0121	0.7	0707	3.2	1332	0.9	1924	3.6
15 M	0218	0.7	0808	3.2	1437	0.8	2028	3.5
16 TU	0322	0.7	0911	3.2	1546	0.7	2133	3.5
17 W	0424	0.6	1009	3.3	1649	0.7	2229	3.5
18 TH	0519	0.5	1100	3.4	1744	0.6	2317	3.5
19 F	0608	0.5	1146	3.5	1834	0.5		
20 SA	0003	3.5	0655	0.4	1229	3.5	1919	0.4
21 SU ●	0046	3.6	0736	0.4	1308	3.6	2000	0.4
22 M	0127	3.6	0813	0.4	1345	3.7	2040	0.3
23 TU	0208	3.6	0851	0.4	1424	3.7	2121	0.3
24 W	0251	3.5	0931	0.4	1504	3.7	2203	0.3
25 TH	0335	3.5	1012	0.4	1546	3.7	2246	0.3
26 F	0421	3.4	1056	0.5	1631	3.8	2334	0.4
27 SA	0512	3.4	1144	0.6	1721	3.7		
28 SU ☽	0025	0.4	0607	3.3	1236	0.6	1816	3.7
29 M	0120	0.4	0705	3.3	1333	0.6	1916	3.7
30 TU	0219	0.5	0808	3.3	1440	0.7	2025	3.6

CUXHAVEN
LAT 53°52′N
LONG 8°43′E

TIMES AND HEIGHTS OF HIGH AND LOW WATER (Heights in Metres)

TIME ZONE –0100 (German Standard Time). **Subtract 1 hour for UT. For German Summer Time (area enclosed in shaded box) add 1 hour**

2020

JULY

Date	Day	Time	m
1	W	0327 0915 1553 2137	0.5 3.4 0.7 3.7
2	TH	0436 1021 1705 2244	0.6 3.6 0.7 3.8
3	F	0541 1119 1810 2345	0.6 3.7 0.6 3.8
4	SA	0639 1213 1909	0.6 3.8 0.5
5	SU O	0041 0732 1304 2002	3.7 0.5 3.8 0.5
6	M	0132 0819 1351 2049	3.7 0.5 3.9 0.5
7	TU	0219 0903 1434 2133	3.7 0.6 4.0 0.5
8	W	0303 0943 1513 2214	3.7 0.6 4.0 0.5
9	TH	0343 1018 1550 2249	3.6 0.6 4.0 0.6
10	F	0419 1050 1626 2324	3.5 0.7 4.0 0.6
11	SA	0456 1125 1706	3.4 0.7 3.9
12	SU	0003 0537 1205 1749	0.7 3.4 0.8 3.8
13	M ☾	0042 0620 1246 1833	0.7 3.3 0.8 3.6
14	TU	0120 0705 1332 1923	0.7 3.3 0.8 3.5
15	W	0207 0758 1431 2023	0.7 3.3 0.8 3.4
16	TH	0308 0901 1541 2130	0.7 3.3 0.8 3.4
17	F	0416 1006 1652 2234	0.7 3.3 0.7 3.4
18	SA	0522 1106 1756 2331	0.6 3.4 0.6 3.5
19	SU	0620 1159 1851	0.5 3.5 0.5
20	M ●	0023 0710 1245 1940	3.5 0.5 3.6 0.4
21	TU	0111 0756 1328 2027	3.6 0.5 3.7 0.4
22	W	0157 0841 1411 2113	3.6 0.5 3.8 0.3
23	TH	0242 0925 1454 2158	3.6 0.4 3.8 0.3
24	F	0327 1007 1536 2241	3.6 0.4 3.9 0.3
25	SA	0412 1049 1621 2326	3.5 0.4 3.8 0.3
26	SU	0459 1135 1709	3.5 0.5 3.8
27	M ☽	0014 0551 1224 1800	0.4 3.4 0.5 3.8
28	TU	0102 0642 1313 1854	0.5 3.4 0.6 3.7
29	W	0151 0738 1411 1959	0.6 3.4 0.7 3.6
30	TH	0253 0843 1523 2114	0.7 3.4 0.8 3.6
31	F	0407 0955 1643 2231	0.8 3.5 0.8 3.6

AUGUST

Date	Day	Time	m
1	SA	0521 1103 1757 2338	0.8 3.7 0.7 3.7
2	SU	0624 1201 1859	0.7 3.8 0.6
3	M O	0034 0719 1253 1952	3.7 0.7 3.9 0.5
4	TU	0124 0807 1340 2039	3.7 0.6 3.9 0.5
5	W	0208 0850 1420 2119	3.7 0.6 4.0 0.6
6	TH	0246 0926 1454 2154	3.7 0.6 4.0 0.6
7	F	0320 0956 1526 2224	3.6 0.6 4.0 0.6
8	SA	0350 1024 1558 2254	3.6 0.6 3.9 0.6
9	SU	0423 1057 1634 2328	3.5 0.6 3.8 0.7
10	M	0459 1132 1711	3.5 0.7 3.7
11	TU ☾	0000 0533 1203 1745	0.7 3.4 0.8 3.6
12	W	0026 0606 1234 1822	0.8 3.4 0.8 3.5
13	TH	0058 0648 1321 1917	0.9 3.3 0.9 3.3
14	F	0154 0753 1435 2032	0.9 3.3 0.9 3.3
15	SA	0314 0912 1603 2154	0.9 3.3 0.8 3.3
16	SU	0439 1029 1724 2306	0.8 3.4 0.7 3.4
17	M	0552 1134 1831	0.7 3.5 0.5
18	TU	0006 0652 1226 1925	3.5 0.6 3.7 0.4
19	W ●	0057 0742 1312 2014	3.6 0.5 3.8 0.4
20	TH	0143 0829 1355 2101	3.6 0.4 3.9 0.3
21	F	0228 0914 1438 2145	3.6 0.4 3.9 0.2
22	SA	0311 0956 1521 2227	3.6 0.3 3.9 0.2
23	SU	0354 1036 1605 2309	3.5 0.3 3.8 0.3
24	M	0438 1118 1650 2350	3.5 0.4 3.8 0.4
25	TU ☽	0524 1202 1737	3.4 0.5 3.7
26	W	0032 0611 1246 1828	0.5 3.4 0.6 3.5
27	TH	0116 0704 1340 1932	0.6 3.4 0.7 3.4
28	F	0218 0812 1456 2054	0.8 3.4 0.8 3.4
29	SA	0340 0933 1627 2222	0.9 3.5 0.9 3.4
30	SU	0506 1053 1751 2335	0.9 3.6 0.8 3.5
31	M	0617 1156 1854	0.9 3.8 0.7

SEPTEMBER

Date	Day	Time	m
1	TU	0030 0709 1243 1941	3.6 0.8 3.9 0.6
2	W O	0113 0752 1324 2022	3.6 0.7 3.9 0.6
3	TH	0151 0831 1400 2058	3.6 0.6 4.0 0.6
4	F	0224 0905 1431 2128	3.7 0.6 4.0 0.6
5	SA	0253 0933 1500 2155	3.7 0.6 3.9 0.6
6	SU	0320 0959 1529 2221	3.6 0.6 3.9 0.7
7	M	0349 1028 1601 2251	3.6 0.7 3.8 0.7
8	TU	0420 1059 1633 2318	3.6 0.7 3.7 0.8
9	W	0449 1125 1702 2339	3.5 0.8 3.6 0.8
10	TH ☾	0516 1148 1734	3.5 0.9 3.4
11	F	0004 0553 1228 1825	0.9 3.4 1.0 3.3
12	SA	0056 0657 1342 1945	1.0 3.3 1.0 3.2
13	SU	0223 0826 1521 2119	1.0 3.2 0.9 3.2
14	M	0402 0955 1657 2244	0.9 3.3 0.7 3.3
15	TU	0528 1109 1811 2349	0.8 3.5 0.5 3.5
16	W	0633 1205 1909	0.6 3.6 0.3
17	TH ●	0039 0725 1252 1957	3.5 0.5 3.8 0.3
18	F	0124 0812 1335 2041	3.6 0.4 3.8 0.2
19	SA	0206 0856 1418 2124	3.6 0.3 3.9 0.2
20	SU	0249 0938 1502 2205	3.6 0.3 3.8 0.2
21	M	0331 1018 1545 2245	3.6 0.3 3.8 0.3
22	TU	0412 1057 1629 2322	3.5 0.3 3.7 0.4
23	W	0453 1137 1714 2358	3.5 0.4 3.5 0.6
24	TH ☽	0538 1219 1804	3.4 0.6 3.4
25	F	0041 0631 1313 1908	0.8 3.3 0.7 3.3
26	SA	0144 0743 1431 2033	1.0 3.3 0.9 3.2
27	SU	0312 0911 1608 2206	1.1 3.4 1.0 3.3
28	M	0448 1038 1738 2325	1.1 3.6 0.9 3.4
29	TU	0604 1143 1842	1.0 3.8 0.8
30	W	0016 0654 1225 1922	3.5 0.9 3.9 0.7

OCTOBER

Date	Day	Time	m
1	TH O	0052 0730 1259 1955	3.6 0.8 3.9 0.7
2	F	0125 0806 1333 2028	3.6 0.7 3.9 0.6
3	SA	0156 0840 1404 2058	3.7 0.6 3.9 0.6
4	SU	0224 0908 1433 2124	3.7 0.6 3.9 0.7
5	M	0250 0934 1501 2149	3.7 0.7 3.8 0.7
6	TU	0316 1000 1530 2214	3.7 0.7 3.7 0.7
7	W	0344 1028 1600 2240	3.6 0.7 3.6 0.8
8	TH	0412 1054 1630 2303	3.6 0.8 3.5 0.9
9	F	0440 1120 1704 2331	3.5 0.8 3.4 1.0
10	SA ☾	0518 1200 1755	3.4 0.9 3.2
11	SU	0022 0621 1311 1913	1.1 3.3 1.0 3.1
12	M	0148 0748 1449 2048	1.1 3.3 0.9 3.2
13	TU	0330 0921 1628 2217	0.9 3.3 0.7 3.3
14	W	0500 1039 1746 2324	0.8 3.5 0.4 3.4
15	TH	0608 1138 1844	0.6 3.6 0.3
16	F ●	0015 0701 1227 1932	3.5 0.5 3.7 0.2
17	SA	0059 0748 1312 2016	3.5 0.3 3.8 0.2
18	SU	0140 0832 1355 2057	3.6 0.3 3.8 0.2
19	M	0222 0915 1439 2139	3.6 0.3 3.8 0.3
20	TU	0305 0957 1525 2219	3.6 0.3 3.7 0.4
21	W	0347 1037 1610 2256	3.6 0.4 3.6 0.5
22	TH	0428 1116 1655 2332	3.5 0.4 3.4 0.7
23	F ☽	0512 1159 1744	3.5 0.6 3.3
24	SA	0014 0605 1252 1846	0.9 3.4 0.8 3.2
25	SU	0114 0714 1405 2005	1.1 3.4 1.0 3.2
26	M	0238 0838 1537 2133	1.2 3.5 1.0 3.2
27	TU	0412 1003 1706 2252	1.2 3.6 1.0 3.3
28	W	0532 1111 1810 2345	1.0 3.7 0.9 3.5
29	TH	0624 1155 1849	0.9 3.8 0.8
30	F	0020 0700 1227 1921	3.6 0.8 3.8 0.7
31	SA O	0052 0735 1301 1954	3.6 0.7 3.8 0.7

NOVEMBER

Date	Day	Time	m
1	SU	0124 0810 1335 2026	3.7 0.7 3.8 0.6
2	M	0154 0841 1405 2053	3.7 0.6 3.8 0.7
3	TU	0220 0908 1434 2118	3.7 0.7 3.7 0.7
4	W	0247 0936 1504 2145	3.7 0.7 3.6 0.7
5	TH	0316 1004 1536 2213	3.7 0.7 3.6 0.8
6	F	0347 1035 1611 2243	3.6 0.7 3.5 0.8
7	SA	0421 1109 1652 2318	3.6 0.8 3.4 0.9
8	SU ☾	0503 1153 1743	3.5 0.9 3.3
9	M	0010 0601 1257 1853	1.0 3.4 0.9 3.2
10	TU	0126 0718 1423 2018	1.0 3.4 0.8 3.2
11	W	0258 0845 1554 2142	0.9 3.4 0.6 3.3
12	TH	0425 1003 1712 2250	0.8 3.5 0.5 3.4
13	F	0534 1106 1813 2344	0.7 3.7 0.4 3.5
14	SA	0631 1159 1904	0.5 3.7 0.3
15	SU ●	0030 0722 1248 1949	3.6 0.4 3.8 0.3
16	M	0114 0808 1333 2031	3.6 0.4 3.8 0.4
17	TU	0157 0852 1420 2114	3.7 0.4 3.7 0.5
18	W	0241 0937 1508 2158	3.7 0.4 3.7 0.5
19	TH	0326 1022 1556 2238	3.7 0.4 3.6 0.6
20	F	0410 1104 1641 2314	3.7 0.5 3.4 0.7
21	SA	0453 1146 1727 2354	3.7 0.7 3.3 0.9
22	SU ☽	0542 1234 1821	3.6 0.8 3.2
23	M	0046 0641 1335 1926	1.1 3.6 1.0 3.2
24	TU	0155 0751 1449 2041	1.1 3.6 1.0 3.2
25	W	0316 0908 1608 2154	1.1 3.6 1.0 3.3
26	TH	0433 1017 1714 2253	1.0 3.6 0.9 3.4
27	F	0534 1110 1802 2337	0.9 3.7 0.8 3.5
28	SA	0619 1149 1841	0.8 3.7 0.8
29	SU	0014 0659 1227 1918	3.6 0.8 3.7 0.7
30	M O	0050 0738 1304 1953	3.6 0.7 3.7 0.6

DECEMBER

Date	Day	Time	m
1	TU	0123 0813 1339 2024	3.6 0.6 3.7 0.7
2	W	0154 0845 1412 2054	3.7 0.6 3.6 0.7
3	TH	0226 0918 1447 2126	3.7 0.7 3.6 0.7
4	F	0259 0952 1524 2200	3.7 0.7 3.6 0.7
5	SA	0334 1028 1603 2236	3.7 0.7 3.5 0.8
6	SU	0412 1108 1647 2317	3.7 0.7 3.4 0.9
7	M	0456 1155 1738	3.7 0.7 3.4
8	TU ☾	0007 0548 1250 1837	0.9 3.6 0.7 3.3
9	W	0109 0652 1358 1947	0.9 3.5 0.7 3.2
10	TH	0224 0807 1515 2101	0.9 3.5 0.6 3.3
11	F	0344 0923 1631 2210	0.8 3.6 0.6 3.4
12	SA	0456 1031 1737 2309	0.7 3.7 0.5 3.5
13	SU	0600 1131 1834	0.6 3.7 0.5
14	M ●	0002 0657 1227 1925	3.6 0.5 3.7 0.5
15	TU	0051 0749 1318 2012	3.6 0.4 3.7 0.5
16	W	0138 0837 1407 2057	3.7 0.4 3.7 0.5
17	TH	0224 0925 1457 2142	3.8 0.4 3.6 0.6
18	F	0311 1012 1544 2224	3.8 0.5 3.6 0.6
19	SA	0355 1054 1626 2300	3.8 0.5 3.5 0.7
20	SU	0435 1133 1707 2336	3.8 0.6 3.4 0.8
21	M	0517 1214 1751	3.8 0.7 3.3
22	TU ☽	0017 0604 1300 1841	0.9 3.7 0.8 3.2
23	W	0107 0658 1352 1937	0.9 3.6 0.9 3.2
24	TH	0208 0800 1453 2039	0.9 3.5 0.9 3.2
25	F	0317 0906 1558 2143	0.9 3.5 0.9 3.3
26	SA	0427 1010 1700 2241	0.9 3.5 0.9 3.4
27	SU	0528 1104 1754 2331	0.8 3.5 0.8 3.5
28	M	0621 1152 1842	0.8 3.6 0.7
29	TU	0016 0707 1235 1923	3.6 0.7 3.6 0.7
30	W O	0056 0748 1317 2001	3.6 0.7 3.6 0.7
31	TH	0133 0827 1357 2038	3.7 0.6 3.6 0.7

HOEK VAN HOLLAND

LAT 51°51'N
LONG 4°03'E
TIMES AND HEIGHTS OF HIGH AND LOW WATER (Heights in Metres)

TIME ZONE –0100 (Dutch Standard Time). **Subtract 1 hour for UT. For Netherlands Summer Time (area enclosed in shaded box) add 1 hour**

2020

JANUARY

Date	Time	m	Date	Time	m
1 W	0141 0636 1154 1902	0.6 1.9 0.2 2.1	**16** TH	0200 0644 1149 1905	0.5 2.0 0.1 2.2
2 TH	0147 0716 1244 1956	0.6 1.9 0.2 2.0	**17** F ☾	0244 0735 1254 2006	0.5 1.9 0.1 2.2
3 F ☽	0227 0813 1344 2050	0.6 1.8 0.2 1.9	**18** SA	0234 0835 1354 2110	0.5 1.9 0.2 2.1
4 SA	0313 0904 1447 2145	0.6 1.8 0.3 1.9	**19** SU	0306 0946 1504 2219	0.5 1.9 0.2 2.0
5 SU	0420 1005 1556 2255	0.6 1.7 0.4 1.9	**20** M	0407 1056 1619 2329	0.5 1.9 0.3 2.0
6 M	0517 1115 1807 2355	0.5 1.8 0.4 2.0	**21** TU	0521 1156 1927	0.5 1.9 0.4
7 TU	0607 1215 1908	0.5 1.9 0.4	**22** W	0039 0838 1255 2057	2.0 0.5 2.0 0.4
8 W	0045 0647 1307 2016	2.0 0.5 2.0 0.4	**23** TH	0134 0939 1349 2200	2.0 0.4 2.1 0.4
9 TH	0129 0704 1349 1915	2.1 0.4 2.1 0.4	**24** F ●	0224 1025 1435 2248	2.1 0.3 2.2 0.5
10 F O	0215 0734 1429 1955	2.2 0.4 2.2 0.4	**25** SA	0308 1105 1518 2328	2.1 0.3 2.3 0.5
11 SA	0257 0809 1511 2025	2.2 0.3 2.3 0.5	**26** SU	0345 0849 1558	2.1 0.3 2.3
12 SU	0337 0845 1555 2349	2.2 0.3 2.4 0.5	**27** M	0012 0424 0918 1637	0.5 2.1 0.2 2.3
13 M	0418 0926 1635	2.1 0.2 2.4	**28** TU	0055 0459 0955 1716	0.5 2.1 0.2 2.2
14 TU	0030 0505 1009 1720	0.5 2.1 0.2 2.4	**29** W	0124 0529 1035 1749	0.5 2.0 0.2 2.2
15 W	0115 0549 1055 1808	0.5 2.0 0.1 2.3	**30** TH	0123 0605 1115 1829	0.6 2.0 0.1 2.1
			31 F	0146 0639 1204 [illegible]	0.5 2.0 0.1 [illegible]

FEBRUARY

Date	Time	m	Date	Time	m
1 SA	0127 0720 1255 1949	0.5 2.0 0.1 2.0	**16** SU	0153 0805 1344 2035	0.5 2.0 0.1 2.0
2 SU ☽	0159 0816 1354 2056	0.5 1.9 0.2 1.9	**17** M	0240 0910 1454 2155	0.4 1.9 0.2 1.8
3 M	0246 0920 1450 2150	0.5 1.8 0.3 1.9	**18** TU	0335 1025 1604 2314	0.4 1.8 0.3 1.8
4 TU	0351 1026 1555 2257	0.5 1.8 0.3 1.8	**19** W	0458 1144 1934	0.4 1.9 0.4
5 W	0530 1140 1725	0.5 1.8 0.4	**20** TH	0025 0554 1249 2115	1.8 0.4 2.0 0.4
6 TH	0010 0617 1235 2007	1.9 0.4 1.9 0.4	**21** F	0125 0935 1344 2212	1.9 0.3 2.1 0.4
7 F	0109 0634 1326 2148	2.0 0.4 2.1 0.4	**22** SA	0215 1014 1435 2247	2.0 0.2 2.2 0.4
8 SA	0155 0714 1411 1935	2.0 0.3 2.2 0.4	**23** SU ●	0305 1105 1505 2320	2.0 0.2 2.2 0.5
9 SU O	0238 0749 1455 2009	2.1 0.3 2.3 0.4	**24** M	0339 0824 1538 2355	2.0 0.2 2.2 0.5
10 M	0321 0826 1535 2327	2.1 0.2 2.4 0.5	**25** TU	0405 0859 1615	2.1 0.2 2.2
11 TU	0404 0905 1618	2.1 0.1 2.4	**26** W	0021 0435 0929 1649	0.5 2.1 0.2 2.2
12 W	0015 0445 0947 1705	0.4 2.1 0.1 2.4	**27** TH	0052 0505 1004 1721	0.5 2.1 0.2 2.2
13 TH	0105 0531 1032 1749	0.4 2.1 0.1 2.3	**28** F	0108 0536 1045 1756	0.4 2.1 0.2 2.1
14 F	0150 0619 1125 1838	0.4 2.1 0.1 2.2	**29** SA	0127 0606 1125 1824	0.4 2.1 0.1 2.1
15 SA ☾	0224 0705 1224 1935	0.5 2.0 0.1 2.1			

MARCH

Date	Time	m	Date	Time	m
1 SU	0004 0639 1205 1855	0.4 2.0 0.1 2.0	**16** M ☾	0052 0736 1334 2009	0.4 2.0 0.2 1.8
2 M ☽	0033 0715 1304 1945	0.4 2.0 0.2 1.9	**17** TU	0207 0839 1435 2125	0.3 1.9 0.2 1.7
3 TU	0200 0804 1418 2100	0.4 1.9 0.2 1.8	**18** W	0310 1011 1559 2308	0.3 1.8 0.3 1.6
4 W	0304 0936 1528 2226	0.4 1.8 0.3 1.7	**19** TH	0425 1126 1857	0.3 1.8 0.4
5 TH	0422 1100 1657 2334	0.4 1.8 0.4 1.7	**20** F	0015 0530 1240 2059	1.7 0.3 2.0 0.3
6 F	0536 1216 2008	0.4 1.9 0.4	**21** SA	0114 0915 1335 2150	1.8 0.2 2.1 0.3
7 SA	0045 0614 1309 2130	1.8 0.3 2.1 0.4	**22** SU	0205 1011 1405 2230	1.9 0.2 2.1 0.3
8 SU	0135 0645 1355 2215	1.9 0.3 2.2 0.4	**23** M	0239 1044 1445 2300	2.0 0.2 2.2 0.4
9 M O	0219 0724 1435 2248	2.0 0.2 2.3 0.4	**24** TU ●	0315 0804 1516 2324	2.0 0.2 2.2 0.4
10 TU	0300 0759 1516 2320	2.1 0.1 2.4 0.4	**25** W	0339 0834 1548 2352	2.0 0.2 2.2 0.4
11 W	0345 0840 1558 2355	2.1 0.1 2.4 0.4	**26** TH	0407 0904 1618	2.1 0.2 2.2
12 TH	0425 0922 1642	2.2 0.0 2.4	**27** F	0007 0435 1229 1651	0.4 2.1 0.2 2.1
13 F	0055 0505 1009 1726	0.4 2.2 0.1 2.3	**28** SA	0038 0506 1259 1722	0.3 2.1 0.2 2.1
14 SA	0140 0548 1103 1812	0.4 2.2 0.1 2.2	**29** SU	0110 0535 1044 1749	0.3 2.1 0.2 2.1
15 SU	0214 0639 1204 1905	0.4 2.1 0.1 2.0	**30** M	0145 0605 1124 1821	0.3 2.1 0.2 2.0
			31 TU	0000 0645 1212 [illegible]	0.3 2.1 0.2 [illegible]

APRIL

Date	Time	m	Date	Time	m
1 W ☽	0036 0729 1352 2004	0.3 2.0 0.3 1.8	**16** TH	0308 0940 1547 2248	0.2 1.8 0.4 1.5
2 TH	0225 0844 1514 2152	0.3 1.8 0.3 1.6	**17** F	0419 1115 1838 2354	0.2 1.8 0.4 1.6
3 F	0325 1036 1622 2310	0.3 1.8 0.4 1.6	**18** SA	0504 1219 2011	0.2 2.0 0.4
4 SA	0446 1145 2000	0.3 1.9 0.4	**19** SU	0045 0559 1305 2115	1.7 0.2 2.1 0.3
5 SU	0015 0534 1245 2110	1.7 0.3 2.1 0.3	**20** M	0135 0935 1345 2205	1.8 0.2 2.1 0.3
6 M	0114 0615 1329 2149	1.8 0.2 2.2 0.3	**21** TU	0209 1004 1419 2238	1.9 0.2 2.1 0.3
7 TU	0155 0656 1411 2228	2.0 0.1 2.3 0.4	**22** W	0234 0754 1446 2302	2.0 0.2 2.2 0.4
8 W O	0235 0735 1455 1959	2.1 0.1 2.4 0.4	**23** TH ●	0305 1034 1519 2326	2.0 0.2 2.2 0.4
9 TH	0319 0815 1535 2345	2.2 0.1 2.4 0.4	**24** F	0337 1108 1552 2348	2.1 0.2 2.2 0.3
10 F	0359 0856 1619	2.2 0.1 2.3	**25** SA	0406 1150 1625	2.1 0.2 2.1
11 SA	0035 0442 0946 1705	0.3 2.2 0.1 2.2	**26** SU	0024 0439 1224 1651	0.3 2.1 0.2 2.1
12 SU	0115 0527 1039 1751	0.3 2.2 0.2 2.1	**27** M	0046 0508 1304 1725	0.3 2.1 0.3 2.0
13 M	0211 0611 1252 1843	0.3 2.2 0.3 1.9	**28** TU	0135 0542 1334 1759	0.3 2.1 0.3 2.0
14 TU ☾	0005 0705 1330 1945	0.3 2.1 0.3 1.7	**29** W	0210 0621 1342 1846	0.2 2.1 0.3 1.9
15 W	0137 0815 1428 2059	0.2 1.9 0.3 1.6	**30** TH ☽	0027 0709 1402 1950	0.2 2.0 0.3 1.7

MAY

Date	Time	m	Date	Time	m
1 F	0149 0824 1507 2120	0.2 1.9 0.3 1.6	**16** SA	0348 1040 1621 2321	0.1 1.8 0.4 1.5
2 SA	0255 1006 1616 2245	0.2 1.9 0.4 1.6	**17** SU	0444 1145 1900	0.1 1.9 0.4
3 SU	0404 1114 1912 2349	0.2 2.0 0.4 1.7	**18** M	0014 0535 1225 2014	1.7 0.2 2.0 0.4
4 M	0456 1216 2035	0.2 2.1 0.3	**19** TU	0055 0614 1305 2112	1.8 0.2 2.0 0.3
5 TU	0045 0545 1304 2130	1.8 0.2 2.2 0.3	**20** W	0130 0716 1346 2200	1.8 0.2 2.1 0.3
6 W	0129 0629 1347 2158	2.0 0.1 2.3 0.4	**21** TH	0204 0911 1416 2233	1.9 0.3 2.1 0.3
7 TH O	0212 0712 1432 1936	2.1 0.1 2.3 0.4	**22** F ●	0235 0955 1449 2303	2.0 0.3 2.1 0.3
8 F	0255 0755 1515 2016	2.2 0.1 2.3 0.3	**23** SA	0306 1038 1525 2340	2.1 0.3 2.1 0.3
9 SA	0337 0839 1600	2.2 0.2 2.2	**24** SU	0339 1120 1556	2.1 0.3 2.1
10 SU	0021 0420 1249 1645	0.3 2.2 0.2 2.1	**25** M	0004 0415 1155 1635	0.3 2.1 0.3 2.0
11 M	0110 0505 1345 1729	0.2 2.2 0.3 2.0	**26** TU	0040 0448 1255 1706	0.2 2.1 0.3 2.0
12 TU	0156 0551 1436 1823	0.2 2.2 0.3 1.8	**27** W	0115 0525 1324 1747	0.2 2.1 0.3 1.9
13 W	0230 0641 1515 1914	0.2 2.1 0.4 1.7	**28** TH	0200 0607 1408 1836	0.2 2.1 0.3 1.8
14 TH ☾	0052 0744 1417 2029	0.1 1.9 0.4 1.6	**29** F	0010 0702 1447 1934	0.1 2.1 0.4 1.7
15 F	0220 0904 1522 2204	0.1 1.8 0.4 1.5	**30** SA ☽	0114 0805 1517 2106	0.1 2.0 0.4 1.6
			31 SU	0229 0943 1718 [illegible]	0.1 2.0 0.4 [illegible]

JUNE

Date	Time	m	Date	Time	m
1 M	0324 1042 1844 2316	0.1 2.0 0.4 1.7	**16** TU	0503 1145 1725	0.2 1.9 0.4
2 TU	0425 1146 1954	0.1 2.1 0.4	**17** W	0005 0604 1225 1815	1.7 0.2 1.9 0.4
3 W	0016 0520 1239 2048	1.8 0.1 2.2 0.4	**18** TH	0045 0654 1305 1856	1.8 0.2 2.0 0.4
4 TH	0105 0609 1326 2134	2.0 0.2 2.2 0.4	**19** F	0127 0726 1346 1926	1.9 0.3 2.1 0.3
5 F O	0148 0656 1415 1923	2.1 0.2 2.2 0.3	**20** SA	0205 0922 1424 1953	2.0 0.3 2.1 0.3
6 SA	0236 0744 1458 2005	2.2 0.3 2.2 0.3	**21** SU ●	0241 1003 1502 2024	2.1 0.4 2.1 0.3
7 SU	0318 0829 1545	2.2 0.3 2.1	**22** M	0316 1052 1538 2055	2.1 0.4 2.1 0.3
8 M	0001 0405 1230 1628	0.2 2.2 0.3 2.0	**23** TU	0355 1148 1616 2129	2.2 0.4 2.0 0.2
9 TU	0055 0447 1317 1718	0.2 2.2 0.4 1.9	**24** W	0432 1224 1656 2209	2.2 0.4 2.0 0.2
10 W	0136 0535 1416 1801	0.1 2.2 0.4 1.9	**25** TH	0514 1315 1739 2255	2.2 0.4 1.9 0.1
11 TH	0220 0625 1455 1849	0.1 2.1 0.4 1.8	**26** F	0557 1405 1829 2345	2.2 0.4 1.9 0.1
12 F	0024 0715 1524 1939	0.1 2.0 0.5 1.7	**27** SA	0649 1440 1925	2.2 0.4 1.8
13 SA ☾	0123 0819 1441 2034	0.1 1.9 0.5 1.6	**28** SU ☽	0049 0755 1513 2025	0.1 2.1 0.4 1.8
14 SU	0307 0925 1547 2134	0.1 1.8 0.4 1.6	**29** M	0155 0906 1634 2140	0.1 2.1 0.5 1.8
15 M	0414 1035 1644 2315	0.1 1.8 0.4 1.6	**30** TU	0255 1010 1603 2246	0.1 2.1 0.5 1.8

SUNRISE AND SUNSET TIMES

HOEK VAN HOLLAND

At 51°51'N 4°03'E

European Standard Time (UT-1)

		Sunrise	Sunset
Jan	01	0852	1643
	15	0845	1702
Feb	01	0824	1731
	15	0759	1757
Mar	01	0730	1823
	15	0659	1848
European Summer Time (UT-2)			
Apr	01	0720	2017
	15	0648	2041
May	01	0615	2108
	15	0551	2131
Jun	01	0530	2154
	15	0523	2205
Jul	01	0528	2207
	15	0541	2157
Aug	01	0605	2134
	15	0627	2108
Sep	01	0655	2032
	15	0718	2000
Oct	01	0744	1922
	15	0808	1851
European Standard Time (UT-1)			
Nov	01	0738	1716
	15	0803	1653

HOEK VAN HOLLAND
LAT 51°51′N
LONG 4°03′E

TIMES AND HEIGHTS OF HIGH AND LOW WATER (Heights in Metres)

TIME ZONE –0100 (Dutch Standard Time). **Subtract 1 hour for UT. For For Netherlands Summer Time (area enclosed in shaded box) add 1 hour**

2020

Low waters - important note. Double low waters often occur. Predictions are for the lower low water which is usually the first.

JULY

Date	Day	Time	m	Time	m	Time	m	Time	m
1	W	0354	0.2	1116	2.1	1904	0.4	2346	1.9
2	TH	0505	0.2	1219	2.1	2016	0.4		
3	F	0041	2.0	0605	0.3	1311	2.1	1834	0.4
4	SA	0135	2.1	0655	0.3	1404	2.1	1915	0.3
5	SU	0220	2.2	1018	0.4	1453	2.1	O 1959	0.3
6	M	0308	2.2	1118	0.4	1535	2.0	2039	0.2
7	TU	0350	2.3	1212	0.5	1625	2.0	2117	0.2
8	W	0435	2.3	1301	0.5	1701	2.0	2205	0.1
9	TH	0518	2.2	1356	0.5	1743	1.9	2255	0.1
10	F	0603	2.2	1430	0.5	1825	1.9	2339	0.1
11	SA	0649	2.1	1504	0.5	1905	1.9		
12	SU	0027	0.1	0735	2.0	1402	0.5	1950	1.8
13	M	0134	0.1	0834	1.9	1452	0.5	☾ 2046	1.7
14	TU	0226	0.2	0924	1.9	1552	0.5	2145	1.7
15	W	0431	0.2	1024	1.8	1700	0.4	2255	1.7
16	TH	0534	0.3	1130	1.9	1758	0.4		
17	F	0000	1.8	0637	0.3	1225	1.9	1834	0.4
18	SA	0049	1.9	0655	0.4	1315	2.0	1904	0.4
19	SU	0139	2.0	0710	0.4	1404	2.0	1929	0.3
20	M	0219	2.1	0743	0.4	1439	2.1	● 1959	0.3
21	TU	0258	2.2	0814	0.5	1525	2.1	2033	0.2
22	W	0337	2.3	1124	0.5	1601	2.1	2109	0.2
23	TH	0417	2.3	1205	0.4	1645	2.0	2146	0.1
24	F	0458	2.3	1255	0.4	1726	2.0	2234	0.1
25	SA	0545	2.3	1335	0.4	1810	2.0	2319	0.1
26	SU	0635	2.2	1416	0.4	1905	1.9		
27	M	0014	0.1	0729	2.2	1500	0.5	☽ 2006	1.9
28	TU	0124	0.1	0836	2.1	1452	0.5	2106	1.9
29	W	0234	0.1	0939	2.0	1534	0.5	2216	1.9
30	TH	0345	0.2	1054	2.0	1636	0.5	2324	1.9
31	F	0454	0.3	1205	2.0	1735	0.4		

AUGUST

Date	Day	Time	m	Time	m	Time	m	Time	m
1	SA	0029	2.0	0554	0.4	1305	2.0	1824	0.4
2	SU	0125	2.1	0935	0.4	1355	2.0	1905	0.3
3	M	0215	2.2	1024	0.5	1449	2.1	O 1949	0.3
4	TU	0258	2.3	1104	0.5	1535	2.1	2025	0.2
5	W	0338	2.3	1155	0.5	1609	2.1	2059	0.2
6	TH	0415	2.3	1245	0.6	1641	2.1	2135	0.2
7	F	0456	2.3	1321	0.5	1715	2.0	2215	0.2
8	SA	0536	2.2	1405	0.6	1752	2.0	2255	0.2
9	SU	0616	2.1	1425	0.6	1825	2.0	2344	0.2
10	M	0656	2.1	1402	0.5	1905	2.0		
11	TU	0034	0.2	0740	2.0	1349	0.5	☾ 1956	1.9
12	W	0124	0.2	0825	1.9	1426	0.5	2056	1.8
13	TH	0239	0.3	0931	1.8	1625	0.5	2200	1.8
14	F	0336	0.4	1035	1.8	1730	0.5	2305	1.8
15	SA	0543	0.4	1144	1.8	1810	0.4		
16	SU	0026	1.9	0633	0.4	1256	1.9	1832	0.4
17	M	0115	2.0	0645	0.5	1339	2.0	1905	0.4
18	TU	0158	2.2	0717	0.5	1424	2.1	1935	0.3
19	W	0238	2.3	0755	0.5	1501	2.1	● 2006	0.2
20	TH	0318	2.4	0825	0.5	1544	2.2	2045	0.2
21	F	0357	2.4	1150	0.5	1624	2.2	2122	0.1
22	SA	0440	2.4	1235	0.5	1705	2.1	2206	0.1
23	SU	0525	2.4	1315	0.5	1748	2.1	2255	0.1
24	M	0610	2.3	1356	0.5	1836	2.1	2345	0.2
25	TU ☽	0705	2.2	1438	0.5	1929	2.1		
26	W	0054	0.2	0804	2.1	1417	0.5	2035	2.0
27	TH	0215	0.3	0916	1.9	1508	0.5	2145	1.9
28	F	0330	0.3	1035	1.8	1619	0.5	2304	1.9
29	SA	0449	0.4	1154	1.8	1714	0.4		
30	SU	0019	2.0	0838	0.5	1255	1.9	1805	0.4
31	M	0125	2.1	0944	0.4	1355	2.0	2155	0.3

SEPTEMBER

Date	Day	Time	m	Time	m	Time	m	Time	m
1	TU	0208	2.2	1037	0.5	1435	2.1	1929	0.3
2	W	0245	2.3	1058	0.6	1515	2.1	O 2009	0.3
3	TH	0324	2.3	1138	0.6	1549	2.1	2035	0.3
4	F	0357	2.3	1210	0.6	1615	2.1	2109	0.2
5	SA	0431	2.3	1249	0.6	1648	2.2	2145	0.2
6	SU	0506	2.2	1321	0.6	1719	2.1	2225	0.3
7	M	0545	2.2	1338	0.6	1752	2.1	2305	0.3
8	TU	0610	2.1	1124	0.5	1824	2.1	2345	0.3
9	W	0635	2.1	1213	0.5	1855	2.1		
10	TH	0036	0.3	0719	2.0	1332	0.5	☾ 1935	2.0
11	F	0158	0.4	0819	1.9	1425	0.5	2105	1.8
12	SA	0308	0.5	0956	1.8	1704	0.5	2235	1.8
13	SU	0435	0.5	1104	1.7	1748	0.5	2349	1.9
14	M	0546	0.5	1225	1.8	1804	0.4		
15	TU	0049	2.1	0900	0.5	1315	2.0	1835	0.4
16	W	0135	2.3	0955	0.5	1355	2.1	1905	0.3
17	TH	0215	2.4	0729	0.5	1438	2.2	● 1939	0.2
18	F	0255	2.5	0804	0.5	1517	2.2	2018	0.2
19	SA	0335	2.5	0838	0.5	1558	2.3	2058	0.1
20	SU	0417	2.5	0918	0.6	1640	2.3	2144	0.2
21	M	0500	2.4	1315	0.6	1725	2.3	2229	0.2
22	TU	0545	2.3	1053	0.5	1809	2.2	2325	0.3
23	W	0637	2.2	1154	0.5	1859	2.2		
24	TH	0040	0.3	0731	2.0	1330	0.5	☽ 2005	2.0
25	F	0208	0.4	0849	1.8	1440	0.5	2125	1.9
26	SA	0315	0.5	1031	1.7	1608	0.5	2254	1.9
27	SU	0648	0.5	1150	1.8	1704	0.4		
28	M	0015	2.1	0828	0.5	1249	1.9	2044	0.4
29	TU	0109	2.2	0930	0.4	1335	2.0	2145	0.3
30	W	0155	2.3	1008	0.5	1419	2.1	2229	0.3

OCTOBER

Date	Day	Time	m	Time	m	Time	m	Time	m
1	TH	0225	2.3	1048	0.6	1455	2.1	O 1945	0.3
2	F	0259	2.3	1112	0.6	1523	2.2	2019	0.3
3	SA	0331	2.3	1143	0.6	1548	2.2	2045	0.3
4	SU	0405	2.3	1220	0.6	1621	2.2	2115	0.4
5	M	0436	2.3	1222	0.6	1649	2.2	2150	0.4
6	TU	0506	2.2	1009	0.5	1719	2.2	2224	0.4
7	W	0536	2.1	1044	0.5	1746	2.2	2305	0.4
8	TH	0605	2.1	1127	0.4	1822	2.2	2350	0.4
9	F	0645	2.1	1208	0.4	1904	2.1		
10	SA	0124	0.5	0729	1.9	1348	0.4	☾ 1955	1.9
11	SU	0244	0.5	0908	1.7	1500	0.5	2159	1.9
12	M	0359	0.6	1035	1.7	1612	0.5	2315	2.0
13	TU	0705	0.6	1150	1.8	1713	0.4		
14	W	0019	2.1	0839	0.5	1245	1.9	1755	0.4
15	TH	0106	2.3	0932	0.5	1331	2.1	1832	0.3
16	F	0149	2.4	0703	0.6	1415	2.2	● 1915	0.2
17	SA	0231	2.5	0736	0.5	1453	2.3	1951	0.2
18	SU	0312	2.5	0815	0.5	1535	2.4	2035	0.2
19	M	0355	2.5	0855	0.5	1617	2.4	2119	0.3
20	TU	0439	2.4	0939	0.5	1659	2.4	2209	0.3
21	W	0525	2.2	1029	0.5	1746	2.3	2304	0.4
22	TH	0615	2.1	1129	0.4	1836	2.2		
23	F	0054	0.5	0709	1.9	1240	0.4	☽ 1934	2.1
24	SA	0154	0.5	0824	1.8	1409	0.4	2110	2.0
25	SU	0304	0.6	1005	1.7	1534	0.4	2240	2.0
26	M	0609	0.6	1125	1.7	1640	0.4	2355	2.1
27	TU	0744	0.5	1219	1.9	1735	0.4		
28	W	0044	2.2	0852	0.5	1314	2.0	2100	0.3
29	TH	0124	2.3	0940	0.5	1349	2.1	2200	0.4
30	F	0159	2.3	1019	0.5	1425	2.1	1926	0.4
31	SA	0234	2.3	1045	0.6	1454	2.2	O 2004	0.4

NOVEMBER

Date	Day	Time	m	Time	m	Time	m	Time	m
1	SU	0305	2.3	1115	0.6	1521	2.2	2024	0.4
2	M	0336	2.3	1150	0.5	1554	2.3	2318	0.4
3	TU	0409	2.3	1202	0.5	1624	2.3		
4	W	0009	0.5	0439	2.2	0945	0.5	1655	2.2
5	TH	0045	0.5	0509	2.2	1015	0.4	1725	2.2
6	F	0115	0.5	0543	2.1	1105	0.4	1759	2.2
7	SA	0140	0.5	0619	2.1	1155	0.3	1845	2.2
8	SU	0036	0.5	0715	1.9	1308	0.4	☾ 1943	2.1
9	M	0237	0.6	0830	1.8	1421	0.4	2125	2.0
10	TU	0325	0.6	1000	1.7	1525	0.4	2246	2.0
11	W	0637	0.6	1112	1.8	1625	0.4	2346	2.2
12	TH	0809	0.5	1216	1.9	1715	0.3		
13	F	0038	2.3	0902	0.5	1305	2.1	1806	0.3
14	SA	0124	2.4	0945	0.5	1347	2.2	1846	0.3
15	SU	0207	2.5	0715	0.5	1430	2.3	● 1932	0.3
16	M	0252	2.4	0755	0.5	1513	2.4	2018	0.3
17	TU	0336	2.4	0836	0.4	1557	2.4	2101	0.4
18	W	0420	2.3	0922	0.4	1640	2.4	2155	0.5
19	TH	0506	2.2	1016	0.4	1727	2.4		
20	F	0210	0.5	0557	2.0	1105	0.3	1815	2.3
21	SA	0300	0.6	0649	1.9	1214	0.3	1915	2.1
22	SU	0125	0.6	0759	1.8	1328	0.3	☽ 2035	2.0
23	M	0236	0.6	0914	1.7	1454	0.3	2154	2.0
24	TU	0545	0.6	1045	1.7	1605	0.3	2315	2.0
25	W	0644	0.6	1145	1.8	1705	0.3		
26	TH	0005	2.1	0754	0.5	1234	1.9	1804	0.3
27	F	0056	2.1	0855	0.5	1315	2.0	1846	0.4
28	SA	0129	2.2	0945	0.5	1348	2.0	1935	0.4
29	SU	0204	2.2	1025	0.5	1424	2.1	2125	0.4
30	M	0239	2.2	1100	0.5	1452	2.2	O 2200	0.4

DECEMBER

Date	Day	Time	m	Time	m	Time	m	Time	m
1	TU	0311	2.2	1118	0.5	1527	2.3	2250	0.5
2	W	0345	2.2	1137	0.4	1559	2.3	2342	0.5
3	TH	0416	2.2	0934	0.4	1634	2.3		
4	F	0013	0.5	0451	2.1	1010	0.4	1709	2.3
5	SA	0102	0.5	0529	2.1	1045	0.3	1746	2.3
6	SU	0150	0.5	0609	2.0	1135	0.3	1835	2.2
7	M	0203	0.6	0706	1.9	1234	0.2	1934	2.1
8	TU	0303	0.6	0806	1.8	1339	0.3	☾ 2056	2.1
9	W	0306	0.6	0930	1.8	1450	0.3	2205	2.1
10	TH	0406	0.6	1040	1.8	1555	0.3	2310	2.2
11	F	0728	0.6	1145	1.9	1647	0.3		
12	SA	0010	2.2	0834	0.5	1235	2.1	1744	0.3
13	SU	0104	2.3	0615	0.5	1325	2.2	1834	0.3
14	M	0149	2.3	0704	0.5	1411	2.3	● 1919	0.4
15	TU	0237	2.3	0745	0.4	1455	2.4	2005	0.4
16	W	0322	2.2	0829	0.4	1541	2.4		
17	TH	0005	0.5	0408	2.2	0915	0.3	1626	2.4
18	F	0055	0.5	0457	2.1	0957	0.3	1715	2.3
19	SA	0145	0.5	0545	2.0	1049	0.2	1800	2.3
20	SU	0238	0.6	0629	2.0	1144	0.2	1855	2.2
21	M	0320	0.6	0719	1.9	1244	0.2	1955	2.1
22	TU	0201	0.6	0815	1.8	1359	0.2	☽ 2045	2.0
23	W	0304	0.6	0918	1.7	1527	0.3	2204	1.9
24	TH	0406	0.6	1045	1.7	1640	0.3	2325	1.9
25	F	0506	0.6	1153	1.8	1736	0.3		
26	SA	0016	2.0	0600	0.5	1236	1.8	1832	0.4
27	SU	0058	2.0	0900	0.5	1315	1.9	2003	0.4
28	M	0139	2.1	0956	0.5	1354	2.0	2057	0.4
29	TU	0215	2.1	1029	0.4	1429	2.1	2128	0.5
30	W	0249	2.2	0814	0.4	1506	2.2	O 2237	0.5
31	TH	0327	2.2	0844	0.4	1545	2.3	2314	0.5

VLISSINGEN (FLUSHING)
LAT 51°27′N
LONG 3°36′E

TIMES AND HEIGHTS OF HIGH AND LOW WATER (Heights in Metres)

TIME ZONE –0100 (Dutch Standard Time). **Subtract 1 hour for UT. For Dutch Summer Time (area enclosed in shaded box) add 1 hour**

2020

JANUARY

Date	Day	Time	m
1	W	0545 1210 1815	4.4 0.8 4.4
2	TH	0015 0626 1256 1900	1.3 4.3 0.9 4.3
3	F ☽	0057 0716 1345 1955	1.4 4.2 1.0 4.1
4	SA	0216 0810 1445 2056	1.4 4.0 1.1 4.0
5	SU	0320 0920 1550 2200	1.4 4.0 1.1 4.1
6	M	0420 1026 1656 2307	1.4 4.1 1.1 4.2
7	TU	0520 1125 1746 2358	1.2 4.3 1.0 4.5
8	W	0613 1216 1836	1.1 4.5 0.9
9	TH	0045 0658 1259 1920	4.6 0.9 4.7 0.8
10	F O	0126 0744 1342 2005	4.8 0.8 4.9 0.7
11	SA	0207 0830 1425 2046	4.9 0.6 5.0 0.7
12	SU	0247 0916 1505 2132	4.9 0.5 5.1 0.7
13	M	0332 1002 1548 2216	4.9 0.4 5.1 0.7
14	TU	0415 1049 1635 2305	4.9 0.4 5.1 0.8
15	W	0500 1140 1723 2355	4.8 0.4 5.0 0.8
16	TH	0550 1229 1818	4.7 0.5 4.8
17	F ☾	0040 0645 1316 1919	0.9 4.6 0.6 4.6
18	SA	0136 0746 1416 2025	1.0 4.5 0.7 4.5
19	SU	0236 0852 1520 2135	1.1 4.3 0.8 4.4
20	M	0350 1000 1635 2245	1.2 4.3 0.9 4.3
21	TU	0510 1109 1746 2351	1.1 4.4 0.9 4.4
22	W	0615 1215 1845	1.0 4.5 0.8
23	TH	0047 0710 1308 1929	4.6 0.8 4.7 0.8
24	F ●	0137 0757 1359 2014	4.7 0.6 4.8 0.8
25	SA	0221 0841 1437 2050	4.7 0.6 4.9 0.9
26	SU	0258 0920 1515 2127	4.8 0.5 4.9 0.9
27	M	0335 0958 1551 2202	4.8 0.5 4.9 0.9
28	TU	0408 1035 1627 2238	4.8 0.5 4.8 1.0
29	W	0441 1110 1705 2310	4.7 0.6 4.7 1.0
30	TH	0516 1145 1739 2340	4.6 0.7 4.6 1.0
31	F	0550 1210 1815	4.5 0.7 4.5

FEBRUARY

Date	Day	Time	m
1	SA	0016 0629 1240 1856	1.1 4.4 0.8 4.3
2	SU ☽	0054 0716 1324 1956	1.1 4.3 0.9 4.2
3	M	0150 0820 1424 2100	1.2 4.1 1.1 4.1
4	TU	0310 0935 1555 2215	1.3 4.0 1.1 4.0
5	W	0436 1045 1704 2322	1.3 4.1 1.1 4.2
6	TH	0545 1146 1810	1.1 4.3 1.0
7	F	0019 0636 1241 1859	4.4 0.9 4.6 0.8
8	SA	0107 0726 1325 1945	4.6 0.7 4.9 0.7
9	SU O	0152 0815 1408 2034	4.8 0.5 5.1 0.6
10	M	0235 0902 1450 2118	4.9 0.4 5.2 0.6
11	TU	0315 0950 1535 2202	5.0 0.3 5.3 0.6
12	W	0357 1036 1616 2248	5.0 0.2 5.2 0.6
13	TH	0441 1120 1706 2332	5.0 0.2 5.1 0.7
14	F	0529 1206 1755	4.9 0.3 4.9
15	SA ☾	0015 0619 1250 1855	0.8 4.8 0.4 4.7
16	SU	0106 0715 1340 1955	0.9 4.6 0.7 4.4
17	M	0205 0824 1444 2105	1.0 4.3 0.9 4.2
18	TU	0315 0936 1605 2226	1.2 4.2 1.1 4.0
19	W	0445 1056 1728 2345	1.2 4.2 1.1 4.2
20	TH	0605 1205 1830	1.0 4.4 1.0
21	F	0043 0705 1308 1916	4.4 0.8 4.6 0.9
22	SA	0128 0746 1353 1959	4.6 0.6 4.8 0.9
23	SU ●	0208 0829 1427 2035	4.7 0.5 4.9 0.9
24	M	0245 0904 1459 2107	4.7 0.5 4.9 0.9
25	TU	0315 0937 1529 2140	4.8 0.5 4.9 0.8
26	W	0343 1012 1602 2216	4.8 0.5 4.9 0.8
27	TH	0415 1045 1635 2245	4.8 0.5 4.8 0.8
28	F	0446 1110 1703 2310	4.8 0.6 4.7 0.9
29	SA	0516 1136 1735 2340	4.7 0.6 4.6 0.9

MARCH

Date	Day	Time	m
1	SU	0545 1206 1805	4.6 0.7 4.5
2	M ☽	0015 0625 1244 1849	0.9 4.5 0.8 4.3
3	TU	0100 0716 1340 2005	1.0 4.2 1.0 4.1
4	W	0205 0846 1455 2126	1.2 4.0 1.2 3.9
5	TH	0345 1010 1635 2245	1.3 4.0 1.2 4.0
6	F	0511 1125 1746 2357	1.1 4.2 1.0 4.2
7	SA	0616 1224 1840	0.9 4.6 0.8
8	SU	0047 0712 1307 1930	4.5 0.6 4.9 0.7
9	M O	0131 0800 1349 2015	4.8 0.4 5.1 0.6
10	TU	0212 0845 1431 2100	5.0 0.3 5.3 0.5
11	W	0253 0930 1513 2143	5.1 0.1 5.3 0.5
12	TH	0335 1015 1557 2227	5.2 0.1 5.3 0.5
13	F	0418 1058 1642 2310	5.1 0.2 5.1 0.5
14	SA	0505 1140 1728 2355	5.1 0.3 4.9 0.6
15	SU	0551 1224 1821	4.9 0.5 4.6
16	M ☾	0040 0645 1313 1925	0.8 4.6 0.7 4.3
17	TU	0134 0755 1414 2036	0.9 4.3 1.0 4.0
18	W	0250 0916 1540 2210	1.1 4.1 1.2 3.8
19	TH	0431 1046 1720 2326	1.1 4.1 1.2 4.0
20	F	0550 1159 1815	0.9 4.4 1.0
21	SA	0026 0646 1252 1905	4.3 0.7 4.6 0.9
22	SU	0112 0735 1331 1939	4.5 0.6 4.8 0.9
23	M	0147 0806 1405 2013	4.6 0.5 4.8 0.8
24	TU ●	0217 0836 1435 2045	4.7 0.5 4.9 0.8
25	W	0245 0910 1503 2115	4.8 0.4 4.9 0.7
26	TH	0316 0945 1535 2146	4.9 0.4 4.9 0.7
27	F	0345 1016 1605 2216	4.9 0.5 4.8 0.7
28	SA	0415 1045 1631 2245	4.8 0.5 4.8 0.7
29	SU	0443 1106 1659 2315	4.8 0.6 4.7 0.8
30	M	0513 1136 1735 2345	4.7 0.7 4.6 0.8
31	TU	0551 1215 1815	4.6 0.8 4.4

APRIL

Date	Day	Time	m
1	W ☽	0035 0637 1306 1915	0.9 4.4 1.0 4.1
2	TH	0136 0806 1425 2055	1.0 4.1 1.2 3.9
3	F	0310 0940 1600 2220	1.1 4.0 1.2 3.9
4	SA	0446 1056 1720 2329	1.0 4.2 1.0 4.2
5	SU	0556 1157 1819	0.8 4.6 0.8
6	M	0022 0655 1246 1910	4.5 0.6 4.9 0.7
7	TU	0106 0740 1328 1956	4.8 0.3 5.1 0.6
8	W O	0148 0825 1410 2038	5.0 0.2 5.3 0.5
9	TH	0229 0908 1451 2123	5.1 0.1 5.3 0.4
10	F	0313 0952 1535 2207	5.2 0.1 5.2 0.4
11	SA	0355 1035 1618 2248	5.2 0.2 5.1 0.5
12	SU	0438 1113 1706 2330	5.1 0.4 4.8 0.5
13	M	0527 1155 1756	4.9 0.6 4.5
14	TU ☾	0020 0621 1246 1856	0.7 4.6 0.9 4.2
15	W	0114 0735 1345 2004	0.9 4.3 1.1 3.9
16	TH	0235 0856 1520 2140	1.0 4.0 1.3 3.7
17	F	0354 1026 1650 2256	1.0 4.1 1.2 3.9
18	SA	0526 1135 1754 2356	0.9 4.3 1.1 4.2
19	SU	0615 1225 1835	0.7 4.5 1.0
20	M	0039 0702 1301 1912	4.4 0.6 4.7 0.9
21	TU	0115 0736 1335 1945	4.5 0.5 4.7 0.8
22	W	0145 0806 1403 2015	4.6 0.5 4.8 0.7
23	TH ●	0216 0840 1435 2048	4.8 0.5 4.9 0.7
24	F	0245 0910 1505 2122	4.9 0.5 4.9 0.6
25	SA	0316 0942 1535 2155	4.9 0.5 4.9 0.6
26	SU	0346 1015 1605 2225	4.9 0.6 4.8 0.7
27	M	0417 1045 1636 2255	4.8 0.7 4.7 0.7
28	TU	0452 1116 1712 2332	4.7 0.7 4.6 0.7
29	W	0531 1156 1756	4.6 0.8 4.4
30	TH ☽	0025 0621 1250 1859	0.8 4.4 1.0 4.1

MAY

Date	Day	Time	m
1	F	0125 0740 1405 2026	0.9 4.2 1.1 3.9
2	SA	0247 0912 1535 2146	1.0 4.2 1.2 4.0
3	SU	0415 1026 1645 2257	0.9 4.3 1.0 4.2
4	M	0530 1129 1755 2352	0.7 4.6 0.9 4.5
5	TU	0626 1221 1848	0.5 4.9 0.7
6	W	0039 0716 1305 1935	4.8 0.3 5.1 0.6
7	TH O	0123 0802 1347 2018	5.0 0.2 5.2 0.5
8	F	0206 0845 1432 2105	5.1 0.2 5.2 0.4
9	SA	0250 0926 1515 2146	5.2 0.3 5.1 0.4
10	SU	0335 1010 1602 2229	5.1 0.4 4.9 0.4
11	M	0420 1051 1647 2315	5.0 0.6 4.7 0.5
12	TU	0509 1132 1736	4.8 0.8 4.5
13	W	0000 0605 1219 1825	0.6 4.6 1.0 4.2
14	TH ☾	0054 0709 1315 1936	0.8 4.3 1.2 3.9
15	F	0205 0815 1438 2056	0.9 4.1 1.3 3.8
16	SA	0315 0946 1544 2215	0.9 4.0 1.3 3.8
17	SU	0435 1049 1654 2315	0.9 4.2 1.2 4.0
18	M	0536 1141 1749 2359	0.8 4.4 1.1 4.2
19	TU	0625 1225 1834	0.7 4.5 0.9
20	W	0036 0659 1301 1910	4.4 0.6 4.7 0.8
21	TH	0109 0734 1335 1945	4.6 0.6 4.8 0.7
22	F ●	0142 0806 1403 2020	4.7 0.6 4.8 0.7
23	SA	0216 0840 1437 2056	4.8 0.5 4.9 0.6
24	SU	0249 0916 1511 2136	4.9 0.6 4.8 0.6
25	M	0325 0952 1545 2210	4.8 0.6 4.8 0.6
26	TU	0359 1028 1619 2250	4.8 0.7 4.7 0.6
27	W	0437 1106 1701 2330	4.8 0.8 4.5 0.7
28	TH	0521 1150 1749	4.7 0.9 4.4
29	F	0025 0615 1245 1855	0.7 4.5 1.0 4.2
30	SA ☽	0120 0730 1354 2006	0.7 4.4 1.1 4.1
31	SU	0236 0848 1505 2116	0.8 4.4 1.1 4.1

JUNE

Date	Day	Time	m
1	M	0346 0956 1615 2225	0.7 4.5 1.0 4.3
2	TU	0454 1059 1726 2323	0.6 4.6 0.9 4.5
3	W	0600 1156 1824	0.5 4.8 0.7
4	TH	0013 0652 1245 1912	4.7 0.4 5.0 0.6
5	F O	0101 0738 1330 2000	4.9 0.4 5.0 0.5
6	SA	0148 0823 1416 2046	5.0 0.4 5.0 0.4
7	SU	0235 0907 1501 2129	5.1 0.5 4.9 0.4
8	M	0320 0947 1547 2215	5.0 0.6 4.8 0.4
9	TU	0406 1029 1634 2259	5.0 0.7 4.7 0.5
10	W	0456 1110 1719 2346	4.8 0.9 4.5 0.6
11	TH	0546 1156 1806	4.6 1.0 4.3
12	F	0036 0639 1246 1855	0.7 4.4 1.2 4.2
13	SA ☾	0130 0736 1345 1950	0.8 4.2 1.3 4.0
14	SU	0230 0844 1456 2100	0.8 4.1 1.3 3.9
15	M	0324 0956 1555 2216	0.9 4.1 1.3 3.9
16	TU	0435 1055 1655 2310	0.9 4.2 1.2 4.1
17	W	0530 1142 1745 2355	0.8 4.3 1.1 4.3
18	TH	0616 1222 1830	0.8 4.5 0.9
19	F	0035 0656 1300 1912	4.4 0.7 4.7 0.8
20	SA	0112 0732 1337 1955	4.6 0.7 4.8 0.7
21	SU ●	0151 0815 1415 2035	4.8 0.7 4.8 0.6
22	M	0227 0849 1450 2111	4.8 0.7 4.8 0.6
23	TU	0306 0932 1529 2158	4.9 0.7 4.8 0.5
24	W	0345 1015 1608 2242	4.9 0.7 4.7 0.5
25	TH	0426 1058 1652 2334	4.9 0.8 4.6 0.5
26	F	0512 1145 1738	4.8 0.9 4.5
27	SA	0020 0606 1236 1837	0.5 4.7 0.9 4.4
28	SU ☽	0116 0711 1334 1942	0.6 4.6 1.0 4.3
29	M	0215 0816 1436 2048	0.6 4.5 1.0 4.3
30	TU	0315 0925 1546 2152	0.6 4.5 1.0 4.4

SUNRISE AND SUNSET TIMES

VLISSINGEN (FLUSHING)
At 51°27′N 3°36′E

		Sunrise	Sunset
European Standard Time (UT-1)			
Jan	01	0851	1648
	15	0844	1706
Feb	01	0824	1735
	15	0759	1801
Mar	01	0731	1826
	15	0700	1850
European Summer Time (UT-2)			
Apr	01	0721	2020
	15	0650	2042
May	01	0618	2109
	15	0554	2131
Jun	01	0534	2153
	15	0528	2204
Jul	01	0533	2206
	15	0546	2156
Aug	01	0610	2133
	15	0631	2108
Sep	01	0658	2032
	15	0721	2000
Oct	01	0746	1923
	15	0810	1852
European Standard Time (UT-1)			
Nov	01	0739	1719
	15	0804	1656

VLISSINGEN (FLUSHING)
LAT 51°27'N
LONG 3°36'E

TIMES AND HEIGHTS OF HIGH AND LOW WATER (Heights in Metres)

TIME ZONE –0100 (Dutch Standard Time). **Subtract 1 hour for UT. For Dutch Summer Time (area enclosed in shaded box) add 1 hour**

2020

JULY

Date	Day	Time	m	Time	m	Time	m	Time	m
1	W	0420	0.7	1031	4.6	1650	1.0	2256	4.5
2	TH	0535	0.6	1135	4.7	1756	0.8	2355	4.6
3	F	0630	0.6	1229	4.8	1856	0.7		
4	SA	0047	4.8	0720	0.6	1319	4.8	1946	0.6
5	SU O	0137	4.9	0806	0.6	1405	4.9	2032	0.5
6	M	0225	5.0	0848	0.7	1455	4.8	2116	0.4
7	TU	0310	5.0	0930	0.8	1535	4.8	2202	0.4
8	W	0355	4.9	1010	0.9	1617	4.7	2245	0.5
9	TH	0436	4.9	1049	1.0	1657	4.7	2325	0.5
10	F	0519	4.7	1129	1.0	1736	4.5		
11	SA	0006	0.6	0605	4.6	1210	1.1	1816	4.4
12	SU	0045	0.7	0649	4.4	1255	1.2	1905	4.3
13	M ☾	0136	0.8	0740	4.2	1359	1.3	1955	4.1
14	TU	0230	0.9	0835	4.1	1504	1.3	2056	4.0
15	W	0336	1.0	0944	4.1	1600	1.3	2206	4.0
16	TH	0436	1.0	1050	4.1	1705	1.2	2310	4.1
17	F	0535	1.0	1142	4.3	1756	1.1		
18	SA	0002	4.3	0619	0.9	1231	4.5	1846	0.9
19	SU	0048	4.5	0706	0.8	1315	4.7	1929	0.8
20	M ●	0131	4.7	0746	0.8	1356	4.8	2015	0.7
21	TU	0209	4.9	0829	0.7	1435	4.9	2100	0.5
22	W	0250	5.0	0915	0.7	1515	4.9	2145	0.5
23	TH	0332	5.1	0958	0.7	1556	4.9	2232	0.4
24	F	0415	5.1	1045	0.7	1637	4.8	2320	0.4
25	SA	0459	5.0	1132	0.8	1726	4.8		
26	SU	0005	0.4	0549	4.9	1216	0.9	1815	4.7
27	M ☽	0055	0.5	0647	4.7	1310	0.9	1912	4.6
28	TU	0142	0.6	0749	4.6	1402	1.0	2015	4.5
29	W	0240	0.7	0856	4.5	1505	1.1	2125	4.4
30	TH	0350	0.8	1008	4.4	1626	1.1	2235	4.4
31	F	0510	0.9	1117	4.4	1740	1.0	2341	4.5

AUGUST

Date	Day	Time	m	Time	m	Time	m	Time	m
1	SA	0615	0.8	1221	4.6	1845	0.8		
2	SU	0041	4.7	0706	0.8	1315	4.7	1935	0.6
3	M O	0135	4.9	0752	0.8	1401	4.8	2024	0.5
4	TU	0218	5.0	0835	0.8	1441	4.8	2105	0.5
5	W	0301	5.0	0911	0.9	1518	4.8	2145	0.5
6	TH	0336	5.0	0946	0.9	1556	4.8	2220	0.5
7	F	0415	4.9	1024	1.0	1629	4.8	2256	0.5
8	SA	0451	4.8	1100	1.0	1706	4.7	2335	0.6
9	SU	0527	4.7	1136	1.1	1739	4.6		
10	M	0006	0.7	0605	4.5	1210	1.1	1816	4.5
11	TU ☾	0040	0.8	0645	4.4	1239	1.2	1905	4.3
12	W	0115	0.9	0736	4.2	1324	1.3	2000	4.1
13	TH	0209	1.1	0836	4.1	1447	1.4	2109	4.0
14	F	0340	1.2	0946	4.0	1620	1.3	2225	4.0
15	SA	0450	1.2	1106	4.1	1726	1.2	2335	4.2
16	SU	0550	1.1	1205	4.3	1820	1.0		
17	M	0026	4.5	0645	0.9	1251	4.6	1910	0.8
18	TU	0111	4.8	0727	0.8	1335	4.8	1956	0.6
19	W ●	0154	5.0	0815	0.7	1415	5.0	2042	0.5
20	TH	0232	5.2	0855	0.7	1455	5.1	2128	0.4
21	F	0313	5.3	0940	0.7	1536	5.1	2212	0.3
22	SA	0355	5.3	1023	0.7	1616	5.1	2258	0.3
23	SU	0438	5.2	1110	0.7	1702	5.0	2342	0.3
24	M	0526	5.0	1152	0.8	1747	4.9		
25	TU ☽	0027	0.5	0618	4.8	1240	0.9	1845	4.7
26	W	0115	0.6	0716	4.6	1336	1.0	1948	4.5
27	TH	0215	0.9	0826	4.3	1446	1.1	2100	4.3
28	F	0325	1.1	0947	4.2	1605	1.2	2219	4.3
29	SA	0456	1.1	1110	4.2	1730	1.0	2339	4.5
30	SU	0606	1.0	1215	4.4	1836	0.8		
31	M	0039	4.7	0659	0.9	1306	4.6	1928	0.6

SEPTEMBER

Date	Day	Time	m	Time	m	Time	m	Time	m
1	TU	0129	4.9	0745	0.9	1347	4.8	2009	0.5
2	W O	0206	5.0	0819	0.9	1425	4.8	2046	0.5
3	TH	0240	5.0	0851	0.9	1455	4.9	2122	0.5
4	F	0315	5.0	0925	0.9	1529	4.9	2155	0.5
5	SA	0347	5.0	0959	0.9	1559	4.9	2226	0.6
6	SU	0421	4.9	1034	0.9	1633	4.9	2300	0.7
7	M	0451	4.8	1100	1.0	1705	4.8	2326	0.8
8	TU	0521	4.6	1125	1.0	1735	4.7	2350	0.8
9	W	0551	4.5	1156	1.1	1807	4.5		
10	TH ☾	0025	0.9	0635	4.3	1240	1.1	1849	4.3
11	F	0110	1.1	0730	4.1	1335	1.3	2014	4.0
12	SA	0224	1.3	0856	3.9	1525	1.4	2145	4.0
13	SU	0410	1.3	1024	4.0	1650	1.3	2305	4.2
14	M	0526	1.2	1136	4.2	1800	1.1		
15	TU	0005	4.5	0619	1.0	1228	4.6	1850	0.8
16	W	0049	4.9	0708	0.8	1309	4.8	1938	0.6
17	TH ●	0128	5.1	0752	0.7	1350	5.0	2022	0.4
18	F	0210	5.3	0833	0.6	1430	5.2	2105	0.3
19	SA	0250	5.4	0918	0.6	1511	5.3	2150	0.3
20	SU	0332	5.4	1005	0.6	1553	5.3	2233	0.3
21	M	0416	5.3	1047	0.7	1636	5.2	2316	0.4
22	TU	0501	5.1	1129	0.7	1722	5.0	2356	0.6
23	W	0550	4.8	1215	0.9	1816	4.8		
24	TH ☽	0042	0.8	0649	4.5	1310	1.0	1915	4.5
25	F	0145	1.1	0800	4.2	1420	1.2	2040	4.3
26	SA	0257	1.3	0926	4.0	1549	1.2	2210	4.2
27	SU	0445	1.3	1055	4.1	1720	1.0	2324	4.4
28	M	0555	1.2	1159	4.4	1826	0.8		
29	TU	0029	4.7	0650	1.0	1248	4.6	1915	0.6
30	W	0111	4.9	0726	1.0	1326	4.8	1949	0.6

OCTOBER

Date	Day	Time	m	Time	m	Time	m	Time	m
1	TH O	0147	5.0	0756	1.0	1359	4.8	2022	0.6
2	F	0217	5.0	0825	0.9	1428	4.9	2053	0.6
3	SA	0248	5.0	0858	0.9	1459	5.0	2126	0.6
4	SU	0317	5.0	0932	0.9	1528	5.0	2158	0.6
5	M	0347	5.0	1005	0.9	1559	5.0	2226	0.7
6	TU	0417	4.8	1030	0.9	1629	4.9	2248	0.8
7	W	0446	4.7	1055	1.0	1658	4.8	2316	0.9
8	TH	0516	4.6	1122	1.0	1731	4.7	2350	1.0
9	F	0552	4.5	1208	1.0	1811	4.5		
10	SA ☾	0038	1.1	0646	4.2	1306	1.2	1914	4.2
11	SU	0145	1.4	0816	3.9	1434	1.4	2106	4.0
12	M	0330	1.4	0942	3.9	1615	1.3	2229	4.2
13	TU	0456	1.3	1105	4.2	1726	1.0	2335	4.6
14	W	0555	1.1	1159	4.5	1826	0.8		
15	TH	0022	4.9	0642	0.9	1242	4.8	1915	0.6
16	F ●	0105	5.2	0726	0.7	1323	5.1	1958	0.4
17	SA	0145	5.4	0812	0.6	1405	5.3	2041	0.3
18	SU	0226	5.4	0856	0.6	1446	5.4	2126	0.3
19	M	0310	5.4	0942	0.6	1529	5.3	2207	0.4
20	TU	0355	5.2	1023	0.6	1613	5.2	2249	0.5
21	W	0439	5.0	1108	0.7	1659	5.1	2335	0.7
22	TH	0527	4.7	1155	0.8	1754	4.8		
23	F ☽	0016	1.0	0626	4.4	1249	1.0	1859	4.5
24	SA	0116	1.2	0735	4.1	1406	1.1	2020	4.2
25	SU	0234	1.4	0900	3.9	1535	1.2	2146	4.2
26	M	0420	1.4	1026	4.0	1656	1.0	2305	4.4
27	TU	0536	1.3	1133	4.3	1756	0.9	2359	4.6
28	W	0615	1.1	1219	4.5	1845	0.7		
29	TH	0045	4.8	0700	1.0	1256	4.7	1920	0.7
30	F	0118	4.9	0730	1.0	1329	4.8	1955	0.7
31	SA O	0149	4.9	0800	0.9	1358	4.9	2022	0.6

NOVEMBER

Date	Day	Time	m	Time	m	Time	m	Time	m
1	SU	0219	5.0	0835	0.9	1429	5.0	2056	0.7
2	M	0249	5.0	0906	0.8	1500	5.0	2125	0.7
3	TU	0319	5.0	0936	0.8	1532	5.0	2155	0.8
4	W	0349	4.9	1006	0.9	1605	4.9	2225	0.9
5	TH	0421	4.8	1036	0.9	1635	4.8	2252	0.9
6	F	0455	4.7	1110	0.9	1709	4.7	2332	1.0
7	SA	0531	4.5	1150	1.0	1755	4.6		
8	SU ☾	0016	1.2	0625	4.3	1244	1.1	1856	4.3
9	M	0124	1.3	0740	4.1	1404	1.2	2035	4.2
10	TU	0250	1.4	0909	4.0	1535	1.1	2155	4.3
11	W	0415	1.3	1025	4.2	1650	1.0	2259	4.6
12	TH	0520	1.1	1125	4.5	1756	0.8	2352	4.9
13	F	0618	0.9	1212	4.8	1845	0.6		
14	SA	0037	5.1	0705	0.8	1258	5.1	1933	0.4
15	SU ●	0123	5.3	0750	0.6	1341	5.2	2018	0.4
16	M	0206	5.3	0837	0.6	1425	5.3	2102	0.4
17	TU	0250	5.3	0922	0.5	1510	5.3	2146	0.5
18	W	0336	5.1	1006	0.6	1556	5.2	2226	0.7
19	TH	0425	4.9	1049	0.6	1645	5.0	2308	0.9
20	F	0515	4.7	1136	0.7	1736	4.8	2355	1.1
21	SA	0605	4.4	1225	0.9	1836	4.5		
22	SU ☽	0045	1.3	0707	4.2	1335	1.0	1950	4.3
23	M	0154	1.5	0815	4.0	1445	1.1	2110	4.2
24	TU	0315	1.5	0940	3.9	1610	1.1	2226	4.2
25	W	0441	1.4	1049	4.1	1720	1.0	2325	4.4
26	TH	0535	1.3	1139	4.3	1808	0.9		
27	F	0009	4.6	0615	1.2	1224	4.5	1845	0.8
28	SA	0047	4.7	0658	1.0	1257	4.6	1920	0.8
29	SU	0119	4.8	0730	0.9	1329	4.7	1955	0.8
30	M O	0151	4.9	0805	0.9	1402	4.9	2026	0.7

DECEMBER

Date	Day	Time	m	Time	m	Time	m	Time	m
1	TU	0225	4.9	0840	0.8	1437	4.9	2056	0.7
2	W	0256	4.9	0915	0.8	1509	4.9	2132	0.8
3	TH	0329	4.9	0950	0.8	1543	4.9	2205	0.9
4	F	0405	4.8	1028	0.8	1617	4.9	2240	0.9
5	SA	0439	4.7	1105	0.8	1657	4.8	2320	1.0
6	SU	0524	4.5	1145	0.8	1745	4.7		
7	M	0006	1.1	0615	4.4	1240	0.9	1845	4.5
8	TU ☾	0106	1.2	0719	4.2	1348	0.9	2005	4.4
9	W	0215	1.3	0838	4.2	1500	0.9	2115	4.4
10	TH	0330	1.2	0945	4.3	1616	0.9	2225	4.6
11	F	0440	1.1	1048	4.5	1720	0.8	2325	4.8
12	SA	0546	1.0	1145	4.7	1821	0.6		
13	SU	0015	4.9	0645	0.8	1235	4.9	1912	0.5
14	M ●	0105	5.0	0735	0.7	1325	5.1	1958	0.5
15	TU	0152	5.1	0820	0.6	1409	5.2	2045	0.6
16	W	0238	5.1	0908	0.5	1456	5.2	2125	0.6
17	TH	0323	5.0	0955	0.5	1545	5.1	2208	0.8
18	F	0409	4.9	1036	0.5	1630	5.0	2249	0.9
19	SA	0457	4.7	1125	0.6	1719	4.8	2335	1.1
20	SU	0545	4.6	1209	0.7	1815	4.6		
21	M	0016	1.2	0635	4.4	1255	0.8	1906	4.4
22	TU ☽	0114	1.3	0726	4.2	1400	0.9	2005	4.2
23	W	0214	1.4	0830	4.0	1455	1.0	2124	4.1
24	TH	0325	1.5	0946	4.0	1605	1.1	2225	4.1
25	F	0424	1.4	1050	4.0	1710	1.1	2325	4.2
26	SA	0530	1.3	1140	4.2	1800	1.0		
27	SU	0010	4.4	0615	1.2	1222	4.4	1842	0.9
28	M	0049	4.5	0705	1.0	1301	4.5	1925	0.9
29	TU	0125	4.7	0740	0.9	1339	4.7	2000	0.8
30	W O	0205	4.8	0820	0.8	1417	4.8	2036	0.8
31	TH	0238	4.8	0900	0.7	1452	4.9	2112	0.8

ZEEBRUGGE
LAT 51°21'N
LONG 3°12'E

TIMES AND HEIGHTS OF HIGH AND LOW WATER (Heights in Metres)

TIME ZONE –0100 (Belgian Standard Time). **Subtract 1 hour for UT. For Belgian Summer Time (area enclosed in shaded box) add 1 hour**

2020

JANUARY

Date	Day	Time	m
1	W	0519 1143 1747 2345	4.2 0.9 4.3 1.3
2	TH	0603 1234 1837	4.1 1.0 4.1
3	F ☽	0037 0655 1336 1935	1.4 4.0 1.1 4.0
4	SA	0150 0758 1438 2039	1.5 3.9 1.2 4.0
5	SU	0302 0903 1537 2142	1.5 3.8 1.2 4.0
6	M	0405 1005 1631 2241	1.4 3.9 1.1 4.1
7	TU	0501 1102 1722 2334	1.3 4.1 1.0 4.3
8	W	0551 1152 1808	1.1 4.3 0.9
9	TH	0021 0635 1237 1851	4.4 0.9 4.4 0.8
10	F ○	0102 0717 1318 1932	4.5 0.8 4.6 0.8
11	SA	0140 0758 1358 2013	4.6 0.7 4.7 0.7
12	SU	0219 0840 1439 2056	4.6 0.6 4.8 0.7
13	M	0300 0924 1523 2141	4.7 0.5 4.9 0.8
14	TU	0343 1010 1609 2227	4.7 0.4 4.9 0.8
15	W	0429 1059 1659 2317	4.6 0.4 4.8 0.9
16	TH	0519 1151 1753	4.6 0.5 4.7
17	F ☾	0010 0614 1247 1854	1.0 4.5 0.6 4.5
18	SA	0108 0717 1347 2000	1.1 4.3 0.7 4.3
19	SU	0213 0825 1454 2111	1.2 4.2 0.8 4.2
20	M	0327 0939 1607 2225	1.2 4.2 0.9 4.2
21	TU	0446 1053 1718 2336	1.2 4.2 0.9 4.3
22	W	0554 1159 1819	1.0 4.4 0.9
23	TH	0031 0647 1250 1907	4.4 0.9 4.5 0.9
24	F ●	0114 0731 1332 1947	4.4 0.7 4.6 0.9
25	SA	0152 0810 1410 2023	4.5 0.6 4.6 0.9
26	SU	0228 0846 1446 2057	4.5 0.6 4.6 0.9
27	M	0303 0922 1523 2130	4.5 0.5 4.6 0.9
28	TU	0338 0958 1559 2202	4.5 0.5 4.6 0.9
29	W	0413 1033 1635 2235	4.5 0.6 4.5 1.0
30	TH	0447 1108 1710 2309	4.5 0.7 4.5 1.0
31	F	0521 1142 1747	4.4 0.8 4.3

FEBRUARY

Date	Day	Time	m
1	SA	0559 1221 1829	4.2 0.9 4.2
2	SU ☽	0029 0646 1311 1923	1.3 4.1 1.1 4.0
3	M	0128 0747 1430 2032	1.4 3.9 1.3 3.9
4	TU	0308 0903 1546 2150	1.5 3.8 1.3 3.8
5	W	0423 1019 1648 2259	1.4 3.9 1.2 3.9
6	TH	0523 1124 1742 2356	1.2 4.1 1.1 4.1
7	F	0614 1216 1830	1.0 4.3 0.9
8	SA	0042 0700 1301 1914	4.3 0.8 4.6 0.8
9	SU ○	0122 0742 1342 1957	4.5 0.6 4.8 0.7
10	M	0202 0825 1424 2041	4.7 0.4 5.0 0.6
11	TU	0243 0910 1508 2126	4.8 0.3 5.0 0.6
12	W	0326 0956 1553 2212	4.9 0.2 5.0 0.6
13	TH	0411 1042 1640 2258	4.9 0.2 5.0 0.7
14	F	0458 1130 1730 2345	4.8 0.3 4.8 0.8
15	SA ☾	0549 1220 1824	4.6 0.4 4.5
16	SU	0036 0645 1316 1926	1.0 4.4 0.7 4.2
17	M	0138 0752 1426 2040	1.2 4.2 0.9 4.0
18	TU	0301 0914 1546 2206	1.3 4.0 1.1 3.9
19	W	0429 1043 1705 2325	1.2 4.0 1.1 4.0
20	TH	0543 1152 1811	1.1 4.2 1.1
21	F	0020 0637 1241 1858	4.2 0.8 4.4 1.0
22	SA	0102 0719 1320 1934	4.3 0.7 4.5 1.0
23	SU ●	0136 0755 1354 2005	4.4 0.6 4.6 0.9
24	M	0208 0828 1426 2035	4.5 0.5 4.7 0.9
25	TU	0240 0900 1459 2104	4.6 0.4 4.7 0.8
26	W	0312 0931 1532 2135	4.6 0.4 4.7 0.7
27	TH	0344 1003 1604 2207	4.6 0.4 4.7 0.7
28	F	0414 1034 1635 2238	4.6 0.5 4.6 0.8
29	SA	0445 1105 1707 2311	4.6 0.6 4.5 0.9

MARCH

Date	Day	Time	m
1	SU	0520 1137 1743 2347	4.5 0.8 4.4 1.0
2	M ☽	0601 1216 1828	4.3 1.0 4.2
3	TU	0032 0652 1311 1928	1.2 4.1 1.2 3.9
4	W	0143 0805 1458 2058	1.4 3.8 1.4 3.7
5	TH	0346 0941 1616 2226	1.4 3.8 1.3 3.7
6	F	0454 1058 1717 2330	1.2 4.0 1.2 4.0
7	SA	0550 1154 1809	1.0 4.3 1.0
8	SU	0018 0639 1240 1855	4.3 0.7 4.6 0.8
9	M ○	0100 0723 1323 1939	4.5 0.4 4.9 0.6
10	TU	0141 0807 1405 2023	4.8 0.2 5.1 0.5
11	W	0222 0851 1448 2107	5.0 0.1 5.2 0.4
12	TH	0305 0936 1532 2152	5.0 0.0 5.1 0.4
13	F	0350 1021 1618 2236	5.0 0.1 5.0 0.5
14	SA	0436 1106 1705 2321	4.9 0.2 4.8 0.7
15	SU	0524 1153 1755	4.7 0.5 4.4
16	M ☾	0008 0616 1247 1853	0.9 4.4 0.8 4.1
17	TU	0108 0722 1400 2009	1.1 4.1 1.1 3.8
18	W	0239 0851 1524 2142	1.3 3.8 1.3 3.6
19	TH	0404 1025 1643 2302	1.2 3.9 1.3 3.8
20	F	0518 1133 1751 2358	1.0 4.1 1.2 4.1
21	SA	0615 1221 1839	0.8 4.4 1.0
22	SU	0039 0658 1258 1913	4.3 0.7 4.5 1.0
23	M	0113 0732 1331 1942	4.4 0.6 4.6 0.9
24	TU ●	0144 0802 1402 2009	4.5 0.5 4.7 0.8
25	W	0214 0832 1433 2037	4.6 0.4 4.7 0.7
26	TH	0244 0902 1503 2108	4.7 0.4 4.7 0.6
27	F	0314 0932 1533 2140	4.7 0.4 4.7 0.6
28	SA	0343 1003 1602 2211	4.7 0.5 4.6 0.7
29	SU	0414 1033 1634 2243	4.6 0.6 4.6 0.7
30	M	0448 1105 1709 2318	4.6 0.7 4.4 0.9
31	TU	0529 1142 1752	4.4 0.9 4.2

APRIL

Date	Day	Time	m
1	W ☽	0618 1233 1848	4.2 1.2 3.9
2	TH	0103 0728 1412 2018	1.3 3.9 1.4 3.6
3	F	0312 0911 1546 2155	1.3 3.8 1.3 3.7
4	SA	0423 1031 1649 2301	1.1 4.1 1.2 4.0
5	SU	0522 1129 1744 2351	0.8 4.4 0.9 4.3
6	M	0613 1217 1833	0.5 4.7 0.7
7	TU	0035 0700 1300 1918	4.6 0.3 5.0 0.6
8	W ○	0117 0745 1343 2002	4.9 0.1 5.1 0.4
9	TH	0200 0829 1426 2046	5.0 0.0 5.2 0.4
10	F	0244 0914 1510 2130	5.1 0.0 5.1 0.4
11	SA	0328 0958 1555 2214	5.1 0.1 4.9 0.4
12	SU	0414 1042 1641 2258	4.9 0.4 4.6 0.6
13	M	0501 1127 1729 2344	4.7 0.7 4.3 0.8
14	TU ☾	0553 1219 1825	4.4 1.0 4.0
15	W	0045 0657 1335 1939	1.1 4.0 1.3 3.7
16	TH	0215 0824 1455 2107	1.2 3.8 1.4 3.6
17	F	0330 0952 1607 2225	1.2 3.8 1.4 3.7
18	SA	0439 1100 1714 2323	1.0 4.0 1.3 4.0
19	SU	0539 1149 1807	0.8 4.3 1.1
20	M	0006 0626 1228 1844	4.2 0.7 4.5 1.0
21	TU	0042 0702 1302 1913	4.4 0.6 4.6 0.8
22	W	0115 0732 1334 1940	4.5 0.5 4.7 0.7
23	TH ●	0145 0800 1404 2009	4.6 0.5 4.7 0.6
24	F	0215 0831 1434 2041	4.6 0.5 4.7 0.6
25	SA	0245 0902 1504 2115	4.7 0.5 4.7 0.6
26	SU	0315 0935 1534 2148	4.6 0.6 4.6 0.6
27	M	0348 1007 1607 2222	4.6 0.7 4.5 0.7
28	TU	0425 1041 1644 2258	4.6 0.8 4.4 0.8
29	W	0507 1121 1729 2343	4.4 1.0 4.2 1.0
30	TH ☽	0559 1214 1826	4.2 1.2 3.9

MAY

Date	Day	Time	m
1	F	0052 0711 1346 1954	1.1 4.0 1.3 3.7
2	SA	0240 0846 1515 2123	1.1 4.0 1.3 3.8
3	SU	0350 1002 1619 2229	0.9 4.2 1.1 4.0
4	M	0450 1101 1716 2322	0.7 4.5 0.9 4.4
5	TU	0545 1151 1808	0.5 4.7 0.7
6	W	0010 0635 1237 1856	4.6 0.3 4.9 0.6
7	TH ○	0055 0722 1322 1942	4.8 0.2 5.0 0.5
8	F	0139 0807 1406 2026	5.0 0.2 5.0 0.4
9	SA	0224 0852 1450 2110	5.0 0.2 4.9 0.4
10	SU	0309 0936 1535 2154	4.9 0.4 4.7 0.5
11	M	0355 1019 1621 2238	4.8 0.6 4.5 0.6
12	TU	0442 1104 1708 2326	4.6 0.9 4.2 0.8
13	W	0533 1154 1800	4.3 1.1 4.0
14	TH ☾	0027 0634 1303 1906	0.9 4.1 1.4 3.7
15	F	0145 0750 1418 2023	1.1 3.9 1.5 3.6
16	SA	0252 0906 1523 2135	1.1 3.8 1.4 3.7
17	SU	0354 1012 1625 2236	1.0 4.0 1.3 3.9
18	M	0453 1106 1721 2325	0.9 4.2 1.2 4.1
19	TU	0543 1151 1805	0.8 4.4 1.0
20	W	0007 0624 1229 1839	4.3 0.7 4.5 0.9
21	TH	0043 0657 1304 1910	4.4 0.6 4.6 0.8
22	F ●	0116 0728 1337 1943	4.5 0.6 4.6 0.7
23	SA	0148 0801 1408 2017	4.5 0.6 4.6 0.6
24	SU	0219 0835 1439 2053	4.6 0.6 4.6 0.6
25	M	0253 0910 1512 2129	4.6 0.7 4.5 0.7
26	TU	0329 0946 1548 2207	4.6 0.8 4.4 0.7
27	W	0409 1025 1629 2248	4.5 0.9 4.3 0.8
28	TH	0454 1109 1716 2339	4.5 1.0 4.2 0.8
29	F	0549 1207 1816	4.3 1.1 4.0
30	SA ☽	0050 0700 1325 1933	0.9 4.2 1.2 3.9
31	SU	0210 0820 1441	0.8 4.2 1.2

JUNE

Date	Day	Time	m
1	M	0317 0931 1546 2156	0.7 4.3 1.1 4.2
2	TU	0419 1032 1647 2254	0.6 4.5 0.9 4.4
3	W	0518 1127 1745 2347	0.5 4.6 0.8 4.6
4	TH	0612 1218 1837	0.4 4.7 0.7
5	F ○	0036 0702 1305 1924	4.7 0.4 4.8 0.6
6	SA	0123 0748 1350 2010	4.8 0.4 4.7 0.5
7	SU	0209 0832 1434 2054	4.8 0.5 4.7 0.5
8	M	0254 0916 1518 2137	4.8 0.6 4.5 0.5
9	TU	0339 0958 1602 2222	4.7 0.8 4.4 0.6
10	W	0425 1041 1647 2309	4.5 1.0 4.3 0.7
11	TH	0513 1126 1735	4.4 1.1 4.1
12	F	0003 0607 1222 1830	0.8 4.2 1.3 4.0
13	SA ☾	0107 0708 1329 1933	0.9 4.0 1.4 3.8
14	SU	0209 0813 1433 2039	1.0 3.9 1.4 3.8
15	M	0307 0917 1533 2141	1.0 4.0 1.4 3.9
16	TU	0403 1015 1630 2237	1.0 4.0 1.3 4.0
17	W	0455 1108 1721 2326	0.9 4.2 1.1 4.1
18	TH	0542 1154 1805	0.9 4.3 1.0
19	F	0009 0621 1235 1843	4.3 0.8 4.4 0.9
20	SA	0048 0658 1311 1919	4.4 0.8 4.5 0.8
21	SU ●	0124 0734 1345 1956	4.5 0.8 4.5 0.7
22	M	0159 0811 1419 2035	4.5 0.8 4.5 0.7
23	TU	0236 0850 1456 2114	4.6 0.8 4.5 0.6
24	W	0315 0930 1535 2157	4.6 0.8 4.5 0.6
25	TH	0358 1014 1618 2243	4.6 0.9 4.4 0.6
26	F	0446 1102 1707 2336	4.6 0.9 4.4 0.6
27	SA	0540 1157 1803	4.6 1.0 4.3
28	SU ☽	0036 0643 1300 1908	0.6 4.5 1.1 4.2
29	M	0140 0751 1406 2016	0.6 4.4 1.1 4.2
30	TU	0244 0859 1513 2123	0.6 4.4 1.1 4.3

SUNRISE AND SUNSET TIMES

ZEEBRUGGE
At 51°21'N 3°12'E

		Sunrise	Sunset
European Standard Time (UT-1)			
Jan	01	0852	1655
	15	0845	1708
Feb	01	0825	1738
	15	0800	1803
Mar	01	0732	1828
		0701	1852
European Summer Time (UT–2)			
Apr	01	0723	2021
	15	0652	2044
May	01	0619	2110
	15	0556	2132
Jun	01	0537	2154
	15	0530	2205
Jul	01	0535	2207
	15	0549	2157
Aug	01	0612	2134
	15	0633	2109
Sep	01	0700	2033
	15	0722	2001
Oct	01	0740	1825
	15	0811	1824
European Standard Time (UT–1)			
Nov	01	0741	1720
	15	0805	1659
Dec	01	0830	1642

ZEEBRUGGE
LAT 51°21′N
LONG 3°12′E

TIMES AND HEIGHTS OF HIGH AND LOW WATER (Heights in Metres)

TIME ZONE
–0100 (Belgian Standard Time).
Subtract 1 hour for UT. For Belgian Summer Time (area enclosed in shaded box) add 1 hour

2020

JULY

Date	Day	Time	m	Time	m	Time	m	Time	m
1	W	0349	0.6	1004	4.4	1620	1.0	2228	4.3
2	TH	0454	0.6	1107	4.4	1726	0.9	2330	4.4
3	F	0554	0.6	1205	4.5	1823	0.8		
4	SA	0025	4.6	0647	0.7	1255	4.5	1913	0.7
5	SU O	0114	4.6	0734	0.7	1339	4.5	1957	0.6
6	M	0158	4.7	0816	0.8	1421	4.5	2040	0.6
7	TU	0241	4.7	0857	0.8	1502	4.5	2122	0.5
8	W	0323	4.7	0937	0.9	1543	4.5	2204	0.5
9	TH	0406	4.6	1016	1.0	1624	4.4	2247	0.5
10	F	0449	4.5	1056	1.0	1706	4.4	2332	0.6
11	SA	0534	4.4	1137	1.1	1750	4.3		
12	SU	0020	0.8	0621	4.2	1224	1.2	1838	4.1
13	M ☾	0113	0.9	0714	4.1	1321	1.4	1934	4.0
14	TU	0212	1.0	0813	4.0	1432	1.4	2036	3.9
15	W	0311	1.1	0915	3.9	1538	1.4	2140	3.9
16	TH	0408	1.1	1018	4.0	1638	1.3	2241	3.9
17	F	0501	1.1	1116	4.1	1731	1.2	2336	4.1
18	SA	0549	1.0	1206	4.2	1818	1.0		
19	SU	0022	4.3	0631	0.9	1248	4.3	1859	0.9
20	M ●	0103	4.4	0711	0.9	1325	4.4	1938	0.7
21	TU	0141	4.6	0751	0.8	1402	4.5	2019	0.6
22	W	0221	4.7	0833	0.8	1440	4.6	2101	0.5
23	TH	0302	4.8	0916	0.7	1521	4.7	2146	0.4
24	F	0346	4.9	1002	0.7	1605	4.7	2233	0.4
25	SA	0433	4.9	1050	0.8	1651	4.7	2322	0.4
26	SU	0523	4.8	1139	0.9	1742	4.6		
27	M ☽	0014	0.4	0618	4.7	1232	1.0	1839	4.5
28	TU	0110	0.5	0719	4.5	1332	1.1	1943	4.4
29	W	0213	0.7	0826	4.3	1441	1.2	2053	4.2
30	TH	0323	0.8	0939	4.2	1558	1.2	2209	4.2
31	F	0435	0.9	1054	4.2	1713	1.1	2321	4.3

AUGUST

Date	Day	Time	m	Time	m	Time	m	Time	m
1	SA	0543	0.9	1158	4.3	1815	0.9		
2	SU	0020	4.5	0638	0.9	1248	4.4	1904	0.8
3	M O	0107	4.6	0723	0.9	1329	4.5	1946	0.6
4	TU	0147	4.7	0801	0.9	1406	4.5	2025	0.5
5	W	0225	4.7	0838	0.9	1443	4.6	2103	0.5
6	TH	0303	4.8	0913	0.9	1520	4.7	2141	0.4
7	F	0342	4.7	0949	0.9	1557	4.7	2219	0.4
8	SA	0420	4.7	1024	0.9	1634	4.6	2256	0.5
9	SU	0458	4.6	1058	0.9	1710	4.5	2331	0.7
10	M	0534	4.5	1133	1.0	1746	4.4		
11	TU ☾	0007	0.9	0613	4.3	1212	1.2	1827	4.2
12	W	0050	1.1	0659	4.1	1300	1.4	1920	4.0
13	TH	0154	1.3	0800	3.9	1429	1.5	2031	3.9
14	F	0320	1.3	0920	3.8	1558	1.5	2153	3.8
15	SA	0425	1.3	1037	3.9	1700	1.3	2304	4.0
16	SU	0520	1.2	1137	4.1	1753	1.1	2358	4.3
17	M	0608	1.0	1224	4.3	1838	0.9		
18	TU	0042	4.5	0651	0.9	1303	4.5	1919	0.7
19	W ●	0122	4.8	0733	0.8	1341	4.7	2001	0.5
20	TH	0203	5.0	0816	0.7	1421	4.9	2045	0.3
21	F	0244	5.1	0900	0.6	1502	5.0	2130	0.2
22	SA	0328	5.2	0945	0.6	1545	5.0	2216	0.2
23	SU	0413	5.1	1031	0.6	1631	5.0	2302	0.2
24	M	0500	5.0	1117	0.7	1719	4.9	2350	0.4
25	TU ☽	0551	4.7	1205	0.9	1811	4.7		
26	W	0041	0.6	0647	4.4	1300	1.1	1911	4.4
27	TH	0144	0.9	0755	4.1	1414	1.3	2027	4.2
28	F	0302	1.1	0918	3.9	1542	1.3	2157	4.1
29	SA	0422	1.2	1044	4.0	1701	1.1	2316	4.3
30	SU	0533	1.1	1149	4.2	1804	0.9		
31	M	0013	4.5	0628	1.1	1235	4.4	1851	0.7

SEPTEMBER

Date	Day	Time	m	Time	m	Time	m	Time	m
1	TU	0055	4.6	0709	1.0	1312	4.5	1931	0.6
2	W O	0131	4.7	0744	0.9	1346	4.6	2006	0.5
3	TH	0206	4.8	0816	0.9	1420	4.8	2040	0.4
4	F	0240	4.9	0848	0.8	1454	4.8	2114	0.4
5	SA	0315	4.9	0920	0.7	1528	4.8	2148	0.4
6	SU	0349	4.8	0953	0.7	1601	4.8	2220	0.5
7	M	0421	4.7	1025	0.8	1632	4.7	2251	0.7
8	TU	0452	4.6	1056	0.9	1704	4.6	2321	0.8
9	W	0525	4.5	1130	1.0	1741	4.4	2356	1.0
10	TH ☾	0605	4.3	1209	1.2	1827	4.2		
11	F	0042	1.3	0656	4.0	1306	1.5	1930	4.0
12	SA	0214	1.5	0817	3.8	1519	1.5	2109	3.8
13	SU	0352	1.5	0959	3.8	1630	1.3	2233	4.0
14	M	0452	1.3	1107	4.0	1725	1.1	2332	4.4
15	TU	0544	1.1	1156	4.3	1814	0.8		
16	W	0019	4.7	0630	0.9	1238	4.6	1857	0.5
17	TH ●	0100	5.0	0713	0.7	1318	4.9	1941	0.3
18	F	0141	5.2	0756	0.5	1358	5.1	2024	0.1
19	SA	0223	5.3	0841	0.5	1440	5.2	2109	0.1
20	SU	0306	5.3	0925	0.4	1524	5.2	2154	0.1
21	M	0351	5.2	1010	0.5	1608	5.1	2239	0.3
22	TU	0437	5.0	1054	0.7	1655	4.9	2324	0.5
23	W	0525	4.7	1140	0.9	1745	4.7		
24	TH ☽	0014	0.8	0618	4.3	1233	1.1	1845	4.3
25	F	0119	1.2	0727	4.0	1354	1.3	2007	4.1
26	SA	0245	1.4	0858	3.8	1524	1.3	2144	4.0
27	SU	0404	1.4	1025	3.9	1639	1.1	2301	4.3
28	M	0515	1.3	1128	4.2	1743	0.9	2355	4.5
29	TU	0610	1.1	1214	4.4	1831	0.7		
30	W	0036	4.7	0650	1.0	1251	4.6	1909	0.6

OCTOBER

Date	Day	Time	m	Time	m	Time	m	Time	m
1	TH O	0110	4.8	0722	0.9	1324	4.7	1943	0.5
2	F	0143	4.9	0752	0.8	1356	4.8	2014	0.4
3	SA	0216	4.9	0821	0.7	1428	4.9	2045	0.4
4	SU	0248	4.9	0853	0.7	1500	4.9	2117	0.5
5	M	0319	4.9	0924	0.7	1530	4.8	2147	0.6
6	TU	0348	4.8	0956	0.7	1559	4.8	2217	0.7
7	W	0417	4.6	1026	0.8	1631	4.7	2246	0.9
8	TH	0450	4.5	1059	1.0	1708	4.5	2320	1.1
9	F	0528	4.3	1137	1.1	1753	4.3		
10	SA ☾	0004	1.3	0617	4.1	1230	1.4	1854	4.1
11	SU	0118	1.5	0734	3.8	1440	1.5	2036	3.9
12	M	0319	1.5	0923	3.8	1557	1.3	2203	4.1
13	TU	0423	1.3	1034	4.0	1655	1.0	2304	4.5
14	W	0517	1.1	1126	4.4	1746	0.7	2353	4.8
15	TH	0606	0.8	1211	4.7	1833	0.4		
16	F ●	0036	5.1	0652	0.6	1253	5.0	1918	0.2
17	SA	0119	5.3	0736	0.5	1336	5.2	2003	0.1
18	SU	0201	5.4	0821	0.4	1419	5.3	2047	0.1
19	M	0245	5.3	0905	0.4	1503	5.3	2132	0.2
20	TU	0329	5.1	0949	0.5	1548	5.1	2216	0.4
21	W	0415	4.8	1033	0.6	1634	4.9	2301	0.7
22	TH	0502	4.5	1119	0.8	1725	4.6	2350	1.0
23	F ☽	0555	4.2	1214	1.1	1826	4.3		
24	SA	0057	1.4	0704	3.9	1338	1.2	1948	4.0
25	SU	0222	1.5	0831	3.8	1458	1.2	2118	4.0
26	M	0335	1.5	0953	3.9	1607	1.1	2232	4.2
27	TU	0444	1.4	1056	4.1	1711	0.9	2326	4.5
28	W	0542	1.2	1145	4.4	1802	0.7		
29	TH	0009	4.7	0624	1.0	1224	4.6	1843	0.6
30	F	0045	4.8	0658	0.9	1258	4.7	1916	0.6
31	SA O	0119	4.9	0727	0.8	1331	4.8	1947	0.6

NOVEMBER

Date	Day	Time	m	Time	m	Time	m	Time	m
1	SU	0151	4.9	0757	0.7	1403	4.8	2017	0.6
2	M	0222	4.9	0827	0.7	1433	4.8	2047	0.6
3	TU	0252	4.8	0859	0.7	1502	4.8	2118	0.7
4	W	0320	4.7	0931	0.8	1533	4.7	2149	0.8
5	TH	0350	4.6	1004	0.8	1606	4.6	2221	1.0
6	F	0424	4.5	1038	0.9	1645	4.6	2257	1.1
7	SA	0504	4.3	1119	1.0	1732	4.4	2344	1.3
8	SU ☾	0555	4.1	1216	1.2	1836	4.2		
9	M	0057	1.5	0711	3.9	1404	1.3	2010	4.1
10	TU	0243	1.5	0848	3.9	1522	1.1	2130	4.3
11	W	0350	1.3	0959	4.1	1622	0.8	2233	4.6
12	TH	0448	1.1	1055	4.4	1717	0.6	2325	4.8
13	F	0541	0.9	1144	4.7	1808	0.4		
14	SA	0013	5.0	0631	0.7	1230	5.0	1856	0.3
15	SU ●	0058	5.1	0717	0.6	1315	5.1	1943	0.3
16	M	0142	5.1	0803	0.5	1400	5.2	2028	0.3
17	TU	0227	5.1	0847	0.5	1445	5.1	2112	0.5
18	W	0312	4.9	0931	0.5	1531	5.0	2156	0.7
19	TH	0357	4.7	1016	0.6	1619	4.8	2241	0.9
20	F	0444	4.4	1104	0.8	1710	4.6	2330	1.2
21	SA	0536	4.2	1201	0.9	1808	4.3		
22	SU ☽	0032	1.4	0638	4.0	1313	1.1	1921	4.1
23	M	0147	1.5	0753	3.9	1424	1.1	2038	4.0
24	TU	0256	1.5	0907	3.9	1528	1.0	2148	4.1
25	W	0401	1.4	1013	4.0	1630	1.0	2247	4.3
26	TH	0502	1.3	1107	4.2	1726	0.8	2336	4.5
27	F	0553	1.1	1152	4.4	1812	0.8		
28	SA	0017	4.6	0632	1.0	1232	4.5	1848	0.7
29	SU	0055	4.7	0704	0.9	1308	4.6	1920	0.7
30	M O	0129	4.7	0735	0.8	1340	4.6	1950	0.8

DECEMBER

Date	Day	Time	m	Time	m	Time	m	Time	m
1	TU	0200	4.7	0806	0.8	1411	4.6	2021	0.8
2	W	0229	4.6	0839	0.8	1441	4.6	2054	0.9
3	TH	0259	4.5	0913	0.8	1514	4.6	2127	0.9
4	F	0331	4.5	0948	0.8	1551	4.6	2203	1.0
5	SA	0409	4.4	1027	0.8	1633	4.6	2244	1.1
6	SU	0452	4.3	1112	0.9	1722	4.5	2334	1.2
7	M	0545	4.2	1213	1.0	1825	4.4		
8	TU ☾	0042	1.3	0653	4.1	1332	1.0	1942	4.3
9	W	0204	1.4	0812	4.1	1445	0.9	2056	4.4
10	TH	0314	1.3	0922	4.2	1548	0.8	2201	4.5
11	F	0417	1.1	1023	4.4	1649	0.6	2259	4.6
12	SA	0518	1.0	1120	4.6	1746	0.6	2353	4.8
13	SU	0613	0.8	1212	4.8	1838	0.5		
14	M ●	0042	4.8	0703	0.7	1301	4.9	1926	0.5
15	TU	0129	4.8	0749	0.6	1348	4.9	2012	0.6
16	W	0214	4.8	0834	0.6	1433	4.9	2055	0.7
17	TH	0258	4.7	0918	0.5	1519	4.8	2139	0.8
18	F	0342	4.6	1003	0.6	1605	4.7	2222	1.0
19	SA	0427	4.5	1050	0.6	1653	4.6	2308	1.1
20	SU	0514	4.3	1142	0.7	1745	4.4		
21	M	1241	0.8	1844	4.2				
22	TU ☽	0101	1.4	0708	4.0	1343	1.0	1949	4.1
23	W	0207	1.5	0814	3.9	1444	1.0	2054	4.0
24	TH	0312	1.5	0919	3.9	1544	1.1	2157	4.1
25	F	0415	1.4	1020	4.0	1643	1.1	2255	4.2
26	SA	0514	1.3	1116	4.1	1735	1.0	2346	4.3
27	SU	0604	1.1	1204	4.2	1819	1.0		
28	M	0031	4.4	0643	1.0	1245	4.3	1854	1.0
29	TU	0109	4.4	0716	0.9	1321	4.4	1927	0.9
30	W O	0142	4.5	0749	0.9	1353	4.5	1959	0.9
31	TH	0212	4.5	0823	0.8	1426	4.6	2034	0.9

DUNKERQUE
LAT 51°03′N
LONG 2°22′E

TIMES AND HEIGHTS OF HIGH AND LOW WATER (Heights in Metres)

TIME ZONE –0100 (French Standard Time). **Subtract 1 hour for UT. For French Summer Time (area enclosed in shaded box) add 1 hour**

2020

SUNRISE AND SUNSET TIMES

DUNKERQUE
At 51°03′N 2°22′E

		Sunrise	Sunset
European Standard Time (UT-1)			
Jan	01	0854	1655
	15	0847	1713
Feb	01	0827	1742
	15	0803	1807
Mar	01	0735	1832
	15	0704	1855
European Summer Time (UT-2)			
Apr	01	0726	2023
	15	0656	2046
May	01	0624	2112
	15	0601	2134
Jun	01	0541	2156
	15	0535	2207
Jul	01	0540	2208
	15	0553	2159
Aug	01	0616	2137
	15	0637	2111
Sep	01	0704	2036
	15	0726	2005
Oct	01	0751	1928
	15	0814	1858
European Standard Time (UT-1)			
Nov	01	0743	1725
	15	0807	1703
Dec	01	0832	1647
	15	0848	1644

JANUARY

Date	Day	Time	m
1	W	0418 1114 1648 2330	5.4 1.2 5.3 1.5
2	TH	0501 1154 1734	5.2 1.4 5.1
3	F ☽	0013 0551 1242 1829	1.7 5.0 1.5 4.9
4	SA	0108 0649 1345 1932	1.8 4.8 1.6 4.8
5	SU	0219 0756 1459 2040	1.9 4.8 1.6 4.8
6	M	0330 0905 1603 2145	1.8 4.9 1.5 5.0
7	TU	0431 1006 1700 2239	1.6 5.1 1.4 5.2
8	W	0525 1057 1750 2325	1.4 5.3 1.2 5.4
9	TH	0613 1141 1836	1.2 5.6 1.0
10	F ○	0006 0658 1221 1920	5.6 0.9 5.8 0.9
11	SA	0046 0742 1303 2004	5.8 0.7 6.0 0.8
12	SU	0127 0827 1346 2049	5.9 0.6 6.1 0.7
13	M	0210 0912 1431 2134	6.0 0.5 6.1 0.7
14	TU	0254 0958 1518 2220	5.9 0.5 6.1 0.8
15	W	0339 1044 1606 2306	5.9 0.5 5.9 0.9
16	TH	0427 1133 1658 2355	5.7 0.6 5.7 1.1
17	F ☾	0519 1226 1756	5.6 0.8 5.5
18	SA	0052 0619 1328 1902	1.3 5.4 1.0 5.3
19	SU	0158 0730 1435 2019	1.4 5.2 1.1 5.2
20	M	0308 0848 1546 2132	1.5 5.2 1.2 5.2
21	TU	0422 0958 1659 2236	1.4 5.3 1.2 5.3
22	W	0531 1059 1801 2332	1.2 5.4 1.1 5.4
23	TH	0626 1152 1850	1.0 5.6 1.0
24	F ●	0018 0712 1237 1932	5.6 0.9 5.7 0.9
25	SA	0058 0753 1318 2011	5.7 0.7 5.8 0.9
26	SU	0135 0832 1357 2046	5.8 0.7 5.9 0.9
27	M	0211 0908 1433 2120	5.8 0.7 5.8 0.9
28	TU	0243 0941 1506 2153	5.8 0.7 5.8 1.0
29	W	0315 1013 1538 2225	5.7 0.8 5.6 1.1
30	TH	0347 1044 1612 2256	5.6 0.9 5.5 1.2
31	F	0422 1116 1650 2331	5.4 1.1 5.3 1.3

FEBRUARY

Date	Day	Time	m
1	SA	0502 1153 1734	5.3 1.2 5.1
2	SU ☽	0011 0550 1238 1829	1.5 5.0 1.4 4.9
3	M	0103 0652 1340 1934	1.7 4.8 1.6 4.7
4	TU	0215 0803 1502 2048	1.8 4.7 1.7 4.7
5	W	0338 0919 1617 2202	1.8 4.8 1.6 4.9
6	TH	0449 1027 1722 2302	1.5 5.1 1.3 5.2
7	F	0549 1122 1818 2350	1.2 5.4 1.0 5.5
8	SA	0642 1207 1906	0.9 5.8 0.8
9	SU ○	0033 0729 1251 1951	5.8 0.6 6.0 0.6
10	M	0113 0814 1333 2036	6.0 0.4 6.2 0.5
11	TU	0155 0859 1417 2120	6.1 0.2 6.2 0.5
12	W	0237 0944 1502 2204	6.1 0.2 6.2 0.5
13	TH	0319 1029 1547 2247	6.1 0.2 6.1 0.7
14	F	0404 1114 1634 2332	6.0 0.4 5.9 0.9
15	SA ☾	0453 1202 1727	5.8 0.6 5.6
16	SU	0022 0548 1257 1828	1.1 5.5 0.9 5.2
17	M	0123 0656 1403 1945	1.4 5.2 1.3 4.9
18	TU	0235 0820 1519 2109	1.6 5.0 1.4 4.8
19	W	0400 0942 1644 2224	1.6 5.0 1.4 5.0
20	TH	0518 1051 1750 2324	1.3 5.2 1.2 5.2
21	F	0614 1146 1838	1.1 5.4 1.1
22	SA	0009 0659 1228 1917	5.4 0.8 5.6 0.9
23	SU ●	0045 0738 1305 1953	5.6 0.7 5.8 0.9
24	M	0118 0813 1339 2025	5.7 0.6 5.8 0.8
25	TU	0150 0845 1411 2057	5.8 0.6 5.9 0.8
26	W	0219 0917 1439 2127	5.8 0.6 5.8 0.8
27	TH	0247 0946 1507 2157	5.8 0.6 5.8 0.9
28	F	0316 1014 1537 2225	5.7 0.7 5.6 0.9
29	SA	0345 1042 1606 2255	5.6 0.9 5.5 1.1

MARCH

Date	Day	Time	m
1	SU	0414 1114 1638 2330	5.5 1.0 5.3 1.3
2	M ☽	0450 1153 1722	5.2 1.3 5.0
3	TU	0014 0545 1245 1837	1.5 4.9 1.5 4.7
4	W	0116 0711 1403 2002	1.7 4.7 1.7 4.6
5	TH	0245 0839 1536 2129	1.8 4.7 1.7 4.7
6	F	0414 1002 1656 2240	1.6 5.0 1.4 5.1
7	SA	0527 1103 1759 2332	1.2 5.4 1.0 5.5
8	SU	0623 1151 1849	0.8 5.8 0.7
9	M ○	0015 0711 1233 1934	5.8 0.4 6.1 0.5
10	TU	0054 0756 1315 2017	6.0 0.2 6.3 0.4
11	W	0133 0840 1357 2100	6.2 0.1 6.3 0.4
12	TH	0214 0923 1439 2142	6.2 0.0 6.3 0.4
13	F	0256 1007 1524 2224	6.2 0.1 6.1 0.5
14	SA	0340 1050 1609 2307	6.1 0.3 5.9 0.7
15	SU	0428 1135 1659 2354	5.9 0.6 5.6 1.0
16	M ☾	0522 1226 1758	5.6 1.0 5.2
17	TU	0051 0629 1331 1915	1.3 5.2 1.4 4.8
18	W	0205 0756 1454 2046	1.6 4.8 1.7 4.6
19	TH	0337 0925 1624 2205	1.6 4.8 1.6 4.8
20	F	0458 1036 1732 2304	1.4 5.1 1.3 5.1
21	SA	0555 1129 1817 2347	1.1 5.4 1.1 5.3
22	SU	0639 1209 1855	0.8 5.6 0.9
23	M	0022 0715 1243 1928	5.6 0.7 5.7 0.8
24	TU ●	0054 0747 1315 1958	5.7 0.6 5.8 0.8
25	W	0124 0817 1344 2028	5.8 0.6 5.9 0.7
26	TH	0151 0847 1410 2059	5.8 0.6 5.8 0.7
27	F	0217 0917 1436 2128	5.8 0.6 5.8 0.7
28	SA	0244 0944 1503 2156	5.8 0.7 5.7 0.8
29	SU	0312 1012 1530 2226	5.7 0.8 5.6 0.9
30	M	0339 1043 1558 2300	5.6 1.0 5.4 1.1
31	TU	0413 1121 1638 2344	5.4 1.2 5.1 1.3

APRIL

Date	Day	Time	m
1	W ☽	0503 1213 1749	5.1 1.5 4.7
2	TH	0044 0635 1328 1929	1.6 4.8 1.7 4.6
3	F	0210 0809 1504 2059	1.7 4.7 1.7 4.7
4	SA	0343 0937 1630 2214	1.5 5.0 1.4 5.1
5	SU	0501 1040 1736 2308	1.1 5.5 1.0 5.5
6	M	0600 1129 1827 2350	0.7 5.9 0.7 5.8
7	TU	0649 1211 1911	0.4 6.1 0.5
8	W ○	0029 0734 1252 1954	6.0 0.2 6.3 0.4
9	TH	0108 0817 1333 2036	6.2 0.1 6.3 0.4
10	F	0149 0900 1416 2119	6.3 0.1 6.2 0.4
11	SA	0233 0943 1501 2201	6.3 0.2 6.1 0.5
12	SU	0318 1026 1547 2244	6.1 0.4 5.8 0.7
13	M	0407 1110 1636 2330	5.9 0.8 5.5 1.0
14	TU ☾	0502 1159 1733	5.5 1.2 5.1
15	W	0024 0607 1301 1845	1.3 5.1 1.5 4.7
16	TH	0136 0730 1423 2015	1.5 4.8 1.8 4.6
17	F	0305 0859 1551 2132	1.6 4.8 1.7 4.7
18	SA	0426 1007 1659 2229	1.4 5.0 1.4 5.0
19	SU	0524 1058 1747 2314	1.1 5.3 1.2 5.3
20	M	0608 1138 1825 2351	0.9 5.5 1.0 5.5
21	TU	0644 1214 1857	0.8 5.7 0.9
22	W	0024 0714 1246 1927	5.6 0.7 5.7 0.8
23	TH ●	0054 0744 1314 1958	5.7 0.7 5.8 0.7
24	F	0121 0816 1340 2030	5.8 0.6 5.8 0.7
25	SA	0148 0848 1407 2102	5.8 0.7 5.8 0.7
26	SU	0217 0918 1436 2133	5.8 0.7 5.7 0.8
27	M	0248 0949 1506 2206	5.7 0.8 5.6 0.9
28	TU	0319 1022 1540 2243	5.6 1.0 5.4 1.0
29	W	0358 1103 1624 2329	5.4 1.2 5.1 1.2
30	TH ☽	0456 1157 1742	5.1 1.4 4.8

MAY

Date	Day	Time	m
1	F	0030 0622 1311 1905	1.4 4.9 1.6 4.7
2	SA	0149 0744 1440 2028	1.5 4.9 1.6 4.8
3	SU	0317 0908 1601 2143	1.3 5.2 1.3 5.1
4	M	0431 1013 1706 2238	0.9 5.5 1.0 5.5
5	TU	0532 1103 1800 2322	0.6 5.8 0.7 5.8
6	W	0623 1146 1846	0.4 6.0 0.6
7	TH ○	0003 0710 1228 1930	6.0 0.3 6.1 0.5
8	F	0044 0754 1311 2014	6.2 0.2 6.2 0.4
9	SA	0128 0837 1355 2057	6.2 0.3 6.1 0.4
10	SU	0214 0921 1442 2141	6.2 0.4 6.0 0.5
11	M	0302 1004 1530 2225	6.0 0.6 5.7 0.7
12	TU	0353 1048 1618 2310	5.8 0.9 5.5 0.9
13	W	0446 1135 1711	5.5 1.3 5.1
14	TH ☾	0001 0544 1231 1812	1.2 5.1 1.5 4.8
15	F	0104 0656 1342 1930	1.4 4.8 1.7 4.6
16	SA	0221 0818 1501 2046	1.5 4.8 1.7 4.7
17	SU	0336 0924 1608 2145	1.4 4.9 1.5 4.9
18	M	0437 1016 1702 2233	1.2 5.1 1.3 5.1
19	TU	0525 1101 1745 2314	1.0 5.3 1.1 5.4
20	W	0604 1139 1821 2351	0.9 5.5 1.0 5.5
21	TH	0638 1214 1854	0.8 5.6 0.9
22	F ●	0023 0712 1244 1929	5.6 0.8 5.7 0.8
23	SA	0053 0746 1313 2004	5.7 0.8 5.7 0.8
24	SU	0124 0822 1344 2041	5.8 0.8 5.7 0.7
25	M	0158 0858 1420 2117	5.8 0.8 5.7 0.8
26	TU	0236 0935 1458 2155	5.7 0.9 5.6 0.8
27	W	0316 1014 1541 2237	5.6 1.0 5.4 0.9
28	TH	0404 1058 1634 2325	5.5 1.2 5.2 1.0
29	F	0504 1152 1737	5.3 1.3 5.0
30	SA ☽	0023 0609 1258 1842	1.2 5.2 1.4 5.0
31	SU	0134 0719 1416 1954	1.2 5.2 1.4 5.0

JUNE

Date	Day	Time	m
1	M	0250 0836 1530 2107	1.1 5.3 1.2 5.2
2	TU	0401 0943 1635 2206	0.9 5.5 1.0 5.5
3	W	0503 1037 1732 2256	0.7 5.7 0.9 5.7
4	TH	0558 1124 1823 2342	0.5 5.9 0.7 5.9
5	F ○	0648 1210 1911	0.5 5.9 0.6
6	SA	0027 0734 1255 1956	6.0 0.5 6.0 0.6
7	SU	0114 0820 1341 2041	6.1 0.5 5.9 0.5
8	M	0203 0904 1430 2125	6.0 0.6 5.8 0.6
9	TU	0252 0947 1516 2209	5.9 0.8 5.7 0.7
10	W	0341 1029 1601 2252	5.7 1.0 5.5 0.9
11	TH	0428 1112 1646 2337	5.5 1.2 5.3 1.1
12	F	0516 1159 1734	5.2 1.4 5.0
13	SA ☾	0027 0611 1253 1831	1.2 5.0 1.6 4.9
14	SU	0128 0716 1400 1940	1.4 4.8 1.7 4.8
15	M	0234 0826 1506 2048	1.4 4.8 1.6 4.8
16	TU	0337 0925 1606 2144	1.4 5.0 1.5 5.0
17	W	0432 1016 1658 2233	1.2 5.1 1.3 5.2
18	TH	0520 1101 1743 2316	1.1 5.3 1.2 5.3
19	F	0603 1141 1824 2354	1.0 5.4 1.1 5.5
20	SA	0643 1217 1903	1.0 5.5 0.9
21	SU ●	0030 0722 1252 1943	5.6 0.9 5.6 0.8
22	M	0106 0803 1329 2024	5.7 0.9 5.7 0.7
23	TU	0146 0844 1409 2106	5.8 0.8 5.7 0.7
24	W	0229 0926 1453 2149	5.8 0.9 5.7 0.7
25	TH	0314 1009 1539 2233	5.8 0.9 5.6 0.7
26	F	0402 1055 1627 2321	5.7 1.0 5.5 0.8
27	SA	0453 1144 1719	5.6 1.1 5.4
28	SU ☽	0013 0550 1241 1816	0.9 5.4 1.2 5.3
29	M	0115 0652 1348 1921	0.9 5.4 1.3 5.3
30	TU	0223 0802 1458 2032	0.9 5.3 1.3 5.3

DUNKERQUE
LAT 51°03′N
LONG 2°22′E

TIMES AND HEIGHTS OF HIGH AND LOW WATER (Heights in Metres)

TIME ZONE –0100 (French Standard Time). **Subtract 1 hour for UT. For French Summer Time (area enclosed in shaded box) add 1 hour**

2020

JULY

Date	Day	Time	m
1	W	0331 0913 1605 2139	0.9 5.4 1.2 5.4
2	TH	0437 1016 1709 2238	0.8 5.5 1.1 5.6
3	F	0539 1111 1807 2331	0.8 5.6 0.9 5.7
4	SA	0634 1202 1859	0.8 5.7 0.8
5	SU O	0021 0723 1249 1946	5.8 0.7 5.8 0.7
6	M	0109 0807 1334 2030	5.9 0.8 5.8 0.6
7	TU	0156 0850 1418 2112	5.9 0.8 5.8 0.6
8	W	0241 0930 1459 2153	5.9 0.9 5.7 0.6
9	TH	0323 1008 1538 2231	5.8 1.0 5.6 0.8
10	F	0403 1046 1615 2309	5.6 1.1 5.5 0.9
11	SA	0443 1124 1655 2348	5.4 1.3 5.3 1.1
12	SU	0525 1206 1739	5.2 1.4 5.1
13	M ☾	0033 0613 1256 1832	1.2 5.0 1.6 5.0
14	TU	0128 0709 1359 1934	1.4 4.9 1.7 4.8
15	W	0233 0815 1507 2042	1.5 4.8 1.7 4.8
16	TH	0338 0922 1609 2147	1.5 4.9 1.6 4.9
17	F	0437 1021 1706 2242	1.4 5.0 1.4 5.1
18	SA	0531 1112 1757 2330	1.3 5.2 1.2 5.4
19	SU	0619 1156 1843	1.1 5.4 1.0
20	M ●	0011 0704 1236 1927	5.6 1.0 5.6 0.8
21	TU	0052 0748 1315 2011	5.8 0.9 5.8 0.6
22	W	0133 0831 1356 2055	5.9 0.8 5.8 0.5
23	TH	0216 0915 1438 2139	6.0 0.7 5.9 0.4
24	F	0259 0959 1521 2223	6.0 0.8 5.8 0.5
25	SA	0345 1042 1605 2308	5.9 0.8 5.7 0.5
26	SU	0433 1128 1653 2356	5.8 1.0 5.7 0.6
27	M ☽	0525 1218 1747	5.6 1.1 5.5
28	TU	0051 0624 1319 1850	0.8 5.5 1.3 5.4
29	W	0155 0732 1428 2003	1.0 5.3 1.4 5.3
30	TH	0305 0850 1541 2121	1.1 5.2 1.4 5.3
31	F	0418 1003 1656 2230	1.2 5.2 1.2 5.4

AUGUST

Date	Day	Time	m
1	SA	0529 1107 1800 2329	1.1 5.4 1.0 5.6
2	SU	0626 1200 1851	1.0 5.5 0.8
3	M O	0020 0713 1244 1936	5.7 0.9 5.7 0.7
4	TU	0103 0755 1323 2017	5.9 0.9 5.8 0.6
5	W	0144 0833 1400 2055	5.9 0.9 5.8 0.6
6	TH	0222 0909 1436 2131	5.9 0.9 5.8 0.6
7	F	0259 0943 1508 2205	5.8 0.9 5.7 0.7
8	SA	0332 1016 1541 2237	5.7 1.0 5.6 0.8
9	SU	0404 1049 1614 2309	5.6 1.1 5.5 1.0
10	M	0439 1122 1652 2343	5.4 1.3 5.3 1.2
11	TU ☾	0521 1200 1738	5.2 1.5 5.1
12	W	0024 0611 1248 1835	1.4 4.9 1.7 4.9
13	TH	0121 0713 1356 1944	1.6 4.7 1.9 4.7
14	F	0238 0826 1518 2101	1.8 4.7 1.9 4.7
15	SA	0355 0942 1631 2212	1.7 4.8 1.7 5.0
16	SU	0503 1046 1734 2308	1.5 5.1 1.3 5.3
17	M	0601 1136 1826 2354	1.2 5.4 1.0 5.6
18	TU	0648 1218 1911	1.0 5.7 0.7
19	W ●	0035 0732 1257 1954	5.9 0.8 5.9 0.5
20	TH	0115 0815 1335 2038	6.1 0.7 6.0 0.3
21	F	0156 0857 1415 2121	6.2 0.6 6.1 0.3
22	SA	0238 0940 1455 2204	6.2 0.6 6.1 0.3
23	SU	0321 1022 1538 2247	6.1 0.7 6.0 0.4
24	M	0407 1105 1625 2333	6.0 0.9 5.9 0.6
25	TU ☽	0458 1152 1719	5.7 1.1 5.7
26	W	0024 0555 1249 1823	0.9 5.4 1.3 5.4
27	TH	0127 0705 1401 1942	1.2 5.1 1.5 5.1
28	F	0243 0832 1524 2110	1.4 4.9 1.6 5.1
29	SA	0408 0955 1648 2226	1.5 5.0 1.4 5.3
30	SU	0523 1102 1751 2326	1.3 5.2 1.1 5.5
31	M	0616 1152 1839	1.1 5.5 0.8

SEPTEMBER

Date	Day	Time	m
1	TU	0012 0659 1230 1920	5.7 1.0 5.7 0.7
2	W O	0050 0737 1304 1958	5.9 0.9 5.8 0.6
3	TH	0124 0811 1336 2032	5.9 0.9 5.9 0.6
4	F	0157 0843 1407 2104	5.9 0.9 5.9 0.6
5	SA	0228 0914 1436 2134	5.9 0.9 5.9 0.7
6	SU	0256 0945 1504 2203	5.8 1.0 5.8 0.8
7	M	0324 1013 1534 2230	5.7 1.1 5.7 1.0
8	TU	0354 1042 1604 2300	5.5 1.2 5.5 1.2
9	W	0426 1115 1639 2336	5.3 1.4 5.2 1.4
10	TH ☾	0506 1156 1729	5.0 1.6 4.9
11	F	0024 0616 1254 1855	1.7 4.7 1.9 4.7
12	SA	0136 0741 1421 2021	1.9 4.6 2.0 4.6
13	SU	0312 0907 1554 2144	1.9 4.7 1.8 4.9
14	M	0436 1020 1709 2246	1.6 5.0 1.4 5.3
15	TU	0540 1114 1804 2334	1.3 5.4 1.0 5.7
16	W	0629 1156 1850	1.0 5.7 0.6
17	TH ●	0014 0711 1233 1933	6.0 0.7 6.0 0.4
18	F	0052 0753 1309 2016	6.2 0.6 6.2 0.3
19	SA	0131 0834 1347 2058	6.3 0.6 6.3 0.2
20	SU	0212 0916 1428 2141	6.3 0.6 6.3 0.3
21	M	0255 0958 1512 2223	6.2 0.7 6.2 0.4
22	TU	0341 1041 1559 2308	6.0 0.8 6.0 0.7
23	W	0431 1127 1654 2358	5.7 1.1 5.7 1.1
24	TH ☽	0529 1223 1801	5.4 1.4 5.4
25	F	0102 0642 1338 1925	1.5 5.0 1.6 5.0
26	SA	0225 0815 1509 2100	1.7 4.8 1.7 5.0
27	SU	0357 0941 1634 2216	1.7 4.9 1.4 5.2
28	M	0510 1046 1735 2312	1.4 5.2 1.1 5.5
29	TU	0559 1132 1821 2354	1.2 5.5 0.8 5.7
30	W	0639 1207 1859	1.0 5.7 0.7

OCTOBER

Date	Day	Time	m
1	TH O	0027 0713 1238 1932	5.9 1.0 5.8 0.7
2	F	0059 0744 1308 2003	6.0 0.9 5.9 0.7
3	SA	0129 0813 1336 2032	6.0 0.9 5.9 0.7
4	SU	0156 0844 1402 2102	5.9 0.9 5.9 0.8
5	M	0221 0913 1429 2130	5.9 1.0 5.9 0.9
6	TU	0247 0941 1457 2156	5.8 1.0 5.8 1.0
7	W	0315 1009 1525 2225	5.6 1.2 5.6 1.2
8	TH	0342 1041 1556 2300	5.4 1.4 5.4 1.5
9	F	0416 1121 1638 2347	5.1 1.6 5.1 1.7
10	SA ☾	0511 1218 1810	4.8 1.8 4.7
11	SU	0057 0704 1340 1947	2.0 4.6 2.0 4.7
12	M	0232 0831 1517 2113	2.0 4.6 1.8 5.0
13	TU	0405 0950 1638 2219	1.7 5.0 1.4 5.4
14	W	0512 1045 1737 2308	1.3 5.4 0.9 5.8
15	TH	0603 1127 1825 2348	1.0 5.8 0.6 6.1
16	F ●	0646 1204 1909	0.7 6.1 0.4
17	SA	0026 0728 1241 1951	6.3 0.6 6.3 0.3
18	SU	0105 0810 1321 2034	6.4 0.6 6.4 0.3
19	M	0147 0852 1404 2117	6.4 0.6 6.4 0.4
20	TU	0231 0935 1450 2200	6.2 0.7 6.3 0.6
21	W	0318 1019 1540 2245	6.0 0.8 6.0 0.9
22	TH	0409 1106 1636 2335	5.7 1.1 5.7 1.3
23	F ☽	0507 1201 1743	5.3 1.4 5.3
24	SA	0038 0617 1315 1905	1.7 4.9 1.7 5.0
25	SU	0201 0749 1444 2037	1.9 4.7 1.7 4.9
26	M	0329 0912 1606 2149	1.8 4.8 1.5 5.1
27	TU	0441 1013 1707 2242	1.6 5.1 1.2 5.4
28	W	0531 1058 1753 2323	1.3 5.4 0.9 5.6
29	TH	0610 1135 1831 2358	1.2 5.6 0.8 5.8
30	F	0644 1208 1902	1.1 5.8 0.8
31	SA O	0030 0713 1239 1931	5.9 1.0 5.9 0.8

NOVEMBER

Date	Day	Time	m
1	SU	0059 0743 1306 2001	5.9 0.9 5.9 0.8
2	M	0124 0814 1333 2032	5.9 0.9 5.9 0.9
3	TU	0150 0846 1401 2102	5.9 1.0 5.9 1.0
4	W	0218 0916 1431 2131	5.8 1.0 5.8 1.1
5	TH	0249 0947 1503 2202	5.7 1.1 5.7 1.3
6	F	0320 1021 1537 2239	5.5 1.3 5.4 1.5
7	SA	0357 1104 1624 2329	5.2 1.5 5.2 1.7
8	SU ☾	0456 1200 1748	4.9 1.7 4.9
9	M	0035 0631 1313 1913	1.9 4.7 1.7 4.9
10	TU	0159 0751 1441 2034	1.9 4.8 1.6 5.1
11	W	0327 0909 1601 2144	1.7 5.0 1.3 5.4
12	TH	0437 1009 1704 2236	1.3 5.4 0.9 5.8
13	F	0532 1055 1757 2320	1.0 5.8 0.6 6.1
14	SA	0619 1136 1843	0.8 6.1 0.5
15	SU ●	0001 0704 1217 1928	6.2 0.7 6.3 0.4
16	M	0043 0748 1300 2012	6.3 0.6 6.3 0.4
17	TU	0127 0832 1347 2057	6.3 0.6 6.3 0.5
18	W	0213 0917 1436 2141	6.1 0.7 6.2 0.8
19	TH	0302 1003 1528 2227	5.9 0.8 6.0 1.0
20	F	0353 1050 1622 2316	5.6 1.0 5.7 1.4
21	SA	0446 1142 1722	5.3 1.3 5.3
22	SU ☽	0011 0546 1245 1833	1.7 5.0 1.5 5.0
23	M	0121 0703 1402 1956	1.9 4.8 1.6 4.9
24	TU	0239 0824 1517 2105	1.9 4.8 1.6 5.0
25	W	0348 0926 1621 2159	1.8 5.0 1.4 5.2
26	TH	0445 1015 1712 2245	1.5 5.2 1.2 5.4
27	F	0531 1058 1754 2324	1.3 5.4 1.1 5.6
28	SA	0609 1136 1828	1.2 5.6 1.0
29	SU	0000 0642 1210 1900	5.7 1.1 5.7 1.0
30	M O	0031 0715 1240 1933	5.7 1.0 5.8 1.0

DECEMBER

Date	Day	Time	m
1	TU	0059 0749 1310 2007	5.8 1.0 5.8 1.0
2	W	0128 0824 1342 2041	5.8 1.0 5.8 1.0
3	TH	0201 0859 1418 2116	5.8 1.0 5.8 1.1
4	F	0237 0935 1455 2152	5.7 1.0 5.7 1.2
5	SA	0315 1014 1537 2233	5.5 1.1 5.5 1.4
6	SU	0358 1058 1627 2320	5.3 1.2 5.3 1.5
7	M	0453 1150 1731	5.1 1.4 5.2
8	TU ☾	0018 0600 1252 1839	1.6 5.0 1.4 5.1
9	W	0128 0709 1407 1952	1.7 5.0 1.4 5.2
10	TH	0247 0821 1523 2104	1.6 5.1 1.2 5.4
11	F	0358 0929 1630 2205	1.4 5.4 0.9 5.6
12	SA	0500 1025 1729 2257	1.2 5.7 0.8 5.8
13	SU	0555 1114 1822 2344	1.0 5.9 0.6 6.0
14	M ●	0645 1202 1911	0.8 6.1 0.6
15	TU	0029 0733 1250 1957	6.0 0.7 6.2 0.6
16	W	0117 0819 1339 2043	6.1 0.6 6.2 0.7
17	TH	0204 0905 1428 2128	6.0 0.6 6.1 0.8
18	F	0251 0950 1518 2212	5.9 0.7 5.9 1.0
19	SA	0337 1035 1606 2255	5.7 0.9 5.7 1.3
20	SU	0422 1120 1655 2340	5.4 1.1 5.4 1.5
21	M	0509 1209 1748	5.2 1.3 5.1
22	TU ☽	0031 0603 1305 1852	1.7 5.0 1.5 4.9
23	W	0132 0710 1410 2003	1.8 4.8 1.6 4.8
24	TH	0239 0823 1515 2105	1.8 4.8 1.6 4.9
25	F	0342 0924 1615 2159	1.7 4.9 1.5 5.0
26	SA	0440 1017 1708 2247	1.6 5.1 1.4 5.2
27	SU	0530 1103 1753 2330	1.4 5.3 1.2 5.4
28	M	0613 1144 1833	1.3 5.4 1.2
29	TU	0007 0652 1220 1911	5.5 1.1 5.6 1.1
30	W O	0041 0730 1254 1949	5.6 1.0 5.7 1.0
31	TH	0115 0809 1331 2028	5.7 0.9 5.8 1.0

CALAIS

LAT 50°58′N
LONG 1°51′E

TIMES AND HEIGHTS OF HIGH AND LOW WATER (Heights in Metres)

TIME ZONE –0100 (French Standard Time). **Subtract 1 hour for UT. For Summer Time (area enclosed in shaded box) add 1 hour**

2020

SUNRISE AND SUNSET TIMES

CALAIS
At 50°58′N 1°51′E

		Sunrise	Sunset
European Standard Time (UT-1)			
Jan	01	0856	1657
	15	0849	1715
Feb	01	0829	1744
	15	0805	1809
Mar	01	0737	1834
	15	0706	1857
European Summer Time (UT-2)			
Apr	01	0728	2026
	15	0658	2048
May	01	0626	2114
	15	0603	2136
Jun	01	0544	2158
	15	0538	2209
Jul	01	0543	2210
	15	0556	2201
Aug	01	0618	2138
	15	0640	2113
Sep	01	0706	2038
	15	0728	2007
Oct	01	0753	1930
	15	0816	1900
European Standard Time (UT-1)			
Nov	01	0745	1727
	15	0809	1705
Dec	01	0834	1649

JANUARY

Date	Day	Time	m	Time	m	Time	m	Time	m
1	W	0354	6.5	1057	1.7	1619	6.4	2316	1.9
2	TH	0435	6.3	1137	2.0	1704	6.1	2359	2.1
3	F ☽	0523	6.1	1229	2.2	1758	5.9		
4	SA	0056	2.3	0621	5.9	1334	2.3	1903	5.8
5	SU	0204	2.4	0730	5.8	1441	2.3	2015	5.8
6	M	0310	2.3	0840	6.0	1544	2.1	2117	6.0
7	TU	0412	2.1	0938	6.2	1644	1.8	2209	6.3
8	W	0510	1.8	1026	6.5	1739	1.6	2254	6.6
9	TH	0601	1.5	1108	6.7	1827	1.3	2335	6.8
10	F O	0647	1.2	1149	7.0	1913	1.1		
11	SA	0015	7.0	0732	1.0	1230	7.2	1958	0.9
12	SU	0058	7.2	0816	0.9	1314	7.3	2043	0.8
13	M	0142	7.3	0901	0.8	1401	7.4	2128	0.8
14	TU	0229	7.2	0946	0.8	1449	7.3	2213	0.9
15	W	0317	7.1	1032	0.9	1539	7.1	2258	1.1
16	TH	0406	7.0	1119	1.0	1633	6.9	2345	1.3
17	F ☾	0458	6.8	1210	1.2	1730	6.6		
18	SA	0037	1.5	0557	6.6	1308	1.5	1837	6.4
19	SU	0139	1.8	0707	6.4	1417	1.6	1952	6.2
20	M	0252	1.9	0824	6.3	1535	1.7	2106	6.3
21	TU	0411	1.8	0936	6.4	1648	1.6	2212	6.4
22	W	0518	1.6	1037	6.6	1748	1.4	2308	6.6
23	TH	0612	1.4	1129	6.8	1838	1.2	2354	6.8
24	F ●	0659	1.2	1212	7.0	1922	1.1		
25	SA	0033	6.9	0741	1.1	1251	7.1	2002	1.0
26	SU	0111	7.0	0821	1.0	1329	7.1	2040	1.0
27	M	0147	7.1	0858	1.0	1405	7.1	2115	1.1
28	TU	0221	7.0	0932	1.1	1439	7.0	2147	1.2
29	W	0252	6.9	1002	1.2	1511	6.8	2216	1.4
30	TH	0323	6.8	1031	1.4	1544	6.6	2245	1.6
31	F	0357	6.6	1101	1.6	1620	6.4	2318	1.8

FEBRUARY

Date	Day	Time	m	Time	m	Time	m	Time	m
1	SA	0435	6.4	1137	1.8	1703	6.1	2357	2.0
2	SU ☽	0522	6.1	1225	2.1	1757	5.9		
3	M	0051	2.3	0621	5.9	1331	2.3	1903	5.7
4	TU	0204	2.4	0734	5.7	1446	2.3	2021	5.7
5	W	0319	2.3	0852	5.8	1559	2.1	2133	5.9
6	TH	0432	2.0	0957	6.2	1709	1.7	2230	6.3
7	F	0537	1.6	1049	6.6	1808	1.4	2319	6.7
8	SA	0631	1.2	1135	6.9	1859	1.0		
9	SU O	0004	7.0	0719	0.9	1219	7.2	1947	0.8
10	M	0047	7.3	0805	0.7	1304	7.4	2033	0.6
11	TU	0133	7.4	0851	0.5	1351	7.5	2117	0.5
12	W	0218	7.5	0936	0.4	1440	7.5	2201	0.6
13	TH	0303	7.4	1020	0.5	1526	7.3	2242	0.7
14	F	0346	7.2	1103	0.7	1612	7.1	2324	1.0
15	SA ☾	0432	7.0	1148	1.0	1702	6.7		
16	SU	0009	1.4	0525	6.7	1240	1.4	1802	6.3
17	M	0104	1.8	0632	6.3	1343	1.8	1918	6.0
18	TU	0216	2.1	0756	6.0	1505	2.0	2045	5.9
19	W	0345	2.1	0920	6.1	1629	1.9	2159	6.1
20	TH	0502	1.8	1028	6.3	1735	1.6	2258	6.3
21	F	0601	1.5	1120	6.6	1827	1.4	2342	6.6
22	SA	0648	1.2	1201	6.8	1910	1.2		
23	SU ●	0018	6.8	0729	1.0	1236	7.0	1948	1.0
24	M	0052	7.0	0806	0.9	1310	7.1	2023	1.0
25	TU	0124	7.1	0840	0.9	1343	7.1	2055	1.0
26	W	0155	7.1	0911	0.9	1413	7.0	2124	1.0
27	TH	0224	7.0	0939	1.0	1442	6.9	2150	1.1
28	F	0252	6.9	1004	1.1	1510	6.8	2216	1.3
29	SA	0321	6.8	1031	1.3	1540	6.6	2244	1.5

MARCH

Date	Day	Time	m	Time	m	Time	m	Time	m
1	SU	0351	6.6	1100	1.6	1613	6.3	2316	1.8
2	M ☽	0427	6.3	1137	1.9	1658	6.0	2359	2.1
3	TU	0522	5.9	1233	2.2	1806	5.7		
4	W	0106	2.4	0640	5.7	1354	2.4	1932	5.5
5	TH	0232	2.4	0811	5.7	1520	2.2	2101	5.7
6	F	0358	2.1	0931	6.0	1645	1.8	2210	6.2
7	SA	0515	1.6	1031	6.5	1751	1.3	2303	6.6
8	SU	0614	1.1	1120	6.9	1843	0.9	2349	7.0
9	M O	0704	0.8	1206	7.3	1932	0.6		
10	TU	0032	7.3	0751	0.5	1251	7.5	2017	0.5
11	W	0116	7.5	0836	0.3	1337	7.6	2100	0.4
12	TH	0200	7.6	0920	0.2	1424	7.6	2141	0.4
13	F	0242	7.5	1001	0.3	1507	7.4	2220	0.6
14	SA	0323	7.4	1042	0.6	1550	7.1	2259	0.9
15	SU	0406	7.1	1124	1.0	1636	6.7	2341	1.4
16	M ☾	0457	6.6	1211	1.5	1733	6.2		
17	TU	0033	1.8	0603	6.1	1313	1.9	1849	5.8
18	W	0147	2.2	0731	5.8	1438	2.2	2021	5.6
19	TH	0321	2.2	0902	5.8	1606	2.1	2141	5.8
20	F	0442	1.9	1012	6.1	1717	1.7	2240	6.2
21	SA	0544	1.5	1103	6.5	1809	1.4	2322	6.5
22	SU	0631	1.2	1141	6.7	1850	1.2	2356	6.8
23	M	0710	1.1	1214	6.9	1926	1.1		
24	TU ●	0027	7.0	0744	0.9	1246	7.0	1958	1.0
25	W	0058	7.0	0815	0.9	1317	7.1	2027	0.9
26	TH	0127	7.1	0844	0.9	1345	7.0	2056	1.0
27	F	0153	7.1	0912	0.9	1411	7.0	2123	1.0
28	SA	0220	7.0	0938	1.0	1438	6.8	2149	1.2
29	SU	0247	6.8	1004	1.2	1504	6.6	2216	1.4
30	M	0312	6.6	1032	1.5	1531	6.4	2247	1.6
31	TU	0345	6.4	1107	1.8	1611	6.1	2328	2.0

APRIL

Date	Day	Time	m	Time	m	Time	m	Time	m
1	W ☽	0437	6.0	1159	2.1	1722	5.7		
2	TH	0032	2.2	0602	5.7	1318	2.3	1858	5.5
3	F	0156	2.3	0740	5.7	1448	2.2	2032	5.7
4	SA	0328	2.1	0906	6.0	1620	1.8	2147	6.2
5	SU	0451	1.6	1011	6.5	1728	1.3	2242	6.7
6	M	0551	1.0	1101	7.0	1822	0.9	2327	7.1
7	TU	0643	0.7	1147	7.3	1909	0.6		
8	W O	0009	7.4	0730	0.4	1231	7.5	1954	0.5
9	TH	0051	7.5	0815	0.3	1317	7.6	2036	0.4
10	F	0134	7.6	0858	0.3	1403	7.5	2117	0.5
11	SA	0218	7.5	0939	0.4	1447	7.3	2156	0.7
12	SU	0301	7.3	1019	0.7	1529	7.0	2234	1.0
13	M	0346	7.0	1100	1.1	1614	6.6	2316	1.4
14	TU ☾	0437	6.5	1146	1.6	1708	6.1		
15	W	0007	1.9	0540	6.1	1246	2.0	1820	5.7
16	TH	0122	2.2	0703	5.7	1408	2.3	1950	5.5
17	F	0250	2.3	0832	5.7	1531	2.2	2107	5.7
18	SA	0408	2.0	0940	6.0	1641	1.9	2204	6.1
19	SU	0510	1.6	1030	6.3	1735	1.5	2247	6.4
20	M	0558	1.3	1110	6.6	1817	1.3	2323	6.7
21	TU	0638	1.2	1145	6.8	1853	1.2	2356	6.8
22	W	0712	1.1	1217	6.9	1925	1.1		
23	TH ●	0027	6.9	0744	1.0	1247	6.9	1955	1.0
24	F	0055	7.0	0813	1.0	1314	6.9	2025	1.0
25	SA	0122	7.0	0843	1.0	1341	6.9	2056	1.0
26	SU	0150	7.0	0914	1.1	1410	6.8	2126	1.1
27	M	0219	6.8	0944	1.2	1439	6.7	2157	1.3
28	TU	0250	6.7	1015	1.4	1511	6.4	2230	1.6
29	W	0327	6.4	1053	1.7	1556	6.1	2315	1.8
30	TH ☽	0424	6.1	1146	2.0	1709	5.8		

MAY

Date	Day	Time	m	Time	m	Time	m	Time	m
1	F	0016	2.1	0546	5.9	1257	2.2	1835	5.7
2	SA	0133	2.1	0714	5.8	1422	2.1	2002	5.8
3	SU	0300	1.9	0838	6.1	1551	1.7	2117	6.2
4	M	0422	1.4	0944	6.6	1659	1.3	2213	6.7
5	TU	0524	1.0	1036	6.9	1754	0.9	2259	7.1
6	W	0617	0.7	1123	7.2	1843	0.7	2341	7.3
7	TH O	0706	0.6	1207	7.3	1928	0.6		
8	F	0024	7.4	0752	0.5	1254	7.4	2011	0.6
9	SA	0109	7.4	0836	0.5	1342	7.3	2053	0.6
10	SU	0157	7.3	0918	0.6	1428	7.2	2133	0.8
11	M	0245	7.2	0958	0.8	1512	6.9	2213	1.1
12	TU	0332	6.9	1039	1.2	1556	6.6	2255	1.4
13	W	0420	6.5	1123	1.6	1645	6.2	2345	1.8
14	TH ☾	0516	6.1	1218	2.0	1746	5.8		
15	F	0052	2.1	0626	5.8	1330	2.3	1904	5.6
16	SA	0208	2.2	0748	5.7	1443	2.3	2019	5.7
17	SU	0318	2.1	0854	5.9	1548	2.0	2117	6.0
18	M	0419	1.8	0946	6.1	1645	1.8	2204	6.2
19	TU	0511	1.6	1030	6.4	1732	1.5	2244	6.5
20	W	0555	1.4	1109	6.6	1812	1.4	2321	6.7
21	TH	0633	1.3	1144	6.7	1848	1.3	2353	6.8
22	F ●	0708	1.2	1215	6.8	1921	1.2		
23	SA	0023	6.8	0742	1.1	1244	6.8	1956	1.1
24	SU	0053	6.9	0816	1.1	1315	6.9	2031	1.1
25	M	0126	6.9	0852	1.1	1349	6.8	2107	1.1
26	TU	0202	6.9	0928	1.2	1427	6.7	2144	1.2
27	W	0242	6.7	1006	1.4	1509	6.5	2223	1.4
28	TH	0328	6.5	1048	1.6	1600	6.3	2310	1.6
29	F	0426	6.3	1140	1.8	1703	6.1		
30	SA ☽	0006	1.8	0534	6.2	1242	1.9	1813	6.0
31	SU	0114	1.8	0649	6.1	1356	1.9	1928	6.1

JUNE

Date	Day	Time	m	Time	m	Time	m	Time	m
1	M	0231	1.7	0805	6.3	1516	1.7	2040	6.4
2	TU	0348	1.4	0913	6.6	1626	1.4	2140	6.7
3	W	0454	1.1	1009	6.8	1724	1.1	2232	6.9
4	TH	0551	0.9	1100	7.0	1816	1.0	2319	7.1
5	F O	0642	0.8	1149	7.1	1904	0.9		
6	SA	0006	7.2	0730	0.8	1237	7.1	1949	0.8
7	SU	0054	7.2	0815	0.8	1325	7.1	2033	0.8
8	M	0143	7.2	0858	0.8	1411	7.0	2115	0.9
9	TU	0230	7.0	0940	1.0	1455	6.9	2156	1.1
10	W	0315	6.8	1020	1.3	1536	6.6	2237	1.4
11	TH	0359	6.5	1101	1.6	1619	6.4	2321	1.7
12	F	0445	6.2	1146	1.9	1705	6.1		
13	SA ☾	0013	1.9	0538	6.0	1241	2.1	1801	5.8
14	SU	0115	2.1	0644	5.8	1344	2.2	1911	5.8
15	M	0218	2.1	0754	5.8	1446	2.2	2018	5.8
16	TU	0318	2.0	0853	5.9	1545	2.1	2113	6.0
17	W	0415	1.8	0944	6.1	1639	1.9	2201	6.2
18	TH	0506	1.7	1029	6.3	1728	1.7	2243	6.4
19	F	0552	1.5	1108	6.5	1811	1.5	2320	6.6
20	SA	0633	1.4	1144	6.6	1850	1.3	2355	6.7
21	SU ●	0713	1.3	1219	6.7	1930	1.2		
22	M	0031	6.9	0753	1.2	1255	6.9	2011	1.1
23	TU	0109	7.0	0834	1.1	1336	6.9	2052	1.1
24	W	0152	7.0	0916	1.1	1420	6.9	2134	1.1
25	TH	0237	6.9	0959	1.2	1506	6.8	2217	1.2
26	F	0325	6.8	1043	1.3	1555	6.6	2303	1.3
27	SA	0418	6.6	1131	1.5	1648	6.5	2355	1.4
28	SU ☽	0517	6.5	1225	1.6	1747	6.4		
29	M	0054	1.5	0621	6.4	1328	1.7	1853	6.4
30	TU	0201	1.5	0731	6.4	1438	1.7	2003	6.4

CALAIS
LAT 50°58′N
LONG 1°51′E

TIMES AND HEIGHTS OF HIGH AND LOW WATER (Heights in Metres)

TIME ZONE –0100 (French Standard Time). **Subtract 1 hour for UT. For Summer Time (area enclosed in shaded box) add 1 hour**

2020

JULY

Date	Day	Time	m
1	W	0314 0842 1551 2111	1.5 6.4 1.6 6.5
2	TH	0425 0947 1657 2212	1.3 6.6 1.4 6.7
3	F	0528 1045 1755 2307	1.2 6.7 1.3 6.9
4	SA	0623 1138 1846 2357	1.1 6.8 1.1 7.0
5	SU ○	0712 1225 1933	1.0 6.9 1.0
6	M	0043 0758 1310 2017	7.1 1.0 7.0 1.0
7	TU	0128 0841 1352 2100	7.1 1.0 7.0 1.0
8	W	0212 0922 1433 2140	7.0 1.1 6.9 1.1
9	TH	0253 1000 1511 2217	6.9 1.3 6.8 1.3
10	F	0332 1035 1547 2252	6.7 1.5 6.6 1.5
11	SA	0409 1110 1624 2330	6.5 1.7 6.4 1.7
12	SU	0449 1149 1706	6.2 1.9 6.2
13	M ☾	0014 0536 1237 1756	1.9 6.0 2.1 6.0
14	TU	0110 0632 1337 1857	2.1 5.8 2.3 5.8
15	W	0212 0740 1441 2008	2.2 5.7 2.3 5.8
16	TH	0314 0848 1543 2112	2.1 5.8 2.2 6.0
17	F	0415 0946 1643 2206	2.0 6.0 2.0 6.2
18	SA	0512 1035 1737 2252	1.8 6.3 1.7 6.5
19	SU	0603 1119 1825 2333	1.6 6.5 1.4 6.7
20	M ●	0650 1159 1910	1.3 6.8 1.2
21	TU	0013 0735 1240 1954	6.9 1.2 6.9 1.0
22	W	0055 0820 1322 2038	7.1 1.0 7.1 0.9
23	TH	0139 0905 1407 2123	7.2 0.9 7.1 0.9
24	F	0225 0949 1453 2207	7.2 0.9 7.1 0.9
25	SA	0313 1032 1539 2252	7.1 1.0 7.0 0.9
26	SU	0402 1116 1627 2338	7.0 1.2 6.9 1.1
27	M ☽	0454 1203 1719	6.8 1.4 6.7
28	TU	0030 0552 1257 1820	1.3 6.6 1.6 6.5
29	W	0130 0659 1402 1931	1.5 6.3 1.8 6.4
30	TH	0243 0816 1521 2050	1.7 6.2 1.9 6.3
31	F	0403 0932 1638 2201	1.7 6.3 1.7 6.5

AUGUST

Date	Day	Time	m
1	SA	0512 1036 1741 2300	1.5 6.5 1.5 6.7
2	SU	0609 1128 1833 2348	1.4 6.7 1.3 6.9
3	M ○	0658 1212 1919	1.2 6.9 1.1
4	TU	0031 0742 1252 2002	7.0 1.1 7.0 1.0
5	W	0110 0823 1330 2042	7.1 1.1 7.1 1.0
6	TH	0149 0901 1406 2119	7.1 1.1 7.1 1.1
7	F	0226 0935 1441 2151	7.0 1.2 7.0 1.2
8	SA	0259 1005 1512 2220	6.9 1.3 6.9 1.3
9	SU	0332 1033 1544 2249	6.7 1.5 6.7 1.5
10	M	0405 1103 1620 2321	6.5 1.7 6.5 1.7
11	TU ☾	0445 1138 1703	6.3 2.0 6.3
12	W	0002 0534 1225 1757	2.0 6.0 2.2 6.0
13	TH	0100 0634 1332 1905	2.3 5.7 2.4 5.8
14	F	0214 0749 1449 2024	2.4 5.7 2.5 5.8
15	SA	0328 0905 1603 2133	2.3 5.8 2.2 6.0
16	SU	0440 1007 1710 2229	2.0 6.1 1.8 6.4
17	M	0541 1058 1805 2315	1.6 6.5 1.5 6.8
18	TU	0632 1142 1852 2357	1.3 6.9 1.1 7.1
19	W ●	0719 1223 1938	1.1 7.1 0.9
20	TH	0039 0804 1305 2023	7.3 0.9 7.3 0.7
21	F	0123 0849 1349 2108	7.5 0.8 7.4 0.6
22	SA	0208 0932 1432 2151	7.5 0.7 7.4 0.6
23	SU	0254 1013 1516 2234	7.4 0.8 7.3 0.7
24	M	0340 1054 1601 2317	7.2 1.0 7.2 1.0
25	TU ☽	0429 1137 1652	7.0 1.3 6.9
26	W	0004 0524 1227 1752	1.3 6.6 1.7 6.5
27	TH	0102 0632 1332 1908	1.7 6.2 2.0 6.2
28	F	0218 0756 1501 2037	2.0 6.0 2.2 6.1
29	SA	0348 0920 1626 2153	2.0 6.1 2.0 6.3
30	SU	0502 1026 1730 2251	1.8 6.4 1.6 6.7
31	M	0559 1116 1822 2336	1.5 6.7 1.3 6.9

SEPTEMBER

Date	Day	Time	m
1	TU	0645 1155 1905	1.3 6.9 1.2
2	W ○	0013 0725 1230 1944	7.1 1.2 7.1 1.0
3	TH	0048 0801 1304 2020	7.2 1.1 7.2 1.0
4	F	0123 0835 1337 2052	7.2 1.1 7.2 1.0
5	SA	0155 0905 1407 2121	7.2 1.1 7.2 1.1
6	SU	0226 0933 1436 2147	7.1 1.2 7.1 1.2
7	M	0254 0959 1505 2213	6.9 1.4 6.9 1.4
8	TU	0324 1025 1536 2241	6.7 1.6 6.7 1.6
9	W	0357 1055 1612 2314	6.5 1.8 6.4 1.9
10	TH ☾	0439 1134 1703	6.1 2.1 6.1
11	F	0002 0543 1233 1818	2.3 5.8 2.5 5.7
12	SA	0117 0704 1359 1945	2.5 5.6 2.6 5.7
13	SU	0246 0831 1526 2105	2.5 5.7 2.4 6.0
14	M	0412 0942 1645 2207	2.1 6.1 1.9 6.5
15	TU	0521 1037 1745 2255	1.6 6.6 1.4 6.9
16	W	0614 1121 1834 2338	1.2 7.0 1.0 7.3
17	TH ●	0700 1201 1920	0.9 7.4 0.7
18	F	0019 0744 1242 2004	7.6 0.7 7.6 0.5
19	SA	0102 0827 1323 2047	7.7 0.6 7.7 0.5
20	SU	0147 0909 1406 2130	7.7 0.6 7.7 0.5
21	M	0231 0949 1449 2211	7.6 0.7 7.5 0.7
22	TU	0317 1029 1535 2253	7.3 1.0 7.3 1.0
23	W	0405 1111 1628 2339	7.0 1.4 6.9 1.4
24	TH ☽	0501 1201 1731	6.5 1.8 6.5
25	F	0037 0610 1310 1851	1.9 6.1 2.2 6.1
26	SA	0200 0739 1446 2024	2.2 5.8 2.3 6.0
27	SU	0333 0905 1611 2140	2.2 6.0 2.0 6.3
28	M	0447 1009 1716 2235	1.9 6.3 1.6 6.6
29	TU	0542 1056 1805 2317	1.5 6.7 1.3 6.9
30	W	0625 1132 1845 2351	1.3 7.0 1.1 7.1

OCTOBER

Date	Day	Time	m
1	TH ○	0701 1204 1920	1.2 7.1 1.0
2	F	0024 0734 1236 1952	7.2 1.1 7.2 1.0
3	SA	0055 0805 1306 2023	7.3 1.1 7.3 1.0
4	SU	0125 0834 1334 2051	7.2 1.1 7.2 1.1
5	M	0152 0902 1401 2118	7.2 1.2 7.2 1.2
6	TU	0219 0929 1429 2144	7.0 1.3 7.0 1.3
7	W	0247 0956 1457 2211	6.9 1.5 6.8 1.6
8	TH	0315 1025 1528 2244	6.6 1.8 6.5 1.9
9	F	0350 1103 1613 2329	6.3 2.1 6.1 2.2
10	SA ☾	0455 1159 1740	5.9 2.4 5.8
11	SU	0039 0631 1321 1913	2.5 5.6 2.6 5.7
12	M	0210 0759 1453 2037	2.5 5.7 2.4 6.0
13	TU	0345 0916 1619 2142	2.1 6.2 1.8 6.6
14	W	0456 1012 1721 2233	1.6 6.7 1.3 7.1
15	TH	0550 1056 1811 2316	1.1 7.2 0.9 7.4
16	F ●	0637 1136 1858 2356	0.8 7.5 0.6 7.7
17	SA	0721 1215 1942	0.7 7.7 0.5
18	SU	0039 0803 1257 2025	7.8 0.6 7.8 0.4
19	M	0124 0845 1341 2108	7.8 0.6 7.7 0.5
20	TU	0210 0926 1428 2150	7.6 0.8 7.6 0.7
21	W	0257 1007 1517 2232	7.3 1.0 7.3 1.1
22	TH	0347 1050 1612 2319	6.9 1.4 6.9 1.6
23	F ☽	0442 1141 1715	6.5 1.9 6.4
24	SA	0017 0549 1253 1833	2.0 6.0 2.2 6.0
25	SU	0139 0715 1424 2002	2.4 5.8 2.3 6.0
26	M	0305 0837 1543 2113	2.3 6.0 2.1 6.2
27	TU	0416 0938 1646 2206	2.0 6.3 1.7 6.6
28	W	0511 1024 1735 2248	1.7 6.6 1.4 6.8
29	TH	0554 1101 1815 2323	1.4 6.9 1.2 7.0
30	F	0630 1135 1850 2356	1.3 7.1 1.1 7.2
31	SA ○	0703 1207 1922	1.2 7.2 1.1

NOVEMBER

Date	Day	Time	m
1	SU	0027 0734 1236 1953	7.2 1.2 7.2 1.1
2	M	0055 0805 1303 2023	7.2 1.1 7.2 1.1
3	TU	0122 0835 1332 2053	7.2 1.2 7.2 1.2
4	W	0151 0906 1402 2123	7.1 1.3 7.0 1.3
5	TH	0221 0936 1433 2154	6.9 1.5 6.8 1.6
6	F	0254 1009 1508 2229	6.7 1.7 6.6 1.8
7	SA	0333 1049 1557 2316	6.3 2.0 6.2 2.1
8	SU ☾	0437 1144 1718	6.0 2.2 6.0
9	M	0020 0603 1256 1843	2.3 5.8 2.3 5.9
10	TU	0141 0726 1421 2005	2.4 5.9 2.2 6.2
11	W	0310 0842 1546 2113	2.1 6.3 1.7 6.6
12	TH	0425 0941 1652 2206	1.6 6.7 1.2 7.0
13	F	0522 1028 1746 2252	1.2 7.2 0.9 7.4
14	SA	0612 1110 1835 2335	0.9 7.5 0.7 7.6
15	SU ●	0658 1152 1921	0.8 7.6 0.6
16	M	0020 0742 1237 2006	7.7 0.7 7.7 0.5
17	TU	0107 0825 1325 2050	7.6 0.7 7.6 0.6
18	W	0156 0908 1416 2133	7.5 0.8 7.5 0.8
19	TH	0245 0951 1507 2217	7.2 1.1 7.2 1.2
20	F	0334 1035 1600 2303	6.9 1.4 6.8 1.6
21	SA	0424 1126 1656 2357	6.5 1.8 6.4 2.0
22	SU ☽	0523 1231 1804	6.2 2.1 6.1
23	M	0106 0636 1346 1923	2.3 5.9 2.2 6.0
24	TU	0219 0753 1457 2032	2.3 5.9 2.1 6.1
25	W	0326 0854 1559 2126	2.2 6.1 1.9 6.3
26	TH	0424 0944 1653 2212	1.9 6.4 1.6 6.6
27	F	0514 1026 1738 2252	1.7 6.7 1.4 6.8
28	SA	0556 1104 1818 2328	1.5 6.8 1.3 6.9
29	SU	0632 1139 1853	1.4 7.0 1.2
30	M ○	0001 0706 1210 1926	7.0 1.3 7.0 1.2

DECEMBER

Date	Day	Time	m
1	TU	0031 0740 1240 1959	7.0 1.2 7.1 1.2
2	W	0101 0814 1312 2034	7.1 1.2 7.1 1.2
3	TH	0134 0849 1347 2109	7.0 1.2 7.0 1.3
4	F	0210 0924 1425 2145	6.9 1.3 6.9 1.5
5	SA	0249 1002 1506 2225	6.7 1.5 6.7 1.7
6	SU	0333 1045 1556 2311	6.5 1.7 6.4 1.9
7	M	0429 1136 1700	6.3 1.9 6.2
8	TU ☾	0007 0536 1237 1813	2.0 6.1 2.0 6.2
9	W	0114 0648 1349 1927	2.1 6.1 1.9 6.3
10	TH	0230 0801 1507 2038	1.9 6.3 1.7 6.5
11	F	0346 0906 1619 2138	1.7 6.7 1.3 6.8
12	SA	0452 1001 1721 2232	1.4 7.0 1.1 7.1
13	SU	0548 1052 1815 2322	1.1 7.2 0.9 7.3
14	M ●	0639 1140 1905	1.0 7.4 0.8
15	TU	0011 0726 1229 1952	7.4 0.9 7.5 0.7
16	W	0100 0811 1319 2037	7.4 0.8 7.5 0.8
17	TH	0148 0856 1409 2122	7.3 0.9 7.4 0.9
18	F	0234 0940 1456 2205	7.2 1.0 7.2 1.1
19	SA	0318 1024 1543 2247	7.0 1.3 6.9 1.5
20	SU	0402 1109 1630 2332	6.7 1.6 6.5 1.8
21	M	0448 1158 1722	6.4 1.8 6.2
22	TU ☽	0022 0541 1255 1825	2.1 6.1 2.1 6.0
23	W	0121 0648 1356 1935	2.3 5.9 2.2 5.9
24	TH	0222 0757 1457 2036	2.3 5.9 2.1 5.9
25	F	0323 0856 1558 2130	2.2 6.0 2.0 6.1
26	SA	0423 0948 1654 2218	2.0 6.2 1.8 6.3
27	SU	0516 1033 1744 2300	1.8 6.5 1.6 6.5
28	M	0602 1114 1826 2338	1.6 6.6 1.5 6.7
29	TU	0642 1150 1904	1.4 6.8 1.3
30	W ○	0013 0719 1224 1941	6.8 1.3 6.9 1.2
31	TH	0047 0757 1259 2020	6.9 1.2 7.0 1.2

DIEPPE

LAT 49°56′N
LONG 1°05′E

TIMES AND HEIGHTS OF HIGH AND LOW WATER (Heights in Metres)

TIME ZONE –0100 (French Standard Time). **Subtract 1 hour for UT. For French Summer Time (area enclosed in shaded box) add 1 hour**

2020

SUNRISE AND SUNSET TIMES

DIEPPE
At 49°56′N 1°05′E
European Standard Time (UT-1)

		Sunrise	Sunset
Jan	01	0854	1705
	15	0848	1723
Feb	01	0829	1750
	15	0806	1814
Mar	01	0739	1838
	15	0709	1901
European Summer Time (UT-2)			
Apr	01	0732	2028
	15	0703	2049
May	01	0632	2114
	15	0610	2135
Jun	01	0552	2156
	15	0546	2206
Jul	01	0551	2208
	15	0504	2159
Aug	01	0625	2138
	15	0646	2114
Sep	01	0711	2039
	15	0732	2010
Oct	01	0756	1934
	15	0818	1905
European Standard Time (UT-1)			
Nov	01	0745	1733
	15	0808	1712
Dec	01	0832	1657
	15	0847	1654

JANUARY

Day	Time	m	Time	m	Time	m	Time	m
1 W	0314	8.1	0956	2.3	1530	7.9	2215	2.2
2 TH	0352	7.7	1034	2.6	1612	7.5	2255	2.5
3 F ☽	0437	7.4	1122	2.8	1702	7.2	2345	2.7
4 SA	0533	7.1	1220	3.0	1805	7.0		
5 SU	0046	2.9	0642	7.1	1328	2.9	1919	7.0
6 M	0156	2.8	0754	7.3	1440	2.7	2027	7.3
7 TU	0306	2.5	0855	7.7	1544	2.3	2123	7.7
8 W	0407	2.1	0946	8.1	1639	1.9	2212	8.2
9 TH	0459	1.8	1032	8.5	1728	1.5	2258	8.6
10 F ○	0548	1.5	1116	8.9	1816	1.2	2342	8.9
11 SA	0634	1.2	1200	9.1	1903	0.9		
12 SU	0026	9.1	0721	1.1	1244	9.3	1949	0.8
13 M	0111	9.3	0807	1.0	1329	9.4	2035	0.7
14 TU	0157	9.3	0852	1.0	1415	9.3	2119	0.8
15 W	0243	9.1	0937	1.1	1502	9.1	2203	1.0
16 TH	0330	8.9	1023	1.4	1550	8.7	2249	1.3
17 F ☾	0420	8.5	1112	1.7	1643	8.3	2338	1.7
18 SA	0516	8.1	1208	2.0	1745	7.9		
19 SU	0038	2.0	0622	7.9	1315	2.2	1857	7.7
20 M	0150	2.2	0737	7.8	1431	2.2	2014	7.7
21 TU	0305	2.2	0849	7.9	1543	2.0	2123	7.9
22 W	0413	2.0	0951	8.2	1646	1.7	2221	8.3
23 TH	0510	1.7	1044	8.6	1739	1.4	2310	8.5
24 F ●	0559	1.5	1128	8.8	1825	1.2	2352	8.8
25 SA	0642	1.4	1208	8.9	1905	1.1		
26 SU	0030	8.9	0720	1.3	1245	9.0	1942	1.0
27 M	0105	8.9	0757	1.3	1320	9.0	2017	1.1
28 TU	0139	8.9	0830	1.4	1354	8.9	2048	1.2
29 W	0212	8.7	0900	1.5	1427	8.6	2116	1.4
30 TH	0244	8.5	0927	1.8	1458	8.3	2143	1.7
31 F	0314	8.2	0957	2.0	1530	8.0	2215	2.0

FEBRUARY

Day	Time	m	Time	m	Time	m	Time	m
1 SA	0347	7.8	1034	2.3	1607	7.6	2253	2.3
2 SU ☽	0427	7.5	1119	2.7	1654	7.2	2342	2.7
3 M	0522	7.1	1217	2.9	1800	6.9		
4 TU	0045	2.9	0639	7.0	1331	2.9	1929	6.9
5 W	0205	2.9	0807	7.2	1456	2.6	2046	7.3
6 TH	0327	2.5	0914	7.7	1606	2.1	2147	7.9
7 F	0432	2.0	1010	8.2	1705	1.6	2239	8.4
8 SA	0528	1.5	1100	8.8	1800	1.1	2328	8.9
9 SU ○	0622	1.1	1147	9.2	1853	0.7		
10 M	0015	9.3	0713	0.8	1233	9.6	1942	0.4
11 TU	0100	9.6	0801	0.6	1319	9.7	2028	0.3
12 W	0144	9.7	0846	0.5	1403	9.7	2110	0.3
13 TH	0228	9.6	0927	0.6	1446	9.5	2150	0.6
14 F	0310	9.3	1008	0.9	1530	9.1	2228	1.0
15 SA ☾	0354	8.8	1049	1.3	1617	8.5	2310	1.5
16 SU	0443	8.2	1137	1.8	1712	7.9		
17 M	0001	2.1	0544	7.7	1238	2.3	1824	7.4
18 TU	0111	2.6	0704	7.3	1359	2.5	1952	7.2
19 W	0238	2.7	0831	7.4	1523	2.3	2113	7.5
20 TH	0358	2.4	0942	7.8	1635	1.9	2213	8.0
21 F	0502	2.0	1034	8.3	1730	1.5	2259	8.4
22 SA	0551	1.6	1117	8.6	1813	1.3	2338	8.7
23 SU ●	0630	1.4	1154	8.9	1850	1.1		
24 M	0012	8.9	0705	1.2	1227	9.0	1924	1.0
25 TU	0044	9.0	0738	1.1	1258	9.1	1955	0.9
26 W	0115	9.0	0808	1.1	1330	9.0	2024	1.0
27 TH	0145	8.9	0835	1.2	1359	8.9	2049	1.2
28 F	0213	8.8	0900	1.4	1428	8.7	2114	1.4
29 SA	0240	8.5	0926	1.7	1456	8.3	2141	1.7

MARCH

Day	Time	m	Time	m	Time	m	Time	m
1 SU	0309	8.2	0957	2.0	1528	7.9	2214	2.1
2 M ☽	0344	7.8	1036	2.4	1608	7.5	2256	2.5
3 TU	0429	7.3	1127	2.7	1704	7.0	2354	2.9
4 W	0536	6.9	1238	3.0	1832	6.7		
5 TH	0115	3.1	0718	6.9	1411	2.8	2013	7.1
6 F	0251	2.7	0845	7.4	1537	2.2	2123	7.7
7 SA	0407	2.0	0948	8.1	1643	1.5	2220	8.5
8 SU	0509	1.4	1042	8.8	1743	0.9	2311	9.1
9 M ○	0607	0.9	1131	9.4	1838	0.5	2357	9.5
10 TU	0659	0.5	1217	9.8	1927	0.1		
11 W	0042	9.8	0747	0.3	1301	10.0	2012	0.0
12 TH	0125	9.9	0830	0.2	1344	9.9	2052	0.1
13 F	0206	9.8	0910	0.4	1426	9.7	2129	0.4
14 SA	0247	9.4	0947	0.7	1507	9.2	2204	0.9
15 SU	0327	8.9	1024	1.2	1551	8.5	2241	1.6
16 M ☾	0412	8.2	1108	1.8	1642	7.8	2329	2.3
17 TU	0509	7.5	1206	2.4	1753	7.1		
18 W	0038	2.8	0633	7.0	1327	2.7	1930	6.9
19 TH	0212	2.9	0813	7.0	1500	2.6	2058	7.3
20 F	0341	2.6	0926	7.5	1616	2.1	2155	7.8
21 SA	0445	2.0	1016	8.1	1710	1.6	2239	8.3
22 SU	0531	1.6	1056	8.5	1751	1.3	2315	8.7
23 M	0608	1.3	1131	8.8	1826	1.1	2347	8.9
24 TU ●	0641	1.2	1202	9.0	1858	1.0		
25 W	0017	9.0	0712	1.1	1232	9.1	1928	0.9
26 TH	0046	9.0	0741	1.1	1302	9.1	1956	0.9
27 F	0115	9.0	0809	1.1	1331	9.0	2022	1.1
28 SA	0143	8.9	0834	1.2	1359	8.8	2047	1.3
29 SU	0210	8.7	0901	1.4	1429	8.5	2114	1.6
30 M	0240	8.4	0930	1.7	1501	8.1	2144	2.0
31 TU	0314	8.0	1006	2.1	1541	7.6	2225	2.4

APRIL

Day	Time	m	Time	m	Time	m	Time	m
1 W ☽	0358	7.5	1055	2.5	1634	7.1	2323	2.8
2 TH	0502	7.0	1205	2.8	1758	6.8		
3 F	0044	3.0	0642	6.9	1339	2.7	1943	7.1
4 SA	0223	2.7	0817	7.4	1510	2.2	2058	7.8
5 SU	0342	2.0	0924	8.1	1619	1.4	2157	8.6
6 M	0446	1.3	1020	8.8	1720	0.8	2248	9.2
7 TU	0545	0.8	1109	9.4	1816	0.4	2335	9.6
8 W ○	0638	0.4	1155	9.8	1905	0.1		
9 TH	0019	9.9	0725	0.2	1240	9.9	1949	0.1
10 F	0101	9.9	0808	0.2	1322	9.9	2028	0.2
11 SA	0142	9.8	0848	0.4	1403	9.6	2105	0.6
12 SU	0222	9.4	0924	0.7	1445	9.1	2139	1.1
13 M	0302	8.8	1001	1.3	1528	8.4	2216	1.8
14 TU ☾	0346	8.1	1043	1.9	1618	7.7	2303	2.4
15 W	0441	7.4	1139	2.4	1726	7.1		
16 TH	0011	2.9	0600	6.9	1255	2.8	1857	6.8
17 F	0139	3.0	0738	6.9	1422	2.7	2025	7.1
18 SA	0303	2.7	0853	7.3	1536	2.2	2123	7.7
19 SU	0407	2.1	0944	7.8	1631	1.8	2206	8.2
20 M	0454	1.7	1025	8.3	1714	1.5	2242	8.5
21 TU	0534	1.4	1100	8.6	1751	1.2	2315	8.7
22 W	0609	1.3	1132	8.8	1825	1.1	2346	8.9
23 TH ●	0642	1.2	1204	8.9	1857	1.1		
24 F	0016	8.9	0713	1.1	1234	8.9	1926	1.1
25 SA	0046	9.0	0742	1.1	1305	8.9	1955	1.1
26 SU	0115	8.9	0811	1.2	1335	8.8	2023	1.3
27 M	0146	8.8	0841	1.3	1408	8.6	2054	1.6
28 TU	0219	8.5	0913	1.6	1444	8.2	2127	1.9
29 W	0256	8.1	0951	2.0	1526	7.8	2210	2.3
30 TH ☽	0343	7.6	1041	2.3	1622	7.3	2309	2.7

MAY

Day	Time	m	Time	m	Time	m	Time	m
1 F	0447	7.2	1148	2.6	1742	7.1		
2 SA	0026	2.8	0619	7.1	1316	2.5	1915	7.4
3 SU	0157	2.4	0746	7.5	1442	2.0	2029	8.0
4 M	0314	1.8	0855	8.2	1551	1.4	2129	8.6
5 TU	0419	1.3	0953	8.8	1652	0.9	2221	9.1
6 W	0518	0.8	1044	9.3	1748	0.6	2309	9.5
7 TH ○	0612	0.6	1132	9.6	1837	0.4	2354	9.7
8 F	0700	0.4	1217	9.7	1922	0.4		
9 SA	0037	9.7	0744	0.4	1300	9.6	2003	0.6
10 SU	0119	9.5	0825	0.6	1343	9.4	2041	0.9
11 M	0200	9.2	0903	0.9	1425	8.9	2117	1.3
12 TU	0241	8.7	0941	1.3	1509	8.4	2156	1.9
13 W	0326	8.1	1023	1.8	1558	7.8	2242	2.4
14 TH ☾	0418	7.5	1114	2.3	1657	7.3	2342	2.8
15 F	0524	7.0	1218	2.6	1808	7.0		
16 SA	0056	2.9	0642	6.9	1331	2.7	1926	7.1
17 SU	0208	2.7	0758	7.1	1438	2.4	2032	7.4
18 M	0311	2.3	0857	7.5	1537	2.1	2121	7.9
19 TU	0404	2.0	0943	7.9	1626	1.7	2202	8.2
20 W	0450	1.7	1022	8.3	1709	1.5	2239	8.5
21 TH	0531	1.5	1059	8.5	1748	1.4	2314	8.7
22 F ●	0608	1.3	1134	8.7	1824	1.3	2347	8.8
23 SA	0644	1.2	1208	8.7	1858	1.3		
24 SU	0020	8.8	0717	1.2	1242	8.8	1931	1.3
25 M	0053	8.8	0752	1.2	1317	8.7	2006	1.4
26 TU	0128	8.8	0827	1.3	1355	8.6	2042	1.5
27 W	0207	8.5	0905	1.5	1435	8.3	2121	1.8
28 TH	0249	8.2	0948	1.7	1522	8.0	2207	2.1
29 F	0339	7.9	1038	2.0	1618	7.7	2303	2.3
30 SA ☽	0442	7.6	1140	2.1	1729	7.6		
31 SU	0012	2.4	0558	7.5	1255	2.1	1845	7.7

JUNE

Day	Time	m	Time	m	Time	m	Time	m
1 M	0130	2.2	0715	7.8	1411	1.8	1956	8.1
2 TU	0244	1.8	0824	8.2	1520	1.4	2058	8.5
3 W	0349	1.4	0925	8.6	1622	1.1	2154	8.9
4 TH	0449	1.1	1020	8.9	1718	0.9	2244	9.2
5 F ○	0545	0.9	1110	9.2	1810	0.8	2331	9.3
6 SA	0635	0.8	1157	9.3	1856	0.8		
7 SU	0016	9.3	0721	0.7	1242	9.2	1940	0.9
8 M	0059	9.2	0804	0.8	1326	9.1	2020	1.1
9 TU	0142	9.0	0845	1.0	1409	8.8	2100	1.4
10 W	0224	8.7	0924	1.3	1452	8.4	2139	1.8
11 TH	0307	8.2	1003	1.7	1536	8.0	2220	2.2
12 F	0353	7.8	1046	2.1	1624	7.6	2308	2.5
13 SA ☾	0445	7.4	1135	2.4	1718	7.3		
14 SU	0004	2.7	0544	7.1	1233	2.6	1819	7.1
15 M	0106	2.7	0650	7.0	1335	2.6	1925	7.2
16 TU	0210	2.6	0756	7.2	1437	2.4	2025	7.5
17 W	0310	2.3	0853	7.5	1535	2.1	2117	7.8
18 TH	0404	2.0	0942	7.9	1626	1.9	2202	8.1
19 F	0452	1.8	1026	8.2	1712	1.7	2243	8.4
20 SA	0536	1.5	1107	8.4	1754	1.5	2321	8.6
21 SU ●	0617	1.4	1146	8.6	1834	1.4	2359	8.7
22 M	0658	1.2	1225	8.7	1913	1.3		
23 TU	0038	8.8	0738	1.1	1305	8.8	1954	1.3
24 W	0118	8.8	0820	1.1	1347	8.8	2036	1.4
25 TH	0201	8.8	0903	1.2	1432	8.6	2119	1.5
26 F	0247	8.6	0948	1.3	1519	8.4	2206	1.7
27 SA	0336	8.3	1035	1.5	1610	8.2	2257	1.8
28 SU ☽	0431	8.1	1129	1.7	1708	8.0	2355	1.9
29 M	0533	7.9	1230	1.8	1813	8.0		
30 TU	0101	2.0	0643	7.9	1338	1.8	1922	8.0

DIEPPE
LAT 49°56′N
LONG 1°05′E

TIMES AND HEIGHTS OF HIGH AND LOW WATER (Heights in Metres)

TIME ZONE –0100 (French Standard Time). **Subtract 1 hour for UT. For French Summer Time (area enclosed in shaded box) add 1 hour**

2020

JULY

Date	Day	Time	m
1	W	0213 0754 1448 2029	1.9 8.0 1.7 8.3
2	TH	0322 0901 1554 2131	1.6 8.2 1.6 8.5
3	F	0425 1001 1654 2226	1.4 8.5 1.4 8.7
4	SA	0523 1055 1748 2316	1.2 8.7 1.3 8.9
5	SU O	0615 1144 1837	1.1 8.9 1.2
6	M	0002 0703 1230 1922	9.0 1.0 9.0 1.2
7	TU	0045 0747 1312 2004	9.0 1.0 9.0 1.2
8	W	0126 0828 1352 2043	8.9 1.0 8.8 1.4
9	TH	0206 0905 1431 2119	8.8 1.2 8.6 1.6
10	F	0245 0940 1509 2153	8.5 1.5 8.3 1.9
11	SA	0324 1013 1547 2228	8.1 1.8 8.0 2.2
12	SU	0403 1049 1627 2309	7.8 2.1 7.6 2.5
13	M ☾	0447 1133 1714 2359	7.4 2.4 7.3 2.7
14	TU	0541 1226 1814	7.1 2.6 7.1
15	W	0100 0648 1330 1924	2.8 7.0 2.7 7.1
16	TH	0209 0801 1440 2031	2.7 7.1 2.6 7.4
17	F	0317 0904 1545 2127	2.5 7.4 2.3 7.7
18	SA	0416 0957 1640 2215	2.1 7.8 2.0 8.1
19	SU	0507 1044 1729 2300	1.7 8.2 1.7 8.5
20	M ●	0555 1128 1816 2343	1.4 8.6 1.4 8.8
21	TU	0643 1212 1902	1.2 8.8 1.2
22	W	0026 0730 1255 1947	9.0 1.0 9.0 1.1
23	TH	0110 0816 1339 2032	9.1 0.8 9.1 1.0
24	F	0154 0900 1423 2116	9.2 0.8 9.1 1.1
25	SA	0238 0942 1507 2159	9.1 0.9 9.0 1.2
26	SU	0323 1025 1552 2244	8.8 1.1 8.7 1.4
27	M ☽	0411 1110 1642 2333	8.5 1.4 8.4 1.7
28	TU	0506 1201 1741	8.1 1.8 8.0
29	W	0032 0613 1306 1851	2.0 7.8 2.1 7.8
30	TH	0144 0730 1422 2007	2.1 7.7 2.2 7.8
31	F	0301 0846 1535 2118	2.0 7.8 2.0 8.1

AUGUST

Date	Day	Time	m
1	SA	0410 0954 1640 2218	1.8 8.1 1.8 8.4
2	SU	0512 1050 1737 2309	1.5 8.5 1.6 8.7
3	M O	0605 1137 1826 2353	1.3 8.7 1.4 8.9
4	TU	0651 1218 1909	1.1 8.9 1.3
5	W	0032 0732 1256 1947	9.0 1.0 9.0 1.2
6	TH	0109 0809 1331 2022	9.0 1.0 9.0 1.3
7	F	0144 0842 1405 2054	8.9 1.1 8.8 1.4
8	SA	0218 0911 1437 2121	8.7 1.3 8.6 1.7
9	SU	0250 0938 1508 2149	8.5 1.6 8.3 1.9
10	M	0321 1006 1539 2221	8.1 1.9 8.0 2.2
11	TU ☾	0354 1040 1615 2302	7.7 2.3 7.6 2.6
12	W	0436 1125 1702 2355	7.3 2.7 7.2 2.9
13	TH	0535 1224 1812	6.9 3.0 6.9
14	F	0104 0701 1342 1942	3.1 6.7 3.1 6.9
15	SA	0230 0828 1507 2055	2.9 7.0 2.8 7.4
16	SU	0344 0931 1613 2152	2.4 7.6 2.2 7.9
17	M	0443 1024 1708 2242	1.8 8.2 1.7 8.5
18	TU	0537 1111 1800 2328	1.4 8.7 1.3 8.9
19	W ●	0630 1156 1850	1.0 9.1 1.0
20	TH	0012 0719 1240 1938	9.3 0.7 9.4 0.8
21	F	0056 0805 1323 2022	9.5 0.5 9.5 0.7
22	SA	0139 0848 1405 2104	9.6 0.4 9.5 0.7
23	SU	0221 0927 1447 2143	9.5 0.6 9.4 0.9
24	M	0304 1005 1529 2223	9.2 0.9 9.0 1.2
25	TU ☽	0348 1045 1614 2308	8.7 1.4 8.5 1.7
26	W	0439 1133 1710	8.1 2.0 7.9
27	TH	0004 0546 1237 1825	2.2 7.5 2.5 7.5
28	F	0120 0713 1403 1954	2.5 7.3 2.6 7.4
29	SA	0248 0842 1527 2113	2.4 7.5 2.4 7.8
30	SU	0404 0950 1636 2212	2.0 8.0 2.0 8.3
31	M	0507 1041 1731 2259	1.6 8.5 1.6 8.7

SEPTEMBER

Date	Day	Time	m
1	TU	0556 1124 1816 2339	1.3 8.8 1.3 8.9
2	W O	0637 1200 1852	1.1 9.0 1.2
3	TH	0014 0712 1233 1926	9.0 1.0 9.1 1.2
4	F	0046 0743 1304 1956	9.1 1.0 9.1 1.2
5	SA	0117 0813 1334 2024	9.0 1.1 9.0 1.3
6	SU	0147 0839 1403 2049	8.9 1.3 8.8 1.5
7	M	0216 0902 1430 2113	8.7 1.5 8.5 1.8
8	TU	0243 0927 1457 2141	8.3 1.8 8.2 2.1
9	W	0312 0957 1528 2216	7.9 2.2 7.8 2.5
10	TH ☾	0349 1036 1610 2304	7.4 2.7 7.3 2.9
11	F	0441 1132 1712	6.9 3.2 6.8
12	SA	0011 0602 1252 1852	3.2 6.6 3.4 6.7
13	SU	0145 0753 1432 2025	3.1 6.8 3.1 7.2
14	M	0315 0906 1548 2128	2.6 7.5 2.4 7.9
15	TU	0420 1001 1647 2220	1.9 8.3 1.7 8.6
16	W	0517 1050 1741 2307	1.2 8.9 1.1 9.1
17	TH ●	0611 1135 1832 2352	0.8 9.4 0.8 9.6
18	F	0701 1218 1920	0.4 9.7 0.5
19	SA	0035 0746 1301 2004	9.8 0.3 9.8 0.4
20	SU	0118 0827 1342 2045	9.9 0.3 9.8 0.5
21	M	0200 0905 1423 2123	9.7 0.5 9.5 0.8
22	TU	0241 0941 1504 2201	9.3 1.0 9.1 1.2
23	W	0325 1020 1548 2244	8.7 1.6 8.5 1.8
24	TH ☽	0415 1107 1643 2339	8.0 2.3 7.7 2.4
25	F	0524 1214 1803	7.3 2.8 7.2
26	SA	0059 0659 1348 1941	2.8 7.0 3.0 7.1
27	SU	0235 0833 1517 2101	2.6 7.4 2.6 7.6
28	M	0353 0935 1624 2156	2.1 8.0 2.0 8.2
29	TU	0450 1022 1714 2239	1.6 8.5 1.6 8.6
30	W	0535 1100 1753 2316	1.3 8.8 1.3 8.9

OCTOBER

Date	Day	Time	m
1	TH O	0611 1134 1827 2348	1.2 9.0 1.2 9.0
2	F	0643 1205 1857	1.1 9.1 1.2
3	SA	0018 0713 1234 1927	9.1 1.1 9.1 1.2
4	SU	0047 0741 1302 1954	9.1 1.1 9.0 1.3
5	M	0116 0807 1329 2019	9.0 1.3 8.9 1.4
6	TU	0144 0831 1356 2044	8.7 1.5 8.7 1.7
7	W	0211 0855 1423 2111	8.5 1.8 8.4 2.0
8	TH	0242 0924 1455 2143	8.1 2.3 7.9 2.4
9	F	0318 1001 1536 2228	7.6 2.7 7.4 2.8
10	SA ☾	0408 1057 1635 2334	7.1 3.2 6.9 3.2
11	SU	0526 1216 1812	6.7 3.4 6.7
12	M	0108 0718 1359 1952	3.2 6.9 3.1 7.2
13	TU	0244 0836 1520 2059	2.6 7.6 2.3 7.9
14	W	0353 0933 1621 2153	1.8 8.4 1.6 8.7
15	TH	0451 1023 1716 2242	1.2 9.1 1.0 9.3
16	F ●	0545 1109 1808 2328	0.7 9.6 0.7 9.7
17	SA	0635 1153 1857	0.4 9.8 0.5
18	SU	0012 0721 1236 1941	9.9 0.3 9.9 0.4
19	M	0055 0803 1317 2022	9.9 0.4 9.8 0.5
20	TU	0137 0841 1359 2101	9.7 0.7 9.5 0.8
21	W	0220 0918 1441 2140	9.3 1.2 9.0 1.3
22	TH	0305 0958 1526 2223	8.6 1.8 8.4 1.9
23	F ☽	0356 1046 1622 2318	7.9 2.5 7.7 2.5
24	SA	0503 1154 1739	7.3 3.0 7.1
25	SU	0035 0632 1324 1912	2.8 7.0 3.1 7.0
26	M	0204 0802 1447 2031	2.8 7.3 2.7 7.4
27	TU	0319 0905 1551 2126	2.3 7.8 2.2 8.0
28	W	0415 0950 1639 2208	1.9 8.3 1.7 8.4
29	TH	0459 1028 1719 2245	1.5 8.7 1.5 8.7
30	F	0535 1102 1754 2317	1.4 8.9 1.3 8.9
31	SA O	0608 1133 1826 2348	1.3 9.0 1.3 8.9

NOVEMBER

Date	Day	Time	m
1	SU	0639 1202 1857	1.2 9.0 1.3
2	M	0018 0709 1231 1926	9.0 1.3 9.0 1.3
3	TU	0048 0738 1300 1954	8.9 1.4 8.9 1.4
4	W	0117 0805 1329 2022	8.8 1.6 8.7 1.6
5	TH	0148 0833 1400 2051	8.5 1.9 8.5 1.9
6	F	0222 0905 1435 2126	8.2 2.2 8.1 2.2
7	SA	0301 0945 1518 2211	7.8 2.6 7.6 2.6
8	SU ☾	0352 1039 1617 2314	7.3 3.0 7.1 2.9
9	M	0505 1153 1743	7.0 3.1 7.0
10	TU	0038 0641 1325 1914	2.9 7.1 2.9 7.3
11	W	0208 0758 1446 2024	2.5 7.7 2.3 8.0
12	TH	0320 0859 1550 2122	1.8 8.4 1.6 8.6
13	F	0420 0952 1647 2214	1.2 9.0 1.1 9.2
14	SA	0516 1041 1741 2303	0.8 9.5 0.8 9.5
15	SU ●	0607 1127 1831 2349	0.6 9.7 0.6 9.7
16	M	0654 1212 1917	0.6 9.8 0.5
17	TU	0034 0738 1255 2001	9.7 0.7 9.7 0.6
18	W	0118 0819 1338 2042	9.5 0.9 9.4 0.9
19	TH	0203 0859 1422 2123	9.1 1.4 9.0 1.3
20	F	0249 0940 1509 2206	8.6 1.9 8.4 1.8
21	SA	0339 1028 1602 2257	8.0 2.4 7.8 2.4
22	SU ☽	0438 1128 1706	7.5 2.8 7.3
23	M	0000 0547 1240 1820	2.7 7.1 3.0 7.1
24	TU	0112 0704 1353 1936	2.8 7.2 2.8 7.2
25	W	0221 0813 1457 2039	2.6 7.5 2.5 7.5
26	TH	0321 0906 1551 2127	2.3 7.9 2.1 7.9
27	F	0411 0949 1637 2208	2.0 8.3 1.8 8.3
28	SA	0454 1026 1717 2244	1.7 8.5 1.6 8.5
29	SU	0533 1100 1754 2319	1.6 8.7 1.5 8.7
30	M O	0608 1134 1829 2353	1.5 8.8 1.4 8.7

DECEMBER

Date	Day	Time	m
1	TU	0642 1206 1902	1.5 8.9 1.4
2	W	0026 0714 1238 1934	8.8 1.5 8.9 1.4
3	TH	0059 0746 1311 2008	8.7 1.6 8.8 1.5
4	F	0134 0821 1347 2043	8.6 1.8 8.6 1.7
5	SA	0212 0858 1427 2122	8.4 2.0 8.3 1.9
6	SU	0255 0940 1512 2207	8.0 2.3 7.9 2.2
7	M	0345 1032 1608 2303	7.7 2.5 7.6 2.4
8	TU ☾	0448 1135 1716	7.5 2.6 7.5
9	W	0011 0603 1249 1833	2.4 7.5 2.5 7.6
10	TH	0127 0717 1406 1946	2.3 7.8 2.2 7.9
11	F	0242 0823 1516 2050	1.9 8.3 1.8 8.4
12	SA	0347 0922 1618 2148	1.5 8.8 1.3 8.8
13	SU	0446 1016 1715 2241	1.2 9.1 1.0 9.1
14	M ●	0541 1105 1808 2331	1.0 9.4 0.8 9.3
15	TU	0631 1153 1857	0.9 9.5 0.7
16	W	0018 0718 1239 1943	9.4 1.0 9.5 0.8
17	TH	0104 0802 1324 2027	9.3 1.1 9.3 0.9
18	F	0149 0844 1408 2109	9.1 1.4 9.0 1.2
19	SA	0234 0926 1452 2149	8.7 1.7 8.6 1.6
20	SU	0318 1008 1538 2230	8.3 2.1 8.1 2.0
21	M	0405 1053 1627 2316	7.8 2.5 7.6 2.4
22	TU ☽	0456 1145 1722	7.5 2.7 7.3
23	W	0008 0555 1244 1826	2.7 7.2 2.9 7.1
24	TH	0109 0701 1349 1934	2.8 7.2 2.8 7.1
25	F	0214 0807 1454 2036	2.7 7.4 2.6 7.4
26	SA	0317 0903 1552 2128	2.5 7.7 2.3 7.7
27	SU	0412 0949 1641 2213	2.2 8.0 2.0 8.0
28	M	0459 1031 1725 2254	2.0 8.3 1.7 8.3
29	TU	0541 1110 1805 2332	1.8 8.5 1.5 8.5
30	W O	0620 1147 1844	1.6 8.7 1.4
31	TH	0010 0658 1224 1922	8.7 1.5 8.8 1.3

LE HAVRE
LAT 49°29'N
LONG 0°07'E

TIMES AND HEIGHTS OF HIGH AND LOW WATER (Heights in Metres)

TIME ZONE –0100 (French Standard Time). **Subtract 1 hour for UT. For French Summer Time (area enclosed in shaded box) add 1 hour**

2020

JANUARY

Date	Day	Time	m	Time	m	Time	m	Time	m
1	W	0218	7.1	0911	2.7	1427	7.1	2129	2.5
2	TH	0258	6.8	0949	2.9	1509	6.8	2209	2.8
3	F ☽	0348	6.6	1035	3.2	1605	6.5	2257	3.1
4	SA	0452	6.5	1128	3.3	1717	6.4	2353	3.2
5	SU	0558	6.5	1229	3.3	1826	6.5		
6	M	0056	3.1	0700	6.7	1341	3.1	1929	6.6
7	TU	0211	2.9	0757	6.9	1455	2.7	2028	6.9
8	W	0318	2.6	0849	7.2	1551	2.3	2118	7.2
9	TH	0410	2.2	0935	7.5	1639	1.9	2204	7.5
10	F O	0458	1.9	1018	7.7	1726	1.6	2248	7.7
11	SA	0544	1.7	1101	7.9	1813	1.3	2332	7.9
12	SU	0630	1.5	1145	8.0	1859	1.2		
13	M	0016	8.0	0716	1.4	1230	8.0	1945	1.1
14	TU	0102	8.0	0802	1.5	1316	8.0	2029	1.2
15	W	0148	7.9	0846	1.6	1403	7.8	2113	1.4
16	TH	0236	7.7	0930	1.8	1451	7.6	2157	1.7
17	F ☾	0327	7.4	1018	2.1	1545	7.3	2247	2.1
18	SA	0424	7.2	1114	2.4	1648	7.1	2348	2.4
19	SU	0533	7.0	1224	2.6	1805	6.9		
20	M	0100	2.6	0647	7.0	1339	2.6	1922	6.9
21	TU	0212	2.5	0755	7.1	1450	2.4	2028	7.1
22	W	0319	2.4	0853	7.3	1555	2.1	2125	7.3
23	TH	0419	2.1	0943	7.5	1651	1.9	2213	7.5
24	F ●	0511	2.0	1027	7.7	1737	1.7	2255	7.6
25	SA	0554	1.8	1106	7.8	1817	1.5	2333	7.7
26	SU	0632	1.7	1142	7.8	1853	1.5		
27	M	0008	7.7	0708	1.7	1216	7.8	1928	1.5
28	TU	0041	7.6	0742	1.8	1250	7.7	2000	1.6
29	W	0114	7.5	0814	2.0	1323	7.6	2030	1.8
30	TH	0146	7.3	0843	2.2	1354	7.4	2058	2.1
31	F	0216	7.1	0911	2.5	1426	7.1	2127	2.4

FEBRUARY

Date	Day	Time	m	Time	m	Time	m	Time	m
1	SA	0249	6.9	0944	2.8	1504	6.8	2202	2.7
2	SU ☽	0332	6.7	1027	3.0	1555	6.5	2250	3.0
3	M	0432	6.5	1123	3.3	1710	6.3	2351	3.2
4	TU	0552	6.5	1232	3.3	1836	6.4		
5	W	0107	3.2	0710	6.6	1402	3.0	1954	6.6
6	TH	0238	2.9	0819	6.9	1519	2.5	2058	7.0
7	F	0344	2.4	0915	7.3	1617	2.0	2148	7.5
8	SA	0439	1.9	1003	7.7	1711	1.5	2234	7.8
9	SU O	0533	1.5	1048	7.9	1804	1.1	2318	8.0
10	M	0625	1.2	1133	8.2	1854	0.8		
11	TU	0003	8.2	0713	1.0	1218	8.3	1940	0.6
12	W	0047	8.2	0757	0.9	1302	8.3	2022	0.7
13	TH	0131	8.2	0838	1.1	1346	8.1	2101	1.0
14	F	0215	7.9	0918	1.4	1431	7.8	2139	1.4
15	SA ☾	0259	7.6	0957	1.8	1517	7.4	2219	2.0
16	SU	0348	7.2	1043	2.3	1614	7.0	2310	2.5
17	M	0452	6.9	1145	2.7	1734	6.7		
18	TU	0022	2.9	0616	6.7	1305	2.9	1905	6.6
19	W	0143	3.0	0737	6.8	1427	2.8	2021	6.8
20	TH	0303	2.8	0842	7.0	1545	2.4	2119	7.1
21	F	0415	2.4	0933	7.2	1646	2.0	2203	7.3
22	SA	0506	2.0	1015	7.5	1729	1.7	2241	7.5
23	SU ●	0545	1.8	1050	7.7	1804	1.5	2314	7.6
24	M	0618	1.6	1123	7.8	1837	1.4	2345	7.7
25	TU	0651	1.5	1154	7.8	1907	1.3		
26	W	0015	7.7	0721	1.5	1225	7.8	1936	1.4
27	TH	0045	7.6	0748	1.6	1255	7.7	2003	1.6
28	F	0114	7.5	0815	1.8	1324	7.5	2028	1.8
29	SA	0142	7.4	0841	2.1	1354	7.3	2054	2.1

MARCH

Date	Day	Time	m	Time	m	Time	m	Time	m
1	SU	0211	7.1	0909	2.4	1428	7.0	2124	2.5
2	M ☽	0245	6.9	0944	2.7	1511	6.6	2205	2.9
3	TU	0334	6.5	1034	3.1	1615	6.3	2303	3.3
4	W	0452	6.3	1142	3.3	1748	6.2		
5	TH	0020	3.4	0626	6.4	1318	3.2	1926	6.5
6	F	0206	3.1	0753	6.7	1451	2.6	2037	7.0
7	SA	0321	2.4	0855	7.2	1555	1.9	2130	7.5
8	SU	0422	1.8	0945	7.7	1655	1.4	2215	7.9
9	M O	0520	1.3	1031	8.0	1750	0.9	2300	8.2
10	TU	0612	0.9	1115	8.3	1840	0.5	2343	8.3
11	W	0659	0.7	1200	8.4	1923	0.4		
12	TH	0026	8.4	0742	0.6	1243	8.4	2004	0.5
13	F	0109	8.3	0821	0.8	1326	8.2	2041	0.8
14	SA	0150	8.0	0858	1.1	1408	7.9	2116	1.4
15	SU	0231	7.6	0934	1.7	1452	7.4	2152	2.0
16	M ☾	0315	7.2	1015	2.3	1545	6.9	2239	2.7
17	TU	0414	6.7	1112	2.8	1709	6.5	2349	3.2
18	W	0547	6.4	1233	3.1	1848	6.4		
19	TH	0117	3.3	0717	6.5	1403	3.0	2009	6.6
20	F	0249	3.0	0828	6.7	1531	2.5	2105	7.0
21	SA	0402	2.5	0917	7.1	1627	2.1	2145	7.3
22	SU	0448	2.0	0955	7.4	1707	1.8	2219	7.5
23	M	0523	1.8	1028	7.6	1740	1.5	2249	7.6
24	TU ●	0556	1.6	1058	7.7	1812	1.4	2318	7.7
25	W	0626	1.5	1128	7.8	1841	1.3	2347	7.7
26	TH	0655	1.4	1159	7.7	1908	1.4		
27	F	0016	7.7	0721	1.5	1229	7.7	1934	1.5
28	SA	0044	7.6	0747	1.6	1259	7.5	2001	1.7
29	SU	0112	7.5	0815	1.8	1330	7.3	2028	2.0
30	M	0143	7.3	0844	2.2	1405	7.0	2059	2.4
31	TU	0216	7.0	0918	2.5	1447	6.7	2136	2.8

APRIL

Date	Day	Time	m	Time	m	Time	m	Time	m
1	W ☽	0302	6.6	1003	2.9	1549	6.4	2231	3.2
2	TH	0417	6.3	1108	3.2	1719	6.3	2349	3.4
3	F	0554	6.3	1249	3.1	1901	6.5		
4	SA	0142	3.1	0726	6.7	1425	2.5	2013	7.0
5	SU	0257	2.4	0831	7.2	1530	1.8	2106	7.6
6	M	0359	1.7	0922	7.7	1632	1.3	2152	7.9
7	TU	0458	1.2	1009	8.0	1728	0.8	2236	8.2
8	W O	0551	0.8	1054	8.3	1817	0.5	2320	8.3
9	TH	0638	0.6	1138	8.4	1901	0.4		
10	F	0003	8.4	0721	0.6	1222	8.3	1941	0.6
11	SA	0045	8.3	0800	0.8	1305	8.1	2018	1.0
12	SU	0126	8.0	0836	1.2	1347	7.8	2052	1.6
13	M	0206	7.6	0912	1.7	1431	7.3	2128	2.2
14	TU ☾	0249	7.1	0951	2.3	1524	6.8	2215	2.9
15	W	0345	6.7	1046	2.8	1645	6.4	2323	3.3
16	TH	0515	6.3	1201	3.1	1818	6.3		
17	F	0045	3.4	0642	6.4	1324	3.1	1940	6.5
18	SA	0210	3.1	0757	6.6	1444	2.7	2036	6.9
19	SU	0320	2.6	0848	6.9	1543	2.3	2115	7.2
20	M	0409	2.2	0926	7.2	1628	1.9	2148	7.4
21	TU	0449	1.9	0958	7.4	1706	1.7	2217	7.6
22	W	0524	1.7	1029	7.6	1740	1.6	2247	7.6
23	TH ●	0557	1.6	1101	7.6	1810	1.5	2317	7.7
24	F	0626	1.5	1132	7.6	1838	1.5	2347	7.7
25	SA	0653	1.5	1204	7.6	1906	1.6		
26	SU	0017	7.6	0722	1.6	1237	7.5	1936	1.8
27	M	0048	7.5	0753	1.8	1312	7.3	2007	2.0
28	TU	0123	7.3	0826	2.0	1352	7.1	2041	2.4
29	W	0202	7.0	0901	2.4	1438	6.8	2121	2.7
30	TH ☽	0252	6.7	0946	2.7	1539	6.6	2214	3.1

MAY

Date	Day	Time	m	Time	m	Time	m	Time	m
1	F	0400	6.5	1050	2.9	1701	6.5	2331	3.2
2	SA	0529	6.5	1227	2.9	1833	6.7		
3	SU	0116	2.9	0655	6.8	1356	2.4	1942	7.1
4	M	0229	2.3	0801	7.2	1501	1.8	2037	7.6
5	TU	0331	1.7	0856	7.6	1602	1.3	2126	7.9
6	W	0430	1.3	0944	7.9	1659	1.0	2211	8.1
7	TH O	0525	1.0	1031	8.1	1750	0.8	2255	8.2
8	F	0614	0.8	1116	8.1	1835	0.8	2339	8.2
9	SA	0657	0.8	1201	8.1	1916	1.0		
10	SU	0021	8.1	0737	1.0	1245	7.9	1954	1.3
11	M	0103	7.8	0815	1.3	1329	7.6	2031	1.8
12	TU	0144	7.5	0852	1.8	1413	7.2	2109	2.3
13	W	0227	7.1	0932	2.3	1505	6.8	2155	2.8
14	TH ☾	0321	6.7	1023	2.7	1614	6.5	2256	3.2
15	F	0436	6.4	1126	3.0	1730	6.4		
16	SA	0005	3.3	0551	6.3	1234	3.0	1842	6.5
17	SU	0114	3.1	0701	6.5	1342	2.9	1946	6.7
18	M	0221	2.8	0800	6.7	1445	2.5	2032	7.0
19	TU	0317	2.4	0845	7.0	1538	2.2	2108	7.2
20	W	0405	2.1	0922	7.2	1623	2.0	2141	7.4
21	TH	0447	1.9	0958	7.3	1702	1.9	2214	7.5
22	F ●	0523	1.8	1033	7.4	1736	1.8	2247	7.6
23	SA	0555	1.7	1108	7.5	1808	1.7	2320	7.6
24	SU	0628	1.6	1143	7.5	1841	1.7	2354	7.6
25	M	0702	1.6	1220	7.5	1916	1.8		
26	TU	0030	7.5	0737	1.7	1300	7.4	1952	2.0
27	W	0110	7.4	0813	1.9	1344	7.2	2030	2.3
28	TH	0155	7.2	0853	2.2	1433	7.0	2112	2.5
29	F	0246	7.0	0939	2.4	1531	6.8	2206	2.8
30	SA ☽	0348	6.8	1040	2.6	1641	6.8	2319	2.9
31	SU	0503	6.8	1204	2.5	1759	6.9		

JUNE

Date	Day	Time	m	Time	m	Time	m	Time	m
1	M	0045	2.7	0620	6.9	1323	2.3	1908	7.2
2	TU	0157	2.3	0729	7.2	1429	1.9	2007	7.5
3	W	0300	1.9	0828	7.5	1530	1.6	2059	7.7
4	TH	0401	1.5	0921	7.7	1629	1.4	2147	7.9
5	F O	0457	1.3	1011	7.8	1722	1.3	2233	8.0
6	SA	0548	1.2	1058	7.9	1810	1.3	2317	8.0
7	SU	0634	1.1	1144	7.8	1853	1.4		
8	M	0001	7.9	0716	1.2	1228	7.7	1933	1.6
9	TU	0042	7.7	0755	1.5	1312	7.5	2012	1.9
10	W	0124	7.5	0834	1.8	1356	7.2	2052	2.3
11	TH	0206	7.2	0913	2.2	1441	6.9	2134	2.7
12	F	0252	6.9	0956	2.5	1534	6.7	2222	3.0
13	SA ☾	0349	6.6	1044	2.8	1635	6.5	2315	3.1
14	SU	0454	6.4	1139	3.0	1736	6.5		
15	M	0014	3.2	0557	6.4	1237	3.0	1835	6.6
16	TU	0116	3.1	0656	6.5	1341	2.9	1931	6.8
17	W	0221	2.8	0753	6.7	1444	2.7	2020	7.0
18	TH	0318	2.5	0843	6.9	1537	2.4	2103	7.2
19	F	0405	2.3	0927	7.1	1623	2.2	2143	7.3
20	SA	0448	2.0	1008	7.3	1703	2.1	2221	7.5
21	SU ●	0527	1.8	1047	7.4	1742	1.9	2259	7.6
22	M	0606	1.7	1127	7.5	1822	1.8	2337	7.6
23	TU	0646	1.6	1208	7.5	1902	1.8		
24	W	0018	7.7	0727	1.6	1251	7.5	1943	1.9
25	TH	0102	7.6	0809	1.7	1337	7.5	2026	2.0
26	F	0149	7.5	0851	1.8	1425	7.3	2110	2.2
27	SA	0238	7.3	0937	2.0	1517	7.2	2200	2.4
28	SU ☽	0332	7.2	1030	2.2	1615	7.1	2300	2.5
29	M	0434	7.0	1135	2.3	1721	7.0		
30	TU	0011	2.5	0545	7.0	1247	2.3	1832	7.1

SUNRISE AND SUNSET TIMES

LE HAVRE
At 49°29'N 0°07'E

Date		Sunrise	Sunset
European Standard Time (UT-1)			
Jan	01	0856	1711
	15	0850	1728
Feb	01	0831	1756
	15	0809	1819
Mar	01	0742	1842
	15	0713	1905
European Summer Time (UT-2)			
Apr	01	0737	2031
	15	0708	2052
May	01	0637	2117
	15	0616	2137
Jun	01	0558	2158
	15	0552	2208
Jul	01	0557	2209
	15	0609	2201
Aug	01	0631	2140
	15	0651	2116
Sep	01	0715	2043
	15	0736	2013
Oct	01	0759	1938
	15	0821	1909
European Standard Time (UT-1)			
Nov	01	0748	1738
	15	0811	1717
Dec	01	0834	1703

LE HAVRE
LAT 49°29′N
LONG 0°07′E

TIMES AND HEIGHTS OF HIGH AND LOW WATER (Heights in Metres)

TIME ZONE –0100 (French Standard Time). **Subtract 1 hour for UT. For French Summer Time (area enclosed in shaded box) add 1 hour**

2020

JULY

Date	Time	m	Date	Time	m
1 W	0124 0658 1357 1938	2.4 7.1 2.2 7.3	16 TH	0108 0658 1336 1929	3.2 6.4 3.1 6.7
2 TH	0231 0805 1501 2036	2.1 7.2 2.0 7.5	17 F	0224 0802 1450 2026	2.9 6.6 2.9 6.9
3 F	0334 0904 1602 2128	1.9 7.4 1.9 7.6	18 SA	0325 0859 1547 2116	2.6 6.9 2.5 7.2
4 SA	0433 0957 1658 2216	1.7 7.5 1.8 7.7	19 SU	0416 0947 1636 2200	2.2 7.2 2.2 7.4
5 SU	0527 1045 1749 O 2301	1.5 7.6 1.7 7.8	20 M	0504 1031 1722 ● 2242	1.9 7.4 2.0 7.6
6 M	0616 1130 1834 2343	1.5 7.6 1.7 7.8	21 TU	0550 1113 1809 2325	1.6 7.6 1.8 7.8
7 TU	0658 1213 1915	1.5 7.6 1.8	22 W	0637 1156 1855	1.4 7.7 1.6
8 W	0024 0737 1254 1954	7.7 1.5 7.5 1.9	23 TH	0008 0723 1240 1940	7.9 1.3 7.8 1.5
9 TH	0103 0814 1332 2030	7.6 1.7 7.4 2.1	24 F	0052 0807 1324 2024	7.9 1.3 7.8 1.6
10 F	0141 0849 1410 2106	7.4 2.0 7.2 2.4	25 SA	0137 0848 1410 2105	7.8 1.4 7.7 1.7
11 SA	0219 0922 1449 2141	7.2 2.3 6.9 2.7	26 SU	0223 0929 1456 2148	7.7 1.6 7.5 2.0
12 SU	0259 0957 1532 2220	6.9 2.6 6.7 2.9	27 M	0311 1011 1545 ☽ 2236	7.5 1.9 7.3 2.2
13 M	0345 1038 1623 ☾ 2307	6.6 2.9 6.6 3.1	28 TU	0404 1103 1644 2337	7.2 2.2 7.1 2.5
14 TU	0445 1127 1725	6.4 3.1 6.5	29 W	0512 1211 1758	6.9 2.5 7.0
15 W	0002 0552 1226 1828	3.2 6.3 3.2 6.5	30 TH	0053 0635 1329 1914	2.6 6.8 2.6 7.0
			31 F	0207 0751 1439 2020	2.5 6.9 2.5 7.2

AUGUST

Date	Time	m	Date	Time	m
1 SA	0314 0855 1544 2117	2.3 7.1 2.3 7.4	16 SU	0252 0835 1520 2053	2.8 6.8 2.7 7.1
2 SU	0418 0949 1646 2205	2.0 7.3 2.1 7.6	17 M	0351 0928 1615 2142	2.3 7.2 2.3 7.5
3 M	0516 1036 1739 O 2248	1.8 7.5 1.9 7.7	18 TU	0444 1013 1707 2226	1.8 7.6 1.9 7.8
4 TU	0604 1117 1821 2327	1.6 7.6 1.8 7.8	19 W	0537 1056 1758 ● 2309	1.4 7.8 1.5 8.0
5 W	0643 1155 1858	1.5 7.6 1.8	20 TH	0627 1139 1846 2353	1.1 8.0 1.3 8.1
6 TH	0003 0718 1229 1933	7.8 1.5 7.6 1.8	21 F	0713 1222 1931	0.9 8.1 1.1
7 F	0037 0750 1303 2004	7.7 1.6 7.5 1.9	22 SA	0036 0755 1305 2012	8.2 0.9 8.1 1.2
8 SA	0111 0819 1335 2033	7.6 1.8 7.4 2.1	23 SU	0120 0834 1348 2051	8.1 1.0 8.0 1.4
9 SU	0143 0846 1405 2100	7.4 2.0 7.2 2.4	24 M	0203 0910 1431 2129	7.9 1.4 7.7 1.7
10 M	0214 0912 1435 2128	7.2 2.3 7.0 2.7	25 TU	0247 0948 1516 ☽ 2210	7.6 1.8 7.4 2.2
11 TU	0247 0941 1511 ☾ 2204	6.9 2.7 6.8 3.0	26 W	0337 1033 1610 2306	7.2 2.4 7.1 2.6
12 W	0332 1023 1602 2256	6.6 3.0 6.6 3.3	27 TH	0446 1139 1730	6.8 2.9 6.8
13 TH	0436 1120 1717	6.3 3.3 6.4	28 F	0026 0621 1307 1859	2.9 6.6 3.1 6.8
14 F	0002 0602 1234 1839	3.4 6.3 3.4 6.4	29 SA	0150 0746 1427 2012	2.8 6.7 2.9 7.0
15 SA	0129 0725 1408 1953	3.3 6.4 3.2 6.7	30 SU	0306 0852 1542 2109	2.5 7.0 2.5 7.3
			31 M	0418 0941 1645 2154	2.1 7.3 2.2 7.5

SEPTEMBER

Date	Time	m	Date	Time	m
1 TU	0510 1022 1730 2232	1.8 7.5 1.9 7.7	16 W	0424 0951 1649 2206	1.7 7.8 1.7 7.9
2 W	0549 1058 1805 O 2306	1.6 7.6 1.8 7.9	17 TH	0518 1034 1741 ● 2249	1.2 8.1 1.3 8.2
3 TH	0622 1130 1836 2338	1.5 7.7 1.7 7.9	18 F	0608 1117 1829 2332	0.9 8.3 1.0 8.4
4 F	0652 1200 1907	1.5 7.7 1.7	19 SA	0654 1200 1913	0.7 8.4 0.9
5 SA	0009 0721 1230 1935	7.9 1.5 7.7 1.7	20 SU	0016 0735 1242 1953	8.4 0.7 8.3 0.9
6 SU	0040 0747 1259 2000	7.8 1.7 7.6 1.9	21 M	0059 0813 1324 2031	8.3 0.9 8.2 1.2
7 M	0109 0811 1326 2024	7.6 1.9 7.4 2.2	22 TU	0142 0848 1405 2107	8.0 1.4 7.8 1.7
8 TU	0137 0835 1353 2049	7.4 2.2 7.2 2.5	23 W	0225 0924 1449 2147	7.6 2.0 7.4 2.2
9 W	0209 0901 1425 2121	7.1 2.6 7.0 2.8	24 TH	0316 1007 1543 ☽ 2241	7.1 2.6 7.0 2.8
10 TH	0249 0937 1509 ☾ 2206	6.7 3.0 6.6 3.2	25 F	0429 1116 1709	6.6 3.2 6.6
11 F	0347 1031 1620 2312	6.4 3.4 6.4 3.5	26 SA	0004 0612 1250 1844	3.1 6.5 3.4 6.6
12 SA	0515 1146 1755	6.2 3.6 6.3	27 SU	0136 0737 1420 1959	3.0 6.7 3.1 6.8
13 SU	0044 0656 1336 1925	3.4 6.4 3.4 6.6	28 M	0300 0840 1535 2054	2.6 7.0 2.6 7.2
14 M	0225 0813 1457 2032	2.9 6.8 2.8 7.1	29 TU	0403 0924 1627 2135	2.2 7.4 2.1 7.5
15 TU	0328 0906 1555 2121	2.2 7.4 2.2 7.6	30 W	0447 1000 1706 2210	1.8 7.6 1.9 7.7

OCTOBER

Date	Time	m	Date	Time	m
1 TH	0521 1031 1738 O 2241	1.6 7.7 1.7 7.9	16 F	0453 1009 1717 ● 2226	1.1 8.2 1.1 8.3
2 F	0552 1100 1808 2310	1.5 7.8 1.6 7.9	17 SA	0543 1052 1806 2310	0.8 8.4 0.8 8.5
3 SA	0622 1129 1837 2340	1.5 7.8 1.6 7.9	18 SU	0629 1135 1851 2355	0.7 8.5 0.8 8.5
4 SU	0650 1157 1904	1.5 7.8 1.7	19 M	0711 1218 1932	0.7 8.4 0.9
5 M	0010 0715 1225 1930	7.8 1.7 7.7 1.8	20 TU	0038 0750 1300 2010	8.3 1.1 8.2 1.2
6 TU	0039 0740 1252 1955	7.7 1.9 7.6 2.0	21 W	0122 0827 1342 2048	8.0 1.6 7.8 1.7
7 W	0109 0806 1321 2023	7.4 2.2 7.4 2.3	22 TH	0208 0904 1427 2128	7.5 2.2 7.4 2.3
8 TH	0143 0835 1353 2055	7.1 2.6 7.1 2.7	23 F	0300 0949 1522 ☽ 2222	7.0 2.8 6.9 2.8
9 F	0224 0910 1438 2137	6.8 3.0 6.7 3.1	24 SA	0416 1058 1648 2341	6.6 3.3 6.6 3.1
10 SA	0322 1001 1546 ☾ 2238	6.5 3.4 6.4 3.4	25 SU	0549 1227 1816	6.5 3.4 6.5
11 SU	0446 1114 1722	6.3 3.6 6.3	26 M	0107 0710 1351 1931	3.1 6.7 3.1 6.7
12 M	0009 0629 1308 1857	3.4 6.5 3.4 6.6	27 TU	0224 0813 1459 2027	2.7 7.0 2.7 7.1
13 TU	0157 0745 1431 2004	2.9 7.0 2.7 7.1	28 W	0322 0856 1549 2108	2.3 7.3 2.3 7.4
14 W	0302 0839 1530 2056	2.2 7.5 2.0 7.7	29 TH	0406 0930 1629 2142	2.0 7.6 2.0 7.6
15 TH	0358 0925 1625 2142	1.5 7.9 1.5 8.1	30 F	0444 1001 1705 2213	1.8 7.7 1.8 7.8
			31 SA	0519 1029 1738 O 2244	1.7 7.8 1.7 7.8

NOVEMBER

Date	Time	m	Date	Time	m
1 SU	0550 1058 1808 2315	1.6 7.8 1.7 7.8	16 M	0604 1113 1828 2336	0.9 8.4 0.9 8.3
2 M	0619 1128 1836 2346	1.7 7.8 1.7 7.7	17 TU	0648 1156 1911	1.0 8.3 1.0
3 TU	0647 1156 1904	1.8 7.8 1.8	18 W	0021 0730 1240 1953	8.2 1.3 8.1 1.3
4 W	0017 0715 1226 1934	7.6 1.9 7.6 1.9	19 TH	0107 0809 1324 2033	7.9 1.7 7.8 1.7
5 TH	0050 0746 1259 2005	7.4 2.2 7.5 2.2	20 F	0154 0850 1409 2115	7.5 2.3 7.4 2.2
6 F	0128 0818 1337 2040	7.2 2.5 7.2 2.5	21 SA	0246 0937 1503 2206	7.1 2.8 7.0 2.7
7 SA	0213 0856 1424 2122	6.9 2.9 6.8 2.9	22 SU	0353 1036 1615 ☽ 2308	6.8 3.2 6.7 3.0
8 SU	0310 0945 1530 ☾ 2219	6.6 3.2 6.6 3.1	23 M	0507 1145 1730	6.6 3.3 6.6
9 M	0426 1054 1654 2343	6.5 3.4 6.5 3.1	24 TU	0016 0617 1256 1839	3.1 6.6 3.2 6.6
10 TU	0557 1235 1822	6.7 3.2 6.7	25 W	0125 0724 1403 1942	2.9 6.8 2.9 6.9
11 W	0122 0711 1358 1931	2.7 7.1 2.7 7.2	26 TH	0227 0815 1500 2031	2.6 7.1 2.6 7.1
12 TH	0230 0808 1500 2027	2.1 7.5 2.0 7.6	27 F	0320 0854 1548 2110	2.3 7.4 2.2 7.3
13 F	0328 0857 1557 2116	1.6 7.9 1.5 8.0	28 SA	0405 0927 1630 2145	2.1 7.5 2.0 7.5
14 SA	0424 0943 1651 2204	1.2 8.2 1.2 8.2	29 SU	0445 1000 1708 2220	2.0 7.6 1.9 7.6
15 SU	0516 1028 1742 ● 2250	1.0 8.3 0.9 8.3	30 M	0520 1032 1741 O 2254	1.9 7.7 1.8 7.6

DECEMBER

Date	Time	m	Date	Time	m
1 TU	0552 1104 1813 2328	1.9 7.7 1.7 7.6	16 W	0629 1140 1855	1.3 8.2 1.1
2 W	0623 1136 1844	1.9 7.7 1.8	17 TH	0009 0714 1224 1939	8.0 1.5 8.0 1.3
3 TH	0002 0657 1210 1919	7.6 2.0 7.7 1.8	18 F	0054 0756 1308 2020	7.8 1.8 7.8 1.6
4 F	0039 0732 1248 1954	7.5 2.1 7.5 2.0	19 SA	0140 0838 1352 2101	7.6 2.1 7.5 2.0
5 SA	0121 0809 1330 2033	7.3 2.4 7.3 2.2	20 SU	0226 0920 1439 2142	7.3 2.5 7.2 2.3
6 SU	0207 0849 1419 2116	7.1 2.6 7.1 2.5	21 M	0317 1005 1532 2228	7.0 2.8 6.9 2.7
7 M	0301 0938 1516 2209	6.9 2.9 6.9 2.7	22 TU	0414 1055 1633 ☽ 2318	6.8 3.1 6.7 2.9
8 TU	0404 1039 1625 ☾ 2318	6.8 3.0 6.8 2.7	23 W	0514 1150 1737	6.6 3.2 6.5
9 W	0519 1157 1741	6.9 2.9 6.9	24 TH	0015 0615 1254 1840	3.1 6.6 3.2 6.6
10 TH	0040 0631 1318 1854	2.6 7.1 2.6 7.1	25 F	0120 0715 1405 1941	3.0 6.8 3.0 6.7
11 F	0153 0735 1427 1958	2.2 7.4 2.2 7.4	26 SA	0229 0809 1506 2035	2.9 7.0 2.7 6.9
12 SA	0257 0830 1529 2054	1.8 7.7 1.8 7.7	27 SU	0325 0854 1556 2120	2.6 7.2 2.4 7.2
13 SU	0356 0920 1626 2145	1.5 8.0 1.4 7.9	28 M	0412 0934 1638 2200	2.3 7.4 2.1 7.3
14 M	0451 1008 1720 ● 2234	1.3 8.1 1.2 8.1	29 TU	0453 1011 1717 2238	2.2 7.5 1.9 7.5
15 TU	0542 1055 1810 2322	1.3 8.2 1.1 8.1	30 W	0530 1047 1754 O 2315	2.0 7.6 1.8 7.6
			31 TH	0607 1123 1832 2353	1.9 7.7 1.7 7.6

CHERBOURG
LAT 49°39'N
LONG 1°38'W

TIMES AND HEIGHTS OF HIGH AND LOW WATER (Heights in Metres)

TIME ZONE
–0100 (French Standard Time). **Subtract 1 hour for UT. For French Summer Time (area enclosed in shaded box) add 1 hour**

2020

JANUARY

Day		Time	m	Time	m	Time	m	Time	m
1	W	0020	5.5	0700	2.4	1232	5.6	1922	2.2
2	TH	0059	5.3	0742	2.6	1314	5.3	2005	2.4
3	F ☽	0145	5.1	0831	2.8	1404	5.1	2057	2.6
4	SA	0242	4.9	0932	2.9	1506	4.9	2200	2.7
5	SU	0349	4.9	1044	2.9	1617	4.9	2311	2.7
6	M	0502	5.1	1153	2.7	1729	5.1		
7	TU	0015	2.5	0603	5.3	1250	2.4	1829	5.4
8	W	0109	2.2	0653	5.6	1341	2.1	1920	5.7
9	TH	0158	1.9	0738	5.9	1427	1.7	2006	5.9
10	F ○	0244	1.7	0821	6.2	1513	1.5	2051	6.1
11	SA	0329	1.5	0903	6.4	1558	1.2	2134	6.3
12	SU	0414	1.4	0946	6.5	1643	1.1	2218	6.4
13	M	0459	1.3	1030	6.6	1728	1.0	2303	6.3
14	TU	0544	1.3	1115	6.5	1814	1.1	2349	6.2
15	W	0630	1.5	1202	6.4	1900	1.3		
16	TH	0037	6.0	0719	1.7	1250	6.1	1949	1.5
17	F ☾	0127	5.8	0811	2.0	1343	5.8	2043	1.8
18	SA	0225	5.5	0911	2.2	1446	5.5	2147	2.1
19	SU	0335	5.4	1022	2.4	1602	5.3	2300	2.3
20	M	0448	5.4	1139	2.3	1719	5.3		
21	TU	0013	2.2	0556	5.5	1249	2.1	1828	5.5
22	W	0117	2.1	0656	5.7	1349	1.9	1928	5.7
23	TH	0212	1.9	0747	5.9	1440	1.7	2018	5.8
24	F ●	0300	1.7	0832	6.1	1525	1.5	2100	6.0
25	SA	0341	1.6	0911	6.2	1604	1.3	2137	6.0
26	SU	0419	1.6	0947	6.3	1640	1.3	2213	6.1
27	M	0454	1.6	1022	6.3	1714	1.3	2245	6.0
28	TU	0527	1.6	1056	6.2	1746	1.4	2318	5.9
29	W	0559	1.8	1129	6.0	1817	1.6	2349	5.7
30	TH	0630	2.0	1200	5.8	1849	1.8		
31	F	0020	5.5	0703	2.2	1232	5.6	1922	2.1

FEBRUARY

Day		Time	m	Time	m	Time	m	Time	m
1	SA	0053	5.3	0740	2.5	1309	5.3	2001	2.4
2	SU ☽	0135	5.1	0826	2.7	1357	5.0	2051	2.6
3	M	0230	4.9	0928	2.9	1503	4.8	2159	2.8
4	TU	0344	4.9	1048	2.9	1629	4.8	2322	2.7
5	W	0513	5.0	1208	2.6	1756	5.0		
6	TH	0035	2.5	0623	5.3	1312	2.2	1858	5.4
7	F	0134	2.1	0716	5.7	1407	1.8	1949	5.8
8	SA	0227	1.7	0804	6.1	1458	1.3	2037	6.2
9	SU ○	0317	1.4	0851	6.4	1547	1.0	2124	6.4
10	M	0404	1.1	0937	6.7	1633	0.7	2209	6.6
11	TU	0450	0.9	1023	6.8	1718	0.6	2254	6.6
12	W	0534	0.9	1107	6.8	1801	0.6	2337	6.5
13	TH	0617	1.0	1150	6.7	1844	0.9		
14	F	0019	6.3	0701	1.3	1232	6.3	1927	1.3
15	SA ☾	0101	6.0	0747	1.7	1317	5.9	2014	1.8
16	SU	0148	5.6	0840	2.1	1411	5.4	2111	2.2
17	M	0250	5.2	0946	2.4	1524	5.1	2226	2.5
18	TU	0413	5.1	1111	2.5	1659	4.9	2352	2.6
19	W	0536	5.1	1233	2.4	1822	5.1		
20	TH	0106	2.4	0645	5.4	1339	2.1	1925	5.4
21	F	0204	2.1	0738	5.7	1430	1.8	2011	5.7
22	SA	0250	1.8	0820	6.0	1512	1.5	2048	5.9
23	SU ●	0328	1.6	0856	6.2	1548	1.3	2121	6.0
24	M	0403	1.5	0930	6.3	1620	1.2	2152	6.1
25	TU	0434	1.4	1002	6.3	1651	1.2	2222	6.1
26	W	0504	1.4	1032	6.3	1720	1.3	2250	6.1
27	TH	0533	1.5	1102	6.2	1748	1.4	2318	5.9
28	F	0600	1.7	1130	6.0	1816	1.6	2345	5.8
29	SA	0629	1.9	1158	5.7	1845	1.9		

MARCH

Day		Time	m	Time	m	Time	m	Time	m
1	SU	0014	5.6	0701	2.1	1229	5.4	1918	2.2
2	M ☽	0047	5.3	0739	2.4	1309	5.1	2001	2.5
3	TU	0132	5.0	0832	2.7	1407	4.8	2103	2.8
4	W	0242	4.8	0952	2.9	1541	4.7	2234	2.9
5	TH	0424	4.8	1130	2.7	1731	4.9		
6	F	0006	2.6	0556	5.1	1247	2.2	1838	5.3
7	SA	0114	2.2	0657	5.6	1347	1.7	1932	5.8
8	SU	0211	1.7	0748	6.1	1441	1.2	2021	6.2
9	M ○	0302	1.2	0836	6.5	1530	0.8	2108	6.6
10	TU	0350	0.9	0923	6.8	1616	0.5	2153	6.8
11	W	0435	0.6	1008	7.0	1700	0.4	2236	6.8
12	TH	0517	0.6	1051	7.0	1742	0.5	2317	6.7
13	F	0559	0.7	1131	6.7	1822	0.8	2355	6.4
14	SA	0640	1.1	1212	6.3	1903	1.3		
15	SU	0033	6.1	0723	1.5	1253	5.8	1946	1.8
16	M ☾	0115	5.6	0812	2.0	1342	5.3	2039	2.4
17	TU	0212	5.2	0914	2.5	1454	4.8	2155	2.8
18	W	0338	4.9	1043	2.7	1644	4.7	2332	2.8
19	TH	0515	4.9	1214	2.5	1816	5.0		
20	F	0051	2.6	0628	5.2	1321	2.2	1911	5.3
21	SA	0148	2.2	0719	5.5	1410	1.8	1951	5.6
22	SU	0232	1.9	0759	5.8	1449	1.6	2025	5.9
23	M	0307	1.6	0834	6.1	1523	1.4	2056	6.0
24	TU ●	0339	1.5	0906	6.2	1554	1.2	2126	6.1
25	W	0409	1.4	0937	6.3	1623	1.2	2154	6.2
26	TH	0438	1.3	1006	6.3	1651	1.2	2221	6.2
27	F	0505	1.4	1034	6.2	1719	1.3	2247	6.1
28	SA	0533	1.5	1102	6.0	1746	1.5	2315	5.9
29	SU	0601	1.7	1132	5.8	1814	1.8	2344	5.7
30	M	0632	1.9	1203	5.5	1847	2.1		
31	TU	0015	5.5	0709	2.2	1241	5.2	1929	2.5

APRIL

Day		Time	m	Time	m	Time	m	Time	m
1	W ☽	0057	5.2	0759	2.5	1337	4.9	2030	2.8
2	TH	0203	4.9	0917	2.7	1513	4.7	2203	2.9
3	F	0348	4.8	1059	2.6	1709	4.9	2340	2.7
4	SA	0529	5.1	1221	2.2	1816	5.4		
5	SU	0052	2.2	0633	5.6	1323	1.6	1909	5.9
6	M	0149	1.6	0725	6.1	1418	1.1	1958	6.3
7	TU	0241	1.1	0814	6.5	1507	0.7	2045	6.7
8	W ○	0329	0.8	0902	6.8	1554	0.5	2130	6.8
9	TH	0414	0.6	0947	7.0	1637	0.4	2212	6.9
10	F	0457	0.6	1030	6.9	1719	0.6	2252	6.7
11	SA	0538	0.7	1110	6.6	1759	0.9	2331	6.4
12	SU	0619	1.1	1151	6.2	1839	1.4		
13	M	0008	6.1	0701	1.5	1232	5.7	1921	2.0
14	TU ☾	0050	5.6	0748	2.0	1321	5.2	2013	2.5
15	W	0144	5.1	0847	2.5	1430	4.8	2126	2.9
16	TH	0304	4.8	1011	2.7	1616	4.7	2302	2.9
17	F	0439	4.8	1139	2.6	1746	4.9		
18	SA	0019	2.7	0554	5.1	1245	2.3	1839	5.2
19	SU	0115	2.3	0646	5.4	1334	2.0	1918	5.5
20	M	0159	2.0	0726	5.7	1414	1.7	1952	5.8
21	TU	0235	1.7	0803	5.9	1449	1.5	2024	6.0
22	W	0308	1.6	0837	6.1	1521	1.4	2055	6.1
23	TH ●	0339	1.4	0909	6.1	1551	1.3	2124	6.2
24	F	0409	1.4	0939	6.2	1621	1.3	2152	6.2
25	SA	0438	1.4	1008	6.1	1651	1.4	2220	6.1
26	SU	0509	1.5	1039	6.0	1720	1.6	2250	6.0
27	M	0539	1.6	1112	5.8	1751	1.8	2323	5.8
28	TU	0612	1.8	1149	5.6	1827	2.1	2359	5.6
29	W	0653	2.1	1232	5.3	1912	2.4		
30	TH ☽	0045	5.3	0746	2.4	1330	5.0	2016	2.7

MAY

Day		Time	m	Time	m	Time	m	Time	m
1	F	0149	5.0	0901	2.5	1459	4.8	2143	2.8
2	SA	0323	4.9	1032	2.4	1640	5.0	2313	2.5
3	SU	0458	5.2	1151	2.0	1747	5.4		
4	M	0023	2.1	0604	5.6	1254	1.6	1841	5.9
5	TU	0122	1.6	0658	6.1	1350	1.2	1931	6.3
6	W	0215	1.2	0749	6.4	1441	0.9	2018	6.6
7	TH ○	0305	0.9	0838	6.6	1529	0.7	2104	6.7
8	F	0351	0.8	0924	6.7	1613	0.7	2147	6.7
9	SA	0435	0.8	1008	6.6	1655	0.9	2228	6.6
10	SU	0518	0.9	1050	6.4	1736	1.2	2307	6.3
11	M	0559	1.2	1131	6.0	1817	1.7	2347	6.0
12	TU	0641	1.6	1215	5.6	1900	2.1		
13	W	0030	5.6	0726	2.0	1303	5.2	1950	2.5
14	TH ☾	0121	5.2	0820	2.4	1403	4.9	2054	2.8
15	F	0228	4.9	0928	2.6	1525	4.7	2215	2.9
16	SA	0346	4.8	1046	2.6	1647	4.8	2328	2.8
17	SU	0500	5.0	1152	2.4	1747	5.1		
18	M	0026	2.5	0558	5.2	1245	2.2	1832	5.4
19	TU	0114	2.2	0645	5.4	1330	2.0	1911	5.6
20	W	0156	2.0	0726	5.7	1410	1.8	1948	5.8
21	TH	0232	1.8	0804	5.8	1445	1.6	2022	6.0
22	F ●	0306	1.6	0840	5.9	1519	1.6	2054	6.1
23	SA	0340	1.5	0913	6.0	1552	1.5	2125	6.1
24	SU	0414	1.5	0946	6.0	1626	1.6	2157	6.1
25	M	0449	1.5	1021	5.9	1701	1.7	2232	6.1
26	TU	0525	1.6	1100	5.8	1737	1.8	2310	5.9
27	W	0603	1.7	1141	5.7	1818	2.0	2353	5.7
28	TH	0648	1.9	1229	5.4	1908	2.3		
29	F	0042	5.5	0742	2.1	1326	5.2	2010	2.5
30	SA ☽	0142	5.3	0849	2.2	1440	5.1	2124	2.5
31	SU	0259	5.2	1004	2.2	1604	5.2	2241	2.4

JUNE

Day		Time	m	Time	m	Time	m	Time	m
1	M	0424	5.4	1118	2.0	1713	5.5	2351	2.1
2	TU	0530	5.6	1223	1.7	1810	5.8		
3	W	0053	1.7	0629	5.9	1321	1.4	1903	6.1
4	TH	0149	1.4	0724	6.2	1415	1.2	1952	6.3
5	F ○	0241	1.2	0815	6.3	1505	1.1	2039	6.4
6	SA	0330	1.1	0904	6.3	1552	1.2	2124	6.5
7	SU	0416	1.0	0951	6.3	1635	1.3	2206	6.4
8	M	0500	1.1	1034	6.1	1717	1.5	2247	6.2
9	TU	0541	1.3	1115	5.9	1758	1.8	2328	6.0
10	W	0622	1.6	1157	5.6	1840	2.1		
11	TH	0011	5.7	0704	1.9	1241	5.4	1925	2.4
12	F	0056	5.4	0749	2.2	1330	5.1	2015	2.6
13	SA ☾	0147	5.1	0840	2.4	1426	4.9	2115	2.8
14	SU	0246	5.0	0940	2.6	1531	4.9	2223	2.8
15	M	0351	4.9	1047	2.6	1639	4.9	2327	2.7
16	TU	0456	5.0	1148	2.5	1737	5.1		
17	W	0023	2.5	0555	5.1	1241	2.3	1826	5.4
18	TH	0112	2.3	0646	5.4	1327	2.1	1910	5.6
19	F	0155	2.0	0731	5.6	1409	1.9	1949	5.8
20	SA	0235	1.8	0812	5.7	1449	1.8	2027	6.0
21	SU ●	0315	1.6	0852	5.9	1528	1.7	2103	6.1
22	M	0354	1.5	0930	5.9	1608	1.6	2140	6.1
23	TU	0435	1.4	1009	6.0	1648	1.6	2219	6.2
24	W	0516	1.4	1051	6.0	1730	1.7	2302	6.1
25	TH	0558	1.5	1135	5.9	1814	1.8	2347	6.0
26	F	0644	1.6	1223	5.7	1903	2.0		
27	SA	0035	5.8	0734	1.7	1315	5.6	1958	2.1
28	SU ☽	0129	5.7	0831	1.9	1415	5.4	2100	2.2
29	M	0232	5.5	0935	2.0	1524	5.4	2209	2.3
30	TU	0345	5.4	1044	2.0	1636	5.4	2320	2.2

SUNRISE AND SUNSET TIMES
CHERBOURG
At 49°39'N 1°38'W

		Sunrise	Sunset
European Standard Time (UT-1)			
Jan	01	0903	1717
	15	0858	1735
Feb	01	0839	1802
	15	0816	1826
Mar	01	0749	1849
	15	0720	1912
European Summer Time (UT-2)			
Apr	01	0744	2038
	15	0714	2100
May	01	0644	2124
	15	0622	2145
Jun	01	0604	2205
	15	0559	2216
Jul	01	0603	2217
	15	0616	2209
Aug	01	0637	2148
	15	0657	2124
Sep	01	0722	2050
	15	0743	2020
Oct	01	0806	1945
	15	0828	1916
European Standard Time (UT-1)			
Nov	01	0755	1744
	15	0818	1724
Dec	01	0842	1709

CHERBOURG

LAT 49°39′N
LONG 1°38′W

TIMES AND HEIGHTS OF HIGH AND LOW WATER (Heights in Metres)

TIME ZONE –0100 (French Standard Time). **Subtract 1 hour for UT. For French Summer Time (area enclosed in shaded box) add 1 hour**

2020

JULY

Day	Time	m	Day	Time	m
1 W	0458 1153 1741	5.5 1.9 5.6	16 TH	0455 1147 1735	4.9 2.6 5.1
2 TH	0026 0605 1257 1839	2.0 5.6 1.8 5.8	17 F	0027 0605 1247 1833	2.5 5.1 2.4 5.3
3 F	0128 0705 1355 1932	1.7 5.8 1.7 6.0	18 SA	0120 0701 1338 1920	2.3 5.3 2.2 5.6
4 SA	0224 0801 1448 2022	1.5 5.9 1.6 6.2	19 SU	0208 0749 1425 2004	2.0 5.6 2.0 5.9
5 SU	0315 0851 1536 O 2107	1.4 6.0 1.5 6.3	20 M	0254 0834 1510 ● 2046	1.7 5.8 1.8 6.1
6 M	0401 0937 1620 2149	1.3 6.0 1.5 6.3	21 TU	0338 0916 1554 2127	1.4 6.0 1.6 6.3
7 TU	0444 1019 1701 2229	1.3 6.0 1.6 6.2	22 W	0423 0959 1638 2209	1.3 6.1 1.5 6.4
8 W	0524 1058 1740 2309	1.3 5.9 1.7 6.1	23 TH	0506 1042 1722 2253	1.1 6.2 1.4 6.4
9 TH	0601 1136 1817 2347	1.5 5.8 1.9 5.9	24 F	0550 1126 1806 2337	1.1 6.2 1.4 6.4
10 F	0637 1213 1854	1.7 5.6 2.1	25 SA	0634 1210 1851	1.2 6.1 1.6
11 SA	0025 0713 1250 1933	5.7 2.0 5.4 2.4	26 SU	0023 0719 1256 1939	6.2 1.4 5.9 1.8
12 SU	0103 0752 1330 2016	5.4 2.2 5.2 2.6	27 M	0110 0808 1345 ☽ 2033	6.0 1.7 5.7 2.0
13 M	0146 0837 1416 ☾ 2109	5.1 2.5 5.0 2.8	28 TU	0204 0904 1445 2137	5.7 2.0 5.4 2.3
14 TU	0238 0931 1514 2215	4.9 2.6 4.9 2.8	29 W	0310 1012 1559 2252	5.4 2.2 5.3 2.3
15 W	0341 1038 1623 2325	4.8 2.7 4.9 2.8	30 TH	0432 1128 1716	5.2 2.3 5.4
			31 F	0007 0549 1240 1823	2.2 5.3 2.2 5.6

AUGUST

Day	Time	m	Day	Time	m
1 SA	0115 0657 1343 1921	2.0 5.5 2.0 5.8	16 SU	0051 0637 1313 1857	2.4 5.2 2.4 5.5
2 SU	0213 0755 1438 2011	1.7 5.7 1.9 6.0	17 M	0146 0729 1406 1944	2.0 5.6 2.0 5.9
3 M	0304 0844 1525 O 2055	1.5 5.9 1.7 6.2	18 TU	0235 0816 1454 2029	1.6 6.0 1.7 6.3
4 TU	0348 0925 1606 2133	1.4 6.0 1.6 6.3	19 W	0322 0901 1540 ● 2113	1.3 6.2 1.4 6.5
5 W	0427 1001 1643 2210	1.3 6.0 1.6 6.3	20 TH	0408 0945 1625 2157	1.0 6.4 1.2 6.7
6 TH	0502 1035 1717 2245	1.3 6.0 1.6 6.2	21 F	0451 1028 1708 2240	0.8 6.5 1.1 6.8
7 F	0535 1108 1749 2318	1.4 6.0 1.7 6.1	22 SA	0534 1110 1750 2322	0.8 6.5 1.1 6.7
8 SA	0606 1139 1820 2350	1.6 5.8 1.9 5.9	23 SU	0615 1151 1833	0.9 6.4 1.3
9 SU	0636 1209 1851	1.8 5.6 2.1	24 M	0004 0657 1232 1917	6.5 1.2 6.1 1.6
10 M	0021 0707 1239 1925	5.6 2.0 5.4 2.4	25 TU	0048 0742 1316 ☽ 2007	6.1 1.7 5.8 2.0
11 TU	0054 0742 1315 ☾ 2007	5.4 2.3 5.2 2.7	26 W	0137 0834 1410 2108	5.7 2.1 5.4 2.4
12 W	0136 0826 1403 2102	5.1 2.6 5.0 2.9	27 TH	0242 0943 1527 2230	5.2 2.5 5.2 2.6
13 TH	0234 0926 1510 2220	4.8 2.9 4.8 3.0	28 F	0416 1112 1658 2357	5.0 2.7 5.2 2.5
14 F	0355 1050 1637 2345	4.7 2.9 4.9 2.8	29 SA	0546 1233 1814	5.1 2.5 5.4
15 SA	0530 1211 1800	4.9 2.7 5.2	30 SU	0109 0657 1338 1913	2.2 5.4 2.2 5.7
			31 M	0205 0750 1429 2000	1.8 5.7 2.0 6.0

SEPTEMBER

Day	Time	m	Day	Time	m
1 TU	0251 0831 1511 2039	1.6 5.9 1.7 6.2	16 W	0214 0754 1435 2009	1.5 6.2 1.5 6.5
2 W	0330 0905 1547 O 2114	1.4 6.1 1.6 6.4	17 TH	0301 0839 1521 ● 2054	1.1 6.5 1.2 6.8
3 TH	0404 0937 1619 2146	1.3 6.2 1.5 6.4	18 F	0347 0923 1605 2138	0.7 6.7 0.9 7.0
4 F	0435 1007 1649 2217	1.3 6.2 1.5 6.4	19 SA	0430 1006 1648 2221	0.6 6.8 0.8 7.0
5 SA	0505 1036 1718 2247	1.3 6.1 1.6 6.3	20 SU	0512 1048 1730 2303	0.6 6.8 0.9 6.9
6 SU	0533 1103 1745 2315	1.5 6.0 1.7 6.1	21 M	0553 1127 1812 2344	0.9 6.6 1.1 6.6
7 M	0600 1129 1813 2343	1.7 5.9 2.0 5.8	22 TU	0634 1207 1855	1.3 6.3 1.5
8 TU	0627 1157 1843	2.0 5.7 2.2	23 W	0026 0717 1249 1944	6.1 1.8 5.8 2.0
9 W	0012 0657 1228 1918	5.5 2.3 5.4 2.5	24 TH	0115 0809 1342 ☽ 2045	5.6 2.4 5.4 2.5
10 TH	0049 0735 1309 ☾ 2006	5.2 2.6 5.1 2.8	25 F	0222 0921 1502 2212	5.1 2.8 5.1 2.7
11 F	0143 0831 1413 2121	4.9 3.0 4.9 3.0	26 SA	0406 1101 1642 2346	4.9 2.9 5.0 2.6
12 SA	0310 0959 1550 2306	4.7 3.1 4.8 2.9	27 SU	0544 1225 1802	5.1 2.7 5.3
13 SU	0504 1141 1732	4.8 2.9 5.1	28 M	0056 0647 1325 1857	2.3 5.4 2.3 5.7
14 M	0025 0616 1251 1835	2.5 5.2 2.5 5.5	29 TU	0147 0730 1410 1939	1.9 5.7 2.0 6.0
15 TU	0123 0707 1346 1923	2.0 5.7 2.0 6.0	30 W	0228 0806 1448 2015	1.6 6.0 1.7 6.2

OCTOBER

Day	Time	m	Day	Time	m
1 TH	0303 0838 1521 O 2048	1.5 6.2 1.6 6.4	16 F	0236 0813 1457 ● 2030	1.0 6.7 1.0 6.9
2 F	0335 0907 1551 2119	1.4 6.3 1.5 6.4	17 SA	0322 0858 1543 2116	0.7 6.9 0.8 7.1
3 SA	0404 0936 1620 2149	1.3 6.3 1.5 6.4	18 SU	0406 0941 1627 2200	0.6 7.0 0.7 7.0
4 SU	0433 1003 1648 2216	1.4 6.3 1.5 6.3	19 M	0448 1023 1710 2243	0.7 6.9 0.8 6.8
5 M	0500 1029 1715 2244	1.5 6.2 1.7 6.1	20 TU	0530 1103 1752 2325	1.0 6.7 1.1 6.5
6 TU	0527 1055 1742 2312	1.7 6.0 1.9 5.9	21 W	0612 1144 1836	1.5 6.3 1.5
7 W	0554 1123 1811 2343	2.0 5.8 2.1 5.6	22 TH	0009 0656 1227 1924	6.0 2.0 5.9 2.0
8 TH	0624 1154 1845	2.3 5.6 2.4	23 F	0059 0749 1321 ☽ 2024	5.5 2.6 5.4 2.5
9 F	0020 0702 1233 1932	5.3 2.6 5.3 2.7	24 SA	0205 0901 1439 2148	5.0 2.9 5.1 2.7
10 SA	0113 0757 1335 ☾ 2044	5.0 3.0 5.0 3.0	25 SU	0346 1038 1613 2318	4.9 3.0 5.0 2.6
11 SU	0242 0926 1515 2230	4.7 3.2 4.8 2.9	26 M	0518 1158 1731	5.1 2.8 5.2
12 M	0439 1112 1703 2356	4.9 3.0 5.1 2.5	27 TU	0024 0616 1254 1826	2.4 5.4 2.4 5.6
13 TU	0550 1225 1808	5.3 2.5 5.6	28 W	0114 0657 1339 1908	2.1 5.7 2.1 5.9
14 W	0056 0641 1321 1858	1.9 5.8 1.9 6.1	29 TH	0155 0732 1416 1945	1.8 6.0 1.8 6.1
15 TH	0148 0728 1410 1945	1.4 6.3 1.4 6.6	30 F	0230 0805 1450 2019	1.6 6.2 1.7 6.2
			31 SA	0302 0836 1521 O 2051	1.5 6.3 1.6 6.3

NOVEMBER

Day	Time	m	Day	Time	m
1 SU	0333 0905 1551 2122	1.5 6.3 1.5 6.3	16 M	0343 0917 1607 2141	0.8 6.9 0.8 6.8
2 M	0402 0933 1621 2150	1.5 6.3 1.6 6.2	17 TU	0428 1001 1652 2225	1.0 6.8 0.9 6.6
3 TU	0432 1000 1650 2219	1.6 6.3 1.6 6.1	18 W	0511 1043 1736 2309	1.2 6.6 1.2 6.3
4 W	0501 1029 1720 2251	1.8 6.1 1.8 5.9	19 TH	0554 1126 1821 2355	1.6 6.3 1.5 5.9
5 TH	0531 1100 1752 2327	2.0 6.0 2.0 5.7	20 F	0640 1211 1908	2.1 5.9 1.9
6 F	0604 1136 1829	2.3 5.7 2.3	21 SA	0045 0731 1303 2002	5.5 2.5 5.5 2.3
7 SA	0008 0646 1219 1918	5.4 2.6 5.4 2.5	22 SU	0144 0833 1408 ☽ 2109	5.1 2.8 5.2 2.6
8 SU	0103 0743 1319 ☾ 2027	5.1 2.9 5.1 2.7	23 M	0302 0952 1524 2226	5.0 3.0 5.1 2.7
9 M	0224 0904 1447 2156	4.9 3.0 5.0 2.7	24 TU	0421 1108 1638 2334	5.0 2.9 5.1 2.5
10 TU	0404 1037 1628 2319	5.0 2.8 5.2 2.4	25 W	0526 1208 1740	5.2 2.6 5.3
11 W	0517 1152 1733	5.4 2.4 5.6	26 TH	0028 0614 1258 1829	2.3 5.5 2.3 5.6
12 TH	0023 0611 1251 1828	1.9 5.9 1.9 6.1	27 F	0114 0654 1340 1911	2.1 5.7 2.1 5.8
13 F	0118 0700 1343 1918	1.4 6.3 1.5 6.5	28 SA	0154 0731 1418 1949	1.9 6.0 1.9 6.0
14 SA	0209 0747 1433 2007	1.1 6.6 1.1 6.8	29 SU	0230 0806 1452 2025	1.8 6.1 1.7 6.1
15 SU	0257 0833 1521 ● 2054	0.9 6.8 0.9 6.9	30 M	0303 0838 1526 O 2059	1.7 6.2 1.7 6.1

DECEMBER

Day	Time	m	Day	Time	m
1 TU	0336 0909 1559 2131	1.7 6.2 1.6 6.1	16 W	0412 0944 1639 2214	1.2 6.7 1.0 6.4
2 W	0410 0939 1633 2204	1.7 6.2 1.6 6.1	17 TH	0457 1028 1724 2259	1.4 6.5 1.2 6.2
3 TH	0443 1012 1707 2240	1.8 6.2 1.7 5.9	18 F	0541 1112 1807 2342	1.6 6.3 1.4 5.9
4 F	0518 1049 1744 2319	2.0 6.1 1.8 5.8	19 SA	0624 1156 1850	1.9 6.0 1.7
5 SA	0556 1129 1825	2.2 5.9 2.0	20 SU	0026 0709 1241 1934	5.6 2.3 5.7 2.1
6 SU	0004 0641 1215 1913	5.6 2.4 5.7 2.2	21 M	0114 0757 1330 2023	5.3 2.6 5.4 2.3
7 M	0056 0736 1310 2013	5.4 2.6 5.4 2.3	22 TU	0206 0852 1426 ☽ 2119	5.1 2.8 5.2 2.6
8 TU	0202 0843 1419 ☾ 2124	5.2 2.7 5.3 2.4	23 W	0308 0957 1530 2224	5.0 2.9 5.0 2.7
9 W	0322 0959 1540 2239	5.2 2.6 5.4 2.2	24 TH	0417 1106 1638 2329	5.0 2.8 5.0 2.6
10 TH	0437 1113 1656 2348	5.4 2.4 5.6 2.0	25 F	0520 1208 1742	5.1 2.7 5.1
11 F	0538 1219 1758	5.8 2.0 5.9	26 SA	0027 0613 1300 1835	2.5 5.4 2.4 5.4
12 SA	0049 0632 1318 1855	1.6 6.1 1.7 6.2	27 SU	0116 0658 1346 1921	2.3 5.6 2.2 5.6
13 SU	0144 0723 1412 1948	1.4 6.4 1.3 6.4	28 M	0159 0739 1426 2003	2.1 5.8 2.0 5.8
14 M	0236 0812 1504 ● 2039	1.2 6.6 1.1 6.5	29 TU	0238 0816 1505 2042	1.9 6.0 1.8 5.9
15 TU	0326 0859 1553 2128	1.2 6.7 1.0 6.5	30 W	0316 0851 1543 O 2118	1.8 6.1 1.6 6.0
			31 TH	0354 0926 1621 2155	1.7 6.2 1.5 6.0

ST PETER PORT
LAT 49°27′N
LONG 2°31′W

TIMES AND HEIGHTS OF HIGH AND LOW WATER (Heights in Metres)

TIME ZONE UT
For Summer Time (area enclosed in shaded box) add 1 hour

2020

JANUARY

Date	Day	Time	m	Time	m	Time	m	Time	m
1	W	0403	3.1	1006	7.8	1633	3.0	2229	7.4
2	TH	0441	3.5	1047	7.4	1715	3.4	2313	7.1
3	F ☽	0528	3.8	1137	7.1	1807	3.6		
4	SA	0009	6.9	0631	4.0	1241	6.9	1910	3.8
5	SU	0120	6.8	0745	4.0	1354	6.9	2018	3.7
6	M	0232	7.0	0854	3.7	1501	7.2	2122	3.4
7	TU	0333	7.4	0955	3.3	1600	7.5	2219	3.0
8	W	0426	7.9	1049	2.8	1651	8.0	2310	2.5
9	TH	0513	8.3	1138	2.3	1740	8.4	2358	2.1
10	F ○	0559	8.8	1226	1.9	1826	8.7		
11	SA	0045	1.7	0643	9.1	1313	1.5	1911	9.0
12	SU	0130	1.5	0727	9.4	1358	1.3	1956	9.1
13	M	0214	1.4	0811	9.5	1442	1.2	2039	9.1
14	TU	0257	1.4	0855	9.4	1525	1.3	2123	9.0
15	W	0341	1.7	0940	9.1	1610	1.6	2208	8.7
16	TH	0426	2.0	1027	8.8	1657	2.0	2257	8.2
17	F ☾	0516	2.5	1119	8.3	1749	2.5	2353	7.8
18	SA	0615	2.9	1220	7.8	1852	2.9		
19	SU	0101	7.5	0727	3.2	1333	7.5	2007	3.1
20	M	0221	7.4	0848	3.2	1453	7.4	2125	3.1
21	TU	0334	7.6	1002	3.0	1603	7.6	2231	2.8
22	W	0434	8.0	1102	2.6	1701	8.0	2326	2.5
23	TH	0525	8.4	1153	2.2	1750	8.3		
24	F ●	0014	2.2	0610	8.7	1239	1.9	1834	8.5
25	SA	0057	2.0	0651	9.0	1320	1.7	1915	8.7
26	SU	0136	1.8	0730	9.1	1358	1.6	1952	8.7
27	M	0211	1.8	0805	9.0	1433	1.7	2025	8.7
28	TU	0242	1.9	0838	8.9	1504	1.9	2056	8.5
29	W	0311	2.2	0909	8.6	1533	2.1	2126	8.2
30	TH	0338	2.5	0939	8.2	1601	2.5	2156	7.9
31	F	0407	2.9	1011	7.8	1631	2.9		

FEBRUARY

Date	Day	Time	m	Time	m	Time	m	Time	m
1	SA	0440	3.2	1046	7.4	1706	3.3	2306	7.2
2	SU ☽	0522	3.6	1132	7.1	1755	3.6	2358	6.9
3	M	0624	3.9	1236	6.8	1905	3.8		
4	TU	0112	6.8	0751	3.9	1401	6.8	2029	3.7
5	W	0241	7.0	0913	3.6	1522	7.1	2143	3.3
6	TH	0353	7.4	1021	3.0	1627	7.6	2246	2.8
7	F	0451	8.0	1119	2.4	1723	8.2	2342	2.2
8	SA	0543	8.7	1212	1.7	1814	8.7		
9	SU ○	0033	1.6	0631	9.2	1302	1.2	1901	9.2
10	M	0120	1.1	0717	9.7	1348	0.8	1946	9.5
11	TU	0205	0.8	0801	9.9	1432	0.6	2028	9.6
12	W	0248	0.7	0844	9.9	1513	0.6	2109	9.5
13	TH	0329	0.9	0925	9.7	1554	1.0	2150	9.2
14	F	0409	1.4	1007	9.1	1634	1.5	2232	8.6
15	SA ☾	0452	2.0	1052	8.5	1718	2.3	2318	7.9
16	SU	0541	2.7	1144	7.7	1811	3.0		
17	M	0016	7.3	0644	3.3	1255	7.1	1923	3.5
18	TU	0142	6.9	0815	3.6	1431	6.8	2101	3.7
19	W	0315	7.1	0948	3.4	1553	7.1	2220	3.3
20	TH	0421	7.5	1052	2.9	1652	7.5	2316	2.9
21	F	0512	8.0	1141	2.4	1739	8.0		
22	SA	0001	2.4	0555	8.5	1225	2.0	1819	8.4
23	SU ●	0042	2.0	0635	8.8	1303	1.7	1857	8.7
24	M	0118	1.7	0711	9.1	1338	1.5	1931	8.9
25	TU	0151	1.6	0745	9.1	1410	1.4	2003	8.9
26	W	0220	1.6	0816	9.1	1439	1.5	2032	8.8
27	TH	0247	1.8	0845	8.8	1505	1.8	2059	8.6
28	F	0312	2.0	0912	8.5	1529	2.1	2124	8.2
29	SA	0337	2.4	0938	8.1	1554	2.5	2151	7.9

MARCH

Date	Day	Time	m	Time	m	Time	m	Time	m
1	SU	0403	2.8	1008	7.7	1624	3.0	2222	7.5
2	M ☽	0437	3.2	1046	7.3	1703	3.4	2305	7.1
3	TU	0526	3.6	1141	6.8	1802	3.8		
4	W	0010	6.8	0647	3.9	1306	6.6	1936	3.9
5	TH	0147	6.7	0835	3.7	1450	6.8	2113	3.6
6	F	0323	7.2	0958	3.1	1608	7.4	2226	2.9
7	SA	0431	7.9	1102	2.3	1707	8.1	2325	2.1
8	SU	0526	8.7	1156	1.5	1758	8.8		
9	M ○	0017	1.4	0615	9.4	1246	0.8	1844	9.4
10	TU	0105	0.8	0701	9.9	1331	0.4	1928	9.9
11	W	0149	0.4	0744	10.2	1414	0.1	2010	10.0
12	TH	0230	0.3	0826	10.2	1454	0.3	2049	9.9
13	F	0310	0.5	0906	9.9	1532	0.7	2127	9.4
14	SA	0348	1.0	0945	9.3	1609	1.4	2205	8.8
15	SU	0427	1.8	1025	8.4	1648	2.3	2246	8.0
16	M ☾	0511	2.6	1112	7.5	1735	3.1	2337	7.2
17	TU	0610	3.4	1218	6.8	1844	3.8		
18	W	0102	6.7	0743	3.8	1410	6.5	2037	4.0
19	TH	0253	6.7	0931	3.6	1539	6.8	2204	3.6
20	F	0403	7.2	1034	3.1	1635	7.3	2257	3.0
21	SA	0452	7.8	1120	2.5	1718	7.9	2340	2.5
22	SU	0533	8.3	1200	2.0	1756	8.3		
23	M	0018	2.0	0610	8.7	1237	1.7	1831	8.7
24	TU ●	0053	1.7	0646	9.0	1311	1.4	1904	8.9
25	W	0125	1.5	0719	9.1	1342	1.3	1935	9.0
26	TH	0154	1.5	0750	9.1	1410	1.4	2004	8.9
27	F	0220	1.6	0818	8.9	1435	1.6	2030	8.7
28	SA	0245	1.8	0844	8.6	1500	2.0	2055	8.5
29	SU	0310	2.1	0911	8.3	1525	2.3	2121	8.1
30	M	0336	2.5	0940	7.9	1554	2.8	2152	7.7
31	TU	0409	3.0	1017	7.4	1632	3.3		

APRIL

Date	Day	Time	m	Time	m	Time	m	Time	m
1	W ☽	0455	3.4	1112	6.9	1728	3.7	2338	6.9
2	TH	0612	3.7	1234	6.6	1900	3.9		
3	F	0110	6.8	0806	3.6	1423	6.8	2046	3.6
4	SA	0253	7.2	0935	3.0	1546	7.5	2203	2.9
5	SU	0407	7.9	1039	2.2	1645	8.2	2303	2.0
6	M	0503	8.7	1133	1.4	1735	9.0	2355	1.3
7	TU	0553	9.4	1222	0.7	1822	9.6		
8	W ○	0042	0.6	0639	9.9	1308	0.3	1905	10.0
9	TH	0127	0.3	0723	10.2	1350	0.1	1946	10.1
10	F	0209	0.2	0805	10.1	1430	0.3	2026	9.9
11	SA	0248	0.5	0844	9.7	1508	0.8	2103	9.5
12	SU	0327	1.0	0923	9.1	1545	1.6	2141	8.8
13	M	0405	1.8	1003	8.3	1623	2.4	2220	8.0
14	TU ☾	0448	2.6	1048	7.4	1708	3.3	2308	7.2
15	W	0546	3.4	1151	6.7	1813	3.9		
16	TH	0025	6.7	0711	3.8	1337	6.4	1958	4.2
17	F	0216	6.6	0856	3.7	1507	6.7	2131	3.8
18	SA	0329	7.0	1000	3.2	1603	7.2	2225	3.2
19	SU	0420	7.6	1047	2.7	1645	7.7	2307	2.7
20	M	0501	8.1	1126	2.2	1723	8.2	2345	2.2
21	TU	0539	8.5	1203	1.8	1758	8.6		
22	W	0020	1.9	0614	8.8	1237	1.6	1832	8.8
23	TH ●	0053	1.6	0649	8.9	1309	1.5	1904	9.0
24	F	0123	1.5	0721	8.9	1338	1.5	1934	8.9
25	SA	0152	1.6	0751	8.8	1406	1.7	2002	8.8
26	SU	0220	1.8	0819	8.6	1434	1.9	2030	8.6
27	M	0248	2.1	0849	8.3	1502	2.3	2059	8.3
28	TU	0318	2.4	0922	7.9	1535	2.7	2134	7.9
29	W	0354	2.8	1004	7.5	1616	3.1	2220	7.5
30	TH ☽	0445	3.2	1101	7.1	1715	3.5	2325	7.2

MAY

Date	Day	Time	m	Time	m	Time	m	Time	m
1	F	0600	3.5	1220	6.9	1841	3.7		
2	SA	0049	7.1	0741	3.3	1355	7.1	2019	3.4
3	SU	0222	7.4	0906	2.8	1515	7.6	2135	2.7
4	M	0335	8.0	1010	2.1	1615	8.3	2235	2.0
5	TU	0434	8.7	1105	1.4	1707	9.0	2328	1.3
6	W	0526	9.3	1155	0.9	1755	9.5		
7	TH ○	0017	0.8	0614	9.7	1242	0.6	1840	9.8
8	F	0103	0.6	0700	9.8	1326	0.5	1922	9.9
9	SA	0147	0.5	0743	9.7	1408	0.7	2003	9.7
10	SU	0228	0.8	0825	9.4	1447	1.2	2042	9.3
11	M	0308	1.3	0905	8.8	1525	1.8	2121	8.7
12	TU	0348	1.9	0946	8.1	1604	2.6	2201	8.0
13	W	0432	2.6	1031	7.5	1648	3.3	2247	7.4
14	TH ☾	0525	3.2	1127	6.9	1746	3.8	2351	6.9
15	F	0635	3.6	1245	6.6	1905	4.0		
16	SA	0116	6.7	0755	3.7	1410	6.7	2031	3.9
17	SU	0235	6.9	0906	3.4	1513	7.0	2135	3.5
18	M	0333	7.3	0959	3.0	1601	7.5	2222	3.0
19	TU	0419	7.7	1042	2.6	1642	7.9	2303	2.6
20	W	0500	8.1	1121	2.2	1720	8.3	2341	2.2
21	TH	0539	8.4	1158	2.0	1757	8.6		
22	F ●	0017	1.9	0616	8.6	1234	1.8	1832	8.8
23	SA	0052	1.8	0652	8.7	1308	1.7	1906	8.8
24	SU	0126	1.7	0726	8.7	1342	1.8	1938	8.8
25	M	0159	1.8	0800	8.6	1415	2.0	2011	8.7
26	TU	0233	2.0	0835	8.4	1449	2.2	2047	8.5
27	W	0310	2.2	0914	8.1	1527	2.5	2127	8.2
28	TH	0352	2.5	1000	7.8	1613	2.9	2217	7.9
29	F	0445	2.8	1057	7.5	1711	3.2	2318	7.6
30	SA ☽	0554	3.0	1206	7.3	1825	3.3		
31	SU	0030	7.5	0714	3.0	1324	7.4		

JUNE

Date	Day	Time	m	Time	m	Time	m	Time	m
1	M	0149	7.7	0831	2.6	1439	7.8	2102	2.7
2	TU	0302	8.0	0938	2.2	1543	8.2	2205	2.2
3	W	0405	8.5	1036	1.8	1638	8.7	2301	1.7
4	TH	0500	8.9	1129	1.4	1729	9.1	2353	1.3
5	F ○	0552	9.1	1218	1.2	1817	9.3		
6	SA	0042	1.1	0640	9.3	1305	1.2	1902	9.4
7	SU	0128	1.0	0726	9.2	1349	1.3	1945	9.3
8	M	0212	1.2	0810	9.0	1430	1.6	2026	9.1
9	TU	0254	1.5	0851	8.6	1510	2.0	2105	8.7
10	W	0334	2.0	0932	8.2	1548	2.5	2144	8.2
11	TH	0416	2.5	1013	7.7	1629	3.0	2226	7.7
12	F	0501	3.0	1059	7.2	1715	3.5	2315	7.3
13	SA ☾	0553	3.3	1153	6.9	1811	3.8		
14	SU	0015	7.0	0652	3.5	1257	6.8	1916	3.9
15	M	0123	6.9	0755	3.5	1403	6.9	2023	3.7
16	TU	0229	7.0	0855	3.3	1503	7.2	2123	3.4
17	W	0327	7.3	0949	3.0	1554	7.5	2214	3.0
18	TH	0417	7.6	1036	2.7	1640	7.9	2300	2.6
19	F	0502	8.0	1120	2.4	1722	8.2	2342	2.3
20	SA	0545	8.2	1202	2.1	1803	8.5		
21	SU ●	0024	2.0	0626	8.5	1243	2.0	1842	8.7
22	M	0105	1.8	0707	8.6	1323	1.9	1920	8.8
23	TU	0146	1.7	0747	8.6	1403	1.9	2000	8.8
24	W	0226	1.7	0828	8.6	1443	2.0	2041	8.8
25	TH	0308	1.9	0911	8.4	1525	2.1	2124	8.6
26	F	0352	2.0	0957	8.2	1611	2.4	2212	8.4
27	SA	0442	2.3	1048	8.0	1703	2.6	2306	8.1
28	SU ☽	0539	2.5	1146	7.8	1804	2.9		
29	M	0008	7.9	0644	2.7	1252	7.6	1914	2.9
30	TU	0117	7.8	0756	2.7	1404	7.7	2028	2.8

SUNRISE AND SUNSET TIMES

ST PETER PORT (GUERNSEY)
At 49°27′N 2°31′W

UT		Sunrise	Sunset
Jan	01	0806	1622
	15	0800	1639
Feb	01	0742	1706
	15	0719	1730
Mar	01	0653	1753
	15	0624	1815
BST (UT-1)			
Apr	01	0647	1942
	15	0618	2003
May	01	0548	2027
	15	0526	2048
Jun	01	0508	2108
	15	0503	2118
Jul	01	0508	2120
	15	0520	2111
Aug	01	0541	2051
	15	0601	2027
Sep	01	0626	1953
	15	0646	1923
Oct	01	0710	1849
	15	0731	1820
UT			
Nov	01	0659	1648
	15	0721	1628
Dec	01	0745	1613

ST PETER PORT
LAT 49°27′N
LONG 2°31′W

TIMES AND HEIGHTS OF HIGH AND LOW WATER (Heights in Metres)

TIME ZONE UT
For Summer Time (area enclosed in shaded box) add 1 hour

2020

JULY

Date	Day	Time	m	Time	m	Time	m	Time	m	Moon
1	W	0231	7.8	0906	2.6	1513	7.9	2138	2.5	
2	TH	0340	8.0	1011	2.3	1615	8.3	2240	2.2	
3	F	0441	8.3	1109	2.1	1710	8.6	2336	1.9	
4	SA	0536	8.5	1201	1.9	1800	8.9			
5	SU	0027	1.6	0627	8.7	1251	1.7	1847	9.1	○
6	M	0115	1.5	0714	8.8	1336	1.7	1930	9.1	
7	TU	0159	1.4	0757	8.8	1417	1.8	2011	9.0	
8	W	0240	1.6	0837	8.6	1455	2.0	2049	8.8	
9	TH	0318	1.8	0914	8.3	1530	2.3	2125	8.4	
10	F	0354	2.2	0949	8.0	1604	2.7	2200	8.1	
11	SA	0429	2.6	1025	7.6	1639	3.1	2238	7.6	
12	SU	0507	3.0	1105	7.3	1718	3.4	2320	7.3	☾
13	M	0552	3.4	1151	7.0	1809	3.7			
14	TU	0013	7.0	0646	3.6	1250	6.9	1912	3.8	
15	W	0119	6.8	0750	3.6	1357	6.9	2021	3.7	
16	TH	0229	6.9	0854	3.5	1503	7.1	2125	3.4	
17	F	0333	7.2	0953	3.2	1601	7.5	2223	3.0	
18	SA	0429	7.6	1047	2.8	1652	7.9	2315	2.6	
19	SU	0520	8.0	1137	2.4	1739	8.4			
20	M	0003	2.1	0607	8.3	1225	2.1	1824	8.7	●
21	TU	0051	1.8	0653	8.7	1311	1.7	1908	9.0	
22	W	0136	1.5	0737	8.9	1355	1.5	1951	9.2	
23	TH	0220	1.3	0820	9.0	1437	1.5	2034	9.3	
24	F	0303	1.3	0903	9.0	1519	1.5	2116	9.2	
25	SA	0345	1.4	0946	8.8	1602	1.8	2200	8.9	
26	SU	0429	1.8	1031	8.5	1647	2.1	2247	8.5	
27	M	0517	2.2	1120	8.1	1738	2.5	2341	8.1	☽
28	TU	0612	2.6	1219	7.7	1840	2.9			
29	W	0045	7.6	0720	3.0	1331	7.4	1957	3.2	
30	TH	0205	7.4	0840	3.1	1450	7.5	2119	3.1	
31	F	0325	7.5	0956	3.0	1601	7.8	2229	2.7	

AUGUST

Date	Day	Time	m	Time	m	Time	m	Time	m	Moon
1	SA	0433	7.8	1059	2.7	1659	8.2	2327	2.3	
2	SU	0529	8.1	1152	2.3	1749	8.6			
3	M	0018	1.9	0617	8.5	1240	2.0	1834	8.9	○
4	TU	0103	1.6	0701	8.7	1323	1.8	1916	9.1	
5	W	0144	1.5	0740	8.8	1401	1.7	1954	9.1	
6	TH	0222	1.5	0816	8.8	1436	1.8	2028	9.0	
7	F	0255	1.7	0849	8.6	1506	2.0	2100	8.7	
8	SA	0325	2.0	0919	8.4	1534	2.3	2130	8.4	
9	SU	0353	2.3	0949	8.0	1601	2.7	2200	8.0	
10	M	0421	2.8	1019	7.7	1630	3.1	2232	7.5	
11	TU	0452	3.2	1053	7.3	1705	3.5	2312	7.1	☾
12	W	0534	3.6	1139	6.9	1758	3.8			
13	TH	0007	6.8	0639	3.9	1245	6.7	1918	4.0	
14	F	0128	6.7	0803	3.9	1411	6.8	2044	3.8	
15	SA	0256	6.9	0918	3.6	1528	7.2	2155	3.3	
16	SU	0405	7.3	1022	3.1	1628	7.7	2255	2.7	
17	M	0502	7.9	1118	2.5	1721	8.3	2348	2.1	
18	TU	0552	8.4	1209	2.0	1809	8.9			
19	W	0037	1.5	0639	8.9	1258	1.5	1854	9.4	●
20	TH	0124	1.1	0723	9.3	1342	1.1	1938	9.7	
21	F	0207	0.8	0806	9.5	1425	0.9	2020	9.8	
22	SA	0248	0.7	0846	9.5	1505	1.0	2101	9.7	
23	SU	0328	1.0	0927	9.3	1545	1.3	2141	9.3	
24	M	0408	1.4	1007	8.8	1626	1.8	2224	8.7	
25	TU	0450	2.1	1052	8.2	1711	2.5	2312	8.0	☽
26	W	0540	2.8	1145	7.6	1809	3.1			
27	TH	0015	7.3	0647	3.4	1302	7.1	1931	3.6	
28	F	0149	6.9	0823	3.7	1438	7.1	2113	3.5	
29	SA	0324	7.1	0952	3.5	1554	7.5	2227	3.1	
30	SU	0430	7.5	1053	3.0	1650	8.0	2320	2.5	
31	M	0520	8.0	1142	2.5	1736	8.5			

SEPTEMBER

Date	Day	Time	m	Time	m	Time	m	Time	m	Moon
1	TU	0005	2.0	0602	8.5	1225	2.0	1817	8.9	
2	W	0046	1.7	0641	8.8	1304	1.7	1855	9.2	○
3	TH	0123	1.5	0717	9.0	1339	1.6	1930	9.2	
4	F	0156	1.4	0749	9.0	1410	1.6	2002	9.2	
5	SA	0226	1.5	0819	8.9	1437	1.8	2031	9.0	
6	SU	0252	1.8	0847	8.7	1502	2.1	2058	8.6	
7	M	0316	2.2	0912	8.3	1525	2.5	2124	8.2	
8	TU	0339	2.6	0938	7.9	1550	2.9	2151	7.8	
9	W	0406	3.1	1006	7.5	1619	3.3	2224	7.3	
10	TH	0440	3.6	1045	7.1	1701	3.8	2313	6.9	☾
11	F	0534	4.0	1145	6.8	1814	4.1			
12	SA	0032	6.5	0711	4.2	1320	6.7	2008	4.0	
13	SU	0225	6.7	0850	3.9	1459	7.0	2133	3.5	
14	M	0347	7.3	1002	3.3	1608	7.7	2237	2.7	
15	TU	0444	8.0	1100	2.5	1702	8.5	2330	1.9	
16	W	0534	8.7	1151	1.8	1750	9.2			
17	TH	0018	1.3	0619	9.3	1239	1.2	1835	9.7	●
18	F	0104	0.7	0703	9.7	1323	0.7	1918	10.1	
19	SA	0147	0.4	0744	10.0	1405	0.5	2000	10.2	
20	SU	0227	0.5	0824	9.9	1445	0.6	2040	10.0	
21	M	0306	0.8	0903	9.6	1524	1.1	2120	9.5	
22	TU	0344	1.4	0942	9.0	1603	1.7	2200	8.7	
23	W	0423	2.2	1024	8.3	1647	2.5	2245	7.8	
24	TH	0511	3.1	1115	7.5	1744	3.4	2348	7.0	☽
25	F	0620	3.8	1237	6.9	1914	3.9			
26	SA	0140	6.6	0815	4.1	1427	6.9	2107	3.7	
27	SU	0318	6.9	0944	3.7	1541	7.3	2215	3.2	
28	M	0417	7.5	1039	3.1	1633	7.9	2302	2.6	
29	TU	0501	8.0	1122	2.6	1715	8.5	2343	2.1	
30	W	0539	8.5	1201	2.1	1753	8.9			

OCTOBER

Date	Day	Time	m	Time	m	Time	m	Time	m	Moon
1	TH	0019	1.8	0614	8.9	1237	1.8	1828	9.1	○
2	F	0054	1.5	0647	9.1	1310	1.6	1902	9.3	
3	SA	0125	1.5	0718	9.1	1340	1.6	1933	9.2	
4	SU	0153	1.6	0747	9.1	1406	1.7	2001	9.0	
5	M	0219	1.8	0814	8.8	1431	2.0	2028	8.7	
6	TU	0242	2.1	0839	8.5	1455	2.4	2053	8.4	
7	W	0306	2.6	0904	8.2	1519	2.8	2120	7.9	
8	TH	0332	3.0	0932	7.8	1548	3.2	2152	7.5	
9	F	0406	3.5	1010	7.3	1629	3.7	2241	7.0	
10	SA	0458	4.0	1109	6.9	1737	4.1	2359	6.6	☾
11	SU	0629	4.3	1241	6.7	1935	4.0			
12	M	0154	6.7	0822	4.0	1428	7.1	2108	3.4	
13	TU	0322	7.3	0939	3.3	1541	7.8	2213	2.6	
14	W	0420	8.1	1037	2.5	1636	8.6	2306	1.8	
15	TH	0509	8.9	1127	1.7	1725	9.3	2354	1.2	
16	F	0554	9.5	1215	1.1	1811	9.9			●
17	SA	0039	0.7	0638	9.9	1300	0.6	1855	10.2	
18	SU	0123	0.5	0720	10.1	1343	0.5	1938	10.2	
19	M	0204	0.5	0800	10.0	1424	0.7	2019	9.9	
20	TU	0243	0.9	0840	9.7	1504	1.1	2059	9.4	
21	W	0322	1.6	0919	9.0	1544	1.8	2140	8.6	
22	TH	0402	2.4	1001	8.3	1629	2.6	2226	7.7	
23	F	0449	3.3	1052	7.5	1726	3.4	2329	6.9	☽
24	SA	0557	4.0	1212	6.9	1853	3.9			
25	SU	0117	6.6	0748	4.2	1358	6.9	2038	3.8	
26	M	0251	6.9	0916	3.9	1511	7.3	2144	3.3	
27	TU	0348	7.4	1010	3.3	1603	7.8	2231	2.8	
28	W	0430	7.9	1052	2.8	1644	8.2	2310	2.4	
29	TH	0507	8.4	1130	2.4	1722	8.6	2346	2.0	
30	F	0542	8.7	1205	2.0	1758	8.9			
31	SA	0020	1.8	0614	9.0	1238	1.8	1831	9.1	○

NOVEMBER

Date	Day	Time	m	Time	m	Time	m	Time	m	Moon
1	SU	0052	1.7	0646	9.1	1308	1.8	1903	9.1	
2	M	0121	1.7	0717	9.1	1337	1.8	1933	8.9	
3	TU	0148	1.9	0745	8.9	1404	2.0	2002	8.7	
4	W	0215	2.2	0812	8.7	1431	2.3	2030	8.4	
5	TH	0242	2.5	0840	8.3	1500	2.7	2100	8.0	
6	F	0312	3.0	0912	8.0	1533	3.1	2137	7.6	
7	SA	0350	3.4	0954	7.6	1617	3.5	2228	7.2	
8	SU	0443	3.8	1054	7.2	1724	3.8	2341	6.9	☾
9	M	0604	4.1	1216	7.0	1902	3.8			
10	TU	0119	6.9	0747	3.8	1350	7.3	2033	3.3	
11	W	0246	7.5	0906	3.2	1506	7.9	2140	2.6	
12	TH	0348	8.2	1007	2.5	1605	8.6	2236	1.9	
13	F	0439	8.8	1100	1.8	1658	9.2	2326	1.4	
14	SA	0527	9.4	1150	1.2	1747	9.6			
15	SU	0014	1.0	0612	9.8	1237	0.9	1833	9.9	●
16	M	0059	0.8	0656	9.9	1322	0.8	1918	9.9	
17	TU	0143	0.9	0739	9.9	1406	0.9	2001	9.6	
18	W	0224	1.3	0821	9.5	1448	1.3	2044	9.1	
19	TH	0305	1.8	0902	9.0	1531	1.9	2126	8.5	
20	F	0346	2.5	0945	8.4	1617	2.6	2213	7.8	
21	SA	0433	3.2	1035	7.7	1710	3.2	2309	7.1	
22	SU	0532	3.8	1139	7.2	1818	3.7			☽
23	M	0026	6.8	0652	4.1	1303	6.9	1938	3.8	
24	TU	0155	6.8	0820	4.0	1420	7.1	2051	3.6	
25	W	0300	7.1	0924	3.7	1518	7.4	2145	3.2	
26	TH	0349	7.6	1011	3.2	1605	7.8	2229	2.8	
27	F	0429	8.0	1052	2.8	1646	8.1	2308	2.5	
28	SA	0506	8.4	1129	2.5	1724	8.4	2344	2.2	
29	SU	0542	8.7	1204	2.2	1801	8.6			
30	M	0018	2.1	0616	8.9	1238	2.0	1836	8.7	○

DECEMBER

Date	Day	Time	m	Time	m	Time	m	Time	m	Moon
1	TU	0052	2.0	0649	8.9	1312	2.0	1910	8.7	
2	W	0124	2.0	0722	8.9	1345	2.1	1943	8.6	
3	TH	0156	2.2	0753	8.7	1417	2.2	2016	8.4	
4	F	0229	2.4	0827	8.5	1452	2.5	2052	8.2	
5	SA	0305	2.7	0905	8.2	1530	2.7	2133	7.8	
6	SU	0346	3.1	0950	7.9	1617	3.0	2223	7.5	
7	M	0437	3.4	1045	7.7	1715	3.2	2326	7.3	
8	TU	0544	3.6	1153	7.5	1829	3.3			☾
9	W	0041	7.3	0706	3.5	1311	7.6	1949	3.1	
10	TH	0202	7.5	0826	3.2	1426	7.9	2102	2.7	
11	F	0311	8.0	0934	2.7	1533	8.3	2205	2.3	
12	SA	0410	8.5	1033	2.1	1632	8.7	2301	1.8	
13	SU	0503	9.0	1127	1.7	1725	9.1	2352	1.5	
14	M	0552	9.4	1218	1.3	1816	9.3			●
15	TU	0041	1.3	0639	9.6	1307	1.2	1904	9.3	
16	W	0127	1.3	0724	9.6	1354	1.2	1949	9.2	
17	TH	0211	1.5	0808	9.4	1438	1.4	2033	8.9	
18	F	0253	1.9	0850	9.1	1521	1.8	2115	8.5	
19	SA	0334	2.3	0932	8.6	1603	2.3	2157	8.0	
20	SU	0415	2.9	1014	8.1	1647	2.8	2241	7.5	
21	M	0500	3.4	1101	7.6	1735	3.2	2331	7.1	☽
22	TU	0553	3.8	1157	7.2	1830	3.6			
23	W	0032	6.9	0656	4.0	1303	7.0	1932	3.7	
24	TH	0142	6.8	0806	3.9	1412	7.0	2036	3.6	
25	F	0248	7.1	0911	3.7	1513	7.2	2134	3.4	
26	SA	0342	7.4	1005	3.3	1605	7.5	2224	3.1	
27	SU	0428	7.8	1051	3.0	1651	7.9	2308	2.7	
28	M	0511	8.2	1133	2.6	1733	8.2	2349	2.4	
29	TU	0551	8.5	1213	2.3	1814	8.4			
30	W	0029	2.2	0629	8.7	1254	2.1	1853	8.5	○
31	TH	0108	2.0	0706	8.8	1333	1.9	1932	8.6	

ST HELIER
LAT 49°11′N
LONG 2°07′W

TIMES AND HEIGHTS OF HIGH AND LOW WATER (Heights in Metres)

TIME ZONE UT
For Summer Time (area enclosed in shaded box) add 1 hour

2020

JANUARY

Date	Day	Time	m	Time	m	Time	m	Time	m
1	W	0407	3.3	0954	9.1	1633	3.3	2217	8.7
2	TH	0444	3.8	1034	8.6	1714	3.7	2301	8.3
3	F ☽	0530	4.2	1124	8.2	1805	4.1	2359	7.9
4	SA	0630	4.4	1231	7.9	1909	4.2		
5	SU	0112	7.8	0744	4.5	1349	7.9	2023	4.1
6	M	0225	8.1	0900	4.1	1456	8.3	2131	3.8
7	TU	0324	8.6	1002	3.6	1552	8.8	2228	3.2
8	W	0414	9.2	1057	3.0	1642	9.4	2320	2.7
9	TH	0502	9.8	1147	2.4	1729	9.9		
10	F O	0008	2.2	0547	10.3	1235	1.9	1815	10.4
11	SA	0055	1.8	0632	10.8	1321	1.6	1901	10.7
12	SU	0140	1.6	0718	11.1	1407	1.3	1947	10.9
13	M	0224	1.5	0802	11.2	1451	1.3	2032	10.9
14	TU	0307	1.5	0847	11.1	1535	1.3	2117	10.6
15	W	0351	1.7	0932	10.8	1619	1.6	2202	10.3
16	TH	0436	2.0	1018	10.3	1704	2.1	2249	9.7
17	F ☾	0524	2.5	1107	9.7	1754	2.6	2342	9.2
18	SA	0619	3.0	1204	9.1	1853	3.1		
19	SU	0045	8.8	0726	3.4	1315	8.7	2005	3.4
20	M	0202	8.6	0842	3.5	1435	8.6	2121	3.4
21	TU	0318	8.8	0957	3.2	1549	8.9	2231	3.1
22	W	0422	9.3	1103	2.8	1651	9.3	2331	2.7
23	TH	0516	9.8	1159	2.4	1742	9.7		
24	F ●	0021	2.3	0601	10.2	1247	2.0	1826	10.0
25	SA	0105	2.1	0642	10.5	1328	1.9	1905	10.2
26	SU	0143	2.0	0720	10.6	1404	1.8	1941	10.3
27	M	0216	2.0	0755	10.6	1437	1.9	2014	10.2
28	TU	0247	2.1	0827	10.4	1507	2.0	2044	10.0
29	W	0315	2.3	0857	10.1	1535	2.3	2114	9.7
30	TH	0343	2.7	0927	9.7	1604	2.7	2143	9.3
31	F	0412	3.1	0956	9.2	1634	3.1		

FEBRUARY

Date	Day	Time	m	Time	m	Time	m	Time	m
1	SA	0445	3.5	1029	8.7	1710	3.6	2251	8.4
2	SU ☽	0525	4.0	1112	8.2	1757	4.1	2343	7.9
3	M	0624	4.4	1218	7.8	1905	4.3		
4	TU	0100	7.8	0747	4.4	1348	7.8	2032	4.2
5	W	0228	8.0	0915	4.0	1511	8.2	2150	3.7
6	TH	0339	8.7	1025	3.3	1616	8.9	2253	3.0
7	F	0438	9.5	1125	2.5	1712	9.7	2349	2.3
8	SA	0531	10.2	1219	1.8	1803	10.4		
9	SU O	0041	1.6	0621	10.9	1311	1.2	1851	10.9
10	M	0131	1.2	0708	11.4	1359	0.8	1937	11.3
11	TU	0216	0.8	0753	11.7	1443	0.6	2021	11.5
12	W	0259	0.7	0836	11.7	1525	0.6	2103	11.3
13	TH	0341	0.9	0918	11.4	1605	1.0	2143	10.8
14	F	0421	1.4	0959	10.8	1644	1.6	2224	10.2
15	SA ☾	0501	2.1	1041	10.0	1725	2.4	2307	9.4
16	SU	0547	2.9	1129	9.1	1814	3.3		
17	M	0002	8.6	0646	3.6	1234	8.3	1923	3.9
18	TU	0121	8.1	0809	3.9	1406	8.0	2055	4.0
19	W	0255	8.2	0939	3.7	1537	8.2	2219	3.6
20	TH	0409	8.7	1053	3.1	1642	8.8	2321	3.0
21	F	0504	9.4	1149	2.5	1732	9.5		
22	SA	0010	2.5	0548	10.0	1234	2.1	1812	9.9
23	SU ●	0052	2.1	0628	10.4	1313	1.8	1849	10.2
24	M	0127	1.9	0703	10.6	1346	1.7	1921	10.4
25	TU	0158	1.8	0735	10.7	1416	1.6	1951	10.5
26	W	0226	1.8	0804	10.6	1443	1.7	2019	10.4
27	TH	0252	1.9	0832	10.5	1509	1.8	2046	10.2
28	F	0318	2.1	0858	10.1	1535	2.2	2111	9.8
29	SA	0345	2.5	0924	9.6	1602	2.7	2136	9.4

MARCH

Date	Day	Time	m	Time	m	Time	m	Time	m
1	SU	0412	3.0	0950	9.1	1630	3.3	2205	8.8
2	M ☽	0443	3.6	1022	8.5	1706	3.8	2245	8.3
3	TU	0528	4.1	1114	7.9	1802	4.3	2351	7.8
4	W	0645	4.4	1246	7.6	1936	4.5		
5	TH	0135	7.8	0830	4.2	1437	7.9	2115	4.0
6	F	0310	8.4	0957	3.4	1556	8.7	2230	3.1
7	SA	0419	9.3	1104	2.5	1656	9.7	2331	2.2
8	SU	0515	10.3	1202	1.6	1748	10.6		
9	M O	0025	1.4	0605	11.1	1255	0.9	1836	11.3
10	TU	0115	0.8	0652	11.7	1343	0.4	1920	11.7
11	W	0201	0.4	0737	12.1	1427	0.2	2002	11.9
12	TH	0244	0.3	0819	12.1	1507	0.3	2042	11.7
13	F	0323	0.5	0859	11.7	1545	0.7	2120	11.1
14	SA	0401	1.1	0937	10.9	1620	1.5	2157	10.3
15	SU	0438	1.9	1015	9.9	1656	2.5	2235	9.4
16	M ☾	0518	2.9	1058	8.9	1739	3.5	2324	8.5
17	TU	0612	3.7	1200	8.0	1846	4.3		
18	W	0044	7.8	0740	4.2	1344	7.6	2031	4.4
19	TH	0234	7.9	0922	4.0	1524	8.0	2203	3.9
20	F	0352	8.5	1036	3.3	1627	8.7	2304	3.2
21	SA	0445	9.2	1128	2.6	1712	9.4	2350	2.6
22	SU	0528	9.8	1211	2.1	1751	9.9		
23	M	0028	2.1	0605	10.3	1248	1.8	1824	10.3
24	TU ●	0103	1.9	0638	10.5	1320	1.6	1855	10.5
25	W	0133	1.7	0709	10.7	1349	1.5	1924	10.6
26	TH	0201	1.6	0738	10.7	1416	1.5	1951	10.6
27	F	0228	1.7	0805	10.6	1443	1.7	2017	10.4
28	SA	0254	1.9	0831	10.3	1509	2.0	2042	10.1
29	SU	0320	2.2	0856	9.9	1535	2.5	2106	9.7
30	M	0347	2.7	0922	9.3	1603	3.1	2134	9.2
31	TU	0417	3.3	0954	8.7	1637	3.7		

APRIL

Date	Day	Time	m	Time	m	Time	m	Time	m
1	W ☽	0500	3.9	1043	8.1	1730	4.2	2315	8.0
2	TH	0611	4.2	1215	7.6	1900	4.4		
3	F	0101	7.8	0756	4.1	1413	7.9	2045	4.0
4	SA	0245	8.4	0930	3.3	1534	8.8	2205	3.1
5	SU	0356	9.4	1039	2.4	1635	9.8	2307	2.1
6	M	0454	10.4	1138	1.5	1727	10.7		
7	TU	0002	1.3	0544	11.2	1232	0.8	1814	11.4
8	W O	0053	0.7	0631	11.8	1320	0.4	1858	11.8
9	TH	0140	0.3	0715	12.0	1404	0.2	1939	11.9
10	F	0222	0.3	0757	11.9	1444	0.4	2019	11.7
11	SA	0302	0.6	0837	11.5	1521	1.0	2056	11.1
12	SU	0339	1.2	0915	10.7	1556	1.8	2132	10.3
13	M	0416	2.0	0952	9.7	1631	2.7	2210	9.3
14	TU ☾	0455	3.0	1035	8.7	1712	3.7	2257	8.4
15	W	0547	3.8	1136	7.8	1816	4.4		
16	TH	0015	7.8	0711	4.3	1318	7.5	1959	4.6
17	F	0203	7.8	0850	4.1	1453	7.9	2130	4.1
18	SA	0320	8.3	1001	3.5	1554	8.6	2230	3.4
19	SU	0413	9.0	1053	2.9	1640	9.2	2316	2.8
20	M	0456	9.6	1135	2.4	1718	9.8	2354	2.3
21	TU	0534	10.0	1212	2.0	1753	10.1		
22	W	0029	2.0	0608	10.3	1246	1.8	1823	10.4
23	TH ●	0102	1.8	0639	10.5	1318	1.7	1853	10.5
24	F	0133	1.7	0709	10.5	1348	1.7	1921	10.6
25	SA	0202	1.7	0738	10.5	1417	1.7	1949	10.5
26	SU	0231	1.8	0807	10.3	1445	2.0	2017	10.3
27	M	0300	2.1	0835	9.9	1514	2.4	2046	9.9
28	TU	0330	2.6	0906	9.4	1546	2.9	2118	9.4
29	W	0405	3.1	0944	8.8	1624	3.5	2201	8.8
30	TH ☽	0451	3.5	1040	8.3	1720	3.9	2307	8.3

MAY

Date	Day	Time	m	Time	m	Time	m	Time	m
1	F	0601	3.8	1207	7.9	1843	4.1		
2	SA	0043	8.2	0733	3.7	1348	8.2	2017	3.7
3	SU	0216	8.7	0900	3.1	1506	9.0	2135	3.0
4	M	0328	9.5	1009	2.3	1607	9.8	2238	2.1
5	TU	0427	10.3	1109	1.6	1700	10.6	2334	1.4
6	W	0519	11.0	1203	1.0	1748	11.2		
7	TH O	0026	0.9	0607	11.4	1253	0.7	1832	11.5
8	F	0115	0.7	0652	11.6	1338	0.7	1915	11.6
9	SA	0159	0.7	0735	11.5	1420	0.9	1955	11.4
10	SU	0240	0.9	0816	11.0	1459	1.4	2034	10.9
11	M	0320	1.5	0856	10.3	1536	2.1	2112	10.2
12	TU	0358	2.2	0935	9.5	1612	2.9	2151	9.3
13	W	0438	3.0	1018	8.7	1653	3.7	2237	8.6
14	TH ☾	0527	3.7	1114	8.0	1749	4.3	2344	8.0
15	F	0634	4.1	1234	7.7	1909	4.5		
16	SA	0112	7.9	0755	4.1	1400	7.9	2034	4.3
17	SU	0230	8.2	0906	3.7	1505	8.4	2138	3.8
18	M	0328	8.7	1002	3.3	1555	8.9	2228	3.2
19	TU	0415	9.2	1048	2.8	1637	9.4	2311	2.8
20	W	0456	9.6	1129	2.4	1714	9.8	2350	2.4
21	TH	0533	9.9	1208	2.2	1749	10.1		
22	F ●	0027	2.1	0607	10.1	1245	2.0	1821	10.3
23	SA	0104	1.9	0641	10.3	1320	1.9	1854	10.5
24	SU	0138	1.9	0714	10.3	1353	1.9	1926	10.5
25	M	0212	1.9	0748	10.2	1426	2.0	2000	10.4
26	TU	0246	2.1	0824	10.0	1501	2.3	2036	10.1
27	W	0322	2.3	0903	9.6	1538	2.7	2117	9.7
28	TH	0402	2.7	0949	9.1	1622	3.1	2205	9.2
29	F	0452	3.0	1046	8.7	1718	3.4	2308	8.9
30	SA ☽	0555	3.3	1157	8.5	1829	3.6		
31	SU	0024	8.7	0711	3.3	1317	8.6		

JUNE

Date	Day	Time	m	Time	m	Time	m	Time	m
1	M	0143	9.0	0827	2.9	1431	9.1	2101	2.9
2	TU	0255	9.4	0936	2.4	1535	9.7	2206	2.3
3	W	0357	10.0	1038	2.0	1631	10.2	2305	1.8
4	TH	0452	10.5	1134	1.6	1722	10.7		
5	F O	0000	1.5	0543	10.8	1227	1.4	1809	11.0
6	SA	0051	1.2	0631	10.9	1315	1.4	1853	11.1
7	SU	0139	1.2	0716	10.8	1359	1.5	1936	11.0
8	M	0222	1.4	0759	10.6	1440	1.8	2016	10.6
9	TU	0304	1.7	0840	10.1	1519	2.3	2056	10.1
10	W	0343	2.2	0920	9.5	1556	2.8	2135	9.5
11	TH	0421	2.8	1000	9.0	1634	3.4	2217	9.0
12	F	0502	3.3	1046	8.4	1717	3.9	2307	8.4
13	SA ☾	0550	3.7	1142	8.1	1811	4.2		
14	SU	0011	8.1	0648	4.0	1251	8.0	1919	4.3
15	M	0124	8.1	0755	3.9	1400	8.1	2029	4.1
16	TU	0230	8.3	0859	3.7	1500	8.5	2130	3.7
17	W	0325	8.6	0955	3.4	1549	8.9	2223	3.3
18	TH	0413	9.0	1044	3.0	1633	9.3	2310	2.9
19	F	0456	9.4	1130	2.6	1713	9.7	2354	2.5
20	SA	0536	9.8	1213	2.3	1752	10.1		
21	SU ●	0037	2.2	0616	10.0	1255	2.1	1830	10.3
22	M	0118	1.9	0656	10.2	1335	2.0	1910	10.5
23	TU	0158	1.8	0737	10.3	1414	2.0	1951	10.5
24	W	0238	1.8	0819	10.2	1454	2.0	2033	10.4
25	TH	0319	1.9	0903	10.0	1536	2.2	2117	10.2
26	F	0402	2.1	0950	9.7	1621	2.5	2205	9.9
27	SA	0450	2.4	1040	9.4	1712	2.8	2258	9.5
28	SU ☽	0544	2.7	1137	9.1	1810	3.0	2359	9.2
29	M	0645	2.9	1242	8.9	1917	3.1		
30	TU	0107	9.1	0753	3.0	1353	9.0	2027	3.0

SUNRISE AND SUNSET TIMES

ST HELIER
At 49°N 2°W

UT		Sunrise	Sunset
Jan	01	0803	1621
	15	0758	1639
Feb	01	0739	1705
	15	0717	1729
Mar	01	0651	1752
	15	0622	1814
BST (UT-1)			
Apr	01	0646	1940
	15	0617	2001
May	01	0547	2025
	15	0526	2045
Jun	01	0508	2105
	15	0503	2115
Jul	01	0508	2117
	15	0520	2109
Aug	01	0541	2048
	15	0600	2025
Sep	01	0625	1951
	15	0645	1921
Oct	01	0708	1847
	15	0729	1818
UT			
Nov	01	0656	1647
	15	0719	1627
Dec	01	0742	1613
	15	0757	1611

ST HELIER
LAT 49°11′N
LONG 2°07′W

TIMES AND HEIGHTS OF HIGH AND LOW WATER (Heights in Metres)

TIME ZONE UT
For Summer Time (area enclosed in shaded box) add 1 hour

2020

JULY

Date	Day	Time	m
1	W	0220 0903 1502 2136	9.1 2.8 9.2 2.8
2	TH	0329 1010 1605 2241	9.4 2.6 9.6 2.4
3	F	0431 1111 1701 2340	9.7 2.3 10.1 2.1
4	SA	0527 1208 1751	10.1 2.1 10.4
5	SU ○	0035 0617 1259 1837	1.8 10.3 1.9 10.6
6	M	0125 0703 1344 1921	1.6 10.4 1.9 10.7
7	TU	0209 0745 1425 2001	1.6 10.3 2.0 10.6
8	W	0249 0824 1502 2039	1.8 10.1 2.2 10.3
9	TH	0325 0901 1536 2114	2.1 9.8 2.6 9.9
10	F	0359 0936 1608 2150	2.5 9.4 2.9 9.4
11	SA	0431 1011 1642 2227	2.9 9.0 3.4 8.9
12	SU ☾	0506 1050 1720 2310	3.3 8.6 3.8 8.5
13	M	0548 1139 1809	3.7 8.2 4.1
14	TU	0006 0641 1242 1912	8.1 4.0 8.0 4.3
15	W	0118 0748 1354 2026	7.9 4.1 8.0 4.2
16	TH	0229 0859 1459 2134	8.1 3.9 8.3 3.8
17	F	0330 1002 1553 2233	8.4 3.5 8.8 3.3
18	SA	0423 1057 1642 2325	9.0 3.0 9.4 2.7
19	SU	0511 1147 1729	9.5 2.5 9.9
20	M ●	0015 0557 1235 1813	2.2 9.9 2.1 10.4
21	TU	0102 0643 1321 1858	1.9 10.3 1.8 10.7
22	W	0148 0728 1405 1942	1.6 10.6 1.6 11.0
23	TH	0232 0812 1448 2026	1.4 10.7 1.5 11.0
24	F	0314 0855 1530 2110	1.3 10.7 1.6 10.9
25	SA	0357 0939 1613 2154	1.4 10.5 1.8 10.6
26	SU	0439 1023 1658 2240	1.8 10.0 2.2 10.1
27	M ☽	0524 1111 1747 2330	2.3 9.5 2.7 9.5
28	TU	0616 1206 1845	2.8 9.0 3.2
29	W	0032 0718 1315 1956	8.9 3.3 8.7 3.4
30	TH	0148 0834 1434 2114	8.6 3.4 8.7 3.3
31	F	0310 0951 1548 2228	8.7 3.3 9.0 3.0

AUGUST

Date	Day	Time	m
1	SA	0421 1100 1649 2332	9.1 2.9 9.6 2.5
2	SU	0519 1158 1741	9.6 2.5 10.1
3	M ○	0026 0608 1248 1825	2.1 10.0 2.2 10.4
4	TU	0114 0651 1331 1906	1.8 10.2 2.0 10.6
5	W	0155 0729 1409 1943	1.7 10.3 1.9 10.7
6	TH	0230 0804 1441 2017	1.7 10.3 2.0 10.5
7	F	0301 0836 1511 2049	1.9 10.2 2.2 10.3
8	SA	0330 0905 1538 2118	2.1 9.9 2.5 9.9
9	SU	0357 0934 1606 2147	2.5 9.5 2.9 9.4
10	M	0425 1004 1636 2218	2.9 9.0 3.4 8.8
11	TU ☾	0458 1037 1713 2256	3.5 8.5 3.9 8.3
12	W	0539 1123 1804 2354	4.0 8.1 4.3 7.8
13	TH	0639 1233 1920	4.4 7.7 4.5
14	F	0123 0802 1405 2048	7.6 4.4 7.9 4.3
15	SA	0252 0924 1520 2202	8.0 4.0 8.4 3.6
16	SU	0358 1030 1619 2302	8.6 3.3 9.2 2.9
17	M	0453 1126 1710 2356	9.4 2.6 9.9 2.2
18	TU	0542 1218 1759	10.1 2.0 10.6
19	W ●	0047 0629 1307 1845	1.6 10.7 1.5 11.1
20	TH	0135 0714 1353 1929	1.1 11.1 1.1 11.5
21	F	0220 0757 1436 2013	0.8 11.3 0.9 11.7
22	SA	0302 0839 1518 2054	0.7 11.3 1.0 11.5
23	SU	0342 0920 1558 2135	0.9 11.0 1.3 11.0
24	M	0421 1000 1638 2216	1.5 10.4 1.9 10.3
25	TU ☽	0500 1041 1721 2301	2.2 9.7 2.6 9.4
26	W	0545 1130 1815 2359	3.0 8.9 3.4 8.5
27	TH	0647 1241 1932	3.8 8.3 3.9
28	F	0125 0815 1418 2104	8.0 4.1 8.2 3.8
29	SA	0306 0946 1542 2225	8.2 3.8 8.7 3.3
30	SU	0419 1056 1642 2326	8.8 3.2 9.4 2.6
31	M	0512 1149 1730	9.4 2.6 10.0

SEPTEMBER

Date	Day	Time	m
1	TU	0015 0555 1234 1810	2.1 10.0 2.2 10.5
2	W ○	0057 0633 1313 1847	1.8 10.3 1.9 10.7
3	TH	0133 0707 1346 1920	1.7 10.5 1.8 10.8
4	F	0204 0738 1415 1951	1.6 10.6 1.9 10.8
5	SA	0232 0806 1441 2019	1.7 10.5 2.0 10.6
6	SU	0257 0833 1506 2046	1.9 10.3 2.2 10.2
7	M	0323 0858 1532 2110	2.2 9.9 2.6 9.7
8	TU	0349 0922 1559 2135	2.7 9.5 3.1 9.1
9	W	0416 0949 1629 2204	3.3 8.9 3.7 8.5
10	TH ☾	0449 1023 1710 2248	4.0 8.3 4.3 7.9
11	F	0541 1122 1823	4.5 7.8 4.7
12	SA	0017 0710 1310 2006	7.4 4.7 7.6 4.5
13	SU	0221 0851 1452 2135	7.7 4.3 8.2 3.8
14	M	0338 1006 1558 2240	8.5 3.5 9.1 2.9
15	TU	0434 1105 1652 2335	9.4 2.6 10.1 2.0
16	W	0524 1158 1741	10.3 1.8 10.9
17	TH ●	0027 0610 1248 1826	1.3 11.0 1.2 11.6
18	F	0116 0654 1334 1911	0.8 11.5 0.8 12.0
19	SA	0200 0737 1417 1953	0.5 11.8 0.6 12.1
20	SU	0242 0817 1458 2034	0.5 11.7 0.7 11.8
21	M	0320 0856 1537 2113	0.8 11.3 1.1 11.1
22	TU	0358 0934 1616 2152	1.5 10.6 1.9 10.2
23	W	0435 1012 1657 2234	2.4 9.7 2.8 9.1
24	TH ☽	0518 1059 1750 2333	3.4 8.7 3.7 8.2
25	F	0621 1214 1915	4.2 8.0 4.2
26	SA	0113 0803 1409 2057	7.6 4.5 7.9 4.1
27	SU	0303 0939 1532 2215	8.0 4.1 8.5 3.4
28	M	0408 1043 1627 2309	8.7 3.3 9.3 2.7
29	TU	0454 1130 1710 2352	9.5 2.6 10.0 2.2
30	W	0533 1211 1748	10.0 2.2 10.5

OCTOBER

Date	Day	Time	m
1	TH ○	0030 0608 1246 1822	1.9 10.4 1.9 10.7
2	F	0104 0639 1317 1853	1.7 10.6 1.8 10.8
3	SA	0133 0708 1344 1922	1.7 10.7 1.8 10.8
4	SU	0159 0735 1411 1949	1.7 10.7 1.9 10.7
5	M	0225 0801 1437 2015	1.9 10.5 2.1 10.4
6	TU	0252 0825 1503 2039	2.2 10.2 2.5 9.9
7	W	0318 0849 1530 2103	2.7 9.7 3.0 9.3
8	TH	0345 0914 1559 2131	3.3 9.2 3.6 8.7
9	F	0416 0947 1638 2213	3.9 8.6 4.2 8.0
10	SA ☾	0505 1041 1745 2337	4.5 8.0 4.6 7.5
11	SU	0632 1228 1931	4.8 7.7 4.5
12	M	0150 0819 1422 2106	7.7 4.4 8.2 3.8
13	TU	0313 0939 1533 2213	8.5 3.5 9.1 2.8
14	W	0410 1039 1628 2309	9.6 2.6 10.2 1.9
15	TH	0500 1133 1717	10.5 1.7 11.0
16	F ●	0001 0546 1223 1803	1.2 11.2 1.1 11.7
17	SA	0050 0630 1310 1848	0.7 11.7 0.7 12.0
18	SU	0135 0712 1354 1930	0.5 11.9 0.6 12.0
19	M	0217 0753 1436 2012	0.6 11.8 0.7 11.7
20	TU	0257 0832 1516 2051	1.1 11.3 1.3 10.9
21	W	0335 0910 1555 2131	1.8 10.6 2.0 10.0
22	TH	0413 0949 1638 2215	2.7 9.6 3.0 8.9
23	F ☽	0456 1037 1733 2314	3.7 8.7 3.8 8.0
24	SA	0601 1151 1856	4.4 8.0 4.3
25	SU	0054 0741 1342 2033	7.6 4.7 7.9 4.2
26	M	0236 0912 1503 2145	7.9 4.2 8.4 3.6
27	TU	0338 1013 1557 2236	8.6 3.5 9.1 2.9
28	W	0424 1059 1640 2318	9.3 2.9 9.8 2.5
29	TH	0502 1137 1718 2355	9.9 2.4 10.2 2.1
30	F	0537 1212 1752	10.3 2.2 10.4
31	SA ○	0028 0607 1244 1823	2.0 10.5 2.0 10.6

NOVEMBER

Date	Day	Time	m
1	SU	0059 0637 1314 1853	1.9 10.6 1.9 10.6
2	M	0128 0705 1343 1921	1.9 10.6 2.0 10.5
3	TU	0157 0732 1412 1949	2.0 10.6 2.1 10.3
4	W	0226 0759 1440 2017	2.2 10.3 2.4 9.9
5	TH	0254 0826 1510 2045	2.6 9.9 2.8 9.4
6	F	0324 0856 1542 2119	3.2 9.4 3.3 8.9
7	SA	0400 0934 1625 2206	3.7 8.9 3.8 8.3
8	SU ☾	0450 1030 1729 2326	4.2 8.3 4.2 7.9
9	M	0608 1202 1900	4.5 8.0 4.2
10	TU	0113 0743 1343 2029	8.0 4.2 8.4 3.6
11	W	0237 0904 1458 2140	8.7 3.5 9.2 2.8
12	TH	0339 1008 1557 2238	9.5 2.6 10.1 2.0
13	F	0431 1103 1650 2332	10.4 1.9 10.8 1.4
14	SA	0520 1155 1739	11.1 1.3 11.4
15	SU ●	0022 0605 1245 1825	1.0 11.5 0.9 11.6
16	M	0109 0649 1331 1910	0.9 11.7 0.8 11.6
17	TU	0154 0731 1415 1953	1.0 11.5 1.0 11.3
18	W	0236 0812 1458 2035	1.4 11.1 1.5 10.6
19	TH	0316 0852 1540 2117	2.0 10.5 2.1 9.8
20	F	0357 0934 1625 2202	2.8 9.7 2.9 9.0
21	SA	0441 1021 1716 2256	3.6 8.9 3.6 8.3
22	SU ☽	0537 1122 1822	4.2 8.3 4.1
23	M	0010 0654 1248 1941	7.8 4.5 8.0 4.2
24	TU	0138 0817 1410 2052	7.9 4.4 8.2 3.9
25	W	0247 0923 1512 2148	8.3 3.9 8.7 3.4
26	TH	0340 1014 1600 2234	8.9 3.4 9.2 3.0
27	F	0423 1057 1642 2314	9.4 3.0 9.6 2.6
28	SA	0501 1135 1719 2351	9.8 2.6 9.9 2.4
29	SU	0535 1211 1754	10.1 2.3 10.1
30	M ○	0027 0607 1246 1826	2.2 10.3 2.2 10.3

DECEMBER

Date	Day	Time	m
1	TU	0102 0638 1320 1859	2.1 10.5 2.1 10.3
2	W	0135 0710 1353 1931	2.1 10.5 2.1 10.2
3	TH	0207 0742 1426 2005	2.3 10.4 2.3 10.0
4	F	0240 0816 1500 2041	2.5 10.1 2.5 9.6
5	SA	0314 0853 1537 2122	2.8 9.8 2.9 9.2
6	SU	0354 0936 1622 2212	3.2 9.4 3.2 8.8
7	M	0444 1030 1719 2315	3.6 8.9 3.5 8.5
8	TU ☾	0548 1140 1830	3.8 8.7 3.6
9	W	0032 0706 1300 1948	8.4 3.8 8.7 3.4
10	TH	0152 0824 1417 2101	8.7 3.4 9.1 3.0
11	F	0301 0932 1523 2205	9.3 2.9 9.7 2.4
12	SA	0400 1033 1622 2303	9.9 2.3 10.2 2.0
13	SU	0454 1130 1716 2358	10.5 1.8 10.7 1.6
14	M ●	0543 1223 1807	10.9 1.4 10.9
15	TU	0048 0630 1314 1854	1.5 11.2 1.3 11.0
16	W	0136 0715 1402 1940	1.5 11.2 1.3 10.8
17	TH	0221 0758 1447 2024	1.7 11.0 1.6 10.5
18	F	0303 0840 1529 2105	2.1 10.6 2.0 9.9
19	SA	0344 0921 1610 2146	2.6 10.0 2.6 9.3
20	SU	0423 1002 1651 2229	3.2 9.4 3.1 8.8
21	M ☽	0505 1048 1736 2319	3.7 8.8 3.6 8.3
22	TU	0554 1144 1830	4.1 8.3 4.0
23	W	0021 0657 1255 1934	8.0 4.4 8.1 4.1
24	TH	0134 0809 1408 2041	8.0 4.3 8.1 4.0
25	F	0241 0915 1510 2141	8.3 4.0 8.4 3.7
26	SA	0337 1011 1602 2232	8.7 3.6 8.8 3.3
27	SU	0423 1058 1646 2318	9.1 3.2 9.2 2.9
28	M	0503 1142 1727	9.6 2.7 9.6
29	TU	0000 0541 1223 1805	2.6 9.9 2.4 9.9
30	W ○	0040 0618 1303 1843	2.3 10.2 2.2 10.1
31	TH	0119 0655 1341 1921	2.2 10.4 2.0 10.2

ST-MALO
LAT 48°38′N
LONG 2°02′W

TIMES AND HEIGHTS OF HIGH AND LOW WATER (Heights in Metres)

TIME ZONE –0100 (French Standard Time). **Subtract 1 hour for UT. For French Summer Time (area enclosed in shaded box) add 1 hour**

2020

SUNRISE AND SUNSET TIMES

ST MALO
At 48°38′N 2°02′W
European Standard Time (UT-1)

		Sunrise	Sunset
Jan	01	0901	1723
	15	0855	1740
Feb	01	0838	1807
	15	0816	1829
Mar	01	0750	1852
	15	0721	1913
European Summer Time (UT-2)			
Apr	01	0746	2039
	15	0718	2100
May	01	0648	2123
	15	0627	2143
Jun	01	0610	2202
	15	0605	2212
Jul	01	0610	2214
	15	0622	2206
Aug	01	0642	2146
	15	0701	2123
Sep	01	0725	2050
	15	0745	2021
Oct	01	0808	1947
	15	0828	1919
European Standard Time (UT-1)			
Nov	01	0755	1748
	15	0816	1728
Dec	01	0839	1715

JANUARY

Date	Day	Time	m
1	W	0506 1039 1731 2301	3.6 10.2 3.6 9.8
2	TH	0540 1118 1808 2343	4.1 9.7 4.1 9.3
3	F ☽	0621 1206 1854	4.6 9.2 4.4
4	SA	0038 0717 1312 1954	8.9 4.8 8.9 4.6
5	SU	0150 0829 1429 2108	8.8 4.9 8.9 4.6
6	M	0305 0947 1539 2220	9.0 4.6 9.2 4.2
7	TU	0408 1053 1637 2320	9.6 4.0 9.8 3.6
8	W	0501 1149 1729	10.2 3.4 10.4
9	TH	0013 0549 1240 1817	3.0 10.9 2.7 11.0
10	F ○	0103 0634 1330 1903	2.5 11.4 2.2 11.4
11	SA	0151 0718 1419 1948	2.0 11.9 1.8 11.8
12	SU	0238 0802 1507 2032	1.7 12.2 1.5 12.0
13	M	0325 0847 1554 2117	1.6 12.4 1.4 12.0
14	TU	0409 0931 1638 2201	1.6 12.3 1.5 11.8
15	W	0453 1016 1722 2246	1.9 12.0 1.9 11.4
16	TH	0538 1102 1807 2333	2.3 11.5 2.4 10.8
17	F ☾	0624 1152 1856	2.9 10.8 3.0
18	SA	0026 0718 1251 1953	10.3 3.4 10.2 3.5
19	SU	0130 0823 1403 2102	9.8 3.8 9.8 3.8
20	M	0247 0939 1522 2218	9.7 3.8 9.7 3.7
21	TU	0403 1054 1635 2328	9.9 3.5 10.0 3.4
22	W	0507 1159 1735	10.4 3.1 10.5
23	TH	0027 0601 1254 1826	3.0 10.9 2.6 10.9
24	F ●	0117 0647 1341 1911	2.6 11.4 2.3 11.2
25	SA	0200 0728 1422 1950	2.3 11.6 2.0 11.4
26	SU	0238 0805 1459 2026	2.2 11.8 1.9 11.5
27	M	0313 0839 1533 2059	2.2 11.8 2.0 11.4
28	TU	0345 0911 1605 2129	2.3 11.6 2.2 11.2
29	W	0414 0941 1634 2159	2.5 11.3 2.5 10.9
30	TH	0441 1011 1701 2228	2.9 10.9 2.9 10.4
31	F	0507 1040 1729	3.4 10.3 3.4

FEBRUARY

Date	Day	Time	m
1	SA	0537 1112 1803 2334	3.9 9.7 3.9 9.4
2	SU ☽	0616 1154 1848	4.4 9.1 4.4
3	M	0025 0711 1301 1951	8.9 4.8 8.7 4.7
4	TU	0146 0831 1438 2118	8.7 4.9 8.6 4.7
5	W	0317 1004 1601 2240	8.9 4.5 9.1 4.1
6	TH	0429 1117 1706 2345	9.6 3.8 9.9 3.4
7	F	0527 1218 1801	10.4 2.9 10.7
8	SA	0044 0619 1316 1851	2.6 11.3 2.1 11.5
9	SU ○	0139 0707 1410 1938	1.9 12.0 1.4 12.1
10	M	0230 0753 1501 2023	1.3 12.6 0.9 12.6
11	TU	0319 0838 1547 2106	0.9 13.0 0.6 12.7
12	W	0403 0921 1630 2148	0.8 13.0 0.7 12.6
13	TH	0445 1003 1710 2228	1.0 12.7 1.1 12.1
14	F	0524 1044 1748 2308	1.6 12.0 1.9 11.3
15	SA ☾	0603 1126 1828 2352	2.4 11.1 2.8 10.5
16	SU	0647 1215 1915	3.2 10.2 3.6
17	M	0047 0744 1322 2021	9.7 3.9 9.4 4.3
18	TU	0208 0904 1456 2147	9.1 4.3 9.0 4.4
19	W	0343 1032 1623 2310	9.2 4.1 9.3 4.0
20	TH	0456 1145 1727	9.8 3.5 10.0
21	F	0014 0549 1240 1815	3.4 10.5 2.9 10.6
22	SA	0104 0633 1326 1856	2.8 11.1 2.4 11.1
23	SU ●	0145 0712 1406 1933	2.4 11.6 2.0 11.4
24	M	0222 0747 1441 2006	2.1 11.8 1.8 11.6
25	TU	0255 0819 1513 2036	1.9 11.9 1.8 11.7
26	W	0325 0848 1542 2104	1.9 11.9 1.8 11.6
27	TH	0351 0916 1608 2131	2.1 11.7 2.1 11.4
28	F	0415 0943 1632 2157	2.4 11.3 2.5 11.0
29	SA	0439 1008 1657 2222	2.8 10.8 3.0 10.5

MARCH

Date	Day	Time	m
1	SU	0504 1034 1725 2250	3.4 10.1 3.6 9.9
2	M ☽	0536 1105 1802 2328	3.9 9.5 4.2 9.3
3	TU	0621 1154 1856	4.5 8.8 4.7
4	W	0031 0731 1333 2023	8.7 4.9 8.4 5.0
5	TH	0226 0920 1532 2207	8.6 4.8 8.7 4.5
6	F	0401 1050 1647 2322	9.2 4.0 9.6 3.6
7	SA	0508 1159 1744	10.2 2.9 10.7
8	SU	0026 0602 1300 1835	2.5 11.3 1.9 11.7
9	M ○	0124 0652 1356 1922	1.6 12.3 1.0 12.5
10	TU	0217 0738 1446 2006	0.9 13.0 0.4 13.0
11	W	0305 0822 1531 2048	0.4 13.4 0.1 13.2
12	TH	0348 0904 1612 2128	0.3 13.4 0.3 13.0
13	F	0428 0944 1650 2206	0.6 13.0 0.9 12.4
14	SA	0504 1022 1724 2242	1.3 12.2 1.8 11.6
15	SU	0540 1101 1759 2321	2.2 11.1 2.8 10.6
16	M ☾	0618 1145 1840	3.2 10.0 3.9
17	TU	0011 0710 1248 1943	9.5 4.1 9.0 4.7
18	W	0133 0831 1433 2120	8.8 4.6 8.5 4.9
19	TH	0323 1011 1611 2252	8.8 4.4 9.0 4.4
20	F	0439 1125 1711 2355	9.5 3.7 9.7 3.6
21	SA	0530 1219 1755	10.3 3.0 10.5
22	SU	0042 0611 1303 1833	2.9 10.9 2.5 11.0
23	M	0122 0648 1341 1907	2.4 11.4 2.1 11.4
24	TU ●	0158 0722 1415 1939	2.1 11.7 1.8 11.7
25	W	0230 0753 1446 2008	1.9 11.9 1.7 11.8
26	TH	0259 0822 1514 2036	1.8 11.9 1.8 11.8
27	F	0325 0849 1540 2102	1.9 11.8 1.9 11.6
28	SA	0350 0915 1605 2128	2.2 11.5 2.3 11.3
29	SU	0414 0941 1629 2153	2.5 11.0 2.8 10.8
30	M	0440 1007 1657 2221	3.1 10.4 3.4 10.2
31	TU	0511 1038 1733	3.7 9.7 4.1

APRIL

Date	Day	Time	m
1	W ☽	0553 1125 1825 2355	4.3 8.9 4.7 8.9
2	TH	0659 1257 1949	4.8 8.4 5.0
3	F	0149 0848 1507 2139	8.6 4.7 8.7 4.6
4	SA	0334 1026 1624 2259	9.2 3.9 9.7 3.6
5	SU	0444 1137 1722	10.3 2.8 10.8
6	M	0004 0540 1239 1812	2.5 11.4 1.7 11.8
7	TU	0103 0630 1335 1859	1.5 12.4 0.9 12.6
8	W ○	0156 0717 1424 1943	0.7 13.1 0.3 13.1
9	TH	0244 0801 1509 2025	0.3 13.4 0.2 13.2
10	F	0327 0843 1549 2104	0.3 13.3 0.4 13.0
11	SA	0406 0922 1625 2141	0.7 12.8 1.1 12.4
12	SU	0442 1000 1658 2217	1.4 12.0 2.0 11.5
13	M	0517 1038 1732 2256	2.3 10.9 3.1 10.5
14	TU ☾	0554 1121 1811 2344	3.3 9.8 4.1 9.5
15	W	0643 1222 1912	4.2 8.9 4.9
16	TH	0103 0759 1403 2048	8.8 4.7 8.4 5.1
17	F	0251 0936 1540 2219	8.7 4.6 8.8 4.6
18	SA	0407 1050 1640 2320	9.3 4.0 9.5 3.8
19	SU	0458 1143 1723	10.0 3.3 10.2
20	M	0007 0539 1227 1800	3.2 10.6 2.7 10.8
21	TU	0048 0616 1306 1835	2.7 11.1 2.3 11.3
22	W	0125 0651 1342 1907	2.3 11.5 2.1 11.5
23	TH ●	0158 0723 1414 1938	2.1 11.6 2.0 11.7
24	F	0229 0753 1444 2006	2.0 11.7 1.9 11.7
25	SA	0258 0822 1513 2034	2.0 11.6 2.0 11.7
26	SU	0326 0851 1540 2102	2.2 11.4 2.3 11.4
27	M	0354 0920 1608 2132	2.5 11.0 2.7 11.0
28	TU	0423 0951 1640 2205	2.9 10.4 3.3 10.4
29	W	0458 1029 1719 2247	3.5 9.8 3.9 9.8
30	TH ☽	0543 1122 1813 2350	4.0 9.1 4.5 9.2

MAY

Date	Day	Time	m
1	F	0650 1252 1935	4.4 8.7 4.7
2	SA	0129 0828 1437 2114	9.0 4.4 9.0 4.3
3	SU	0303 0958 1553 2232	9.5 3.7 9.9 3.4
4	M	0413 1109 1653 2337	10.4 2.7 10.8 2.5
5	TU	0511 1211 1745	11.4 1.8 11.7
6	W	0036 0603 1308 1832	1.7 12.1 1.2 12.4
7	TH ○	0130 0652 1358 1917	1.1 12.7 0.8 12.8
8	F	0219 0737 1443 2000	0.8 12.8 0.8 12.8
9	SA	0303 0820 1523 2040	0.8 12.7 1.0 12.6
10	SU	0343 0901 1600 2119	1.1 12.3 1.6 12.1
11	M	0420 0941 1634 2157	1.7 11.6 2.4 11.4
12	TU	0456 1020 1709 2237	2.5 10.7 3.2 10.5
13	W	0534 1103 1749 2324	3.3 9.8 4.1 9.7
14	TH ☾	0620 1158 1843	4.0 9.1 4.7
15	F	0030 0722 1315 2001	9.0 4.5 8.6 5.0
16	SA	0156 0842 1443 2125	8.8 4.6 8.7 4.8
17	SU	0314 0955 1550 2229	9.0 4.3 9.2 4.2
18	M	0411 1053 1638 2320	9.6 3.7 9.8 3.7
19	TU	0457 1141 1719	10.1 3.2 10.4
20	W	0005 0537 1224 1757	3.2 10.6 2.8 10.8
21	TH	0045 0615 1303 1833	2.8 11.0 2.5 11.2
22	F ●	0123 0651 1340 1906	2.5 11.2 2.3 11.4
23	SA	0159 0726 1415 1939	2.3 11.3 2.3 11.6
24	SU	0233 0759 1448 2011	2.2 11.3 2.3 11.6
25	M	0307 0832 1521 2044	2.3 11.2 2.4 11.5
26	TU	0341 0908 1556 2121	2.5 11.0 2.7 11.2
27	W	0417 0947 1633 2201	2.8 10.6 3.1 10.7
28	TH	0457 1032 1717 2250	3.2 10.1 3.6 10.2
29	F	0546 1129 1812 2351	3.6 9.6 4.0 9.8
30	SA ☽	0650 1241 1924	3.9 9.4 4.2
31	SU	0108 0808 1402	9.6 3.8 9.5

JUNE

Date	Day	Time	m
1	M	0227 0926 1515 2159	9.9 3.5 10.0 3.4
2	TU	0338 1037 1619 2306	10.4 2.9 10.7 2.7
3	W	0440 1140 1715	11.0 2.3 11.3
4	TH	0007 0536 1238 1806	2.1 11.6 1.8 11.8
5	F ○	0103 0628 1331 1853	1.7 11.9 1.6 12.1
6	SA	0154 0716 1417 1938	1.5 12.1 1.6 12.2
7	SU	0240 0801 1459 2020	1.4 12.0 1.7 12.1
8	M	0321 0844 1537 2100	1.6 11.7 2.1 11.8
9	TU	0400 0925 1614 2140	2.0 11.3 2.6 11.3
10	W	0437 1004 1650 2220	2.5 10.7 3.1 10.7
11	TH	0515 1044 1728 2302	3.1 10.1 3.8 10.0
12	F	0555 1128 1811 2351	3.7 9.5 4.3 9.5
13	SA ☾	0641 1221 1905	4.2 9.1 4.7
14	SU	0050 0738 1325 2011	9.1 4.5 8.8 4.8
15	M	0200 0844 1436 2122	8.9 4.5 8.9 4.6
16	TU	0307 0950 1539 2223	9.1 4.3 9.3 4.2
17	W	0405 1047 1631 2316	9.5 3.9 9.8 3.8
18	TH	0454 1138 1717	9.9 3.5 10.3
19	F	0004 0539 1224 1759	3.3 10.4 3.1 10.7
20	SA	0048 0622 1308 1838	2.9 10.7 2.8 11.1
21	SU ●	0130 0702 1349 1916	2.6 11.0 2.5 11.4
22	M	0212 0741 1430 1955	2.4 11.2 2.4 11.5
23	TU	0253 0821 1510 2034	2.3 11.3 2.4 11.6
24	W	0335 0902 1551 2116	2.3 11.2 2.4 11.5
25	TH	0417 0946 1633 2200	2.4 11.1 2.6 11.3
26	F	0501 1032 1718 2248	2.6 10.8 2.9 10.9
27	SA	0549 1123 1809 2341	2.9 10.4 3.3 10.5
28	SU ☽	0641 1219 1906	3.2 10.1 3.6
29	M	0042 0742 1324 2013	10.2 3.4 9.9 3.7
30	TU	0151 0851 1435 2125	10.1 3.4 9.9 3.5

ST-MALO
LAT 48°38′N
LONG 2°02′W

TIMES AND HEIGHTS OF HIGH AND LOW WATER (Heights in Metres)

TIME ZONE –0100 (French Standard Time). **Subtract 1 hour for UT. For French Summer Time (area enclosed in shaded box) add 1 hour**

2020

JULY

Date	Day	Time	m
1	W	0303 1002 1545 2236	10.2 3.3 10.3 3.2
2	TH	0412 1110 1649 2341	10.5 3.0 10.7 2.7
3	F	0515 1213 1746	10.8 2.6 11.2
4	SA	0041 0611 1308 1836	2.4 11.1 2.4 11.5
5	SU ○	0134 0702 1357 1923	2.1 11.4 2.2 11.7
6	M	0221 0748 1440 2006	2.0 11.4 2.2 11.8
7	TU	0304 0830 1520 2045	2.0 11.4 2.3 11.7
8	W	0342 0909 1556 2123	2.1 11.3 2.5 11.5
9	TH	0419 0945 1630 2159	2.4 11.0 2.9 11.1
10	F	0453 1020 1703 2234	2.8 10.6 3.3 10.6
11	SA	0525 1054 1735 2310	3.2 10.1 3.8 10.0
12	SU	0558 1131 1810 2351	3.7 9.6 4.2 9.5
13	M ☾	0637 1216 1855	4.2 9.2 4.6
14	TU	0043 0726 1315 1957	9.1 4.5 8.9 4.9
15	W	0152 0832 1428 2114	8.8 4.6 8.9 4.8
16	TH	0306 0947 1539 2227	8.9 4.5 9.2 4.4
17	F	0412 1054 1638 2326	9.3 4.1 9.7 3.8
18	SA	0507 1150 1729	9.8 3.6 10.3
19	SU	0018 0557 1241 1816	3.3 10.4 3.1 10.9
20	M ●	0108 0644 1329 1900	2.8 10.9 2.6 11.4
21	TU	0157 0729 1417 1943	2.3 11.3 2.3 11.8
22	W	0245 0812 1503 2026	2.0 11.6 2.0 12.1
23	TH	0331 0855 1548 2109	1.7 11.8 1.8 12.2
24	F	0415 0939 1631 2153	1.7 11.8 1.9 12.1
25	SA	0458 1022 1713 2236	1.8 11.6 2.2 11.7
26	SU	0540 1105 1756 2322	2.2 11.1 2.6 11.2
27	M ☽	0623 1152 1843	2.7 10.6 3.1
28	TU	0013 0713 1247 1941	10.6 3.3 10.1 3.6
29	W	0116 0815 1357 2052	10.0 3.7 9.7 3.9
30	TH	0232 0930 1517 2211	9.7 3.9 9.7 3.8
31	F	0353 1048 1633 2324	9.8 3.7 10.1 3.3

AUGUST

Date	Day	Time	m
1	SA	0504 1156 1735	10.2 3.3 10.7
2	SU	0026 0602 1254 1826	2.8 10.6 2.9 11.2
3	M ○	0120 0652 1343 1911	2.4 11.0 2.6 11.6
4	TU	0207 0735 1426 1951	2.2 11.3 2.3 11.8
5	W	0248 0813 1503 2028	2.0 11.5 2.2 11.8
6	TH	0323 0848 1537 2101	2.0 11.5 2.3 11.8
7	F	0356 0920 1607 2132	2.1 11.3 2.5 11.5
8	SA	0425 0950 1633 2202	2.4 11.0 2.8 11.1
9	SU	0451 1018 1658 2230	2.8 10.6 3.3 10.5
10	M	0516 1047 1723 2300	3.3 10.2 3.8 9.9
11	TU ☾	0545 1118 1757 2336	3.9 9.6 4.3 9.3
12	W	0623 1201 1844	4.4 9.1 4.8
13	TH	0032 0718 1311 1956	8.7 4.8 8.7 5.1
14	F	0205 0840 1446 2136	8.5 5.0 8.7 4.9
15	SA	0336 1012 1606 2254	8.8 4.6 9.3 4.2
16	SU	0444 1121 1706 2354	9.5 3.9 10.0 3.4
17	M	0539 1219 1758	10.3 3.2 10.9
18	TU	0050 0628 1313 1845	2.7 11.0 2.5 11.6
19	W ●	0144 0715 1405 1930	2.0 11.7 1.9 12.3
20	TH	0235 0759 1454 2014	1.4 12.2 1.4 12.7
21	F	0321 0841 1538 2056	1.0 12.5 1.1 12.9
22	SA	0404 0923 1620 2137	0.9 12.5 1.2 12.8
23	SU	0444 1003 1659 2218	1.2 12.2 1.6 12.3
24	M	0522 1042 1737 2259	1.8 11.7 2.2 11.5
25	TU ☽	0559 1123 1818 2345	2.5 10.9 3.0 10.6
26	W	0642 1213 1910	3.4 10.1 3.8
27	TH	0043 0741 1323 2023	9.7 4.2 9.4 4.3
28	F	0209 0905 1500 2155	9.1 4.5 9.2 4.3
29	SA	0346 1035 1625 2315	9.2 4.3 9.7 3.7
30	SU	0459 1147 1726	9.9 3.6 10.5
31	M	0016 0553 1242 1813	3.0 10.5 3.0 11.2

SEPTEMBER

Date	Day	Time	m
1	TU	0106 0637 1328 1854	2.5 11.1 2.5 11.6
2	W ○	0149 0716 1407 1931	2.1 11.5 2.2 11.9
3	TH	0226 0750 1442 2004	1.9 11.7 2.1 12.0
4	F	0259 0822 1512 2035	1.9 11.7 2.1 12.0
5	SA	0328 0850 1539 2103	1.9 11.7 2.2 11.8
6	SU	0354 0917 1602 2129	2.2 11.5 2.5 11.4
7	M	0417 0942 1624 2154	2.6 11.1 3.0 10.9
8	TU	0439 1007 1646 2218	3.1 10.6 3.5 10.3
9	W	0504 1032 1715 2246	3.6 10.0 4.1 9.6
10	TH ☾	0537 1105 1755 2328	4.3 9.4 4.7 8.9
11	F	0625 1200 1858	4.9 8.7 5.2
12	SA	0058 0743 1356 2047	8.3 5.3 8.4 5.2
13	SU	0308 0937 1539 2227	8.5 5.0 9.0 4.4
14	M	0424 1057 1645 2333	9.4 4.1 10.0 3.4
15	TU	0519 1159 1738	10.4 3.1 11.0
16	W	0031 0609 1255 1826	2.4 11.4 2.2 12.0
17	TH ●	0126 0655 1348 1911	1.5 12.2 1.4 12.8
18	F	0217 0739 1437 1955	0.9 12.8 0.9 13.3
19	SA	0303 0821 1521 2037	0.5 13.1 0.6 13.4
20	SU	0345 0901 1602 2117	0.5 13.0 0.8 13.1
21	M	0423 0939 1639 2156	1.0 12.6 1.3 12.5
22	TU	0459 1017 1716 2236	1.7 11.9 2.1 11.5
23	W	0534 1056 1754 2319	2.7 10.9 3.1 10.4
24	TH ☽	0614 1144 1844	3.7 9.9 4.0
25	F	0018 0711 1258 1959	9.4 4.6 9.1 4.6
26	SA	0154 0845 1448 2142	8.7 5.0 9.0 4.5
27	SU	0339 1025 1613 2301	9.0 4.5 9.6 3.8
28	M	0446 1131 1708 2357	9.8 3.7 10.4 3.1
29	TU	0533 1221 1751	10.6 3.0 11.1
30	W	0043 0613 1303 1829	2.5 11.2 2.5 11.7

OCTOBER

Date	Day	Time	m
1	TH ○	0122 0649 1340 1904	2.1 11.6 2.2 12.0
2	F	0157 0721 1413 1936	1.9 11.8 2.1 12.1
3	SA	0228 0751 1442 2006	1.9 11.9 2.0 12.0
4	SU	0256 0819 1509 2032	1.9 11.9 2.1 11.9
5	M	0322 0844 1533 2058	2.1 11.7 2.4 11.5
6	TU	0345 0909 1555 2123	2.5 11.4 2.8 11.1
7	W	0409 0934 1619 2147	3.0 10.9 3.3 10.5
8	TH	0434 1000 1648 2216	3.5 10.3 3.9 9.8
9	F	0507 1032 1727 2257	4.2 9.6 4.5 9.0
10	SA ☾	0554 1124 1827	4.9 8.9 5.0
11	SU	0019 0710 1315 2011	8.4 5.3 8.5 5.1
12	M	0241 0905 1509 2158	8.6 5.0 9.1 4.4
13	TU	0358 1031 1617 2308	9.5 4.1 10.1 3.3
14	W	0454 1134 1712	10.6 2.9 11.2
15	TH	0007 0543 1230 1801	2.2 11.6 1.9 12.2
16	F ●	0102 0629 1324 1848	1.3 12.5 1.2 13.0
17	SA	0152 0714 1414 1932	0.7 13.1 0.7 13.4
18	SU	0239 0756 1459 2015	0.4 13.3 0.5 13.4
19	M	0321 0837 1540 2056	0.6 13.1 0.8 13.0
20	TU	0359 0916 1618 2136	1.1 12.7 1.4 12.3
21	W	0435 0954 1655 2216	1.9 11.9 2.2 11.3
22	TH	0510 1034 1735 2300	2.9 10.9 3.2 10.2
23	F ☽	0551 1123 1824 2359	4.0 9.9 4.1 9.2
24	SA	0648 1238 1936	4.8 9.1 4.7
25	SU	0133 0820 1423 2112	8.7 5.1 8.9 4.6
26	M	0313 0956 1544 2229	8.9 4.7 9.5 4.0
27	TU	0417 1059 1638 2323	9.6 3.9 10.2 3.3
28	W	0503 1148 1720	10.4 3.2 10.9
29	TH	0008 0541 1229 1758	2.8 11.0 2.7 11.4
30	F	0047 0616 1306 1834	2.4 11.4 2.4 11.7
31	SA ○	0122 0649 1340 1906	2.2 11.7 2.2 11.8

NOVEMBER

Date	Day	Time	m
1	SU	0155 0720 1411 1937	2.1 11.8 2.2 11.8
2	M	0225 0749 1440 2005	2.1 11.8 2.2 11.7
3	TU	0253 0816 1508 2033	2.2 11.7 2.4 11.5
4	W	0320 0843 1535 2101	2.5 11.5 2.7 11.1
5	TH	0347 0911 1603 2131	2.9 11.1 3.1 10.6
6	F	0417 0943 1635 2206	3.4 10.6 3.7 9.9
7	SA	0453 1021 1717 2252	4.0 9.9 4.2 9.2
8	SU ☾	0542 1116 1817	4.6 9.3 4.7
9	M	0012 0655 1250 1947	8.7 5.0 8.9 4.7
10	TU	0203 0834 1430 2123	8.9 4.7 9.3 4.1
11	W	0322 0957 1542 2236	9.6 3.9 10.2 3.2
12	TH	0422 1103 1641 2337	10.6 2.9 11.2 2.2
13	F	0514 1202 1733	11.6 2.0 12.1
14	SA	0033 0602 1257 1822	1.5 12.3 1.3 12.7
15	SU ●	0126 0648 1349 1909	1.0 12.8 0.9 13.0
16	M	0213 0732 1436 1954	0.8 13.0 0.8 13.0
17	TU	0257 0815 1519 2038	1.0 12.9 1.0 12.6
18	W	0337 0856 1600 2120	1.5 12.5 1.5 12.0
19	TH	0415 0937 1639 2202	2.2 11.8 2.2 11.2
20	F	0452 1019 1719 2247	3.0 10.9 3.1 10.3
21	SA	0534 1108 1806 2340	3.8 10.1 3.8 9.4
22	SU ☽	0626 1210 1905	4.5 9.4 4.4
23	M	0051 0737 1332 2020	8.9 4.9 9.0 4.6
24	TU	0217 0900 1453 2134	8.9 4.8 9.2 4.3
25	W	0328 1009 1553 2234	9.3 4.3 9.7 3.8
26	TH	0420 1102 1641 2323	9.9 3.8 10.2 3.3
27	F	0503 1148 1723	10.4 3.3 10.7
28	SA	0007 0541 1229 1801	2.9 10.9 2.9 11.1
29	SU	0046 0617 1307 1837	2.6 11.3 2.6 11.3
30	M ○	0123 0651 1343 1911	2.4 11.5 2.4 11.4

DECEMBER

Date	Day	Time	m
1	TU	0157 0723 1416 1944	2.3 11.6 2.4 11.4
2	W	0230 0755 1450 2016	2.4 11.6 2.4 11.3
3	TH	0303 0827 1523 2050	2.5 11.5 2.6 11.1
4	F	0336 0901 1557 2127	2.8 11.3 2.9 10.7
5	SA	0411 0939 1635 2208	3.1 10.9 3.2 10.3
6	SU	0452 1023 1720 2257	3.6 10.4 3.6 9.8
7	M	0541 1117 1816	4.0 9.9 4.0
8	TU ☾	0001 0644 1227 1926	9.4 4.3 9.6 4.1
9	W	0120 0800 1347 2045	9.4 4.2 9.7 3.8
10	TH	0237 0919 1502 2158	9.7 3.8 10.1 3.3
11	F	0344 1029 1608 2305	10.4 3.1 10.8 2.6
12	SA	0443 1133 1706	11.1 2.4 11.4
13	SU	0005 0537 1232 1801	2.0 11.8 1.8 12.0
14	M ●	0100 0627 1326 1852	1.6 12.2 1.5 12.2
15	TU	0151 0714 1416 1940	1.5 12.5 1.3 12.3
16	W	0237 0800 1502 2025	1.5 12.5 1.4 12.1
17	TH	0320 0843 1545 2109	1.8 12.2 1.6 11.8
18	F	0400 0925 1625 2150	2.2 11.8 2.1 11.2
19	SA	0439 1007 1705 2232	2.8 11.2 2.7 10.6
20	SU	0517 1049 1745 2314	3.4 10.5 3.3 9.9
21	M	0558 1134 1828	4.0 9.9 3.9
22	TU ☽	0002 0646 1229 1919	9.4 4.5 9.3 4.3
23	W	0101 0746 1336 2020	9.0 4.8 9.0 4.5
24	TH	0212 0856 1449 2128	8.9 4.8 9.1 4.4
25	F	0321 1004 1552 2231	9.2 4.5 9.4 4.1
26	SA	0418 1102 1644 2325	9.6 4.0 9.8 3.6
27	SU	0505 1152 1730	10.2 3.5 10.3
28	M	0012 0548 1237 1812	3.2 10.7 3.1 10.7
29	TU	0055 0627 1318 1852	2.9 11.1 2.7 11.0
30	W ○	0135 0705 1359 1930	2.6 11.4 2.5 11.2
31	TH	0214 0742 1439 2007	2.4 11.5 2.3 11.3

BREST

LAT 48°23′N
LONG 4°30′W

TIMES AND HEIGHTS OF HIGH AND LOW WATER (Heights in Metres)

TIME ZONE –0100 (French Standard Time). **Subtract 1 hour for UT. For French Summer Time (area enclosed in shaded box) add 1 hour**

2020

SUNRISE AND SUNSET TIMES

BREST
At 48°23′N 4°30′W
European Standard Time (UT-1)

		Sunrise	Sunset
Jan	01	0910	1735
	15	0905	1752
Feb	01	0847	1818
	15	0826	1841
Mar	01	0800	1903
	15	0732	1924
European Summer Time (UT-2)			
Apr	01	0757	2049
	15	0729	2110
May	01	0700	2133
	15	0639	2152
Jun	01	0622	2212
	15	0617	2222
Jul	01	0622	2223
	15	0633	2215
Aug	01	0654	2156
	15	0713	2133
Sep	01	0736	2100
	15	0756	2031
Oct	01	0818	1958
	15	0839	1930
European Standard Time (UT-1)			
Nov	01	0805	1759
	15	0826	1740
Dec	01	0849	1726

JANUARY

Date	Day	Time	m	Time	m	Time	m	Time	m
1	W	0245	2.4	0841	6.0	1509	2.4	2103	5.6
2	TH	0328	2.7	0926	5.7	1554	2.7	2152	5.4
3	F ☽	0418	2.9	1020	5.5	1648	2.8	2253	5.3
4	SA	0518	3.0	1125	5.4	1751	2.9		
5	SU	0001	5.3	0625	3.0	1233	5.4	1857	2.8
6	M	0107	5.4	0731	2.8	1337	5.6	1957	2.6
7	TU	0205	5.7	0829	2.5	1433	5.9	2050	2.3
8	W	0256	6.0	0920	2.2	1522	6.2	2138	2.0
9	TH	0343	6.4	1007	1.8	1608	6.5	2223	1.7
10	F O	0427	6.7	1051	1.5	1652	6.7	2307	1.5
11	SA	0510	7.0	1135	1.3	1735	6.9	2351	1.3
12	SU	0554	7.2	1219	1.1	1819	7.0		
13	M	0036	1.2	0638	7.2	1303	1.0	1904	7.0
14	TU	0121	1.2	0723	7.2	1350	1.1	1951	6.8
15	W	0208	1.4	0811	7.0	1438	1.3	2040	6.6
16	TH	0258	1.6	0900	6.7	1530	1.6	2132	6.3
17	F ☾	0351	1.9	0955	6.4	1627	2.0	2231	6.0
18	SA	0451	2.2	1058	6.0	1731	2.2	2338	5.8
19	SU	0559	2.4	1210	5.8	1841	2.4		
20	M	0051	5.8	0712	2.4	1326	5.8	1952	2.3
21	TU	0201	6.0	0823	2.2	1434	6.0	2055	2.1
22	W	0302	6.2	0924	2.0	1530	6.2	2149	1.9
23	TH	0353	6.5	1015	1.7	1618	6.4	2236	1.7
24	F ●	0438	6.7	1100	1.5	1700	6.5	2318	1.6
25	SA	0518	6.9	1140	1.4	1738	6.6	2356	1.5
26	SU	0555	6.9	1216	1.4	1812	6.6		
27	M	0032	1.6	0629	6.9	1251	1.5	1845	6.5
28	TU	0106	1.6	0702	6.8	1324	1.6	1917	6.4
29	W	0139	1.8	0734	6.6	1357	1.8	1949	6.2
30	TH	0212	2.0	0807	6.3	1430	2.1	2022	6.0
31	F	0247	2.3	0841	6.0	1506	2.3	[illegible]	[illegible]

FEBRUARY

Date	Day	Time	m	Time	m	Time	m	Time	m
1	SA	0325	2.6	0921	5.7	1548	2.6	2144	5.5
2	SU ☽	0412	2.8	1013	5.4	1641	2.9	2245	5.3
3	M	0512	3.0	1122	5.3	1748	3.0		
4	TU	0000	5.2	0628	3.0	1242	5.3	1904	2.9
5	W	0116	5.4	0745	2.8	1356	5.5	2014	2.6
6	TH	0224	5.8	0851	2.4	1458	5.9	2112	2.2
7	F	0320	6.2	0945	1.9	1550	6.4	2204	1.7
8	SA	0410	6.7	1034	1.4	1637	6.8	2251	1.3
9	SU O	0457	7.1	1120	1.0	1722	7.1	2337	1.0
10	M	0542	7.4	1205	0.7	1806	7.3		
11	TU	0022	0.8	0626	7.6	1250	0.6	1850	7.4
12	W	0107	0.7	0710	7.6	1334	0.7	1933	7.2
13	TH	0152	0.9	0754	7.4	1419	1.0	2018	6.9
14	F	0239	1.2	0839	7.0	1506	1.4	2105	6.5
15	SA ☾	0327	1.6	0927	6.5	1557	1.9	2158	6.1
16	SU	0422	2.1	1023	6.0	1657	2.4	2302	5.7
17	M	0527	2.5	1136	5.6	1809	2.7		
18	TU	0021	5.5	0645	2.7	1304	5.4	1931	2.7
19	W	0143	5.6	0808	2.5	1425	5.6	2043	2.5
20	TH	0250	5.9	0914	2.2	1523	5.9	2139	2.1
21	F	0342	6.3	1005	1.9	1608	6.2	2224	1.9
22	SA	0425	6.6	1047	1.6	1647	6.4	2303	1.6
23	SU ●	0502	6.8	1123	1.5	1720	6.6	2338	1.5
24	M	0535	6.9	1156	1.4	1751	6.7		
25	TU	0010	1.4	0606	6.9	1227	1.3	1820	6.7
26	W	0041	1.5	0636	6.9	1257	1.4	1849	6.6
27	TH	0111	1.6	0705	6.8	1326	1.6	1917	6.5
28	F	0141	1.7	0735	6.5	1356	1.8	1946	6.3
29	SA	0212	2.0	0805	6.3	1427	2.1	2017	6.0

MARCH

Date	Day	Time	m	Time	m	Time	m	Time	m
1	SU	0246	2.3	0839	5.9	1504	2.4	2056	5.7
2	M ☽	0327	2.6	0922	5.6	1550	2.7	2148	5.4
3	TU	0420	2.9	1025	5.3	1652	3.0	2302	5.2
4	W	0533	3.0	1152	5.1	1815	3.0		
5	TH	0031	5.3	0703	2.9	1324	5.3	1940	2.8
6	F	0154	5.6	0823	2.5	1436	5.8	2049	2.3
7	SA	0258	6.1	0924	1.9	1531	6.4	2144	1.7
8	SU	0351	6.7	1015	1.3	1619	6.9	2233	1.2
9	M O	0439	7.2	1102	0.8	1704	7.3	2320	0.7
10	TU	0524	7.6	1147	0.4	1747	7.6		
11	W	0005	0.5	0608	7.8	1231	0.3	1830	7.6
12	TH	0049	0.4	0650	7.8	1314	0.5	1911	7.5
13	F	0132	0.6	0732	7.5	1357	0.8	1953	7.1
14	SA	0217	1.0	0815	7.0	1441	1.4	2037	6.6
15	SU	0304	1.5	0900	6.4	1529	2.0	2127	6.1
16	M ☾	0356	2.1	0953	5.8	1626	2.5	2230	5.6
17	TU	0459	2.6	1106	5.3	1740	2.9	2353	5.4
18	W	0620	2.8	1245	5.2	1911	2.9		
19	TH	0123	5.5	0750	2.7	1411	5.4	2027	2.6
20	F	0232	5.8	0857	2.4	1508	5.8	2121	2.3
21	SA	0322	6.1	0945	2.0	1550	6.1	2204	1.9
22	SU	0403	6.4	1025	1.7	1625	6.4	2241	1.7
23	M	0438	6.7	1059	1.5	1656	6.6	2313	1.5
24	TU ●	0510	6.8	1130	1.4	1725	6.7	2344	1.4
25	W	0539	6.9	1159	1.3	1753	6.8		
26	TH	0013	1.4	0608	6.9	1228	1.4	1820	6.7
27	F	0042	1.5	0637	6.8	1256	1.5	1847	6.6
28	SA	0112	1.6	0706	6.6	1325	1.7	1915	6.5
29	SU	0142	1.8	0736	6.4	1356	2.0	1946	6.2
30	M	0217	2.1	0810	6.0	1433	2.3	2024	5.9
31	TU	0258	2.4	0852	5.7	1518	2.6	[illegible]	[illegible]

APRIL

Date	Day	Time	m	Time	m	Time	m	Time	m
1	W ☽	0351	2.7	0953	5.3	1619	2.9	2227	5.3
2	TH	0502	2.9	1120	5.1	1740	3.0	2359	5.3
3	F	0632	2.8	1256	5.3	1911	2.8		
4	SA	0126	5.6	0756	2.4	1411	5.8	2024	2.2
5	SU	0233	6.2	0859	1.8	1508	6.4	2121	1.6
6	M	0328	6.8	0952	1.2	1557	7.0	2211	1.1
7	TU	0416	7.3	1039	0.7	1642	7.4	2258	0.6
8	W O	0502	7.6	1125	0.4	1725	7.6	2343	0.4
9	TH	0546	7.8	1208	0.4	1807	7.6		
10	F	0027	0.4	0628	7.7	1251	0.6	1848	7.5
11	SA	0111	0.7	0710	7.3	1334	1.0	1929	7.1
12	SU	0155	1.1	0752	6.8	1417	1.5	2013	6.6
13	M	0242	1.6	0837	6.3	1504	2.1	2102	6.1
14	TU ☾	0333	2.1	0930	5.7	1559	2.6	2203	5.6
15	W	0434	2.6	1041	5.2	1711	3.0	2324	5.3
16	TH	0552	2.8	1214	5.1	1840	3.0		
17	F	0050	5.4	0717	2.8	1340	5.3	1956	2.8
18	SA	0159	5.6	0824	2.5	1437	5.6	2051	2.4
19	SU	0250	6.0	0913	2.2	1519	6.0	2133	2.1
20	M	0331	6.2	0952	1.9	1554	6.3	2210	1.8
21	TU	0406	6.5	1027	1.7	1626	6.5	2243	1.6
22	W	0439	6.6	1058	1.5	1655	6.6	2314	1.5
23	TH ●	0510	6.7	1129	1.4	1724	6.7	2345	1.5
24	F	0540	6.8	1159	1.4	1752	6.7		
25	SA	0016	1.5	0610	6.7	1229	1.5	1821	6.7
26	SU	0047	1.6	0641	6.6	1300	1.7	1851	6.5
27	M	0120	1.8	0714	6.3	1334	1.9	1925	6.3
28	TU	0157	2.0	0752	6.0	1413	2.2	2005	6.0
29	W	0241	2.3	0838	5.7	1500	2.5	2058	5.7
30	TH ☽	0336	2.5	0941	5.4	1601	2.8	2210	5.5

MAY

Date	Day	Time	m	Time	m	Time	m	Time	m
1	F	0445	2.7	1102	5.3	1719	2.9	2336	5.5
2	SA	0608	2.6	1228	5.5	1844	2.6		
3	SU	0057	5.8	0727	2.2	1342	5.9	1956	2.2
4	M	0205	6.3	0831	1.7	1440	6.4	2054	1.6
5	TU	0301	6.7	0925	1.2	1531	6.9	2146	1.1
6	W	0351	7.2	1014	0.8	1617	7.3	2235	0.8
7	TH O	0439	7.4	1101	0.7	1702	7.4	2321	0.6
8	F	0524	7.5	1146	0.7	1745	7.5		
9	SA	0007	0.7	0607	7.3	1229	0.9	1827	7.3
10	SU	0051	0.9	0650	7.0	1312	1.2	1909	7.0
11	M	0136	1.2	0733	6.6	1356	1.7	1953	6.6
12	TU	0222	1.7	0818	6.1	1442	2.2	2041	6.1
13	W	0312	2.1	0909	5.7	1535	2.6	2138	5.7
14	TH ☾	0408	2.5	1012	5.3	1639	2.9	2247	5.4
15	F	0515	2.8	1128	5.1	1753	3.0		
16	SA	0001	5.4	0627	2.8	1245	5.2	1906	2.9
17	SU	0109	5.5	0734	2.6	1348	5.5	2005	2.6
18	M	0204	5.7	0827	2.4	1436	5.7	2052	2.3
19	TU	0250	6.0	0911	2.1	1515	6.0	2132	2.1
20	W	0329	6.2	0949	1.9	1550	6.3	2209	1.9
21	TH	0405	6.4	1024	1.7	1623	6.5	2244	1.7
22	F ●	0440	6.5	1058	1.6	1656	6.6	2318	1.6
23	SA	0514	6.6	1132	1.6	1728	6.7	2352	1.6
24	SU	0548	6.6	1206	1.6	1801	6.6		
25	M	0027	1.6	0623	6.5	1241	1.7	1836	6.6
26	TU	0105	1.7	0701	6.3	1319	1.9	1914	6.4
27	W	0146	1.9	0744	6.1	1402	2.1	1959	6.2
28	TH	0233	2.1	0834	5.9	1452	2.3	2054	5.9
29	F	0328	2.2	0934	5.7	1550	2.5	2159	5.8
30	SA ☽	0432	2.4	1044	5.6	1700	2.6	2313	5.8
31	SU	0544	2.3	1158	5.7	1815	2.4		

JUNE

Date	Day	Time	m	Time	m	Time	m	Time	m
1	M	0026	5.9	0656	2.1	1308	6.0	1925	2.1
2	TU	0134	6.2	0801	1.8	1410	6.3	2027	1.7
3	W	0233	6.5	0858	1.5	1504	6.7	2122	1.4
4	TH	0327	6.8	0950	1.2	1554	6.9	2214	1.1
5	F O	0417	7.0	1039	1.1	1641	7.1	2302	1.0
6	SA	0505	7.0	1126	1.1	1726	7.1	2349	1.0
7	SU	0550	6.9	1211	1.2	1810	7.0		
8	M	0034	1.1	0633	6.7	1254	1.5	1852	6.8
9	TU	0118	1.4	0716	6.4	1337	1.8	1935	6.5
10	W	0202	1.7	0759	6.1	1421	2.1	2019	6.2
11	TH	0248	2.0	0844	5.8	1508	2.4	2107	5.9
12	F	0336	2.4	0935	5.5	1559	2.7	2202	5.6
13	SA ☾	0429	2.6	1033	5.3	1658	2.9	2303	5.4
14	SU	0529	2.7	1138	5.2	1802	2.9		
15	M	0006	5.4	0630	2.7	1242	5.3	1905	2.8
16	TU	0107	5.5	0729	2.6	1340	5.5	2001	2.6
17	W	0201	5.6	0822	2.4	1429	5.7	2050	2.4
18	TH	0249	5.9	0908	2.2	1512	6.0	2134	2.1
19	F	0332	6.1	0950	2.0	1552	6.2	2215	1.9
20	SA	0413	6.3	1030	1.8	1630	6.4	2254	1.7
21	SU ●	0452	6.4	1109	1.7	1708	6.6	2333	1.6
22	M	0531	6.5	1147	1.6	1746	6.7		
23	TU	0013	1.5	0611	6.5	1227	1.6	1826	6.7
24	W	0054	1.5	0653	6.5	1309	1.7	1909	6.6
25	TH	0138	1.6	0738	6.3	1354	1.8	1956	6.5
26	F	0225	1.7	0827	6.2	1443	1.9	2047	6.3
27	SA	0317	1.8	0921	6.0	1537	2.1	2144	6.1
28	SU ☽	0414	2.0	1021	5.9	1638	2.2	2247	6.0
29	M	0518	2.1	1126	5.8	1745	2.3	2354	6.0
30	TU	0625	2.1	1235	5.9	1855	2.2		

BREST
LAT 48°23′N
LONG 4°30′W

TIMES AND HEIGHTS OF HIGH AND LOW WATER (Heights in Metres)

TIME ZONE –0100 (French Standard Time). **Subtract 1 hour for UT. For French Summer Time (area enclosed in shaded box) add 1 hour**

2020

JULY

Day	Time	m	Time	m	Time	m	Time	m
1 W	0104	6.0	0732	2.0	1341	6.1	2001	2.0
2 TH	0210	6.2	0834	1.8	1442	6.3	2103	1.7
3 F	0309	6.4	0932	1.7	1537	6.6	2158	1.5
4 SA	0403	6.5	1023	1.5	1626	6.8	2249	1.4
5 SU ○	0452	6.6	1111	1.5	1712	6.9	2335	1.3
6 M	0536	6.6	1155	1.5	1755	6.9		
7 TU	0019	1.3	0618	6.5	1237	1.5	1836	6.8
8 W	0100	1.4	0658	6.4	1317	1.7	1915	6.6
9 TH	0140	1.6	0735	6.2	1356	1.9	1953	6.4
10 F	0219	1.9	0813	6.0	1436	2.2	2032	6.1
11 SA	0258	2.1	0852	5.7	1517	2.4	2113	5.8
12 SU	0340	2.4	0936	5.5	1602	2.7	2201	5.6
13 M ☾	0428	2.6	1028	5.3	1656	2.9	2258	5.4
14 TU	0524	2.8	1131	5.2	1758	2.9		
15 W	0003	5.3	0627	2.8	1237	5.3	1904	2.9
16 TH	0109	5.3	0730	2.7	1340	5.4	2006	2.7
17 F	0209	5.5	0828	2.5	1435	5.7	2101	2.4
18 SA	0302	5.8	0919	2.3	1524	6.0	2149	2.1
19 SU	0350	6.1	1005	2.0	1609	6.3	2234	1.8
20 M ●	0434	6.3	1049	1.7	1652	6.6	2317	1.5
21 TU	0517	6.6	1132	1.5	1734	6.8	2359	1.3
22 W	0559	6.7	1215	1.4	1816	7.0		
23 TH	0042	1.2	0642	6.8	1258	1.3	1900	7.0
24 F	0126	1.1	0726	6.7	1343	1.3	1944	6.9
25 SA	0211	1.2	0812	6.6	1429	1.5	2031	6.7
26 SU	0259	1.5	0900	6.4	1519	1.7	2121	6.5
27 M ☽	0351	1.8	0953	6.1	1614	2.0	2218	6.1
28 TU	0449	2.1	1054	5.9	1717	2.2	2323	5.9
29 W	0555	2.3	1204	5.8	1828	2.4		
30 TH	0038	5.7	0708	2.4	1319	5.8	1942	2.3
31 F	0155	5.8	0819	2.3	1429	6.0	2051	2.1

AUGUST

Day	Time	m	Time	m	Time	m	Time	m
1 SA	0301	6.0	0921	2.0	1527	6.3	2149	1.8
2 SU	0355	6.2	1013	1.8	1616	6.6	2239	1.6
3 M ○	0442	6.4	1059	1.6	1700	6.8	2323	1.4
4 TU	0523	6.5	1141	1.5	1740	6.9		
5 W	0002	1.4	0600	6.6	1218	1.5	1816	6.9
6 TH	0039	1.4	0634	6.5	1254	1.6	1850	6.8
7 F	0113	1.5	0706	6.4	1327	1.7	1922	6.6
8 SA	0146	1.7	0737	6.2	1401	1.9	1954	6.4
9 SU	0219	1.9	0809	6.0	1434	2.2	2028	6.1
10 M	0253	2.2	0843	5.7	1511	2.5	2105	5.7
11 TU ☾	0331	2.5	0924	5.5	1554	2.8	2152	5.4
12 W	0418	2.8	1019	5.3	1650	3.0	2256	5.2
13 TH	0521	3.0	1132	5.1	1803	3.1		
14 F	0015	5.1	0636	3.0	1251	5.2	1923	2.9
15 SA	0133	5.3	0750	2.8	1402	5.5	2031	2.6
16 SU	0237	5.6	0851	2.4	1500	5.9	2126	2.1
17 M	0330	6.1	0943	2.0	1549	6.4	2214	1.7
18 TU	0416	6.5	1030	1.6	1635	6.8	2259	1.3
19 W ●	0500	6.8	1115	1.3	1718	7.1	2342	0.9
20 TH	0543	7.1	1158	1.0	1801	7.4		
21 F	0025	0.8	0625	7.2	1241	0.9	1843	7.4
22 SA	0108	0.7	0707	7.2	1325	0.9	1926	7.3
23 SU	0152	0.9	0750	7.0	1410	1.1	2010	7.0
24 M	0237	1.3	0835	6.6	1457	1.5	2056	6.6
25 TU ☽	0325	1.7	0925	6.2	1550	1.9	2150	6.1
26 W	0421	2.2	1025	5.8	1651	2.4	2256	5.7
27 TH	0529	2.6	1140	5.6	1807	2.6		
28 F	0022	5.4	0651	2.7	1307	5.6	1932	2.6
29 SA	0150	5.5	0811	2.5	1421	5.9	2045	2.3
30 SU	0257	5.8	0913	2.2	1518	6.3	2141	1.9
31 M	0347	6.2	1002	1.9	1604	6.6	2227	1.6

SEPTEMBER

Day	Time	m	Time	m	Time	m	Time	m
1 TU	0429	6.4	1044	1.7	1644	6.8	2306	1.4
2 W ○	0505	6.6	1121	1.5	1719	6.9	2341	1.3
3 TH	0537	6.7	1155	1.5	1751	6.9		
4 F	0012	1.3	0606	6.7	1226	1.5	1821	6.9
5 SA	0042	1.4	0634	6.6	1256	1.6	1850	6.8
6 SU	0112	1.6	0702	6.5	1326	1.8	1919	6.5
7 M	0141	1.8	0730	6.3	1356	2.0	1948	6.2
8 TU	0211	2.1	0800	6.0	1429	2.4	2021	5.9
9 W	0245	2.5	0835	5.7	1507	2.7	2101	5.5
10 TH ☾	0328	2.8	0922	5.4	1558	3.0	2200	5.2
11 F	0426	3.1	1034	5.2	1710	3.2	2327	5.0
12 SA	0546	3.2	1208	5.2	1842	3.1		
13 SU	0101	5.2	0716	3.0	1332	5.5	2003	2.7
14 M	0214	5.6	0826	2.5	1436	6.0	2102	2.1
15 TU	0308	6.2	0921	2.0	1527	6.5	2152	1.5
16 W	0355	6.7	1009	1.4	1614	7.1	2237	1.0
17 TH ●	0439	7.1	1054	1.0	1657	7.5	2321	0.7
18 F	0521	7.4	1138	0.7	1740	7.7		
19 SA	0004	0.5	0603	7.6	1221	0.6	1822	7.7
20 SU	0046	0.5	0644	7.5	1304	0.7	1904	7.5
21 M	0129	0.8	0726	7.2	1349	1.0	1947	7.1
22 TU	0213	1.3	0810	6.8	1435	1.5	2033	6.6
23 W	0301	1.9	0859	6.3	1528	2.0	2126	6.0
24 TH ☽	0356	2.4	1000	5.8	1630	2.5	2236	5.5
25 F	0507	2.9	1122	5.5	1751	2.8		
26 SA	0012	5.3	0637	3.0	1254	5.6	1921	2.7
27 SU	0142	5.4	0759	2.7	1407	5.9	2032	2.4
28 M	0244	5.8	0858	2.3	1500	6.2	2123	2.0
29 TU	0329	6.2	0943	1.9	1543	6.6	2205	1.7
30 W	0407	6.5	1022	1.7	1620	6.8	2241	1.5

OCTOBER

Day	Time	m	Time	m	Time	m	Time	m
1 TH ○	0440	6.7	1056	1.5	1652	6.9	2313	1.4
2 F	0509	6.8	1127	1.5	1722	7.0	2343	1.4
3 SA	0537	6.8	1157	1.5	1751	6.9		
4 SU	0012	1.4	0604	6.8	1226	1.6	1819	6.8
5 M	0040	1.6	0631	6.7	1255	1.7	1848	6.6
6 TU	0109	1.8	0658	6.5	1325	2.0	1917	6.3
7 W	0139	2.1	0727	6.2	1357	2.3	1949	6.0
8 TH	0212	2.4	0802	5.9	1437	2.6	2029	5.6
9 F	0255	2.8	0847	5.6	1527	2.9	2127	5.3
10 SA ☾	0352	3.1	0957	5.3	1636	3.1	2254	5.1
11 SU	0510	3.2	1133	5.2	1808	3.0		
12 M	0030	5.2	0643	3.0	1302	5.6	1933	2.6
13 TU	0146	5.7	0758	2.5	1408	6.1	2034	2.0
14 W	0242	6.3	0855	1.9	1501	6.7	2125	1.4
15 TH	0330	6.9	0944	1.3	1549	7.2	2212	0.9
16 F ●	0415	7.3	1030	0.9	1634	7.6	2257	0.6
17 SA	0458	7.6	1115	0.6	1717	7.8	2341	0.5
18 SU	0540	7.7	1200	0.5	1800	7.8		
19 M	0024	0.6	0622	7.6	1244	0.7	1843	7.5
20 TU	0107	0.9	0704	7.3	1329	1.0	1927	7.1
21 W	0152	1.4	0748	6.8	1416	1.5	2014	6.5
22 TH	0240	2.0	0838	6.3	1509	2.1	2108	5.9
23 F ☽	0335	2.6	0940	5.8	1612	2.6	2219	5.4
24 SA	0446	3.0	1100	5.5	1730	2.8	2350	5.2
25 SU	0613	3.0	1227	5.6	1855	2.8		
26 M	0115	5.4	0731	2.8	1338	5.8	2003	2.5
27 TU	0215	5.8	0829	2.4	1430	6.1	2053	2.1
28 W	0259	6.1	0914	2.1	1513	6.4	2134	1.9
29 TH	0337	6.4	0953	1.8	1549	6.6	2210	1.7
30 F	0409	6.6	1027	1.7	1622	6.8	2242	1.6
31 SA ○	0439	6.7	1059	1.6	1653	6.8	2313	1.5

NOVEMBER

Day	Time	m	Time	m	Time	m	Time	m
1 SU	0508	6.8	1129	1.6	1723	6.8	2343	1.6
2 M	0537	6.8	1200	1.6	1754	6.8		
3 TU	0013	1.7	0606	6.7	1231	1.8	1824	6.6
4 W	0043	1.8	0635	6.6	1302	1.9	1855	6.4
5 TH	0115	2.1	0706	6.4	1338	2.2	1930	6.1
6 F	0152	2.3	0743	6.1	1419	2.5	2014	5.7
7 SA	0237	2.6	0831	5.8	1510	2.7	2112	5.4
8 SU ☾	0333	2.9	0938	5.5	1616	2.9	2231	5.3
9 M	0445	3.0	1104	5.5	1737	2.8	2357	5.4
10 TU	0610	2.9	1227	5.7	1857	2.5		
11 W	0111	5.8	0725	2.4	1335	6.2	2002	2.0
12 TH	0211	6.3	0825	1.9	1432	6.7	2056	1.5
13 F	0302	6.8	0918	1.4	1522	7.1	2146	1.0
14 SA	0349	7.3	1007	1.0	1610	7.5	2233	0.8
15 SU ●	0435	7.5	1054	0.7	1656	7.6	2319	0.7
16 M	0519	7.6	1140	0.7	1741	7.5		
17 TU	0004	0.8	0603	7.5	1226	0.8	1826	7.3
18 W	0049	1.1	0647	7.3	1313	1.1	1911	6.9
19 TH	0134	1.6	0733	6.9	1400	1.6	1959	6.4
20 F	0222	2.0	0822	6.4	1452	2.0	2051	5.9
21 SA	0315	2.5	0919	6.0	1549	2.5	2154	5.5
22 SU ☽	0417	2.8	1026	5.7	1656	2.7	2308	5.3
23 M	0530	3.0	1140	5.6	1808	2.8		
24 TU	0024	5.3	0643	2.9	1250	5.7	1916	2.7
25 W	0128	5.6	0746	2.7	1348	5.9	2011	2.4
26 TH	0218	5.8	0836	2.4	1435	6.1	2056	2.2
27 F	0300	6.1	0918	2.2	1515	6.3	2135	2.0
28 SA	0336	6.4	0956	2.0	1552	6.5	2211	1.8
29 SU	0410	6.5	1031	1.8	1627	6.6	2245	1.7
30 M ○	0443	6.7	1105	1.7	1700	6.7	2318	1.7

DECEMBER

Day	Time	m	Time	m	Time	m	Time	m
1 TU	0515	6.7	1139	1.7	1734	6.6	2351	1.7
2 W	0547	6.7	1213	1.7	1808	6.5		
3 TH	0025	1.8	0621	6.6	1249	1.8	1844	6.4
4 F	0102	2.0	0657	6.5	1327	2.0	1923	6.2
5 SA	0141	2.1	0738	6.3	1410	2.2	2008	6.0
6 SU	0227	2.4	0826	6.1	1500	2.4	2103	5.7
7 M	0320	2.6	0925	5.9	1559	2.5	2209	5.6
8 TU ☾	0423	2.7	1034	5.8	1707	2.5	2321	5.6
9 W	0535	2.6	1148	5.9	1820	2.3		
10 TH	0032	5.9	0648	2.4	1259	6.1	1927	2.0
11 F	0136	6.2	0753	2.0	1402	6.5	2027	1.7
12 SA	0234	6.6	0852	1.6	1459	6.8	2121	1.4
13 SU	0327	7.0	0946	1.3	1551	7.1	2213	1.2
14 M ●	0416	7.2	1037	1.0	1640	7.2	2301	1.1
15 TU	0504	7.3	1126	1.0	1728	7.2	2349	1.1
16 W	0550	7.3	1213	1.0	1814	7.0		
17 TH	0034	1.3	0635	7.2	1259	1.2	1859	6.8
18 F	0119	1.6	0719	6.9	1345	1.5	1943	6.4
19 SA	0205	1.9	0804	6.6	1431	1.9	2029	6.1
20 SU	0251	2.2	0851	6.2	1519	2.2	2118	5.7
21 M	0341	2.5	0942	5.9	1611	2.5	2213	5.5
22 TU ☽	0437	2.8	1040	5.6	1709	2.7	2316	5.3
23 W	0539	2.9	1144	5.5	1812	2.8		
24 TH	0022	5.3	0644	2.9	1249	5.5	1914	2.8
25 F	0124	5.5	0746	2.8	1348	5.7	2009	2.6
26 SA	0217	5.7	0839	2.5	1439	5.9	2057	2.4
27 SU	0303	6.0	0925	2.3	1523	6.1	2140	2.2
28 M	0343	6.2	1006	2.1	1604	6.3	2220	2.0
29 TU	0421	6.4	1045	1.9	1642	6.4	2258	1.8
30 W ○	0458	6.6	1123	1.7	1719	6.5	2335	1.7
31 TH	0535	6.7	1200	1.6	1757	6.6		

POINTE DE GRAVE
LAT 45°34'N
LONG 1°04'W

TIMES AND HEIGHTS OF HIGH AND LOW WATER (Heights in Metres)

TIME ZONE –0100 (French Standard Time). **Subtract 1 hour for UT. For French Summer Time (area enclosed in shaded box) add 1 hour**

2020

JANUARY

Date	Day	Time	m	Time	m	Time	m	Time	m
1	W	0233	1.9	0856	4.7	1458	1.9	2121	4.3
2	TH	0319	2.1	0945	4.5	1546	2.1	2218	4.2
3	F	0413	2.2	1043	4.3	1643	2.2	☽ 2324	4.1
4	SA	0515	2.3	1147	4.3	1747	2.3		
5	SU	0032	4.2	0620	2.3	1254	4.3	1851	2.2
6	M	0134	4.3	0720	2.2	1356	4.4	1948	2.1
7	TU	0227	4.5	0815	2.0	1450	4.6	2038	1.9
8	W	0313	4.7	0905	1.8	1538	4.8	2125	1.7
9	TH	0356	5.0	0953	1.6	1622	5.0	2210	1.5
10	F	0438	5.2	1039	1.4	1705	5.2	○ 2254	1.3
11	SA	0521	5.3	1124	1.2	1748	5.3	2339	1.2
12	SU	0605	5.4	1209	1.1	1832	5.3		
13	M	0023	1.1	0650	5.4	1254	1.0	1918	5.2
14	TU	0108	1.2	0737	5.4	1339	1.1	2006	5.1
15	W	0154	1.2	0827	5.3	1426	1.2	2057	4.9
16	TH	0242	1.4	0921	5.1	1516	1.4	2155	4.8
17	F	0335	1.6	1022	4.9	1612	1.6	☾ 2301	4.6
18	SA	0436	1.7	1132	4.7	1717	1.8		
19	SU	0012	4.5	0545	1.9	1246	4.6	1828	1.9
20	M	0122	4.6	0659	1.9	1357	4.6	1940	1.9
21	TU	0225	4.7	0809	1.8	1459	4.7	2043	1.7
22	W	0319	4.9	0910	1.6	1552	4.8	2136	1.6
23	TH	0406	5.0	1002	1.5	1637	4.9	2223	1.4
24	F	0448	5.1	1047	1.4	1717	5.0	● 2305	1.4
25	SA	0527	5.2	1128	1.3	1753	5.0	2344	1.3
26	SU	0603	5.2	1206	1.3	1826	5.0		
27	M	0020	1.3	0637	5.2	1241	1.3	1857	4.9
28	TU	0054	1.4	0709	5.1	1314	1.4	1927	4.8
29	W	0127	1.5	0742	5.0	1347	1.5	1958	4.7
30	TH	0201	1.7	0816	4.8	1421	1.7	2032	4.5
31	F	0236	1.8	0855	4.7	1457	1.9	2113	4.4

FEBRUARY

Date	Day	Time	m	Time	m	Time	m	Time	m
1	SA	0316	2.0	0940	4.4	1539	2.1	2205	4.2
2	SU	0405	2.2	1038	4.3	1634	2.2	☽ 2314	4.1
3	M	0512	2.3	1150	4.2	1746	2.3		
4	TU	0032	4.1	0627	2.3	1310	4.2	1900	2.2
5	W	0146	4.3	0737	2.2	1420	4.4	2004	2.1
6	TH	0246	4.6	0839	1.9	1516	4.7	2101	1.8
7	F	0336	4.9	0934	1.6	1605	4.9	2153	1.5
8	SA	0422	5.2	1024	1.3	1651	5.2	2241	1.2
9	SU	0508	5.4	1112	1.0	1735	5.4	○ 2327	1.0
10	M	0553	5.6	1157	0.8	1819	5.5		
11	TU	0012	0.9	0638	5.7	1241	0.8	1903	5.5
12	W	0056	0.9	0723	5.6	1324	0.8	1948	5.3
13	TH	0139	0.9	0809	5.5	1407	1.0	2034	5.1
14	F	0223	1.1	0858	5.2	1452	1.2	2123	4.9
15	SA	0311	1.4	0952	4.9	1542	1.6	☾ 2223	4.6
16	SU	0407	1.7	1058	4.5	1643	1.9	2338	4.4
17	M	0516	1.9	1222	4.3	1759	2.1		
18	TU	0100	4.4	0637	2.0	1346	4.3	1921	2.1
19	W	0212	4.5	0757	1.9	1455	4.4	2031	1.9
20	TH	0310	4.7	0901	1.7	1547	4.6	2126	1.7
21	F	0356	4.9	0951	1.5	1628	4.8	2211	1.5
22	SA	0435	5.0	1034	1.4	1703	4.9	2251	1.4
23	SU	0510	5.2	1112	1.3	1734	5.0	● 2327	1.3
24	M	0541	5.2	1146	1.2	1802	5.0	2359	1.3
25	TU	0611	5.2	1217	1.3	1829	5.0		
26	W	0030	1.3	0641	5.2	1247	1.3	1856	5.0
27	TH	0100	1.4	0710	5.1	1316	1.4	1923	4.9
28	F	0129	1.5	0740	5.0	1345	1.5	1952	4.7
29	SA	0158	1.6	0813	4.8	1415	1.7	2026	4.6

MARCH

Date	Day	Time	m	Time	m	Time	m	Time	m
1	SU	0232	1.8	0852	4.5	1451	1.9	2107	4.4
2	M	0313	2.0	0942	4.3	1537	2.1	☽ 2206	4.2
3	TU	0409	2.2	1054	4.1	1642	2.3	2330	4.1
4	W	0533	2.3	1226	4.1	1811	2.4		
5	TH	0105	4.2	0701	2.2	1352	4.3	1932	2.2
6	F	0218	4.5	0815	1.9	1454	4.6	2038	1.9
7	SA	0315	4.8	0914	1.5	1545	5.0	2134	1.5
8	SU	0404	5.2	1006	1.2	1632	5.3	2224	1.2
9	M	0450	5.5	1054	0.9	1716	5.5	○ 2310	0.9
10	TU	0535	5.7	1139	0.7	1800	5.6	2355	0.7
11	W	0619	5.8	1222	0.6	1842	5.6		
12	TH	0038	0.7	0703	5.7	1303	0.7	1925	5.5
13	F	0119	0.8	0747	5.5	1344	0.9	2008	5.2
14	SA	0202	1.0	0833	5.2	1426	1.2	2053	4.9
15	SU	0247	1.3	0922	4.8	1513	1.6	2147	4.6
16	M	0340	1.6	1027	4.4	1612	2.0	☾ 2302	4.3
17	TU	0448	2.0	1200	4.1	1731	2.2		
18	W	0035	4.2	0615	2.1	1334	4.1	1901	2.2
19	TH	0154	4.4	0740	2.0	1443	4.3	2013	2.0
20	F	0253	4.6	0843	1.8	1532	4.5	2106	1.8
21	SA	0337	4.8	0931	1.6	1609	4.7	2150	1.6
22	SU	0413	4.9	1011	1.4	1639	4.9	2228	1.4
23	M	0445	5.1	1047	1.3	1707	5.0	2302	1.3
24	TU	0514	5.2	1119	1.3	1733	5.0	● 2333	1.3
25	W	0543	5.2	1148	1.3	1759	5.1		
26	TH	0003	1.3	0612	5.2	1217	1.3	1825	5.0
27	F	0031	1.3	0640	5.1	1245	1.3	1852	5.0
28	SA	0059	1.4	0710	5.0	1312	1.5	1920	4.9
29	SU	0128	1.5	0741	4.8	1342	1.6	1952	4.7
30	M	0201	1.7	0819	4.6	1418	1.8	2033	4.5
31	TU	0241	1.9	0909	4.3	1502	2.0	2129	4.3

APRIL

Date	Day	Time	m	Time	m	Time	m	Time	m
1	W	0334	2.1	1020	4.1	1603	2.3	☽ 2249	4.2
2	TH	0454	2.3	1155	4.1	1732	2.3		
3	F	0028	4.2	0629	2.2	1324	4.3	1859	2.2
4	SA	0149	4.5	0747	1.9	1428	4.6	2010	1.8
5	SU	0249	4.9	0849	1.5	1521	5.0	2109	1.5
6	M	0341	5.2	0942	1.1	1608	5.3	2201	1.1
7	TU	0428	5.5	1030	0.8	1653	5.5	2248	0.8
8	W	0513	5.7	1115	0.7	1736	5.6	○ 2333	0.7
9	TH	0558	5.8	1158	0.7	1819	5.6		
10	F	0016	0.7	0641	5.7	1239	0.8	1901	5.5
11	SA	0058	0.8	0725	5.4	1319	1.0	1944	5.2
12	SU	0139	1.0	0809	5.1	1401	1.3	2028	4.9
13	M	0224	1.3	0857	4.6	1447	1.7	2119	4.6
14	TU	0314	1.7	1000	4.3	1543	2.0	☾ 2229	4.3
15	W	0419	2.0	1132	4.0	1659	2.3	2357	4.2
16	TH	0544	2.2	1305	4.0	1828	2.3		
17	F	0118	4.3	0708	2.1	1412	4.2	1940	2.1
18	SA	0219	4.4	0811	1.9	1500	4.4	2035	1.9
19	SU	0305	4.6	0859	1.7	1536	4.6	2119	1.7
20	M	0342	4.8	0939	1.5	1606	4.8	2157	1.5
21	TU	0414	5.0	1014	1.4	1634	4.9	2231	1.4
22	W	0444	5.1	1046	1.3	1701	5.0	2302	1.3
23	TH	0514	5.1	1116	1.3	1729	5.1	● 2333	1.3
24	F	0544	5.1	1145	1.3	1757	5.1		
25	SA	0003	1.3	0615	5.1	1215	1.3	1826	5.0
26	SU	0034	1.4	0646	5.0	1246	1.4	1857	4.9
27	M	0106	1.4	0721	4.8	1318	1.5	1932	4.8
28	TU	0141	1.6	0802	4.6	1356	1.7	2017	4.6
29	W	0224	1.8	0855	4.4	1443	1.9	2115	4.4
30	TH	0319	1.9	1004	4.2	1545	2.1	☽ 2230	4.3

MAY

Date	Day	Time	m	Time	m	Time	m	Time	m
1	F	0434	2.1	1132	4.2	1706	2.2	2359	4.4
2	SA	0559	2.0	1255	4.4	1828	2.1		
3	SU	0118	4.6	0715	1.7	1359	4.7	1938	1.8
4	M	0221	4.9	0818	1.4	1453	5.0	2039	1.4
5	TU	0315	5.2	0913	1.1	1542	5.2	2133	1.1
6	W	0404	5.4	1003	0.9	1628	5.4	2223	0.9
7	TH	0451	5.6	1049	0.8	1713	5.5	○ 2309	0.8
8	F	0536	5.6	1133	0.8	1756	5.5	2354	0.8
9	SA	0621	5.4	1215	0.9	1840	5.4		
10	SU	0037	0.9	0705	5.2	1256	1.1	1923	5.2
11	M	0119	1.1	0750	4.9	1338	1.4	2008	4.9
12	TU	0203	1.3	0837	4.6	1423	1.7	2057	4.7
13	W	0252	1.6	0934	4.3	1516	2.0	2156	4.4
14	TH	0350	1.9	1048	4.0	1623	2.2	☾ 2308	4.3
15	F	0501	2.1	1210	4.0	1740	2.3		
16	SA	0020	4.2	0616	2.1	1320	4.1	1851	2.2
17	SU	0125	4.3	0722	2.0	1412	4.3	1949	2.0
18	M	0218	4.5	0815	1.9	1453	4.5	2037	1.8
19	TU	0300	4.6	0858	1.7	1527	4.6	2118	1.7
20	W	0338	4.8	0935	1.6	1558	4.8	2155	1.6
21	TH	0413	4.9	1010	1.5	1630	4.9	2230	1.5
22	F	0447	5.0	1043	1.4	1702	5.0	● 2304	1.4
23	SA	0521	5.0	1117	1.4	1734	5.0	2339	1.3
24	SU	0556	5.0	1151	1.4	1807	5.0		
25	M	0014	1.3	0632	4.9	1226	1.4	1843	5.0
26	TU	0052	1.4	0711	4.8	1304	1.5	1924	4.9
27	W	0132	1.5	0756	4.6	1346	1.6	2012	4.7
28	TH	0217	1.6	0849	4.5	1435	1.8	2109	4.6
29	F	0312	1.7	0953	4.4	1534	1.9	2217	4.5
30	SA	0418	1.8	1109	4.4	1644	2.0	☽ 2334	4.6
31	SU	0530	1.8	1224	4.5	1757	1.9		

JUNE

Date	Day	Time	m	Time	m	Time	m	Time	m
1	M	0048	4.7	0641	1.6	1329	4.7	1906	1.7
2	TU	0152	4.9	0746	1.5	1426	4.9	2009	1.5
3	W	0249	5.1	0844	1.3	1517	5.1	2107	1.2
4	TH	0342	5.2	0937	1.1	1605	5.2	2159	1.1
5	F	0432	5.3	1025	1.0	1652	5.3	○ 2248	1.0
6	SA	0519	5.3	1111	1.0	1737	5.3	2335	0.9
7	SU	0605	5.2	1154	1.1	1822	5.3		
8	M	0019	1.0	0650	5.0	1237	1.2	1906	5.1
9	TU	0102	1.2	0733	4.8	1319	1.4	1949	5.0
10	W	0145	1.3	0816	4.5	1402	1.6	2033	4.7
11	TH	0229	1.6	0902	4.3	1450	1.8	2121	4.5
12	F	0318	1.8	0955	4.2	1544	2.0	2216	4.4
13	SA	0413	2.0	1058	4.0	1645	2.1	☾ 2316	4.3
14	SU	0516	2.1	1204	4.0	1750	2.2		
15	M	0018	4.2	0620	2.1	1307	4.1	1851	2.1
16	TU	0119	4.3	0719	2.0	1400	4.3	1946	2.0
17	W	0213	4.4	0810	1.9	1444	4.5	2035	1.9
18	TH	0300	4.5	0855	1.7	1524	4.6	2118	1.7
19	F	0343	4.7	0936	1.6	1601	4.8	2200	1.6
20	SA	0423	4.8	1015	1.5	1638	4.9	2240	1.4
21	SU	0503	4.9	1054	1.4	1716	5.0	● 2320	1.3
22	M	0542	4.9	1133	1.3	1755	5.0		
23	TU	0001	1.3	0622	4.9	1213	1.3	1836	5.0
24	W	0043	1.2	0704	4.9	1255	1.3	1920	5.0
25	TH	0126	1.3	0750	4.8	1339	1.4	2009	4.9
26	F	0212	1.3	0840	4.7	1427	1.5	2102	4.8
27	SA	0302	1.4	0937	4.6	1521	1.6	2202	4.7
28	SU	0358	1.5	1042	4.5	1622	1.7	☽ 2308	4.7
29	M	0501	1.6	1153	4.5	1728	1.7		
30	TU	0019	4.7	0609	1.6	1300	4.6	1837	1.7

SUNRISE AND SUNSET TIMES

POINTE DE GRAVE
At 45°34'N 1°04'W

		Sunrise	Sunset
European Standard Time (UT-1)			
Jan	01	0845	1731
	15	0841	1747
Feb	01	0825	1811
	15	0806	1831
Mar	01	0743	1851
	15	0717	1910
European Summer Time (UT-2)			
Apr	01	0745	2033
	15	0719	2051
May	01	0652	2111
	15	0634	2128
Jun	01	0619	2146
	15	0615	2155
Jul	01	0619	2157
	15	0630	2150
Aug	01	0648	2132
	15	0705	2112
Sep	01	0726	2042
	15	0743	2015
Oct	01	0803	1945
	15	0821	1919
European Standard Time (UT-1)			
Nov	01	0744	1751
	15	0804	1734
Dec	01	0824	1722

POINTE DE GRAVE
LAT 45°34′N
LONG 1°04′W

TIMES AND HEIGHTS OF HIGH AND LOW WATER (Heights in Metres)

TIME ZONE –0100 (French Standard Time). **Subtract 1 hour for UT. For French Summer Time (area enclosed in shaded box) add 1 hour**

2020

JULY

Day	Time	m
1 W	0127	4.7
	0716	1.6
	1402	4.7
	1944	1.6
2 TH	0230	4.8
	0820	1.5
	1458	4.9
	2046	1.4
3 F	0327	4.9
	0917	1.4
	1549	5.0
	2142	1.3
4 SA	0419	4.9
	1009	1.3
	1637	5.1
	2234	1.2
5 SU	0507	5.0
	1056	1.2
	1723	5.2
O	2321	1.1
6 M	0552	5.0
	1140	1.2
	1806	5.2
7 TU	0005	1.1
	0634	4.9
	1222	1.3
	1847	5.1
8 W	0047	1.2
	0713	4.8
	1301	1.4
	1926	5.0
9 TH	0126	1.3
	0749	4.6
	1341	1.5
	2003	4.8
10 F	0204	1.5
	0824	4.5
	1420	1.7
	2042	4.7
11 SA	0244	1.6
	0903	4.3
	1503	1.8
	2126	4.5
12 SU	0327	1.8
	0950	4.2
	1551	2.0
	2216	4.3
13 M	0417	2.0
	1049	4.1
	1648	2.1
☾	2315	4.2
14 TU	0515	2.1
	1155	4.0
	1752	2.2
15 W	0019	4.2
	0619	2.1
	1302	4.1
	1855	2.2
16 TH	0125	4.2
	0721	2.1
	1402	4.3
	1954	2.0
17 F	0225	4.3
	0817	1.9
	1452	4.5
	2046	1.8
18 SA	0317	4.5
	0906	1.7
	1537	4.7
	2135	1.6
19 SU	0403	4.7
	0952	1.6
	1619	4.9
	2221	1.4
20 M	0446	4.8
	1036	1.4
	1701	5.0
●	2306	1.3
21 TU	0528	5.0
	1119	1.3
	1743	5.2
	2350	1.1
22 W	0611	5.0
	1203	1.2
	1826	5.2
23 TH	0033	1.0
	0653	5.1
	1246	1.1
	1911	5.3
24 F	0116	1.0
	0738	5.0
	1329	1.2
	1957	5.2
25 SA	0200	1.1
	0824	4.9
	1414	1.2
	2047	5.1
26 SU	0245	1.2
	0915	4.7
	1502	1.4
	2141	4.9
27 M	0335	1.4
	1013	4.6
	1557	1.5
☽	2242	4.7
28 TU	0432	1.6
	1122	4.5
	1701	1.7
	2354	4.5
29 W	0540	1.8
	1236	4.4
	1813	1.8
30 TH	0109	4.5
	0654	1.8
	1346	4.5
	1928	1.7
31 F	0220	4.5
	0805	1.7
	1447	4.7
	2036	1.6

AUGUST

Day	Time	m
1 SA	0321	4.6
	0907	1.6
	1540	4.9
	2135	1.4
2 SU	0413	4.7
	1000	1.4
	1627	5.0
	2226	1.3
3 M	0458	4.8
	1046	1.3
	1709	5.1
O	2311	1.2
4 TU	0538	4.9
	1128	1.2
	1748	5.2
	2351	1.2
5 W	0614	4.9
	1206	1.2
	1824	5.2
6 TH	0028	1.2
	0646	4.8
	1242	1.3
	1857	5.1
7 F	0103	1.3
	0715	4.8
	1315	1.4
	1929	5.0
8 SA	0136	1.4
	0744	4.6
	1349	1.5
	2002	4.8
9 SU	0208	1.5
	0816	4.5
	1423	1.7
	2038	4.6
10 M	0242	1.7
	0853	4.3
	1500	1.9
	2121	4.4
11 TU	0321	1.9
	0940	4.2
	1545	2.1
☾	2214	4.2
12 W	0409	2.1
	1043	4.0
	1646	2.3
	2321	4.1
13 TH	0515	2.3
	1202	4.0
	1804	2.3
14 F	0040	4.0
	0633	2.3
	1322	4.1
	1918	2.2
15 SA	0155	4.2
	0742	2.1
	1425	4.4
	2021	2.0
16 SU	0254	4.4
	0841	1.9
	1515	4.6
	2115	1.7
17 M	0343	4.7
	0932	1.6
	1601	4.9
	2204	1.4
18 TU	0428	4.9
	1020	1.4
	1644	5.2
	2250	1.1
19 W	0511	5.1
	1105	1.1
	1727	5.4
●	2335	0.9
20 TH	0554	5.3
	1149	1.0
	1810	5.5
21 F	0018	0.8
	0636	5.3
	1231	0.9
	1854	5.5
22 SA	0059	0.8
	0719	5.3
	1313	0.9
	1939	5.4
23 SU	0141	0.9
	0803	5.1
	1356	1.1
	2026	5.2
24 M	0223	1.1
	0850	4.9
	1441	1.3
	2117	4.9
25 TU	0310	1.4
	0944	4.6
	1533	1.5
☽	2218	4.6
26 W	0405	1.7
	1054	4.4
	1637	1.8
	2336	4.3
27 TH	0515	2.0
	1219	4.3
	1757	2.0
28 F	0104	4.3
	0639	2.1
	1338	4.4
	1921	1.9
29 SA	0220	4.4
	0759	2.0
	1442	4.6
	2032	1.7
30 SU	0320	4.5
	0900	1.7
	1533	4.8
	2128	1.5
31 M	0407	4.7
	0949	1.5
	1615	5.0
	2214	1.3

SEPTEMBER

Day	Time	m
1 TU	0444	4.8
	1032	1.3
	1651	5.1
	2254	1.2
2 W	0517	4.9
	1110	1.3
	1724	5.2
O	2330	1.2
3 TH	0547	5.0
	1145	1.2
	1755	5.2
4 F	0003	1.2
	0614	5.0
	1217	1.3
	1824	5.2
5 SA	0034	1.3
	0640	4.9
	1247	1.4
	1854	5.1
6 SU	0103	1.4
	0707	4.8
	1315	1.5
	1924	4.9
7 M	0131	1.5
	0735	4.7
	1344	1.6
	1956	4.7
8 TU	0201	1.7
	0807	4.5
	1416	1.8
	2033	4.5
9 W	0234	1.9
	0845	4.3
	1454	2.1
	2121	4.2
10 TH	0315	2.1
	0939	4.1
	1546	2.3
☾	2230	4.0
11 F	0413	2.4
	1102	4.0
	1709	2.4
12 SA	0002	4.0
	0543	2.4
	1242	4.1
	1845	2.3
13 SU	0128	4.2
	0709	2.3
	1357	4.4
	1956	2.0
14 M	0230	4.5
	0815	2.0
	1452	4.7
	2053	1.7
15 TU	0320	4.8
	0910	1.6
	1539	5.1
	2143	1.3
16 W	0406	5.1
	0959	1.3
	1623	5.4
	2229	1.0
17 TH	0449	5.3
	1045	1.0
	1707	5.6
●	2313	0.8
18 F	0531	5.5
	1129	0.9
	1750	5.7
	2356	0.7
19 SA	0614	5.5
	1212	0.8
	1833	5.7
20 SU	0037	0.8
	0656	5.5
	1253	0.8
	1918	5.6
21 M	0118	0.9
	0739	5.3
	1335	1.0
	2004	5.3
22 TU	0200	1.2
	0826	5.0
	1420	1.3
	2054	4.9
23 W	0245	1.5
	0919	4.7
	1511	1.6
	2157	4.5
24 TH	0340	1.9
	1031	4.4
	1616	1.9
☽	2328	4.2
25 F	0454	2.2
	1205	4.3
	1743	2.1
26 SA	0102	4.2
	0626	2.3
	1327	4.4
	1912	2.0
27 SU	0214	4.4
	0745	2.1
	1429	4.6
	2019	1.8
28 M	0308	4.6
	0843	1.8
	1517	4.9
	2110	1.6
29 TU	0349	4.7
	0929	1.6
	1555	5.0
	2152	1.4
30 W	0421	4.9
	1009	1.4
	1627	5.2
	2229	1.3

OCTOBER

Day	Time	m
1 TH	0449	5.0
	1045	1.3
	1657	5.2
O	2303	1.3
2 F	0516	5.1
	1118	1.3
	1726	5.3
	2333	1.3
3 SA	0542	5.1
	1148	1.3
	1754	5.2
4 SU	0002	1.3
	0608	5.1
	1216	1.4
	1823	5.1
5 M	0030	1.4
	0635	5.0
	1244	1.5
	1852	5.0
6 TU	0057	1.5
	0702	4.9
	1313	1.6
	1923	4.8
7 W	0126	1.7
	0733	4.7
	1344	1.8
	1959	4.6
8 TH	0200	1.9
	0810	4.5
	1422	2.0
	2046	4.3
9 F	0241	2.1
	0902	4.3
	1511	2.2
	2156	4.1
10 SA	0337	2.4
	1022	4.1
	1628	2.4
☾	2331	4.0
11 SU	0503	2.5
	1205	4.2
	1810	2.3
12 M	0100	4.2
	0634	2.3
	1326	4.5
	1926	2.0
13 TU	0203	4.6
	0744	2.0
	1424	4.8
	2024	1.6
14 W	0254	4.9
	0841	1.7
	1514	5.2
	2115	1.3
15 TH	0340	5.2
	0933	1.3
	1600	5.5
	2202	1.0
16 F	0424	5.5
	1020	1.0
	1644	5.7
●	2247	0.8
17 SA	0507	5.6
	1106	0.8
	1728	5.8
	2331	0.7
18 SU	0550	5.7
	1149	0.8
	1813	5.8
19 M	0013	0.8
	0634	5.6
	1232	0.8
	1858	5.5
20 TU	0054	1.0
	0718	5.4
	1315	1.0
	1945	5.2
21 W	0137	1.3
	0806	5.1
	1400	1.3
	2037	4.8
22 TH	0223	1.7
	0900	4.8
	1451	1.7
	2142	4.4
23 F	0318	2.0
	1011	4.5
	1555	2.0
☽	2313	4.2
24 SA	0431	2.3
	1140	4.4
	1719	2.2
25 SU	0042	4.2
	0600	2.3
	1300	4.4
	1845	2.1
26 M	0150	4.4
	0716	2.2
	1402	4.6
	1951	1.9
27 TU	0241	4.6
	0814	1.9
	1450	4.8
	2040	1.7
28 W	0319	4.7
	0900	1.7
	1527	5.0
	2122	1.6
29 TH	0350	4.9
	0940	1.6
	1559	5.1
	2158	1.5
30 F	0418	5.0
	1015	1.5
	1628	5.2
	2230	1.4
31 SA	0445	5.1
	1047	1.4
	1658	5.2
O	2301	1.4

NOVEMBER

Day	Time	m
1 SU	0513	5.1
	1118	1.4
	1728	5.2
	2330	1.4
2 M	0541	5.1
	1148	1.4
	1759	5.1
3 TU	0000	1.5
	0610	5.1
	1219	1.5
	1830	5.0
4 W	0030	1.6
	0639	5.0
	1250	1.6
	1903	4.8
5 TH	0102	1.7
	0713	4.8
	1324	1.8
	1941	4.6
6 F	0138	1.9
	0754	4.6
	1405	1.9
	2031	4.4
7 SA	0222	2.1
	0848	4.5
	1456	2.1
	2138	4.2
8 SU	0318	2.3
	1001	4.3
	1606	2.3
☾	2304	4.2
9 M	0435	2.4
	1131	4.4
	1733	2.2
10 TU	0027	4.4
	0557	2.3
	1251	4.6
	1847	2.0
11 W	0131	4.7
	0707	2.0
	1353	4.9
	1949	1.6
12 TH	0225	5.0
	0808	1.7
	1447	5.2
	2044	1.3
13 F	0314	5.3
	0903	1.3
	1536	5.5
	2134	1.1
14 SA	0400	5.5
	0954	1.1
	1623	5.7
	2221	0.9
15 SU	0445	5.6
	1042	0.9
	1709	5.7
●	2306	0.9
16 M	0530	5.6
	1128	0.8
	1756	5.6
	2351	1.0
17 TU	0616	5.6
	1213	0.9
	1842	5.4
18 W	0034	1.1
	0702	5.4
	1258	1.1
	1931	5.1
19 TH	0118	1.4
	0750	5.2
	1344	1.3
	2022	4.8
20 F	0205	1.7
	0843	4.9
	1434	1.6
	2123	4.5
21 SA	0258	2.0
	0945	4.6
	1532	1.9
	2238	4.2
22 SU	0402	2.2
	1057	4.5
	1641	2.1
☽	2356	4.2
23 M	0516	2.3
	1210	4.4
	1757	2.2
24 TU	0105	4.3
	0629	2.2
	1315	4.5
	1905	2.1
25 W	0158	4.4
	0731	2.1
	1408	4.6
	2000	1.9
26 TH	0240	4.6
	0821	1.9
	1451	4.8
	2044	1.8
27 F	0315	4.8
	0904	1.8
	1527	4.9
	2123	1.7
28 SA	0346	4.9
	0942	1.7
	1601	5.0
	2157	1.6
29 SU	0417	5.0
	1017	1.6
	1635	5.1
	2230	1.5
30 M	0449	5.1
	1051	1.5
	1709	5.1
O	2303	1.5

DECEMBER

Day	Time	m
1 TU	0521	5.1
	1125	1.5
	1742	5.0
	2336	1.5
2 W	0553	5.1
	1200	1.5
	1817	5.0
3 TH	0011	1.5
	0628	5.0
	1236	1.5
	1854	4.9
4 F	0048	1.6
	0706	4.9
	1315	1.6
	1935	4.7
5 SA	0127	1.8
	0750	4.8
	1358	1.8
	2024	4.6
6 SU	0212	1.9
	0842	4.7
	1447	1.9
	2123	4.4
7 M	0306	2.0
	0945	4.6
	1547	2.0
	2234	4.4
8 TU	0411	2.1
	1058	4.6
	1657	2.0
☾	2349	4.5
9 W	0522	2.1
	1213	4.7
	1807	1.9
10 TH	0057	4.7
	0630	1.9
	1321	4.9
	1913	1.7
11 F	0156	4.9
	0735	1.7
	1421	5.1
	2013	1.5
12 SA	0249	5.1
	0835	1.4
	1516	5.3
	2108	1.3
13 SU	0339	5.3
	0931	1.2
	1607	5.4
	2159	1.1
14 M	0428	5.5
	1023	1.1
	1656	5.4
●	2247	1.1
15 TU	0515	5.5
	1112	1.0
	1744	5.4
	2334	1.1
16 W	0602	5.5
	1159	1.0
	1831	5.3
17 TH	0019	1.2
	0649	5.4
	1245	1.1
	1918	5.1
18 F	0103	1.4
	0735	5.2
	1330	1.3
	2005	4.8
19 SA	0148	1.6
	0821	5.0
	1415	1.5
	2052	4.6
20 SU	0235	1.8
	0910	4.8
	1503	1.8
	2144	4.4
21 M	0326	2.0
	1003	4.6
	1557	2.0
	2244	4.2
22 TU	0425	2.2
	1102	4.4
	1657	2.1
☽	2349	4.2
23 W	0529	2.2
	1206	4.4
	1802	2.2
24 TH	0055	4.2
	0633	2.2
	1310	4.4
	1905	2.2
25 F	0151	4.4
	0733	2.2
	1408	4.5
	1959	2.0
26 SA	0237	4.5
	0825	2.0
	1456	4.6
	2046	1.9
27 SU	0317	4.7
	0910	1.9
	1538	4.7
	2127	1.8
28 M	0355	4.8
	0951	1.7
	1617	4.9
	2205	1.7
29 TU	0431	5.0
	1030	1.6
	1654	4.9
	2243	1.5
30 W	0507	5.1
	1109	1.5
	1731	5.0
O	2320	1.5
31 TH	0543	5.1
	1148	1.4
	1808	5.0
	2359	1.4

LISBON

LAT 38°42′N
LONG 9°08′W

TIMES AND HEIGHTS OF HIGH AND LOW WATER (Heights in Metres)

TIME ZONE UT (Portuguese Standard Time) **For Portuguese Summer Time (area enclosed in shaded box) add 1 hour**

2020

JANUARY

Date	Day	Time	m	Time	m	Time	m	Time	m
1	W	0023	1.3	0652	3.2	1258	1.2	1920	2.9
2	TH	0109	1.4	0737	3.1	1347	1.3	2013	2.8
3	F ☽	0206	1.5	0832	2.9	1446	1.4	2118	2.8
4	SA	0313	1.6	0938	2.9	1550	1.4	2227	2.8
5	SU	0422	1.5	1046	2.9	1653	1.4	2328	3.0
6	M	0524	1.4	1148	3.0	1748	1.3		
7	TU	0022	3.1	0619	1.3	1242	3.1	1837	1.1
8	W	0110	3.3	0707	1.1	1332	3.3	1923	0.9
9	TH	0156	3.5	0754	0.9	1420	3.4	2008	0.8
10	F ○	0241	3.6	0839	0.7	1506	3.5	2052	0.7
11	SA	0326	3.8	0923	0.6	1552	3.6	2135	0.6
12	SU	0411	3.9	1007	0.5	1637	3.6	2219	0.6
13	M	0455	3.9	1051	0.5	1722	3.6	2303	0.6
14	TU	0540	3.9	1137	0.5	1808	3.5	2349	0.7
15	W	0627	3.8	1224	0.6	1857	3.4		
16	TH	0039	0.8	0718	3.6	1316	0.8	1951	3.3
17	F ☾	0134	1.0	0815	3.4	1415	1.0	2053	3.2
18	SA	0239	1.1	0921	3.3	1522	1.1	2203	3.1
19	SU	0353	1.2	1034	3.2	1635	1.2	2314	3.2
20	M	0510	1.2	1146	3.2	1744	1.1		
21	TU	0019	3.3	0619	1.1	1250	3.2	1844	1.0
22	W	0116	3.4	0717	1.0	1345	3.3	1935	0.9
23	TH	0206	3.5	0807	0.8	1433	3.4	2020	0.9
24	F ●	0251	3.6	0850	0.7	1515	3.4	2100	0.8
25	SA	0332	3.7	0929	0.7	1554	3.4	2137	0.8
26	SU	0409	3.7	1005	0.7	1629	3.4	2212	0.8
27	M	0443	3.7	1038	0.7	1702	3.4	2245	0.8
28	TU	0515	3.6	1111	0.8	1733	3.3	2317	0.9
29	W	0546	3.5	1143	0.9	1804	3.2	2350	1.0
30	TH	0618	3.3	1216	1.0	1838	3.1		
31	F	0026	1.2	0653	3.2	1253	1.1	1917	2.9

FEBRUARY

Date	Day	Time	m	Time	m	Time	m	Time	m
1	SA	0108	1.3	0736	3.0	1338	1.3	2007	2.8
2	SU ☽	0201	1.5	0831	2.9	1437	1.4	2112	2.8
3	M	0313	1.5	0942	2.8	1549	1.5	2228	2.8
4	TU	0433	1.5	1100	2.8	1703	1.4	2340	3.0
5	W	0545	1.3	1211	3.0	1807	1.2		
6	TH	0042	3.2	0645	1.1	1312	3.1	1902	1.0
7	F	0136	3.4	0738	0.9	1405	3.3	1952	0.8
8	SA	0225	3.6	0826	0.6	1453	3.5	2039	0.6
9	SU ○	0312	3.8	0911	0.4	1539	3.7	2123	0.5
10	M	0358	4.0	0954	0.3	1624	3.8	2207	0.4
11	TU	0442	4.1	1037	0.3	1707	3.8	2250	0.4
12	W	0526	4.1	1120	0.3	1751	3.7	2333	0.5
13	TH	0611	3.9	1204	0.5	1836	3.6		
14	F	0019	0.6	0658	3.7	1250	0.7	1924	3.4
15	SA ☾	0109	0.9	0750	3.4	1343	1.0	2021	3.2
16	SU	0210	1.1	0852	3.2	1448	1.2	2130	3.0
17	M	0326	1.3	1009	3.0	1608	1.4	2249	3.0
18	TU	0454	1.3	1131	2.9	1729	1.3		
19	W	0004	3.1	0613	1.2	1241	3.0	1835	1.2
20	TH	0105	3.3	0712	1.1	1336	3.2	1926	1.1
21	F	0155	3.4	0759	0.9	1421	3.3	2009	0.9
22	SA	0237	3.6	0837	0.8	1500	3.4	2046	0.8
23	SU ●	0315	3.6	0912	0.7	1535	3.5	2119	0.8
24	M	0349	3.7	0943	0.6	1607	3.5	2151	0.7
25	TU	0420	3.7	1013	0.6	1637	3.5	2221	0.7
26	W	0450	3.6	1042	0.7	1705	3.4	2250	0.8
27	TH	0518	3.5	1110	0.8	1734	3.3	2319	0.9
28	F	0548	3.4	1139	0.9	1804	3.2	2351	1.0
29	SA	0620	3.3	1211	1.0	1838	3.1		

MARCH

Date	Day	Time	m	Time	m	Time	m	Time	m
1	SU	0026	1.2	0657	3.1	1248	1.2	1919	3.0
2	M ☽	0111	1.3	0744	2.9	1338	1.4	2015	2.8
3	TU	0215	1.5	0851	2.8	1451	1.5	2133	2.8
4	W	0346	1.5	1020	2.7	1622	1.5	2301	2.9
5	TH	0514	1.4	1146	2.9	1740	1.3		
6	F	0015	3.1	0624	1.1	1253	3.1	1843	1.1
7	SA	0115	3.4	0719	0.8	1347	3.4	1935	0.8
8	SU	0207	3.7	0807	0.6	1436	3.7	2021	0.6
9	M ○	0254	4.0	0852	0.3	1521	3.8	2106	0.4
10	TU	0340	4.1	0935	0.2	1604	4.0	2149	0.3
11	W	0424	4.2	1016	0.2	1647	4.0	2231	0.3
12	TH	0507	4.2	1058	0.3	1729	3.9	2313	0.4
13	F	0551	4.0	1140	0.5	1812	3.7	2357	0.6
14	SA	0635	3.7	1223	0.8	1858	3.5		
15	SU	0046	0.9	0725	3.4	1313	1.1	1950	3.2
16	M ☾	0144	1.1	0826	3.0	1416	1.4	2059	3.0
17	TU	0304	1.4	0947	2.8	1542	1.5	2225	2.9
18	W	0440	1.4	1117	2.8	1712	1.5	2345	3.0
19	TH	0601	1.3	1228	3.0	1820	1.4		
20	F	0047	3.2	0657	1.1	1320	3.1	1909	1.2
21	SA	0135	3.4	0739	1.0	1402	3.3	1949	1.0
22	SU	0215	3.5	0814	0.8	1438	3.4	2023	0.9
23	M	0250	3.6	0846	0.7	1510	3.5	2055	0.8
24	TU ●	0323	3.7	0915	0.7	1540	3.5	2125	0.7
25	W	0353	3.7	0943	0.7	1609	3.6	2154	0.7
26	TH	0422	3.7	1010	0.7	1637	3.5	2222	0.8
27	F	0451	3.6	1038	0.8	1705	3.5	2251	0.8
28	SA	0521	3.5	1107	0.9	1735	3.4	2322	0.9
29	SU	0553	3.3	1137	1.0	1809	3.3	2357	1.1
30	M	0629	3.2	1213	1.2	1848	3.1		
31	TU	0040	1.3	0714	3.0	1301	1.4	1940	3.0

APRIL

Date	Day	Time	m	Time	m	Time	m	Time	m
1	W ☽	0142	1.4	0819	2.8	1412	1.5	2054	2.9
2	TH	0312	1.5	0952	2.8	1548	1.5	2227	3.0
3	F	0445	1.4	1123	2.9	1713	1.4	2347	3.2
4	SA	0557	1.1	1230	3.2	1818	1.1		
5	SU	0050	3.5	0654	0.8	1324	3.5	1911	0.8
6	M	0143	3.8	0743	0.5	1413	3.8	1959	0.5
7	TU	0231	4.0	0828	0.3	1458	4.0	2044	0.3
8	W ○	0318	4.2	0911	0.2	1542	4.1	2127	0.3
9	TH	0402	4.2	0953	0.2	1624	4.1	2210	0.3
10	F	0446	4.1	1034	0.4	1706	4.0	2253	0.4
11	SA	0529	3.9	1115	0.6	1748	3.8	2337	0.6
12	SU	0614	3.6	1158	0.9	1833	3.5		
13	M	0026	0.9	0702	3.3	1246	1.2	1923	3.3
14	TU ☾	0123	1.2	0801	3.0	1347	1.5	2029	3.0
15	W	0241	1.4	0922	2.8	1511	1.6	2153	3.0
16	TH	0412	1.5	1051	2.8	1640	1.6	2314	3.0
17	F	0530	1.4	1201	2.9	1748	1.5		
18	SA	0016	3.2	0625	1.2	1251	3.1	1839	1.3
19	SU	0104	3.3	0707	1.1	1332	3.3	1919	1.1
20	M	0143	3.4	0742	0.9	1406	3.4	1953	1.0
21	TU	0218	3.5	0813	0.8	1438	3.5	2025	0.9
22	W	0251	3.6	0842	0.8	1509	3.6	2055	0.8
23	TH ●	0322	3.6	0911	0.7	1539	3.6	2126	0.8
24	F	0353	3.6	0940	0.8	1609	3.6	2156	0.8
25	SA	0425	3.6	1009	0.8	1640	3.6	2228	0.8
26	SU	0458	3.5	1040	0.9	1713	3.5	2302	0.9
27	M	0533	3.3	1114	1.0	1749	3.4	2340	1.0
28	TU	0612	3.2	1153	1.2	1830	3.3		
29	W	0026	1.2	0700	3.0	1242	1.3	1922	3.1
30	TH ☽	0128	1.3	0804	2.9	1353	1.5	2033	3.0

MAY

Date	Day	Time	m	Time	m	Time	m	Time	m
1	F	0251	1.4	0930	2.9	1521	1.5	2158	3.1
2	SA	0415	1.3	1054	3.0	1642	1.3	2316	3.3
3	SU	0526	1.0	1201	3.3	1748	1.1		
4	M	0020	3.5	0624	0.8	1256	3.5	1843	0.8
5	TU	0116	3.8	0715	0.6	1346	3.8	1934	0.6
6	W	0206	4.0	0802	0.4	1433	3.9	2021	0.4
7	TH ○	0254	4.1	0846	0.4	1518	4.0	2106	0.3
8	F	0340	4.1	0929	0.4	1602	4.0	2150	0.4
9	SA	0425	3.9	1011	0.5	1644	3.9	2235	0.5
10	SU	0509	3.7	1053	0.7	1727	3.8	2320	0.7
11	M	0553	3.5	1136	0.9	1811	3.6		
12	TU	0008	0.9	0640	3.2	1223	1.2	1859	3.3
13	W	0103	1.2	0735	3.0	1320	1.4	1957	3.1
14	TH ☾	0210	1.4	0845	2.8	1432	1.6	2110	3.0
15	F	0326	1.5	1005	2.8	1550	1.6	2225	3.0
16	SA	0438	1.4	1115	2.9	1700	1.5	2329	3.1
17	SU	0537	1.3	1209	3.0	1755	1.4		
18	M	0021	3.2	0623	1.2	1251	3.2	1839	1.2
19	TU	0103	3.3	0701	1.1	1328	3.3	1917	1.1
20	W	0141	3.4	0734	0.9	1403	3.4	1952	1.0
21	TH	0216	3.5	0807	0.9	1436	3.5	2026	0.9
22	F ●	0251	3.5	0839	0.8	1509	3.6	2100	0.8
23	SA	0326	3.5	0912	0.8	1544	3.6	2135	0.8
24	SU	0403	3.5	0946	0.8	1620	3.6	2211	0.8
25	M	0440	3.5	1022	0.9	1657	3.6	2249	0.9
26	TU	0520	3.4	1100	1.0	1737	3.5	2332	1.0
27	W	0603	3.2	1143	1.1	1821	3.4		
28	TH	0021	1.1	0653	3.1	1235	1.2	1914	3.3
29	F	0120	1.1	0755	3.0	1339	1.3	2018	3.2
30	SA ☽	0230	1.2	0908	3.0	1455	1.3	2132	3.2
31	SU	0343	1.1	1023	3.1	1609	1.2	[illegible]	[illegible]

JUNE

Date	Day	Time	m	Time	m	Time	m	Time	m
1	M	0452	1.0	1129	3.3	1716	1.1	2351	3.5
2	TU	0553	0.8	1227	3.5	1816	0.9		
3	W	0049	3.7	0647	0.7	1320	3.7	1910	0.7
4	TH	0143	3.8	0737	0.6	1410	3.8	2001	0.6
5	F ○	0234	3.8	0824	0.6	1457	3.9	2049	0.5
6	SA	0322	3.8	0909	0.6	1542	3.9	2135	0.5
7	SU	0408	3.7	0952	0.7	1626	3.8	2220	0.6
8	M	0452	3.6	1034	0.8	1709	3.7	2305	0.8
9	TU	0535	3.4	1117	1.0	1752	3.6	2350	0.9
10	W	0618	3.2	1201	1.1	1835	3.4		
11	TH	0038	1.1	0705	3.0	1249	1.3	1923	3.2
12	F	0130	1.3	0759	2.9	1346	1.4	2019	3.1
13	SA ☾	0230	1.4	0903	2.8	1451	1.5	2123	3.0
14	SU	0334	1.4	1011	2.8	1559	1.5	2228	3.0
15	M	0435	1.4	1112	2.9	1701	1.5	2326	3.0
16	TU	0529	1.3	1202	3.0	1753	1.4		
17	W	0016	3.1	0615	1.2	1245	3.2	1838	1.2
18	TH	0101	3.2	0655	1.1	1326	3.3	1919	1.1
19	F	0143	3.3	0734	1.0	1405	3.4	1959	1.0
20	SA	0224	3.4	0812	0.9	1444	3.5	2039	0.9
21	SU ●	0305	3.4	0850	0.9	1524	3.6	2119	0.8
22	M	0346	3.5	0929	0.8	1604	3.7	2159	0.8
23	TU	0428	3.5	1010	0.8	1646	3.7	2241	0.8
24	W	0511	3.4	1052	0.9	1729	3.6	2325	0.8
25	TH	0556	3.4	1137	0.9	1814	3.6		
26	F	0013	0.8	0645	3.3	1226	1.0	1905	3.5
27	SA	0105	0.9	0740	3.2	1323	1.1	2002	3.4
28	SU ☽	0205	1.0	0842	3.2	1427	1.2	2106	3.3
29	M	0311	1.0	0951	3.2	1538	1.2	2216	3.3
30	TU	0420	1.0	1058	3.3	1648	1.1	2325	3.4

SUNRISE AND SUNSET TIMES

LISBON
At 38°42′N 9°08′W

Portuguese Time UT

		Sunrise	Sunset
Jan	01	0755	1726
	15	0753	1739
Feb	01	0742	1758
	15	0727	1814
Mar	01	0709	1829
	15	0648	1844
Portuguese Summer Time (UT-1)			
Apr	01	0721	2000
	15	0700	2013
May	01	0639	2029
	15	0624	2042
Jun	01	0614	2055
	15	0611	2103
Jul	01	0616	2105
	15	0624	2101
Aug	01	0638	2047
	15	0650	2031
Sep	01	0706	2007
	15	0718	1945
Oct	01	0732	1919
	15	0746	1858
Portuguese Standard Time (UT)			
Nov	01	0703	1736
	15	0719	1723
Dec	01	0736	1715
	15	0747	1716

LISBON
LAT 38°42′N
LONG 9°08′W

TIMES AND HEIGHTS OF HIGH AND LOW WATER (Heights in Metres)

TIME ZONE UT (Portuguese Standard Time) **For Portuguese Summer Time (area enclosed in shaded box) add 1 hour**

2020

JULY

Day	Time	m	Time	m	Time	m	Time	m
1 W	0525	1.0	1201	3.4	1754	1.0		
2 TH	0029	3.4	0625	0.9	1259	3.5	1854	0.9
3 F	0127	3.5	0719	0.8	1352	3.6	1948	0.8
4 SA	0219	3.5	0808	0.8	1441	3.7	2038	0.7
5 SU	0308	3.6	0854	0.8	1528	3.8	O 2124	0.6
6 M	0354	3.5	0937	0.8	1611	3.8	2207	0.7
7 TU	0436	3.5	1018	0.8	1652	3.7	2248	0.7
8 W	0516	3.4	1057	0.9	1731	3.6	2328	0.8
9 TH	0554	3.3	1136	1.0	1808	3.5		
10 F	0007	1.0	0631	3.1	1215	1.1	1847	3.3
11 SA	0047	1.1	0712	3.0	1259	1.3	1928	3.2
12 SU	0132	1.3	0758	2.9	1350	1.4	☾ 2017	3.0
13 M	0225	1.4	0855	2.8	1451	1.5	2117	2.9
14 TU	0326	1.5	1001	2.8	1559	1.5	2223	2.9
15 W	0430	1.4	1105	2.9	1704	1.5	2326	2.9
16 TH	0528	1.4	1201	3.0	1801	1.4		
17 F	0023	3.0	0619	1.2	1251	3.2	1852	1.2
18 SA	0114	3.2	0706	1.1	1338	3.4	1938	1.0
19 SU	0202	3.3	0751	1.0	1423	3.5	2022	0.9
20 M	0248	3.4	0834	0.9	1507	3.7	● 2105	0.7
21 TU	0333	3.5	0916	0.8	1551	3.8	2148	0.6
22 W	0416	3.6	0959	0.7	1634	3.8	2230	0.6
23 TH	0500	3.6	1041	0.7	1718	3.9	2313	0.6
24 F	0544	3.6	1125	0.7	1802	3.8	2357	0.6
25 SA	0630	3.5	1211	0.8	1849	3.7		
26 SU	0045	0.8	0719	3.4	1302	0.9	1941	3.5
27 M	0138	0.9	0815	3.3	1401	1.1	☽ 2041	3.3
28 TU	0240	1.1	0920	3.2	1510	1.2	2151	3.2
29 W	0351	1.2	1032	3.2	1627	1.2	2306	3.2
30 TH	0505	1.2	1142	3.3	1742	1.2		
31 F	0017	3.2	0612	1.1	1246	3.4	1848	1.0

AUGUST

Day	Time	m	Time	m	Time	m	Time	m
1 SA	0118	3.3	0710	1.0	1341	3.5	1943	0.9
2 SU	0211	3.4	0759	0.9	1430	3.7	2031	0.8
3 M	0257	3.5	0843	0.9	1514	3.7	O 2113	0.7
4 TU	0339	3.5	0922	0.8	1555	3.8	2151	0.7
5 W	0417	3.5	0959	0.8	1632	3.8	2226	0.7
6 TH	0452	3.5	1034	0.8	1706	3.7	2259	0.8
7 F	0525	3.4	1107	0.9	1738	3.6	2332	0.9
8 SA	0556	3.3	1140	1.0	1810	3.4		
9 SU	0005	1.0	0628	3.2	1215	1.2	1843	3.3
10 M	0040	1.2	0704	3.0	1255	1.3	1923	3.1
11 TU	0122	1.4	0750	2.9	1346	1.5	☾ 2013	2.9
12 W	0216	1.5	0850	2.8	1454	1.6	2121	2.8
13 TH	0328	1.6	1004	2.8	1614	1.6	2239	2.8
14 F	0443	1.5	1118	2.9	1728	1.5	2352	2.9
15 SA	0549	1.4	1221	3.1	1829	1.3		
16 SU	0053	3.1	0644	1.2	1315	3.3	1920	1.1
17 M	0145	3.3	0733	1.0	1404	3.6	2006	0.8
18 TU	0232	3.5	0818	0.8	1450	3.8	2049	0.6
19 W	0316	3.7	0901	0.6	1534	4.0	● 2131	0.5
20 TH	0400	3.8	0943	0.5	1618	4.1	2212	0.4
21 F	0443	3.9	1025	0.5	1701	4.1	2254	0.4
22 SA	0525	3.8	1107	0.5	1745	4.0	2336	0.5
23 SU	0609	3.7	1151	0.7	1830	3.8		
24 M	0020	0.7	0655	3.5	1239	0.9	1919	3.6
25 TU	0110	1.0	0748	3.3	1336	1.1	☽ 2018	3.3
26 W	0211	1.3	0852	3.2	1448	1.3	2132	3.1
27 TH	0328	1.4	1011	3.1	1616	1.4	2256	3.0
28 F	0454	1.5	1130	3.2	1741	1.3		
29 SA	0012	3.1	0607	1.3	1237	3.3	1847	1.1
30 SU	0112	3.3	0703	1.2	1331	3.5	1937	1.0
31 M	0201	3.4	0748	1.0	1417	3.7	2018	0.8

SEPTEMBER

Day	Time	m	Time	m	Time	m	Time	m
1 TU	0242	3.5	0828	0.9	1457	3.8	2054	0.8
2 W	0319	3.6	0903	0.8	1533	3.8	O 2127	0.7
3 TH	0353	3.6	0936	0.8	1606	3.8	2158	0.7
4 F	0424	3.6	1007	0.8	1637	3.7	2227	0.8
5 SA	0453	3.5	1037	0.9	1706	3.7	2256	0.9
6 SU	0521	3.5	1106	1.0	1735	3.5	2324	1.0
7 M	0550	3.4	1137	1.1	1805	3.3	2355	1.2
8 TU	0622	3.2	1211	1.3	1841	3.2		
9 W	0030	1.4	0701	3.1	1254	1.5	1926	3.0
10 TH	0117	1.5	0754	2.9	1356	1.6	☾ 2029	2.8
11 F	0227	1.7	0909	2.9	1527	1.7	2158	2.8
12 SA	0401	1.7	1037	2.9	1657	1.6	2326	2.9
13 SU	0521	1.5	1152	3.1	1805	1.3		
14 M	0032	3.1	0621	1.3	1251	3.4	1858	1.0
15 TU	0124	3.4	0711	1.0	1341	3.7	1944	0.8
16 W	0211	3.7	0757	0.8	1428	4.0	2027	0.5
17 TH	0255	3.9	0840	0.6	1513	4.2	● 2108	0.4
18 F	0338	4.0	0922	0.4	1557	4.3	2149	0.3
19 SA	0420	4.1	1004	0.4	1640	4.2	2230	0.4
20 SU	0503	4.0	1046	0.4	1724	4.1	2312	0.6
21 M	0545	3.9	1130	0.6	1809	3.9	2355	0.8
22 TU	0631	3.7	1218	0.9	1858	3.5		
23 W	0044	1.1	0722	3.4	1315	1.2	1957	3.2
24 TH	0145	1.4	0827	3.2	1431	1.4	☽ 2116	3.0
25 F	0309	1.6	0952	3.1	1608	1.5	2247	3.0
26 SA	0443	1.6	1116	3.2	1734	1.4		
27 SU	0003	3.1	0555	1.5	1222	3.3	1835	1.2
28 M	0058	3.3	0648	1.3	1313	3.5	1919	1.0
29 TU	0142	3.4	0730	1.1	1355	3.7	1956	0.9
30 W	0219	3.6	0806	0.9	1432	3.8	2028	0.8

OCTOBER

Day	Time	m	Time	m	Time	m	Time	m
1 TH	0253	3.7	0838	0.9	1506	3.8	O 2058	0.8
2 F	0324	3.7	0909	0.8	1537	3.8	2127	0.8
3 SA	0353	3.7	0938	0.8	1606	3.8	2154	0.8
4 SU	0421	3.7	1007	0.9	1635	3.7	2221	0.9
5 M	0449	3.6	1036	1.0	1704	3.6	2249	1.0
6 TU	0518	3.5	1106	1.1	1735	3.4	2319	1.1
7 W	0550	3.4	1140	1.2	1810	3.2	2353	1.3
8 TH	0628	3.2	1221	1.4	1853	3.0		
9 F	0037	1.5	0716	3.1	1318	1.6	1954	2.9
10 SA	0143	1.7	0827	3.0	1447	1.7	☾ 2124	2.8
11 SU	0321	1.7	0959	3.0	1622	1.6	2257	2.9
12 M	0448	1.6	1120	3.2	1733	1.3		
13 TU	0005	3.2	0552	1.3	1222	3.5	1828	1.0
14 W	0058	3.5	0645	1.0	1314	3.8	1916	0.7
15 TH	0145	3.8	0731	0.7	1403	4.0	2000	0.5
16 F	0230	4.0	0816	0.5	1449	4.2	● 2043	0.4
17 SA	0314	4.1	0900	0.4	1534	4.3	2125	0.3
18 SU	0357	4.2	0943	0.4	1619	4.2	2207	0.4
19 M	0440	4.1	1027	0.4	1703	4.0	2249	0.6
20 TU	0523	3.9	1112	0.6	1749	3.8	2332	0.9
21 W	0608	3.7	1200	0.9	1838	3.5		
22 TH	0021	1.2	0659	3.5	1258	1.2	1937	3.2
23 F	0121	1.5	0803	3.2	1413	1.4	☽ 2055	2.9
24 SA	0244	1.7	0926	3.1	1545	1.5	2224	2.9
25 SU	0414	1.7	1048	3.2	1706	1.4	2337	3.0
26 M	0526	1.5	1153	3.3	1805	1.3		
27 TU	0031	3.2	0619	1.4	1244	3.4	1848	1.1
28 W	0113	3.4	0701	1.2	1325	3.6	1924	1.0
29 TH	0149	3.5	0737	1.0	1402	3.6	1956	0.9
30 F	0222	3.6	0809	0.9	1435	3.7	2026	0.9
31 SA	0253	3.7	0840	0.9	1506	3.7	O 2054	0.8

NOVEMBER

Day	Time	m	Time	m	Time	m	Time	m
1 SU	0322	3.7	0910	0.9	1536	3.7	2123	0.9
2 M	0351	3.7	0940	0.9	1607	3.6	2152	0.9
3 TU	0422	3.7	1012	0.9	1639	3.5	2222	1.0
4 W	0453	3.6	1044	1.0	1713	3.4	2254	1.1
5 TH	0528	3.5	1121	1.2	1750	3.2	2330	1.3
6 F	0607	3.3	1203	1.3	1835	3.1		
7 SA	0015	1.5	0655	3.2	1300	1.4	1934	2.9
8 SU	0119	1.6	0800	3.1	1417	1.5	☾ 2055	2.9
9 M	0245	1.6	0922	3.1	1542	1.4	2221	3.0
10 TU	0409	1.5	1042	3.3	1654	1.2	2330	3.2
11 W	0517	1.3	1148	3.5	1754	1.0		
12 TH	0026	3.5	0614	1.0	1245	3.7	1845	0.7
13 F	0117	3.8	0705	0.7	1336	4.0	1933	0.5
14 SA	0204	4.0	0753	0.5	1426	4.1	2018	0.4
15 SU	0250	4.1	0839	0.4	1513	4.1	● 2102	0.4
16 M	0335	4.1	0925	0.4	1600	4.0	2146	0.6
17 TU	0420	4.1	1011	0.5	1645	3.9	2229	0.7
18 W	0504	3.9	1058	0.7	1732	3.6	2314	0.9
19 TH	0550	3.7	1147	0.9	1820	3.4		
20 F	0002	1.2	0639	3.5	1242	1.1	1915	3.1
21 SA	0057	1.4	0737	3.3	1346	1.3	2023	2.9
22 SU	0206	1.6	0847	3.1	1500	1.5	☽ 2141	2.9
23 M	0325	1.6	1002	3.1	1614	1.5	2252	2.9
24 TU	0438	1.6	1109	3.1	1717	1.4	2350	3.1
25 W	0537	1.4	1203	3.2	1806	1.3		
26 TH	0035	3.2	0624	1.3	1248	3.3	1846	1.1
27 F	0114	3.4	0704	1.2	1326	3.4	1920	1.0
28 SA	0149	3.5	0739	1.0	1402	3.5	1953	0.9
29 SU	0221	3.6	0813	1.0	1436	3.5	2025	0.9
30 M	0254	3.6	0847	0.9	1511	3.5	O 2057	0.9

DECEMBER

Day	Time	m	Time	m	Time	m	Time	m
1 TU	0327	3.7	0921	0.9	1546	3.5	2130	0.9
2 W	0402	3.7	0956	0.9	1622	3.5	2204	0.9
3 TH	0437	3.6	1032	0.9	1659	3.4	2240	1.0
4 F	0515	3.5	1111	1.0	1740	3.3	2320	1.1
5 SA	0556	3.4	1156	1.1	1826	3.2		
6 SU	0006	1.3	0644	3.3	1248	1.2	1920	3.0
7 M	0103	1.4	0741	3.3	1351	1.2	2028	3.0
8 TU	0213	1.4	0850	3.2	1502	1.2	☾ 2142	3.1
9 W	0328	1.4	1004	3.3	1613	1.1	2252	3.2
10 TH	0440	1.2	1114	3.4	1718	1.0	2354	3.4
11 F	0543	1.0	1216	3.6	1816	0.8		
12 SA	0050	3.6	0641	0.8	1314	3.7	1909	0.7
13 SU	0142	3.8	0734	0.6	1407	3.8	1958	0.6
14 M	0231	3.9	0825	0.5	1457	3.8	● 2045	0.6
15 TU	0319	4.0	0913	0.5	1546	3.8	2131	0.6
16 W	0405	3.9	1001	0.5	1632	3.7	2215	0.7
17 TH	0450	3.9	1047	0.6	1717	3.5	2259	0.9
18 F	0534	3.7	1133	0.8	1802	3.3	2343	1.0
19 SA	0619	3.6	1220	1.0	1849	3.2		
20 SU	0030	1.2	0706	3.4	1310	1.1	1940	3.0
21 M	0123	1.4	0759	3.2	1406	1.3	☽ 2040	2.9
22 TU	0225	1.5	0900	3.0	1508	1.4	2147	2.8
23 W	0334	1.5	1006	3.0	1612	1.4	2252	2.9
24 TH	0441	1.5	1108	3.0	1711	1.4	2347	3.0
25 F	0539	1.4	1202	3.0	1801	1.3		
26 SA	0034	3.1	0628	1.3	1249	3.1	1844	1.2
27 SU	0115	3.3	0711	1.2	1332	3.2	1923	1.1
28 M	0153	3.4	0751	1.0	1412	3.3	2001	1.0
29 TU	0231	3.5	0829	0.9	1452	3.4	2038	0.9
30 W	0310	3.6	0907	0.9	1531	3.4	O 2115	0.9
31 TH	0348	3.6	0945	0.8	1611	3.4	2153	0.8

GIBRALTAR
LAT 36°08′N
LONG 5°21′W

TIMES AND HEIGHTS OF HIGH AND LOW WATER (Heights in Metres)

TIME ZONE
−0100
Subtract 1 hour for UT. Summer Time (area enclosed in shaded box) add 1 hour

2020

JANUARY

Date	Day	Time	m	Time	m	Time	m	Time	m
1	W	0019	0.2	0706	0.8	1242	0.3	1931	0.7
2	TH	0108	0.3	0754	0.7	1340	0.3	2021	0.7
3	F	0210	0.3	0847	0.7	1445	0.3	☽ 2118	0.7
4	SA	0321	0.3	0945	0.7	1556	0.3	2225	0.7
5	SU	0433	0.3	1048	0.7	1703	0.3	2334	0.7
6	M	0532	0.3	1147	0.8	1757	0.2		
7	TU	0030	0.7	0618	0.2	1237	0.8	1841	0.2
8	W	0116	0.8	0658	0.2	1323	0.9	1922	0.1
9	TH	0200	0.8	0737	0.2	1408	0.9	2002	0.1
10	F	0242	0.9	0817	0.1	1454	0.9	O 2043	0.1
11	SA	0325	0.9	0859	0.1	1539	1.0	2125	0.0
12	SU	0408	1.0	0943	0.1	1624	1.0	2207	0.0
13	M	0452	1.0	1028	0.1	1710	1.0	2250	0.1
14	TU	0537	1.0	1115	0.1	1756	0.9	2335	0.1
15	W	0625	0.9	1207	0.1	1847	0.9		
16	TH	0025	0.1	0718	0.9	1306	0.2	1942	0.8
17	F	0123	0.2	0817	0.9	1413	0.2	☾ 2043	0.8
18	SA	0232	0.2	0923	0.8	1527	0.2	2153	0.7
19	SU	0353	0.2	1035	0.8	1649	0.2	2312	0.7
20	M	0515	0.2	1146	0.8	1800	0.2		
21	TU	0024	0.7	0618	0.2	1247	0.8	1854	0.1
22	W	0122	0.8	0707	0.2	1339	0.8	1940	0.1
23	TH	0211	0.8	0750	0.1	1426	0.9	2022	0.1
24	F	0255	0.8	0830	0.1	1510	0.9	● 2100	0.0
25	SA	0335	0.9	0908	0.1	1551	0.9	2136	0.0
26	SU	0412	0.9	0945	0.1	1629	0.9	2210	0.0
27	M	0447	0.9	1020	0.1	1705	0.8	2243	0.1
28	TU	0520	0.8	1054	0.1	1740	0.8	2315	0.1
29	W	0553	0.8	1128	0.1	1815	0.8	2347	0.1
30	TH	0627	0.8	1204	0.2	1851	0.7		
31	F	0021	0.2	0705	0.7	1244	0.2		

FEBRUARY

Date	Day	Time	m	Time	m	Time	m	Time	m
1	SA	0101	0.2	0750	0.7	1332	0.3	2019	0.6
2	SU	0154	0.3	0843	0.7	1437	0.3	☽ 2117	0.6
3	M	0312	0.3	0946	0.7	1603	0.3	2232	0.6
4	TU	0446	0.3	1100	0.7	1728	0.2	2352	0.6
5	W	0553	0.3	1208	0.7	1825	0.2		
6	TH	0052	0.7	0642	0.2	1304	0.8	1910	0.1
7	F	0143	0.8	0725	0.1	1354	0.9	1952	0.1
8	SA	0229	0.9	0808	0.1	1443	0.9	2035	0.0
9	SU	0313	0.9	0851	0.0	1529	1.0	O 2117	0.0
10	M	0357	1.0	0936	0.0	1615	1.0	2159	0.0
11	TU	0440	1.0	1020	0.0	1659	1.0	2240	0.0
12	W	0523	1.0	1105	0.0	1745	1.0	2321	0.0
13	TH	0609	1.0	1151	0.0	1832	0.9		
14	F	0005	0.1	0658	0.9	1241	0.1	1923	0.8
15	SA	0054	0.1	0752	0.9	1339	0.2	☾ 2019	0.8
16	SU	0153	0.2	0854	0.8	1452	0.2	2125	0.7
17	M	0314	0.3	1008	0.7	1629	0.2	2248	0.7
18	TU	0502	0.3	1131	0.7	1755	0.2		
19	W	0014	0.7	0617	0.2	1242	0.7	1852	0.2
20	TH	0118	0.7	0706	0.2	1336	0.8	1935	0.1
21	F	0206	0.8	0746	0.1	1421	0.8	2013	0.1
22	SA	0247	0.8	0822	0.1	1501	0.8	2047	0.1
23	SU	0322	0.8	0856	0.1	1538	0.9	● 2120	0.0
24	M	0354	0.9	0929	0.1	1611	0.9	2151	0.0
25	TU	0424	0.9	1001	0.1	1643	0.9	2221	0.0
26	W	0453	0.9	1031	0.1	1714	0.8	2249	0.1
27	TH	0521	0.8	1100	0.1	1744	0.8	2316	0.1
28	F	0551	0.8	1129	0.1	1816	0.8	2345	0.1
29	SA	0624	0.8	1201	0.2	1852	0.7		

MARCH

Date	Day	Time	m	Time	m	Time	m	Time	m
1	SU	0016	0.2	0704	0.7	1239	0.2	1936	0.7
2	M	0056	0.3	0754	0.7	1332	0.3	☽ 2032	0.6
3	TU	0158	0.3	0857	0.6	1459	0.3	2144	0.6
4	W	0354	0.3	1017	0.6	1659	0.3	2315	0.6
5	TH	0531	0.3	1142	0.7	1808	0.2		
6	F	0029	0.7	0627	0.2	1247	0.8	1855	0.1
7	SA	0124	0.8	0712	0.1	1340	0.8	1938	0.0
8	SU	0211	0.9	0756	0.0	1428	0.9	2020	0.0
9	M	0255	1.0	0839	0.0	1515	1.0	O 2102	0.0
10	TU	0339	1.0	0923	-0.1	1600	1.0	2143	-0.1
11	W	0422	1.1	1006	-0.1	1644	1.0	2222	-0.1
12	TH	0505	1.0	1048	-0.1	1728	1.0	2302	0.0
13	F	0549	1.0	1131	0.0	1814	0.9	2342	0.0
14	SA	0636	0.9	1216	0.1	1904	0.9		
15	SU	0026	0.1	0728	0.8	1308	0.2	1958	0.8
16	M	0121	0.2	0828	0.8	1418	0.2	☾ 2102	0.7
17	TU	0240	0.3	0942	0.7	1605	0.3	2224	0.7
18	W	0450	0.3	1116	0.7	1742	0.3	2358	0.7
19	TH	0611	0.3	1232	0.7	1837	0.2		
20	F	0102	0.7	0655	0.2	1325	0.8	1916	0.2
21	SA	0148	0.8	0731	0.2	1406	0.8	1950	0.1
22	SU	0224	0.8	0803	0.1	1442	0.8	2022	0.1
23	M	0257	0.9	0835	0.1	1515	0.9	2054	0.1
24	TU	0326	0.9	0906	0.1	1547	0.9	● 2124	0.1
25	W	0355	0.9	0936	0.1	1617	0.9	2153	0.1
26	TH	0422	0.9	1004	0.1	1646	0.9	2220	0.1
27	F	0450	0.9	1032	0.1	1716	0.9	2247	0.1
28	SA	0520	0.8	1100	0.1	1747	0.8	2315	0.2
29	SU	0552	0.8	1130	0.1	1824	0.8	2346	0.2
30	M	0631	0.8	1205	0.2	1908	0.7		
31	TU	0024	0.3	0720	0.7	1254	0.3		

APRIL

Date	Day	Time	m	Time	m	Time	m	Time	m
1	W	0123	0.3	0823	0.7	1419	0.3	☽ 2115	0.6
2	TH	0317	0.3	0945	0.6	1627	0.3	2243	0.7
3	F	0505	0.3	1117	0.7	1743	0.2		
4	SA	0002	0.7	0606	0.2	1227	0.8	1832	0.1
5	SU	0059	0.8	0653	0.1	1320	0.8	1915	0.1
6	M	0147	0.9	0738	0.0	1408	0.9	1957	0.0
7	TU	0232	1.0	0821	0.0	1454	1.0	2038	0.0
8	W	0316	1.0	0904	-0.1	1540	1.0	O 2119	0.0
9	TH	0400	1.1	0947	-0.1	1624	1.0	2159	0.0
10	F	0443	1.0	1028	0.0	1709	1.0	2239	0.0
11	SA	0527	1.0	1109	0.0	1755	0.9	2319	0.1
12	SU	0614	0.9	1152	0.1	1844	0.9		
13	M	0002	0.2	0705	0.8	1241	0.2	1938	0.8
14	TU	0055	0.3	0805	0.7	1347	0.3	☾ 2040	0.7
15	W	0211	0.3	0917	0.7	1526	0.3	2155	0.7
16	TH	0413	0.3	1046	0.7	1703	0.3	2321	0.7
17	F	0542	0.3	1204	0.7	1800	0.3		
18	SA	0026	0.7	0627	0.3	1257	0.7	1840	0.2
19	SU	0112	0.8	0701	0.2	1337	0.8	1915	0.2
20	M	0148	0.8	0733	0.2	1412	0.8	1947	0.1
21	TU	0220	0.9	0805	0.1	1445	0.9	2019	0.1
22	W	0250	0.9	0836	0.1	1516	0.9	2051	0.1
23	TH	0320	0.9	0907	0.1	1547	0.9	● 2121	0.1
24	F	0351	0.9	0937	0.1	1618	0.9	2151	0.1
25	SA	0422	0.9	1006	0.1	1650	0.9	2220	0.2
26	SU	0454	0.9	1036	0.1	1724	0.8	2251	0.2
27	M	0529	0.8	1108	0.2	1803	0.8	2325	0.2
28	TU	0610	0.8	1146	0.2	1850	0.8		
29	W	0008	0.3	0659	0.7	1237	0.3	1946	0.7
30	TH	0113	0.3	0803	0.7	1400	0.3	☽ 2054	0.7

MAY

Date	Day	Time	m	Time	m	Time	m	Time	m
1	F	0252	0.3	0920	0.7	1548	0.3	2213	0.7
2	SA	0429	0.3	1047	0.7	1705	0.2	2329	0.8
3	SU	0537	0.2	1159	0.8	1800	0.2		
4	M	0028	0.9	0628	0.1	1255	0.8	1845	0.1
5	TU	0118	0.9	0714	0.0	1344	0.9	1929	0.0
6	W	0204	1.0	0759	0.0	1431	1.0	2011	0.0
7	TH	0250	1.0	0843	0.0	1517	1.0	O 2053	0.0
8	F	0335	1.0	0926	0.0	1603	1.0	2135	0.0
9	SA	0420	1.0	1008	0.0	1648	1.0	2216	0.1
10	SU	0506	1.0	1049	0.0	1735	0.9	2258	0.1
11	M	0553	0.9	1131	0.1	1824	0.9	2342	0.2
12	TU	0644	0.8	1218	0.2	1918	0.8		
13	W	0033	0.3	0742	0.7	1318	0.3	2016	0.8
14	TH	0142	0.3	0846	0.7	1437	0.3	☾ 2119	0.7
15	F	0311	0.3	0959	0.7	1559	0.3	2228	0.7
16	SA	0439	0.3	1114	0.7	1705	0.3	2332	0.7
17	SU	0539	0.3	1212	0.7	1754	0.3		
18	M	0022	0.8	0621	0.2	1257	0.8	1833	0.2
19	TU	0102	0.8	0657	0.2	1335	0.8	1909	0.2
20	W	0137	0.9	0731	0.2	1409	0.8	1943	0.2
21	TH	0211	0.9	0805	0.1	1444	0.9	2017	0.2
22	F	0245	0.9	0838	0.1	1518	0.9	● 2050	0.2
23	SA	0320	0.9	0911	0.1	1552	0.9	2123	0.2
24	SU	0356	0.9	0944	0.1	1628	0.9	2158	0.2
25	M	0433	0.9	1018	0.1	1706	0.9	2234	0.2
26	TU	0512	0.9	1054	0.2	1747	0.9	2314	0.2
27	W	0556	0.8	1135	0.2	1835	0.8		
28	TH	0002	0.3	0646	0.8	1229	0.2	1930	0.8
29	F	0106	0.3	0747	0.8	1342	0.3	2033	0.8
30	SA	0227	0.3	0857	0.7	1505	0.3	☽ 2142	0.8
31	SU	0348	0.3	1014	0.7	1620	0.2		

JUNE

Date	Day	Time	m	Time	m	Time	m	Time	m
1	M	0501	0.2	1127	0.8	1723	0.2	2356	0.9
2	TU	0601	0.1	1227	0.8	1816	0.1		
3	W	0049	0.9	0651	0.1	1319	0.9	1902	0.1
4	TH	0138	1.0	0738	0.0	1408	0.9	1947	0.1
5	F	0226	1.0	0824	0.0	1456	0.9	O 2032	0.1
6	SA	0313	1.0	0908	0.0	1544	0.9	2116	0.1
7	SU	0400	1.0	0951	0.0	1630	0.9	2159	0.1
8	M	0447	0.9	1032	0.1	1716	0.9	2241	0.1
9	TU	0534	0.9	1113	0.1	1804	0.9	2325	0.2
10	W	0623	0.8	1157	0.2	1853	0.8		
11	TH	0012	0.2	0715	0.8	1247	0.2	1944	0.8
12	F	0108	0.3	0810	0.7	1346	0.3	2036	0.8
13	SA	0212	0.3	0908	0.7	1451	0.3	☾ 2130	0.7
14	SU	0322	0.3	1011	0.7	1557	0.3	2228	0.7
15	M	0432	0.3	1115	0.7	1658	0.3	2323	0.8
16	TU	0532	0.3	1210	0.7	1749	0.3		
17	W	0011	0.8	0618	0.2	1255	0.8	1831	0.3
18	TH	0054	0.8	0658	0.2	1334	0.8	1910	0.2
19	F	0134	0.9	0735	0.2	1413	0.8	1946	0.2
20	SA	0213	0.9	0811	0.2	1451	0.9	2023	0.2
21	SU	0254	0.9	0848	0.1	1530	0.9	● 2101	0.2
22	M	0335	0.9	0925	0.1	1609	0.9	2140	0.2
23	TU	0417	0.9	1003	0.1	1650	0.9	2221	0.2
24	W	0500	0.9	1043	0.1	1732	0.9	2305	0.2
25	TH	0545	0.9	1126	0.2	1819	0.9	2354	0.2
26	F	0635	0.9	1216	0.2	1911	0.9		
27	SA	0051	0.2	0730	0.8	1316	0.2	2008	0.9
28	SU	0158	0.2	0833	0.8	1424	0.2	☽ 2110	0.8
29	M	0310	0.2	0942	0.8	1536	0.2	2218	0.8
30	TU	0426	0.2	1056	0.8	1649	0.2	2325	0.9

SUNRISE AND SUNSET TIMES

GIBRALTAR
At 36°08′N 5°21′W

		Sunrise	Sunset
European Standard Time (UT-1)			
Jan	01	0832	1818
	15	0832	1830
Feb	01	0822	1848
	15	0809	1903
Mar	01	0752	1916
	15	0732	1929
European Summer Time (UT-2)			
Apr	01	0808	2043
	15	0748	2055
May	01	0729	2109
	15	0715	2121
Jun	01	0706	2133
	15	0704	2140
Jul	01	0708	2142
	15	0716	2139
Aug	01	0729	2126
	15	0740	2111
Sep	01	0753	2049
	15	0804	2029
Oct	01	0816	2005
	15	0828	1945
European Standard Time (UT-1)			
Nov	01	0744	1825
	15	0758	1814
Dec	01	0814	1807

GIBRALTAR
LAT 36°08′N
LONG 5°21′W

TIMES AND HEIGHTS OF HIGH AND LOW WATER (Heights in Metres)

TIME ZONE –0100
Subtract 1 hour for UT. Summer Time (area enclosed in shaded box) add 1 hour

2020

JULY

Date	Time	m	Date	Time	m
1 W	0537 1203 1752	0.2 0.8 0.2	**16** TH	0538 1213 1758	0.3 0.7 0.3
2 TH	0024 0635 1301 1845	0.9 0.1 0.8 0.2	**17** F	0012 0628 1302 1842	0.8 0.2 0.8 0.3
3 F	0118 0725 1353 1933	0.9 0.1 0.9 0.1	**18** SA	0102 0710 1346 1923	0.8 0.2 0.8 0.2
4 SA	0209 0812 1442 2019	0.9 0.1 0.9 0.1	**19** SU	0148 0749 1428 2003	0.9 0.2 0.9 0.2
5 SU	0258 0855 1530 O 2103	0.9 0.1 0.9 0.1	**20** M	0234 0828 1510 ● 2044	0.9 0.1 0.9 0.2
6 M	0346 0937 1615 2145	0.9 0.1 0.9 0.1	**21** TU	0319 0908 1552 2126	1.0 0.1 1.0 0.1
7 TU	0431 1015 1657 2225	0.9 0.1 0.9 0.1	**22** W	0403 0948 1633 2209	1.0 0.1 1.0 0.1
8 W	0514 1053 1739 2305	0.9 0.1 0.9 0.2	**23** TH	0447 1029 1716 2253	1.0 0.1 1.0 0.1
9 TH	0557 1130 1820 2346	0.8 0.1 0.9 0.2	**24** F	0532 1111 1800 2340	1.0 0.1 1.0 0.1
10 F	0641 1210 1902	0.8 0.2 0.8	**25** SA	0619 1156 1848	0.9 0.1 1.0
11 SA	0028 0726 1254 1945	0.2 0.8 0.2 0.8	**26** SU	0030 0711 1247 1941	0.2 0.9 0.2 0.9
12 SU	0117 0814 1345 2030	0.3 0.7 0.3 0.8	**27** M	0129 0809 1347 ☽ 2040	0.2 0.8 0.2 0.9
13 M	0211 0906 1444 ☾ 2120	0.3 0.7 0.3 0.7	**28** TU	0236 0915 1458 2146	0.2 0.8 0.3 0.8
14 TU	0315 1007 1553 2216	0.3 0.7 0.3 0.7	**29** W	0356 1029 1622 2300	0.3 0.8 0.3 0.8
15 W	0430 1114 1702 2317	0.3 0.7 0.3 0.7	**30** TH	0522 1147 1740	0.2 0.8 0.3
			31 F	0010 0628 1252 1839	0.8 0.2 0.8 0.2

AUGUST

Date	Time	m	Date	Time	m
1 SA	0109 0719 1346 1927	0.9 0.1 0.9 0.2	**16** SU	0036 0650 1323 1904	0.8 0.2 0.9 0.2
2 SU	0201 0803 1434 2010	0.9 0.1 0.9 0.2	**17** M	0129 0730 1407 1946	0.9 0.2 0.9 0.2
3 M	0249 0842 1517 O 2051	0.9 0.1 0.9 0.1	**18** TU	0216 0809 1450 2027	1.0 0.1 1.0 0.1
4 TU	0332 0919 1557 2129	0.9 0.1 0.9 0.1	**19** W	0302 0849 1532 ● 2110	1.0 0.1 1.1 0.1
5 W	0413 0954 1634 2205	0.9 0.1 0.9 0.1	**20** TH	0347 0930 1614 2153	1.1 0.1 1.1 0.1
6 TH	0450 1027 1708 2240	0.9 0.1 0.9 0.1	**21** F	0431 1010 1655 2236	1.1 0.1 1.1 0.1
7 F	0526 1059 1741 2314	0.9 0.1 0.9 0.2	**22** SA	0514 1051 1738 2320	1.1 0.1 1.1 0.1
8 SA	0602 1131 1814 2348	0.8 0.2 0.9 0.2	**23** SU	0600 1133 1824	1.0 0.1 1.0
9 SU	0638 1205 1849	0.8 0.2 0.8	**24** M	0006 0650 1219 1914	0.1 1.0 0.2 1.0
10 M	0025 0718 1243 1928	0.2 0.8 0.3 0.8	**25** TU	0059 0745 1313 ☽ 2011	0.2 0.9 0.3 0.9
11 TU	0107 0804 1330 ☾ 2015	0.3 0.7 0.3 0.8	**26** W	0203 0850 1424 2118	0.3 0.8 0.3 0.8
12 W	0202 0901 1438 2110	0.3 0.7 0.4 0.7	**27** TH	0332 1008 1604 2242	0.3 0.8 0.4 0.8
13 TH	0319 1011 1610 2219	0.4 0.7 0.4 0.7	**28** F	0517 1137 1738	0.3 0.8 0.4
14 F	0458 1130 1728 2334	0.3 0.7 0.4 0.8	**29** SA	0005 0623 1248 1836	0.8 0.3 0.8 0.3
15 SA	0604 1233 1821	0.3 0.8 0.3	**30** SU	0108 0709 1339 1919	0.9 0.2 0.9 0.2
			31 M	0156 0748 1421 1957	0.9 0.2 0.9 0.2

SEPTEMBER

Date	Time	m	Date	Time	m
1 TU	0237 0822 1459 2032	0.9 0.1 1.0 0.2	**16** W	0158 0747 1426 2008	1.0 0.1 1.1 0.1
2 W	0314 0855 1532 O 2106	0.9 0.1 1.0 0.1	**17** TH	0243 0827 1508 ● 2050	1.1 0.1 1.1 0.0
3 TH	0348 0926 1603 2139	1.0 0.1 1.0 0.1	**18** F	0327 0907 1551 2133	1.1 0.0 1.2 0.0
4 F	0421 0956 1633 2210	1.0 0.1 1.0 0.1	**19** SA	0410 0947 1633 2215	1.1 0.1 1.2 0.0
5 SA	0451 1025 1701 2240	0.9 0.1 1.0 0.2	**20** SU	0454 1027 1715 2257	1.1 0.1 1.1 0.1
6 SU	0521 1054 1729 2310	0.9 0.2 0.9 0.2	**21** M	0539 1107 1800 2340	1.1 0.1 1.1 0.1
7 M	0552 1123 1759 2340	0.9 0.2 0.9 0.2	**22** TU	0627 1151 1849	1.0 0.2 1.0
8 TU	0627 1154 1835	0.8 0.3 0.8	**23** W	0028 0721 1243 1945	0.2 0.9 0.3 0.9
9 W	0015 0710 1233 1920	0.3 0.8 0.4 0.8	**24** TH	0131 0826 1356 ☽ 2055	0.3 0.8 0.4 0.8
10 TH	0101 0808 1331 ☾ 2019	0.3 0.7 0.4 0.8	**25** F	0311 0948 1552 2229	0.4 0.8 0.4 0.8
11 F	0216 0919 1521 2132	0.4 0.7 0.4 0.7	**26** SA	0505 1125 1730	0.4 0.8 0.4
12 SA	0424 1048 1701 2301	0.4 0.7 0.4 0.8	**27** SU	0000 0608 1234 1822	0.8 0.3 0.9 0.3
13 SU	0542 1205 1800	0.3 0.8 0.3	**28** M	0059 0649 1320 1900	0.9 0.3 0.9 0.3
14 M	0015 0629 1258 1844	0.8 0.2 0.9 0.2	**29** TU	0141 0723 1357 1933	0.9 0.2 1.0 0.2
15 TU	0110 0709 1343 1926	0.9 0.2 1.0 0.2	**30** W	0216 0754 1430 2005	0.9 0.2 1.0 0.2

OCTOBER

Date	Time	m	Date	Time	m
1 TH	0248 0824 1500 O 2037	1.0 0.2 1.0 0.2	**16** F	0220 0801 1443 ● 2027	1.1 0.1 1.1 0.0
2 F	0319 0854 1529 2108	1.0 0.2 1.0 0.1	**17** SA	0304 0841 1526 2109	1.1 0.1 1.2 0.0
3 SA	0348 0924 1557 2138	1.0 0.2 1.0 0.1	**18** SU	0348 0922 1609 2152	1.1 0.1 1.2 0.0
4 SU	0416 0953 1624 2207	1.0 0.2 1.0 0.2	**19** M	0432 1002 1652 2233	1.1 0.1 1.1 0.1
5 M	0445 1021 1653 2236	1.0 0.2 1.0 0.2	**20** TU	0517 1044 1737 2316	1.1 0.2 1.0 0.2
6 TU	0515 1049 1723 2305	0.9 0.3 0.9 0.2	**21** W	0605 1127 1827	1.0 0.3 1.0
7 W	0549 1120 1759 2337	0.9 0.3 0.9 0.3	**22** TH	0002 0659 1219 1924	0.3 0.9 0.3 0.9
8 TH	0633 1156 1844	0.8 0.4 0.8	**23** F	0103 0804 1333 ☽ 2035	0.4 0.8 0.4 0.8
9 F	0019 0730 1251 1944	0.4 0.8 0.4 0.8	**24** SA	0241 0922 1526 2205	0.4 0.8 0.4 0.8
10 SA	0130 0842 1444 ☾ 2059	0.4 0.7 0.5 0.8	**25** SU	0429 1052 1700 2336	0.4 0.8 0.4 0.8
11 SU	0352 1010 1632 2231	0.4 0.8 0.4 0.8	**26** M	0534 1201 1753	0.4 0.8 0.4
12 M	0514 1132 1734 2352	0.3 0.8 0.3 0.8	**27** TU	0033 0616 1247 1830	0.8 0.3 0.9 0.3
13 TU	0603 1229 1821	0.3 0.9 0.2	**28** W	0114 0650 1323 1903	0.9 0.3 0.9 0.2
14 W	0048 0643 1316 1903	0.9 0.2 1.0 0.1	**29** TH	0147 0721 1355 1935	0.9 0.2 1.0 0.2
15 TH	0135 0722 1400 1945	1.0 0.1 1.1 0.1	**30** F	0219 0752 1425 2007	1.0 0.2 1.0 0.2
			31 SA	0248 0823 1454 O 2038	1.0 0.2 1.0 0.2

NOVEMBER

Date	Time	m	Date	Time	m
1 SU	0317 0854 1524 2109	1.0 0.2 1.0 0.2	**16** M	0327 0900 1547 2132	1.1 0.1 1.1 0.0
2 M	0347 0924 1554 2140	1.0 0.2 1.0 0.2	**17** TU	0412 0943 1633 2215	1.1 0.1 1.1 0.1
3 TU	0417 0954 1626 2210	1.0 0.2 1.0 0.2	**18** W	0458 1026 1720 2258	1.0 0.2 1.0 0.2
4 W	0449 1024 1700 2240	0.9 0.3 0.9 0.2	**19** TH	0546 1111 1810 2344	1.0 0.2 0.9 0.2
5 TH	0526 1057 1738 2314	0.9 0.3 0.9 0.3	**20** F	0640 1203 1906	0.9 0.3 0.8
6 F	0610 1136 1824 2356	0.9 0.4 0.8 0.3	**21** SA	0040 0740 1311 2010	0.3 0.8 0.4 0.8
7 SA	0706 1234 1922	0.8 0.4 0.8	**22** SU	0159 0848 1440 ☽ 2123	0.4 0.8 0.4 0.7
8 SU	0104 0814 1415 ☾ 2033	0.4 0.8 0.4 0.8	**23** M	0328 1002 1605 2244	0.4 0.8 0.4 0.7
9 M	0307 0933 1553 2157	0.4 0.8 0.4 0.8	**24** TU	0440 1110 1707 2350	0.4 0.8 0.3 0.8
10 TU	0434 1054 1700 2320	0.3 0.8 0.3 0.8	**25** W	0533 1203 1753	0.3 0.8 0.3
11 W	0530 1156 1753	0.3 0.9 0.2	**26** TH	0037 0614 1243 1831	0.8 0.3 0.9 0.2
12 TH	0021 0615 1247 1838	0.9 0.2 1.0 0.1	**27** F	0115 0650 1318 1907	0.9 0.2 0.9 0.2
13 F	0111 0656 1332 1922	1.0 0.1 1.1 0.1	**28** SA	0149 0724 1351 1941	0.9 0.2 0.9 0.2
14 SA	0157 0737 1417 2005	1.0 0.1 1.1 0.0	**29** SU	0221 0757 1424 2014	0.9 0.2 1.0 0.2
15 SU	0242 0818 1502 ● 2049	1.1 0.1 1.1 0.0	**30** M	0253 0829 1458 O 2047	0.9 0.2 1.0 0.2

DECEMBER

Date	Time	m	Date	Time	m
1 TU	0325 0902 1533 2120	0.9 0.2 1.0 0.2	**16** W	0400 0932 1620 2205	1.0 0.1 1.0 0.1
2 W	0359 0934 1609 2153	0.9 0.2 0.9 0.2	**17** TH	0446 1016 1707 2247	1.0 0.1 0.9 0.1
3 TH	0435 1009 1647 2227	0.9 0.2 0.9 0.2	**18** F	0532 1101 1755 2331	0.9 0.2 0.9 0.2
4 F	0513 1046 1727 2304	0.9 0.3 0.9 0.2	**19** SA	0621 1149 1846	0.9 0.2 0.8
5 SA	0557 1129 1813 2348	0.9 0.3 0.8 0.3	**20** SU	0018 0712 1245 1940	0.2 0.8 0.3 0.8
6 SU	0648 1226 1907	0.8 0.3 0.8	**21** M	0115 0808 1349 2037	0.3 0.8 0.3 0.7
7 M	0049 0749 1346 2010	0.3 0.8 0.3 0.8	**22** TU	0222 0906 1459 ☽ 2139	0.3 0.8 0.3 0.7
8 TU	0216 0859 1509 ☾ 2123	0.3 0.8 0.3 0.8	**23** W	0332 1007 1608 2249	0.3 0.7 0.3 0.7
9 W	0341 1012 1622 2242	0.3 0.8 0.3 0.8	**24** TH	0440 1107 1711 2352	0.3 0.8 0.3 0.7
10 TH	0450 1121 1724 2351	0.3 0.9 0.2 0.8	**25** F	0537 1200 1802	0.3 0.8 0.3
11 F	0546 1218 1817	0.2 0.9 0.1	**26** SA	0041 0622 1244 1843	0.8 0.3 0.8 0.2
12 SA	0047 0634 1308 1905	0.9 0.1 1.0 0.1	**27** SU	0123 0701 1323 1922	0.8 0.2 0.8 0.2
13 SU	0137 0719 1356 1952	0.9 0.1 1.0 0.0	**28** M	0200 0737 1402 1958	0.8 0.2 0.9 0.2
14 M	0225 0803 1444 ● 2037	1.0 0.1 1.0 0.0	**29** TU	0236 0812 1441 2033	0.9 0.2 0.9 0.1
15 TU	0313 0847 1532 2122	1.0 0.1 1.0 0.0	**30** W	0312 0847 1520 O 2109	0.9 0.2 0.9 0.1
			31 TH	0348 0923 1559 2144	0.9 0.2 0.9 0.1

BREST — TIDAL COEFFICIENTS 2020

The tidal co-efficients for Brest are used in many marinas in N and NW France to denote the time of opening of lock gates.
Mean spring tides have co-efficient of 95, average tides 70, mean neaps 45.
Tidal streams and heights vary in proportion to the co-efficient.

	January		February		March		April		May		June	
Day	am	pm	am	pm	am	pm	am	pm	am	pm	am	pm
1	56	51	49	45	57	52	40	36	41	42	57	62
2	47	43	41	38	46	41	35	36	46		67	73
3	40	38	36		37	34	41		52	60	78	83
4	37		35	37	33		48	57	68	76	87	91
5	37	39	41	46	35	41	66	76	84	91	93	95
6	42	46	52	59	47	56	85	94	97	102	95	95
7	50	55	66	73	64	74	101	107	106	108	94	91
8	60	66	80	87	82	91	112	115	108	107	88	84
9	71	76	93	98	99	105	117	116	105	101	80	74
10	80	85	103	106	110	114	114	110	96	90	69	64
11	88	91	108	108	116	117	104	97	83	76	59	53
12	93	95	107	105	115	111	89	80	69	61	49	45
13	95	95	101	95	106	100	71	62	54	48	42	40
14	93	91	89	81	92	83	53	45	43	39	39	
15	88	83	74	66	74	64	40	36	37		39	41
16	79	73	58	52	56	47	35		38	39	43	46
17	69	63	47		41	38	38	42	43	46	50	53
18	59	56	44	44	37		47	52	51	55	57	61
19	54		47	50	40	45	58	62	59	63	64	67
20	54	55	55	60	51	56	67	71	67	70	70	73
21	58	61	66	70	62	67	75	78	73	75	75	77
22	65	69	75	78	72	76	81	82	77	79	79	80
23	72	76	81	84	80	82	84	85	80	80	80	80
24	79	81	85	86	85	86	85	85	80	80	79	78
25	83	84	87	87	87	88	84	82	78	77	76	74
26	84	84	86	84	87	86	79	77	74	71	72	69
27	84	82	82	79	85	83	73	69	68	64	66	63
28	80	78	75	72	79	76	64	59	60	57	61	60
29	74	71	67	62	72	67	54	49	54	51	59	59
30	67	63			62	56	45	42	51	51	60	
31	58	54			50	45			51	54		

	July		August		September		October		November		December	
Day	am	pm	am	pm	am	pm	am	pm	am	pm	am	pm
1	62	65	64	68	78	81	84	86	85	84	80	79
2	68	71	72	75	84	85	87	88	84	82	79	78
3	75	78	78	81	86	87	87	87	80	78	76	74
4	80	83	83	84	87	86	85	83	75	71	71	68
5	84	85	84	84	84	81	81	78	67	62	64	61
6	85	85	83	81	78	75	74	69	58	52	57	54
7	84	82	79	76	71	66	65	59	48	43	51	49
8	80	77	73	69	61	56	54	48	40	38	49	50
9	74	70	65	60	51	45	43	37	38	42	52	
10	66	61	56	51	40	35	33	31	47		56	61
11	57	53	46	42	35	32	32		54	62	67	73
12	49	45	38	35	31		36	43	71	79	79	84
13	42	39	33		35	42	51	60	87	93	89	93
14	38		33	35	49	58	70	79	100	104	96	98
15	37	38	39	45	67	75	88	96	107	109	99	99
16	40	43	51	57	84	91	103	108	109	108	97	95
17	47	51	64	71	98	104	112	115	105	101	92	88
18	56	61	78	84	109	112	115	114	96	89	83	78
19	65	70	90	94	113	113	111	107	82	75	72	67
20	74	78	99	101	111	107	100	93	67	60	61	56
21	82	85	103	104	101	95	84	76	53	47	51	47
22	87	89	103	100	87	78	66	58	43	41	43	41
23	90	90	96	91	69	60	50	43	40		40	
24	90	88	85	78	52	45	39	38	41	44	40	42
25	85	82	71	63	40		40		47	52	44	47
26	78	73	56	50	39	41	44	49	56	60	50	54
27	68	64	46		45	51	54	60	63	67	58	62
28	60	56	44	46	57	63	64	69	70	73	65	69
29	54		49	53	68	73	73	77	75	77	71	74
30	53	54	59	64	77	81	79	82	79	79	76	78
31	57	60	69	74			83	84			79	80